ORACLE®

Oracle Press™

W9-AKW-063

Oracle9*i* JDeveloper Handbook

ORACLE®   *Oracle Press*™

Oracle9*i* JDeveloper Handbook

Peter Koletzke
Dr. Paul Dorsey
Dr. Avrom Faderman

McGraw-Hill/Osborne

New York   Chicago   San Francisco
Lisbon   London   Madrid   Mexico City   Milan
New Delhi   San Juan   Seoul   Singapore   Sydney   Toronto

The McGraw·Hill Companies

McGraw-Hill/Osborne
2600 Tenth Street
Berkeley, California 94710
U.S.A.

To arrange bulk purchase discounts for sales promotions, premiums, or fund-raisers, please contact **McGraw-Hill**/Osborne at the above address. For information on translations or book distributors outside the U.S.A., please see the International Contact Information page immediately following the index of this book.

Oracle9*i* JDeveloper Handbook

1234567890 DOC DOC 0198765432

ISBN 0-07-222384-7

Publisher Brandon A. Nordin	**Technical Readers** Dede Moyse, David Parker, Joel Thompson
Vice President & Associate Publisher Scott Rogers	**Technical Contributor** David Brown
Acquisitions Editor Lisa McClain	**Copy Editor** Jan Jue
Project Editor Jody McKenzie	**Proofreaders** Susan Carlson Green, Susie Elkind
Acquisitions Coordinator Athena Honore	**Indexer** Caryl Lee Fisher
Technical Editor Leslie Tierstein	**Computer Designers** Tara A. Davis, Kathleen Fay Edwards
Technical Reviewers Srinivasan Arun, Dominic Battiston, Dai Clegg, Robert Clevenger, Simon Day, Mike De Groot, Susan Duncan, Charles Gayraud, Ted Farrell, Brian Fry, Raghu Kodali, Amy Kucera, Stuart Malkin, Steve Muench, Juan Oropeza, Versha Pradhan, Pete Pressley, Guus Ramackers, Blaise Ribet, Grant Ronald, Jon Russell, Chris Schalk, J.R. Smiljanic, Roel Stalman, Hans van der Meer	**Illustrators** Melinda Moore Lytle, Michael Mueller, Lyssa Wald **Series Design** Jani Beckwith **Cover Designer** Damore Johann Design, Inc.

This book was composed with Corel VENTURA™ Publisher.

To Marilyn, whose courage is an inspiration.
—Peter Koletzke

In memory of my long-time canine companion, Popper.
He was truly a "golden" retriever, in spirit as well as in breed.
—Dr. Paul Dorsey

To my parents, with love and gratitude.
—Dr. Avrom Faderman

About the Authors

Peter Koletzke is a technical director and principal instructor for the Enterprise e-Commerce Solutions practice at Quovera, in San Jose, California, and has 18 years of industry experience. Peter has presented at various Oracle users group conferences more than 100 times in the past seven years and has won awards such as Pinnacle Publishing's Technical Achievement, Oracle Development Tools Users Group (ODTUG) Editor's Choice, ECO/SEOUC Oracle Designer Award, and the ODTUG Volunteer of the Year. He is an Oracle Certified Master and coauthor, with Dr. Paul Dorsey, of other Oracle Press books: *Oracle JDeveloper 3 Handbook, Oracle Developer Advanced Forms and Reports, Oracle Designer Handbook, 2nd Edition,* and *Oracle Designer/2000 Handbook.* http://ourworld.compuserve.com/homepages/Peter_Koletzke.

Quovera is a business consulting and technology integration firm that specializes in delivering solutions to high technology, telecommunications, semiconductor, manufacturing, and financial services industries. It deploys solutions that deliver optimized business processes quickly and economically, driving increased productivity and improved operational efficiency. Quovera has an eight-year track record of delivering more than 300 strategy, design, and implementation projects to over 250 Fortune 500, high-growth mid-market, and emerging-market companies. Quovera's client list includes notable companies such as Cisco Systems, Sun Microsystems, Nortel Networks, Seagate, Handspring, Verisign, Visa, Charles Schwab, Providian, Lucas Digital, and Best Buy. www.quovera.com.

Dr. Paul Dorsey is the founder and president of Dulcian, Inc., an Oracle consulting firm specializing in business rules and web based application development. Paul is the co-author of five Oracle Press books on Designer, Developer, JDeveloper, and Database Design, which have been translated into six languages. He is president of the New York Oracle Users Group and a contributing editor of IOUG's SELECT Journal. Dr. Dorsey was honored by IOUG in 2001 as volunteer of the year and by Oracle as one of the six initial honorary Oracle9i Certified Masters. Paul is also the founder and Chairperson of the ODTUG Business Rules Symposium, now in its fourth year. You can email Paul at paul_dorsey@dulcian.com.

Dulcian, Inc. specializes in Oracle client/server and web custom application development using object-oriented thinking implemented in a traditional relational database. The company provides a wide variety of consulting services, customized training, and products for the Oracle development environment. Dulcian builds business rule–based systems using its business rules repository manager (BRIM™) product suite. The company website can be found at www.dulcian.com.

Dr. Avrom Faderman is a senior technical writer in the Application Development Tools group at Oracle Corporation. He has been documenting JDeveloper since 1999 and BC4J since 2000. He demos JDeveloper and BC4J at OracleWorld conferences and has served as an expert on JDeveloper panels at a conference of the Oracle Development Tools Users Group. You can email Avrom at avrom.faderman@oracle.com.

Before joining Oracle, Avrom served on the Philosophy Department faculties at Stanford University and the University of Rochester, specializing in mathematical logic and the philosophy of language. He holds a B.S. in Mathematics with a Specialization in Computer Science and a B.A. in Philosophy from UCLA, and a Ph.D. in Symbolic Systems and Philosophy from Stanford University.

NOTE
Sample code for the hands-on practices in this book as well as errata are available from the company websites mentioned here.

Contents at a Glance

PART I
Overview

1	Overview of JDeveloper	3
2	The Integrated Development Environment	39
3	Creating BC4J Applications with the IDE Tools	95
4	Java Language Concepts for JDeveloper Work	135
5	Naming Conventions	167
6	Debugging the Code	181
7	J2EE Architectures and Deployment Alternatives	221
8	The Class Modeler	259

PART II
Business Components for Java

9	Introducing Business Components for Java	303
10	Representing Data	327
11	Modeling Business Components and Generating Database Tables	355
12	Adding Business Rules	375
13	Working with Queries	413
14	Working with Queries at Runtime	461
15	Managing Multiple Transactions	505
16	Deploying Business Components	531

PART III

Java Client Applications

17	Java Client Overview	561
18	User Interface Components	577
19	Menus and Toolbars	623
20	Layout Managers	659

PART IV

JavaServer Pages Applications

21	JSP Development	713
22	Constructing JSP Pages with BC4J Data Tags	751
23	BC4J Data Tag Techniques	787
24	A Closer Look at BC4J Data Tags	813

PART V

APPENDIXES

A	Wizards and Dialogs	843
B	Other Resources	857
C	UML Class Diagram Syntax	861
D	Overview of HTML and Cascading Style Sheets	875

Contents

Foreword xxiii
Acknowledgments xxvii
Hands-on Practices at a Glance xxxi
Introduction xxxiii

PART I
Overview

I Overview of JDeveloper 3
    JDeveloper: Past, Present, and Future 5
        Past: Product History and Roots 5
        Present: Where Is JDeveloper Now? 6
        Future: The Vision 7
    Business Components for Java 8
        Java and XML 8
        BC4J Structure 9
        The BC4J Components 10
        Logical Architecture of BC4J 12
        Using BC4J 15
        Approaches for Using BC4J 15
        Building Applications Using BC4J 18
    Creating Application Code in JDeveloper 19
        Workspaces 20
        Projects 20
        JDeveloper Directory Structure 20
        File Management in JDeveloper 21
        High-Level and Low-Level Wizards 21
        Development Steps 21
    Hands-on Practice: Build Applications Using the JDeveloper Wizards 22
        I. Create the Workspace and Database Connection 23
        II. Create a BC4J Project 27
        III. Create a Java Application 32
        IV. Create a JSP Project 34

2 The Integrated Development Environment 39
  What's the Big IDEa? 40
  The JDeveloper Environment 42
    IDE Window 43
    Main Work Areas 47
    Wizards and New File Dialogs 82
    The Help System 86
    Software Configuration Management 89

3 Creating BC4J Applications with the IDE Tools 95
  About the BC4J Project 96
  About the Java Application Project 97
  About the JSP Project 98
  Hands-on Practice: Create a BC4J Project Manually 98
    I. Create a Workspace, Project, and Connection 99
    II. Create Entity Objects and View Objects 102
    III. Delete and Create an Association 104
    IV. Create a View Link 106
    V. Create an Application Module 107
    VI. Test the Application 108
  Hands-on Practice: Create a Master-Detail Java Application Manually 111
    I. Create a Java Application Project 112
    II. Create the Locations Portion of the Application 113
    III. Create the Application-Level Panel 119
    IV. Test and Modify the Locations Portion of the Application 121
    V. Create the Departments Portion of the Application 122
    VI. Modify the Application 125
  Hands-on Practice: Create a JSP Application Manually 129
    I. Set Up the Project and Attach the Application Module 129
    II. Add a Data Source and Data Tags 131
    III. Modify the Display 132

4 Java Language Concepts for JDeveloper Work 135
  Why Java? 136
    Benefits 136
    Drawbacks 138
    Transitioning to Java 139
  Object-Orientation Concepts 140
    Handling and Storing Data 141
    Inheritance 142
  Java Language Review 143
    Annotated Java Code Example 143
    Annotated Use of the Box Example Class 147
    Other Java Language Concepts 149
  Hands-on Practice: Create Java Class Files 161
    I. Make a Workspace and Project 161
    II. Create and Test Java Class Files 162

5 Naming Conventions 167
The Importance of Using Naming Conventions 168
Types of Objects to Name 169
    The Consistency Issue 170
General Naming Convention Considerations and Guidelines 171
    Use Suffixes to Imply Type 172
    Consider the Capabilities of the Language 172
    Be Aware of Case Sensitivity 172
    Use a Dictionary of Allowable Words 173
    Use Abbreviations Carefully 173
Recognized Naming Conventions in Java 174
    Constants (Final Variables) 174
    Classes 174
    Class Instances, Exceptions, Methods, and Variables 174
    Packages 175
JDeveloper-Specific Naming Conventions 175
    Workspaces 176
    Projects 177
    Class Source Files 177
    Libraries 177
    JClient Data Models 178
    Connections 178
    Business Components for Java 178
    UI Components 180
    Java Application Files 180
    UML Diagram Elements 180
    Other Components 180

6 Debugging the Code 181
Overview 182
    Types of Program Errors 183
    Debugging Activities 186
Do You Really Have to Run the Debugger? 186
    Apply General Troubleshooting Techniques 187
    Test and Edit the Connection 187
    Test and Edit the BC4J View Object 188
    Test the BC4J Application Module 188
    Displaying Messages 188
The JDeveloper Debugger 192
    Starting a Debugging Session 193
    The Debug Toolbar Buttons 196
    The Debug Menu Items 197
    Controlling Program Execution 197
    Examining Program Data Values 201
Remote Debugging 203
    More Information 203

The Profiler 203
    Running the Profiler 204
    Event Profiler 205
    Execution Profiler 205
    Memory Profiler 205
Hands-on Practice: Debug a Java Application 207
    I. Create a Buggy Application 208
    II. Prepare for the Debugging Session 211
    III. Control Program Execution 212
    IV. Examine Data Values 216

7 J2EE Architectures and Deployment Alternatives **221**
A Summary of J2EE 222
    J2ME 223
    J2SE 223
    J2EE 223
JDeveloper and J2EE 225
    Deploying J2EE Applications in JDeveloper 226
Java Client Architectures 226
    Java Applications 226
    Applets 230
JavaServer Pages Architecture 233
    JSP Technology Overview 234
    Where Does OC4J Fit? 237
Hands-on Practice: Deploy a Java Application 238
    I. Prepare a Simple Java Application 238
    II. Create a Java Application JAR File 239
    III. Install and Test the JAR File 243
Creating and Deploying Applets 245
    Creating the Applet 245
    Creating the HTML File 246
    Deploying the Applet 246
    Running the Applet 247
Hands-on Practice: Deploy a JSP Application 247
    I. Set Up OC4J 248
    II. Create a JSP Application 251
    III. Deploy the JSP Application 252

8 The Class Modeler **259**
Background 261
The UML in Systems Development 261
JDeveloper Class Modeler Overview 262
    Starting a Diagram 263
    Class Diagram Component Palettes 264

Model Menu 271
Diagram Visual Properties 273
Publishing a Diagram 273
Importing a Diagram 274
Using the Class Modeler as an Analysis Tool 274
Class Modeler for BC4J 274
Class Modeler Window for BC4J Diagrams 276
Class Diagram Behavior 278
BC4J Associations 278
Hands-on Practice: Build a BC4J Class Diagram 279
I. Create the Class Diagram 280
Class Modeler for Java Elements 283
Java Code Generation 283
Java Classes 284
Interfaces 286
Realizations 286
Packages 287
Associations 289
Hands-on Practice: Build a Java Class Diagram 291
I. Create a Class Diagram 291
II. Create an Association Between Two Classes 296
III. Add a Generalization 297
IV. Change a Generalization into an Interface 298
Using the UML Class Modeler for Database Design 298
How Can the UML Be Extended to Support the Elements Necessary
for Physical Database Design? 299

PART II
Business Components for Java

9 Introducing Business Components for Java 303
Why Use Business Components for Java? 304
Entity Objects and Associations 305
Associations 307
View Objects and View Links 307
View Links 308
Application Modules 308
Domains 309
Business Components, Java, and XML 310
Hands-on Practice: Examine a Default BC4J Layer 311
I. Create a BC4J Layer 312
II. Explore a Default Entity Object and a Default Association 314
III. Explore a Default View Object and a Default View Link 318
IV. Explore the Default Application Module 322
V. Test the Default Business Components 323

10 Representing Data **327**
    Entity Attributes 328
        Adding and Deleting Attributes 328
        Changing Datatypes 329
        Representing Column Constraints 330
        Synchronizing Entity Objects with the Database 332
    Representing Foreign Key Relationships 332
        Creating an Association 333
        Compositions 335
    One-to-One, One-to-Many, and Many-to-Many Relationships 335
        Creating One-to-One Associations 337
        Creating Many-to-Many Associations 337
    Representing Oracle Object Types 338
        Using Custom Domains 338
        Using Oracle Object Types 339
    Hands-on Practice: Represent the HR Schema 339
        I. Create a Workspace and Empty Project 340
        II. Create Default Entity Objects 340
        III. Change the Attributes 341
        IV. Create a Many-to-Many Association 343
        V. Create Default View Objects and View Links and a Simple
           Application Module 346
        VI. Test the Entity Object Layer 352

11 Modeling Business Components and Generating Database Tables **355**
    The Class Modeler and BC4J 356
        Starting a Class Model 357
        Modeling a New Entity Object 357
        Modeling New Associations 358
    Generating Database Tables 359
    Generating Table Constraints 361
        Generating PRIMARY KEY, NOT NULL, and Single-Column
           UNIQUE Constraints 362
        Generating Foreign Key Constraints 363
        Entity Constraints 364
    Hands-on Practice: Try Out Class Modeling and Database Generation 365
        I. Create a Workspace, Project, and Class Model 366
        II. Create Entity Objects and Associations 366
        III. Define Constraints 369
        IV. Generate the Table and Constraints 371
        V. Populate the BONUSES Table 371

12 Adding Business Rules **375**
    Overview of Entity Classes 376
        Entity Object Classes 376
        Entity Definition Classes 377
        Entity Collection Classes 378
        Generating Entity Object Classes 378

Validation Rules 378
   The CompareValidator 379
   The ListValidator 382
   The RangeValidator 383
   The MethodValidator 384
   When Validation Fails 385
Adding Business Rules to Source Code 386
   MethodValidators vs. Business Logic in Setters 387
   Coding with Domains 388
Adding Business Logic Using Domains 390
   The validate() Method 391
   Validation Domains and Column Constraints 392
The validateEntity() Method 392
Hands-on Practice: Add Simple Validation to the HR Business Model 394
   I. Add a Validation Rule 395
   II. Enforce Business Logic at the Domain Level 396
   III. Test the Business Logic 397
Adding Default Values to Entity Attributes 398
   Static Default Values 399
   Dynamically Calculated Default Values 399
   The SequenceImpl Class and the DBSequence Domain 400
Calculated Transient Attributes 400
Traversing Associations 401
   Getting a Unique Associated Entity 401
   Getting Many Associated Entities 402
Using Discriminator Columns 402
Hands-on Practice: Refine the HR Business Model 405
   I. Populate an Attribute from a Database Sequence 406
   II. Calculate an Attribute 407
   III. Add Validation Logic that Traverses a One-to-Many Association 409
   IV. Test the Business Logic 411

13 Working with Queries 413
The Types of View Attributes 414
Caching 416
   How Persistent View Attributes are Populated 416
   How SQL-Only Attributes are Populated 418
   How Entity-Derived and Transient Attributes Are Set 420
   The Advantages of Maintaining Data in Entity Objects 421
Refining a View Object's Query 423
   Changing the WHERE and ORDER BY Clauses 424
   Expert Mode 424
Hands-on Practice: Create View Objects for HR 426
   I. Remove the Default View Object Layer 427
   II. Plan the View Objects 428
   III. Create a Simple View Object 429
   IV. Create a SQL-only View Object 431

V. Create a View Object Based on Two Entity Objects 432
VI. Create a View Object Based on an Entity Object Using Expert Mode 436
VII. Test the View Objects 438
Representing Relationships Between Query Result Sets 441
View Link SQL 441
Effects of Creating a View Link 442
Entity Objects and View Link Accessors 443
View Link Directionality and Cardinality 443
Bidirectional View Links 445
One-to-One, One-to-Many, and Many-to-Many View Links 445
Data Models 446
Detail View Usages 447
Nested Application Modules 447
Polymorphic View Objects 448
Hands-on Practice: Create View Links and Application Modules for HR 449
I. Plan the Data Models 450
II. Create One-to-Many View Links 452
III. Create a Many-to-Many, Bidirectional View Link 454
IV. Create and Test CareerPathListerModule 455
V. Create and Test AccountantPromotionModule 459

14 Working with Queries at Runtime **461**
Overview of View Classes 462
View Object Classes 463
View Row Classes 463
Generating the View Classes 464
The Application Module Class 464
Interfaces, Implementation Classes, and Exported Methods 465
Custom Interfaces and Exported Methods 466
Instantiating an Application Module and View Usages 468
The createRootApplicationModule() Method 468
The findApplicationModule() Method 468
The findViewObject() Method 469
Navigating Through Result Sets 469
Stepping Through a Query's Result Set 469
first(), last(), and previous() 469
Row Keys 470
Hands-on Practice: Create Simple Batch Clients 471
I. Create View Row Classes and Interfaces 472
II. Create a Project for AccountantPromotionClient 473
III. Add Code to Begin AccountantPromotionClient 474
IV. Create a Project for CareerPathLister 476
V. Add Code to CareerPathLister 477
Manipulating Data 480
Reading and Changing Attribute Values 480
Creating and Deleting Rows 481

Traversing View Links 482
    Traversing a View Link Through the Data Model 482
    Traversing a View Link Through an Accessor 482
    The Data Model vs. Accessors 482
Changing a View Usage's WHERE Clause at Runtime 483
    Using setWhereClause() 483
    Parameterized WHERE Clauses 484
    Abstract View Objects 485
Hands-on Practice: Traverse View Links and Change Data 487
    I. Create and Export Service Methods 488
    II. Refine AccountantPromotionClient 490
    III. Refine CareerPathLister 493
    IV. Create a Silent Accountant Promotion Client 495
Changing the Data Model at Runtime 498
    Adding a Usage of a Predefined View Object to the Data Model 498
    Creating a SQL-Only View Object 499
    Creating a View Object Based on an Entity Object 499
    Linking View Usages at Runtime 500
Secondary Row Set Iterators 502
Optimizing Query Caching 503
    Forward-Only Mode 503
    Ranges 504

15 Managing Multiple Transactions **505**
The Transaction and DBTransaction Interfaces 506
    The Transaction Interface 506
    The DBTransaction Interface 507
Committing and Rolling Back Changes 507
    The Commit Cycle 507
    The Rollback Cycle 509
Locking 509
    Pessimistic Locking 509
    Optimistic Locking 510
    Explicitly Locking Rows 510
    Change Indicators 511
Hands-on Practice: Commit Changes and Customize the Commit Cycle 512
    I. Test Pessimistic and Optimistic Locking 512
    II. Use Optimistic Locking 514
    III. Attempt to Commit Changes 515
    IV. Provide Reports on the Commit Operation 516
    V. Test the Batch Client 517
    VI. Modify the promoteAccountants() Method to Commit Data 518
Application Module Pooling 519
    Creating an Application Module Pool and a SessionCookie 520
    Checking Application Modules Into and Out of the Pool 522
    Stateless Release Mode 524
    Reserved Release Mode 524

Stateful Release Mode 525
Letting Application Module Instances Expire 528
Connection Pooling 528

16 Deploying Business Components **531**
J2EE Containers 532
Deployment Configurations for Java Clients 533
Java Clients in Local Mode 533
Java Clients in Remote Mode 533
Java Clients: Local Mode vs. Remote Mode 535
Deployment Configurations for JSP Clients 535
JSP Clients in Web Module Mode 535
JSP Clients in Remote Mode 536
JSP Clients: Web Module Mode vs. Remote Mode 537
Configurations 538
Creating and Editing Configurations 538
Using a Configuration to Instantiate an Application Module 540
The BC4J Client-Side Architecture 542
Service Session Facades 542
Web Services 544
Advantages and Disadvantages of Deploying BC4J as a Web Service 544
Hands-on Practice: Deploy a BC4J Application 545
I. Deploy CareerPathLister and Its BC4J Layer in Local Mode 546
II. Deploy CareerPathListerModule as a Session Facade 549
III. Deploy CareerPathLister in Remote Mode 552
IV. Create and Use a Web Service 554

PART III
Java Client Applications

17 Java Client Overview **561**
Java Applications and Applets in JDeveloper 563
Java Client Architecture Decisions 565
Should You Build a Java Application or Applet? 565
How Many Independent Programs Will You Use? 565
How Many Directories, Workspaces, and Projects Will You Create? 565
What Is the BC4J and Data Validation Strategy? 566
What Type of Container Layout Should Be Used? 566
How Many Packages Will You Create and How Will You Name Them? 566
Other Issues 566
JClient Architecture 567
Developing a Client Data Model 568
Binding Swing Components to BC4J 569
Binding Panels 569
Hands-on Practice: Create a Basic JClient Java Application 570
I. Create the Panel Class 570
II. Add Interface Components 572
Getting the Right Information 575

18 User Interface Components **577**
   The Component Palette 578
      AWT 579
      Code Snippets 581
      JClient Controls 582
      Swing 584
      Swing Containers 588
   Working with Swing Components in JDeveloper 589
      Using Swing Components 590
      Adding Swing Components to a Program 590
      Categories of Swing Components 591
      Container Objects 591
      Modifying Swing Components 595
   Binding a Swing Component to BC4J 596
   Defining Events 596
   Hands-on Practice: Create a Tabbed User Interface Application 598
      I. Create the BC4J Project 599
      II. Create the Java Application Project 600
      III. Create a Three-Tab User Interface 601
   Hands-on Practice: Customize the Component Palette and Create a JavaBean 612
      I. Create and Deploy a JavaBean 613
      II. Create a Library for the JavaBean 615
      III. Add a Component Palette Page and a Custom JavaBean 616
      IV. Test the Custom Component 618

19 Menus and Toolbars **623**
   Design Considerations 624
      What Do You Put on a Menu? 625
      Other Menu Features 626
      What Do You Put on the Toolbar? 630
      Other Toolbar Features 630
      Summary of User Access Methods 631
   Menus and Toolbars in JDeveloper 631
      Menu Objects 633
      Toolbar Objects 634
   Hands-on Practice: Prepare a Sample Application 635
   Hands-on Practice: Build a Menu 637
      I. Lay Out the Menu Elements 638
      II. Set the Menu Element Properties 641
      III. Write the Menu Item Code 643
   Hands-on Practice: Build a Popup Menu 646
      I. Lay Out the Elements 647
      II. Write the Menu Code 648
   Hands-on Practice: Build a Toolbar 650
      I. Lay Out the Toolbar Elements 651
      II. Set the Button Properties 654
      III. Write the Button Code 657

20 Layout Managers 659
   Layout Manager Concepts 660
      Laying Out a User Interface 661
      Assigning a Layout Manager 663
      Setting Layout Manager Properties 664
      UI Editor Tools 664
      Layout Managers in JDeveloper 665
   Overview of the Layout Managers 666
      BorderLayout 667
      BoxLayout2 668
      CardLayout 671
      FlowLayout 672
      GridBagLayout 674
      GridLayout 682
      null Layout 683
      OverlayLayout2 686
      PaneLayout 687
      VerticalFlowLayout 689
      XYLayout 691
      Layout Manager Usage 691
   Multiple Layouts 692
   Hands-on Practice: Work with Layouts 695
      Hands-on Practice Sample Application 695
      I. Use the BorderLayout Manager 696
      II. Use the FlowLayout Manager 699
      III. Use the GridBagLayout Manager 703

PART IV
JavaServer Pages Applications

21 JSP Development 713
   Basic JSP Tags 715
      Processing of Standard Tags 715
   Custom Tag Libraries 728
      JSP Tag Library Support 729
   JSP Development Requirements 731
      Required Language Skills 731
      Understanding JSP Compilation and Runtime 731
   Developing JSP Pages in the JDeveloper IDE 732
      Editing JSP Files 733
      Setting Up an External HTML Editor 734
      JSP Viewer 736
      BC4J Admin Utility 737
      JDeveloper JSP Directory Structure 739

Hands-on Practice: Build a Simple JSP Page 740
    I. Create a Workspace, Project, and Default JSP Page 741
    II. Modify the JSP Page 742
    III. Apply a Cascading Style Sheet 743
    IV. Run the JSP Page 745
Hands-on Practice: Create a Simple JSP Form 746
    I. Create a Default JSP Page and Add Form Code 746
    II. Add Table Logic and Run the JSP Page 748

22 Constructing JSP Pages with BC4J Data Tags **751**
Introduction to the BC4J Data Tags Library 752
Development Methods Using the BC4J Data Tags Library 753
    General Development Steps 753
    JSP Wizards and Dialogs 755
    Working with BC4J Data Tags in the Code Editor 759
Hands-on Practice: Build JSP Pages Using BC4J Data Tags 762
    I. Set Up the Workspace and Projects 763
    II. Create the Browse Page Using the Component Palette 764
    III. Create an Edit Page Using the JSP Data Binding Tool 774
Hands-on Practice: Build Query and Details Pages 778
    I. Create a Query Page 778
    II. Add a Details Page 785

23 BC4J Data Tag Techniques **787**
BC4J Data Tags Library Development Techniques 788
    Ordering Connection Tags and Component Tags 788
    Working with Data Tag Component JSP Files 789
    Modifying JSP Attribute Behavior and Appearance 794
    Formatting Data 798
    The BC4J Cascading Style Sheet 800
Hands-on Practice: Modify a Data Page Wizard JSP Page 801
    I. Add to the BC4J Project 801
    II. Create Employee Browse and Edit Forms 803
    III. Modify the Edit Page 805

24 A Closer Look at BC4J Data Tags **813**
BC4J Data Tags Library 814
    BC4J JSP Page Concepts 814
    Quick Tour of the BC4J Data Tags 820
Hands-on Practice: Experiment with Form and Data Access Tags 828
    I. Create the JSP File and Add Data Sources 829
    II. Define the HTML Form and Fields 831
    III. Refine the Edit Page 836
    IV. Construct a Data Table 838

PART V
APPENDIXES

A Wizards and Dialogs 843
  The New Gallery 844
  Wizards and Dialogs 846

B Other Resources 857
  Books 858
  Websites 858

C UML Class Diagram Syntax 861
  Classes 862
  Attributes 862
  Associations 862
    Association Roles 863
    Naming Associations 863
    Association Cardinality (Multiplicity) 864
    Close Associations 865
    Generalization 870
  Extending the UML 872
    Stereotypes 873
    Constraints 873
    Keywords (Tagged Values) 873
    Interfaces and Realizations 873

D Overview of HTML and Cascading Style Sheets 875
  HTML 876
    Editing HTML 876
    HTML Tags 876
    Sample HTML Code 879
    JavaScript in HTML 880
  Cascading Style Sheets 883
    Building a Cascading Style Sheet 883
    Using a Cascading Style Sheet 885

  Index 887

Foreword

There is something very powerful here which I think many of us are missing completely...
—kkirk, JDeveloper Forum, posted February 09, 2001 11:58 A.M.

t was the fall of 1999 at the Oracle Open World conference and I was lurking in the back of the room of a packed technical session. The speaker was one of the most prominent and experienced users in the Oracle Tools community: Paul Dorsey. Never known for mincing words, Paul was summing up the last three releases of my product: "JDeveloper 1.0—useless. JDeveloper 2.0—useless. JDeveloper 3.0—now that's interesting!" Ouch. I wasn't sure whether to slink out of the room over the first two pronouncements or to hold my head up high because of the third.

From the perspective of somebody accustomed to the maturity and productivity of traditional client-server database tools like Oracle Forms, PowerBuilder, and VisualBasic, I knew that Paul was absolutely right about the first two releases of the product. Prior to 3.0, JDeveloper was easily dismissed as yet another Java IDE (Integrated Development Environment). Despite its numerous powerful and innovative capabilities for Java programmers (such as the fastest debugger on the market and the unique CodeCoach feature that catches and corrects suboptimal Java coding practices), the early versions of JDeveloper did very little to simplify the critical task of building a scalable multi-tier database application on the J2EE platform. This fact certainly was not going to escape someone like Paul.

Fortunately, the fact that JDeveloper 3.0 was fundamentally different from its predecessors had not escaped Paul either. The inclusion of Business Components for Java—our new component-based J2EE application framework—plugged the hole that Paul had identified and spurred the quantum leap from "useless" to "interesting." Now we were finally able to demonstrate our vision of providing *both* a powerful programming environment *and* a productive J2EE application framework. This was something that Paul, an experienced database application developer applying his skills in the new Internet era, could appreciate.

In the years following the debut of JDeveloper 3.0 and the first edition of this book, we have substantially refined both the framework and the development environment. In fact, the recent transition from JDeveloper 3.0 to Oracle9i JDeveloper represents yet another quantum leap, if not several. First of all, Oracle9i JDeveloper is a complete re-write of the product in pure Java. This marks the transition from a Windows-only development environment to a fully cross-platform solution. Second, Oracle9i JDeveloper introduces completely new areas of capability such as integrated performance profiling, software configuration management, and UML modeling.

This marks major advances in our ongoing quest to cover the complete development lifecycle in a single integrated environment. And third, Oracle9i JDeveloper provides a comprehensive extension API. This transforms JDeveloper from just another standalone tool into an open, extensible design-time platform—a development hub into which other Oracle development teams, partners, and even customers can plug their own domain specific capabilities to form a complete development solution. With all of these recent advances, I think you will find that the product has progressed well beyond "interesting." Those who take the time to learn JDeveloper by reading books like this one and experimenting with the product will discover that we have produced something very powerful.

Before you delve in for yourself, allow me to highlight just a few of the key ingredients that make JDeveloper and Business Components for Java particularly compelling:

- **Standard platform** The IDE and the framework are built from the ground up on J2EE and Internet standard protocols, languages, and APIs. Java itself is an immensely popular and powerful modern object-oriented programming language that is uniquely tailored for the Internet. Having a standard platform means that educational resources for the underlying technologies are readily available, the skills you will develop while using JDeveloper are broadly applicable, and the applications you deploy will be highly interoperable.

- **"White box" framework** Unlike the traditional black box 4GL engines of the client-server era that are largely opaque to the developer, component frameworks implemented in a standard object-oriented language like Java provide a "white box" environment in which the inner workings can be examined, debugged, and even specialized or overridden when necessary. This approach yields the ultimate balance between the flexibility of a 3GL programming environment and the productivity of a 4GL Rapid Application Development tool.

- **Multi-tier component-based architecture** The framework is designed to encourage a clean logical separation between the client, application, and database tiers. This is particularly crucial in the Internet environment where massive throughput requirements typically demand independent scaling of the application tier. The clean separation also enables the reuse of complex, expensive-to-develop business components across the ever-expanding array of Internet clients—from desktops to browsers to mobile devices to web services.

- **Flexible deployment** Determining the optimal deployment configuration for a multi-tier Internet application can be immensely complex. Do I really need a separate remote EJB server? Or should I just deploy my application logic locally within the same Java Virtual Machine as my servlet engine or Java UI? The framework eases these tough decisions by separating deployment considerations from application logic design. The same business components can be deployed in a variety of configurations. This allows you to start with the simplest or cheapest configuration first and evolve it later without recoding.

In this book, Paul, Peter, and Avrom delve into these key elements of JDeveloper and much, much more. The book provides an excellent cross-section of the knowledge you will need to be successful with JDeveloper. It covers the underlying Internet technologies, the application framework, and the IDE that houses them all. Most importantly, it is written from the perspective of client-server database application development experts who have made their own journey to the brave new multi-tier, component-based world of the Internet.

As the quote at the opening of this foreword indicates, there is indeed "something very powerful here." Don't miss it. Read this book and discover how to harness the power of JDeveloper and Business Components for Java. Then please come share and expand your newfound wisdom with the rest of the JDeveloper community on http://otn.oracle.com.

Bill Dwight
Vice President, Application Development Tools
Oracle Corporation

Acknowledgments

or me, this book project was a lot like a bicycle tour. You look at the map and get an idea of the terrain and distance, but never know what is in store until you are on the road. Somewhere around Mile 5, you look up and there is a really steep hill to climb. Wait! That was not on the map. Around the next turn, the sky opens up and you are drenched with rain. Nothing like that in the weather report. The road is really bumpy around Mile 11, and you run over some glass around Mile 28. Fixing the flat tire takes some valuable riding time. Who would have known? You keep going because turning back is not allowed (Cyclist Rule #3) and because there is something in you that kind of enjoys the surprises. Around Mile 35, the headwind coming in from the bay is so fierce that it slows you to a crawl. There is no way any map could have told you that. You never get off the bike (Cyclist Rule #12). There are many times when you are tired and discouraged and cranky, but the finish line is nearly in sight. Finally, there is a downhill ride into the end of the tour. Also not on the map, but what a relief!

The secret of success in completing a bike tour or in writing a book is partially endurance and dedication with a large measure of stubbornness and a little bit of luck. However, even with those qualities, success is not ensured. You need help, and we had lots of it on this book. It is necessary to thank all those in our peloton (pack of cyclists that provides wind resistance, pacing, and moral and technical support).

First, many thanks to Caryl Lee Fisher, Paul's assistant, who is unsurpassed in her abilities to edit, debug code, encourage, as well as to organize Paul's time in the direction of book work. Thanks also to Charlie Fisher who assisted his mom in creating the index. I must thank Paul profusely, too, for hiring Caryl Lee and for finding time to work on his chapters despite the pressures of running a company. I'd also like to express my appreciation to Avrom, who was amazingly patient when Paul and I forgot to tell him about yet another one of those (unwritten) standards that we have developed over the years. Avrom quickly adapted to our style and a book process with which we are very familiar. He also steered me in the correct direction for many Java and J2EE topics and kept us up-to-date with inside information from the Oracle JDeveloper team.

It was a pleasure to work again with my friend Leslie Tierstein, our main technical editor. Leslie has served in this capacity for many Oracle Press books, and her comments always add to the quality and completeness of the finished product. Thanks, Leslie, for questioning the forest issues when I wrote about the trees and for filling in some sentences and crossing out others that I wrote when I was clearly asleep at the keyboard.

The many members of our peloton from Oracle deserve special thanks. Their work on the book was often outside of business hours and provided an additional pressure to their normal task of product development. Their names appear in the credits at the beginning of the book. Paul and Avrom have also listed some of these team members, and I would like to add to and repeat some of those names. Roel Stalman was our main liaison with the JDeveloper product team. Roel assisted greatly by filtering our requests to the proper resources. Srinivasan Arun helped organize the many chapter reviews that the JDeveloper team provided and gave us some excellent technical information.

I really appreciate the help that Chris Schalk gave us to guide and review the chapters in Part IV as well as to spend much time on the phone answering questions. Chris as well as Avrom also kept us current with the recent JDeveloper builds. Brian Fry also assisted us greatly outside of his role as reviewer for a number of chapters. Brian followed up on some of our sticky problems with the development team. David Brown kindly assisted by supplying material about the Software Configuration Manager features accessible in JDeveloper. There were many Oracle folks who responded quickly to our questions, and I would like to express gratitude for that service to Kishore Bhamidipati, Ted Farrell, Pascal Gibert, Christophe Job, Stuart Malkin, Blaise Ribet, Grant Ronald, Odile Sullivan-Tarazi, and Hans van der Meer.

We also received technical assistance from non-Oracle employees. Dede Moyse, David Parker, and Joel Thompson reviewed chapters and gave us comments from their expert in-the-trenches standpoint. Rob Weaver of Quovera and Will Andrews also answered some of my bothersome questions about Java. Gnana Supramaniam supplied material on CodeCoach and the debugger that carried over from our previous edition of this book.

I also extend my thanks for the patient, expert, and cheerful help we received from our McGraw-Hill/Osborne editorial staff—Lisa McClain, Jody McKenzie, Jan Jue, Athena Honore, and Pamela Woolf.

When working on a book, as with any other major project, you also rely on family and friends for support, sympathy, and advice. Alice Rischert, who was also writing an Oracle-related book at the time, helped by comparing notes on her progress and by listening to me relate my challenges. Douglas Scherer, author of many Oracle-related books, also kept in touch with our progress and gave useful advice. My parents and sister, also recreational cyclists, cheered me on throughout the long months of writing and editing, and I am very appreciative of that support.

Finally, to my wife, Anne, whom I love very much—thank you for your patience and understanding, and I promise we will now have a few weekends together to fix up the living room.

Peter Koletzke
San Carlos, California
November 2002

In 1996, Peter Koletzke and I published the *Designer/2000 Handbook.* Little did I dream that this was the start of a publishing cycle that would produce a book almost every year or so for a total of 3596 pages to date (not counting this tome).

At the end of every project, we ask ourselves why we do this. It certainly can't be the money (we could make more per hour flipping burgers). It isn't the rave reviews we get for all the work that goes into these projects. (I am particularly fond of the review from an alleged 12-year-old who said that he knew more about the Developer product than we did.)

I used to think that the main deliverable from writing a book was what we learned about the subjects of the books. Clearly, we learn a lot by working on these books. However, on this project, I think that the main payback for me was the actual process of working on the book with the other people who made this project possible. It gave me a chance to spend time with some really wonderful people with whom I would otherwise not have spent as much time.

The people whom I acknowledge here helped with more than just the book. I thank them for their friendship, their understanding, and their support. I am proud to have been associated with them.

Of the six books I have coauthored, I have had the good fortune to have Peter Koletzke as my coauthor on five of them. Peter's unfailing attention to detail, amazing ability to absorb and recall a myriad of details about every Oracle product he writes about, and his willingness to help keep all of these projects on track make him the ideal coauthor. Why he agreed to work with me on yet another project is a testament to his true generosity of spirit.

Avrom Faderman joined us for this project. His in-depth coverage of BC4J added much to the value of this book as a JDeveloper resource. Also, the fact that he works for Oracle helped greatly when we needed access to additional resources, updates, information, and help from the people actually building the tool we were trying to write about. He was more than patient with me as I slowly grew to understand his vision of BC4J.

My sincere thanks to Ileana. Building a new relationship while having to compete with a book is above and beyond the call of duty.

Caryl Lee Fisher is the unacknowledged fourth author of the book. Her contribution is more than I can easily express. Suffice it to say that I would not have completed what I needed to on this book without her support. Others have come and gone over the years. Caryl Lee is my oldest friend.

Finally, there is one who prefers to not be acknowledged for his contribution. Even if I can't acknowledge your contribution by name here, you know I couldn't have done it without you. Thanks.

Our technical editor, Leslie Tierstein of STR, LLC, trained her ever-critical eye on our text, helping to make sure that all three authors presented a coherent and cohesive story about how to use JDeveloper to its best advantage.

On this project, we received exceptional cooperation from the JDeveloper team at Oracle, namely, Bill Dwight, Roel Stalman, Simon Day, Srinivasan Arun, Dai Clegg, Steve Muench, Brian Fry, Blaise Ribet, Chris Schalk, and Guus Ramackers, who helped answer our many questions, fixed problems as we encountered them, and reviewed chapters for us. We greatly appreciated all of the time and effort they devoted to this project.

Thanks to the McGraw-Hill/Osborne team, Lisa McClain, Athena Honore, Jody McKenzie, and Jan Jue, for patiently adjusting their schedules to cope with the seemingly endless outline changes and deadline adjustments encountered on this project.

In my last five books, I have always given mention to my dog, Popper. Sadly, Popper passed away this past year. He will be missed for years to come.

Dr. Paul Dorsey
Colonia, New Jersey
November 2002

Being the new kid is always a strange experience.

When OMH first approached me about integrating my plans for a book about BC4J into an update of the *JDeveloper 3 Handbook,* I have to admit I was wary. It was, I thought, a daunting enough prospect to settle in to write a first book, but to collaborate on it with strangers—strangers who had written several books together before, who almost assuredly had their own set of protocols and secret codes—struck me as more daunting still. But I can now say that I'm immensely happy I joined up, thanks in no small part to Peter, Paul, and (perhaps especially) Paul's assistant, Caryl Lee Fisher, who kept the gears turning even when it seemed the oil was running low. (Yes, there were protocols and secret codes, as in any club of grand tradition. But Peter, Paul, and Caryl Lee tirelessly showed me the ropes, and soon even the most obscure rituals were laid bare.)

This book has also benefited greatly from having been under the watchful eye of our technical editor, Leslie Tierstein. And of course, it couldn't have existed at all without the tireless efforts of the McGraw-Hill/Osborne team—Lisa McClain, Athena Honore, Jody McKenzie, Jan Jue, and Pamela Woolf.

Perhaps the people who most helped my work on this book are my teammates in Oracle's Application Development Tools Group. My manager, Steve Anderson, and the management chain above him, Roel Stalman, Christophe Job, and Bill Dwight, granted me the release time that made the book merely very, very hard (as opposed to a complete impossibility). The other writers of JDeveloper documentation, Orlando Cordero, Cathy Godwin, David Goering, Ralph Gordon, Mario Korf, Susan Leveille, Robin Merrin, Mysti Rubert, and Odile Sullivan-Tarazi, picked up the inevitable slack I left when book deadlines pressed.

We also had excellent support from the product management, development, and quality assurance teams, who all chipped in to provide additional technical reviews. We all owe them a great debt, but I can speak specifically about those who worked with me on the material of Part II: Dai Clegg, Simon Day, Mike De Groot, Susan Duncan, Steve Muench, Juan Oropeza, Versha Pradhan, Pete Pressley, Blaise Ribet, and J.R. Smiljanic. Blaise deserves special mention here—as the BC4J product manager, she was the first target of nearly all my questions, and over the course of the book, I had many, many questions. In addition, the process of recruiting Oracle reviewers and organizing the reviews would have been a nightmare without the help of our Group Product Manager, Srinivasan Arun.

Of course, writing a book doesn't just require a lot of input and direct assistance. It's a draining endeavor, and it requires a lot of emotional support as well. Lots of people helped in that capacity—providing comfort, motivation, and distraction when each was most needed. A few names from the preceding fall into this category too, especially Steve Anderson, Mario, Odile, Susan Leveille, David, and Orlando. Richard Barrick and Yuni Jiang, who welcomed me back to California so warmly when I returned in 1999, maintained that sunny warmth throughout this grueling process. My parents, Lillian Faderman and Phyllis Irwin, contributed in more ways than I can count: as inspirations, as rocks in crises, as counselors, as sources of unconditional love. And finally, a special gem, discovered all too recently: Ina Roy, who has nurtured, refreshed, and loved me—and whom I love in return. I owe her a greater debt than words can tell.

Avrom Faderman
Redwood City, California
November 2002

Hands-on Practices at a Glance

This book contains many hands-on practices to help you learn about the myriad features and functions of Oracle9i JDeveloper. The following is a quick reference list to enable you to find a specific practice. Search within the following categories for a practice that addresses the subject with which you need to experiment:

- BC4J
- Debugging
- Java Client (Java application and applet)
- Java Concepts
- JSP Pages
- UML Modeling

If you have questions about the purpose of a particular practice, review the description and list of steps at the beginning of the practice.

Category	Practice Name	Chapter	Page
BC4J	Examine a Default BC4J Layer	9	311
BC4J	Represent the HR Schema	10	339
BC4J	Add Simple Validation to the HR Business Model	12	394
BC4J	Refine the HR Business Model	12	405
BC4J	Create View Objects for HR	13	426
BC4J	Create View Links and Application Modules for HR	13	449
BC4J	Create Simple Batch Clients	14	471

Category	Practice Name	Chapter	Page
BC4J	Traverse View Links and Change Data	14	487
BC4J	Commit Changes and Customize the Commit Cycle	15	512
BC4J	Deploy a BC4J Application	16	545
BC4J	Create a BC4J Project Manually	3	98
BC4J, Java Client, JSP Pages	Build Applications Using the JDeveloper Wizards (BC4J project, Java application, JSP application)	1	22
Debugging	Debug a Java Application	6	207
Java Client	Create a Basic JClient Java Application	17	570
Java Client	Customize the Component Palette and Create a JavaBean	18	612
Java Client	Create a Tabbed User Interface Application	18	598
Java Client	Prepare a Simple Application	19	635
Java Client	Build a Menu	19	637
Java Client	Build a Popup Menu	19	646
Java Client	Build a Toolbar	19	650
Java Client	Work with Layouts (BorderLayout, FlowLayout, and GridBagLayout)	20	695
Java Client	Create a Master-Detail Java Application Manually	3	111
Java Client	Deploy a Java Application	7	238
Java Concepts	Create Java Class Files	4	161
JSP Pages	Build a Simple JSP Page	21	740
JSP Pages	Create a Simple JSP Form	21	746
JSP Pages	Build JSP Pages Using BC4J Data Tags	22	762
JSP Pages	Build Query and Details Pages	22	778
JSP Pages	Modify a Data Page Wizard JSP Page	23	801
JSP Pages	Experiment with Form and Data Access Tags	24	828
JSP Pages	Create a JSP Application Manually	3	129
JSP Pages	Deploy a JSP Application	7	247
UML Modeling, BC4J	Try Out Class Modeling and Database Generation	11	365
UML Modeling	Build a BC4J Class Diagram	8	279
UML Modeling	Build a Java Class Diagram	8	291

Introduction

This is not a novel to be tossed aside lightly.
It should be thrown with great force.

—Dorothy Parker (1893–1967)

 his is not the only book you will need to learn how to create Java-based web applications. After reading this book, you will not be able to build all types of Java applications using the full power of JDeveloper. We thought that you should know that up front.

JDeveloper's current Oracle9i incarnation offers an enormous amount of functionality, and discussing all of it is beyond the scope of any one printed book. Therefore, this book is a "handbook," not in the sense of a complete guide to all areas of the tool but, as the cover indicates, a guide for creating Java-based web applications. It provides you with solid techniques to maximize your efficiency when developing applications with JDeveloper. This introduction will give you a good picture of the contents of the book so you can determine whether this is the book for you.

 NOTE
This book was written using a pre-production release of Oracle9i JDeveloper 9.0.3 (build 988). Some material was checked with later builds, but you may need to adapt to slightly different names and features if you are using a different build or version of Oracle9i JDeveloper.

Should I Read This Book?

We set the scope of this book to satisfy an audience of traditional Oracle developers who have had little or no exposure to Java. That said, the book does not explain the Java language in any detail, because the pages are filled with specific information about JDeveloper. Chapter 4 provides an overview of some of the necessary Java concepts in case you have not been exposed to Java; or you need a review; or you need a bit of background before taking your first formal training class in Java.

The book is also aimed at those who have been in the Java world for some time and need to learn how JDeveloper can make them more productive in creating solid, working, high-performance, easy-to-maintain code. We expect that this group will be able to skim over most of the introductory material aimed at non-Java developers, but that much of the book will also provide new and helpful information.

Do I Have to Know Java?

Since JDeveloper generates 3GL Java code, it is important that you have a basic understanding of the Java language before beginning serious development work. As mentioned, if you do not have a background in the Java language, Chapter 4 will explain some of the concepts and elements of Java. However, you will also want to obtain some training or to study one or more of the basic Java books listed in Appendix B. The Sun Microsystems Java website (java.sun.com) contains a wealth of free introductory and advanced information including self-directed tutorials that you can use to become familiar with Java.

The JDeveloper wizards create a lot of code for you. This code is completely functional and well formatted. You can learn a lot by examining and analyzing the code that the wizards create. If you are new to Java, after reading through Chapter 4, you can look at the generated code and test your understanding of Java concepts.

Part II is considerably more Java-intensive than the rest of the book. Some sections of Part II (particularly Chapters 12, 14, and 15) describe features of JDeveloper that require some understanding of object-oriented programming and some hand-coding in Java. We expect that the background provided in Chapter 4 will be enough to make these chapters useful, but some further training in Java may make some subtleties expressed in those chapters clearer. Parts I, III, and IV do not rely as heavily upon fluency in Java.

What Will I Find in This Book?

We believe that the best way to learn a new tool is with a combination of overview information and annotated hands-on practices. We have included both types of sections in almost every chapter. The overview material orients you to the tasks and the ways in which they are performed in JDeveloper. The hands-on practices help you to understand the JDeveloper environment and the basics of building applications. Although you will not be able to reach the goal of creating entire production systems by reading the whole book or completing all of the hands-on practices, the book will take you some distance down that road.

If you just purchase JDeveloper, load it, and begin working, you may end up like many developers, playing with the product for weeks, if not months, trying to make it do something useful. This book will hold your hand and help you take the first few steps in learning about and using JDeveloper. It will provide a foundation for becoming skilled in this new environment and will point you to features that you may miss with self-directed study. We encourage you to go through the chapters sequentially to help build the skills necessary to begin creating systems. We also strongly encourage you to complete the hands-on practices. You would even be well served to go through each one several times to best assimilate the concepts and to become familiar with the operations.

The best way to learn a new product is to use it to solve a real problem. Once you have mastered the material well enough to make your way through the tutorials without difficulty, select a small project and use the product to build the project. If you have no experience in this environment, we recommend that you build your first project as a Java client. Novices will find building client/server Java applications not much different from building in other products with which they may already be familiar.

What Is JDeveloper?

Before explaining details of the book's contents, we need to explain a bit about the tool itself. JDeveloper is a development environment designed to help you design, develop, debug, and deploy

Java code of different types and build an object layer that accesses the database. The tool does these things very well. It also helps you create other types of files (such as XML) that support the Java environment. Although products such as IBM's Visual Age or Borland's JBuilder are also good products, what makes JDeveloper stand head and shoulders above other web development tools is the database objects layer—Oracle Business Components for Java (BC4J). The wizards in JDeveloper allow you to quickly and easily build Java applications that will connect to a relational database. Prior to BC4J, building Java applications for a relational database was a challenging experience.

In addition to BC4J, JDeveloper offers a feature called JClient that allows you to connect a Java application Swing component to a database object (through BC4J) with a single property setting. This feature is found only in JDeveloper and is extremely useful and highly productive. JClient has a counterpart in the BC4J Data Tags Library that provides the same easy-to-use connection for JavaServer Pages HTML-based applications.

Book Overview

As mentioned, the chapters in the book build on one another and are intended to be read in order. In Part I, we introduce the JDeveloper development environment with overviews of the IDE. A typical approach for a Java development book is to introduce how to create code without the complication of connecting to a database and accessing the data layer. However, in this book, you will work with database objects right away because, as a developer of Oracle web applications, you need to access data. The hands-on practices in Part I show how to develop basic applications with the wizards. Part I also discusses the important topic of naming conventions. It provides an overview of the Java language, the JDeveloper debugger, Java deployment alternatives, and JDeveloper's UML Class Modeler. This overview material is intended to orient you to the most important topics of Java development in general and JDeveloper specifically.

Part II builds on this overview material and explains the strategies, techniques, and best practices for working with BC4J. In this part, you learn how to represent data in BC4J objects, how to deploy BC4J code to servers, how to code business rules into BC4J, how to work with queries at design time and at runtime, how to manage and tune the data cache that BC4J offers, and more about how to use the Class Modeler to work with BC4J objects. Part II provides a solid background in BC4J that will allow you to understand where and how to place business logic and database access code.

Although BC4J offers complete support of database and business logic, it does not provide a user interface. Parts III and IV explain how to work with two popular types of Java-based user interface code—Java client (Java applications and applets) and JavaServer Pages. Part III explains how you would make the right decisions in structuring a Java client application. It also describes the JClient architecture and techniques as well as some of the user interface components available in JDeveloper. To complete the Java client discussion, Part III provides details about the Java client application design feature, layout managers, and the user interface features, menus, and toolbars.

Part IV focuses on similar aspects in the JavaServer Pages (JSP) style of application. Since the JSP environment is relatively new, Part IV starts by explaining how JSP pages work and how to code them. It then introduces the BC4J Data Tags Library, a set of customized JSP tags, and shows how to create JSP pages that easily connect to database objects. Finally, Part IV goes under the covers in the BC4J Data Tags Library and looks at how some of the low-level custom tags work so that you can use them in your own JSP applications.

The appendixes contain supplemental information about JDeveloper-related subjects. In addition to reference information such as a list of JDeveloper wizards and dialogs and a list of additional resources, the appendixes provide necessary background information for those who are new to the subjects of UML class modeling syntax, HTML, and cascading style sheets.

There is no book so bad that some part is not profitable.
—Pliny, the Younger (A.D. 62–113)

What Will I Not Find in This Book?

As mentioned, this book is not a one-stop shop for all of the information that you will need to create an enterprise-class Java application. The purpose of the book is to get you started developing Java applications that use BC4J to access a database. Each chapter contains a brief description of the contents of the chapter and the topics that are out of scope. Some of the important features of JDeveloper that are not covered in the book include the following:

- **Non-Oracle9iAS deployment options** The book provides some detail about deploying code to the Oracle Containers for J2EE (OC4J) feature of Oracle9iAS, but does not discuss in depth how to deploy to other servers.

- **Java stored procedures** The book contains no discussion about writing Java code that is stored and run in the database, even though JDeveloper is capable of writing and debugging such code.

- **XML code** The support for writing and checking XML files within JDeveloper is omitted.

- **Enterprise JavaBean development** Although the topic of Enterprise JavaBeans (EJB) is mentioned in several places in the book, and the book discusses how to deploy BC4J as an EJB session bean, we do not provide detailed descriptions of how to develop EJB applications.

- **Web services** You can create web services easily with JDeveloper but, other than a brief discussion and hands-on practice in Chapter 16, this topic is not discussed in the book.

- **Security topics** The topic of security is quite important for a production application. The book does not provide material about this subject.

- **Non-BC4J database connection methods** The authors believe that BC4J offers the easiest solution to the problem of connecting Java to an Oracle database. Therefore, the book presents only BC4J as the connection method. Some development shops have used SQLJ, pure Java Database Connectivity (JDBC) or additional frameworks as their standard, and this work is fully supported in JDeveloper.

- **Configuration management** JDeveloper has integrated support for several configuration management tools, including Oracle's Software Configuration Manager (SCM) product. This topic is not discussed other than in an introduction at the end of Chapter 2.

- **UML Activity Modeler** The UML Activity Modeler is a new feature to JDeveloper that is still evolving. We only briefly mention it.

Topics that are out of scope for this book are likely covered in the JDeveloper online help system or on the Oracle otn.oracle.com website, and these should be your starting point for obtaining information about JDeveloper that is not in this book.

About the Hands-on Practices

At first glance, the hands-on practices in this book may look similar to tutorials that you have seen elsewhere. The difference with the practices in this book is that they are annotated. That is, they contain extensive explanations to help you understand the purpose of the steps you are taking. Each major section (called a "phase") contains a summary so that you can relate the instructions to the task at hand. By the time you complete the practice, with a little review, you should be able to accomplish the same task in a real work situation.

JDeveloper and the Hands-on Practices

The practices are intended to be hands-on, so it does not make sense to read through the practices without trying the steps. If you do not read the hands-on practices, you will be missing some key information, because some topics are discussed only in the context of particular hands-on steps. You learn more if you interact with something new in different ways. Since experience is the best teacher, you should follow all of the practices to receive the full benefit from this book.

As mentioned, the book was written using a pre-production release of JDeveloper 9.0.3 (build 988 with some material checked with production build 1035). Since each release is slightly different, you may have to adjust some steps for the version and build you are using. The authors' websites may contain some information about changes that require adjustments for particular releases.

Installing and Running JDeveloper

JDeveloper is distributed on the Oracle9iDS (Developer Suite) install CD. You may also download a trial version of the JDeveloper install file from the Oracle Technology Network (OTN) website at otn.oracle.com. The download file is currently less than 200MB—less than 100MB if you already have a copy of the Java SDK and are willing to use documentation hosted on OTN. After downloading the file, unzip it into a new directory. (The examples in this book were built with JDeveloper installed into C:\JDev9i.) To run JDeveloper, navigate to the JDEV_HOME\jdev\bin directory and double click jdevw.exe. You can also create a shortcut that uses this executable file to start JDeveloper. The next section explains the abbreviation "JDEV_HOME."

Under the "Getting Started with JDeveloper" node in the help system Contents tab, you can find instructions about how to upgrade existing workspaces and projects from an earlier JDeveloper release.

NOTE
The jdev.exe file in the JDEV_HOME\jdev\bin directory also starts up JDeveloper. However, this executable also opens a separate command-line window, which does not appear when you run jdevw.exe. If you use jdev.exe, closing this command-line window will close JDeveloper.

What Is JDEV_HOME?

When you install JDeveloper, you place all files in a single root directory such as C:\JDev9i. Since you may choose to use a different name, this book often refers to that directory as "JDEV_HOME" (as mentioned, we used "C:\JDev9i" as the JDEV_HOME). For example, if a practice instructs you to create a file in the JDEV_HOME\jdev\mywork subdirectory, and your JDeveloper installation is in the C:\JDev9i directory, the file should be created in the C:\JDev9i\jdev\mywork directory.

NOTE
*All sample code in this book is created in the mywork directory under
JDEV_HOME\jdev. Although this is the default directory for workspaces
and projects, you can change this when you create a project or
workspace.*

The Sample Schema

All hands-on practices use a common set of human resources tables that are contained in a schema
called "HR." The tables (such as EMPLOYEES, DEPARTMENTS, and LOCATIONS) and other database
objects are included with sample schemas in Oracle9i JDeveloper and also with the Oracle9i
database. The sample schema will run in an Oracle8i environment as well, but the sample tables
included with Oracle8i are slightly different. The reason these tables are used in this book is that they
are familiar to most Oracle developers and are simple enough that no time needs to be spent
explaining the data model. There are four different ways to install this sample schema:

- **Follow the instructions in the help system topic** "Creating and Populating the Sample
  Schema Tables," which is available under the Tutorials node in the Contents tab. This
  installs more objects than are required for the practices in this book, but is the simplest
  to explain and will always be synchronized with the JDeveloper files. This method
  creates a user called "HR8" (whereas the book shows samples with the user HR).

- **Use a sample schema already installed in an Oracle9i database.** The HR schema may
  already be installed in an available Oracle9i database to which you have access.

- **Use the SQL*Plus script.** The authors' websites, listed in the author biographies at the
  beginning of the book, contain sample files for the practices as well as a SQL*Plus script
  that you can use to create the required objects. This script is a variation of the scripts
  included with JDeveloper, but it only contains the objects required for this book.

- **Run selected scripts in the JDeveloper tutorial directories.** The
  JDEV_HOME\jdev\tutorials\sample_schema_scripts directory contains the SQL*Plus
  scripts you need. Run the following scripts in this order to create the required objects for
  the hands-on practices in this book. Note that you first need to create the HR user and
  grant CONNECT and RESOURCE to that user.

  ```
  hr8_cre.sql
  hr8_popul.sql
  hr8_idx.sql
  hr8_code.sql
  hr8_comnt.sql
  ```

CAUTION
*The sample schema created by the Oracle9i and JDeveloper scripts
contains a trigger called "SECURE_EMPLOYEES" on the EMPLOYEES
table that prevents you from committing an INSERT, UPDATE, or DELETE
operation on the EMPLOYEES table after business hours. You can disable
this trigger by issuing the following statement in a SQL*Plus session:
ALTER TRIGGER secure_employees DISABLE;*

Supported Operating Systems

The authors used MS Windows 2000 to construct the example code, figures, and illustrations in this book. JDeveloper is also certified under Windows NT or XP, Linux, Solaris, and HP/UX. You may need to adjust some steps in the practices if you are not using a Windows operating system. In addition, the CodeCoach feature described in Chapter 2 will only work on a Windows operating system.

The authors used the Oracle look-and-feel for the screenshots in the book. The look-and-feel environment setting is described in Chapter 2.

CAUTION
If you are using the Oracle look-and-feel and a feature is not working as documented, switch back to Windows look-and-feel and try the feature again.

Which Database to Use?

The database drivers distributed with Oracle9i JDeveloper 9.0.3 support access to Oracle8i (8.1.7), Oracle9i Release 1 (9.0.1), and Oracle9i Release 2 (9.2). You can also connect to any database that offers a JDBC driver.

NOTE
This book uses the term "right-click menu" to mean the context menu or pop-up menu that appears when you click the alternate mouse button. Some users set the alternate mouse button as the left-hand button, and this is the button they would press when the instruction for "right-click" appears in the text.

What if the Practices Do Not Work?

Although it is not expected that you will have problems with the hands-on practices, there is always a risk in basing book material heavily on hands-on practices, because version-specific features may be added or changed. With the variable conditions that are possible in system configurations, you may experience a problem (or even a bug in the practice description) at some point. While the authors or publisher cannot personally support your work in the practices, here are some ideas for resolving any problems that you experience in the practices:

- **Slow down.** Read the instructions carefully to determine the exact operation that you need to perform. The authors and technical reviewers have run the practices many times to ensure that they work and that the instructions are clear. However, as is true with most programming languages, Java is not forgiving if you skip a step or miss a setting. If you slow down and assimilate the meaning of the step, you are more likely to experience success.

- **Start over with a new project or workspace.** Sometimes a wrong step early in the practice can cascade into a larger problem later. You may even want to restart your system in case you have a memory area that has not been cleared correctly. Starting over is described more in the next section.

- **Use the debugging techniques described in Chapter 6.** Some of these techniques do not require running the JDeveloper debugger.

- **Step back and look at the process** to see if it makes sense from what you know. If there is a wrong step in the practice, try to skip or work around it.

- **Download the sample solution** from the authors' websites (listed in the author biographies at the beginning of the book). Compare your code with the solution (using a file comparison utility such as Microsoft Word's file comparison tool), and determine where the differences occur.

- **Consult the list of other resources** (in the next section) for more help. Particularly helpful will be discussion forums where you can compare notes with other users.

Starting Over

At this point, you will probably not have worked through any practices. However, when you do follow the practices and experience difficulties that require starting over, you can use one of the following methods:

- Delete the old files and directories

- Rename the files and directories

NOTE
All of the hands-on practices in Part II (except those in Chapters 9, 10, and 11) are cumulative. That is, they build on previous practices. If you want to start over on a cumulative practice, you will need to download the previous practice's solution from the authors' websites.

Delete the Old Files and Directories   If you want to delete a file, select it in the Navigator and select **File | Erase from Disk** in the menu.

If you want to remove a workspace or project and have stored the workspace file and all project files inside a single workspace directory with nested project directories, you can start over by removing the workspace or project from the IDE by selecting it in the Navigator and clicking "Remove from" in the Navigator toolbar. (Workspaces and projects are explained in Chapter 1.) Then delete the directory that contains the workspace or project by using Windows Explorer. Although you can delete files in JDeveloper using the **File | Erase from Disk** menu item, it is faster to use an operating system utility.

If you are deleting a workspace that contains no projects used by projects in other workspaces, you do not need to do anything else.

Searching for Related Files   If you want to delete a project, check whether any other workspaces use the project by following these steps (written for Windows 2000):

1. In JDeveloper, select **Search | Search Files** to display the Search Files dialog. In the *Search Text* field, enter the name of the project file (for example, "EmpDeptJA.jpr").

2. In the *File Type(s)* field, enter "*.jws" (indicating all workspace files). In the *Search Path(s)* field, enter "JDEV_HOME\jdev\mywork" (the top-level workspace directory).

3. Uncheck the *Use Active Project Source Path by Default* checkbox so the dialog matches the dialog in Figure i-1. Click OK.

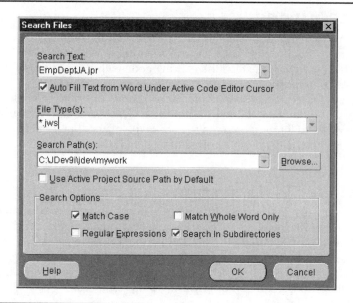

FIGURE i-1. *Search Files dialog*

If any workspace files include the file name of the project (indicating that the project is also part of those other workspaces), the list in the Log window will indicate their names. If you find any references to the project file, you need to decide whether the workspaces referencing that project directory require the project. If the references to the directory are not important, or if you found no references, you may delete the directory using Windows Explorer.

Rename the New Files and Directories   If you want to keep the old files and directories, but still want to start over with a practice, you can leave the original files and follow the practice steps as written. When you reach a step where you need to name the workspace directory, add a number to the name (for example, "EmpWS2"). The main part of the name will be recognizable, but you will be able to start fresh in a particular practice. While this is not a recommended production practice, it will suffice for the purposes of learning JDeveloper.

CAUTION
Be aware that JDeveloper automatically writes the names of files and directories into the project and workspace files (described in Chapter 1). Therefore, if you rename a file or directory outside of JDeveloper, a reference in a JDeveloper file may no longer be valid. Therefore, use JDeveloper to rename project and workspace files whenever possible.

Other Resources

By spending the time to search out what has already been written, you will probably find that others have spent many hours doing just what you want to do. With the extensibility of Java classes, you can use, modify, and extend the existing code with a fraction of the effort that would be required to develop it from scratch.

In addition to the sources of additional information summarized in Appendix B, the book contains references throughout to online websites, both Oracle and others, that you can visit, and books that you can refer to for more information about the material introduced in the text. There are several other resources generic to the topics of Java and JDeveloper that are worth special mention here.

The JDeveloper Help System

The JDeveloper help system (introduced in Chapter 2) contains a wealth of information. There are low-level details such as Javadoc references about the Java language and Oracle-created classes used in various files. There are also descriptions of the steps used to create specific components or full applications. The help system is a good companion to this book because, although there is some overlap, each contains different tutorial and descriptive material. You will be exposed to many of the tasks that you need to perform by using both resources.

CAUTION
References to help system topics appear throughout the book. The references often include the location or name of the help topic; however, this is subject to change as JDeveloper is upgraded. The best strategy is to use the Search or Index tab in the help system if you cannot find a help topic in the referenced location.

JDeveloper Tutorials

The help system contains some key tutorials under the Contents node "Tutorials."

JDeveloper Samples

The best way to learn a technique is to examine a sample application to determine how its creator solved a specific problem. You can find sample code on OTN (otn.oracle.com).

JDeveloper Readme (Release Notes)

Additional notes about JDeveloper are installed with the product and are available by selecting **Help | Release Notes** from the menu. The Release Notes contain useful information that is not included in other sources, and you should be familiar with them. Some of the notes refer to limitations or workarounds that you might not know about otherwise.

Oracle User Groups

One resource of which you must avail yourself is other users of Java and JDeveloper. The process of learning and using these tools is a challenging one, and it is likely that another user somewhere has already solved a problem you may be having. There are many online forums where the experts congregate, particularly, the International Oracle Users Group – Americas (IOUG-A) discussion forums (www.ioug.org), where users discuss Oracle web development topics. In addition, the Oracle Development Tools User Group (ODTUG) hosts list servers for a wide range of Oracle development topics, including web applications and Java (www.odtug.com). You will also want to hook up with your local Oracle users group (the IOUG-A office can help you locate the nearest group, or you can find one in your area at www.dbdomain.com/user_grps.htm) and discuss issues face-to-face with Oracle users in your area. OTN also has an active JDeveloper forum (otn.oracle.com) that the JDeveloper product team contributes to and monitors.

PART
I

Overview

CHAPTER
1

Overview of
JDeveloper

If you give someone a program, you will frustrate them for a day;
if you teach them how to program, you will frustrate them for a lifetime.

—Anonymous, from the "Computer Quotes" webpage of Guillaume Dargaud

 Developer is an integrated development environment (IDE) for Java programming. It offers a rich set of features for designing, developing, debugging, and deploying all types of 3GL Java and other related files that are part of the Java 2 Platform, Enterprise Edition (J2EE) strategy. JDeveloper contains many wizards and code generators that make the internal mechanisms of Java easier, enabling you to concentrate on solving business problems with Java. It also offers strong code organization and configuration management. The Oracle9i release of JDeveloper represents a giant leap forward from past versions of the product.

This part of the book provides an overview of JDeveloper and introduces you to its various features and functions.

This chapter introduces one of JDeveloper's major features—Business Components for Java (BC4J) and summarizes how to develop applications with JDeveloper. It also provides some simple hands-on practices so that you can start generating some code. More detailed information about BC4J is contained in Part II. Chapter 2 explains the components of the JDeveloper IDE, and Chapter 3 discusses how the IDE is used in building BC4J applications. For those new to Java, Chapter 4 provides a brief overview of important concepts needed to work effectively with JDeveloper. Chapter 5 discusses the importance of consistent naming conventions and gives suggestions about how to name the many elements needed to develop applications with JDeveloper. Debugging by using JDeveloper's debugging features is discussed in Chapter 6. Chapter 7 outlines approaches to deploying Java client (Java applications and applets) and JavaServer Pages (JSP) applications. Finally, Chapter 8 looks at one of the new features of the 9i release, the Class Modeler, and how it can assist in your application development.

This book often refers to creating "applications." The following sidebar will help clarify the authors' use of this word in the book.

What Is an "Application?"

Many people in the IT industry use the word "application." However, it can mean different things in different contexts. Some people use the word "application" to refer to an entire computer system. Others use it to refer to a portion of a computer system that is physically implemented within a single program. In this book, the second definition will be used to refer to a logical portion of the overall system, usually implemented in a single JDeveloper workspace.

Other usages of the word "application" include *Java application,* a type of Java program deployed with the Java Virtual Machine (JVM) on the client, requiring no browser involvement. In this book, "Java application" refers only to that specific type of program.

An *application module* is a BC4J component that makes a set of view objects and view links available to a client program.

JDeveloper: Past, Present, and Future

JDeveloper's roots go back to 1997, when Oracle licensed Java-based tools from Borland International to be integrated with Oracle's databases and applications tools for both Internet and traditional client/server platforms. At the time, Borland's JBuilder was a strong Java development tool. Purchasing the rights to the JBuilder source code allowed Oracle to jump-start its entry into the Java development environment. The initial JDeveloper 1.0 release (called "AppBuilder for Java") in 1998 was quite close to its JBuilder foundation. Later in 1998, it was renamed JDeveloper. This original similarity continued through the 2.0 release in 1999. In these early versions, you can see the tool's maturation in the Java environment. While only releasing cosmetic changes to the product, behind the scenes Oracle was working on elegantly solving the problem of Java programs connecting to relational database objects.

Past: Product History and Roots

While JDeveloper releases 1.0 and 2.0 were useful Java development products, they provided little support for building applications that would interact with an Oracle database. To be fair, this was the state of the art at that time. Hardy C++ and Java programmers routinely took up the task of writing code to access Oracle databases. Unfortunately, this coding required a great deal of effort, even on the part of a skilled programmer. Therefore, the early JDeveloper adopters were primarily Java developers who were looking for ways to create applications that would interact with Oracle databases. Oracle professionals who were used to products that interacted easily with the database and who built applications efficiently using tools such as Forms Developer did not rapidly adopt this new product.

Oracle's project strategy did not make the situation any easier. In addition to JDeveloper, Oracle has a number of products that enable developers to build applications and deploy them over the Web:

- **Oracle Forms Developer** (sometimes called "Web Forms") continued to mature. With the 9i release, the Web is now the only way to deploy Oracle forms. This tool is based on applet technology that has largely been abandoned by the broader development community for Internet applications due to issues related to firewalls and performance.

- **PL/SQL Web Toolkit** (mod_plsql) had its origins in the early releases of the Oracle Application Server, and Oracle Designer uses it to generate HTML client code. The PL/SQL Toolkit allows you to write PL/SQL in the database that can output HTML to a browser.

- **PL/SQL Server Pages (PSPs)** allow you to embed PL/SQL within HTML. PSPs leverage the concept of server pages in a similar way to JavaServer Pages.

- **Oracle Portal** was originally designed as a simple utility to allow ad hoc access to a database and was marketed as "WebDB." Portal has slowly evolved into a useful website development tool.

Why JDeveloper?

With all of these alternatives, why has Oracle seemingly decided to pursue JDeveloper as the primary development platform? The answer demonstrates long-range planning on Oracle's part. Oracle9i JDeveloper is built upon Java 2 Platform, Enterprise Edition. As such, JDeveloper sits on a stronger foundation than any other product in Oracle's history. All of Oracle's earlier products had to make compromises based upon existing technologies, accommodations to backward compatibility, and internal Oracle politics. JDeveloper is based upon a relatively new technology that has vast support from other vendors and the backing of recognized standards.

The evolution of JDeveloper from release 1.0 to 9i has devoted much more attention to the intellectual and architectural foundation of the product than to the UI components. Even now with the 9i release, portions of the product, still in their fledgling stages, point to the ultimate primary focus of creating a firm foundation for the long term.

Introducing Business Components for Java

This long-term design philosophy, although correct from an architectural perspective, frustrated traditional Oracle development community members, who were often impatient with the poor efficiency of building applications in JDeveloper. Not until the 3.0 release of JDeveloper did Oracle's direction for building Java applications to access an Oracle database become clearer through its introduction of BC4J. BC4J helped to automate most of the difficult work required to make Java code interact with relational database tables. BC4J is a framework to support Java interaction with a database. The BC4J wizards automatically generate the code necessary to allow Java applications to safely interact with the database, solving the security, locking, and performance problems that had hindered earlier efforts.

The generated code relies heavily on an Oracle-supplied Java library. Therefore, the actual amount of code generated by the BC4J wizards is small.

To enable developers to create Java applications with a user interface, Oracle supplied extensions to selected Swing components that attached directly to the BC4J-generated elements. While BC4J proved to be conceptually solid, and able to handle complex applications, the Data Aware Components (DACs) built on Sun's InfoBus architecture proved problematic. After the industry abandoned the InfoBus architecture, Oracle also abandoned all of the InfoBus technology in favor of JDeveloper version 9i's support for Sun's Model-View-Controller (MVC) architecture (implemented in JDeveloper as the client data model). A more detailed description of BC4J appears later in this chapter. Also, Part II of this book goes into detail about the use and structure of BC4J.

Present: Where Is JDeveloper Now?

Currently, JDeveloper includes the very stable Business Components for Java and has solved many of the v. 3.2 performance problems with the 9i release. The MVC architecture allows developers to build Java applications or JavaServer Pages to access an Oracle database with much more confidence.

Oracle9i JDeveloper provides a solid Java development environment. A web search for articles mentioning JDeveloper yields many positive reviews from the Java community. For writing Java to interact with an Oracle database, JDeveloper is a clear winner because of the BC4J layer.

Creating JSP Pages

A JSP file produces an HTML page that is sent to the client. It is compiled into a *servlet,* which is a pure Java program. Though most of the business logic can be written in Java, the UI portion is usually created in HTML.

As a web application development tool for the building of JSP pages, JDeveloper is not the complete solution for a traditional Oracle developer who is used to the simple "one product development environment" of Forms Developer. As of this writing, JDeveloper's support for the visual design of the HTML page is still quite limited compared with a tool such as Microsoft FrontPage. Support for code highlighting, code completion, structure display, and debugging is quite complete, as is the support for running and debugging JSP code inside JDeveloper.

Developers currently using Forms Developer and PL/SQL cannot simply replace those with JDeveloper and Java to create complex client/server–style applications deployed over the Web. Building fully featured web applications that allow customers to safely and efficiently interact with the database is a much more complex task. This is discussed more fully in Chapter 7.

Creating Java Applications

The situation for Java application development deployed in a client/server or intranet environment is quite different from that of deploying JSP pages, because JDeveloper provides complete support for Java applications, including visual editing and property setting in a Forms-like interface. You can build applications of the same or greater complexity and sophistication as was possible using products such as Forms Developer. However, you will not be able to build as quickly using JDeveloper as you can with Forms Developer. The JDeveloper wizards are not sufficiently mature for JDeveloper to compete effectively with Forms Developer as a RAD development tool.

While Forms Developer is a true 4GL, where properties of objects are stored in an internal repository, JDeveloper is actually a code generator and code organizer.

Although you interact with the JDeveloper wizards and IDE areas as in a 4GL environment, you are really generating Java code. Frequently, the application development process goes beyond the capabilities of the JDeveloper wizards, and manual intervention is required to modify property settings that the wizard assigns or to add code that the wizard does not generate.

Future: The Vision

In the 9i release, Oracle's grand vision for JDeveloper is visible, indicating a much broader scope than the earlier versions. The inclusion of limited use Unified Modeling Language (UML) diagrams, a full-featured software configuration management (SCM) repository, and some ability to generate Data Definition Language (DDL) point to Oracle's commitment to this product over the long term.

The ultimate goal is a single, integrated development environment for all Oracle systems. Design, creation, and maintenance of both database and applications will all be handled using one product. JDeveloper may eventually include the functionality of other products such as Oracle Designer and Oracle Forms Developer as well as third-party products such as Quest Software's TOAD or SQL Navigator. The realization of this vision is still a few years away. When Oracle brings this vision to fruition, Oracle professionals will have the integrated design and development environment they have dreamed of.

Short-Term and Long-Term View

What will the short- and long-term future hold for JDeveloper? In the short term, Oracle is justifiably satisfied with the core architecture of the product. Now they are working to improve the product's application development efficiency.

Future JDeveloper improvements may eventually deliver improved wizards to help automate many of the tasks currently required to develop applications and to help close the gap between JDeveloper and Forms Developer for intra-company application development.

A second short-term improvement will focus on JDeveloper as a modeling and design tool. The current Class Modeler reflects Oracle's interest in using UML to design databases. By the end of 2003, JDeveloper will be effectively competing with Designer as a data modeling tool. Other parts of the UML will also be incorporated into JDeveloper to support more of the software development lifecycle. Use cases (UML format for representing business requirements) will likely be included to help support the analysis process.

As mentioned earlier, the long-term move toward a "one-stop" development environment is clear. In a methodical and unhurried fashion, features will be added to JDeveloper to meet all of the changing design and development tasks associated with building Oracle systems.

Business Components for Java

JDeveloper's main advantage over other Java development tools is its Business Components for Java (BC4J) framework and associated code generators. BC4J is the heart of the JDeveloper product that sets it apart as the tool of choice for Oracle developers building Java or web-based applications. At its roots, BC4J is supported by a programming protocol or standard that describes how to build classes that will interact with a relational database.

JDeveloper uses BC4J as the primary way of handling database DML operations (queries, inserts, updates, and deletes). Before BC4J and similar products, connecting a Java-based application to the database was an extraordinarily difficult task. You needed to write complex Java Database Connectivity (JDBC) and/or SQL embedded in Java (SQLJ) code in order to coordinate your Java front-end with the database. In addition, you had to maintain your own data caching, batch your own updates, and keep track of table locks and commits. This complex interface with the database has proven to be one of the biggest hurdles to building web-based applications. Organizations that attempted application projects without a product such as JDeveloper were frequently over budget and found their applications difficult to maintain. The BC4J components in JDeveloper provide a functional interface to the database and can be constructed using the built-in code generators or wizards.

This chapter presents only an overview of the BC4J components. Part II of the book provides in-depth discussion of BC4J, and hands-on practices in that part and in other chapters demonstrate how BC4J components can be used in conjunction with Swing components, JavaServer Pages applications, and other JDeveloper-generated code.

Java and XML

BC4J components are built using a combination of Java and XML. Both XML and Java are open-source (nonproprietary) languages. Since both languages are operating-system and platform independent, they interface well with networks and operate effectively across the Web. Each of these languages has unique strengths that complement the other. Java is a modular and portable language that is ideal for communicating between business applications due to its built-in security and Internet capabilities. Yet Java lacks an effective way of exchanging data across different platforms and applications. This is where Extensible Markup Language (XML) becomes useful. *XML* is a tag or markup language that is similar to HTML; however, the XML tags are much more powerful because the basic tags can be extended to meet your evolving needs. In HTML, you use tags to describe how you want things displayed; while in XML, you create tags to describe the structure and content of the text or data. It should be noted that XML is case sensitive just like Java.

XML is used to define the data, and Java is used to operate on the data. You will find that the BC4J components will have both XML and Java files associated with them. The XML file holds the metadata that defines the business component, and the Java file holds the methods that implement the business component. The Java file contains get() and set() methods, which dynamically generate insert, update, and delete statements at runtime. Also, the XML and Java files can contain more than just database table references. They may define and implement validation rules as well.

BC4J Structure

BC4J is a well-constructed and carefully thought-out component of JDeveloper. Only the sophisticated JDeveloper user will be aware of any of the underlying structure since the BC4J wizards provide a simple mechanism for modifying the underlying Java classes and XML documents.

From the developer's perspective, you will only need to think in terms of logical BC4J objects. You manipulate the Java classes only where complex validation or coding capability beyond what the wizards can handle is required.

The BC4J components allow you to conceptually divide your application into two major parts, as shown in the following illustration:

■ User interface and client logic

■ Database interface and business logic

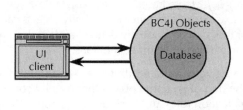

Using this object-oriented framework will help you create reusable business components that can effectively communicate between the database and your user interface (UI). The BC4J wizards read the Oracle system views to obtain metadata representing the database structure. Using this metadata, the wizards generate XML and Java code that provides a customizable framework to which you can add data validation or other business logic.

The BC4J components provide a number of benefits. First, simplicity and organization are easier to achieve using these components. The inclusion of a BC4J project in an application means you can optimize overall performance and reusability of code depending upon where you choose to deploy your BC4J components. Second, you can improve code maintainability by moving shared code such as data validation into the BC4J layer. Third, BC4J classes can be deployed on the database server, application server, or locally on the client. This portability can have a significant performance benefit for applications that are validation intensive.

BC4J enables Java applications to easily communicate with a relational database. By interacting with the BC4J wizards, you can generate XML files and Java classes. Application developers can then write Java code, which will interact with the BC4J-generated classes that handle communication with the database. These generated classes function because of an Oracle-supplied Java library containing all of the complex database interaction routines. Before BC4J, writing Java applications to communicate with a relational database was an extraordinarily complex task, beyond the skills of most developers. The few intrepid pioneers who tried to accomplish this on their own will be pleased at how easily they can now perform this task.

The BC4J Components

The BC4J components fit into three major groups: data definition and validation components, data manipulation and filtering components, and storage locations and containers.

For those readers familiar with data modeling, Figure 1-1 will be helpful in understanding the relationships and cardinality associated with each of the BC4J components. If you are not familiar with UML modeling, the figures can simply be viewed as block diagrams that illustrate the overall relationships in the BC4J layer. (Appendix C explains the symbols used in this type of UML diagram.) This information will help you visualize how these components relate to each other and how they are organized as a group.

Data Definition and Validation Components

The following are descriptions of the components used in data definition and validation:

- **Entity objects** *Entity objects* are based on database tables, views, snapshots, or synonyms and include the database storage requirements. Entity objects can be generated from existing database objects, or they can be manually defined and used to create new database tables. Entity objects contain attribute (column) definitions.

- **Attributes** There are two types of attributes: entity attributes and view attributes. An *entity attribute* is the part of an entity object that usually corresponds to a table column and may include validation rules and business logic. Some attributes, such as BLOB types, cannot be queried and should be identified by unchecking the *Queriable* checkbox in the

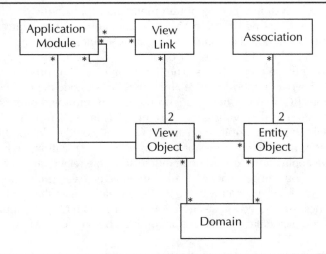

FIGURE 1-1. *Using BC4J components in a multi-tier framework*

Entity Object Wizard. A *view attribute* is simply one of the entity attributes. You can create additional view attributes for items such as calculated columns.

- **Association**   An *association* defines the relationship between a pair of entity objects. Typically, associations represent a foreign key constraint from the database, but they may be defined for any pair of entity object attribute components. You can also specify more than one attribute on each side of the association, as long as you have the same number of attributes on each side. The association is bidirectional.

- **Domain**   A *domain* is a user-defined type representing the type of values an attribute can have. For example, you could create a domain to ensure that you have entered nine digits for your Social Security number. When you write the validation logic for this component, you must put it in a method named `validate()` that is called in the constructor of the domain's Java file. Each time you instantiate a new object using this domain, the constructor will call the `validate()` method to ensure that the new attribute meets your defined criteria.

- **Property**   Within the context of a BC4J component, a *property* is a name/value pair of type String. Properties are used to store text strings. These text strings can be used to display information at runtime, for example, to define a user's access level, to specify what type of UI control to use, and to set a domain's format mask. You can define properties for domains, entity objects, view objects, entity attributes, view attributes, and application modules. The BC4J properties are stored in the associated component's XML file.

Data Manipulation or Filtering Components

View objects and view links provide the appropriate data to support your UI by filtering the data defined by the entity objects.

- **View objects**   View objects use SQL queries to specify and filter data that is defined in the entity objects. Client applications can navigate, update, insert, and delete data using the view object's `get()` and `set()` methods.

- **View links**   *View links* are used to express the relationships between view objects. These relationships are only implemented in one direction. Thus, in a master-detail relationship (the master being the source and the detail being the destination), only the source objects have get/set accessor methods defined. View links provide the filtered rows for the detail table, for the current row selected in the master table.

View links link view objects in the same way that associations link entity objects. However, there is no programmatic connection between view links and associations. Associations can be used to generate view links, or view links can be created independently of the associations.

Storage Locations and Containers

There are two types of locations/containers for placing elements in the BC4J layer:

- **Packages**   Java classes are grouped by categories in *packages*. During development, these packages are equivalent to the subdirectories or folders on the hard disk where your source code is stored.

■ **Application modules** The *application module* defines the BC4J view objects and view links with which the client applications will interact. It is possible to have multiple application modules within the same BC4J layer. It is also possible to nest application modules within other application modules.

You may want to use multiple application modules to implement the business logic for a particular application screen or task, giving each logical part its own module. Typically, an application module would contain three to four view objects and links, though it might contain many more. A large application could have 20 or more application modules, each containing the appropriate view objects and view links for a given task.

Logical Architecture of BC4J

Logically, the objects built with BC4J fall into two categories: database-interface objects and application-side objects. On the database side, BC4J includes entity objects and associations. The application-side objects include view objects, view links, and application modules.

Entity Objects and Associations

Entity objects and associations correspond more or less to tables and foreign key constraints. However, an entity object is not necessarily structured the same way as a table. As a novice interacting with BC4J, you will create a default entity object that is merely an image of a table. Default associations will be generated from the foreign key constraints in the database so that you end up with an exact image of your database in the BC4J layer.

However, entity objects need not be structured like their underlying database tables. They can differ in a number of ways:

■ **You can define an entity object that does not represent all columns in a table.**
If developers never need to interact with columns such as CREATED_DATE, CREATED_BY, MODIFIED_DATE, and MODIFIED_BY, there is no reason to clutter the application with these columns. Also, if you have very wide (many column) tables in your database, including all of the columns in the BC4J layer will make the entity objects difficult to work with.

■ **You can have columns in the entity objects that are not in the database.** Examples include a TOTAL column on a purchase order detail showing Quantity multiplied by Price, or a display function associated with the table such as a display name in the EMP table that concatenates the first and last names for display purposes. This enables developers to merely access the attribute when they want to display a particular employee record rather than each developer having to decide which columns to use when displaying the record.

■ **You can define entity attributes that update different columns in the database.** This can be as simple as renaming an existing column, which can be used to either clarify/obfuscate the database or can be used to simplify the development environment. For example, BC4J entity attributes such as "Birthday" and "Age" can be used together to populate the "Date of Birth" column in the physical database.

- **You can perform additional validation in the entity object.** You can do this by copying business logic from the relational database into the BC4J layer to support check constraints or trigger-based validation. You could even place additional validation in the BC4J layer. However, use caution. If any rule validation exists in the entity object and not in the database, any applications that bypass the BC4J layer will also bypass any validation contained there.

- **You can define entity objects that behave in a way similar to views with INSTEAD OF triggers.** You can bypass the standard INSERT, UPDATE, and DELETE logic and execute whatever code you desire instead. However, the same caution applies to this type of BC4J view object: applications that directly access the tables will bypass the trigger code on the database view.

- **An entity object need not be associated with any table.** The entity object may be a completely artificial construct, which, from the developer's standpoint, looks just like a table, but may be interacting with an alternative data source, flat file, or Java code that is entirely local to the application.

Just as entity objects are typically generated from relational database tables, associations are typically generated from foreign key constraints. However, associations in BC4J can differ from referential integrity constraints in the database. You can change the cardinality of the association from what is in the database, keeping in mind that, even if the BC4J layer allows in data, the BC4J rules can never weaken the rules of the underlying database. You can only strengthen the rules. You can also build BC4J associations that have no underlying foreign key constraints in the database.

The Layer of Abstraction
Entity objects and associations are the developer's view of the physical database. As mentioned earlier, this perception may not be identical to the actual physical database. Thus, entity objects are a layer of abstraction between the developer and the database.

This layer has some minor limitations. An entity object can never directly point to more than one table or view. This is not to say that entity objects cannot be made to interact with multiple tables or views in the database. This can actually be accomplished in two different ways, as mentioned earlier:

- You can override the default INSERT, UPDATE, and DELETE behavior of an entity object and have it do something more complex.

- You can use database views with INSTEAD OF triggers. This strategy permits complex views that can query any number of tables, and use INSTEAD OF insert, update, and delete triggers to implement any desired behavior.

With entity objects and associations, Oracle has effectively duplicated the capability present in database views with INSTEAD OF triggers. You risk placing your code where it can possibly be bypassed rather than in the database where it is possible to reuse it with different platforms or tools without rewriting the code. Also, as a designer, if you choose to use BC4J as a place for your business logic, you are committing yourself to the product architecture. Why, then, would anyone want to make an entity object anything other than an exact image of the underlying table or view? The reasons for this follow:

- **Performance improvements** You can choose to place validation in the BC4J layer to achieve performance improvements. In some applications, it may be possible to achieve dramatic improvements because code is applied at the business logic level instead of at the database level, which requires network messaging.

- **Support for overloaded tables** You can have multiple entity objects pointing to the same table. This can be useful for developers trying to support abstract data models containing overloaded tables. For example, in the classic single table implementation of an Employee supertype with Salaried and Hourly subtypes, you have a single Employee table with a Type column. Both hourly and salaried employees are stored in the same table. In BC4J, you can create independent entity objects for salaried and hourly employees with attributes pointing to the appropriate columns in each. However, the same functionality can be achieved just as easily with views in the database.

The entity object layer provides yet another layer of abstraction on top of the database. However, this is not what the applications interact with directly. Another layer of abstraction, namely view objects and view links, exists on top of the entity objects and associations.

View Objects and View Links

View objects and view links may correspond to entity objects and associations, respectively. However, much more can be done with view objects.

When you run the BC4J wizards and accept the default settings, there is a one-to-one correspondence between view objects and entity objects and view links and associations. However, just as entity objects and associations do not have to be exactly the same as tables and foreign key constraints, view objects and view links do not need to correspond exactly to entity objects and associations. In fact, view objects are even less tightly linked to entity objects than entity objects are to tables.

The main characteristic of view objects is that they are exactly the data needed to support the application. A view object is simply a query used to access the relational tables. The relationship between a view object and a entity object can be many-to-many. View links are relationships between view objects.

You can also use the structure of the view object to interact directly with the tables or with any other data structures without using an entity object. As long as the code behaves appropriately, it is not necessary for the view objects to interact with any outside data containers.

All of the flexibility of entity objects also applies to view objects. You can have display attributes, calculation attributes, and so on. You can also place validation logic in view objects; however, validation logic should usually be placed in the database and/or entity objects because those locations are more centralized. You might want to have validation logic in the view objects to enforce an application-specific validation rule.

Application Modules

View objects and view links are used in collections called *application modules*. To support a master-detail application, the master-detail view link must be set up before creating the application module. The application module also contains a definition of the database connection that will be used for data access.

Using BC4J

When you create application-specific BC4J, you are building a set of Java classes that wrap the DML commands and that reference an XML document that stores the data structure definition. These Java classes extend the base BC4J library classes that make the JDBC calls to the database that take over all of the insert, update, delete, and lock functions required to make the applications run. This enables you to completely encapsulate the logic associated with database access. It also provides developers an ease of application development similar to that of basing blocks on tables in Oracle Forms Developer.

However, BC4J does more than this. Frequently, complex validation is placed in database locations such as triggers on tables or views with INSTEAD OF triggers. *INSTEAD OF trigger views* are Oracle views that replace the default insert, update, and delete behavior with user-supplied triggers.

Complex data validation can also be implemented within BC4J classes. Despite this additional option, it is still difficult to set guidelines for what circumstances lead you to place data validation logic in the database as opposed to placing it in the BC4J components. In an environment that is not 100 percent Java, placing validation in BC4J components may be dangerous. Some applications will access the validation through BC4J, while other applications written in different products may be unable to access the validation logic through BC4J. If you are working in a completely Java-based environment, JDeveloper makes the creation and manipulation of BC4J components easy enough that you may choose to use BC4J over server-side validation because reduced development time means lower costs. However, this is only appropriate if you can guarantee that all data-modifying DML operations will use the BC4J components.

BC4J classes can also cache data to be shared among multiple users, providing performance benefits since no access to the database is required.

Approaches for Using BC4J

With Oracle9i JDeveloper and J2EE, you can now build an application in many ways. System business rules may now reside in any of the following places:

- Core database procedures and triggers
- Database views with INSTEAD OF triggers
- BC4J entity objects and associations
- BC4J view objects and view links
- Application logic

There are several schools of thought about how to use BC4J in your applications. Business rules should not be placed in application logic or view objects. They are only listed here because it is possible to place the logic in those locations.

Some assert that all business logic should reside in the database, with subsets used as needed for applications. Others say that virtually all business logic should be stored in the BC4J layer, with the database used as nothing more than a place to hold persistent copies of the data in the classes. The proponents of each strategy adhere to their development style with great tenacity.

This section discusses the pros and cons of these two approaches. Keep in mind that these approaches depend on JDeveloper's ability to support them. As JDeveloper's capabilities expand and evolve, the advantages and disadvantages may shift, and approaches that are barely workable now may become much more viable in future releases.

Database-Centric Approach

The database-centric approach assumes that you are starting with a complete, functioning Oracle database. As you are logically designing applications, it will be evident that they can be built more easily with database views corresponding to the user interface elements. You should build these views using INSTEAD OF triggers to support insert, update, and delete functionality.

All fields to be displayed in the view objects are columns of the database views. For each program, you build a small BC4J project including entity objects and associations that have a one-to-one relationship with the tables, views, and foreign key references necessary to build that program. Next, you create a default view object and view link for each entity object and association. These are then assembled into an application module to support the front-end program. Validation logic is added to the entity objects only for the purpose of enhancing performance, since all business logic is already validated within the database. Only rarely are additional attributes added to entity objects or view objects since these attributes are already included in the foundation views located in the database.

Each program has its own BC4J project. BC4J projects are not shared by other programs. Application modules are kept relatively small, encompassing more or less the same scope as an Oracle Forms Developer file.

Advantages of a Database-Centric Approach   Using a database-centric approach to creating applications has the following advantages:

- **This approach is the most comfortable for existing Oracle developers.** It uses basically the same philosophy as creating any front-end application for an Oracle database.

- **The system is not closely tied to a single product (BC4J).** Most of the non-UI code resides in the database. For example, programs that do not access the BC4J layer will still use the code in the database, because all of the business rules reside in the database.

- **Almost all BC4J work can be supported through the JDeveloper wizards.** Little hand-coding is required. The BC4J project for an application module can be built in a few hours or less because you are only using one default entity object definition for each database view.

Disadvantages of a Database-Centric Approach   The following are some of the disadvantages of creating applications using a database-centric approach:

- **This approach ignores all of the power and flexibility of BC4J.** With entity objects and view objects, two new layers of abstraction are sitting on top of the database that are not used by this development strategy.

- **This approach does not support BC4J reuse.** One of the key elements of the BC4J architecture is the ability to build and reuse BC4J projects.

■ **You do not take full advantage of the BC4J cache.** This is one of the main strengths of BC4J, because it offloads database activity to another location and thus saves the CPU cycles of the database server to fulfill its primary purpose—to manage data. The BC4J layer can cache rows and maintain consistency with the database. This reduces the number of network messages and the amount of database activity required to serve data that has already been served.

■ **You do not take advantage of BC4J's support of Web Tier and Business Tier servers.** BC4J supports the J2EE notion that there is a benefit in splitting out some of the application code to another server. If the database is called upon to handle application code, its efficiency to fulfill the primary directive will be compromised by having to handle complex business logic.

■ **Your application is heavily tied to the Oracle DBMS idea of views with INSTEAD OF triggers.** You cannot use this approach to build cross-database applications unless the other database provides a structure similar to views with INSTEAD OF triggers.

■ **You need talented PL/SQL developers.** If your organization is primarily a Java shop, this approach makes little sense.

Business-Logic Tier Approach

The business-logic tier approach also assumes that you are starting with a complete, functioning Oracle database. The main difference with this approach is that the business logic is contained in Java class files that reside outside of the database. Carried to extremes, this approach would mean creating only one BC4J package, containing entity objects and associations, to support an entire enterprise data model. One entity object is created for each table in the database. Separate projects containing view objects, view links, and application modules can then be built to correspond to the structures that the program requires. A BC4J application module is then built for each program. Business rules are added to the entity objects, possibly backed up by redundant rules in the database for added robustness.

In the case of a large enterprise data model, it can make sense to partition the entity objects and associations created from the database into smaller subsets, to make handling them at design time easier. For example, the 300 entity objects corresponding to a 300-table system could be partitioned into approximately 10 application modules of 30 tables each. Sets of tables with many relationships between them should be placed in a single package together with associations representing those relationships. Cross-package relationships should be represented by associations in the same package as the view objects, view links, and application modules that use them. One entity project will then be shared.

As mentioned earlier, view objects are not simply default images of the entity objects, but often gather information from multiple entity objects simultaneously. In fact, view objects need not be based on entity objects at all, but can instead cache database data directly themselves. For more information, see Chapter 13.

One entity object and association will then be shared by many (5–20) different packages containing extra associations, view objects, view links, and application modules. Simple programs usually have one application module for each program, but it is not uncommon for a program to have more than one application module, or for two programs that accomplish similar tasks to use the same application module.

Using this approach, validation resides in the BC4J layer, and possibly redundantly in the database.

Advantages of the Business-Logic Tier Approach   The following advantages can be gained using this approach:

- **BC4J caching, project reuse, and independence** from the database are useful aspects of this approach.

- **This approach, if used correctly, will afford the greatest development efficiencies** because of the improved modularity of the persistence/business logic layer.

- **You take advantage of BC4J's ability to offload activity from the database server** as mentioned in the disadvantages of the previous approach.

Disadvantages of the Business-Logic Tier Approach   The following are some of the disadvantages of this approach:

- **It is a conceptually difficult approach because business rules of the system may reside in different places.** For example, the rules may reside in tables, entity objects, or view objects. Standards and guidelines for the use of the different code locations must be developed and enforced.

- **Organizations embracing this strategy should be careful to formalize the rules.** The rules apply to the database, entity objects, and view objects. They need to answer questions such as, "How will objects be constructed and how will they interact?"

- **Without careful planning, the additional flexibility afforded by BC4J can result in systems where bugs are difficult to track down.** This is because the logic error may reside in many places. Well-designed error messages can assist in reducing this problem.

Building Applications Using BC4J

You can quickly build an entire application by connecting your user interface to BC4J objects. In the past, the client and database were required to communicate many times to complete even the simplest transaction. However, with today's web and wide area networks, this style of high-volume system traffic is not practical.

The BC4J components solve this problem by providing alternative locations for the traditional client/server logic, resulting in shorter data paths to your business rules and data validation code. Using a BC4J layer is like having a virtual database (tables, columns, synonyms, and metadata) adjacent to the client application. You can think of BC4J as simply a black box database. It can interact with one or more clients to synchronize data, manage the cache, and implement the basic functionality of your data model.

Once you investigate the extensibility of the BC4J components, you will realize that they can provide more functionality than just acting as a virtual repository. BC4J provides an extensible framework that can take you far beyond the traditional relational database constructs by including elements such as complex business rules. For example, you can implement logical "OR" constraints without the need for BEFORE INSERT triggers. By including a bit of extra code and leveraging the deployment options, you can optimize the overall performance of a system.

Virtually every application will need some modification to the basic BC4J components. Thus, it is very important to understand how the BC4J components are designed and interfaced.

Creating Application Code in JDeveloper

JDeveloper is an application development tool that can support your first steps in the Java world. It can act as a blank sheet of paper for the sophisticated do-it-yourselfer, or as a code generator for those who prefer developing applications by using 4GL techniques such as drag and drop. JDeveloper can also automatically generate basic database interface code, allowing you to customize the results to your heart's content.

Coming to an understanding of Java and JDeveloper is like trying to learn English and a computer word processing program at the same time. You should have some experience with other computer languages and application conventions before you leap into this type of effort. It is a good idea to actually build the items and structures in the hands-on practices presented in this book as you read the chapters. In this way, you can quickly get a feel for the development environment by trying out real code.

The first major difference between the traditional environments and the JDeveloper environment is that in some development environments, the user interface and its interaction with the database are inseparable. In JDeveloper, you create files in logical containers called *projects*. Each program will usually consist of two types of JDeveloper projects:

- **Business Components for Java** built and written using Java and XML to provide the database interaction components

- **User interface components and logic** built and written mainly using Java and Java-related languages

JDeveloper is optimized to assist you in producing a multi-tier architecture for your database applications. The power behind JDeveloper to produce a multi-tier application is centered on BC4J. A multi-tier architecture encourages the logical separation of the following elements:

- **Client tier**   The client tier supports the data access requirements of the end user. Complex GUIs can be supported using application code over the Internet, browser-scripting capabilities, and/or by installing application code on the client's desktop and running it outside of the browser.

- **Application tier**   The application tier is where the business logic is generally enforced and data access is coordinated. Application servers contain business logic that can be reused across a wide variety of clients and applications, thus making it possible to share physical and logical resources across multi-tier architectures. The application tier can also contain specialized reporting and analysis tools to handle complex business intelligence requirements. In addition, the application tier (which contains the Web Tier and Business Tier of the J2EE architecture) can serve HTML user interface code that displays in a browser.

■ **Database tier** The database tier is where the data is stored and queried. This layer may also contain links to other external data sources and applications, which may be members of the overall architecture.

The following sections describe the way in which JDeveloper structures and organizes the code needed to support your applications.

Workspaces

A *workspace* is the highest-level container within JDeveloper. All code other than connections must be contained in a workspace. A single workspace corresponds more or less in size and scope to a .fmb file in Forms Developer. Each workspace is implemented with a single file that has a .jws extension. This is an XML file that contains the names of the project files that comprise it. A workspace file contains pointers to the project files that it organizes.

Projects

A *project* is the next level of container in JDeveloper that contains code files. You can think of a project as a major portion of an application. Typically, an application is partitioned across two projects: one for the BC4J components and one for the UI components. One project can reside in the same or different workspaces. A project represents a number of code files that are deployed together. It is implemented in a single file that has a .jpr extension. This is an XML file that contains the names of the code files that comprise it.

JDeveloper Directory Structure

Applications built using JDeveloper will be partitioned across multiple directories. Typically, the workspace is stored in one directory and the projects within that workspace are stored in subdirectories underneath the workspace directory.

Within each project directory, JDeveloper generates two additional directories for Java source code and compiled code. The source code is contained in the folder labeled "src," and compiled code is contained in the "classes" folder. Within each of these directories, additional subdirectories correspond to any defined packages, as shown here:

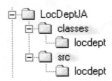

Within a BC4J project's package directory, an additional folder called "common" stores the generated BC4J configuration files.

The JSP project directory shown next resides in the JDEV_HOME\jdev\mywork\LocDeptWS directory and has a different structure because the directories correspond to J2EE standards. In addition to the classes and src subdirectories, the source code is stored in the public_html subdirectory. The WEB-INF folder stores the XML files, while its lib subdirectory stores the executable jar file. This directory structure is further described in Chapter 21.

File Management in JDeveloper

Once you have created workspaces and projects, you may change your mind about the names of the files. You can rename a workspace or project file by selecting it in the Navigator and selecting **File | Rename**. This will not rename the directory for the workspace or project files. To rename the directory, select the workspace or project and click the "Remove from" button in the Navigator toolbar. Than rename the directory using the operating system utilities and add the workspace back to the IDE.

You can use the same renaming technique for code files, but be careful about references. If other files use or reference the file you are renaming, those files may no longer work after renaming. You can select the file and select **Tools | Refactor** to cascade a renaming operation through all dependent files. This is useful if you rename a Java class that you have subclassed, because all the child classes contain an "extends" clause with the name of the class that you renamed. Refactoring will change those references.

High-Level and Low-Level Wizards

JDeveloper includes many different wizards. Some of them build substantial portions of an application. Others build a single component such as a class, entity object, or even a single UI component field. In some chapters of this book, wizards that are broader in scope and that build multiple components forming a significant portion of a project (such as a BC4J project containing many objects) are referred to as *high-level wizards*. The book uses the term *low-level wizards* to represent the wizards that only build single components such as an entity object.

In learning JDeveloper's basic architecture, use the high-level wizards to help you build working applications quickly. However, for real production applications, the high-level wizards frequently do not build applications as desired. You will either need to use the low-level wizards and dialogs to set more specific preferences and functionality, or modify the code that the high-level wizards create.

Development Steps

The general steps you go through to create application code in JDeveloper follow:

1. Create a workspace.

2. Create a BC4J project if the application will connect to the database.

3. Define and test the BC4J objects.

4. Create an application user interface project.

5. Add code for forms and other user interface objects. This code uses objects in the BC4J project.

6. Test the user interface code with the BC4J project.

7. Deploy the BC4J project and the user interface project.

The practices throughout the book provide specifics about each of these steps and give you experience in creating different styles of application code.

Hands-on Practice: Build Applications Using the JDeveloper Wizards

JDeveloper is a 3GL environment. All actions involve generating or writing code. As a result, JDeveloper workspaces and projects can contain an arbitrarily determined group of items.

This practice shows you how to use the wizards to create a BC4J project and two user interface projects: a client/server–style Java application project and a JSP project that can be deployed over the Internet. Detailed information about BC4J may be found in Part II of this book. Part III contains detailed information about Java applications, and Part IV provides more detailed information involving JSP pages. This practice also provides an introduction to working with JDeveloper and gives you a basic understanding of its primary components. Although this practice introduces the main application development features of JDeveloper, Chapter 2 provides details about those and other features.

Since the focus in this chapter is to familiarize you with the BC4J architecture, you will only use the high-level wizards in this hands-on practice. Normally, you would modify the code created by the high-level wizards or just use the low-level wizards to create the code. In Chapter 3, similar BC4J objects and user interface applications will be built using the low-level wizards to give you a feel for building actual production applications with JDeveloper.

The two applications created in this practice could be placed in any number of workspaces with any number of projects. This decision of partitioning into projects and workspaces is similar to the one made about placing PL/SQL programming units in single or multiple packages. You must decide what and how much to place in each structure. For this practice, one workspace will be created to hold all projects. Three separate projects will be used: one for the BC4J components, a second for the Java application, and a third for the JSP UI. Each project represents a number of files that will be deployed as a unit.

This practice consists of the following phases:

    I. Create the workspace and database connection

       ■ Prepare a new workspace

       ■ Create a connection

    II. Create a BC4J project

       ■ Create the project

       ■ Test the BC4J code

    III. Create a Java application

       ■ Create the project

- Create the client data model
- Create the JClient form

IV. Create a JSP project

I. Create the Workspace and Database Connection

After you open the JDeveloper executable file (jdevw.exe), your screen will look like Figure 1-2. The main window has several areas:

- **The System Navigator** (or Navigator) displays all of the workspace folders and project file nodes. By expanding all of the nodes, you can view the contents of your projects. The Navigator also includes the Connections node discussed later in this practice.

- **The Structure window** is used to display the contents of the object selected in the System Navigator.

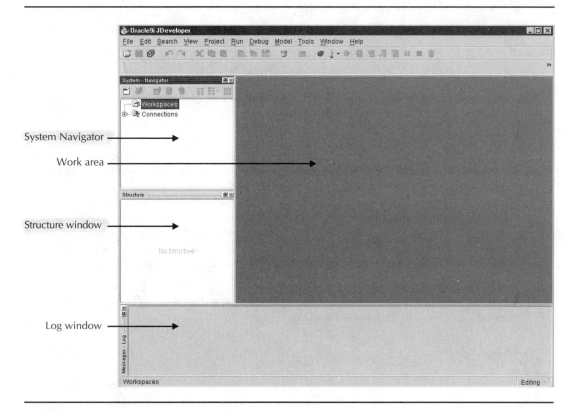

FIGURE 1-2.   *JDeveloper screen layout*

- **The Log window** (titled "Messages – Log") is used to display runtime messages including errors and system processing messages.

- **The work area** is usually used to display the editors, viewers, and the Property Inspector.

Prepare a New Workspace

By default, JDeveloper places all workspaces within the JDEV_HOME\jdev\mywork subdirectories structure. (As mentioned in the Introduction, this book refers to the directory in which you have installed JDeveloper as "JDEV_HOME.") Use the following steps to create the workspace:

1. On the Workspaces node, select New Workspace from the right-click menu.

2. In the Workspace dialog, change the last part of the directory name (which defaults to something like "Workspace1") to "LocDeptWS."

NOTE
Practices in this book instruct you to fill in workspace or project directory names. The directory name replaces only the default name in the directory path, not the entire directory path. For example, a default project directory will appear in the New Project dialog with a name such as "C:\JDev9i\jdev\mywork\LocDeptWS\Project1." When the practice instructs you to change this to "LocDeptBC4J," it is referring to the final part of that string ("Project1"). You will then end up with the directory name "C:\JDev9i\jdev\mywork\LocDeptWS\LocDeptBC4J."

3. Change the *File Name* to "LocDeptWS."

   Additional Information: JDeveloper automatically fills in the appropriate file extension (in this case, ".jws"). It is a good practice to specify both a directory and file name for your workspace. When writing a Java program, you will usually be creating a large number of files. Unlike Forms Developer, where your entire application is stored in a single .fmb file, JDeveloper applications will involve many different files. Therefore, for ease of maintenance of the many files in the workspace, the authors recommend storing each workspace in its own directory. It is good practice to use the same name for both the directory and file of the workspace. See Chapter 5 for more details about naming conventions.

4. Uncheck the *Add a New Empty Project* checkbox. The dialog should look like the following. Click OK to dismiss the dialog:

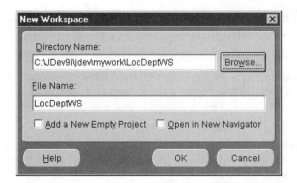

Additional Information: You will notice that the LocDeptWS workspace has been added to the System Navigator. The name of the workspace appears in italics, which indicates that the file has not yet been saved. Clicking the Save All icon in the toolbar will remove the italics, indicating that all new or modified files have been saved.

Create a Connection

If you expand the Connections node in the Navigator, note that there are different types of connections such as Application Server, Database, and SOAP Server. More information about these connection types can be found in Chapter 2. For the purposes of this hands-on practice, you will create a database connection to the HR schema.

The HR schema is one of the demonstration schemas supplied with JDeveloper. Details about setting up the HR database to work with the hands-on practices in this book can be found in the Introduction to this book.

1. On the Database node, select New Connection from the right-click menu to access the Connection Wizard. Click Next if the Welcome page appears.

NOTE
The Welcome page appears by default in many wizards. This page explains the purpose of the wizard and is useful to read when you are learning the product. You can turn off the Welcome page for a particular wizard by unchecking the "Show this page next time" checkbox on the Welcome page.

2. On the Type page, name your connection. Since this practice will use the HR schema supplied with JDeveloper, enter "HR" in the *Connection Name* field. Leave the *Connection Type* as the default, "Oracle (JDBC)." Click Next.

3. On the Authentication page, type "HR" in both the *User Name* and *Password* fields. Leave the *Role* field blank.

4. Check the *Deploy Password* checkbox. Click Next.

Additional Information: When checked, the *Deploy Password* checkbox ensures that the password is included in the IDEconnections.xml file. If you do not check this checkbox, you will need to enter a valid user name and password each time the connection to the database is attempted.

5. On the Connection page, you will need to explicitly set the *Host Name, JDBC Port,* and *SID.* Contact your network administrator or DBA if you are unsure of the appropriate settings. Click Next.

6. Click the Test button on the Test Page to check your connection definition. If the settings were correct, you will see a "Success" message in the status field. If you receive an error message, check the settings on the previous pages by clicking the Back button to return to those pages.

Additional Information: A successful test does not necessarily mean that the database will allow you to correctly build your application. The connection will be successful even if you have no privileges to any table in the system. This test only verifies that you can connect to the specified account.

7. Click Finish. Check that the new connection is listed under the Connections\Database node in the Navigator. The connection has been saved at this point. You do not need to explicitly save it.

Additional Information: Explore the HR node. Examine the various objects to see what is contained in the Oracle-supplied HR schema. You also have the ability to drop existing objects or to create new PL/SQL program units and database users. JDeveloper includes a simple and convenient utility, the SQL Worksheet described in Chapter 2, which may save you from having to use another tool to work with database structures.

What Just Happened? You created a workspace and database connection in preparation for building your JDeveloper application projects. The New Workspace dialog and Connection Wizard are typical of many of the other dialogs and wizards you will encounter in JDeveloper.

Notice how the connection and workspace are completely independent at this point. The workspace is a logical container for building your application and specifies the primary directory where that application will reside. The database connection created a text string entry in the IDEConnections.xml file that can be called where appropriate. Therefore, any workspace can use the connection that you just created.

II. Create a BC4J Project

In this phase, you will build the BC4J layer to support both the Java application and JSP projects. Although the HR schema has numerous tables, you will only be defining BC4J objects for the tables necessary to make the practice applications run. This represents just one style of application development. As previously mentioned, some developers build the entity objects to support a large portion, if not all, of the database and then build separate view objects and application modules for each project. For additional information about BC4J, see Part II of this book.

Create the Project

Use the following steps to create the BC4J project:

1. On the LocDeptWS.jws node, select New Project from the right-click menu.

2. The General category node of the New gallery will be expanded, and Projects will already be selected. Select Project Containing New Business Components from the Items area as shown here. Click OK to start the Business Components Project Wizard.

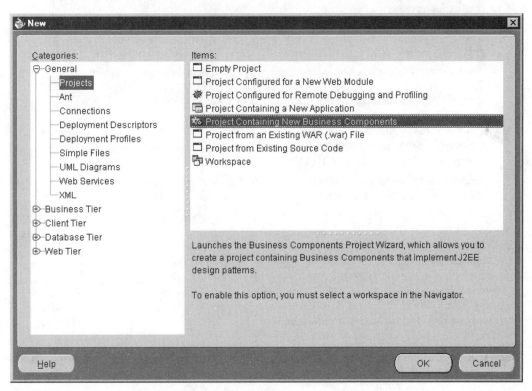

3. Click Next if the Welcome page appears. On the Location page, enter "LocDeptBC4J" as both the *Directory Name* and *File Name* as shown here. The wizard will fill in the file extension of ".jpr" automatically. Click Next.

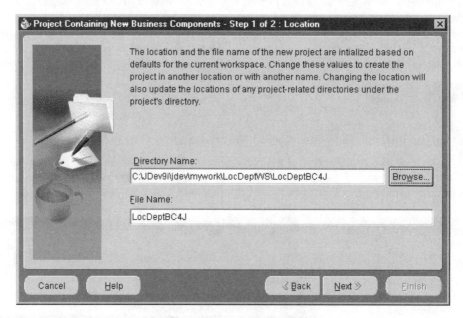

4. On the Paths page, enter "locdept" in the *Default Package* field. Leave the default settings for *Java Source Path* and *Output Directory*. Leave the *Scan source paths to determine project contents* checkbox unchecked. Click Next and Finish.

Additional Information: When you create a project with business components, the Business Components Package Wizard will automatically open after the project is created.

NOTE
A "package" is a logical container for a number of class files. It is represented in the file system by a single directory. Java code references this package name in the class file and in fully qualified names for a method. Chapters 4 and 5 contain more information about packages and how they are named.

5. Click Next if the Welcome page appears. On the Package Name page, "locdept" should already be filled in the *Package Name* field. Leave the default radio group selection "Entity Objects." Click Next.

6. On the Connection page, if HR is not displayed as the *Connection Name,* use the pulldown list to select it. Leave the other settings as is and click Next.

7. On the Business Components page, hold down the CTRL key and select DEPARTMENTS and LOCATIONS from the Available pane. Click the right arrow to move them to the Selected pane as shown here:

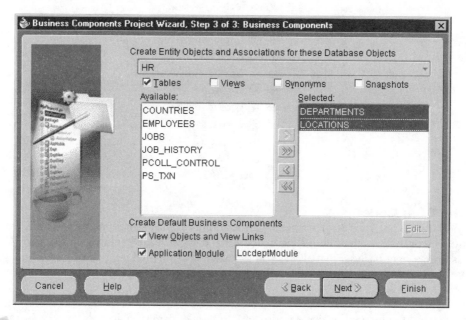

8. Click Next to display the Summary page. Examine it to verify your selections and click Finish.

9. Click Save All.

NOTE
*This book abbreviates the file save process by instructing you to click the Save All icon in the JDeveloper toolbar. You can also select **File |***
Save All.

If you expand the LocDeptBC4J project and locdept package nodes, the Navigator should look like this:

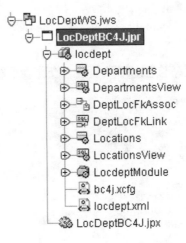

Test the BC4J Code

It is a good idea to test your BC4J project at various points to make sure that everything is working properly. The problem is that there is no user interface for BC4J. JDeveloper includes the Oracle Business Component Browser that allows you to test your BC4J application module without having to create a user interface on top of it. Use the following steps to run the Business Component Browser:

1. Expand the locdept package node, and on the LocdeptModule node, select Test from the right-click menu.

2. When the Connect dialog appears, make sure that "HR" appears in the *Connection Name* pulldown. Click Connect. The Oracle Business Component Browser will open.

3. Select DeptLocFkLink1 and select Show from the right-click menu. Scroll through the departments. You should see something like Figure 1-3.

4. Close the tester by selecting **File | Exit**.

What Just Happened?   In this phase, you made a few simple selections and allowed the JDeveloper wizards to create a BC4J project including information from the DEPARTMENTS and LOCATIONS tables of the HR schema.

Using the default wizards, you created entity objects that are exact images of the underlying DEPARTMENTS and LOCATIONS tables of the HR schema. Because there was a foreign key constraint on the DEPARTMENTS table pointing back to the LOCATIONS table, the wizard generated a BC4J association between the corresponding Departments and Locations entity objects. All of the columns in these tables became entity attributes.

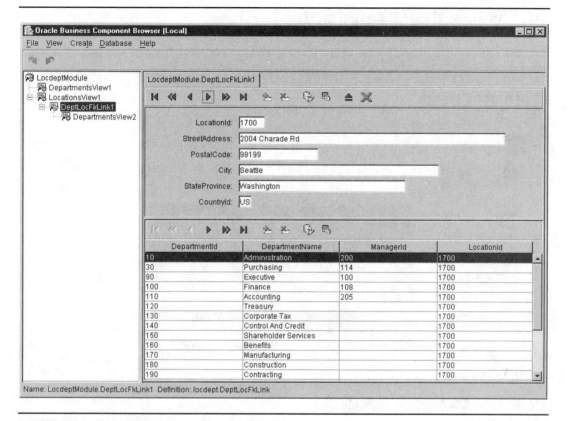

FIGURE 1-3. *Testing the BC4J application module*

In most cases, the BC4J wizards will map tables to entity objects, columns to attributes, and foreign key constraints to associations. The wizards then generate default view objects for the entity objects and view links for the associations. Finally, JDeveloper generates an application module with view object usages called LocationsView1 and DepartmentsView1 for the LocationsView and DepartmentsView view objects and an additional view object usage called DepartmentsView2, which is a filtered view only showing the departments associated with the current LocationsView record. The application module also contains a reference to the DeptLocFkLink view link that joins the LocationsView to the DepartmentsView.

> **NOTE**
> *DepartmentsView1 is not an additional Departments view object. It only exists as a "usage"—a structural component of the application module. It can be viewed in the Structure window by selecting the application module node in the Navigator.*

III. Create a Java Application

In this phase, you will create an application project and link it to the BC4J project created earlier. You will also create a data form that interacts with the database through the BC4J objects. For more information about Java applications, see Part III of this book.

Create the Project

Use the following steps to create a simple application project using the high-level wizards:

1. On the LocDeptWS workspace node, select New Empty Project from the right-click menu.

2. In the New Project dialog, type "LocDeptJA" for both the directory and file names as shown here:

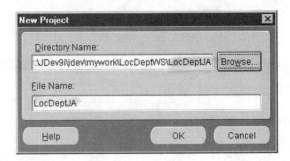

3. Click OK. Click Save All.

Create the Client Data Model

For the user interface project to have access to the BC4J objects, you create a client data model (.cpx file) at design time using the BC4J Client Data Model Definition Wizard. You must already have a BC4J project in the same workspace before you can complete this wizard. The client data model binds the BC4J application module to the user interface project. Data binding in JDeveloper allows you to partition the client application so that different user interface styles can use the same data layer.

1. Select the LocDeptJA.jpr node and select New from the right-click menu.

2. Expand the Client Tier node under Categories, and select Swing /JClient for BC4J. Select Business Components Client Data Model under Items, as shown here, to start the BC4J Client Data Model Definition Wizard:

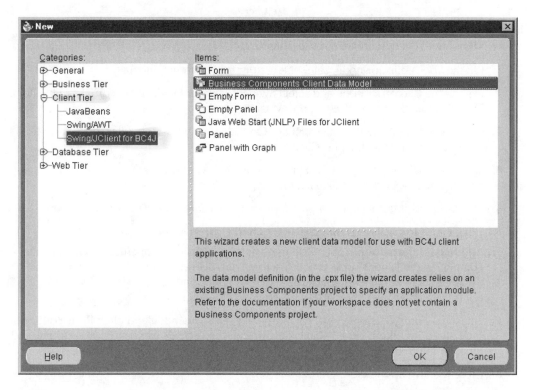

3. Click Next if the Welcome page appears. On the Application Module page of the BC4J Client Data Model Definition Wizard, ensure that the LocDeptBC4J project is showing in the *Business Components Project* field. Accept the other default settings and click Next.

4. On the Definition Name page, LocdeptModule should already be entered in the *Application Module* field. Change that to "LocDeptModel." Click Next and Finish. The LocDeptJA.cpx file containing the definition will appear under the project node in the Navigator.

5. Click Save All.

NOTE
You can also start the BC4J Client Data Model Definition Wizard from the New button on the Data Definition page of wizards that require the client data model. This means that you do not need to create the client data model before you start wizards that require it.

Create the JClient Form

The next steps are needed to create the user interface:

1. On the LocDeptJA.jpr node, select New from the right-click menu.

2. Expand the Client Tier node and select Swing/JClient for BC4J. Select Form from the Items list. Click OK to start the JClient Form Wizard.

3. Click Next if the Welcome page appears. On the Form Types page, select the Master-Detail Tables and Form radio buttons. Click Next.

4. Accept the default settings on the Form Layout, Data Model, Panel View, and both Attribute Selection pages. Click Next on each one.

5. On the File Names page, enter "locdept" in the *Package name* field. Click Next.

6. Click Finish to create the application files and click Save All.

   Additional Information: If you do not want the UI Editor to open automatically after completing the JClient Form Wizard, select **Tools | Preferences** and on the JClient\ Code Generation page, uncheck the *Open UI Editor on Every Newly Generated Form/Data Panel* checkbox. Click OK to accept the change.

7. Select the FormLocationsView1DepartmentsView2.java node and click Run. You should see something like Figure 1-4. Scroll through the records to see the department and location information.

8. Close the Java application.

What Just Happened?   In this phase, you created a simple Java application. You allowed the JDeveloper wizards to create all of the code and viewed the results of using the default settings for creating the application.

The first thing you did in this phase was to create a separate project for the application files; you then attached the application module to the Java application project by creating a client data model. You then ran the wizard to create a default user interface application that looks similar to a page in the BC4J tester. This is not a fully functional production application, but if you carefully review the generated objects, you can use this to get an idea of how you should structure a Java application that interacts with the BC4J components.

To summarize the process of creating a Java application using the wizards:

1. Create an image of the database using entity objects and associations.

2. Create application-specific sets of view objects and view links, which are then assembled into one or more application modules.

3. Create a client data model for binding the BC4J application module to the user interface.

4. Create the user interface application.

IV. Create a JSP Project

In this practice, you will create a JSP application that allows you to view database information in a web browser such as Internet Explorer or Netscape. For additional information about JSP pages, see Part IV of this book.

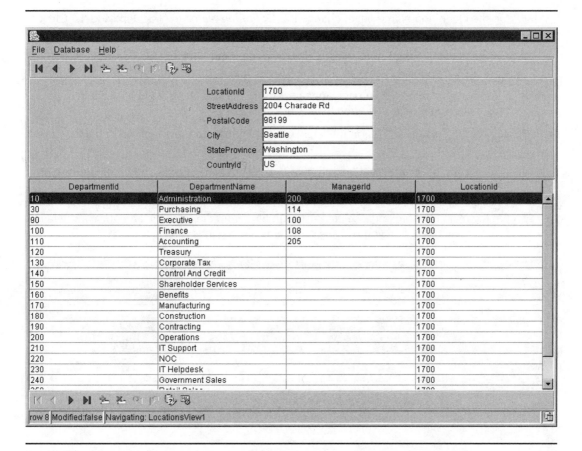

FIGURE 1-4.   *Wizard-generated Java application*

1. On the LocDeptWS workspace node, select New Empty Project from the right-click menu. Click OK.

2. In the New Project dialog, enter "LocDeptJSP" for both the *Directory Name* and *File Name.* Click OK to create the project.

3. Click Save All.

4. On the LocDeptJSP.jpr node, select New from the right-click menu. Expand the Web Tier node, and select the JSP for Business Components category and the Business Components Client Data Model item. Click OK.

5. Click Next if the Welcome page appears. On the Application Module page of the BC4J Client Data Model Definition Wizard, ensure that the LocDeptBC4J project is showing in the *Business Components Project* field. Accept the other default settings and click Next.

6. On the Definition Name page, change the *Definition Name* to "LocDeptModel." Click Next and Finish.

7. On the LocDeptJSP.jpr node, select New from the right-click menu. Select the JSP for Business Components category and the Complete JSP Application item. Click OK.

8. Click Next if the Welcome page appears. Ensure that LocDeptModel appears in the *Select the data model definition* field. Click Next.

9. Accept the default settings on the View Object Forms and View Link Form pages. Click Next on each.

10. Click Finish. Many files will be added to the System Navigator as shown in Figure 1-5.

11. Click Save All.

12. On the main.html file node, select Run main.html from the right-click menu. Your default browser will open, and you will see something like the following:

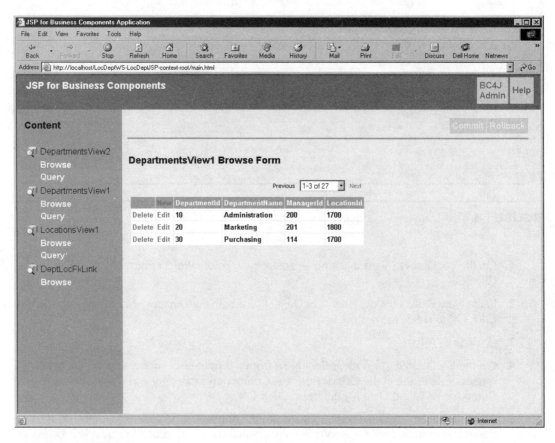

13. Click the links and test the application to see what JDeveloper generates for you.

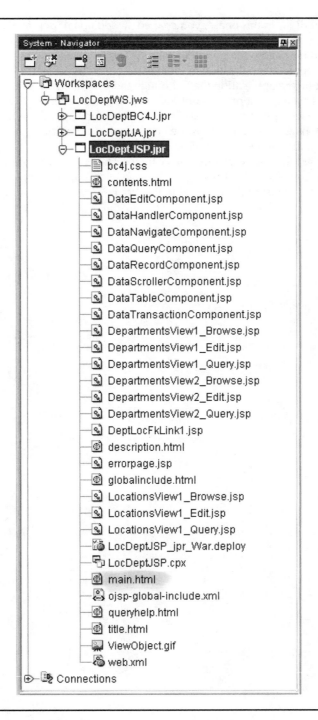

FIGURE 1-5. *JSP project files*

What Just Happened?   In this phase, you created an additional user interface project in the same workspace. This demonstrates the power and flexibility of BC4J, which can be used for both Java applications and JSP pages with no modifications. The JSP application wizard generated a full set of JSP pages to support the application module.

Notice from testing the application that, although the generated JSP user interface contains all the functions of the Java application, it is not nearly as sophisticated. For example, there are separate screens for each operation (such as browse, delete/edit, and query). This is indicative of the limitations of JSP pages. Designers must be very creative in designing applications that hide these limitations from the users.

The authors suggest that you carefully follow the practice steps and examine the generated structures and code. Understanding how JDeveloper generates application elements will enhance your understanding of the rest of the material in this book.

CHAPTER
2

The Integrated
Development
Environment

Beware the ides of March.

—William Shakespeare (1564–1616), *Julius Caesar* (I, ii, 18)

 ntegrated development environments (IDEs) are available for all serious development languages. IDEs allow developers to quickly produce massive amounts of code that are already debugged and optimized. The generated code is available to be modified or used as is. In general parlance, an *integrated development environment* is a cohesive set of programs that automate and centralize the lifecycle of program code creation and deployment. As with all third-generation languages, you can create Java programs using a text editor, and there is no requirement for using an IDE for Java development.

You need to choose which tool and development method to use at the start of a project. Therefore, this chapter starts by briefly examining the benefits that an IDE offers should you need to evaluate different tools. The chapter then examines some of the important work areas and features of JDeveloper, so that you can see how it fulfills all the requirements of a Java IDE.

NOTE
The authors' websites contain a sample project that will allow you to browse the nodes of the Navigator and try out the features mentioned in this chapter.

What's the Big IDEa?

When examining what benefits IDEs offer, it is useful to explore the alternatives. The standard Java development process without using an IDE consists of the following steps:

1. Write the source code (.java file) in a text editor such as Notepad.

2. Compile the source code at the command line using the javac.exe program. If there are compilation errors, fix the code and repeat this step until the code compiles without errors.

3. Run the compiled .class file using the java.exe runtime program.

4. Make note of the Java error dump, or use the debugger, jdb.exe, to determine the causes.

5. Repeat steps 1 through 4 until the code works satisfactorily.

6. Package the program file with the libraries it requires, and deploy the package to a client or server machine.

This is the traditional method that some developers start with because it is a no-cost path. The *Software Development Kit* (SDK, also called the *Java Development Kit* or JDK) that is available as a free download includes a command-line compiler, runtime program, and debugger as well as standard class library files. Therefore, however ponderous the steps are, there is no cost for the required tools. Countless Java programmers today still use this "traditional," bare-bones method with variations, such as using a more programmer-oriented text editor.

The development path is different with a Java IDE. It consists of the same steps (create the source code, compile, test, and debug), but all of these steps are accomplished with an easy-to-use windowed environment. Java development using an IDE is different from the traditional path for the following reasons:

- **You do not need to be an expert in the language to create basic applications.** Proponents of IDEs argue that IDEs allow novice developers to be more effective in creating code. Critics of IDEs argue that they separate the developer from immediate access to code and command-line switches. They think that if the programmer is not fully aware of all of the detailed ramifications of the generated code, he or she will not be able to make decisions about how to modify it or enhance it.

- **You can do everything within the tool.** The major steps of compile, run, and debug are available with a click of a button. There is no need to type commands at the command line.

- **You can work on different levels.** In addition to being able to write lines of code within the tool's code editor, you can use the declarative style of development, in which you define an object by name and assign values to its properties. These definitions will create source code. The code and declarative areas will stay in sync so that when you change one, the other changes. In addition, the tool may offer wizards that will generate large amounts of code that you can use as a starting point to which you add your own code.

- **You can easily visualize the code structure.** Many IDEs include navigator interfaces that allow you to see the numerous files that are required to implement a full Java application. It is difficult to keep track of these files without an IDE.

IDEs may not be right for all developers. Some experts in the language may have developed techniques that help quickly create efficient and complete code. The code that the expert creates has few bugs because it is written with care and an awareness of the libraries and other files that are required to place the code in production. This type of user may not require an IDE to assist in the familiar tasks of creating and compiling code. Although many may claim to have this status, this type of expert is rare in the industry. In addition, many expert developers rely on enhanced tools. For example, instead of using Notepad to write code, the developer will use a more fully featured text editor that can automate some of the tasks. The more automated the text editor becomes, the closer it gets to a full IDE such as JDeveloper.

A traditional measurement for the output of a developer in "heads-down" development mode (when the developer is just writing code based upon a set of requirements) is the number of lines of code produced. In the past, the rule of thumb was that the developer was sufficiently productive if she or he created 100 lines of debugged code a day. Creating code in an IDE has a much greater output because much of the manual effort that coding requires is automated. As a comparison, the hands-on practice in Chapter 3 takes an hour or two to create more than 1800 lines of working code—the equivalent of 18 days of effort by the old rule. Although the comparison between hand coding and code generation is not completely fair, the increased productivity of the code generators is an important benefit.

If the developer's skills are anything less than expert, an IDE will assist greatly. After learning the language, a novice programmer can take advantage of all areas of the IDE and become extremely productive. An IDE can even make an expert more efficient by off-loading some of the tedious manual tasks such as tracking the source code required for a project and building command-line scripts to facilitate the compile and build process. In addition, the code that an IDE generates can assist this type of expert user because it is generated from completely debugged templates and is integrated with the other components that the application requires. The IDE will create a complete set of files that are required for deployment and track them effectively. Those tasks are difficult and tedious in a manual situation.

The JDeveloper Environment

The key to working with the JDeveloper IDE is in knowing how it is organized and what facilities it offers. If you understand the setup of the major areas of the tool, you will be able to work more efficiently when creating code.

For the 9*i* release, JDeveloper's IDE was completely rewritten in Java. The choice of language is natural, because this is a Java development tool. Many other Java development tools are also written in Java. The choice of Java also means that JDeveloper may be run in the Java Virtual Machines (JVMs) of different operating systems with few, if any, changes. This makes JDeveloper extremely portable.

The redesign of the 9*i* release did not change the basic concepts of working with the tool. However, the interface that resulted from the rewrite is friendlier, often faster, and more consistent than previous releases. If you are accustomed to working with earlier releases, this release requires some changes in the operations that you use. You will also find that release 9*i* offers more consistency in the IDE work areas.

This chapter introduces the major development features of the tool. The "getting started" material in this chapter is not available in this form in the JDeveloper help system. However, further details about each feature as well as features not explained in this chapter are supplied in the help system. The following main development features are introduced in this chapter:

- IDE window
- Main work areas
- Wizards
- Help system
- Software configuration management

TIP
*You can reduce the number of features loaded when JDeveloper is started by using the Extension Manager page of the Preferences dialog (**Tools | Preferences**). This page allows you to deselect features that you do not use or use infrequently. JDeveloper will load faster if a reduced set of features is enabled. The Extension Manager page allows you to create and manage sets of extensions as named "configurations," and you can switch from one configuration to another as needed.*

IDE Window

The IDE window shown in Figure 2-1 appears when you start the jdevw.exe executable from a shortcut or from the command line. The IDE window contains a number of work areas that are discussed in the section "Main Work Areas" later in this chapter. There are two types of windows, which exhibit different behaviors in the IDE as follows:

- **Dockable windows**   These work areas may be anchored (docked) to the top, bottom, or sides of the outer IDE window. They can also be pulled out of the docked position and will then float inside or outside of the IDE frame. If they share the same area, a tab control will allow you to switch between them. These windows can be displayed or hidden using the View menu options. You manipulate the docking or floating operations using the double lines in the window title.

- **Viewer and editor windows**   These work areas (named with the noun "Viewer" or "Editor") float inside the IDE frame under the dockable windows. These windows (also called *MDI editor windows*) focus on displaying or editing a single file, and display the file name and path in the window title. The viewer and editor windows can be displayed for a file selected in the System Navigator by selecting the viewer or editor from the right-click menu on the file, selecting **View | Display With**, or double clicking the file in the System Navigator.

TIP
The ability to change the look-and-feel of an application is a feature of Java. As a result, you can define the look-and-feel that you use to access JDeveloper. The sidebar "Modifying the Look-and-Feel" provides details about this feature.

CAUTION
It is possible that you will experience some differences between the look-and-feel environments. If a feature in the IDE does not work as you would expect, try switching the environment to another look-and-feel such as "Windows" and try the feature again.

Docking and Undocking a Window

Docking a dockable window requires a special technique. If the window is floating (not docked), it will have a standard window title bar. Grab the title bar and move the window to one side (or to the bottom or top) until the mouse cursor reaches the border of the outer window. You will see the window outline click into place on that side of the outer IDE window. Release the mouse button and the window will stick.

To remove a window from a docked position, drag the window from its title bar (double lines on the top or left side) so that its outline appears in the middle of the outer window.

When a window is docked, a *pin icon* (with the point of the pin to the left) appears in the window's upper-right-hand corner (next to the "x" close button). Clicking the pin icon causes the window to close and a button with the window name to appear in the nearest margin.

Component   Toolbar
Palette

Menu   System   Document Bar   UI Editor   Property Inspector
        Navigator

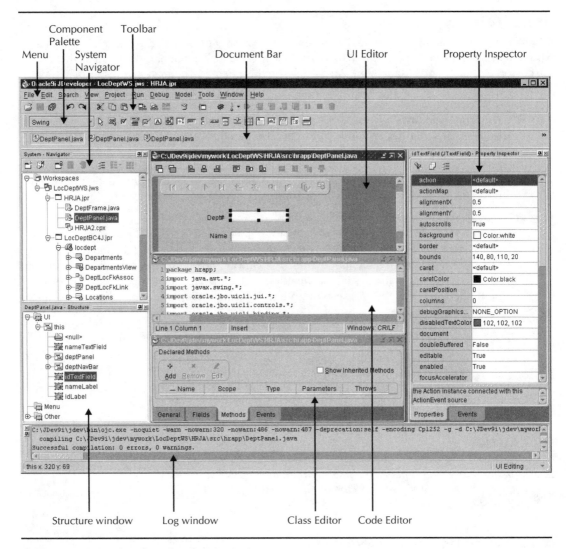

FIGURE 2-1. *The JDeveloper IDE window*

Clicking that button opens the window. Clicking the button again closes the window. Normally, windows resize based on the type of file being edited. However, when the window is pinned, it maintains its size and location regardless of which type of file is selected. When a window is pinned, the *unpin icon* (which shows a pin pointed down) appears next to the "x" button. Clicking the unpin icon removes the button from the margin and allows the window to change size based on the type of file being edited.

NOTE
As mentioned, you can dock more than one window to the same area of the IDE window. Drag the window into the area until the window outline appears inside the area, and then release the mouse button to drop it. This causes the windows to share the same area. A tab control will appear that allows you to switch between windows. You can also dock one window next to another so that they sit side by side or above and below each other. To accomplish this, drag the window into the area, and release the mouse button when the window outline is at one side (or top or bottom) of the area. Dragging the window out of the window area by its tab or title bar undocks that window.

Arranging the JDeveloper Windows

When you work with the JDeveloper IDE, you have to handle many work area windows. You will waste time arranging windows if you do not have a scheme for how windows should be placed in the tool. The following, which is the default used by JDeveloper, is one suggestion for that kind of scheme. You can adjust it as required. An example of how the windows appear is shown in Figure 2-1.

This arrangement docks the System Navigator to the left side of the dockable window and the Property Inspector to the right side of the IDE window. The Log window appears at the bottom of the IDE window. The area in between these windows is reserved for the editors (Code Editor, UI Editor, and Class Editor). Each editor can take up the entire area between docked windows because you usually work on only one editor at a time. You can create and save individual layouts for each editor type as described next.

Modifying the Look-and-Feel

You can change the IDE *look-and-feel* (the style in which the IDE is presented) using the Preferences dialog (**Tools | Preferences**). Although the look-and-feel does not affect functionality, you may prefer one style over another. Experimenting with the options will help you make the decision about look-and-feel.

To change the look-and-feel, select the Environment node in the Preferences navigator, and change the *Look and Feel* field to "CDE/Motif," "Metal," "Oracle," or "Windows." Click OK and close and restart JDeveloper for the modification to take effect.

The Oracle look-and-feel (used in screenshots for this book) is supplied by an Oracle library. The other options are supplied by Swing libraries. You can use any of these look-and-feel options in your Java client applications (Java application or applet). See the help topic "Developing Java GUI Clients\About the Look and Feel of a Swing Application" for the required code. Note that the Oracle look-and-feel is new to JDeveloper. If any IDE function does not work as expected, switch to Windows look-and-feel and try the function again.

Using Layouts to Save the Window Arrangement

You can use a JDeveloper feature called *layouts* to save and restore a particular window arrangement. There are standard layouts supplied with the tool, and you can modify these layouts or create your own. In design mode (not debugging), the layout automatically selected depends upon the file that is open in the editor. In debug mode, the layout automatically selected depends upon the most recently used debug layout.

Understanding Layouts   The easiest way to understand how layouts work is to open several types of editors at the same time, for example, a Java class file in the Code Editor, a JSP file in the Code Editor, and a Java application file in the UI Editor. As you click among these windows, the arrangement of the windows will change to the default layout for that style. If you view the Preferences dialog (**Tools | Preferences**) when the cursor is in a particular editor, you will see the name of the layout for that editor in bold on the Layouts page.

The checkbox fields are checked for using the editor's preferred layout and for using the active layout as the current editor's preferred layout.

Saving a New Layout   To save a layout for a particular editor or viewer, arrange the windows, select **Tools | Preferences**, select the Layouts node, click New, and name the layout. Check both checkbox fields and click OK to close the dialog.

Activating the Layout   To activate a layout for a particular file type, select the file in the editor, and select the layout in the Preferences dialog. Click the Activate button (the name will be shown in italics) and the OK button to close the preferences. In addition, you can select a particular layout in the pulldown list in the bottom right corner of the IDE window. This list contains all default and user-defined layouts.

NOTE
You can set a default layout for all file types and perform other layout functions not mentioned here. The help system contents node "Getting Started with JDeveloper\Customizing the IDE\Working with Layouts in the IDE" contains more information about different layout operations.

Monitor Size and Resolution

There are many work area windows in JDeveloper, and you will probably want to have many of them open at the same time. Using a monitor set to a high resolution such as 1280×1024 (or 1600×1200) gives you more screen real estate in which you can place windows. Figure 2-2 shows JDeveloper running in this resolution. Compare that with Figure 2-1, where the screen is running a 1024×768 resolution.

As in most modern GUI development tools, a large monitor and high resolution are best. Although most of the screenshots in this book use a 1024×768 resolution for clarity, you will be more productive with a higher resolution, such as 1280×1024, because you will be able to open more windows and leave them arranged in a more productive way. With lower resolutions, you will spend time moving windows around on the screen so they are visible or sized correctly. This is time that you could spend on other tasks. As a rule, a 19-inch monitor is a minimum size

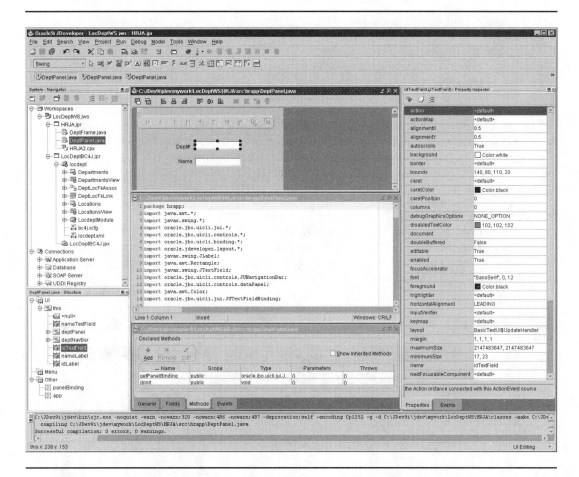

FIGURE 2-2. *JDeveloper running in a 1280×1024 resolution*

for 1280×1024 resolution. 1600×1200 works on a good 21-inch monitor, but may not be comfortable for some people.

NOTE
If possible, set the number of colors option (on the Windows Control Panel's Display application Settings tab) to greater than 256 to avoid color problems.

Main Work Areas

This section introduces the major work areas or features, some of which are shown in Figure 2-1. The practices in other chapters will allow you to try out some of the features mentioned in this section while accomplishing a real task. The more familiar you are with the operations in the IDE, the faster you will be able to complete a particular task.

This section will give you a basic understanding of the range of features and functions available in the tool. The JDeveloper help system discusses the exact actions you need to perform in each area.

Preferences

The behavior of most of the work areas may be modified using the Preferences dialog (**Tools | Preferences**) as shown in Figure 2-3. This dialog contains a navigator for different categories of settings (such as the Code Editor node in Figure 2-3). Changing a setting in this dialog changes the behavior in the tool. Most changes are immediate, although some require exiting and reloading JDeveloper.

System Navigator

Most work in JDeveloper starts in the *System Navigator* (or *Navigator window*), because this window is where you view and interact with workspaces, projects, files, and other components. The System Navigator offers a hierarchical view of the files that you are working on. You can expand and collapse nodes as in any navigator such as Windows Explorer.

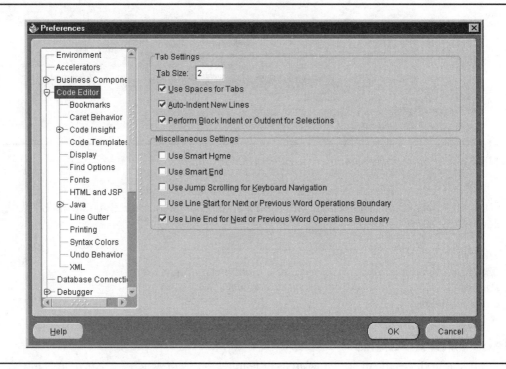

FIGURE 2-3. *Preferences dialog*

For example, the following illustration shows a portion of the hierarchy that appears when you expand a business components package:

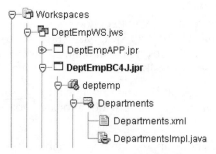

The top nodes are the workspace, DeptEmpWS.jws, and projects such as DeptEmpAPP.jpr. The bottom levels are the .xml and .java files for an entity, Departments, under a package, deptemp. Each listed item type has a specific icon associated with it. If you hold the mouse cursor over the icon, a tooltip will pop up indicating the object type or file name. The file name also appears in the IDE status bar when you select the file in the Navigator.

NOTE
JDeveloper release 9i allows you to open more than one workspace at the same time. Previous releases were limited to one workspace at a time. This is just another organizational feature that you can use if needed, but one workspace will suffice for most purposes.

Other top-level nodes in the System Navigator are the Miscellaneous Files node and the Connections node.

Miscellaneous Files   The Miscellaneous Files node contains files that you have opened (using **File | Open**), but have not assigned to a specific project. This node is saved when you exit JDeveloper, so that when you restart JDeveloper, the files under this node will be reloaded. This node is useful for files that you want to view or copy from but do not want to include in a project.

Connections   The Connections node displays a list of external servers that JDeveloper can access. This node contains the following server types:

- ■ **Application Server**   This node lists the middle-tier servers that you use for Java services. You can define Oracle9iAS Containers for J2EE (OC4J) or BEA WebLogic 6.x servers into which you can automatically deploy using the JDeveloper IDE. Deployment from JDeveloper is discussed in Chapters 7 and 16.

- ■ **Database**   You can define database connections using this node. Each connection uses a single database user's schema and allows you to browse the objects that the user owns or has access to. (The sidebar "Database Connections Node Object Access" further explains which objects appear in this node.) When you are defining data access using Business Components for Java (BC4J), you can select any object to which the user has been granted access, regardless of owner. The JDeveloper Release Notes (**Help** | **Release Notes**) describe how to define connections that access non-Oracle databases through JDBC.

- **SOAP Server**   This node allows you to define connections to *Simple Object Access Protocol* (SOAP) servers. SOAP is an XML-based protocol that accesses applications that have been set up as web services. You can define a connection to a SOAP server in this node so that JDeveloper can easily access the web service.

- **UDDI Registry**   This node allows you to define a Universal Description, Discovery, and Integration (UDDI) connection that provides a location for lists of web services that you can use in your applications.

- **(source control)**   This node appears after you enable source code control. The name of this node depends on the type of source control you define, for example "Oracle9i SCM." This node provides a connection to an Oracle Software Configuration Manager (SCM) repository for file versioning, parallel development, and central storage of all JDeveloper code. This feature is described further in the later section "Software Configuration Management."

- **WebDAV**   This optional node defines connections to Web-based Distributed Authoring and Versioning (WebDAV) servers that allow access to files stored on web servers. You need to first install the WebDAV extension (available on otn.oracle.com) and define the connection. Then you can use JDeveloper to open, edit, and save the files on these servers.

All connections may be created, tested, and edited using the right-click menu options on the Connections and specific server nodes. You can also open and close connections using the

---

Database Connections Node Object Access

By default, the Database Connections node does not display objects in other schemas that are granted to the connection user. For example, if the HR user grants SELECT on the EMPLOYEES table to SCOTT, that table will not be displayed under the Scott connection Tables node. As expected, if the SCOTT account creates a private synonym for that table, the table will appear under the synonyms node.

You can display other schemas by checking the *Show All Database Schemas* checkbox in the Database Connections node of the Preferences dialog. Then, after refreshing a specific Database Connections node, such as Scott, nodes will appear for all database user accounts. The objects visible under these accounts will only be those to which the connection user has been granted access. No synonyms are required in this case. In the previous example, the Tables node under the HR schema in the Scott connection will display the EMPLOYEES table. Scott will be able to see the table structure but not view the data.

Also, as of the 9.0.3 release, public synonyms and objects with public grants do not appear under the Database Connections node, regardless of the preference setting.

right-click menu options on a specific server name. Expanding the navigator node for the specific server name will also open the connection.

In addition to defining servers, you can perform a number of other operations in the Navigator.

Adding and Removing Files   You can use the Add To button in the Navigator toolbar to load a file to a workspace or project. The Remove from button hides the file from the navigator nodes. Removing a file from the IDE does not delete the file from the file system. A menu selection, **File | Erase from Disk**, allows you to delete a file from the file system.

CAUTION
If you select Erase from Disk for a workspace or project that has a dedicated directory, JDeveloper will remove the workspace or project file but not the directory.

Editing Items   Double clicking an item in any of these tabs opens it in the appropriate tool; for example, if you double click a .java file, the Code Editor will open the file. If the item is a graphics file (such as a .gif or .jpg), the Image Viewer will display the file in read-only mode. The sidebar "Opening a File Using Drag and Drop" explains alternative methods for opening files.

Searching for Items in the Navigator   If you need to search for a specific item in the Navigator, click somewhere in the Navigator, and start typing the name of the item. The cursor will jump to the first occurrence of that name if the node that contains that item has already been opened. Press DOWN ARROW to find the next occurrence of the name. If you type the asterisk wildcard character ("*") inside or at the beginning of the search string, the Navigator will match item names containing the characters around the wildcard character. Press ESC to exit search mode.

NOTE
You can also search for files containing a text string by using the **Search | Search Files** *feature described later in the "Search" menu section.*

Modifying the Display   Clicking the Show Categories button in the Navigator toolbar with a project selected displays a list of file types such as shown in the following:

```
⊖─☐ DeptEmpBC4J.jpr
    ⊕──🔳 Sources
    ⊕──🔳 Business Components
    ⊕──🔳 Deployment
```

When you expand these categories, additional categories and files will appear. The categories allow you to easily find a file of a certain type and are useful if the project contains a large number of files. Clicking Show Categories again switches the display back to the list of files.

Opening a File Using Drag and Drop

The Add To toolbar button in the Navigator opens files inside a project node. To open files outside of a project (in the Miscellaneous Files node described earlier in this chapter), select **File | Open** from the menu, and uncheck the *Add to project* checkbox in the File Open dialog.

You can also open a file by dragging it from the System Navigator to an open space in the IDE window. The mouse cursor will change to the following icon if you have reached an open space in the IDE:

Releasing the mouse button will open the appropriate editor or viewer for the file. You can also open files by dragging them from Windows Explorer into the open editor area or onto the Document Bar (if there is no open space available). If you drag the file from Windows Explorer, it will be displayed under the Miscellaneous Files node instead of under a project node, even if that file also appears within a project that is available in the System Navigator.

You can also open more than one file at a time by grouping the files together in the System Navigator and dragging them as a group. Use the CTRL key to group files in the Navigator, and drag and drop the group to an open area. If the group becomes unselected when you do this, hold the CTRL key on the last file in the group as you drag to the open area. Release the mouse button first, and then release the CTRL key to open the files.

NOTE
In previous JDeveloper releases, you were able to create "folders" in the Navigator to organize the files that you created. The current release automatically provides folders and sorts the files as described in this section.

The two rightmost buttons in the Navigator toolbar are activated when you click a category after showing the categories. The File List button is actually a pulldown list button. If you click the down arrow, you will be able to assign a different organization method (File List, Package Tree, Package List, or Directory Tree) to the button. Clicking the button after selecting a category will apply that organization scheme to the category.

The Refresh button allows you to renew the display if it is out of sync. This button is also enabled when categories are displayed. The Show All Files button displays all files in the directory or package that is selected in the Navigator, not just the files in the project.

TIP
The Navigator toolbar has a Project Settings button. Clicking that button opens the Project Settings dialog for the project for the selected file. Using this button could save you a little time because it is not necessary to click the project node first as you must with the menu and right-click menu methods of opening this dialog.

New Navigator   The default Navigator is called the System Navigator. It contains all open workspaces and connections. You can display a new navigator for a specific workspace or project by clicking the Display in New Navigator button of the System Navigator toolbar (or **View | Display in New Navigator**) after selecting a workspace or project. This action will open a new window for the node. This is handy if you want to work on a smaller part of a set of workspaces but still want to leave the rest of the files open.

The new Navigator window will initially display as a tab in the existing Navigator window, but you can drag that tab out of the window to create a separate window.

NOTE
When you start a process such as an OC4J server instance to run a JSP page, a Run Manager tab appears in the System Navigator area. This is a separate window that displays the running process so that you can track the active processes. You can terminate the process using the right-click menu option Terminate.

Structure Window

The Structure window contains a view of the objects within the file or node selected in the System Navigator if the System Navigator has cursor focus. If an editor window has focus, the Structure window displays the objects within the file in the editor. The form that this view takes depends upon the selected file type and the editor that has focus. The following examples demonstrate some of the different displays for files and editors:

Display

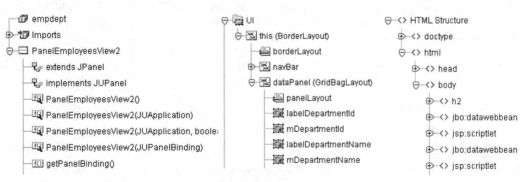

File type	Java application	Java application	JavaServer Page (HTML)
Editor	Code Editor	UI Editor	Code Editor

When a Java application is open in the Code Editor, the Structure window displays details of the class, such as the imports, methods, superclass, and properties. When you are using the UI Editor to edit a Java application, the Structure window displays a hierarchy of the UI objects. You can drop components from the Component Palette into the Structure window, and they will be added to the code and the UI Editor. For an HTML file such as a JavaServer Page file, the Structure window shows the structure of the HTML with its attributes and nested structures. Other file type and editor combinations have appropriate structure displays. For example, if you select a database connection under the Connections node, the Structure window will display details about the connection such as the Type, Driver, User, and URL.

If you are editing a file in the Code Editor, the Structure window will also show errors such as mismatched tags in HTML files and mismatched curly brackets in Java files. The errors are displayed as you move the cursor in the editor and do not require a compilation step. The following example shows how editing errors will be displayed in the Structure window:

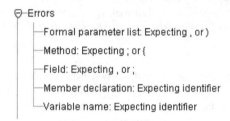

NOTE
In previous JDeveloper releases, the Structure Pane (now called "Structure window") allowed you to edit the names of objects directly in the window. In release 9i, you accomplish this task by using the Property Inspector to edit the "name" property.

Using the Structure Window to Navigate the Code   Double clicking a code item (such as a method name) in the Structure window will move the focus and highlight the applicable line of code in the Code Editor. If the Code Editor is not open, it will be opened as a result of this action. If the UI Editor is open and you click a user interface component (such as a text field or button) in the Structure window, that object will be selected in the UI Editor, and its properties will be loaded into the Property Inspector (if that window is open).

Toolbar
The top IDE toolbar contains frequently accessed commands in the following categories:

- ■ **File operations**   For opening a file, saving a file, and saving all changed files.

- ■ **Edit operations**   For undo, redo, cut, copy, and paste.

- ■ **Compile and run operations**   For making a project, building a project, running a file, and running the Profiler as explained in Chapter 6. Compiling is explained further in the sidebar "Compiling with Make and Rebuild." There is also an icon, Cancel Build, that stops a running compile process. This is useful for a long-running compile that has frozen or that you need to abort.

■   **Debug operations**   For running the debugger, also explained in Chapter 6.

All toolbar buttons provide tooltip hints that appear when the mouse cursor is held over the button.

Menu

The main IDE menu bar contains a large number of selections. In addition, JDeveloper uses right-click (context) menus extensively. Almost everything in the IDE offers right-click menu operations for frequently used operations. These options are numerous and many are contained in the main IDE menu. Therefore, instead of listing and explaining all of the right-click menu selections, it is more useful to explore some of the unusual options in the main menu.

TIP

Always be aware that an operation you may want to perform on a particular object in the IDE may be more easily accessible in a right-click menu than in a pulldown menu.

Compiling with Make and Rebuild

The toolbar and menu contain options for two kinds of compiling. *Make* compiles modified files on the selected node; it also compiles modified files that have been imported by those files (referenced in the import sections). *Rebuild* (called *Build* in some versions of JDeveloper) compiles all files in the selected node; it also compiles files that have been imported by those files. It is useful when you want to force all files in that node to be compiled (for example, if you have replaced a file with an older file and that older file needs to be recompiled). Selecting a node in the Navigator allows you to make or rebuild all files under it. Since Rebuild compiles all files in the selected node, it is slower than Make.

If you select the workspace node and select **Project | Make <workspace>**, all modified files (and modified imported files) in all projects within that workspace will be compiled. If you select a single file in the Navigator and click the Rebuild button in the toolbar, only that file (and its imported files) will be compiled. The Project menu contains options for making and rebuilding the selected object, its project, and its workspace. You can also "make" a file that is open in the editor by selecting Make from the right-click menu in the editor.

When you make or rebuild files, check the Log window for messages about the compilation. This window will indicate if the compilation has been successful or, if there were errors, what went wrong.

File This menu contains common operations such as opening and closing files. The open file dialog (**File | Open**) contains shortcut buttons that allow you to jump to directories defined for the JDeveloper home, workspace, project, and user. The File menu also allows you to remove a file from the project but not delete it from the file system (Remove from <node>) or to delete the file from the file system (Erase from Disk). The New option (discussed later in the "New Gallery" section) creates a file.

A Rename option changes the name of a file. If you want to rename a class file that is used by other class files, use the **Tools | Refactor** menu items. Refactoring will cascade the name change to all dependent classes. It will also change the class declaration code (for example `public class TestClass`) so that it references the new file name. Renaming the file will not automatically change the class declaration or other files that reference it.

CAUTION
If you rename a Java file that has already been compiled, the compiled .class file will not be renamed. This can cause side effects if there are references to the old file name, so it is a good idea to delete the compiled file after renaming a Java file that has been compiled.

The Reopen menu item shows a list of all objects recently opened. You can select from that list and load projects into the IDE more quickly because you do not have to browse the file system.

You can add an existing file to the opened (working) set using the Open item in this menu. For example, you can add a project to a workspace by selecting the workspace, selecting **File | Open**, and finding the project file in the dialog. In this dialog is a checkbox for *Add to project <project name>* that you can check to open a file into the chosen project. If you uncheck this checkbox, the file will open into the Miscellaneous Files node.

To add a copy of an existing file into your project directory, use the Import menu option. You can include a file inside a WAR or EAR file as well as an existing file. The Import item can also just include the file without copying it.

CAUTION
If you use Windows Explorer or another utility to change a file listed in a project or a project file in a workspace, that file name will not be updated automatically in JDeveloper. Although the old file name will show in the System Navigator, there will be no file in the file system to support it. Therefore, when you open that workspace or project, you have to remove the old file and open the new file so that the project is properly updated.

Edit The Edit menu provides the standard Windows editing features. Many items here have keypress shortcuts (such as CTRL-Z for Undo) that are faster to use than the menu selections. The Properties item allows you to modify properties of an object such as a database connection node that has properties.

NOTE
*The keyboard shortcuts mentioned in this book are based upon the default key assignments. You can modify the key assignment scheme by loading another scheme such as the key assignments for Visual C++. To reassign the keyboard shortcuts, select **Tools | Preferences** and click the Load Preset button on the Accelerators page. This page contains a number of preset selections.*

Search   This menu contains standard search features for text searches in source code such as Find, Replace, Search Forward, and Search Backward. Most items have shortcut keys (such as CTRL-F for Find). Selecting text to search will load it into the *Text to Search For* field in the Find Text dialog. There is a Bookmarks submenu that allows you to define places in the code to which you want to return. There are also selections for navigating through messages in the Log window (Go to Next Message and Go to Previous Message). You can jump to a specific line number using Go to Line Number. Some other Search menu selections follow:

- **Clear Highlighting**   If you check the *Highlight all Occurrences* checkbox in the Find Text dialog, all text that matches the search word or phrase will be highlighted throughout the document. This item unhighlights words or phrases highlighted by this mechanism.

- **Incremental Search Forward** and **Incremental Search Backward**   These selections (CTRL-E and CTRL-SHIFT-E) are extremely handy for finding text in a large body of code. After selecting one of these options, you can start typing, and the tool will find the first or last occurrence (for forward and backward searches, respectively) of whatever you type. Pressing F3 will repeat the find.

CAUTION
Pressing ENTER in the Find Text (CTRL-F) window will find the specified text. Pressing ESC will cancel the dialog. You can also just use the OK and Cancel buttons to find the text or cancel the dialog, respectively.

- **Locate in Navigator**   This selection will find the file node in the System Navigator that corresponds to a file that is open in an editor window.

- **Go to Java Class**   Previously called "Browse Symbol", this selection (CTRL--) displays a dialog where you enter or find a class name. When you click OK in that dialog, the source code file for that class is loaded into a Code Editor window (but not into the System Navigator). You can view the code and comments in read-only mode. The Structure window shows the contents of the source code file. This feature is useful for determining which parent methods and attributes are available to a subclassed class.

  The Go to Declaration (previously called "Browse Symbol at Cursor") option in the Code Editor's right-click menu has a similar effect, but loads the source file of the item at the cursor location. If the item is a class name, this option loads the source file for the class; if the cursor item is a primitive variable or object, this option displays the declaration of that variable or object; if the cursor item is a method, this option displays the method declaration.

NOTE
JDeveloper will try to reverse-engineer the code for a class that has no available source code. If it is not able to determine the code, it will display a message in the status bar of the IDE.

■ **Search Files**   This selection opens a dialog that allows you to search for files containing text that you specify, even if the text is within a .zip or .jar file. This is similar to the Windows Explorer file search feature. However, it is platform independent, so that you can use this dialog regardless of the operating system in which you are running JDeveloper.

View   Normally, the IDE displays the editors and windows appropriate to a certain task. The View menu allows you to override or supplement the choices that the IDE makes about which areas to display. You can check or uncheck the menu items to display or hide a feature, respectively. For example, to hide or display one or more toolbars, such as the toolbar in the System Navigator, check or uncheck the appropriate checkbox in the Toolbars submenu of the View menu.

You can open a file using the options in the Display With submenu. Selecting an option from Display With opens the editor or viewer (described later) for the file selected in the System Navigator.

The dockable windows are available as separate items in the View menu. You can open a new Navigator window using the Display in New Navigator item.

The Refresh option is enabled when you select a schema name (such as "SCOTT") or database object type name (such as "Tables") under the Connections\Database node in the System Navigator. This option rereads the Oracle data dictionary for objects that have been added or dropped outside of the tool since the connection was made. Refresh is also available when you are displaying the categories view of a project. In this case, it redisplays the contents of the categories nodes under the project.

Project   The Project menu repeats the Make and Rebuild commands from the toolbar (see the sidebar "Compiling with Make and Rebuild" for more information). The menu also contains items that repeat the System Navigator toolbar items for adding files to the workspace or project, showing categories or all files, and organizing the files in different ways.

The Project menu also contains an item, Project Settings, for displaying the Project Settings dialog, as shown in Figure 2-4. This dialog allows you to change characteristics of the project with which you are working. The properties you set here are stored in the project .jpr file. Use the Default Project Settings item in the Project menu to set characteristics for new project files. This is useful if you need to change a particular setting for all projects. The sidebar "Project Setting Configurations" describes how to define multiple sets of project properties.

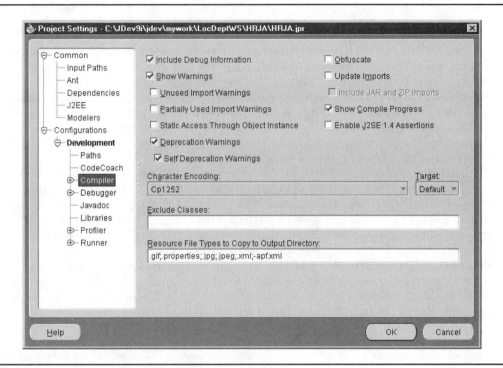

FIGURE 2-4.   *Project Settings dialog*

One of the functions available in the Project Settings dialog is the ability to define settings for the Javadoc that you generate for your Java code. The sidebar "About Javadoc" contains more information about.

TIP
Double clicking a node in the System Navigator displays the default editor for that node. For example, if you double click a project node, the Project Settings node will be displayed for that project. Alternatively, the right-click menu on the project node offers a Project Settings item. Double clicking a .java file in the Navigator opens the Code Editor for that file.

Run   The Run menu contains items for running the project or file that is selected. There is an option to run the CodeCoach feature (described later in this chapter), which analyzes the code and makes suggestions for improvement.

Project Setting Configurations

You can define project setting *configurations,* named sets of properties, and switch back and forth between them as required. The properties that you set for a configuration are contained in the Paths, Libraries, Compiler, Runner, Debugger, Javadoc, Profiler, and CodeCoach nodes of the Configurations\<configuration name> node of the Project Settings dialog. Multiple configurations can be useful if you often change the output directories or classpath directories for the same project (for example, for test and production environments). Instead of typing the new names into the Project Settings dialog, you can set up a configuration to hold the special settings.

To define a new configuration, open the Project Settings dialog, and click New on the Configurations page. You can copy an existing configuration by checking the checkbox in the New Configuration dialog that appears. After you click OK, the Project Settings dialog tree area will contain a new configuration under the old one. This new configuration will contain all of the nodes mentioned earlier, and you can set the properties on those pages differently. The active configuration name is shown in bold in the tree control. If you set up additional configurations in the default project settings dialog (**Project | Default Project Settings**), those configurations will be available to all new projects.

To switch to a different configuration, select it from the pulldown on the Configurations page. You can also delete and rename configurations on this page.

This menu also contains selections to run the Profiler (further described in Chapter 6), which provides details about runtime memory, events, and execution. The Terminate item stops a running program.

NOTE
When you run a file, all changed files in the project will be recompiled automatically. If you prefer to control compilation more closely, you can turn off this behavior by selecting **Project | Project Settings** *and unchecking the "Make Project" field in the Before Running section of the Configurations\Development\Runner\Options page.*

Debug   The Debug menu contains items used during debugging. Debug <project> starts a debugging session and executes the code until the first breakpoint. In the debugging session, many of the items in this menu will become enabled.

Clicking the Debug toolbar icon or pressing SHIFT-F9 will also run the file in debug mode. Chapter 6 describes the debugger in detail.

About Javadoc

Javadoc is a standard feature of the Java language that allows you to generate an HTML help file from your Java source code. The help file will include any text contained within special code comments (delimited with a "/**" at the start and "*/" at the end) as shown next. JDeveloper provides automated support of Javadoc viewing and creation.

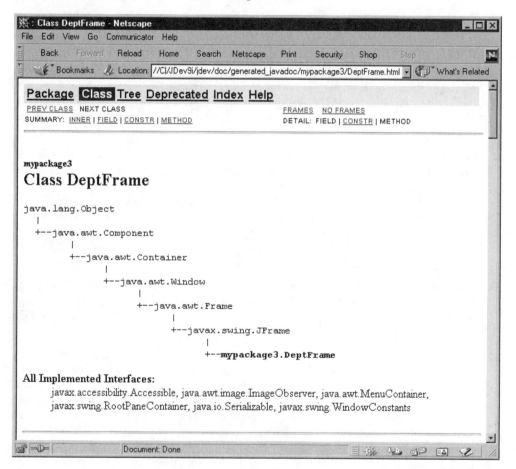

To view previously generated Javadoc for a library class or application class that you created, click the cursor on a class name in the Code Editor, and select Browse Javadoc from the right-click menu. Alternatively, you can press the help key (F1) after placing the cursor in a class name.

To generate Javadoc for a project, select the project node in the System Navigator, select **Generate Javadoc** from the right-click menu. You can set properties about the Javadoc before generating using the Project Settings dialog (**Project | Project Settings**) Configurations\
Development\Javadoc page. Be sure that your code contains Javadoc comments so that the output is useful. The Javadoc you create can become part of the deployment package that you provide to users.

Model   The Model menu contains options that affect the Class Modeler (discussed in Chapters 8 and 11) and the Activity Modeler. The Publish Diagram item allows you to create a .jpg or .svg file from the diagram.

Tools   The Tools menu contains the following items:

- **Configure Palette**   This item displays the *Configure Component Palette* dialog that is also available from the right-click menu on the Component Palette. This dialog allows you to add to or modify the contents of the Component Palette toolbar (discussed later in this chapter).

- **Manage Libraries**   This item opens the Manage Libraries dialog where you can create, modify, and remove groups of files that are organized into libraries. You can also manipulate libraries in the Libraries page (under the Configurations\Development node) of the Project Settings dialog.

- **Refactor** (Rename Class, Move Classes, and Extract Method)   These menu items solve the problem of renaming a class that has dependent classes. For example, normally if you reference Class1 in Class2 and rename Class1, the reference in Class2 will fail. The Rename Class option (available when you click a Java class node in the Navigator) changes the name of the file and modifies all dependent references to that file. The Move Classes option (available when you click one or more Java classes in the Navigator) allows you to change the package in which the classes are stored. This utility will change all references in dependent classes to reference the new package.

- **Show Dependencies**   This item starts a utility that examines the parent and child classes to the file you have selected. The report of "Uses" and "Used by" appears in the Log window. This function is also available from the right-click menu on a Java class file in the Navigator.

- **SQL*Plus**   This starts the SQL*Plus command-line SQL tool. You must select a specific database connection node in the Navigator before this menu item is enabled. If you have not defined the location of the SQL*Plus executable, a dialog will prompt you for the name and location. You can also explicitly define the executable by first navigating to the Database Connections page of the Preferences dialog (**Tools | Preferences**). Then you enter (or browse to find) the name and path of SQL*Plus—usually in the ORACLE_HOME\bin directory file sqlplus.exe or sqlplusw.exe. If your directory names contain spaces, put the entire directory and file name string inside double quotes (for example, "C:\Program Files\oracle\bin\sqlplusw.exe" including the quotes).

TIP
*You can also open SQL*Plus from the right-click menu on a specific Connections node.*

- **Override Methods**   You can use this menu item to add method stubs for methods in the parent that you want to replace. For example, you might want to override a parent set() method in your class file. This menu item adds a code stub for the parent set() method for which you can write code to replace (or supplement) the parent's method.

■ **Implement Interface** This option displays a dialog where you can browse and select an interface file that your class will implement. After you select one or more interfaces and click OK, JDeveloper will add the `implements` clause to your class definition and will add method stubs for which you will need to write code. You can also use this to make an interface extend other interfaces.

■ **Web Object Manager** This option allows you to register HTML Web Beans and data Web Beans so that they are easily available to JSP development in JDeveloper. You select a category (Web Bean or data Web Bean) in the Web Object Manager and select Register to specify the class name of the bean. This process will add items to the list that you see when you select an object from the BC4J Web Beans page of the Component Palette when you are editing a JSP page.

■ **TCP Packet Monitor** This checkbox item opens or closes the TCP Packet Monitor window (by default in the Log window area of the IDE). This monitor captures information about TCP activity in JDeveloper such as interactions with the Embedded OC4J Server or calls to web services.

■ **Convert HTML** This item calls a standard Java utility (Java Plug-in HTML Converter) that converts an HTML file containing applet tags to a file that supports a plugin (for Swing classes, for example). Since this is an external utility, you need to select this menu option before accessing help text about the utility.

■ **External Tools** This item allows you to add programs that are called from the JDeveloper Tools menu, right-click menu, and IDE toolbar. Chapter 21 contains more information and an example in the "Setting Up an External HTML Editor" section.

■ **Preferences** This item displays the Preferences dialog where you can modify the characteristics of the IDE. Figure 2-3 earlier in this chapter shows an example of a page in this dialog.

NOTE
You can add items to right-click menus and to the JDeveloper IDE menu using the Addin API. For more information, look in the "Extending JDeveloper" node in the Contents page of the help system.

Window   The Window menu contains items for switching focus to one of the open windows, editors, or work areas. It also allows you to arrange the windows (tiled vertically, tiled horizontally, or cascaded). The Close All Editors item is handy for clearing out the editor workspace and starting over.

Help   This menu contains expected items—Help Topics, which displays the opening page of the online documentation, and About, which displays version and trademark information. It also contains access to the Release Notes stored locally. Two items, Oracle Technology Network and Oracle Java Education, link to the appropriate Internet sites.

NOTE
The first time you access a help topic in a JDeveloper session, the help system will be initialized in memory. Once that is completed, subsequent calls to the help system will respond more quickly. Another effect you will notice about the help system is that the Help buttons in various dialogs in JDeveloper open the help system in a modal window, so you cannot continue the task until you close the help window.

Component Palette

The Component Palette contains controls you use in the UI Editor for Java client code and in the Code Editor for JSP code. These controls are arranged into pages based on the control's source. For example, there is a Swing tab that contains controls from the Swing libraries. You can add to and modify the contents of these pages using Configure Component Palette dialog (**Tools | Configure Palette** or on the Component Palette, select Properties from the right-click menu). Chapter 18 contains a hands-on practice that steps through adding an icon to the Component Palette.

The tooltips for these icons contain the library information for the class name (such as javax.swing) as well as the class name (such as JButton). You can also display a text label for each icon by selecting List View from the right-click menu on the Component Palette.

The Component Palette changes contents depending upon the file that is being edited. For example, if the cursor is in the UI Editor for a Java application, the Component Palette contains applicable controls from the Swing and AWT libraries. If the cursor is in the Code Editor for a JSP file, the Component Palette contains applicable controls from the various tag libraries supplied with JDeveloper. If a modeler is active, the Component Palette contains diagram components.

NOTE
You cannot add to diagram Component Palette pages as you can to the other pages.

Snippets   The Component Palette contains a page, called Snippets, which you can use to store frequently used blocks of code. The Snippets page is different for Java client (Java applications and applets) and for web client (JSP pages and HTML). You can use selections from the right-click menu in the Snippets page of the Component Palette to add, edit, or remove snippets. When you click a snippet icon in the Component Palette, the code written into the snippet is added at the cursor location in the Code Editor. Chapter 18 contains further discussion of this feature as it relates to Java client programming.

TIP
You can also use Code Completion Templates to quickly add frequently used code to the file you are editing. This feature is described in the "Code Completion Templates" section later in this chapter.

Property Inspector

The Property Inspector window is automatically displayed when the UI Editor is displayed. This window contains two tabs—Properties and Events.

The Properties tab shows a list of properties for the class that is selected in the Structure window. Selecting a property displays a description of that property in the lower pane of the Property Inspector window. When you modify the property value of a component, the code will be changed to reflect the new value. There are various ways to change a value based on the property. Some properties allow you to type in a value; other properties supply a fixed list of values from which to select; still others present a "..." ellipsis button in the property value area. Clicking this button displays another dialog where you set the required values.

When you change a value in the Property Inspector, pressing ENTER will make the change permanent. If you just click on another property or area of another window, the new value may not be entered.

NOTE
You can create "customizers" that handle a number of properties in a single interface. You can define a customizer that works like a wizard or like a dialog with a set of properties. You can also define your own "property editors" for editing individual properties. The help system contains further information about customizers and property editors.

The Events tab displays a list of events for the component that is selected in the Structure window or UI Editor. You can add code to handle any event in this tab by typing an event name as the value for an event in the list and pressing ENTER. The Code Editor will open and navigate to the code stub that was added, so you can type in an event handler. Instead of typing a name, you can click the "..." button in the event property. A dialog such as the following will open, allowing you to rename the event handler and showing the code stub that will be created:

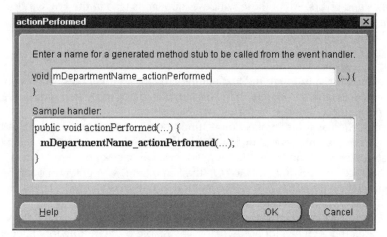

The properties and events in these tabs appear in alphabetical order, but you can click the Categories button in the Property Inspector toolbar to order the properties by types (such as General and Visual). To set a property value, first click the property name; then type in a value, select from the pulldown, or click the ellipsis button as appropriate to the property. To finalize the property value, press ENTER or click another property. The code will be changed to reflect the new value.

NOTE
You can group objects together in the UI Editor using SHIFT-click and CTRL-click and examine properties of the group. Properties with different values will be displayed with the values italicized. You can modify simple (single-valued) properties of those objects as a group, and the modification will be applied to all objects in the group.

TIP
If you group dissimilar objects together, the Property Inspector will display the "intersection"—only the properties that have the same names in all objects. If you click the Union button in the Property Inspector toolbar, all properties of all objects will be displayed, regardless of the property names. Click the Union button again to return to the intersection view of the properties.

Log Window

This window shows messages that are generated when you run, debug, or compile your code. If the message is an error, you can double click on the error text in this window, and the problem code will be highlighted in the Source tab. This gives you a quick way to navigate to the problem area. The right-click menu in the Log window allows you to select and save the text into a file for later use.

The Log window area opens new windows for different types of activities. For example, generating Javadoc opens a new window. Compiling a Java application uses the window to present messages and errors. All of these windows appear as tabs in the Log window area and will move with the Log window if you undock it. You can close and clear them separately using options from the right-click menu.

Code Editor

The Code Editor supplies a full-featured text editing area for all code files. You open the Code Editor by double clicking any code file in the System Navigator or by selecting Code Editor from the right-click menu for a file node in the System Navigator.

Characteristics such as fonts, syntax colors, undo behavior, and tab size are customizable using selections from the Preferences dialog (**Tools | Preferences**) as shown in Figure 2-5. One of the preferences you can set in the Code Editor\Java page of the Preferences dialog is Preferred Open Brace Style. Setting this to "On the Same Line" will enter an opening curly bracket "{" character on the same line as the method signature whenever the editor adds brackets automatically, (for example "`public static main(String[] args) {`").

The Code Editor uses standard shortcut keys such as CTRL-C for Copy and CTRL-V for Paste. The help topic "Reference: JDeveloper Keymaps" (available by searching for "JDeveloper keymaps" in the Search tab) provides lists of the shortcuts for various key mappings.

You can drag and drop selected text in the Code Editor by highlighting it with the mouse and dragging and dropping it into the new location. The right-click menu contains actions that you would use frequently (for example, Cut, Copy, Paste, and Undo). The right-click menu also contains a submenu for sorting import statements in a Java class file. For class files with many import statements, this can help make the code more readable.

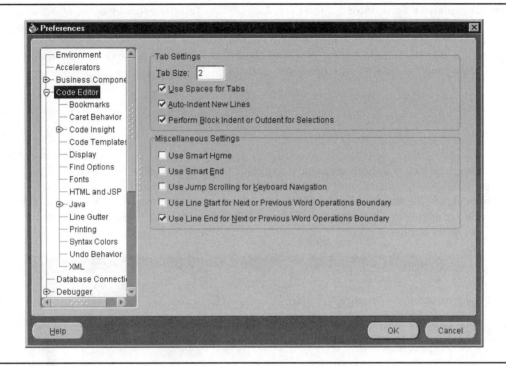

FIGURE 2-5. *Preferences dialog for the Code Editor*

TIP
The file name and path of the file open in the editor are shown in the window title bar. You also see the file name and path in the IDE status bar when you click the file node in the System Navigator.

File Type-Specific Editing Behavior   The Code Editor may be used to edit text files of various types such as Java, HTML, and JSP page. The features are similar for these types of files, but the Component Palette, Code Insight, syntax colors, and automatic completion features are specific to the file type.

For example, when you edit an HTML file in the Code Editor, the editor fills in ending tags (such as "`</table>`") as you type beginning tags (such as "`<table>`"). This behavior is defined by the Preferences dialog's "Code Editor\HTML and JSP" page. The editor determines the file type (by the file extension) and applies this behavior to the editor.

NOTE
Syntax highlighting is available for Java, PL/SQL, SQL, XML, JSP, HTML, C++, and IDL files. You can modify the colors in the Preferences page "Code Editor\Syntax Colors."

Code Completion Templates   The Code Completion Template feature of the editor allows you to create shortcut text strings that can trigger a block of code to be entered automatically. The easiest way to explain this feature is with a demonstration.

Enter the text "for" in the Code Editor, and press CTRL-ENTER (using the default keymap). The following will be entered into the editor window:

```
for ( ; ; )
{

}
```

The symbol "for" is a shortcut for the code block that was entered into the editor. The keypress CTRL-ENTER (called CodeTemplate.EXPAND in the keymap lists available in the help system) activated the shortcut and transformed it into the code template text. You view, define, and modify shortcuts in the Preferences dialog (**Tools | Preferences**) Code Editor\Code Templates as shown here:

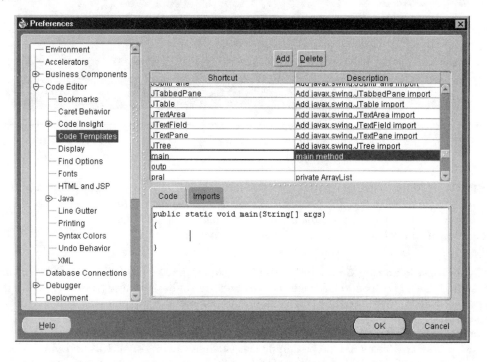

In addition to defining text blocks that will be inserted into the code, you can define import statements that will appear in the imports section. The Imports tab in the Code Templates preferences page allows you to define the import statements that will be inserted. If your code already contains import statements for the parent package, the import code will not be inserted.

TIP
*Although the JDeveloper Code Editor is flexible and fully featured,
you may want to use another editor. You can save a file in JDeveloper
and edit that file with an external editor. When you save the file and
return to JDeveloper, you can reload that file automatically (with or
without a confirmation dialog) based upon settings on the
Environment page of the Preferences dialog. As mentioned, Chapter
21 contains details about how to link an external program into the
JDeveloper toolbar and menus.*

Code Insight   JDeveloper offers another feature to help you write code for Java, JSP, XML,
XSL, UIX, and HTML source files. This feature, called *Code Insight,* pops up context-sensitive lists
of elements that are appropriate to the type of file you are editing. For example, for Java class
files, Code Insight presents lists of methods, constants, imports, and method parameters. The list
appears after you type a period and pause or press CTRL-SPACEBAR in the default keymap. An
example of a Code Insight list is shown here:

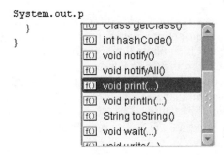

You can select from the list and press ENTER to enter the selected text. Alternatively, you can
keep typing and navigate to a match in the list. Clicking outside the pulldown list (or pressing
ESC) will dismiss the list. This style of Code Insight is called *completion insight* because it assists
you in completing code that you are writing.

Another style of Code Insight, called *parameter insight,* displays a list of valid parameters.
Parameter insight presents a list of valid arguments for a method after you type an open
parenthesis "(" as shown here:

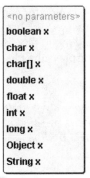

You do not select from this list, but use it as a reminder of the types of objects or variables that can act as parameters to the method. This list will automatically appear when you type an opening parenthesis character or if you press CTRL-SHIFT-SPACEBAR.

Use the Code Editor\Code Insight page of the Preferences dialog to modify the time delay before Insight appears or to turn the feature off and on. Regardless of the settings in this dialog, Code Insight will appear if you press the appropriate key combinations (CTRL-SPACEBAR or CTRL-SHIFT-SPACEBAR).

CAUTION
The classes you want to use to provide Insight must be defined in the classpath of the project's settings. (The classpath is discussed further in Chapter 4.) You also need to compile your code if you want Code Insight to find its members. In addition, insight may not work if the file has compile errors. If Code Insight is not available, an appropriate message will appear in the editor's status bar.

Editing PL/SQL   You can also use the Code Editor to edit PL/SQL database code. Navigate to the database object (function, procedure, package, or package body) that you want to edit by expanding the Connections\<specific connection>\<user> nodes in the System Navigator. Double click the object to open it in the Code Editor.

You can create database code with the New option from the right-click menu on a code object node (such as Package). You can also select New PL/SQL Subprogram from the right-click menu on the user node.

When you save, make, or build a PL/SQL program, it is written to the database. Any compile errors will show in the Log window.

NOTE
You can debug PL/SQL code stored in an Oracle8i or Oracle9i database even if you did not create the code in JDeveloper. The help system topic available from the Index tab "PL/SQL, debugging" entry will get you started.

Document Bar
The Document Bar contains a tab button for each open editor. It allows you to quickly change the cursor focus to an open editor or viewer so that you can work on or view its contents. The list of windows available in the Window menu provides the same functionality but requires more movement. The Document Bar displays the file name and an icon optionally containing a number.

TIP
You can close an editor that is shown in the Document Bar even if it does not have current focus by selecting Close Editor from the right-click menu on the corresponding tab button.

Document Icons   These icons are slightly suggestive of the type of editor. For example, the icon for a Code Editor window is a text document with a pencil; the icon for a UI Editor window is the same icon with a bit of color in the background (denoting a visual editor). The icon contains a number corresponding to the number of the window in the Window menu. The following illustration shows some of the document icons:

Code Editor

UI Editor

Class Editor

Class Model

Activity Model

JDeveloper displays other icons for other types of windows, editors, or viewers such as the Table Viewer.

TIP
The double arrow at the right side of the Document Bar is a pulldown list of open editor documents. Selecting a document from that list makes it the active document.

Document Numbers   Editor documents that you open are designated as *explicit documents* and assigned a number from one to nine. The number is echoed in the Window menu and Document Bar icon. Files that the tool opens automatically are not assigned numbers and are designated as *implicit documents.* You can assign them numbers, and they then become *explicit documents.*

The difference between explicit and implicit documents is that you can toggle between explicit documents using ALT-<#> where "<#>" is the document number. This makes navigation among the open editors quick and easy.

To assign a specific number to an editor (explicit or implicit), click the Document Bar tab button for the editor, and press CTRL-SHIFT-<#> where "<#>" is the number you want to assign the document.

TIP
*You can close all implicit windows using **Window | Close Implicit**.*

UI Editor

The UI Editor shows a graphical view of the layout for rich-client classes such as Java frames and applets. You open the UI Editor for an appropriate file by selecting UI Editor from the right-click menu on the file in the System Navigator or Code Editor.

When you need to add objects to the layout, you can drop them into the parent node of the Structure window or onto the UI Editor. When you make a change to the layout, the Code Editor and Structure window views of the code will be updated appropriately.

The UI Editor also allows you to edit menu bars and popup menus (as described in Chapter 19). The UI Editor offers a number of features that assist in accurate layout of a user interface as follows:

- **Right-click menu** This menu contains editing, alignment, sequencing (Bring to Front and Send to Back), and other options appropriate to the layout manager applied to the container. For example, a null layout manager applied to a panel will cause a number of alignment menu items to appear in the right-click menu when a component within that panel is selected. (Layout managers are explained in Chapter 20.) There is also an option for *Serialize* that creates a .ser file that is a special representation of the state of the object (JavaBean) that you clicked on. The .ser file can be loaded back into JDeveloper to load the property values of the original object to another object.

- **Layout grid** In some layout managers, as you drag in or move components, a grid appears temporarily to help you line up the object with another object. This grid is customizable using the Preferences dialog.

- **Status bar** As you move the mouse cursor over objects in the UI Editor, the JDeveloper IDE status bar displays the object name and, in some cases, its constraints (details about placement).

- **Toolbar** The toolbar in the UI Editor provides functions that are available in the right-click menu such as Bring to Front and Send to Back. As with the right-click menu, the toolbar changes based on the layout manager applied to the container that has focus.

Chapter 3 contains hands-on practice to demonstrate the typical layout activities you would perform in this editor.

NOTE
The help system topic "Developing Java GUI Clients\About JDeveloper's User Interface Design Tools" contains the requirements for files to be displayed in the UI Editor. The rich-client wizards and code generators in JDeveloper create code that fulfills these requirements. However, you might want to load a file created in a different tool and need to be sure that it meets these requirements.

Other Editors

In addition to the Code Editor, JDeveloper offers several editors for creating source code files.

XML Editor   The XML Editor option on the right-click menu for an XML file in the Structure window opens the XML Editor. The XML Editor is a schema-driven editor for editing files in XML languages such as UIX, UIT, XSQL, XSL, XSD, XHTML, and WSDL. The editor supports syntax highlighting, the Structure window view, and the Property Inspector.

If the XML language has an XML schema associated with it, Tag Insight and End Tag Completion are also available. *End Tag Completion* (where the ending tag is automatically inserted when you complete a starting tag) is activated using the Code Editor\XML page of the Preferences dialog. *Tag Insight* is activated when you pause after opening a tag by typing a "<" character. Tag Insight pops up a list of available tags in the same way as Code Insight. It also pops up available attributes when you enter a space after a tag name. In addition, you can activate *Required Attribute Insertion* in the Preferences dialog. This feature adds attribute stubs for the required attributes of a tag (such as "name=" "") after you start typing that tag (such as "xsl:attribute").

If the file is a read-only file (such as a BC4J or other XML file that uses a dialog for editing), the right-click menu contains an option for Code Editor. Selecting this option opens the editor in *protected* (read-only) mode as noted by "Protected" in the editor's status bar. For example, the Code Editor selection on the XML file of a BC4J view object will run the XML Editor in protected mode; to edit this file, you select Edit <view object name> from the right-click menu on the view object parent node in the System Navigator. This opens a dialog with which you interact to change the contents of the XML file. You do not edit the XML file directly inside the tool. The reason for this protection is that the XML structure is specific to the editors in JDeveloper. If you were able to edit the file and mistyped a value or tag, the editors might not work.

You can import an XML schema (.xsd file) for a specific file type using the Preferences dialog's "XML Schemas" page. If the schema is registered in this way, the XML Editor will provide Code Insight and validation for the elements that you enter.

Class Editor   The Class Editor displays Java classes in a more structured way than the Code Editor. Figure 2-6 shows a sample page from the Class Editor for a Java application file.

You manipulate the file by entering definitions into the following tab pages:

- **General**   Using the button in this page, you can create a standard BeanInfo file from your class file so that the class can be used as a JavaBean.

- **Fields**   This page allows you to enter and edit attributes (fields). You can declare that get() and set() method stubs be created when you define a new field.

- **Methods**   You can declare methods in this class using this page. If you click the Add button, you enter details about the method. A method stub will be added to the source file, and you can enter the code details in the Code Editor.

- **Events**   As the name implies, this page is used to enter and modify the events in your class. There is an area to define the events that are fired and the event listeners that will be created.

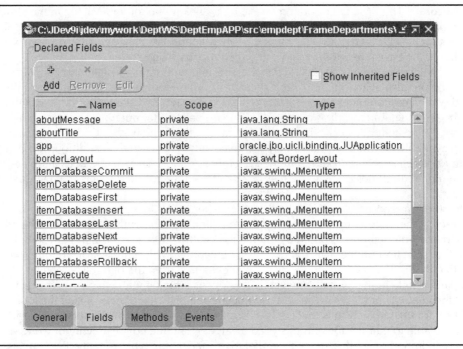

FIGURE 2-6. *Class Editor window*

NOTE
Chapter 4 contains an overview of Java elements such as fields, methods, and events.

The definitions you enter in this dialog immediately create code that you can view in the Code Editor. The Class Editor is handy for quickly entering basic definitions and structures of a class before you fill in the code using the Code Editor.

EJB Module Editor   When you create an Enterprise JavaBean (EJB) from the New dialog (**File | New**), the EJB Module Editor opens to allow you to change characteristics about the files. You can also open this editor by double clicking an EJB node in the Navigator. The editor looks similar to the Class Editor, and it allows you to edit the EJB fields, methods, environment, references, and other details. When you accept the changes in this editor, the appropriate EJB class files will be updated.

The EJB Module Editor is used to manipulate the EJB Java files. If you need to change deployment descriptor characteristics, open the Settings dialog by selecting Settings from the right-click menu on the orion-ejb-jar.xml file in the System Navigator.

NOTE
*The EJB node in the System Navigator for a specific EJB offers
a right-click menu option for Edit EJB that displays the EJB
Module Editor.*

Viewer Windows

For most file types, double clicking the file name in the System Navigator will open the
appropriate editor. For nontext files, an appropriate viewer will open so that you can look at,
but not edit, the file. As with editors, the file name and path appear in the window title.
You can also open a viewer for a file using the selections in the View menu's Display With
submenu. For files that require a viewer, you can select the viewer from the right-click menu
on the file node in the System Navigator.

The following viewer windows are available in the JDeveloper IDE:

HTML Viewer   This viewer displays the HTML code as it would appear in the browser.
Although there is no visual editor for HTML code in JDeveloper, this viewer helps, because
you can open both the Code Editor and the HTML Viewer for the same HTML file. As you
make changes to the HTML code in the Code Editor, the HTML Viewer will update to reflect
the changes.

The HTML Viewer functions as a browser and will load pages that are linked through
hypertext references. The toolbar contains browser buttons such as Go Back, Go Forward,
Refresh, Go to Starting Page, Stop, and Find. A pulldown in the toolbar area shows the names
of files that have been displayed.

NOTE
*If you need a full-featured HTML editor, you can load an HTML file
into a tool such as Macromedia Dreamweaver or Microsoft
FrontPage, edit, and save the file. When you return to JDeveloper,
the modified file will be reloaded into the Code Editor.*

JSP Viewer   The JSP Viewer shows JavaServer Pages code as it would appear in the browser.
This viewer works in the same way as the HTML Editor described earlier and has the same
toolbar. However, this viewer does not run the code in a server container, so the only thing that
is displayed is output of the HTML code with icons for the JSP tags. You will be able to see the
basic layout of the page, but will not see the data and other HTML output by Web Beans or data
Web Beans.

Image Viewer   Double clicking an image file (.gif, .jpg, .jpeg, or .png) in the System
Navigator will display the Image Viewer. This viewer displays the image in a graphical format.
You can select this viewer from the right-click menu on an image file or by selecting the Image
Viewer option from the View menu Display With submenu.

Archive Viewer   You can view the contents of a .zip or .jar file by opening the file in JDeveloper (**File** | **Open**). The Archive Viewer will be displayed automatically as shown here:

Path	Date	Size	Compressed
src/com/sun/image/codec/jpeg/ImageFormatException.java	11/13/01 4:22 PM	1,971	1,971
src/com/sun/image/codec/jpeg/JPEGCodec.java	11/13/01 4:22 PM	5,925	5,925
src/com/sun/image/codec/jpeg/JPEGDecodeParam.java	11/13/01 4:22 PM	13,777	13,777
src/com/sun/image/codec/jpeg/JPEGEncodeParam.java	11/13/01 4:22 PM	10,728	10,728
src/com/sun/image/codec/jpeg/JPEGHuffmanTable.java	11/13/01 4:22 PM	8,787	8,787
src/com/sun/image/codec/jpeg/JPEGImageDecoder.java	11/13/01 4:22 PM	5,908	5,908
src/com/sun/image/codec/jpeg/JPEGImageEncoder.java	11/13/01 4:22 PM	9,220	9,220
src/com/sun/image/codec/jpeg/JPEGQTable.java	11/13/01 4:22 PM	5,071	5,071
src/com/sun/image/codec/jpeg/TruncatedFileException.java	11/13/01 4:22 PM	3,045	3,045
src/com/sun/java/swing/plaf/motif/MotifBorders.java	11/13/01 4:22 PM	24,128	24,128
src/com/sun/java/swing/plaf/motif/MotifButtonListener.java	11/13/01 4:22 PM	1,720	1,720
src/com/sun/java/swing/plaf/motif/MotifButtonUI.java	11/13/01 4:22 PM	3,262	3,262
src/com/sun/java/swing/plaf/motif/MotifCheckBoxMenuItemUI....	11/13/01 4:22 PM	2,884	2,884
src/com/sun/java/swing/plaf/motif/MotifCheckBoxUI.java	11/13/01 4:22 PM	1,760	1,760
src/com/sun/java/swing/plaf/motif/MotifComboBoxRenderer.j...	11/13/01 4:22 PM	2,656	2,656
src/com/sun/java/swing/plaf/motif/MotifComboBoxUI.java	11/13/01 4:22 PM	11,405	11,405
src/com/sun/java/swing/plaf/motif/MotifDesktopIconUI.java	11/13/01 4:22 PM	10,437	10,437
src/com/sun/java/swing/plaf/motif/MotifDesktopPaneUI.java	11/13/01 4:22 PM	4,802	4,802
src/com/sun/java/swing/plaf/motif/MotifEditorPaneUI.java	11/13/01 4:22 PM	1,537	1,537

You can double click a file name in this viewer, and the file will be opened in the appropriate editor or viewer. The file will not be added to the System Navigator, so that when you exit and return to JDeveloper, that file will not automatically load.

Table Viewer   The Table Viewer displays the structure of a table or view as shown here:

PK	Name	Type	Size	Scale	Allow nulls
✓	EMPLOYEE_ID	NUMBER	6	0	✗
✗	FIRST_NAME	VARCHAR2	20		✓
✗	LAST_NAME	VARCHAR2	25		✗
✗	EMAIL	VARCHAR2	25		✗
✗	PHONE_NUMBER	VARCHAR2	20		✓
✗	HIRE_DATE	DATE	7		✗
✗	JOB_ID	VARCHAR2	10		✗
✗	SALARY	NUMBER	8	2	✗
✗	COMMISSION_PCT	NUMBER	2	2	✓
✗	MANAGER_ID	NUMBER	6	0	✓
✗	DEPARTMENT_ID	NUMBER	4	0	✓
✗	DN	VARCHAR2	300		✓

Structure   Data

You can also view the table's data, as shown next, by clicking the Data tab.

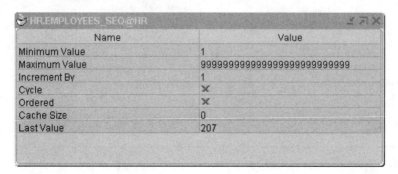

The Data tab allows you to reorder columns by dragging and dropping their headers, but the settings are not saved for the next time you open the viewer.

To activate the Table Viewer for a particular table, navigate to the Database node under Connections in the System Navigator. Find the connection and expand the user name and Tables node (or Views node for database views). Double click the table or select Table Viewer from the right-click menu on the table. You can also open the Table Viewer for tables under the Synonyms node. Views under the Synonyms node do not display the structure although they do display the data. Sequences under the Synonyms node do not display a viewer.

TIP
When you select a table name in the Tables node of the System Navigator, the Structure window will display the columns and indexes for that table.

Sequence Viewer   You can view database sequences in the same way that you view tables. Click the sequence in the System Navigator, and select Sequence Viewer from the right-click menu on the sequence name. The following dialog will appear:

Name	Value
Minimum Value	1
Maximum Value	9999999999999999999999999999
Increment By	1
Cycle	X
Ordered	X
Cache Size	0
Last Value	207

The viewer shows the standard properties for sequences and includes the last value that the sequence retrieved.

TIP
*Although the viewers do not allow you to modify their contents, you can delete some of the files (using **Files** | **Erase from Disk**) and the database object (using Drop from the right-click menu on the database object's node).*

The Modelers

There are two Unified Modeling Language (UML) modelers included with JDeveloper—the Class Modeler and the Activity Modeler. Figure 2-7 shows a sample of the Class Modeler window. These modelers allow you to represent business data and processes diagrammatically. They also allow you to generate Java code that implements the diagrammed elements. Although the topic of the Activity Modeler is out of scope for this book, further details about the Class Modeler are contained in Chapters 8 and 11.

SQL Worksheet

The SQL Worksheet was introduced with the 9.0.2 release of JDeveloper. It supplements the SQL*Plus option in the right-click menu of a connections node. The SQL Worksheet presents a window (as shown in Figure 2-8) where you can enter and execute SQL statements through a database connection that you have defined in the Connections node.

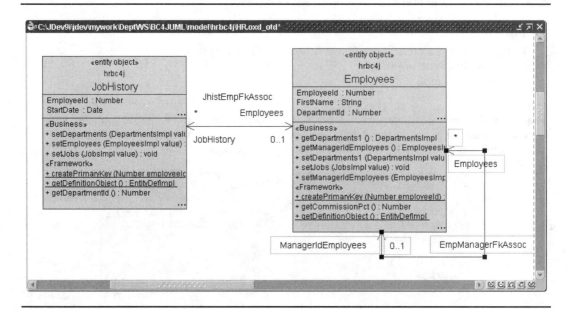

FIGURE 2-7. *Sample class model*

```
 HR                                                                        ⌐ ⅂ X
 Enter SQL Statement:

 ⅏  ⅈ  ⅀

  1 SELECT employee_id, last_name, first_name,
  2        phone_number, email,
  3        hire_date "Started"
  4 FROM   employees
  5 ORDER BY last_name
```

Results:

Fetch Size: 100   Fetch Next   Refresh

EMPLOYE...	LAST_NAME	FIRST_NAME	PHONE_NUMBER	EMAIL	Started
174	Abel	Ellen	011.44.1644.429267	EABEL	1996-05-11 00:00:00.0
166	Ande	Sundar	011.44.1346.629268	SANDE	2000-03-24 00:00:00.0
130	Atkinson	Mozhe	650.124.6234	MATKINSO	1997-10-30 00:00:00.0
105	Austin	David	590.423.4569	DAUSTIN	1997-06-25 00:00:00.0
204	Baer	Hermann	515.123.8888	HBAER	1994-06-07 00:00:00.0
116	Baida	Shelli	515.127.4563	SBAIDA	1997-12-24 00:00:00.0
167	Banda	Amit	011.44.1346.729268	ABANDA	2000-04-21 00:00:00.0
172	Bates	Elizabeth	011.44.1343.529268	EBATES	1999-03-24 00:00:00.0
192	Bell	Sarah	650.501.1876	SBELL	1996-02-04 00:00:00.0
151	Bernstein	David	011.44.1344.345268	DBERNS	1997-03-24 00:00:00.0

FIGURE 2-8.   *SQL Worksheet*

Open the SQL Worksheet by selecting SQL Worksheet from the right-click menu on a database connection name in the Server Navigator. The top pane of the window allows you to enter SQL statements. When you click the "Execute the statement" (the left-hand) button, the statement is executed and the results are displayed in the bottom pane. If the result is data (such as for a SELECT statement), the bottom pane will display the rows of data in a scrollable table.

You can enter more than one command in the SQL Worksheet and execute them one at a time by selecting the command and clicking the "Execute the statement" button.

Another feature of the SQL Worksheet is the ability to display the execution path for the SQL statement. To display the execution plan for a statement, click the "Explain how the statement will be executed" button (the middle button). The "View SQL history dialog" (right-hand) button shows a list of the commands you have used in this session. You can select from the list and the text will be written into the command area.

CodeCoach

CodeCoach is a JDeveloper feature offered if the IDE is running in a Windows environment. CodeCoach provides hints about how to optimize your code. When you activate CodeCoach, your program will run as usual. After you exit the program, you will find a list of suggestions for improving your code in the Log window. You can run CodeCoach on Java code if it runs within the Oracle JVM, is executed locally, and has been compiled with the Oracle Java Compiler. (JDeveloper uses this compiler automatically.) If you work within JDeveloper on Windows, all of these requirements will be met.

Setting Up CodeCoach You can customize the way CodeCoach runs by using the CodeCoach page of the Configurations\Development node in the Project Settings dialog (**Project | Project Settings**), as shown here:

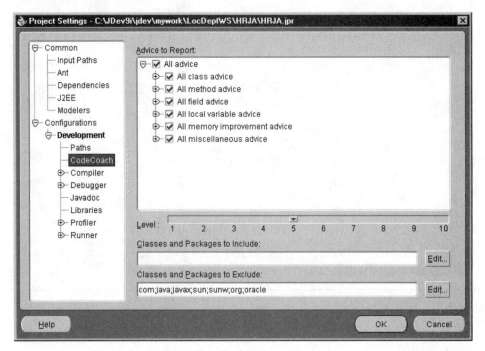

You can request advice in different categories by checking the appropriate checkboxes. The level of help that you request indicates whether CodeCoach will offer advice for the most important findings (1), on all findings (10), or something in between.

Each advice type has a keyword with which it is associated, for example, "CFIN" for "Possible final class" advice or "LFIN" for "Possible final local variable." These keywords are displayed in the Log window after you run the program. Refer to the help system topic "CodeCoach Keywords" (found in the help system index) for a listing of keywords.

This dialog also allows you to exclude classes that you do not want to be CodeCoached (for example, the Java Swing classes). Except for the classes you exclude, CodeCoach will run on all classes in your project and on all classes that those classes reference. You can include classes specifically if needed, but leaving the *include* field blank implies including all classes in the project.

CAUTION
If you fill in the blank include field, be sure to add your project's package name if you also want those files CodeCoached. Otherwise, your project files will not be included in the CodeCoach run.

You can override or refine the CodeCoach settings by inserting pragmas in your code. *Pragmas* are comments that are specially formatted and start with the symbol " / / @" for each pragma line.

When setting up CodeCoach for a project, you also need to check the *Include Debug Information* checkbox on the Compiler page in the Configurations\Development node of Project Settings.

Running CodeCoach   To start CodeCoach, select the project file in the Navigation window, and select **Run | CodeCoach** *<appname>* (where "appname" is the program name). If you receive a warning stating that a class must be compiled with debug information, check the setup requirements described earlier.

As you run the program, test all features of the application so that the CodeCoach can receive a full view of all aspects of the application.

NOTE
You can also run CodeCoach from the command line. The command-line syntax is documented in the "Ways to Start CodeCoach" topic of the "Testing and Optimizing Application Code\CodeCoaching a Project" node in the help system Contents page.

Output from a CodeCoach Session   Upon completion of a CodeCoach session, a results window (tab) will be displayed in the Log window area as shown here:

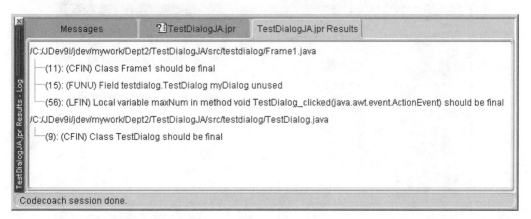

The right-click menu for a line of advice (such as "(CFIN) Class Frame1 should be final") contains options to find the line of source code for this advice; to apply a fix to the problem source code; to ignore the message; to hide messages of this type; and to show messages that you have hidden. Double clicking a message will display the referenced line of code in the Code Editor.

TIP
*The help system Contents page node "Testing and Optimizing
Application Code\CodeCoaching a Project" contains more
information about CodeCoach.*

Wizards and New File Dialogs

One of the main strengths of using an IDE such as JDeveloper is its ability to generate large
amounts of error-free code that you can edit and use. The wizard is one of the main interfaces
that JDeveloper uses to collect settings from you that will determine how it generates a file.
JDeveloper also offers new file dialogs that create starting code for a specific kind of new file.
Appendix A contains a list of all wizards and dialogs that you use to create files.

Wizards

JDeveloper offers wizards to assist in defining new files with features that are relatively complex.
A *wizard* is a dialog that leads you through the steps of creating a type of file or other object.
Typically, a wizard presents the required properties in an easy-to-understand way, supplies default
values where appropriate, and ensures that the values you enter are appropriate and complete.

The wizard dialog usually presents a series of pages that step you through the process of
creating an object. Next and Back buttons allow you to navigate between pages. A Finish button
closes the dialog and accepts all values. A Cancel button exits the dialog, and a Help button
presents specific instructions on the step you are performing. The following shows these features
in the JClient Form Wizard:

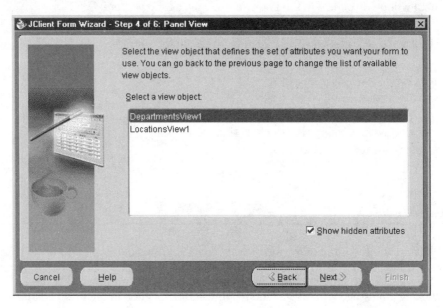

Most wizards are *re-entrant.* That is, once you run the wizard to create the file, you can also edit that file (using an Edit right-click menu option) by using the wizard. The edit version of the wizard does not offer Next and Previous buttons. Instead it allows you to navigate among the pages using a tab or hierarchical tree interface. The pages are usually the same in the creation version of the wizard and the edit version of the wizard, but there may be extra pages in one or the other.

New File Dialogs

JDeveloper also offers *dialogs,* single-page property windows that allow you to specify characteristics of files that do not have complex needs. For example, the following is the New Application dialog, where you can define the name and other properties of the application file. As with the wizards, settings in the dialog affect the code that is generated.

Sometimes a dialog starts up another dialog based upon the settings. For example, in the previous illustration, the Optional Attributes area contains an option to create a new frame file. If you select that option and click OK, the New Application dialog will create the application file and automatically open the New Frame dialog where you define the frame file.

TIP
You can resize wizards, dialogs, and user interface windows in this release of JDeveloper. In addition, some dialogs and wizards have multi-pane areas, which you can resize if something that you need to see is not visible.

New Gallery

Most wizards and dialogs start from the *New gallery* that you access using **File | New**, or by selecting New from the right-click menu on various nodes in the System Navigator. You use the New gallery (shown here) to supply default code for new files.

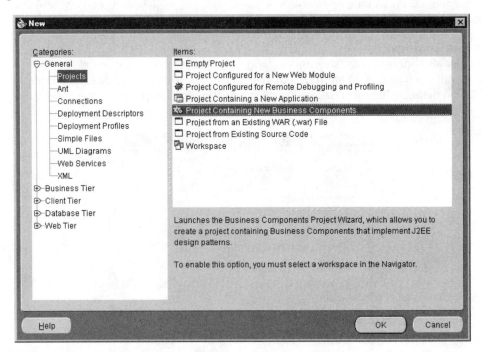

If you select a project node before displaying the New gallery, only items that can be placed into a project will be enabled in the dialog. After you select an object from one of the categories and click OK, the file node will be created in the System Navigator under the project that you selected. Depending on the object, the appropriate wizard or dialog may appear and prompt you for properties.

When you save a file that has been changed, the name of the file in the Navigator window changes from an italicized font to a non-italicized font. Also, the asterisk ("*") that is appended to the file name in the editor window title bar for a modified file is removed.

TIP
Some developers find keypresses more efficient than menu selections. Instead of selecting New from the right-click menu, you can alternatively press CTRL-N.

CAUTION

Wizards hide the complexity of the code they are creating. While this is the main purpose of the wizard interface, it is important that you have an understanding of what you are creating and how it fits into the general context of the application. It also helps to study the code created by the wizards so that you understand its contents and structure. The contents list that is available in the Structure window for a particular file can help you with both contents and structure.

Modifying What the Wizard Creates

The details that you enter in a wizard are translated to code or project properties. Although some wizards are not re-entrant, you can always change the generated code. When you select an edit option from the right-click menu on the file's node in the System Navigator, a dialog with tab or hierarchical tree pages opens. The pages in this dialog are the same as or similar to the pages in the wizard that created the object. When you modify the settings in this dialog and click OK, the file will be updated.

For example, the Business Components Package Wizard creates a large number of code files to access the database. Although you cannot modify the business components project in the same way after the wizard is finished, you can double click any object that it creates (such as the package node or the .jpx file) in the System Navigator and adjust the properties. The following shows a dialog that appears when you double click the application module node in the business components project. You can also load this dialog by selecting Edit from the right-click menu on the application module node. Other types of objects have similar menus, although the actual dialog looks different.

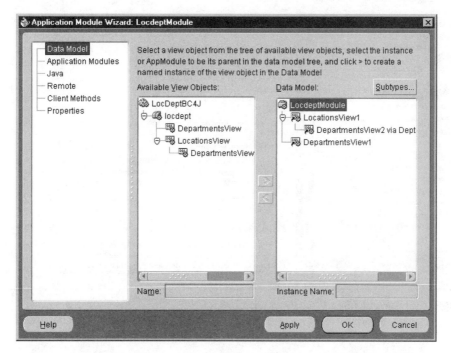

NOTE
*You can create your own wizards using the JDeveloper Addin API
if you do not like the way a wizard works or need to repetitively
perform a task for which there is no wizard. The JDeveloper help
system Contents tab node "Extending JDeveloper" contains more
information about creating JDeveloper wizards and other extensions.*

The Help System

The JDeveloper help system (shown in Figure 2-9) was built using Oracle Help for Java. The main
benefit of this system is that it is platform independent, so the help system will work in any operating
system that supports the JDeveloper IDE. Finding a topic in the help system is relatively easy for
anyone who has used a modern help system such as those built using WinHelp or HTML Help.

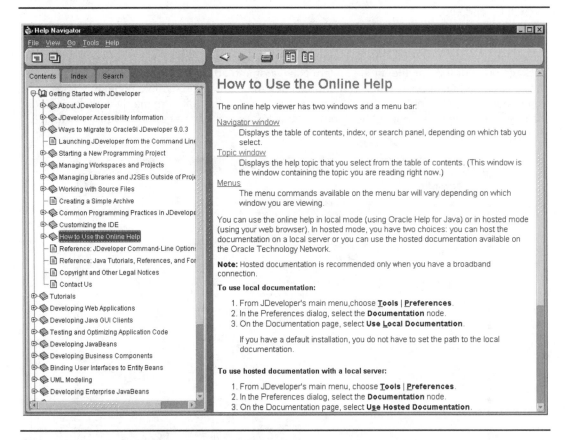

FIGURE 2-9. *Sample page from the help system*

However, if the help engine is unfamiliar to you, it is worth mentioning some of its features so that you can be as productive as possible.

NOTE
The help system contents page node "Getting Started with JDeveloper\How to Use the Online Help" contains details about basic help system operations.

Navigator Window

When the help system appears, it presents a Navigator window with three tabs as follows:

- ■ **Contents**   This tab displays a list of topics. The topics are arranged hierarchically in books that you can expand and in leaf nodes that represent topic pages. Double clicking a book icon expands or collapses the node and displays the topic associated with the book (usually a page with links to the child nodes); double clicking a topic node displays that topic.

- ■ **Index**   This tab contains a list of keywords that are associated with one or more help topics. Typing the text navigates to a match in the keyword list. Clicking a keyword displays a list of topics and if you double click the topic name (or click the Display button), the topic page will be displayed. This behavior is identical to other styles of help engines such as WinHelp.

- ■ **Search**   You can search for text strings on this page. When you click Search, the matching list of topics will appear in the list. The list contains a Rank column that displays a dark circle for a likely match, a half-dark circle for a partial match, and a light circle for a slight match. The Source column displays the node under which the topic appears on the Contents page. If you display a topic that has a source, you can return to the Contents page, and the current page will be selected in the navigator.

The toolbar in this window contains buttons for displaying a selected topic in the topic window and for displaying the topic in a separate topic window. Using the latter button allows you to open more than one topic at the same time.

NOTE
*When you close the help system and reopen it (using **Help | Help Topics**) in the same JDeveloper session, the last open topic will be displayed.*

Topic Window

The help system does not display the topic window until you double click a topic. The topic window appears as a separate window. You can close either the Navigator window or the topic window, and the other window will remain open.

You can dock or detach the help topic window to the Navigator window using buttons in the topic window toolbar. There are also buttons to view the next and previous topics that you have viewed. Other buttons display the Navigator window and print the topic.

You can select text in the help system (by dragging the mouse from left to right across the text), press CTRL-C to copy, and press CTRL-V to paste the text into another editor.

NOTE
You can use Oracle Help for Java to develop help systems for your applications. The help system Contents tab node "Developing Help With Oracle Help for Java" contains the details that you will need to get started.

How to Display the Help System
You can display the help viewer using a number of methods:

- **Selecting Help | Help Topics** will display the last help topic that was open in that session.

- **Pressing F1** at any time in the tool will show a help topic that is related to what you are doing. For example, if the Code Editor is open and you press F1, the help system will display an overview topic about the Code Editor. Pressing F1 when the cursor is inside a class name in the Code Editor will display the Javadoc for that class, if any. Pressing F1 when the cursor is inside the name of a JSP tag (such as "`<jbo:DataSource>`") in the Code Editor will display the help topic for that tag.

- **Clicking the Help button** in a dialog will show context-sensitive help.

Use the Index or Search tab features if those methods yield unsatisfactory results.

TIP
You can download an Adobe Acrobat .pdf file version of the help documentation from Oracle Technology Network (otn.oracle.com). This file offers a format that you might find easier to use for searching and printing text.

Locating Help Centrally
You can run the help system from a centralized server (called *hosted documentation*) so that the help files do not need to be loaded on each developer's hard drive. This requires installing the help files on the server and defining the location of the help files in the Documentation page of the Preferences dialog (**Tools | Preferences**). This page also allows you to define the source of the documentation as the Oracle Technology Network website (otn.oracle.com). Text searches in the hosted documentation environment can be slow, so weigh the convenience of this option with the need for developers to search for text using the Search tab.

Software Configuration Management

Developing software rarely involves one developer, a single application, and a one-time release. Typically, teams of developers produce many integrated applications with releases appearing regularly over time. A software configuration management (SCM) system is designed to track and identify changes to development objects over time and to allow the developers to not only edit the latest version of a program, but also to go back to previous releases and work in parallel with a more current release.

JDeveloper addresses these requirements by providing access to source control systems such as Oracle SCM, Rational ClearCase 4.0, and Concurrent Versions System (CVS). You can also write your own source control system (considered a *plugin* to JDeveloper) and connect it to JDeveloper. More information is available in the help system node "Using Source Control Support."

This section explores the Oracle SCM option since Oracle SCM (formerly called "Repository") is included with Oracle Internet Developer Suite (*i*DS), which also contains JDeveloper. The other SCM solutions are not included with *i*DS or with JDeveloper.

NOTE
In the name of the Oracle SCM product, the "SCM" stands for "Software Configuration Manager." When the acronym "SCM" is used alone, it refers to "software configuration management" in general.

Oracle SCM Features

Oracle SCM provides isolated working areas, controlled access to software configuration management functions, and a range of utilities to enable the following:

- **Object version control** through check-in and check-out procedures
- **Parallel development** through branching
- **Comparison and merging** of object versions
- **Creation of coherent sets** of selected object versions

Workareas, configurations, branches, versioning, and access control provide this functionality in Oracle SCM. This section discusses and demonstrates these concepts and how they integrate with Oracle JDeveloper. It assumes that you have already installed and set up the Oracle SCM repository in an Oracle database.

Enabling Source Control

By default, source control is not active in JDeveloper. You enable this by selecting the active plugin in the Preferences dialog (**Tools | Preferences**) node, Source Control. (You can also select **File | Source Control | Enable** to open this dialog.) When you select a plugin, the page displays fields specific to the plugin. After you fill in the fields and click OK, source control will be enabled.

You then create a connection to the SCM repository using the Connections Wizard (started from the right-click menu on the Oracle9i SCM node in the System Navigator). The last step for setting up source control is using the Oracle9i SCM Workarea Wizard (shown next) to create a workarea to hold the files.

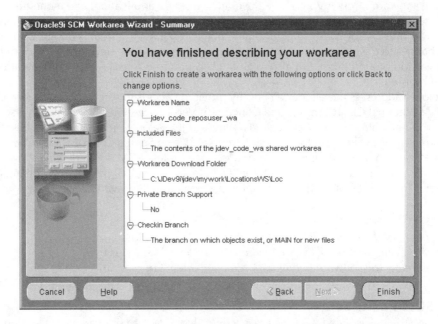

The result of creating the workarea is that files will be downloaded into the local file system from a particular workarea in the SCM repository. If there are no files in the repository, you will be able to add them into the new workarea (by selecting **Source Control | Add** from the right-click menu on a file in the System Navigator). The files may then be opened using the JDeveloper **File | Open** menu option or included in the current project. All types of files are supported.

The SCM Repository

Oracle SCM requires an underlying repository structure. This repository resides within an Oracle9i (or Oracle8i) database, with the database providing services such as backup, restore, and security. The repository is created using the Oracle SCM Repository Administration Utility (RAU); RAU is a utility of Oracle Designer and Oracle SCM (in the same suite of products as JDeveloper). Oracle database users are created outside of the utility and then given access to the repository using RAU. Each developer is given a unique repository user account. The JDeveloper user connects to the repository using this account.

Workareas

Workareas (logical containers for repository objects) permit one and only one version of any repository object to be viewed at any time. They provide a view of the underlying repository and contain pointers to a particular version of a file. They considerably simplify access to files and ensure that developers work with the correct version of a file. Workareas are defined via a set of rules, the simplest being "latest(MAIN)," where "MAIN" represents a branch of code development, and "latest" is the most recent version of a file.

Workareas are dynamic; that is, the version of a file within a workarea obeys a rule and, as development occurs, the version of the file will change. A JDeveloper project usually starts with some code; therefore, source code must be loaded into the SCM repository, given an initial version, and made available via a workarea to developers. This can be achieved via the JDeveloper IDE, from the Repository Object Navigator (RON, in Oracle Designer), or by using an Oracle SCM command-line tool script.

For example, a command-line script to upload Java files into the repository for the first time might look like the following:

```
connect  repos_user/passwd@database
-- create a workarea with simple rule latest(MAIN)
Makewa jdev_code_wa -rulatest(MAIN)
-- set this workarea as the current default
set wa jdev_code_wa
-- upload from a local directory into the SCM repository
upload d:\base_java_source\* jdev_source_fldr -s
-- check in and create first version of all uploaded files & folders
ci * -s
-- lastly commit all changes - this is a database transaction
commit
```

From the RON, grant access to this workarea to the PUBLIC role. You usually define a private workarea for each developer. The private workarea gives you individual control over the files you will modify. You can access Java files stored and versioned in the SCM repository using the JDeveloper client as described later.

NOTE
The concepts of the Oracle SCM "workarea" and JDeveloper "workspace" are similar because they are files that are grouped for convenient access. However, it is important to understand the distinction. A JDeveloper workspace defines one or more projects that you open in JDeveloper—each project representing a number of files in the local file system. An Oracle SCM workarea is a collection of files in the repository (database) that you check in and check out.

Code Editing
Once the repository workarea is defined, the developer can add a file from the local file system to a JDeveloper project within a JDeveloper workspace. The source code is considered "checked in" and is locked in the SCM repository and in the local file system. This prevents the files from being changed. You can check the file out using a right-click menu option on the file. This unlocks the file so that you can modify it. If you specify a *strict locking policy,* checkouts of the file or versions of that file on the same branch are not permitted. A nonstrict policy means that others can check out and modify the code. Once the code is edited and tested, it is checked back into the SCM repository.

If changes are made in the code, a new version is created. You can use the Version History viewer (available from the Source Control submenu of the File menu or the right-click menu) to display the various versions that were checked in. This viewer and the comparison utility that shows the exact changes made to the file (also available in the Source Control submenu of the File menu or right-click menu) are shown here:

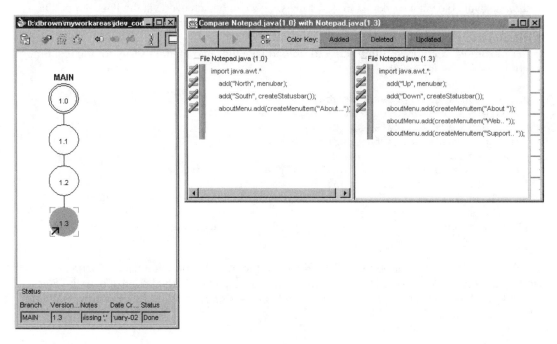

The history shows versions 1.0 through 1.3, and the comparison shows the difference between 1.0 and 1.3.

Parallel Development

Not all development situations are as simple as the preceding example. Teams might require different versions of a file for the following requirements:

- They are working on different tasks such as bug fixes or multi-language usage.

- They are running different operating systems.

- They have distributed development teams.

- They are working on different releases (for example, testing and production versions).

In the previous example, version 1.1 of the file Notepad.java may be part of the current production release. If a bug is found, it must be fixed in version 1.1 and in the latest version using a merge operation. Oracle SCM permits merge operations using branches. To make a fix to the current production version 1.1, a *configuration* (static set of specific file versions that are part of a release) is created from all files belonging to the production version. Normally a configuration is created each time a release is completed.

A workarea rule called INCLUDE_CONFIG(notepad_ver1_cfg{1.0}= Configuration gives developers access to the production file versions; these are not usually the latest files in development. To edit the production code file, each developer creates a private workarea from the shared workarea containing the file and works on the file in that workarea. This isolates changes from other developers while the bug is fixed. The branching allows parallel development with isolation from other releases or developers. Merging the file back to the main integration branch ends the private branch and adds the changes to the main branch.

For example, version 1.1 and 1.1.1.0 would be merged. In the previous case, this would not be required. A merge utility enables all files on a private branch to be merged to the files made available in any other workarea. In this case, a merge to version 1.3 is required, resulting in the following version history:

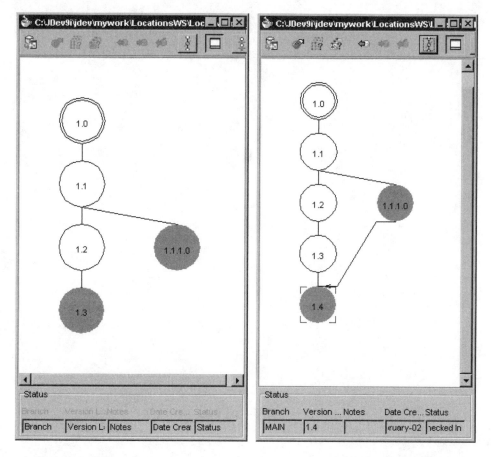

Other SCM Options
Other SCM options within the JDeveloper IDE include listing checked-out and nonversioned files and synchronization between the file system and the SCM repository.

CHAPTER
3

Creating BC4J
Applications with
the IDE Tools

Programmers are tools for converting caffeine into code.

—Unattributed, from a compilation of
humorous computer quotes by Guillaume Dargaud

he JDeveloper Integrated Development Environment (IDE) tools can be used to create applications without relying on the wizards. At times this is necessary because the wizards do not always produce the desired results. In this chapter you will build three projects: a BC4J project, a Java application, and a JSP application. These projects are similar to projects you create with the wizards in Chapter 1. Part II contains more detailed information about working with BC4J projects.

The goal of this chapter is to provide you with a feel for the kinds of activities required and a sense of how long the process of creating a BC4J application will take, but will not necessarily give you a thorough understanding of how to build an application.

You may notice that many of the activities in these practices require significantly more work in JDeveloper than in products such as Oracle Developer or PowerBuilder. Because of the BC4J components, it is probably not as much work as building similar applications in C++ or Visual Basic; however, it is certainly more labor intensive to build simple applications using JDeveloper than it is using Oracle Developer. The justification for the additional effort is that JDeveloper is so much more flexible and fully featured. Be aware that the JDeveloper environment is somewhat more complex than that of traditional Oracle client/server development tools.

Working with JDeveloper means working with Java in a 3GL environment. However, the JDeveloper IDE and wizards allow you to write 3GL code using a 4GL-like environment. Because JDeveloper allows you to "go behind" the code generator and write your own Java code, your applications will not suffer from any of the functional limitations that 4GL applications usually have. Such limitations do not exist in building Java applications. Virtually anything you can imagine can be supported with a proportionate amount of effort. However, the underlying business logic is still very flexible. As with any other tool, once you become familiar with the JDeveloper IDE, learning to use the features of JDeveloper will be straightforward.

About the BC4J Project

In the hands-on practice in Chapter 1, you build a basic BC4J Java application using JDeveloper's powerful high-level wizards. In Chapter 22, you build a basic BC4J JavaServer Page (JSP) application also using the wizards. With just a few clicks in a wizard, you are able to build a functioning master-detail application. If you try to generate a BC4J project using the high-level wizards, your project may not be exactly what you want. For example, some foreign key constraints between the tables in your database may not be relevant in a particular application. You may need to go back and modify an existing application by adding or modifying a component.

Another problem is that the JDeveloper default form generator only generates single master-detail relationships. Anything like a master-detail-detail relationship will require some hand modification.

CAUTION
The renaming of a BC4J object requires modifications to be made in many places within the application. There have been intermittent problems with renaming objects. Care should be taken when doing this, particularly with BC4J components. If the application starts behaving erratically or generating unexplainable error messages, one thing to try is to delete any renamed BC4J components and re-create them with the correct names. This may not always work cleanly because the files you are deleting may be related to other files.

For normal production use of JDeveloper, you may start with the high-level wizards for the first few application objects. However, you may soon find that the wizards have limited functionality and cannot generate the code required by your application. Consequently, you will need to add components manually, integrating them to components generated by the wizards.

About the Java Application Project

In this practice, you will create a simple master-detail application using the Location and Department tables from the HR sample database. (Detailed instructions about how to set up the HR schema are discussed in the Introduction.)

In the hands-on practice in Chapter 1, you created a workspace, LocDeptWS.jws. You used the wizards to create this workspace and the two projects it contains. In this chapter, you will be building the same application as in Chapter 1 without using the wizards in a second workspace, LocDept2WS.jws.

The LocDeptBC4J project supports the connection to the database, and the LocDeptJA application project includes the user interface components. Within the BC4J project, you will see its association to the connection in the Structure window after clicking the jpx file under the BC4J project. A single package—locdept—holds all of the BC4J objects. The LocDept application holds the client data model (LocDeptJA.cpx) and four classes. This application allows you to look at the Department and Location information in the HR schema included with Oracle9i JDeveloper.

Using the high-level wizards is not the only way to build the application. In this practice, you will create a functionally equivalent application by building all of the structures for the LocDept application using lower-level wizards. As you build the application, you can see what additional steps you take, and what additional flexibility these steps add to the application. For example, although the original application included four classes, this one will be structured differently. Deciding how much information should go into a class is like deciding how many procedures to use in coding. Everything may be placed in one large procedure or divided into multiple procedures that call each other.

The JClient Form Wizard built the application using four classes. For those familiar with JDeveloper 3.2, you may remember that using the wizards to generate the same application created only two classes (a frame class and an application class to call it). Deciding how to divide your code into classes is a question of style and may affect performance.

To be able to periodically examine your application and to compare your progress to what was generated by the JDeveloper wizards, this practice will stay as close as possible to the way that the wizards generate code.

About the JSP Project

For web-based applications, most developers will want to build a JSP. In this chapter, you will get a taste of how easy it is to build JSP pages. You will find that many of the development techniques are quite similar to the ones you used to build the other projects, but there are some significant differences. You should pay particular attention to how data tags are built and used.

You will be able to use the same BC4J project as you did for the Java application. This will help to demonstrate the power and flexibility of BC4J.

Hands-on Practice: Create a BC4J Project Manually

The goal of this practice is to build an application using techniques that are akin to those required for building production applications, but kept at a simple level so as not to overwhelm you with too much complexity.

For this practice, you will build the same application that you created in Chapter 1. However, this time, only the lower-level wizards will be used. The rest of the application will be built manually, using the UI Editor.

This practice consists of the following phases:

    I. Create a workspace, project, and connection

        ■ Prepare a new workspace

        ■ Create a project for the business components

        ■ Create or select a connection

    II. Create entity objects and view objects

    III. Delete and create an association

    IV. Create a view link

    V. Create an application module

    VI. Test the application

In this book, references to building applications "by hand" without using the wizards do not mean writing hundreds of lines of Java code. As mentioned in Chapter 1, there are many different wizards within JDeveloper. Some of these can be termed "high level" and enable you to build whole applications or substantial portions of applications with a few mouse clicks and entered properties. Other "low-level" wizards can be employed to create or modify a single program element. These wizards allow you to quickly build components as in a 4GL environment without having to write the necessary 3GL code. The high-level wizards will give you a jumpstart on building your application but the low-level object wizards generate parts of the code.

One of the strengths of JDeveloper is that experienced programmers can edit the Java code directly for any application components. Even the XML generated from BC4J can be edited. Advanced developers have found that the ability to manipulate the BC4J code is a very powerful and desirable feature. However, for most applications, the BC4J wizards are powerful enough that you will not need to manually edit the XML.

I. Create a Workspace, Project, and Connection

In this phase, you will create a workspace and project and connect to the HR sample schema.

Prepare a New Workspace

To create a workspace, use the following steps:

1. On the Workspaces node, select New Workspace from the right-click menu.

2. In the New Workspace dialog, change the default name (such as "Workspace1") in the *Directory Name* field, to "LocDept2WS."

   Additional Information: The workspace directory was created as a subdirectory of the JDeveloper "mywork" folder. This workspace could be placed in any directory, but for all of the hands-on practices in this book, the mywork directory will be used.

3. In the *File Name* field, change the default workspace name to "LocDept2WS" as shown here. JDeveloper will automatically add the appropriate file extensions.

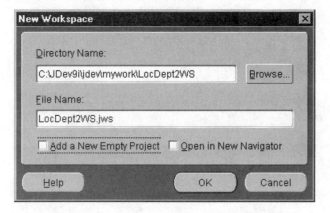

NOTE
Chapter 5 contains detailed information about the naming conventions used in the hands-on practices for this book.

4. Uncheck the *Add a New Empty Project* checkbox and leave the *Open in New Navigator* checkbox unchecked. Click OK.

   Additional Information: You will see a new workspace displayed in the System Navigator. Notice that it is shown in italics. This means that it has not yet been saved.

5. Click Save All.

TIP
*Running a project in JDeveloper will also automatically
compile it. This behavior is set by the* Make Project *checkbox in the
Configurations\Development\Runner\Options page of the Project
Settings dialog (***Project** | **Default Project Settings** *for all future projects
or* **Project** | **Project Settings** *for a specific project). Compiling a file
or project automatically saves it. This behavior is controlled in the
Environment page of the Preferences dialog (***Tools** | **Preferences***).*

Create a Project for the Business Components

Now you need to create the BC4J project within the LocDept2WS workspace.

1. In the Navigator on the LocDept2WS node, select New Project from the right-click menu. Select "Project Containing New Business Components" from the Projects category. Click OK.

2. Click Next if the Welcome page appears. On the Location page, in the *Directory Name* field, change the default name (such as "Project1") to "LocDeptBC4J." In the *File Name* field, type "LocDeptBC4J" as shown here. Click Next.

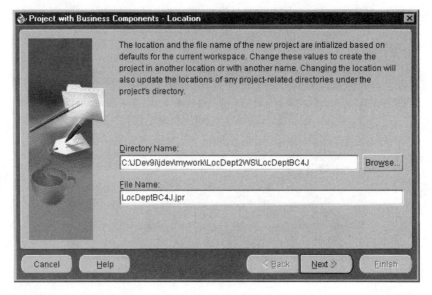

Additional Information: The BC4J project directory is a subdirectory under the LocDept2WS workspace directory.

3. On the Paths page, change the name of the *Default Package* to "locdept."

Additional Information: *Packages* refer to the subdirectory where your code will be stored. Large applications may require partitioning into several subdirectories. However, when doing this, if a class residing in one package (directory) needs to access a class in a different package (directory), you will need to explicitly reference that class using the notation "directory name.class name." To simplify the hands-on practices, the same package name will be used throughout.

The *Java Source Path* is a subdirectory under the package directory to store the source code. The *Output Directory* will store the compiled code. Both of these subdirectories sit conveniently underneath the BC4J project directory.

NOTE
The directory structure is a change in architecture from JDeveloper 3.2. In v. 3.2, JDeveloper took the hierarchical structure of your entire application and duplicated it, storing the generated classes in one structure and the source code in another. This new architecture is much more convenient and simplifies deployment. Chapter 1 explains this directory structure further.

  4. Click Next and Finish to complete the Project Wizard and to display the Business Components Package Wizard. Click Next if the Welcome page appears.

NOTE
The first time you enter any wizard, you will see a Welcome page. If you do not want to see this page each time you enter the wizard, uncheck the Display this page next time *checkbox.*

Create or Select a Connection
If you haven't already done so, you will need to create a connection for your project. (See Chapter 1 for details about creating a connection to the HR schema.)

  1. On the Package Name page of the Business Components Project Wizard, ensure that the *Package Name* field shows "locdept." Leave the default radio group selection. Click Next.

  2. Ensure that "HR" appears in the *Connection Name* field and click Next.

  3. Click Finish. Normally, you would click Next to fill out additional properties of the BC4J package but this practice will show you how to build the components by hand.

  4. Click Save All.

What Just Happened?   You created a new workspace directory, BC4J project directory with a package, and database connection for the BC4J project. These structures serve as logical containers for the files that you will create in this practice.

If the application you built by hand in this practice does not work, you may be able to find errors by comparing your application to the one generated by the wizards that you created in the Chapter 1 hands-on practice. If necessary, compare the files in the Navigator for the two projects.

II. Create Entity Objects and View Objects

In this phase you will add business components to the project that you created in Phase I. Note that the Navigator window now displays an association to the connection in the LocDeptBC4J.jpx file. If you double click the .jpx file, the Business Components Project Wizard will open, and you can change the connection for your project.

1. In the System Navigator, on the LocDeptBC4J.jpr project node, select New from the right-click menu.

TIP

*This "New" gallery will be used often in building applications with JDeveloper. It can be accessed by right clicking a workspace or project in the Navigator, selecting **File | New** from the pulldown menu, or pressing CTRL-N on the keyboard. Some developers find the keypresses more efficient.*

2. Expand the Business Tier and select Business Components (BC4J). Select Entity Object from the Items list. Click OK. The Entity Object Wizard will open.

   Additional Information: Until you have associated the BC4J project with a connection, you cannot select any other object in this area. If you are unable to select an Entity Object, it is because you have not created the appropriate association to a connection. This is important since it is a common error to select Finish too soon when creating the BC4J project. If you do, only the Business Components will be available in this dialog. If this is the case, select Business Components Package and follow the wizard to the same point where the connection has been defined for this project.

3. Click Next if the Welcome Page appears to display the Name page.

4. On the Name page, select "LOCATIONS" from the *Schema Object* pulldown. This will automatically populate the *Name* field with "Locations" as shown here. Click Next.

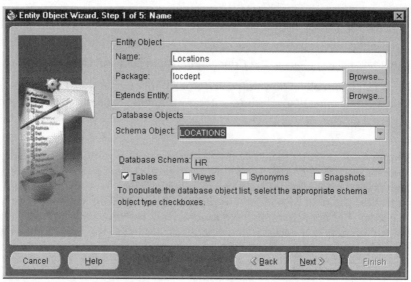

5. On the Attributes page, all of the entity attributes derived from the LOCATIONS table columns will be displayed. You may change the order of the attributes, add a new attribute, or a remove an attribute. For now, just click Next.

Additional Information: Changing the order or the available attributes in the entity object has little effect on the running of the application. The application will be based upon a view object that has an entity object at its core, but the view object can have a different attribute list or attribute order. Physically, the order of the attributes in the generated code will be changed as well as their appearance order in the subsequent steps. In general, when building applications, unless the table has a very large number of attributes, it is common practice to include all of them whether or not they will ultimately be deployed.

CAUTION
If you remove attributes here, they will not exist in the BC4J layer and will not be available in your application. However, if you remove an attribute, you can always re-enter the Entity Object Wizard and add the attribute back.

6. On the Attribute Settings page, ensure that the *Persistent, Primary Key, Mandatory,* and *Queriable* checkboxes are all checked for the LocationId attribute. Accept all of the default attribute settings.

Additional Information: The *Primary Key* and *Mandatory* checkbox information is retrieved from the database when the project is run. When checked, the *Mandatory* option causes the enforcement of a NOT NULL constraint in the BC4J layer, which does not require any database access.

The Entity Object Wizard automatically makes changes to the attribute names. For example, the database column name LOCATION_ID is transformed to LocationId. Select each attribute using the pulldown on the *Select Attribute* field, and observe the checkbox settings used by default.

7. Click Next. Accept all of the default settings on the Java page. Click the Help button for more information about the options on this page. Click Next.

8. For simple applications, the default view object is adequate, and you can create this view object by checking the *Generate Default View Object* checkbox on the Generate page. However, in order to practice creating the view object outside of the wizard, uncheck the *Generate Default View Object* checkbox. Click Next and Finish to create the Locations entity object. Additional information about view objects can be found in Chapters 10 and 13.

9. To create the default view object, expand the LocDeptBC4J.jpr and locdept nodes. On the Locations node, select New Default View Object from the right-click menu.

10. Click Save All.

11. Repeat steps 1–10 in this section to add an entity object and associated view for the DEPARTMENTS table, selecting "DEPARTMENTS" from the *Schema Object* field pulldown.

Additional Information: When you are finished, under the LocDeptBC4J project, you should have created new business components: an entity object for the Departments table and a corresponding view object. There will also be an association called "DeptLocFkAssoc."

12. To save your work, click the Save All icon.

At this point, your Object Navigator should look something like this (you may or may not see a bc4j.xcfg file):

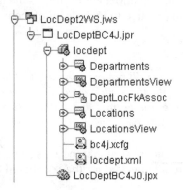

What Just Happened? By creating Location and Department BC4J entities, BC4J also automatically generates an association between them based on the foreign key constraint in the database. All of the necessary Java classes and XML files are created to support the Java application's interaction with the database.

In this phase, you also generated default BC4J view objects that correspond to the BC4J entity objects. View objects are the application interface layer with which your UI components will interact.

III. Delete and Create an Association

When you created the Departments entity, JDeveloper automatically generated an association to Locations from the foreign key constraint in the database. If necessary, you can delete the automatically generated associations and create the desired associations by hand.

Associations can be identified in the System Navigator by an icon with small red arrows between two small squares. If you hold the mouse cursor above the icon, a tooltip will appear that identifies the object type. For this simple example, the generated associations are correct. However, to practice this operation, you will delete a generated association and create it manually. You would have to create an association manually if no corresponding constraint exists in the database.

1. To delete the generated association, select the DeptLocFkAssoc node, and then select Erase DeptLocFkAssoc from disk from the right-click menu. Click Yes on the confirmation dialog.

2. To create an association between the Departments and Locations entities, click either the Departments or the Locations node within the LocDeptBC4J.jpr project. Select New

Association from the right-click menu. Click Next to advance to the Name page if the Welcome page appears.

3. On the Name page, change the name to "LocDeptFkAssoc." Ensure that "locdept" appears in the *Package* field. Click Next.

4. On the Entity Objects page, expand the Locations node under *Select Source Attribute* on the left and the Departments node under *Select Destination Attribute* on the right as shown here.

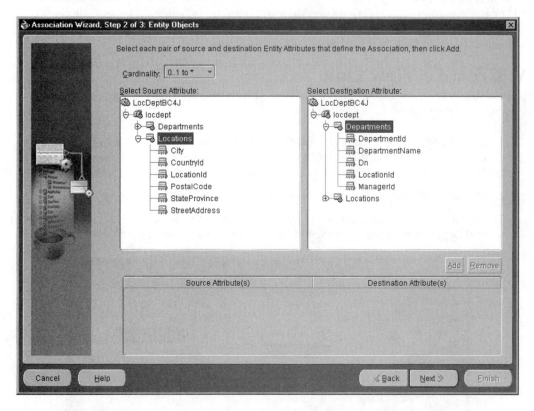

Additional Information: The source object represents the master in a master-detail relationship and the destination represents the detail.

5. Note that the attribute names on this page are the BC4J entity attribute names and not the column names. Select LocationId under Locations on the left and LocationId under Departments on the right. Click Add. You will see the Source and Destination Attributes added at the bottom of the Entity Objects page.

6. Ensure that the *Cardinality* pulldown is set to "0..1 to *". Change it if necessary.

   Additional Information: The cardinality settings of "0..1 to *" are usually displayed as the default cardinalities. If the column is mandatory, the cardinality will still be "0..1 to *" (rather than "1 to *" as you would expect).

7. Leave the default settings on the Association Properties page.

8. Click Next. Examine the Summary page to see that the appropriate association object will be generated. Make alterations if needed by clicking the Back button to return to the appropriate page. Click Finish.

9. Click Save All.

What Just Happened? In this phase, you created associations between the Departments and Locations entities. You will often need to insert, modify, or delete BC4J associations. If your database does not have the requisite foreign key constraints, the appropriate BC4J associations can be created using the wizard, as described in this phase.

IV. Create a View Link

The next step is to create a view link for the view objects to correspond to the LocDeptFkAssoc association for the entities.

1. On the LocDeptFkAssoc node, select New View Link from the right-click menu to access the View Link Wizard. Click Next if the Welcome page appears to display the Name page.

2. On the Name page, change the *Name* to "LocDeptFkLink." Click Next.

3. On the View Objects page, select LocationsView in the *Select Source View Object* area and DepartmentsView in the *Select Destination View Object* area as shown here.

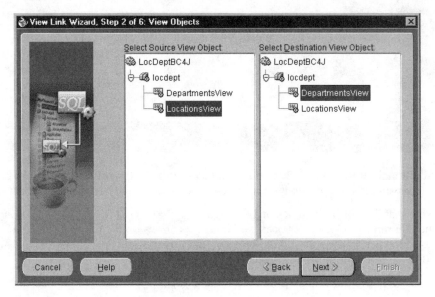

4. Click Next. On the Source Attributes page, select LocDeptFkAssoc and click the right-arrow button. Click Next.

5. On the Destination Attributes page, the LocationId will already appear in the *Selected Attributes* list because you selected the association on the preceding page. Click Next.

6. On the View Link SQL page, click Test to ensure that the query is valid. Click OK on the confirmation message. You can also click Explain Plan to show the explain plan information. The first time you run this in a schema, the wizard may need to create the PLAN_TABLE. Click Next.

7. On the View Link Properties page, ensure that the *Source Cardinality* is set to "0..1," and that the *Destination Cardinality* is set to "*." Accept the other default selections. Click Next.

8. The Summary page will display a structure similar to the Summary page for the association created previously. Click Finish to create the association.

9. Click Save All.

What Just Happened?   In this phase, you deleted and created a view link between the Locations and Departments view objects. A master-detail relationship was created between the two view objects to enable you to build an application that supports the master-detail relationship.

V. Create an Application Module

At this point, you must create an application module for the BC4J project. The application module provides a connection point for the application to the BC4J view objects and view links.

1. On the locdept package node in the System Navigator, select New Application Module from the right-click menu to start the Application Module Wizard. Click Next if the Welcome page appears to display the Name page.

2. Type "LocDeptModule" in the *Name* field. Click Next.

3. On the Data Model page, since departments are always maintained within the context of their location, you are going to define the LocationsView as the parent and DepartmentsView as its child. To do this, select LocationsView under *Available Objects* and click the right-arrow button. "LocationsView1" will appear in the Data Model pane. This represents a view usage.

4. Click the "DepartmentsView via LocDeptFkLink" (you may have to scroll right to see the whole name) under Available View Objects, and click LocationsView1 under Data Model.

5. Click the right-arrow button so that the Data Model page of the Application Module Wizard looks like this.

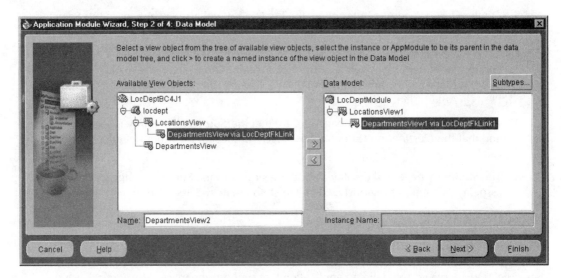

Additional Information: Note that you did not move the second DepartmentsView to the Data Model since it is unnecessary for this application.

6. Click Next. No actions are required on the Application Modules page. Click Next.

7. Accept the default *Generate Java File(s)* checkbox selection on the Java page and click Next.

8. The Summary page should look like Figure 3-1. Click Finish.

9. Click Save All.

What Just Happened? In this phase, you created an application module for the BC4J components. This application module is a structured collection of view objects, which is then attached to the user interface project and defines the interaction between the UI components and the BC4J layer.

VI. Test the Application

It is always important to test your application at different points in the development process. Once you have an application module defined, you can use the following steps to do this:

1. On the LocDeptModule node in the Navigator, select Test from the right-click menu.

2. On the Oracle Business Component Browser – Connect dialog, ensure that the HR connection is selected. Click Connect.

Additional Information: If necessary, you can change your connection at this point to complete the test process.

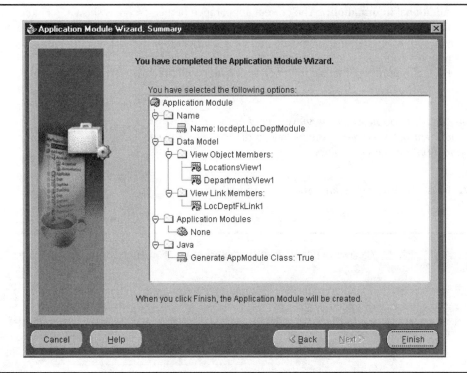

FIGURE 3-1. *Application Module Wizard—Summary page*

TIP
*If you want to use the default connection, click Run in the IDE toolbar
after selecting the application module node. The Business Component
Browser will open without displaying the Connect dialog. Chapter 16
contains more information about connections.*

3. You will now see the Oracle Business Component Browser displaying a default
   application based upon your selected BC4J components.

4. On the LocationsView1 node, select Show from the right-click menu.

5. Scroll through the records in the Locations table using the blue arrows in the toolbar.

6. On the LocDeptFkLink1 node, select Show on the right-click menu to display a default
   master-detail application as shown in Figure 3-2. Scrolling through records should
   display the appropriate detail departments for the selected master location.

TIP
Seattle (LocationId 1700) has many departments.

Additional Information: The correct appearance of this screen as shown in Figure 3-2 validates that the BC4J components have been built correctly. For every project you build, you should test the Insert, Update, and Delete functionality of all view objects. If you cannot perform a specific operation required by your user interface application at this point with the BC4J components, the user interface application will not function properly.

TIP
You can also double click the view object name in the Business Component Browser view objects tree to display the browser application for that view object.

7. Close the Business Component Browser window.

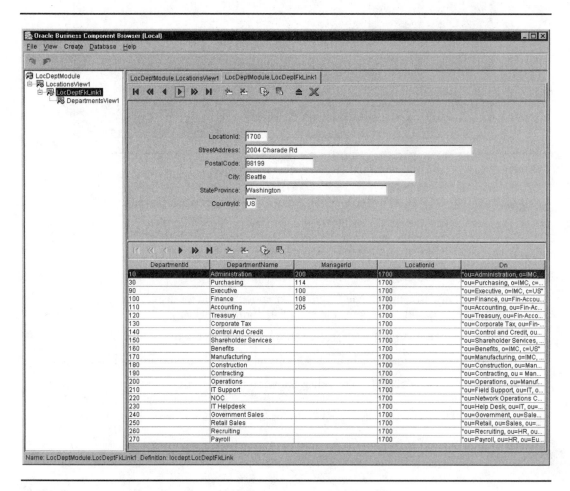

FIGURE 3-2. *Locations and Departments business components test*

What Just Happened?   In this phase of this hands-on practice, you tested the application that you created to ensure that the BC4J components have been created correctly and that the Insert, Update, and Delete functionality of the application work correctly.

Hands-on Practice: Create a Master-Detail Java Application Manually

Now that you have created a BC4J project, you need to create an application that uses the BC4J components. This hands-on practice will demonstrate how to build and modify a typical application. In production application development, you will frequently start with a wizard-generated application and begin modifying it. At other times, you will need to build the application components yourself.

This practice will help to illustrate how to build manually what the wizards build automatically. It is important to understand how the wizards work. The way in which the JDeveloper wizards generate applications is not the only way to build the same applications. Even the panels and frames built here are not strictly necessary, nor are they even necessarily the way you would build an application if left to your own design. The algorithms that the wizards use have slightly changed from the 3.2 to the 9i releases of JDeveloper.

The application in this practice purposely attempts to stay very close to the way in which the JDeveloper wizards generate the application. This will be helpful in case you run into any problems during the practice since you will be able to look at the code that the wizards generated in Chapter 1 and compare it with the code that you create here.

Programming style in any language can be vigorously debated. How you perform specific tasks will evolve as your understanding of Java and JDeveloper deepens. This chapter will illustrate the way that one developer has come up with to build applications. The authors do not suggest that this is necessarily the easiest or best way, but it has been used successfully to build working applications.

This practice session consists of the following phases:

I. Create a Java application project

II. Create the Locations portion of the application

- Add a panel for Locations

- Add a JPanel container

- Add a navigation bar

- Add labels

- Add fields

III. Create the application-level panel

- Add an outer panel

- Modify the Java code

IV. Test and modify the Locations portion of the application

V. Create the Departments portion of the application

■ Add a panel for Departments

■ Add a JPanel container

■ Add a ScrollPane

■ Add a Table Component

VI. Modify the application

■ Modify the size of the application window

■ Change the column headings and widths

I. Create a Java Application Project

Since you will need to connect your application to the BC4J project created in the first hands-on practice in this chapter, you will use the same workspace to create the application.

Create a project within the LocDept2WS workspace using these steps.

I. In the System Navigator, on the LocDept2WS.jws node, select New Empty Project from the right-click menu.

2. In the New Project dialog, change the *Directory Name* to "LocDeptJA" (keeping the rest of the directory path intact) and the *File Name* to "LocDeptJA." Click OK.

Additional Information: At this point, you need to associate this project with the BC4J project created in the first hands-on practice in this chapter. You must provide this visibility, or you will not be able to attach the objects in the new project to the BC4J components.

3. On the LocDeptJA.jpr node and select New from the right-click menu. Expand the Client Tier node. Select Swing/JClient for BC4J and Business Components Client Data Model under Items. Click OK.

4. In the BC4J Client Data Model Definition Wizard, click Next if the Welcome page appears to display the Definition page. Accept the defaults and click Next.

5. On the Definition Name page, JDeveloper will automatically fill in LocDeptModule. Accept this default. Click Next and Finish.

Additional Information: You should see a LocDeptJA.cpx file under the LocDeptJA.jpr node as shown in Figure 3-3. You will only see the .cpx file in the LocDeptJA project that you just created. The .cpx file is a container that stores the *client data model,* named connections to the BC4J application module in the middle tier. You can modify this definition. The Java code will only reference the name. This allows you to redeploy or change definitions without changing any of the code.

6. Click Save All.

What Just Happened? In this phase, you created a project and associated it with the BC4J project created in the earlier hands-on practice in this chapter. The rest of this hands-on practice

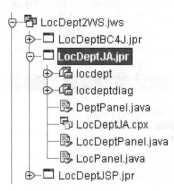

FIGURE 3-3. *Navigator showing Java application*

will demonstrate how to build a complete working application to show Departments and Locations information.

The client data model is further explained in Chapter 17.

II. Create the Locations Portion of the Application

This phase will create the Location portion of the application including a panel, scroller (ScrollPane), navigation bar, labels, and fields.

Add a Panel for Locations

1. Click the LocDeptJA.jpr node in the Navigator and press CTRL-N. Select Empty Panel from the Swing/JClient for BC4J category. Click OK.

2. If the Welcome page appears, click Next to display the Data Model page. In the JClient Empty Panel Wizard, since there is only one data model, the data model will default to the LocDeptModule. Click Next.

3. On the "File names" page, change the package name to "locdept." Change *Panel name* to "LocPanel." Leave the *Generate a runnable panel* checkbox unchecked. Click Next and Finish. You will now see a LocPanel.java file under the LocDeptJA.jpr node and the UI Editor will open automatically.

   Additional Information: On the LocPanel.java node, select Code Editor from the right-click menu. Notice that this panel class is an implementation of the JPanel interface. JPanel is an Oracle-supplied panel that is an extension of the Swing JPanel, modified to support BC4J.

   At this point, you will add some objects to the newly created panel.

   Additional Information: Note that the Structure window on the lower left corner of the IDE displays different information when the UI Editor is active from when the

Code Editor is active. When the UI Editor is active, the Structure window shows the UI perspective of the panel object. If you expand the UI node, you will see the object "this," which refers to the LocPanel file selected in the Navigator. You will also see the name of the object at the top of the Structure window as shown here:

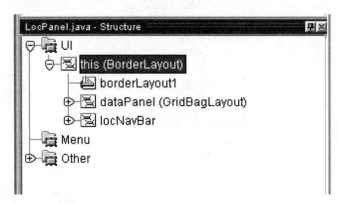

4. Click the "this" node in the Structure window. In the Property Inspector, set the *layout* property to BorderLayout. Layouts are explained in Chapter 20.

5. Click Save All.

Add a JPanel Container

You will now add a JPanel container to your application.

TIP
A reliable way to add objects to the Structure window is to click where the object should be added (usually under the "this" node). Then click the icon on the Component Palette for the object to be added. Finally, click back in the Structure window where you want the object to be inserted. Sometimes you will have to wait a moment before the object appears.

1. On the Component Palette pulldown, select Swing Containers.

2. Click the JPanel icon on the Component Palette. In the Structure window, click "this (Border Layout)," and you should see the new panel (jPanel1) below the borderLayout1 node.

3. Select JPanel1 in the Structure window. The following steps involve making changes in the JPanel Property Inspector.

4. On the Property Inspector, change the *name* property to "dataPanel." Note that the default *constraints* property for the data panel is Center so that the new JPanel object fills the center of the outer window.

NOTE

When filling in any information on the Property Inspector, be sure to press Enter when finished to ensure that your changes are made.

5. Set the *layout* property to "GridBagLayout."

   Additional Information: Here you have been instructed to use GridBagLayout. This is a layout where objects are placed into cells, and their position is determined by a set of properties. You may find this layout confusing until you have had some experience with it. Many developers advocate laying out their screens using the "null" layout, which allows them to position the items on the screen simply by dragging them to the correct position and then converting to grid layout at a later point in the design process. This method allows the layout conversion software to select the correct grid properties. Further discussion of the various layout managers such as GridBagLayout can be found in Chapter 20.

6. Click Save All.

Add a Navigation Bar
The following steps can be used to add a navigation bar to the application.

1. Select the "this (BorderLayout)" node in the Structure window. On the Component Palette, select JClient controls from the pulldown. Click the JUNavigationBar icon.

2. Click the "this"node to add the navigation bar object. In the UI Editor, you should see a navigation bar with grayed out icons in the center of the panel.

3. In the JUNavigationBar1 Property Inspector, set the *constraints* property to "North" and change the *name* property to "locNavBar." You must now attach the navigation bar to a BC4J component. You will see the navigation bar move to the top of the window in the UI Editor.

4. Set the *model* property to "JClient View Binding." In the model dialog, select LocationsView and click OK.

5. Click Save All. Your screen should look like Figure 3-4.

Add Labels
You now need to add labels to your application.

1. With LocPanel.java selected in the System Navigator, select Swing on the Component Palette pulldown.

2. Click the JLabel icon and click the dataPanel node in the Structure window to add the JLabel object.

3. In the JLabel1 object Property Inspector, change *name* to "locIdLabel."

4. Access the *constraints* property dialog by selecting clicking the "…" button in the *constraints* property field. Change the *constraints* dialog to match the settings in

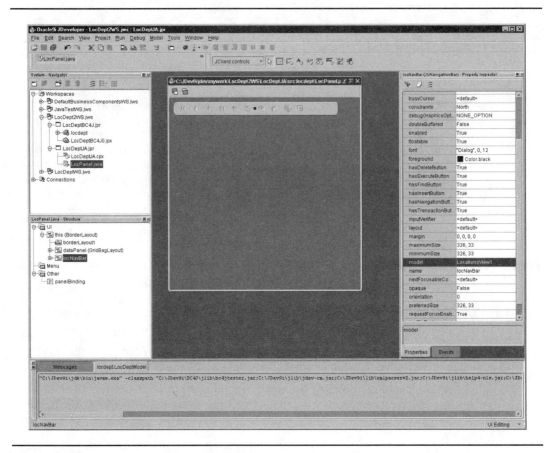

FIGURE 3-4. *Application with navigation bar*

Figure 3-5. For an explanation of the *constraints* settings, refer to the discussion of GridBagLayout in Chapter 21.

You should now see a label in the center of the panel in the UI Editor.

NOTE
If the label appears in the upper-left corner or elsewhere, you need to reset the data panel constraints property. Dismiss the constraints dialog. Select dataPanel in the Structure window, and reset the constraints property to Center.

   5. In the locIdLabel Property Inspector, change the *text* property to "Loc ID."

FIGURE 3-5.   *Constraints property setting for the LocId label*

Additional Information: The wizard does not fill in the property name. Instead, if you look at the generated code from the wizard application, it will take the label text directly from the BC4J attribute name. Explicitly setting the text overrides the BC4J name.

6. Now, you need to add a second label for City. With LocPanel.java selected in the System Navigator, make sure that Swing is selected on the Component Palette pulldown.

7. Click the JLabel icon and click the dataPanel node in the Structure window to add the JLabel object to the dataPanel(GridBagLayout) node.

8. In the jLabel1 object Property Inspector, change *name* to "cityLabel."

9. Change the *constraints* property as shown in Figure 3-5 with the exception that Y = 2. Click OK.

10. Change the *text* property to City.

11. Click Save All.

TIP
If the Structure window does not display the UI node, click an object in the UI Editor.

Add Fields
You now need to add the associated field for the LocId label.

1. Click the JTextField icon in the Component Palette.

2. Click the dataPanel in the Structure window to add the text field as a sibling to the label.

3. In the JTextField Property Inspector, change the *constraints* settings as shown in Figure 3-5 with the following exceptions: X = 2, Y = 1.

4. Change *name* to "locIdField." The JTextField should now appear just to the right of the label in the UI Editor.

5. Select JClient Attribute Binding from the *document* property pulldown. In the document dialog that pops up, under *Select a view*, select LocationsView and under *Select an attribute*, select LocationId. Click OK.

    Additional Information: This uses the *document* property to attach (bind) the object to the BC4J component.

CAUTION
Be sure to set the document *property last since after setting the* document *property, you may see that the field shrinks down to a very narrow one. Set the columns property to "10." The* columns *property sets the width of the field. The number roughly corresponds to the number of characters to be displayed. However, you may need to adjust this number by trial and error.*

6. This same process must be repeated for the *City* field. You must create a label and field for every attribute that you want to display. Click the JTextField icon in the Component Palette.

CAUTION
You might be tempted to copy and paste the existing JLabel objects and then make the appropriate modifications. Until you are more familiar with JDeveloper, do not do this. The copy-and-paste functionality copies all of the Java code, and not all of the properties will stay linked to the generated Java code, causing unexpected application bugs.

7. Click the dataPanel in the Structure window to add the text field as a sibling to the labels. That is, both should be directly under the dataPanel node.

CAUTION
If you inadvertently place an object under the wrong structure node, do not cut and paste it. Delete it and re-add the object.

8. In the JTextField1 Property Inspector, change the *constraints* settings to match those shown in Figure 3-6 with the following exceptions: X = 2, Y = 2.

9. Change *name* to "cityField."

10. Select JClient Attribute Binding from the pulldown in the *document* property pulldown. In the document dialog select the LocationsView1 and the City attribute. Click OK.

11. Set the *columns* property to "10."

12. Click Save All.

The Structure window and UI Editor should now look like Figure 3-6.

What Just Happened?   In this phase, you created the Locations portion of the application by adding panels, a navigation bar, labels, and fields. This should already give you some sense of the amount of manual effort required to build a Java application. For example, notice that labels and fields must be handled independently.

III. Create the Application-Level Panel

This panel will be used for the entire application encompassing both the Location and Department panels. The reason for creating the larger panel at this point is to allow you to test the Location portion of the application and its objects to make sure that these work before building the Department portion.

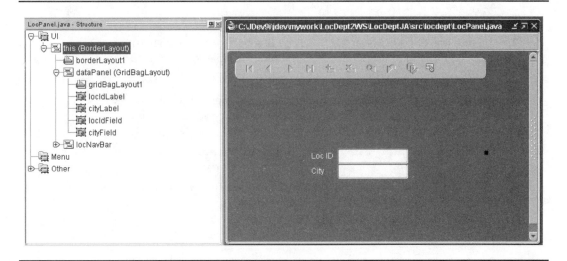

FIGURE 3-6.   *UI Editor and Structure window showing labels and fields*

Add an Outer Panel

The following steps are used to create the application-level panel.

1. On the LocDeptJA.jpr node, select New from the right-click menu. Select Empty Panel from the Swing/JClient for BC4J category. Click OK.

2. If the Welcome page appears, click Next to display the Data Model page of the JClient Empty Panel Wizard. LocDeptModule should be shown in the *Select the data model definition* field. Click Next.

3. On the File names page, ensure that the *Package name* field shows "locdept" and change the Panel name to "LocDeptPanel." Check the *Generate a runnable panel* checkbox.

4. Click Next and Finish. The UI Editor will open automatically.

5. In the this (JPanel) Property Inspector, set the *layout* property to BorderLayout.

6. With LocDeptPanel.java selected in the Navigator, select Swing Containers from the Component Palette pulldown. Click the JScrollPane icon and click the "this" node in the Structure window.

7. Click the new jScrollPane1 node under the "this" node in the Structure window.

8. In the Property Inspector, change *constraints* to North and *name* to "masterScroller."

9. Click Save All.

Modify the Java Code

At this point, you must add three lines of code to the LocDeptPanel.java file.

1. Double click LocDeptPanel.java to open the Code Editor.

2. Add one line of code under the "`JScrollPane masterScroller = new JScrollPane();`" line in the BC4J binding variable section:

   ```
   private LocPanel locPanel;
   ```

3. Add the following lines of code to the `jbInit()` method section under the "`this.add(masterScroller, BorderLayout.NORTH);`" line:

   ```
   locPanel = new LocPanel(panelBinding);
   masterScroller.getViewport().add(locPanel);
   }
   ```

4. In the Code Editor, select Make LocDeptPanel.java from the right-click menu to compile the file and check the syntax of the code you added.

5. Click Save All.

What Just Happened?   In this phase, you created a panel to hold the Location and Department portions of the application and attached the panel to the BC4J components. This gave you an introduction to working with frames and panels as well as writing code without the wizards. Note that some of the work done by hand in this phase may not be necessary as JDeveloper continues to evolve.

IV. Test and Modify the Locations Portion of the Application

At this point, the application is complete enough to run. When you generated the panel LocDept, you specified that it should create an associated application frame using the checkbox. The application frame file contains a main() method and is executable.

1. Select LocDeptPanel.java and click Run. The following will appear:

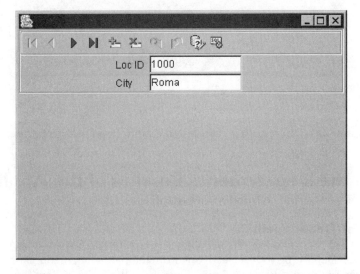

    Additional Information: As you scroll through the records, you will notice that the *City* field is too narrow. You can modify this using the following steps:

2. Close the application window. On the LocPanel.java node, select UI Editor from the right-click menu. In the Structure window, expand the UI, "this," and dataPanel nodes to find the cityField object.

3. Select the cityField object and in the Property Inspector, change the *columns* property to "15."

    Additional Information: This property sets the width of the field. The number roughly corresponds to the number of characters to be displayed. However, you may need to adjust this number by trial and error.

4. Run the application again to see that the *City* field has been expanded. The application should look something like this:

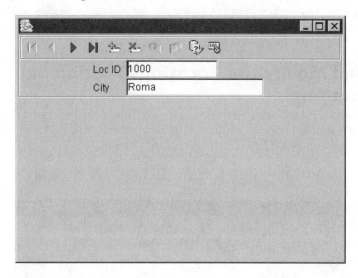

5. Click Save All.

What Just Happened?   In this phase, you tested a portion of the application and made modifications to a field.

V. Create the Departments Portion of the Application
Now you will add the Departments portion of the application.

Add a Panel for Departments

1. On the LocDeptJA.jpr node, select New from the right-click menu. If necessary, expand the Client Tier node and select Empty Panel from the Swing/JClient for BC4J category. Click OK.

2. Click Next if the Welcome page of the JClient Empty Panel Wizard appears.

3. Click Next on the Data Model page.

4. On the "File names" page, if necessary, change the *Package name* field to "locdept." Change the *Panel name* field to "DeptPanel." Leave the *Generate a frame that runs this panel* checkbox unchecked. Click Next and Finish. You should now see a DeptPanel.java file under the LocDeptJA.jpr node.

5. In the Property Inspector, set the *layout* property for "this" to BorderLayout.

6. Expand the "this" node in the Structure window. Select BorderLayout1. In the Property Inspector, change the name to "deptLayout."

7. Click Save All.

Add a JPanel Container
To add a panel to this frame, use the following steps:

1. On the Component Palette, select Swing Containers from the pulldown.

2. Click the JPanel icon. In the Structure window, click "this," and you should see the new panel below the deptLayout node.

3. In the Structure window, make sure that JPanel1 is selected. In the Property Inspector, change the *name* property to "dataPanel."

4. Verify that the *constraints* property is set to "Center."

5. Set the *layout* property to GridBagLayout.

6. Set the *minimum size* property to "100, 100" to ensure that it is always displayed.

7. Click Save All.

Add a ScrollPane
To add a scroller to the data panel object, use the following steps:

1. Select dataPanel(GridBagLayout) in the Structure window. On the Component Palette pulldown, select Swing Containers and click the JScrollPane icon. Click dataPanel in the Structure window.

2. In the Property Inspector for the JScrollPane, change the *name* to "deptScroller."

Add a Table Component
Add a Swing JTable to the Department ScrollPane to display multiple department records using the following steps:

1. Select deptScroller in the Structure window. On the Component Palette pulldown, select Swing and click the JTable icon, and click the deptScroller node in the Structure window. You may need to resize the table in UI Editor by dragging the handles.

2. In the jTable1 Property Inspector, change *name* to "deptViewTable."

3. Set the *model* property to "JClient Attribute list binding" from the pulldown. In the model dialog, select DepartmentsView1 in the *Select a view* area. All attributes appear in the *Selected attributes* area. Move all but the DepartmentId and DepartmentName back to the left. Click OK.

4. Click Save All.

5. You will now add a ScrollPane to the panel. On the LocDeptPanel.java node, select UI Editor from the right-click menu.

NOTE
*This file may already be open. Check the Document Bar in the IDE
toolbar area for the LocDeptPanel.java file name and click that icon.
UI Editors in this bar have an icon with a pencil and colored "page."
Code Editors in this bar have an icon with a pencil and several lines
of text on the "page." You can also press the* ALT *key and the number
key written into the icon in the Document Bar. If the Document Bar is
not visible, select* **View | Document Bar**. *Chapter 2 contains more
information about the Document Bar.*

6. Expand the UI node and select the "this" node in the Structure window.
   On the Component Palette pulldown, select Swing Containers and click the
   JScrollPane icon. Click the "this" node again, and you will see a JScrollPane
   added to the Structure window.

7. In the Property Inspector, change the *name* property to "detailScroller."

8. Verify that the *constraints* property is set to "Center."

   Additional Information: Notice that if you click on the masterScroller in
   the Structure window, its *constraints* property is set to North.

9. Click Save All.

   At this point, you need to return to the Code Editor for the LocDeptPanel.java
   class where the lines of code were added before. Similar lines of code must
   now be added here.

10. Click the Code Editor for the LocDeptPanel.java file in the Document Bar.

11. Under the BC4J binding variable comment, after the "`private JScrollPane`
    `detailScroller = new JScrollPane();`" line, add the following code:

    ```
    private DeptPanel deptPanel;
    ```

12. In the `jbInit()` method, under "`locPanel = new LocPanel(panelBinding);`"
    insert a blank line and add the following code:

    ```
    deptPanel = new DeptPanel(panelBinding);
    ```

13. Also in the `jbInit()` method, under "`masterScroller.getViewport()`
    `.add(LocPanel);`" insert a blank line and add the following code:

    ```
    detailScroller.getViewport().add(deptPanel);
    ```

14. In the Code Editor window, select Make LocDeptPanel.java from the right-click menu to
    compile the file and check the syntax.

15. Click Save All.

16. Test your application by selecting the LocDeptPanel.java node and clicking the Run
    icon. You should see something like Figure 3-7.

17. After checking the application, close the application window.

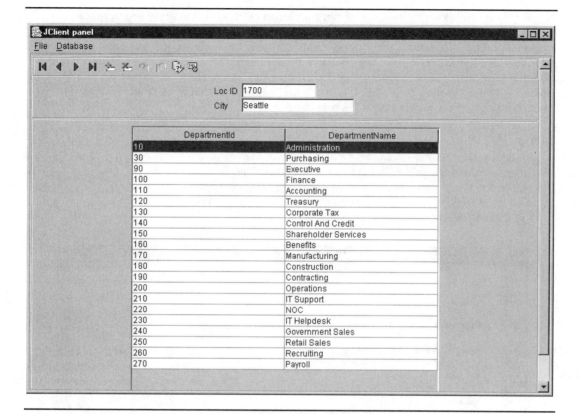

FIGURE 3-7. *Application test*

What Just Happened?   In this phase, you added the Department components to the application, including panels and a ScrollPane. These are the objects necessary to show a multi-record department display as a detail to a master location record.

VI. Modify the Application

In this phase, you will test and modify the application to make it more visually appealing. In looking at the application, you may notice that there are some things that should be modified:

- The overall application window is too small.
- The column headings are not user friendly.
- The DepartmentId column is too wide.

In other products such as Oracle Forms, everything you could manipulate on an object is visible in its associated Property Palette. In the Java environment, this is not the case. The JDeveloper Property Inspector is really nothing more than a limited functionality wizard for your Swing components. A host of other things can be modified in these structures beyond what is shown in the Property Inspector. These modifications must be made in the code itself.

Some of the modifications mentioned earlier can only be made by adding code. It is strongly recommended that you purchase the official Sun reference manual so that you can understand this code (*The Java™ Class Libraries, Second Edition,* by Patrick Chan, Rosanna Lee, Doug Kramer; Addison-Wesley, 1998; ISBN: 0201310023). Be aware that as these libraries evolve, the functionality of the components will change somewhat.

TIP
To see what methods are available for an object, while in the Code Editor, on a new line in the jbInit() *method, type "this." (including the period). Wait a moment and you will see a popup window with a list of all the available methods for the object in question as shown here. This feature, called Code Insight, is explained further in Chapter 2.*

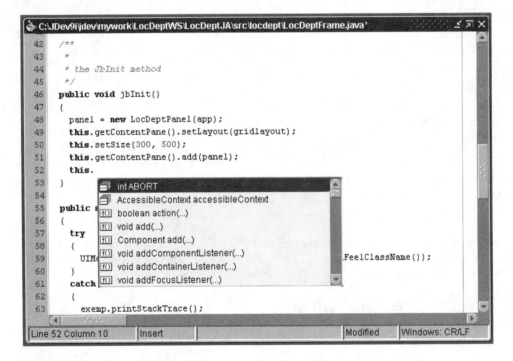

Modify the Size of the Application Window
Use the following steps to make the window size more compatible with the information displayed.

    1. To verify that you can change the size of the application window only by modifying the code, on the LocDeptPanel.java node select UI Editor from the right-click menu. None of the properties listed in the Property Inspector will allow you to modify the application window size.

2. Double click the LocDeptPanel.java node to open the Code Editor. Find the `jbInit()` method (at approximately line 39).

Additional Information: At approximately line 64, you will see that there is already a line of generated code:

```
JUTestFrame.testJClientPanel(panel, panel.getPanelBinding(), new
Dimension(400, 300));
```

This line governs the size of the application window. Change the numbers in parentheses to "500, 300."

3. Click Save All.

4. Run the application to verify the application window size change.

Change the Column Headings and Widths
The next two modifications can be made at the same time.

1. To verify that you can change the column headings and widths only by modifying the code, on the DeptPanel.java node select UI Editor from the right-click menu. If you explore the properties, you will find that none of the properties listed in the Property Inspector will allow you to modify the headings and widths of the columns in the table component.

Additional Information: The most likely place to do this would have been the deptViewTable object visible in the Structure window using the *model* property in the Property Inspector.

2. Double click the DeptPanel.java in the Navigator to open the Code Editor.

3. Find the `jbInit()` method by double clicking the method named in the Structure window (it is at approximately line 49) and add these four lines of code under the "`this.add(dataPanel, BorderLayout.CENTER);`" line:

```
deptViewTable.getColumn("DepartmentId").setMaxWidth(60);
deptViewTable.getColumn("DepartmentId").setHeaderValue("ID");
deptViewTable.getColumn("DepartmentName").setMaxWidth(200);
deptViewTable.getColumn("DepartmentName").setHeaderValue
("Department");
```

Additional Information: Because the attribute names are within quotes, the compiler will not find an error in spelling. Therefore, it is important that the names of the attributes are spelled correctly. To avoid typing errors, you may want to copy and paste the names from the panel binding code immediately preceding.

Unfortunately, there is no visual editor to show the appropriate column width of the JTable component, so setting the widths is somewhat of a trial-and-error process. The numbers used here, 60 and 200, can be set to whatever widths the columns should be in your application.

The `setHeaderValue()` method takes a Java object as its parameter, so the argument passed here could be text or anything else.

   4. Click Save All.

   5. Run the LocDeptPanel.java again to confirm the changes. It should look something like Figure 3-8.

What Just Happened?   In this last phase of the hands-on practice, you were able to modify the application you created earlier using the Code Editor and adding lines of Java code. This was necessary since there are no properties available in the Property Inspectors for the relevant objects to make these modifications.

   The first two hands-on practices in this chapter used some of the basic skills needed to build applications in JDeveloper. You built a BC4J project and an application project, and made them interact. This chapter has not touched on several important other areas of application development (menus and toolbars) since these are discussed in detail in Chapter 20.

   You may have come to the conclusion that building applications by hand in JDeveloper is somewhat more labor intensive than working with other 4GL products such as Oracle Forms. However, in return, JDeveloper grants much greater flexibility to the application programmer. It is a relatively common problem when developers want their tools to do something but are

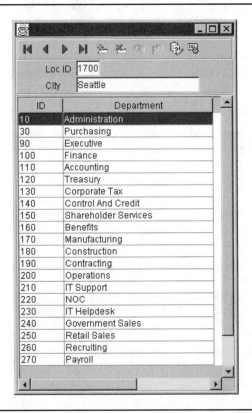

FIGURE 3-8.   *Completed application*

hampered by a product's limitations. Such frustrations are far less likely with JDeveloper. However, there will still be times when you will want to make user interface decisions to minimize the amount of work required in the JDeveloper product. In every product, developers have to balance their desire for the ultimate UI with what the product can easily support.

Hands-on Practice: Create a JSP Application Manually

The BC4J, Java application, and JSP projects you created in Chapter 1 use the high-level wizards. In this practice, you will build a similar application using the low-level wizards and some hand coding. This will give you a feel for how to build JSP applications. Chapters 21-24 provide further discussion of JSP development.

This practice steps you through the following phases:

    I. Set up the project and attach the application module

    II. Add a data source and data tags

    III. Modify the display

- Apply a style sheet
- Modify the label properties

This practice creates a page that displays one record at a time from the department table. It uses BC4J data tags to navigate through the records and to display records. You enter the components using the Component Palette, which prompts you for the BC4J data specifics and other properties such as names.

I. Set Up the Project and Attach the Application Module

The following steps show how to create a JSP project and application. This practice requires you to have created the BC4J project in the first hands-on practice in this chapter.

    1. On the LocDept2WS.jws node, select New Empty Project from the right-click menu.

    2. Enter "LocDeptJSP" for *Directory Name* and "LocDeptJSP.jpr" for *File Name* and click OK.

    3. Click the LocDeptJSP.jpr node and select New from the right-click menu. Expand the Web Tier node and select JSP Page from the JavaServer Pages (JSP) category. Click OK.

    4. In the New JSP dialog, leave the default setting for the *Directory Name* field. Enter "LocDept" in the *File Name* field and click OK. The Code Editor and Component Palette will open automatically and you should now see the LocDept.jsp file added to the project.

NOTE

The Component Palette for JSP files appears on the right side of the IDE by default.

5. In the Code Editor, change "Hello World" under <TITLE> to "Department Locations".

6. In between the <H2> tags, replace "the current time is:" with "Department Locations".

7. Delete everything between the </H2> and </BODY> tags, including the "P" tags. The Code Editor should now look like the following:

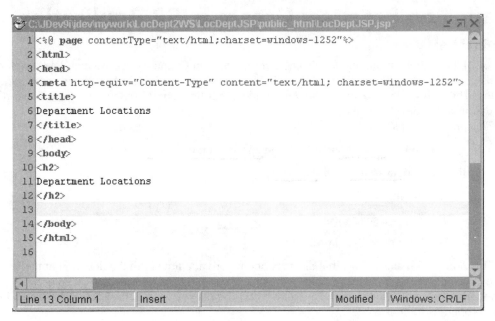

```
C:\JDev9i\jdev\mywork\LocDept2WS\LocDeptJSP\public_html\LocDeptJSP.jsp
 1 <%@ page contentType="text/html;charset=windows-1252"%>
 2 <html>
 3 <head>
 4 <meta http-equiv="Content-Type" content="text/html; charset=windows-1252">
 5 <title>
 6 Department Locations
 7 </title>
 8 </head>
 9 <body>
10 <h2>
11 Department Locations
12 </h2>
13
14 </body>
15 </html>
16
```

Line 13 Column 1   Insert   Modified   Windows: CR/LF

8. Position the cursor in the blank line before the </BODY> tag (add a blank line if there is none). Select BC4J Connections in the Component Palette pulldown.

9. Click ApplicationModule in the Component Palette. In the ApplicationModule dialog, if a data model definition appears, select LocDeptModule from the pulldown.

Additional Information: If no data model definition is present, click New to start the BC4J Client Data Model Definition Wizard. Click Next on the Welcome page. Accept the defaults on the Definition page. Ensure that LocDeptModule appears in the *Definition Name* field. Click Next and Finish.

10. Click Next and Finish to complete the Application Module Wizard. The source code editor will now show the ApplicationModule tag.

11. Click Save All.

What Just Happened?   You created the project and added a reference to the BC4J application module. This phase created a shell JSP and attached it to the same application module used for the Java application in the previous hands-on practice. The JSP is now ready to have UI components added to it that will connect to your BC4J application in the same way that the Java application did.

II. Add a Data Source and Data Tags

Just as you did in the BC4J and Java application projects, you will use the Locations and Departments information in the HR schema for your JSP project. Now that you have defined the BC4J application module, you can define which view objects you will use in this JSP. The data tag that points to a view object is called DataSource and you will add a data source for the LocationsView and another data source for the DepartmentsView.

You will also add data tags to display navigation buttons that are associated with a view object. To display the data, you will add a data tag to display a single Locations record and another data tag to display multiple Departments records. The functionality for retrieving the data and constructing the HTML display is built into the data tag code and the representation of that code in the JSP is relatively simple.

1. Make sure that the cursor in the Code Editor is on a blank line after the jbo:ApplicationModule line. Click DataSource on the BC4J Connections Component Palette page. Select LocationsView1 and click Next.

2. Enter "locationsData" in the *id* field. Leave the other values blank. Click Finish. The Code Editor will now show the DataSource tag.

3. Click DataSource on the BC4J Connections page of the Component Palette. Select DepartmentsView1 (the child under the LocationsView1 node) and click Next.

4. Enter "departmentsData" in the *id* field and "8" in the *rangesize* field. Leave the other values blank. Click Finish. The Code Editor will now show the DataSource tag.

5. Select the BC4J Component Tags page from the Component Palette pulldown. Click DataHandler in the Component Palette. Select "LocDeptModule" in the *appid* pulldown and click Finish. The DataHandler tag will be added to the code. This tag manages the updating of the display when you click the Next and Previous links.

6. Click Save All.

7. You can now add the display data tags to the JSP. Click DataNavigate in the Component Palette. Select "locationsData" in the *datasource* pulldown. Click Finish to add the tag to the code.

8. Click DataRecord. In the *datasource* field, select "locationsData" from the pulldown. Click Finish. Another tag will be entered into the JSP.

9. Click Save All.

10. Add a line under the last DataRecord tag and type "<h2>Departments</h2>."

11. In a blank line after the </h2> tag, click DataTable in the Component Palette.

12. Click in the *datasource* field and select "departmentsData." Leave the other default settings. Click Finish.

13. Click Save All.

14. Select LocDept.jsp in the Navigator and click the Run icon. If you see the Default Run Target dialog, select the LocDept.jsp file from the pulldown (this associates the file that will be run when you run the project) and click OK.

Additional Information: Your default browser will open, and an application such as the one in Figure 3-9 will appear. This may take some time.

15. Try the Next and Previous browse links in the Locations area to see how the navigation data tag works and how the data table will display department records appropriate to the location.

16. Close the browser window.

What Just Happened? In this phase, you added a number of UI components to support a simple master-detail JSP. If you compare this to the JSP pages generated in Chapter 1, you will see that this is only a small part of a full JSP application.

III. Modify the Display

In this phase, you will see the effects of using a style sheet to determine the look and feel of the JSP page. You will also see how data tags can be added or changed to alter the JSP page's behavior.

Apply a Style Sheet

You can modify the look and feel of your JSP by using a predefined style sheet. You can also create your own style sheets to give a more distinctive look to your applications. For this practice you will apply the same style sheet used by the JSP wizards.

1. Add the following line in the heading section after the <meta> tag:

   ```
   <LINK REL=STYLESHEET TYPE="text/css" HREF="bc4j.css">
   ```

2. Select the LocDeptJSP.jpr project node and select **File | Import** to access the Import dialog. Select Existing Sources and click OK to start the Import Existing Sources Wizard.

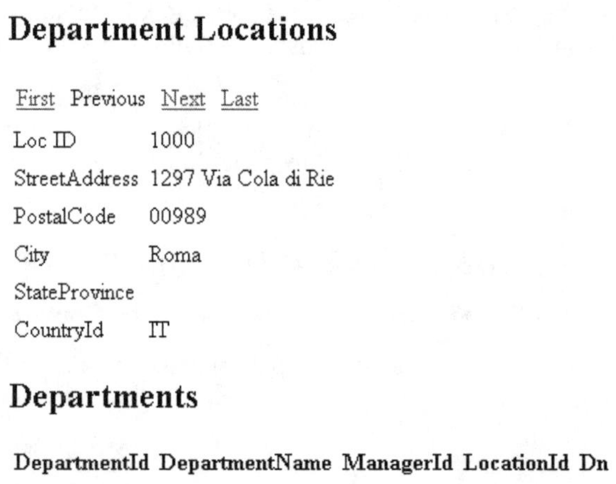

Department Locations

First Previous Next Last

Loc ID	1000
StreetAddress	1297 Via Cola di Rie
PostalCode	00989
City	Roma
StateProvince	
CountryId	IT

Departments

DepartmentId DepartmentName ManagerId LocationId Dn

FIGURE 3-9. *Generated JSP*

3. Click Next if the Welcome page appears. Click Add and navigate to the JDEV_HOME\jdev*systemXX*\templates\common\misc directory where the "XX" in *systemXX* represents a number.

4. Select the bc4j.css file in this directory and click Open.

5. Check the *Copy Files to Project Directory* checkbox. Enter the directory path JDEV_HOME\jdev\mywork\LocDept2WS\LocDeptJSP\public_html.

6. Click Next and Finish to close the wizard. The file will be copied to the project.

7. Click Save All.

8. Select the LocDept.jsp node and click Run. Your default browser will open, and you will see something like Figure 3-10.

Modify the Label Properties

By default, the labels for the fields use the attribute names from the view object in the BC4J layer. These labels are not necessarily the most intuitive to the user. However, there is a way to modify the display value associated with the attribute so that the data tag will use a friendlier label. This technique requires modification of the BC4J layer because the data tag reads all information about the data elements from that layer. The benefit of this technique is that all applications that use the same BC4J project will be able to take advantage of the prompt property because it is part of the common layer.

1. Open the LocDeptBC4J.jpr node in the LocDept2WS.jws workspace and navigate to LocationsView under the locdept package node.

2. Double click the LocationId object icon in the Structure window to display the Attribute Wizard for LocationId.

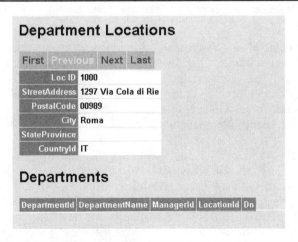

FIGURE 3-10. *JSP with style sheet applied*

3. Click the Control Hints node. Type "Loc ID" in the *Label Text* field as shown here:

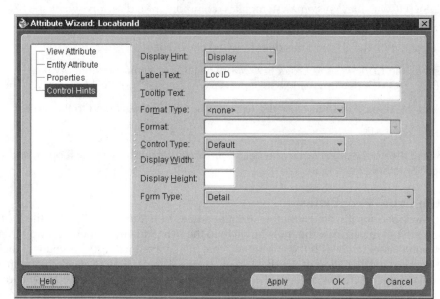

4. This property holds the text that is used when the data tag displays the attribute. Click Apply and OK.

5. Click Save All.

6. Close the browser and click the Run Manager tab in the Navigator. If the Run Manager is not displayed, select **View | Run Manager**.

7. On the Embedded OC4J Server node, select Terminate from the right-click menu. This stops the OC4J server. You need to restart the server because the changes in the BC4J objects will not be read otherwise.

8. Click the System tab in the Navigator and select the LocDept.jsp node in the LocDept2WS.jws workspace. Click the Run icon to run the JSP page and verify the change.

You can modify the label properties of the other attributes in the same way. This does not require changing any code in the application, and any other JSP applications that use these same data tags will pick up the change automatically.

What Just Happened?　　You created an empty JSP application and added BC4J data tags for displaying a master-detail application showing a single location record and multiple department records. In addition, you altered the label of an attribute using BC4J properties.

When you use data tags, adding a data source to a JSP page is just a matter of being sure that your BC4J layer is set up. The database connection and table details are stored in the BC4J layer, which simplifies the code you have to write for the user interface. The data tag is attached to BC4J with the application module name. Chapters 21–24 explore JSP pages in more detail.

CHAPTER
4

Java Language
Concepts for
JDeveloper Work

I love coffee, I love tea
I love the java jive and it loves me.

—The Ink Spots (1940), *The Java Jive*,
music by Ben Oakland, lyrics by Milton Drake

Developer is primarily a Java development environment. JDeveloper is a tool that helps you create and manage 3GL Java code and code written in supporting languages such as XML and HTML. Although you can create sophisticated application code using the wizards, a production system will always require extensive supplementation of this code. You cannot avoid knowing about the Java language if you want to be productive using JDeveloper. The requirement of knowing the language is central to all IDEs. For example, Oracle Forms Developer requires you to be conversant in the PL/SQL language. However, with JDeveloper, Java is central and the result of all activity in the tool instead of an ancillary scripting language (as PL/SQL is in Forms Developer).

This chapter examines some of the reasons why the Java language is important for developing modern systems. Since Java is based upon object orientation concepts, a review of those concepts is provided for those readers who are not using object orientation regularly. The chapter then reviews the fundamentals of Java for readers who need a refresher. Readers who are using Java now will be able to skim this chapter quickly. The hands-on practice at the end of the chapter demonstrates some of the language principles discussed as well as how to create a basic Java class file in JDeveloper.

CAUTION
Although this book is aimed at those who may not be using Java as their main language for development, it assumes that you have already been trained in or have studied the Java language. The overview in this chapter is not a substitute for learning the language outside of the context of this book. Appendix B contains some resources for further study.

Why Java?

Java is a relatively new language (officially launched in 1995) that provides many advantages over other programming languages. It offers a fully object-oriented development and deployment environment. Object orientation provides benefits in analysis and design because business concepts are more easily matched with objects than with standard relational structures. These concepts map easily to programming elements if the language has object orientation at its core.

If you are in the process of examining the Java language for use in a production environment, you need to consider both its benefits and drawbacks as well as what you will need to make the transition should you decide to launch into the Java environment.

Benefits

The IT industry is proceeding at a breakneck speed into Java technologies because of the perceived benefits. It is useful to examine some of the main strengths that Java offers.

Flexibility

Java is flexible enough to support many variations on deployment and development environments. Extensions to the base language are easily made and distributed because Java is built upon an object-oriented foundation.

Java supports light-client applications (through strategies such as JavaServer Pages technology), which only require a browser on the client side. Running the client in a browser virtually eliminates runtime concerns, which were a stumbling point with client/server application environments such as Forms (before it could be web deployed).

Java also supports deployment as a standalone application with a runtime (JVM) on the client. It solves the problem of supporting different screen resolutions with layout managers (further explained in Chapter 20) that are part of the basic libraries.

Strategies such as Sun's Model-View-Controller (MVC) architecture provide layers that can be swapped out when the needs of the enterprise change. With MVC, the view (presentation) layer can be implemented as a Java application running on the client with Swing components or as HTML elements presented in a browser. Although these views are different, they can share the same model (data definition and access) and controller (behavior and operation) layers. This is the kind of flexibility possible with current Java technology.

Current strategies for deployment of Java code emphasize multi-tier architectures that provide one or more application servers in addition to client and database server tiers. Although this feature is not unique to Java environments, it is one of the main design features of current Java web architectures. The application server approach offers flexibility and better scalability as the enterprise grows. For example, to add support for more clients, it is only necessary to add application servers and software that distribute the load among servers. The client and database tiers are unaffected by this scaling. A multi-tier approach also offers a central location to support business logic that is common to many applications.

NOTE

Another characteristic that makes Java attractive is its relative ease of use. Memory management and garbage collection are automatically handled by the Java engine. Also, Java supports multitasking so that you can write a program in Java that has multiple simultaneous threads of execution.

Wide Support from Vendors

A compelling reason to use Java is that it is widely supported by vendors. Instead of one main vendor, as with other technologies (for example, Microsoft's .NET framework), hundreds of companies produce and support Java products. Oracle is one of the companies that has a large stake in the Java world and continues to offer its customers guidance and product support for Java application development. There is strength in numbers in this case because the choice of Java as the language is not strongly tied to a vendor who may not be viable or strong in the future.

Wide Support from Users

Another source of wide support is the user community. Java has a well-established user base that is not necessarily tied to a particular company. The Java community is reminiscent of the early days of Unix, when users made their work available to other users on a not-for-profit basis. The concept of *open source* (www.opensource.org) defines free access to the source code, no-cost licenses, and the ability for others to extend the product. For example, the Linux operating system started and continues to be enhanced through open-source channels.

Although the Java language is not an open-source venture, there are some Java products, such as the Apache web server, that are open-source products. Sample Java code is readily available from many sources on the Internet. In addition, many freeware (with no-cost licenses) or shareware (try before you buy) utility libraries and much application code is available to Java developers.

Platform Independence

Java source code and runtime files are not specific to a particular operating system. Therefore, you can create and compile Java class files in a Windows environment and deploy the same files in a Unix environment without any changes. This aspect of Java, sometimes referred to as *portability,* is important to enterprises that find themselves outgrowing a particular operating environment but that need to support previously created systems.

Drawbacks

Many of Java's drawbacks are derived from the same features as its benefits and result from the newness of the language.

Rapidly Changing Environment

The Java environment is less mature than traditional environments that access a relational database. This immaturity has two main effects: frequent updates that add significant new features, and shifts in technologies that occur more rapidly than in traditional environments. For example, when Java was first released, the main deployment environment was within a Java Virtual Machine (JVM) running on the client machine. As that environment matured, there were features added and features *deprecated* (supported, but specially marked as being removed or replaced in future releases).

In addition to updates in the known environments, additional environments and technologies were added to the mix. For example, in addition to the environment of Java running on the client, there are now many variations on web-deploying a system developed in Java. In fact, the Java web-deployment landscape is so complex that as part of the Java 2 Platform, Enterprise Edition (J2EE), Sun Microsystems has created *blueprints* (also called *design patterns*), which are descriptions of proven techniques and best practices for deploying applications.

Multi-Vendor Support

There is not just one vendor to rely on for support. Although this was listed as one of Java's strengths, it can also be thought of as a drawback. You may need to merge Java technologies from different vendors, and each vendor is responsible only for their part. Oracle offers a complete solution for development (JDeveloper) and deployment (*i*AS), but you may find yourself in a multi-vendor situation if Oracle products were not selected or were extended with components from other vendors.

Requires Significant Language Skills

The Java language is relatively stable and easy to learn. It is an object-oriented language as is C++, but does not require that the developer think about memory management and pointers as in C++.

However, Java developers do need to think in an object-oriented way as well as to understand all aspects of the language and how the code pieces tie together in a production application. Java coding is largely a 3GL effort at this point. The IDEs assist (as mentioned in Chapter 2), but developers also need to have solid programming skills to be effective in the environment.

In addition, for web-deployed Java, developers need to have skills in other languages and technologies such as HTML, XML, and JavaScript. These skills are easily obtained, but are essentially prerequisites to effective work in the Java web environment.

If developers are to be completely effective, they must also have knowledge of database languages. For example, SQL skills are essential for database access, though with JDeveloper's BC4J framework, most SQL statements are hidden from the developers. Although database stored code (packages, procedures, functions, and triggers) can be coded in Java, developers may still need to interface with existing code built in PL/SQL and, therefore, will need to understand PL/SQL.

Transitioning to Java

Working in a Java environment is very different from working with traditional database development environments such as Oracle Forms Developer or Visual Basic (VB). If the benefits of Java have convinced you of the need to make the transition to Java, you'll need to plan that transition carefully.

It will take time to learn the nuances of a Java environment. If you are committed to creating an organization-wide Java environment, building a traditional client/server application may still make sense if your application is used in a small group or departmental situation.

If your development team has skills in another language, Java will require some retraining and ramp-up time. However, building client/server applications directly in Java is a good first step. This method leverages the improved flexibility of Java and its ability to build sophisticated applications. It also makes the transition of your business to the Web easier because Java is a primary language of the Web. The smaller the application, the easier it will be to concentrate on the language and not the application. A prototype or internal administrative application that will not see extensive use might be a good candidate for this first effort.

Another variation on this transition advice is to develop a small web application in Java. This can be the next step after building a client/server application, or it can be the first step. Web applications add the complexity of application and web servers, and this will give you a taste of this extra layer of software.

Making the Leap

The transition to Java may not need to be (and probably should not be) a big bang where you move all new development to Java and start converting existing applications to Java. Although you want to minimize the number of tools and environments that you support, it is likely that you will have to support existing applications in the environments in which they were written. With all current development tools trying to improve their web-enabled capabilities, it becomes increasingly difficult to make a compelling argument for abandoning these technologies. For example, following a long evolution, Oracle Forms Developer running over the Web is now a stable and viable environment.

Therefore, the best approach is to leave the core application development in whatever legacy environment you are comfortable with and to build a few systems of limited scope in the Java environment using JDeveloper as the tool of choice. Once you have some experience in building and deploying applications, you can make an informed decision about whether your organization is ready to make the transition to an entirely Java-based environment. There may still be good reasons to stick with your legacy environment for core applications and only to use a Java-based environment for e-commerce and other web-based applications.

As you become more comfortable with working in Java and have more new Java projects under way, you can think about migrating current applications. However, some applications may never need to make the transition.

NOTE
As with many shops that support legacy COBOL-based programs, it is likely that you will have to support your current development environment for large enterprisewide applications for some time.

Object-Orientation Concepts

Although many people notice cosmetic similarities between Java and the C++ language, there are enough differences between Java and C++ that it is worth reviewing the basics of the language even if you understand the concepts behind C++. Understanding Java requires a comfort level with the concepts of object orientation.

The fundamental building block of an object-oriented language like Java is a structure called a *class*. The class acts as a pattern or blueprint from which *objects* are built. In object-speak, "an object is an instance of a class." An object is built from a class and has an identity (or name). This means that the class is actually not used in a program; it is used as a pattern for an object that appears in a program. For example, an object called "usefulBox" can be instantiated from a class called "Box." In this example, usefulBox is created out of the pattern defined by the Box class.

The concept of class and object loosely parallels the concept of datatyping (and record variable definition) in programming languages such as PL/SQL. In PL/SQL, a datatype is a pattern upon which variables are built. If the datatype concept were expressed in object-oriented terms, a variable would be the object that instantiates the datatype (acting as a class).

A class contains both data (in variables) and behavior (application code logic). This makes it different from anything in the world of relational databases. The closest concept to the class data and behavior characteristics is a relational table with a dedicated package of procedures that are used for SQL operations such as INSERT, UPDATE, DELETE, and SELECT. In this case, the combination of relational table and procedural package contains data (in the table) and behavior (procedures and functions in the package assigned to the table).

The difference between this example from the relational/procedural world and the object-oriented paradigm is that there is only a conceptual link or loose coupling between the table and the code package. The table and package exist as separate objects and can be used separately. In object orientation, the class is inherently both data and behavior; the link is tight and perfectly integrated. The class is used as a pattern to create objects that contain data and pointers to the code in the class. Figure 4-1 depicts this difference.

NOTE
Java programmers sometimes refer to an object by its class name. For example, if you create an object from the Box class, you could refer to the object as "the Box" or "the Box object."

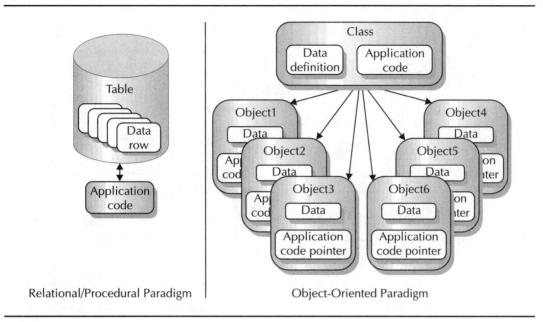

FIGURE 4-1. *Relational/procedural and object-oriented paradigms*

Handling and Storing Data

The ways in which data is handled in an object-oriented language such as Java and in a relational database system are also fundamentally different. Data is not inherently persistent in Java. Therefore, data is available for the time in which the Java program is running. There are ways to store data in between program sessions; the method included as part of the base language is *object serialization.* Object serialization includes the ability to write object values to and read object values from an output stream (such as a file system). You include serialization features in a class by implementing the Serializable interface. (Interfaces are explained later in this chapter.) You can then write and read the class, class signature, and values to a persistent stream such as a file.

Object serialization is the main Java way to handle persistence. However, many programmers of Java and other languages have become accustomed to using a fully featured relational database management system (RDBMS) to handle data persistence. An RDBMS provides solid facilities for fast and safe storage, retrieval, backup, and recovery of mission-critical data. However, the RDBMS, by definition, is built around the concept of storing data in relational tables. This concept does not correspond to the way in which the Java language handles data in objects. Figure 4-2 shows a conceptual mapping that you can make between relational and object-oriented data storage.

This diagram shows how a row in a table roughly corresponds to the data in an object. You can describe a table in object-oriented terms as a collection of records representing instances of related data that are defined by the structure of the table. The problem is that there is a difference in the the way that data appears in the two paradigms. A table contains rows that are accessible

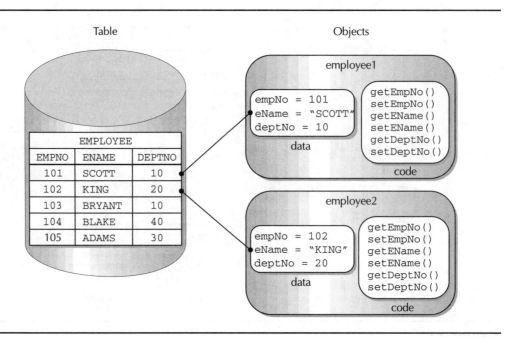

FIGURE 4-2. *Mapping between relational and object data storage*

using a relational database language such as SQL which addresses requests for sets of data to the table. Objects contain data and you address requests for that data directly to the object. You cannot use SQL in an object-oriented environment because the source structure of the data is different; data is distributed across many objects.

Therefore, there are basic differences between the relational and the object paradigms in the areas of persistence, data structures and access code, and conceptual foundations. Using Java code to access a relational database is a common requirement, and there are many solutions to making an effective map between relational tables and objects. For example, architectures such as JDeveloper's Business Components for Java (BC4J) hide the complexity of the relational-object mapping and provide programmers with object-oriented, Java-friendly structures that can be easily incorporated into application programs. Other strategies, such as Java Database Connectivity (JDBC) and SQLJ (SQL embedded in Java), ease the burden of the relational-object mapping problem facing Java developers.

Inheritance

One of the key characteristics of object orientation is the ability of a class to automatically assume the data and methods of another class. This is the concept of *inheritance,* where one class is a parent of another. The parent, also called the *superclass* (base class or generalization), contains elements (data and behavior) that are available in the *subclass* (child class or specialization). The lines of inheritance can be deep, with one class acting as the grandparent or great-grandparent of another. To base a class on a parent class, you *extend* the parent class. The child class can then supplement, modify, or disable the data and behavior of the parent class.

The other main characteristics of object orientation follow:

- **Polymorphism** The ability of an object to modify or override its inherited attributes or behavior. This is a key feature of the Java programming language allowing the developer to create template classes as well as extensions to these classes, which may (but are not required to) inherit attributes and methods from the generalization class.

- **Encapsulation** Only the important characteristics of an object are revealed, but the internals are hidden.

Java Language Review

High-level, theoretical discussions of object orientation often glaze the eyes of the audience. The theory may make more sense when it is demonstrated using some code examples. The following section shows a code sample and explains its contents. Even if you do not have extensive Java experience but have been exposed to other programming languages, you will be able to identify some of the language elements as well as the structure of a typical source code file. The example also demonstrates, in the context of the Java language, the key object-oriented concepts just explained.

TIP

This chapter is not intended as a comprehensive overview of the Java language. If you do not have formal training or experience with the Java language, a good place to start is the free, self-guided Java Tutorial available online at java.sun.com.

Annotated Java Code Example

The ideas of class and object are central to the Java language. All Java code is contained in class files. A class file is made up of a number of standard elements. The following is a representative class file that contains standard elements. The hands-on practice at the end of this chapter shows how to create and work with this class in JDeveloper. The line numbers in the code listing appear for the purpose of reference and would not appear in the actual code file.

```
01: package shapes;
02: import java.lang.*;
03:
04: /*
05:    This class provides a third dimension to Rectangle
06: */
07: public class Box extends Rectangle {
08:   int height;    // override the Rectangle height
09:   int depth;     // unique to Box
10:
11:   public Box() {
12:     height = 4;
13:     width = 3;    // the width from Rectangle
14:     depth = 2;
15:   }
```

```
16:
17:    public int getDepth() {
18:       return depth;
19:    }
20:
21:    public void setDepth(int newDepth) {
22:       depth = newDepth;
23:    }
24:
25:    // width is the same as super.width
26:    public int getVolume() {
27:       return height * width * depth;
28:    }
29: }
```

NOTE
The first rule of the Java language is that all code is case sensitive.
Therefore, a class called "BOX" is different from a class called "Box."
By convention, class names are mixed case, with each word in the
name initial capped. For example, a class that defines salary history
would be called "SalaryHistory." Chapter 5 contains further
guidelines for naming conventions.

Line 01 identifies the directory (package) in which this file is located. *Packages* are
collections of class files in subdirectories in a file system. Packages can be archived into a
.zip or .jar file, and the Java runtime can search in this archive (sometimes called a *library*)
for a specific class file. The *CLASSPATH* operating system environment variable contains a list
of these archive files separated by colons (for Unix) or semicolons (for Windows), for example:
"C:\JDev9i\jdk\jre\lib\rt.jar;C:\JDev9i\jdk\jre\lib\jce.jar;C:\JDev9i\jdk\jre\lib\charsets.jar;C:\
JDev9i\jdk\jre\classes;C:\JDev9i\jdev\lib\jdev-rt.jar."
Line 01 ends with a semicolon, as do all Java statements.

Line 02 defines an *import* (called an "include" in other languages such as C++), specifying
the classes required for the code to execute. Imports are identified by class name as well as
by the directory in which they reside. Many import statements may appear if more than one
directory structure is required. The import statement can reference a single class file or an entire
directory (package) as in line 02. The directory is listed using dot syntax (directory.subdirectory
.subdirectory.*), with "*" indicating that all classes in that directory will be available to the class.
This example is provided for discussion purposes. Normally, the java.lang classes are
automatically available without an import statement.

Lines 04–06 show a multi-line *comment* (using the beginning and ending symbols "/*" and
"*/"). Line 08 shows a single-line comment (using the beginning symbol "//") at the end of the
line. This style of comment can also be used on a line by itself. Java also offers special multi-line
comments that start with "/**" and end with "*/" and are used to generate Javadoc. Chapter 2
contains a sidebar about Javadoc that describes these comments.

Line 07 is the class definition. It includes the keyword `public` indicating that this class is
available to all other classes. The keyword `public` is called an *access specifier* (or *access
modifier*). Other choices for access specifiers are `private` (where access to the class member

is limited to other members of the same class) and `protected` (where you cannot access the class from outside the package unless the calling class is a subclass). If you do not use a specifier keyword, this indicates the *default specifier,* where members are available only to code in the same package.

The end of this line contains an opening curly bracket "{" indicating the start of a *block of code.* Between this and the matched closing curly bracket "}" are code elements and other blocks of code. The code blocks do not need to contain any code (unlike blocks in PL/SQL). Blocks of Java code may be nested. Blocks define the scope of variables as discussed later.

TIP
Always use curly brackets to contain code in code structures (such as if and for). Technically, you do not need curly brackets if there is only one statement to execute. However, it is easy to make the mistake of adding a line of code under an if statement that has no curly brackets and assume that it will execute conditionally. Since only the first line of code under the if statement is part of the conditional logic, the next statement would always be executed if no curly brackets contain the statements. Always using curly brackets will prevent this type of error.

This code defines a class called Box that is built (subclassed) from a class called Rectangle. The `extends` keyword declares that Rectangle is Box's parent and defines the inheritance for Box. The Rectangle class might be defined as follows:

```java
package shapes;

public class Rectangle  {
  int height;
  int width;

  public Rectangle() {
    height = 1;
    width = 1;
  }

  public int getHeight() {
    return height;
  }

  public void setHeight(int newHeight) {
    height = newHeight;
  }
  // getWidth() and setWidth() methods go here
}
```

NOTE
A Java source code file can contain only one public class. The file name is the name of the public class in that file (with a .java extension).

Lines 08–09 declare two variables (as `int` types). These constitute the data (also called *attributes* or *fields*) for the class that was mentioned in the discussion of object-oriented concepts. Since the variables of the parent class are available in the child class, the Rectangle variables `height` and `width` are available to the Box class. However, the Box class also declares a `height` variable, and this overrides the parent's `height` variable. You can still access the parent's `height` variable using the symbol `super.height` (the superclass's or parent's `height` variable). This code also declares a new variable: `depth`. Variable names are formatted the same way as class names: initial cap for all words except the first.

Technically, *variables* in Java are typed from primitive datatypes such as `int`, `float`, or `boolean`. Other data resides inside objects that are instantiations of classes such as `String` or `StringBuffer`. Datatypes are discussed in more detail later in this chapter.

NOTE
Methods from the parent class are available in the subclass using the specifier "super." For example, the Rectangle class contains a `setDepth()` *method. If you wanted the Box class to supplement (not override) this code, you would write a* `setDepth()` *method in the Box class that calls the parent class's method using the expression "super.setDepth()." If you wanted to override the code, you would omit the call to super.setDepth().*

Lines 11–28 define a constructor and methods. The standard unit of code in Java is called a *method.* The first line of the method is called the *method signature* or *signature* because it contains the characteristics of this code such as the arguments, access specifier, and return type.

You can use the same name for more than one method in the class if the methods with that name all have different argument lists (for example, `showWidth(int width)` and `showWidth(String widthUnit)`). Methods with the same name but different arguments are referred to as *overloaded methods.*

Methods implement the object-oriented concept of behavior in a class. All code in a Java class is contained within methods. Java does not distinguish between code units such as functions that return a value and procedures that do not return a value. It has only one unit of code—the method. Methods must declare a return type. They can return a primitive or class—as with functions in other languages—or they can return *void* (nothing)—as with procedures in other languages. Methods can only return one thing, but that thing could be an array or an object, which could be made up of many values.

Lines 11–15 define a unit of code called "Box," that has the same name as the class. This unit is called a *constructor* and is not a method. Constructors use the same syntax as methods, but do not return anything (not even `void`). (If there is a return type declared, the signature identifies a method not a constructor.) Usually, they are used to define an object that is based upon the class (using the keyword `new`); in this case, the constructor just sets values for the variables in the class. The constructor code is contained within a block of code delimited by curly brackets. If you do not define a constructor, you can still create an object from the class because there is an implicit constructor that is available to calling programs.

Method names are, by convention, mixed case, with each word except for the first one initial capped. Constructors must have the same name as the class. Since class names usually begin with an initial-capped word, the constructor also begins with an initial-capped word.

Lines 17–28 define getters and setters (also called *accessors* or *accessor methods*). A *getter* is a method that is usually named with a "get" prefix and variable name suffix. It returns the value of the variable for which it is named. Although this is a standard and expected method that you would write for each property or variable, it is not required if there is a variable that you do not want to expose. Getters are typically as simple as this example because they just return the value of a single variable. In this example, the getDepth() method returns the value of the variable, and the getVolume() method calculates the volume based upon the three dimensions of the box.

A *setter* is a method that is named with a "set" prefix and is normally used to change the value of the property for which it is named. As with the getter, there may be cases where you would not write the setter for a particular variable, but it is normally an expected method. Setters are also often as simple as this example because they just assign a value to a variable.

In this example, the Box class contains no setters and getters for the height and width variables. These would be defined in the parent class, Rectangle, and are available to Box.

Line 29 is the closing bracket for the class definition.

NOTE
Java is a case-sensitive language. If you are transitioning from a non–case-sensitive language, it is useful to keep reminding yourself of this fact.

Annotated Use of the Box Example Class

Code that uses a class such as Box demonstrates some other principles of the Java language. Consider the following example usage:

```
01: package shapes;
02:
03: public class TestBox  {
04:
05:   public static void main(String[] args) {
06:     // this creates an object called usefulBox
07:     Box usefulBox = new Box();
08:     // getHeight() is the getHeight from Rectangle
09:     // height shows the height variable from Box
10:     System.out.println (
11:       "The height of Rectangle is " + usefulBox.getHeight() +
12:       " and of usefulBox is " + usefulBox.height);
13:
14:     // getDepth and getVolume are from Box
15:     System.out.println (
16:       "The depth of usefulBox is " + usefulBox.getDepth() +
17:       " and the volume of usefulBox is " + usefulBox.getVolume());
18:   }
19: }
```

The output for the main method will be the following:

```
The height of Rectangle is 1 and of usefulBox is 4
The depth of usefulBox is 2 and the volume of usefulBox is 24
```

Lines 01–03 state the package and declare the class TestBox.

Lines 05–18 define a method called `main()`. This is a specially named method that executes automatically when the JVM runs the class from the command line (for example: `java.exe shapes.TestBox`). The `main()` method can execute any kind of code; in this case, it shows messages in the Java console (that displays in the JDeveloper Log Window).

The keyword `static` indicates that `main()` is a *class method* that can be run without declaring an instance of the class. That is, you can still run the `main()` method without having to create an object from the TestBox class. Class methods cannot access *instance variables* (variables defined on the class level outside of a method without the keyword `static` and available to objects created from the class), but can access *class variables* (variables declared on the class level using the keyword `static`, for example, `static int boxDepth;`).

The `main()` method signature also includes an argument within the parentheses that follow the method name. This argument is a String datatype and is named "arg." The square brackets [ ] after arg indicate that arg is a String array. *Arrays* are collections of similar objects. The String array arg is used to pass any command-line arguments available when the class is executed. You can also use the expression "`String args[]`" to represent an array of strings.

Line 07 creates an object called usefulBox based upon the Box class. The object is made from the class and, therefore, has the same variables (such as `usefulBox.width`) and methods (such as `usefulBox.getVolume()`) as the class. Line 07 accomplishes two tasks: it declares an object of type Box and creates the object. This line could also be expanded into the following two lines to separate the tasks:

```
Box usefulBox;
usefulBox = new Box();
```

Lines 10–12 output a message (using the `System.out.println()` method) that will be displayed in the Java console window. If you run a Java program from the command line, the Java console window will be the command-line window. If you run a Java program in JDeveloper, the message will appear in the Log window. You can concatenate literal strings (in quotes) and variables with the "+" operator regardless of type.

Line 11 references `getHeight()`, which is a method from the Rectangle class. Since this method displays the value of the `height` variable in `Rectangle`, the value will be 1 (the default for that class). In actual practice, this construct would be a bit confusing and is only shown here to demonstrate that a subclass can override a parent class's variable.

Line 12 references the `height` variable of usefulBox (which was built from the Box class). In this case, the `height` variable will be displayed as the default from the Box class ("4").

Lines 15–19 display the results of usefulBox method calls. Both `getDepth()` and `getVolume()` are declared in the Box class and will be output as 2 and 24, respectively. Lines 18 and 19 close the method and class.

NOTE
*When naming Java elements, you may use a combination of uppercase
and lowercase letters, numbers, the underscore, and the dollar sign.
However, you may not begin names with a number. There is no limit
on the number of characters that you can use in a name.*

Other Java Language Concepts

There are some other Java language concepts that were not demonstrated in the examples but
that are useful to review.

The Code Development and Deployment Process
The typical Java development process, if you are not using an IDE such as JDeveloper, follows:

1. Write a source code file with a text editor, and name it using the name of the class that
   the file represents and a .java extension, for example, TestBox.java.

2. Compile the source code using the javac.exe executable (included in the Java SDK).
   If there are no syntax errors, the compiler creates a file with the same name and a class
   extension, for example, TestBox.class. This binary compiled file (called *bytecode*)
   is interpreted by the Java runtime engine when the program is executed. Java is
   compiled in this way, but it is considered an interpreted language.

3. Test the class file using the java.exe executable (also included in the Java SDK). If the
   Java code is a Java application, the command line is as simple as the following example:

   ```
   java shapes.TestBox
   ```

4. Repeat steps 1–3 until the program performs as required.

5. Package the program file with the library files that it uses (libraries or classes declared
   in the import statements at the beginning of the program), and install the package on a
   client machine that has a Java runtime environment installed (containing the Java
   runtime engine—java.exe—and the base Java libraries such as java.lang.*).

Although an IDE such as JDeveloper automates many of these steps, the tasks are the same
inside and outside an IDE. Also, different types of Java programs have different requirements
for the compile and runtime steps, but the concepts are the same. For example, working with
JavaServer Pages (JSP) files requires the development of a .jsp file that is generated automatically
into a .java file and is compiled automatically into a .class file by a special Java runtime engine.
The subject of deployment is further discussed in Chapters 7 and 15.

Control Statements
The idea of control statements is familiar to anyone who has written program code. This section
reviews only the basic structures, since most structures are similar to those in other programming
languages. You can refer to a standard Java language text to understand the variations and usage
requirements for these control statements. (See Appendix B for Java language resources.)

Sequence   One of the main concepts of control statements is sequence, and Java code is executed in the order in which it appears in the file. The method that is executed first varies with the style of Java program; for example, a Java application executes the `main()` method first, and a Java applet executes the `init()` method first. The commands within these methods are executed in the order in which they appear in the code file. As in other languages, calls to other methods execute the method and return to the line of code after the method call. The keyword `return` jumps out of the current method and returns control to the statement in the calling unit after that method was called.

Conditional Branching   Java uses the statements `if-else` and `switch` to branch the code based upon a condition as follows:

```
class ShowQuarter {
    public static void main (String args[]) {
       int taxMonth = 10;
       String taxQuarter;

       if (taxMonth == 1 || taxMonth == 2 || taxMonth == 3)
          taxQuarter = "1st Quarter";
       else if (taxMonth == 4 || taxMonth == 5 || taxMonth == 6)
          taxQuarter = "2nd Quarter";
       // more conditions would appear here
       else
          taxQuarter = "Not Valid";
       System.out.println("Your current Tax Quarter is: " + taxQuarter );
    }
}
```

This is a branching statement that uses multiple `if` statements. The "||" symbol is a logical OR operator ("&&" is the logical AND). Logical conditions are enclosed in parentheses. The "==" symbol is the equality comparison operator. Each condition is followed by a single statement or block of code. As mentioned before, it is a good idea to always define a block of code enclosed in curly brackets under the `if` statement.

The `switch` statement is an alternative to multiple `if` statements that test the same value. The following example could be used instead of the `if-then` example:

```
class ShowQuarter2 {
    public static void main (String args[]) {
       int taxMonth = 10;
       String taxQuarter;
       // The break statement jumps out of the conditional testing
       switch (taxMonth) {
         case 1:    case 2:    case 3:
           taxQuarter = "1st Quarter";
           break;
         case 4:    case 5:    case 6:
           taxQuarter = "2nd Quarter";
           break;
```

```
      // more conditions would appear here
      default:
        taxQuarter = "Not Valid";
    }    // end of the switch
    System.out.print("Your current Tax Quarter is: " + taxQuarter);
  }        // end of the main() method
}          // end of the class
```

Iteration or Looping   There are three loop statements: `for`, `while`, and `do-while`. The `for` loop controls loop iteration by incrementing and testing the value of a variable as shown in the following example:

```
class TestLoops
{
  public static void main (String args[]) {
    for (int i = 1; i <= 10; i++) {
        System.out.println("Loop 1 count is " + i);
    }
  }
}
```

The `while` and `do-while` loops test a condition at the start or end of the loop, respectively. Refer to a Java language reference, such as The Java Tutorial at java.sun.com, for more examples of loop structures.

Exception Handling   Exceptions can occur in the Java runtime environment when undefined conditions are encountered. To catch exceptions, you enclose the code in a block defined by the keywords `try`, `catch`, and `finally` as in the following example:

```
public class TestException {
   public static void main(String[] args) {
      int numerator = 5, denominator = 0;
      int ratio;
      try {
         ratio = numerator / denominator ;
         System.out.println("The ratio is " + ratio);
      }
      catch (Exception e)   {
         // This shows an error message on the console
         e.printStackTrace();
      }
      finally {
         System.out.println("The end.");
      }
   }
}
```

The message in the `finally` block will be executed regardless of whether an exception is thrown. You may also raise an exception by using the keyword `throw` anywhere in the code.

NOTE
The preceding example shows how you can declare more than one variable (numerator and denominator in this example) of the same type on the same line.

Variable Scope

Variables can be declared and objects can be created anywhere and are available within the block in which they are declared. For example, the following example shows a variable currentSalary that is available throughout the main() method. Another variable, currentCommission, is available only within the if block in which it is declared. The last print statement will cause a compilation error because the variable is out of scope for that statement.

```java
class TestScope {

  public static void main (String[] args) {
    int currentSalary = 0;
    if (currentSalary < 0) {
      int currentCommission = 10;
      System.out.println("No salary but the commission is " + currentCommission);
    }
    else {
      System.out.println("Salary but no commission.");
    }
    // This will cause a compilation error.
    System.out.println(currentCommission);
  }
}
```

NOTE
Although Java does not use the concept of a variable declaration section (such as the DECLARE section of PL/SQL), it is good programming practice to put all variable declarations for a method at the beginning of the method. If you are declaring classwide variables, place all declarations in a section under the class declaration statement. Positioning the variable declarations in this way makes the code easier to read.

In addition to the scope within a block, variable scope is affected by where and how the variable is declared in the class file. The following example demonstrates these usages:

```java
class ShowSalary {
  static int previousSalary = 0;
  int commission = 10;

  public static void main (String[] args) {
    int currentSalary = 100;
```

```
    if (currentSalary == 0) {
      System.out.println("There is only a commission.");
    }
    else {
      System.out.println("Current salary is " + currentSalary);
    }
    System.out.println("{Previous salary is " + previousSalary);

    // The following would cause a compile error.
    // System.out.println(commission);
  }
}
```

This example demonstrates three variables usages—instance variables, class variables, and member variables.

Instance Variables   These are variables created under the class declaration and outside of any method. In this example, the variable `commission` is an instance variable. It does not use the keyword `static` in the declaration and is not available to class methods (that are declared with the keyword `static`). Therefore, the variable `commission` is not available to the `main()` method in this example. Instance variables are available to objects created from the class. For example, you could create an object (instance) from this sample class using "`ShowSalary calcSalary = new ShowSalary();`", and the variable `calcSalary.commission` would be available in the class that contained the object. Each object receives its own copy of the class variable. Therefore, if you create object1 and object2 from the ShowSalary class, `object1.commission` and `object2.commission` are different variables.

Class Variables   Class variables, such as `previousSalary` in this example, are declared using the `static` keyword and are available to class methods (also declared with the keyword `static`). There is only one copy of the class variable regardless of the number of objects that have been created from the class. Therefore, if you create `salary1` and `salary2` from the `ShowSalary` class, the same variable `previousSalary` will be available from both objects (as `salary1.previousSalary` and `salary2.previousSalary`). If `salary2` changes the value of this variable, `salary1` will see that new value because there is only one variable. The following is an example that demonstrates this principle:

```
class TestShowSalary
{
  public static void main(String[] args)
  {
    ShowSalary salary1 = new ShowSalary();
    ShowSalary salary2 = new ShowSalary();
    //
    System.out.println("From salary1, it is " + salary1.previousSalary);
    salary2.previousSalary = 300;
    System.out.println("After salary2 changed it, it is " +
      salary1.previousSalary);
  }
}
```

The output from this program follows:

```
From salary1, it is 0
After salary2 changed it, it is 300
```

Member Variables   This variable usage is declared inside a method. In the sample
`ShowSalary` class, `currentSalary` is a member variable because it is declared inside a
method (`main()`). The variable is available only within the scope of that method.

Constants and "final"

A variable can be marked as `final`, which means that its value cannot change. Since you
cannot change the value, you must assign a value when you declare the variable. This is similar
to the idea of a constant in other languages. The following is an example of a final "variable."
Final variables use all uppercase characters by convention (as mentioned in Chapter 5).

```
final int FEET_IN_MILE = 5280;
```

You can also mark methods with `final`, which means that you cannot override the method
in a subclass. Thus, if class A has a `final` method B( ), and if class C extends A, then you cannot
override the inherited method B( ) in class C. For example:

```
final int getCommission () {
... }
```

Classes may be marked with `final` to indicate that they cannot be subclassed. That is, no
class may extend that class. For example:

```
class final CalcSalary {
... }
```

CAUTION
*The keyword `final` stops inheritance (subclassing) of classes, but
does not stop the overriding of a variable (constant).*

Primitive Datatypes

Variable types fall into two categories: primitive and reference. Primitive datatypes can hold only
a single value and cannot be passed by reference or pointers. Primitives are not based upon
classes. The primitive datatypes include `boolean` (for true and false values), several number
types differentiated by the magnitude and precision of data they can represent (`byte`, `short`,
`int`, `long`, `float`, `double`), and `char`.

A `char` is a single byte number between 0 and about 65,000 that is used to represent
the Unicode international character set. A char datatype can be declared in a number of
ways as follows:

```
// decimal equivalent of the letter 'a'
char charDecimal = 97;
// using an actual character inside single quotes
```

```
char charChar = 'a';
// octal equivalent of the letter 'a'
char charOctal = '\141';
// Hex value for the letter 'a'
char charHex = 0x0061;
// Unicode (hex) value for the letter 'a'
char charUnicode = '\u0061';
```

Reference Datatypes

Reference datatypes represent a memory location for a value or set of values. Since Java does not support pointers or memory addresses, you use the variable name to represent the reference. You can type an object using these reference datatypes, and the object instantiated in this way will have available to it the members in the class or referenced element. Reference datatypes may be arrays, interfaces, or classes.

Arrays   *Collections* are programmatic groups of objects or primitives. There are various types of collections available in Java, such as arrays, sets, dynamic arrays, linked lists, trees, hash tables, and key-value pairs (maps). This section discusses arrays. You will find information about the other categories of collections in Java language references.

Arrays in Java are collections of objects or primitives of similar type and may have one or more dimensions. Arrays are the only type of collection that can store primitive types. Elements within an array are accessed by indexes, which start at zero ([0]). To create an array, you declare it, allocate memory, and initialize the elements. These operations can be performed in two basic steps as shown here:

```
String animals[];
animals = new String[10];
```

The first line of code creates the array variable by adding a pair of square brackets to the end of the declaration. The second line sets the size of the array (in this case, 10), which allocates memory and initializes the elements. Arrays must be declared with a fixed number of members. This code could be condensed into the following line:

```
String animals[] = new String[10];
```

The next step is to store values in the array. In this example, the index numbers run from 0 to 9, and you store a value using that number as follows:

```
animals[3] = "Cat";
```

In Java, you can create arrays of arrays, more commonly known as *multi-dimensional arrays*. Since each array can be independently created, you can even create irregular combinations where array sizes vary within a given dimension. The more complex the array, the harder it is to keep track of, so moderation is advised. The following is a shorthand method for creating and assigning a two-dimensional array that stores pet owner names and the pet types:

```
class PetNames {
  public static main (String args[]) {
```

```
      String petFriends[ ][ ] = {
        {"George", "Snake", "Alligator" },
        {"Denise", "Butterfly"},
        {"Christine", "Tiger"},
        {"Robert", "Parrot", "Dove", "Dog", "Cat"}
      };
  }
}
```

NOTE
*If you need to store unlike objects in an array, you can use "vectors,"
which are collections that permit elements to be of differing types.
The size of a vector can grow or shrink to match the number of
elements. The drawback to vectors is that all operations work with the
Object class so that you need to cast elements in the vector back to
their original type when you retrieve them.*

Interfaces   An interface is somewhat like a PL/SQL package specification because it lists
method signatures and constants without any code body. Classes that *implement* (or inherit)
from the interface must include all methods in the interface. Interfaces are useful for providing
a common type for a number of classes. For example, if you have a method that needs to return a
type that will be manipulated by three different classes (that execute slightly differently), you can
use an interface as the return type. Each of the three classes would implement the interface and,
therefore, be able to be used in the same way by the method.

You can base a class on one or more interfaces, and this also provides a form of multi-parent
inheritance. For example, if you had interfaces called SalaryHistory and CommissionHistory, you
could define a class as follows:

```
public class HistoryAmounts extends CalcSalary implements SalaryHistory,
  CommissionHistory {
... }
```

The HistoryAmounts class is a subclass of the CalcSalary class and will implement (provide
method code for) the SalaryHistory and CommissionHistory interfaces. If you did not want to
provide the code for the methods, you could declare HistoryAmounts as abstract (for example,
`abstract class HistoryAmounts`).

Classes   You can use any class to "type" an object (with the exception of abstract classes
and classes with private constructors). The object becomes an instantiation of the class and has
available to it the methods, class variables, and instance variables defined by the class. Therefore,
classes can be used to create objects with the data and behavior characteristics defined in the class.

There are some wrapper classes, included with the Java language, that are commonly used
as types for variables. When a variable is based upon one of these classes, technically it is an
object, not a variable, but the term "variable" is commonly used to include these objects.

The Java language includes classes, such as Boolean, Byte, Character, Double, Float, Integer,
Long, and Number, that implement primitive datatypes. These classes include methods that
act upon the objects, such as a Long method that converts to an int. For example, using a Long

object called `longVar`, the int value is `longVar.intValue()`. Two commonly used classes are String and StringBuffer.

String Class   A String object can be assigned a set of characters as follows:

```
String stringVar = "This is a Java test string";
```

Objects built from String can take advantage of the methods in the String class. The methods provide functions to create strings from literals, chars, char arrays, and other string reference objects. The following Java Strings store the value "Java" by assigning a value to one String object and concatenating that object to another string using the `concat()` method.

```
String startingLetters = "Ja";
String newString = startingLetters.concat("va");
```

TIP

To view the Javadoc for a basic Java class such as String, type "String" into the Code Editor, place the cursor in the word, and select Browse Javadoc from the right-click menu. A Browse Window will appear with the Javadoc containing methods and constants available to objects built from the String class.

You can compare, concatenate, change the case of, find the length of, extract characters from, search, and modify strings. Although strings cannot be changed in Java, whenever you alter a string through a string operation, the result is a new String object that contains the modifications. You can take advantage of the overloading of the concatenation operator "+" to assign string values from number literals as in the following example:

```
// This assigns "The age is 235" to age.
String age = ("The age is " + 2 + 35);
// This assigns "The age is 37" to age.
String age = "The age is " + (2 + 35);
```

NOTE

In Java, the method `substring(int startIndex, int endIndex)` *returns a portion of a string from the startIndex to the (endIndex –1). As with arrays, the index numbers start with zero. The following example will assign "This is a Java" to the stringVar variable:*

```
String baseString = "This is a Java string";
String newString = baseString.substring(0, 15);
```

StringBuffer Class   `StringBuffer` is a sister class to `String` and represents character sequences that can change size and/or be modified. What this means to the developer is that methods such as `append()` and `insert()` are available to modify a `StringBuffer` variable (that is, it is *mutable*), whereas in `String` you cannot modify the string (that is, the variable is *immutable*) and are limited to the concatenation operator (+). Thus, the `StringBuffer` class may be used when the character sequences being stored need to have substrings inserted or appended. The following shows an example usage of the `append()` method available to StringBuffer:

```
class StringAppend {
  public static void main (String args[]) {
    String stringVar = "A string";
    StringBuffer stringBuff = new StringBuffer(50);
    stringVar = stringBuff.append(stringVar).append(
      " is appended.").toString();
    System.out.println(stringVar);
  }
}
```

Datatype Matching

Java is a semi-strongly typed language—every variable has a type, and every type is strictly defined. Type matching is strictly enforced in cases such as the following:

- The arguments passed to a method must match the argument types in the method's signature.

- Both sides of an assignment expression must contain the same datatype.

- Both sides of a Boolean comparison, such as an equality condition, must match datatypes.

There is no automatic conversion of one variable type to another. However, in practice, Java is not as restrictive as you might think, since most built-in methods are heavily overloaded (defined for different types of arguments). For example, you can combine strings, numbers, and dates using a concatenation operator (+) without formal variable type conversion, because the concatenation operator is overloaded.

In addition to overloading, an exact match is not always required, as shown in the following example:

```
public class TestCast {
  public static void main (String args[]) {
    byte smallNumber = 10;
    int largeNumber;
    largeNumber = smallNumber * 5;
    System.out.println("largeNumber is " + largeNumber);
    // smallNumber = largeNumber;
    smallNumber = (byte) largeNumber;
    System.out.println("smallNumber is " + smallNumber);
  }
}
```

The assignment starting with `largeNumber` assigns the `byte` variable `smallNumber` (times five) to the `int` variable. In this case, there is a datatype mismatch, but the code will compile without a problem because you are storing a smaller type (`byte`) in a larger type (`int`).

Rounding errors can occur from misuse of datatypes. The following shows an example of one of these errors:

```
int numA = 2;
int numB = 3;
System.out.println(numB/numA);
```

Although the division of these two variables results in "1.5," the print statement shows "1" because the output of the operator is the same type as the variables: `int`.

Casting Variables   In the preceding example (TestCast), the statement that is commented out will generate a compile error because it tries to store a larger-capacity datatype in a smaller-capacity datatype (even though the actual value of 50 is within the range of the `byte` datatype).

You can *cast* (explicitly convert) one type to another by preceding the name with the datatype in parentheses. The statement after the commented lines in this example corrects the typing error by casting `largeNumber` as a `byte` so that it can be stored in the `smallNumber` `byte` variable. The disadvantage of casting is that the compiler will not catch any type mismatch as it will for explicit, non-cast types. Another disadvantage is performance—the cast takes time although the more updated JDKs minimize this overhead somewhat.

Casting Objects   You can also cast objects to classes and interfaces so that you can take advantage of the methods defined for the classes and interfaces. Casting allows you to match objects of different, but related, types. For example, the Integer class is a subclass of the Number class. The following code creates an object called `numWidth` as a cast from an Integer object. The cast is required because you cannot instantiate the Number class. The code then creates an object called `width` and assigns it the value of `numWidth`. Since `numWidth` is a Number object, which is more restrictive (or narrower), this code needs to cast it to match the new object.

```
Number numWidth = (Number) new Integer(10);
Integer width = (Integer) numWidth;
```

If the example were reversed so that the Integer was created first and the Number second, casting would not be required. Consider the following example:

```
Integer width2 = new Integer(10);
Number numWidth2 = width2;
```

Casting the Integer (`width2`) into the Number (`numWidth2`) is not required because Number is less restrictive (or wider). Casting to interfaces works in the same way.

Casting Literals   Floating-point literals (such as the value 34.5) default to the `double` datatype. If you want to assign a datatype of `float` to the literal, you must add an "f" suffix (for example, 34.5f). Alternatively, you may cast the literal using an expression such as `(float) 34.5`. Some examples for assigning datatypes to literals follow. ("L" is used for a `long` datatype, and "f" is used for a `float` datatype. It does not matter whether the suffix letters are upper- or lowercase.)

```
long population = 1234567890123456789L ;
int age = 38 ;
float price = 460.95f;
float price = (float) 460.95;
double area, length = 3.15, width = 4.2 ;
area = length * width;
```

Non-floating literals (such as 3) will be assigned an `int` datatype. This can make an expression such as the following fail at compile time:

```
smallNumber = 5 + smallNumber;
```

The right side of the expression (5 + smallNumber) is assigned an `int` type, which does not match the byte type of `smallNumber`. Casting will solve the problem if you apply the cast to the entire side of the expression as follows:

```
smallNumber = (byte) (5 + smallNumber);
```

The Typesafe Concept   *Typesafe* is an important type matching concept in Java. At compile time, the compiler checks the type of a return with the method signature to ensure a match of types. Coding to a more specific (lower) level ensures that tighter matches are enforced by the compiler. For example, an object of type RowSet can be returned by a method that is declared to have a return of Object. However, that same method can return other class types and the method could lead to type problems in the calling program that the compiler will not catch. If the method were declared with a RowSet return, the compiler will ensure that the correct type is returned to the caller.

For example, the following code represents two different ways to declare an object and assign it a value from a view object attribute:

```
Number empId = (Number) newView.getAttribute("EmployeeId");
Number empId = empView.getEmployeeId();
```

The first line casts the return of `getAttribute()` from an Object (the return type for `getAttribute()`) to a Number. If `getAttribute("EmployeeId")` returned something other than a number there would be a runtime error. The compiler cannot catch errors that occur because of the contents of quoted strings (`"EmployeeId"` in this case).

The second line requires no casting because `getEmployeeId()` returns a Number. The compiler will catch any mismatches of type and so this method is an example of a typesafe method.

Chapter 11 contains some more examples of typesafe methods. The use of interfaces (as described earlier) assists in creating typesafe code that ensures correct type matching. Using and creating typesafe methods will reduce the amount of casting needed for type matching. Since there is also some overhead associated with casting, the use of typesafe methods leads to better-performing code.

Hands-on Practice: Create Java Class Files

This practice demonstrates how to create three Java class files using JDeveloper. You can use this method to test the examples in this chapter and to experiment with variations on your own. The examples shown in this practice are the sample class, parent class, and test program shown in the "Java Language Review" section of this chapter. This practice contains the following phases:

> **I. Make a workspace and project**
>
> **II. Create and test Java class files**
>
> > ■ Build the parent class file
> >
> > ■ Build the subclass file
> >
> > ■ Build the test program

I. Make a Workspace and Project

This phase builds a workspace and an empty project for the class files. You will not use the JDeveloper wizards to create the project and application. You will use the New Class dialog as a starting point for most of the objects in this practice. The right-click menus contain the common operations, and it is faster to create some objects by using those menus. This strategy is used in this practice and throughout the book. All files created in this and other practices are available for download from the authors' websites (mentioned in the author biographies at the beginning of the book).

1. On the Workspaces node, select New Workspace from the right-click menu.

2. In the New Workspaces dialog, enter the following:

   Directory Name as "JDEV_HOME\jdev\mywork\JavaTestWS"
   File Name as "JavaTestWS"
   Add a New Empty Project (checked)

   Additional Information: JDEV_HOME is the directory in which you installed JDeveloper. This creates a directory just for this workspace. It also creates a workspace file. Since you checked the *Add a New Empty Project* checkbox, the New Project dialog will appear next.

3. Click OK to create the workspace and display the New Project dialog.

4. Fill in the following fields:

   Directory Name as "JDEV_HOME\jdev\mywork\JavaTestWS\ShapesJA"
   File Name as "ShapesJA"

   Additional Information: The project will hold all classes that relate to the rectangle and box example. The "JA" suffix indicates that most of the files in this project will be Java applications (class files that run from the command line and contain a `main()` method).

5. Click OK to create the project file.

6. Click the Save All button in the toolbar.

What Just Happened? You created a workspace and project to hold the sample class files in this practice. If you want to test other files in the chapter, you can use the same workspace and project, or you can create projects in the same workspace. To create a project, select New Empty Project from the right-click menu on the Workspace node, and follow steps 4 and 5 with a new project file name and directory name.

II. Create and Test Java Class Files

This phase creates the files and allows you to test the interaction between a parent and a subclass. It is good practice to compile each file after creating it so that the final test will require less debugging.

Build the Parent Class File

The first class you need to build is the parent upon which the other files are based. This parent is the Rectangle class that contains some variables and basic methods.

   1. On the ShapesJA project node, select New Class from the right-click menu. The New Class dialog will appear as follows:

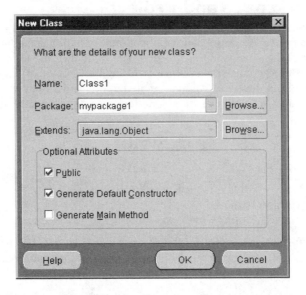

   2. Fill in the field values as follows:

      Name as "Rectangle"
      Package as "shapes"
      Public (checked)
      Generate Default Constructor (checked)
      Generate Main Method (unchecked)

      Additional Information: Adding a default constructor is standard practice even if it remains empty. You do not need a `main()` method because you will not be executing this class from the command line.

3. Click OK to create the file and open the file in the Code Editor.

4. Replace the text in the file with the following:

```
package shapes;

public class Rectangle {
   int height;
   int width;

   public Rectangle() {
     height = 1;
     width = 1;
   }

   public int getHeight() {
     return height;
   }

   public void setHeight(int newHeight) {
      height = newHeight;
   }
   public int getWidth() {
     return width;
   }

   public void setWidth(int newWidth) {
      width = newWidth;
   }
}
```

5. In the Code Editor, Select Make from the right-click menu. The file will be compiled, and messages will appear in the Log Window. If the Log Window is not open, select **View | Log Window**. If you see errors or warnings, correct the code and repeat this step until you have no errors or warnings.

Additional Information: The Log Window shows error and warning messages. The message usually includes the line number in which the error occurred. If you double click an error message, the cursor will jump to the appropriate line of code in the Code Editor.

6. Click Save All.

Additional Information: Since this file has no main() method, you cannot run it, but compiling it successfully will suffice for now.

Build the Subclass File

This section creates a file that subclasses (extends) the Rectangle class. It demonstrates how some variables and methods in a parent can be overridden and how some variables and methods can be added.

I. On the ShapesJA project node, select New Class from the right-click menu. The New Class dialog will appear.

2. Fill in the field values as follows:

Name as "Box"
Package as "shapes"
Extends (Click Browse and select Rectangle under the shapes node in the Class Browser. Then click OK to load "shapes.Rectangle" into the *Extends* field.)
Public and *Generate Default Constructor* (checked)
Generate Main Method (unchecked)

3. Click OK to create the file and open the file in the Code Editor.

Additional Information: The file contains code based upon the fields you filled out in the New Class dialog. Indicating shapes.Rectangle as the superclass (in the *Extends* field) adds the extends clause to the class declaration. Checking the *Public* checkbox adds the keyword public; and checking *Generate Default Constructor* creates a code stub for the Rectangle() constructor.

4. Replace the text in the file with the following:

```
package shapes;
public class Box extends Rectangle {
   int height;    // override the Rectangle height
   int depth;     // unique to Box

   public Box() {
     height = 4;
     width = 3;    // the width from Rectangle
     depth = 2;
   }

   public int getDepth() {
     return depth;
   }

   public void setDepth(int newDepth) {
     depth = newDepth;
   }

    // width is the same as super.width
   public int getVolume() {
     return height * width * depth;
   }
 }
```

5. In the Code Editor, select Make from the right-click menu. If you see errors or warnings in the Log Window, correct the code and repeat this step until you have no errors or warnings.

6. Click Save All.

Additional Information: You cannot run this file either, because it contains no `main()` method, but compiling it successfully will suffice for now.

Build the Test Program

This section builds a program that you can use to test the two class files. It shows how you can build and run a class file based upon other class files. This file instantiates the Box class which, in turn, calls the Rectangle constructor (because Box is a subclass of Rectangle). It also contains a `main()` method so that you can run the class from the command line.

1. Repeat steps 1 and 2 in the previous section and name the file "TestBox." Leave the package as "shapes," and uncheck *Generate Default Constructor.* Check *Generate Main Method.* Click OK.

2. Replace the text in the file with the following:

```java
package shapes;

public class TestBox  {

  public static void main(String[] args) {
    // this creates an object called usefulBox
    Box usefulBox = new Box();
    // getHeight() is the getHeight from Rectangle
    // height shows the height variable from Box
    System.out.println (
      "The height of Rectangle is " + usefulBox.getHeight() +
      " and of usefulBox is " + usefulBox.height);

    // getDepth and getVolume are from Box
    System.out.println (
      "The depth of usefulBox is " + usefulBox.getDepth() +
      " and the volume of usefulBox is " + usefulBox.getVolume());
  }
}
```

3. In the Code Editor, select Make from the right-click menu and correct errors or warnings.

4. Click Save All.

5. In the Code Editor, select Run TestBox.java from the right-click menu to run the program. You will see a ShapesJA.jpr window (tab) appear in the Log Window area.

Additional Information: This tab displays messages about the code run in the ShapesJA project, such as the command line that runs the javaw.exe runtime. You will also see messages in the ShapesJA.jpr window that are output from the TestBox.java program.

6. Study the output and verify that you understand the principles of class inheritance and instantiation as described in the "Annotated Java Code Example" and "Annotated Use of the Box Example Class" sections earlier in this chapter.

What Just Happened?   You created three class files that represented a parent class, a subclass, and a test program. The first two files contained no `main()` method. You can compile but not test this type of program without creating a `main()` method or another class file to test it. The test program you created contained a `main()` method, so you ran it within the JDeveloper Java runtime (JVM).

This demonstrates how to build simple programs that you can use to test the syntax and principles of the Java language. As mentioned, you can use this routine to test and try variations on the other examples in this chapter. The same steps work for other Java applications or other class files.

CHAPTER
5

Naming Conventions

Java, Java bo bava
Banana Fanna fo fava
Fee Fi Mo mava
Java.

— Apologies to Shirley Ellis, *The Name Game*, 1965

onsistently applied naming conventions are critical for the success of any system. Given the enormous number of elements available in the Java and JDeveloper environments, it is even more important to have a clearly defined set of conventions to follow. Unlike many previous development environments that included a relatively finite set of components to name, the Java environment includes almost limitless possibilities. All of these possibilities are advantageous for development, but pose special challenges for developing consistent naming standards. Using previously developed Java elements from different sources yields a hodgepodge of naming standards because the standards of those sources may be quite diverse. In addition, even elements from the same manufacturer may not be named consistently.

This chapter provides some insights into what standards have been used by others as well as some recommendations for structuring your own naming conventions. This chapter also discusses how to create naming standards for the elements you will use when developing applications with Oracle JDeveloper. This chapter suggests the types of names you need to consider and provides examples to help in developing your own standards.

The Importance of Using Naming Conventions

Creating naming conventions for your Java applications has several benefits. First, when you review your own or other people's code, you can quickly grasp the meaning of a particular element simply by seeing its name. Also, by knowing how elements are named, you can locate specific elements more efficiently, making your applications easier to maintain. Another benefit of using a naming convention is that it frees you from having to re-create ways to name elements. By having a naming framework, you will not have to stop and think about how to name each new element.

Consistently named elements applied throughout an organization also make it easier for developers to work on each other's code.

Though elements imported from other sources may not adhere to these conventions, enforcing a naming standard makes it easier to identify those elements that are imported from outside sources and better organizes those created internally.

The goals you strive for should follow the four Cs adapted from *Oracle Developer Advanced Forms & Reports,* Koletzke and Dorsey (Oracle Press, 2000), and be:

- **Consistent**   The way in which you name elements should remain the same within an application and throughout all of your applications. You should create complete naming standards for everything at the same time. You should not create database-naming standards and then later create development standards since these two standards categories interact. The standards must be set for the entire development environment and lifecycle.

- **Concise**   The names that you give elements should be short, but not so short that their meaning is not quickly understood. Short names make repeated typing easier and less prone to errors. Also, short names ease the burden on others who may need to read your code. If you use concise and consistent names, you will be able to scan through your code quickly, find the necessary elements, and determine their basic functions.

JDeveloper allows you to select classes, methods, and parameters from lists that pop up automatically (or by using a keypress such as CTRL-SPACEBAR to display a list of available variables and methods for the class). You can save the typing necessary for long names using these features. However, it is usually faster to type a shorter name than to browse or select from a list. If you use shorter names, you can still use the automatic completion features.

- **Complete**   If you use naming conventions at all, you should use them for every element type that needs a name. This means that you need to adopt or develop a naming standard before any coding begins. If you leave out a particular element from your standard, when it comes to your attention, you should develop a standard for that element before including it in your development effort.

- **Clear**   Select meaningful names for your variables to aid in the "self-documentation" of your programs. For example, when naming Boolean methods, use a name beginning with "is," such as "isOpen."

Naming conventions are an important part of an overall standards effort and, as such, should be included in your standards strategy. As with other components of your standards strategy, you have to consider how to document your naming conventions, train developers how and why to use them, and use code reviews to enforce the naming conventions that you develop.

Ultimately, consistent naming conventions in a Java environment are even more important than they were in traditional development environments such as Oracle Developer. Not only is there a wider variety of elements from which to choose, but behind the scenes, you are working in a straight 3GL environment. This means that, at some point, you will be opening up large blocks of code to edit. All of your program elements may not be neatly organized into an object navigator. They might be organized into a structure navigator like the UI components in the Structure window. If you do not use precise naming conventions, you may end up spending time unnecessarily searching for a particular element.

There are some naming conventions imposed by the Java language such as lower case keywords and constructor method names. Since these are not optional, this chapter does not mention them. Any naming standards document you create will probably not contain these.

You want to be able to scan through the code and quickly identify the type of element you are looking for. By using distinctive naming conventions with consistent prefixes or suffixes for the elements, you can quickly and easily search all of the elements of a particular type by using an automated search routine.

Types of Objects to Name

The elements being named fall into several categories that are different from those used to working with Form Builder. In Form Builder, every element created is physically stored in a single .fmb file. These elements are then only visible through the Form Builder Object Navigator in the appropriate place in the product. For example, LOVs appear under the LOV node and blocks appear under the block node. Using indicators within LOV or block names to identify the object type is usually redundant. This is not the case in JDeveloper.

Some of the objects you name within JDeveloper (such as packages) will be physically implemented as directory names in your operating system file structure. Other objects such as class names will appear as file names within those file directories. Swing components and other objects of that type will appear in the Structure window only and are also Java language elements.

Finally, within the Java routines themselves, you may be creating Java elements that only exist within your code. Some objects such as connections will appear in the System Navigator, but are not visible or editable in any other context.

BC4J objects (such as entity objects and view objects) are similarly only visible and editable through the System Navigator. Therefore, in setting naming conventions, you need some understanding of how objects are physically implemented since you may want to identify the type of object clearly in whatever context it can be viewed.

In products such as Form Builder, using suffixes to clearly identify the type of item as a record group or block is usually unnecessary because the contexts in which the object appeared or is used are quite limited. As the previous discussion indicated, in JDeveloper objects may exist as directory names, file names, code object names, and so on, and having some sort of linguistic cue to indicate the object type can make it easier for developers to work with the code.

Since you are probably working in an Oracle environment, case sensitivity may be new to you. This leads to some complications. Unlike Java, the Oracle database languages such as SQL and PL/SQL are not case sensitive. The normal standard for naming objects in Oracle is to use all capitalized words with underscore separators such as the table "LOC_DEPT." In Java, the naming convention would use initial capital, mixed-case format to name this object "LocDept." BC4J's wizards try to encourage this shift. They rename Oracle tables and columns by removing underscores and changing the names to initial caps, mixed-case words.

As long as you understand the algorithm behind the BC4J wizards, understanding the naming conventions will be less confusing. It is important to keep in mind that the name of a table or column in the database may not be exactly the same as its associated BC4J entity or view object. This may actually cause difficulties in some applications since you cannot count on being able to directly map Oracle object names to BC4J names.

If you rarely use underscores in your column names, you may not even be aware that BC4J strips them out. It may be tempting to write code using the BC4J attribute name as the column name, erroneously assuming that they are always identical (with the exception of case). Your code would always work, except when the database column name contained an underscore which was removed by the BC4J layer.

The Consistency Issue

As you develop Java applications, you will use elements from libraries that someone else created. You will also allow the JDeveloper code generators to write code. Both of these sources use some type of naming convention. For consistency, it would make sense when you are writing your own code to use naming conventions that are similar to those employed by these sources. The good news is that there is some consistency regarding the general structure of a name. For example, a fully qualified name such as `java.lang.String.trim()` is consistent among all Java vendors. (This structure is discussed further in the section "Packages" later in this chapter.)

While most vendors try to be concise and clear when naming code elements of the fully qualified name, there is inconsistency among them as to how to name those elements. You will find naming inconsistencies in how code is generated, even within JDeveloper. In addition, there is inconsistency regarding how concise the names will be. For example, you will encounter the use of acronyms, full names, and abbreviations for conciseness. Some names are only marginally understandable.

Generally you can identify the library author by looking at the way its components are named. The following are some examples of how various companies name their code groupings:

■ **Sun Microsystems** java.io, java.lang, java.math, java.net, java.text, java.util, java.applet, java.awt, java.beans, java.rmi, java.security, javax.accessibility, javax.swing, javax.crypto, javax.servlet, javax.infobus, javax.ejb, org.omg.CORBA

■ **Oracle** oracle.jbo, oracle.dacf, oracle.jdeveloper, oracle.sqlj, oracle.jdbc

■ **Borland** borland.jbcl, borland.sql, borland.javaport, borland.jbuilder

By looking at the groups of names each company uses, note that most use more or less the same convention. Sun Microsystems owns the core Java classes, and they simply use the names "java" or "javax" to identify their code. The code they implement outside of the core language is named according the standards they preach; for example, sun.rmi.*.

Other companies do not necessarily adhere to this standard. Even within the Sun Microsystems names, some of the libraries start with "java" and some start with "javax." CORBA appears in upper case with an "org" prefix. Specialized libraries from smaller providers may use other naming conventions.

When you are creating your own naming conventions, you need to examine the names that are used for existing code and to apply general rules that you create to come up with a fully defined naming convention of your own. It is useful to start your naming conventions with the ones that are generally recognized by Java programmers. This should be familiar territory if you have studied the Java language.

General Naming Convention Considerations and Guidelines

The task of defining and implementing a standard of your own can be formidable. It is easy to espouse the principle of using a naming standard, but attempting to encompass all of the possibilities can be very difficult if you try to create a list of naming methods for each element used in your development effort. Many developers attempting their first Java project have expressed their frustration when trying to apply what they have done in the past to the Java environment. Numerous projects have fallen behind schedule and exceeded their budgets with little to show in terms of completed work. Of course, it is unlikely that projects have failed because of a lack of good naming standards; but in the Java environment, there are many different types of elements and maintaining consistency helps code to be more readable. In the Java environment, it is clear that you must be ready to change the way you think and work, or you may find yourself buried in so many details that you cease to make any headway with your overall project.

It is a good idea to learn and use the current conventions for the major items as just discussed. To complete your naming convention, you need to add some general guidelines and specific rules to the conventions for naming all elements.

It is best to use a predefined, structured approach for your standard. By defining a simple naming structure that fits most situations, you will be free to add new components to your design without having to stop and think about how to name them.

Standards that you create could use the following statements.

Use Suffixes to Imply Type

Some elements are more clearly named if they contain the class or type that they belong to. For example, a panel that you create in the JDeveloper design area to hold information about the master table of a master-detail form would be called "masterPanel." The suffix indicates the type. This makes the code easier to read because you can distinguish the category that the component fits into by looking at the suffix. Without the type, you might have both a master panel and a master navigation bar that use the word "master," but do not imply the element type. A reader might be confused if the name has no suffix.

Using a suffix instead of a prefix is an arbitrary decision, but it follows the naming convention that JDeveloper most commonly uses when its wizards generate code. If you are using a combination of wizard code and self-named code, there may be a disparity of suffixes and prefixes in your application. However, the reader will be able to rely on the fact that your code always uses suffixes.

CAUTION
Naming elements with a suffix that denotes the component type, such as deptnoTextField, has a potential danger. If you decide to change the item type after you have written code based on the component name, you will either need to rename the item and update all of its references, or leave the item with a wrong and potentially confusing name. JDeveloper may not make all of the code changes automatically if you change the name in the UI Editor.

There are several different issues to be considered when developing a set of naming conventions within an organization. It is useful to discuss the main categories of names and apply these general guidelines to describe how you might assign specific naming conventions to these categories.

Consider the Capabilities of the Language

When you are making decisions about what standards to create for naming JDeveloper elements, you will need to consider the capabilities of the language. For example, Java *identifiers* (names) are limited to strings that include characters, numbers, underscores (_), and dollar signs ($). These identifiers can be any length but cannot begin with a number or contain any white spaces.

Be Aware of Case Sensitivity

As previously mentioned, even though Java is case sensitive, keep in mind that the Oracle database is not. "EMP," "Emp," and "emp" are the same in the Oracle database but different in Java. When dealing with Java objects that will be mapped into PL/SQL elements because of function calls to database tables or columns, remember that the Oracle database is case insensitive. However, Oracle string comparisons are case sensitive. If you query any system tables in Oracle, the names of the Oracle elements will always be returned in uppercase. For those developers experienced in the Oracle environment, this will be routine. Java developers should take special care with any elements that will be translated into Oracle elements.

In addition to establishing how things will be named, you also need to decide how they will be capitalized, because of Java's case sensitivity.

Use a Dictionary of Allowable Words

One of the most important issues to ensure consistency of names is to start from a dictionary of allowable words. Therefore, you need to determine how this dictionary will be constructed, either using whole words or abbreviations. Code becomes much less readable if employees are referred to as "Employee," "EMPL," "EMP," or any other variations throughout a system rather than using the same term in all contexts.

Use Abbreviations Carefully

Because of the length limitation of Oracle objects (32 characters), it is frequently impractical to use full words for Oracle objects, so some type of abbreviation mechanism is necessary. A useful abbreviation standard is to select a fixed number of characters (usually five or six) as an abbreviation limit. Whenever possible when abbreviating, use the same number of characters, making exceptions only for industry standards such as "DEPT" for Department.

As an alternative, you can choose to use a more abbreviated set of words for Oracle objects and to spell out words for non-Oracle objects. It is not uncommon for applications to maintain dual names for objects. One shorter name can be used in contexts where the name length is restricted and a more readable verbose name is used where length is unrestricted. Although verbose names for code elements may make each element more readable, they may actually make it more difficult to read the entire code. Use a naming convention that allows you to stay within the Oracle length limitations for all objects.

In order to enforce naming standards, all words and abbreviations that can be used in your code elements should be maintained in a list. Developers can use this list to make sure that only accepted words are used for object names. It is possible to write a program to check the code against the list and validate that only acceptable words are used in the code.

You must be somewhat careful about the abbreviations you select. Otherwise you may end up with undecipherable elements in your system. Under no circumstances should you adopt a naming standard with fewer than five characters since it is too hard to figure out what some of these represent. One of the authors worked on a system where three- to four-character abbreviations had been used. By the time they got to the months of the year, "APR" and "DEC" had already been used for "Annual Percent Rate" and "Declined."

The following discussion of naming elements is divided into two parts: elements in the Java code and elements specific to JDeveloper. This separation is made for several reasons. First, a number of the objects discussed in the second section are unique to JDeveloper, and even experienced Java developers will be unfamiliar with these objects. Second, Java developers may already have their own consistent naming conventions for Java code.

Recognized Naming Conventions in Java

Most Java professionals follow established conventions for naming basic Java elements. By following similar patterns in your own code, you will be able to produce a final product that is not only functional but also integrates well with established conventions.

The following sections examine basic Java code elements and explain the generally recognized naming conventions for those elements. These conventions usually define case usage (uppercase or lowercase). There are a number of categories of elements, each of which has a recognized naming convention.

Constants (Final Variables)

Constants are identified by all uppercase letters. When the name of the constant contains more than one word, the words are separated using the underscore character (_), for example, MAX_LOAD and MIN_SIZE. It is important to follow this standard when you define your own constants.

Classes

Classes use an initial capital letter for each word in the class name, for example, JavaFirstClass, EmployeeHistory, and CustomerOrder. Note that there are no spaces between the words making up the class names.

Class Instances, Exceptions, Methods, and Variables

These elements all use mixed case and always start with the first letter in lowercase and the remaining words using an initial capital letter. There are no white spaces or underscores between words, for example, javaFirstObject, printHistory(), and customerName.

NOTE
You should avoid starting names with an underscore because this is often used for internal operations. This applies to classes, class instances, exceptions, methods, and variables.

A common practice among Java programmers is to use short, meaningless variable names such as "x" or "y." This is not useful and violates the goal of clarity in naming elements. Meaningful names such as "price" or "totalPrice" can make the usage clear. An exception to this rule might be loop counter variables. A common practice in most languages is to use "i" as the name of an integer counter in a loop, for example, for "(int i=0; i < 10; i++)". If there is a nested loop, you would use "j" as the counter for the inner loop. Although these variable names are uninformative, they are generally recognized in the programming community, and your standard could document them. Using descriptive counter names is a good idea. For example, if you are looping through all employee records, the loop counter could be named "countEmp."

Some methods are named to comply with standards in the language. For example, if you had a class called Address that contained methods for assigning a city name and retrieving a city name from an object instantiation, you would name the methods getCity() and setCity(), respectively. These implement a standard feature of the language—getters and setters that the language knows how to handle. The names of these methods use the "get" and "set" verbs combined with the property name (city) with an initial capital letter.

Packages

Physically a package is a file folder or directory in the operating system. Programmatically, a "package" refers to a folder of grouped classes and related files that end up in deployed code. In JDeveloper, compiled class files (.class) are stored in folders referred to as "packages" in the default "classes" folder within each project.

Generally, packages are named using all lowercase letters, but you will find many exceptions to this convention because the package naming standards have continued to change as the popularity of Java has grown. Follow the all-lowercase standard when you create code. There is also a recognized standard of how a fully qualified name is constructed. A *fully qualified name* contains the names of all elements that specifically locate it. For example, `java.lang.String.trim` points to the method `trim()` that is part of the class `String`. The class is contained in a package `java.lang`. The name also indicates (because of the word "java") that the vendor for this library is Sun Microsystems.

This type of fully qualified name is logical and universally recognized. Since the Java naming standards just described are well established, the remaining topic of discussion is how you name the components you create in JDeveloper that make up the fully qualified name (for example, the actual object or method). A sensible strategy is to start with some general guidelines and to add specific rules for each type of element that needs to be named.

JDeveloper-Specific Naming Conventions

JDeveloper uses a multiple-directory structure on your hard drive to store Java-related code. Separate structures exist for source code, compiled code, documentation, and HTML files. To keep all of these files in sync, JDeveloper creates several overhead files as well. Since many of these files are automatically named for you, it is necessary to understand their naming conventions so that you can quickly locate, view, and/or edit them as necessary. As you become more proficient in using JDeveloper, you will be creating and naming many of these files on your own. A quick review of the structure is useful at this point. The directories mentioned here are described further in Chapter 1.

The basic JDeveloper directory structure is as follows (where JDEV_HOME is the directory in which you installed JDeveloper):

```
JDEV_HOME\jdev\mywork\workspace\project\src\package\*.java
```

When compiled, these files are compiled into .class files in the following directory structure:

```
JDEV_HOME\jdev\mywork\workspace\project\classes\package\*.class
```

The source and overhead files use different file extensions to distinguish them, as shown in Table 5-1.

JDeveloper will present a default name (such as Workspace1.jws) when you first create a file. Be sure to change this to a descriptive name in this dialog or when you save the file. JDeveloper will fill in the file extension automatically in most cases. This feature saves you from having to type in the name and worry about the exact extension. Using the default extensions allows you to use the file filters in the save and open dialogs to help locate a file. The descriptions and suggested standards for each file type follow.

File Type	Extension
Workspace	.jws
Project	.jpr
Class source	.java
Libraries	.jar or .zip
Business components	.xml and .java
HTML and XML files	.html and .xml, respectively
Connections and other properties	connections.xml, .properties, etc.

TABLE 5-1. *Developer File Extensions*

NOTE
JDeveloper usually fills in the file extensions for you so you do not need to type an extension such as "jpr" for a project file. If a file extension is required, JDeveloper will warn you before you click the OK or Save button in the dialog.

Workspaces

A workspace in JDeveloper is a file containing a list of projects. It is good practice to have a separate folder to hold the .jws files. A workspace should be stored in its own directory. Therefore, when naming a workspace, you are also naming the directory. For the hands-on practices in this book, the authors have used the following convention for naming workspaces: Initial capital letter, mixed-case words, and a WS suffix. For example, a master-detail DeptEmp workspace directory would be named DeptEmpWS, and the workspace file name would also be named DeptEmpWS. The WS suffix is useful to clearly indicate that the item is a workspace and is helpful when looking at a long list of directories in the file system.

NOTE
When typing workspace and project names in the JDeveloper wizards, the appropriate file extensions are added automatically. (For example, ".jws" is added to all workspace files.)

It could be argued that the WS suffix is superfluous for naming workspaces; however, it is useful for the file name. To minimize errors and inconsistencies, the WS suffix is used on both the file and directory names.

Projects

Project files (.jpr) contain lists of files and some properties. As with workspaces, it is good practice to leave all files in a project within the same folder.

There are several types of projects such as applets, BC4J, Java applications, and JavaServer Pages (JSP). Each is named using the same multi-word, initial capital letter as used in workspaces. The suffix is dependent upon the type of project as follows:

- BC4J suffix is for BC4J projects. With BC4J projects, an additional *.jpx file is also created.

- JA suffix is for a Java application project

- AP suffix is for applet projects.

- JSP suffix is for JSP projects.

- CODE suffix is for Java projects with no UI components (projects holding raw calculation Java classes)

Class Source Files

JDeveloper's wizards create class files for you. If you need to create your own class file, the file name must have the same name and case assignment as the class name. It is a well-established Java standard to use an initial capital letter, mixed case. For example, the Employee History class file would be named EmployeeHistory.java.

Libraries

Publicly distributed libraries are typically zipped (compressed) collections of classes that are stored in files with the extension .jar or .zip. As mentioned, libraries from different vendors do not necessarily have consistent naming conventions.

Aliasing Library Names

In JDeveloper, you can give each library a name that is more readable than the individual files that comprise it. The library list for a project is available in the **Project | Project Settings** dialog; navigate to the Configurations/Development/Libraries page. Since the library file names must follow the naming conventions of your operating system (such as upper and lower case use), you will find that the alias provides a user-friendly way to identify your library.

The alias may also refer to a group of library files, allowing you to store a single logical library in multiple physical files. For example, the Business Components runtime library for JDeveloper has the alias BC4J Runtime. This library alias includes the following physical files: bc4jmt.jar, bc4jct.jar, collections.jar, xmlparserv1.jar, and jndi.jar. Name library files with lowercase names, using an acronym or abbreviation with the same pattern. The abbreviation or acronym must be documented if it is specific to your application or enterprise. Library file names need no suffix because they are distinguished in the context of their usage.

If you work in an area with wide Internet visibility, you should adhere to the practice used by vendors of naming the libraries so that readers can tell the exact source of the code. To avoid conflicts with packages created by other developers, the current convention is to use your reversed Internet domain name as the package root in the library. For example, if you wanted to store the `doJob()` method, from class `MyBusTask`, in the `businessutil` package, use the following naming structure in your library: `com.company.businessutil.BusTask.doJob()`, where "com.company" is a reversed domain name such as "com.mcgrawhill."

If your code has more limited visibility, as in an intranet system, you should keep the names as short as possible to make the typing easier and faster. By convention, library names use all lowercase.

JClient Data Models

JClient Data Models are an internal JDeveloper object referred to by various JDeveloper elements. An initial capital letter, mixed case, and suffix Model are used in the hands-on practices in this book. For example, the Location/Department application data model is called "LocDeptModel."

Connections

For connection names, no suffix is needed. In this book, the authors have used a mixed-case descriptive name for the application or user like "Scott" or "HR."

There are a number of different types of connections such as: Application Server, Database, SOAP Server, and UDDI Registry. In some environments, you will only be using database connections, in which case a suffix or prefix is irrelevant. If you are working in a more complex environment, a suitable suffix indicating the type of connection, such as APPSER, DB, or SOAP, could be used.

Business Components for Java

The JDeveloper BC4J wizards create and automatically name the .xml and .java files for business components. There are several elements within BC4J that require setting naming conventions if you are creating business components outside of the wizards. The following discussion uses the same kind of naming conventions as the wizards use so that your code will be consistent with the wizard-generated code. Part II of this book provides examples of names for other BC4J objects.

Entity Objects

Entity objects in BC4J correspond more or less directly to database tables and views. The same name as the database table is used with the exception of case. Initial capital letters are used, and all underscores are removed. For example, the CUST_HIST table would be CustHist in BC4J.

Entity Attributes

The same naming convention applies to entity attributes as applies to entities. Use an initial capital letter and no underscores. For example, "EMP_NAME" becomes "EmpName."

Entity Associations

The generated name for an association is a concatenation of the foreign key constraint name and "Assoc." Entity associations represent foreign key referential integrity constraints at the BC4J level. These should be named in the same way as foreign key constraints, that is, using the master entity/detail entity/Fk with an "Assoc" suffix (if that is your foreign key naming convention). You may have to shorten the entity names to keep the association name from getting too long. For example, the master-detail association between Location and Department would be LocDeptFKAssoc if the foreign key constraint were called LOC_DEPT_FK

Domains

Domains are user-defined. Replace the default name "Domain" to reflect its intended usage. Use initial uppercase and a suffix of Domain, for example, MaxSalaryDomain. The Domain will have two files associated with it—an .xml file for data definition and a .java file for the object-specific behavior. These associated files are named automatically with the name of the domain, for example, MaxSalaryDomain.xml and MaxSalaryDomain.java.

Application Modules

The generated name for an application module is a concatenation of the package name and the word "Module" in mixed case, for example, empappletModule. As with other BC4J objects, there is an .xml and a .java file that have the same base name with appropriate file extensions.

View Objects

The BC4J generator convention is used to name view objects. View objects should be named like the entity object with the suffix "View."

View Attributes

View attributes should be named the same as their associated entity attributes. If the column you are retrieving is not in a base table that is represented by an entity, you need to construct a name. The value could be derived from a function or subquery embedded in the SELECT list. For example, you may have a business component that includes a query such as the following:

```
SELECT empno,
       ename,
         (SELECT dname
          FROM   dept
          WHERE  dept.deptno = emp.deptno)
       as  dsp_dept_name
FROM   emp
```

The "Dsp" prefix denotes that this is a display-only column. The view attribute name for this column would be DspDeptName.

View Links
View links should be named the same as their corresponding entity associations with a "Link" suffix instead of "Assoc."

UI Components
Java has hundreds of prebuilt classes available for your use. When the code generators (wizards) in JDeveloper add UI components to your project, they will include a default name that you will override. The default name is usually a number added to the component name, for example, jPanel1. After adding several components of the same type, you will find it nearly impossible to distinguish them unless you rename them.

In general, it is good practice to use a suffix to define the type or class of object. This is particularly important for UI components. For example, if you were to add a component from the Swing library javax.swing.JButton as an "Exit" button, it would be named exitButton.

Java Application Files
Part of the naming convention document you create should list the names used to distinguish various files for a Java application. Some examples include the following:

- **Frame**   DeptEmpFrame.java
- **Panel**   DeptPanel.java
- **Master-detail panel**   DeptEmpPanel.java

UML Diagram Elements
No special naming convention is needed for elements appearing on UML class diagrams. You are actually creating and naming already existing elements such as BC4J entity objects, Java classes, or packages. For example, when you create a diagram element that is a Java class, you are actually creating a Java class file and not just the diagram element.

The only remaining naming standard is for the diagrams themselves. You can use descriptive initial-capped names similar to the ones used for a class with an added "CUML" for a UML class diagram or "AUML" for a UML activity diagram. For example, the class diagram for the Human Resources System might be called "HRCUML" or "HumanResourceCUML. An activity diagram modeling the process of hiring an employee might be called HireEmpAUML."

Other Components
Depending upon your project, there are many other different types of components that may be used to create applications using JDeveloper. For example, none of the new features such as naming EJBs have been discussed in this chapter. You can use the suggested naming conventions and strategies in this chapter as a starting point and extend them to suit your project's requirements.

CHAPTER
6

Debugging the Code

Debugging is anticipated with distaste,
performed with reluctance,
and bragged about forever.

—Anonymous

he concept of software testing is broader than just debugging your programs. You need to think critically about testing long before you get to the point of developing and implementing your applications. This type of awareness and planning will go a long way toward ensuring that your applications can be brought quickly to production quality.

Finding design and coding defects early in the development lifecycle can result in huge benefits. Perhaps you will only need to spend hours correcting code errors that are discovered early in the process, rather than the days to weeks otherwise required to retrofit code errors discovered after a product is deployed or shipped to a customer.

In other words, testing, quality assurance, and other configuration-management methods should pervade your system development process from start to finish. These measures will help you to ensure that the highest quality software product is delivered using Oracle9*i* JDeveloper.

It is not the intent of this chapter to discuss the topic of software quality in general. Rather, this chapter discusses some of the techniques that can be easily used within JDeveloper to help you unit-test Java code as it is being written. The chapter explains how the major features of JDeveloper's native debugger handle the debugging process and the essential debugging activities—program control and value checking. It also provides an overview of the Profiler that you can use to understand low-level details about the code as it is executing. The chapter concludes with a hands-on practice that applies these concepts to correcting a simple logic error.

Most of the techniques in this chapter apply equally to debugging a Java application, applet, EJB, servlet, or JSP application that is running in the client machine's Java Virtual Machine (JVM). When you deploy and run JSP, servlet, or EJB code, you may need to perform additional debugging on the server. Although this chapter does not explain remote debugging in detail, the section called "Remote Debugging" explains where to find more information on the subject of debugging code on the server.

Overview

Debugging is the process of locating and fixing errors in software programs. Most developers would readily agree that debugging source code, regardless of the language, is tedious and time-consuming. The objective of debugging is to find and fix the problem as quickly and easily as possible. A number of ways exist to debug a program, many of which do not involve a dedicated debugging tool. However, Java includes a full-featured debugger that helps you to find problems in the code. JDeveloper provides a graphical interface for this debugger and adds many features to assist in the debugging process.

Before explaining how debugging works in a JDeveloper environment, it is useful to review the types of program errors and the activities required in the debugging process to understand where the errors occur. This discussion will provide a context for the description of debugging in JDeveloper.

Types of Program Errors

There are four general types of program errors that you will run into:

- **Syntax errors**   These are the result of incorrectly formed statements. They are easily detected by the JDeveloper compiler, which displays errors in the Log window. You can just double click an error in this window, and the Code Editor will highlight the problem line of code.

- **Data condition errors**   These are a result of inputting or passing a value to the program that causes the program to abort, such as a divide-by-zero error. The error is reported by the Java runtime system (JVM). Data condition errors are more difficult and challenging than syntax errors because testing may miss the data value that causes the error. Developer experience and better program design can eliminate these errors. The watch feature of the debugger assists in fixing this type of bug.

- **Logic errors**   This type of error also shows up only at runtime. A logic error is a result of poor design or of coding mistakes and often manifests itself if the program does something that it is not intended to do. This type of error is the most difficult to catch because it may not occur consistently or early in the development process. In fact, these errors can occur for the first time long after a program is released for production use. The best guard against logic errors is a thorough test plan and testing cycle. Once you experience this type of error, the debugger will help you locate the problem by allowing you to step through the code and to set conditional breakpoints.

- **Resource errors**   This type of error occurs due to lack of a required resource such as network availability, server availability, memory, disk space, or other "physical" (nonprogrammatic) resource. In Oracle9i JDeveloper, you can use the Profiler (described later) to assist in solving resource error problems.

Correcting Syntax Errors

Of course, little advice for fixing a syntax error is necessary. Developers normally read the error text carefully and closely examine the code based on that text.

If an error indicates that a method that you call does not exist, check the spelling and use of upper- and lowercase because the Java language is case sensitive. If the spelling is correct, you should check to see that you are passing the correct argument types. The Javadoc for a method will indicate which arguments are expected and allowed. If the spelling and arguments are correct, you may be missing an import statement. You also need to be sure that the appropriate package is accessible by including it as a library in the Project Settings dialog (**Project | Project Settings** or select Project Settings from the right-click menu on a project node).

Other common errors that are easy to check for include the following:

- Mismatched curly brackets or parentheses

- Misuse of upper- and lowercase

- Argument datatype problems

■ Unmatched or incorrect single or double quotation marks

■ Missing semicolons at the end of an executable line

Some of these errors are visible in the Code Editor. For example, when you place the cursor next to a paired symbol such as a curly bracket or parenthesis, the editor highlights (in a color such as light blue) the nearest match as follows:

```
if (storeIndex != i) {
  numList[storeIndex] = numList[i];
  numList[i] = storeMax;
}
```

If you do not see the match that you were expecting, you can fix the mistake. The Code Editor also indicates a missing paired symbol using a red highlight in the same way as shown here for a missing close parenthesis:

```
catch(Exception ex)
{
    ex.printStackTrace();
}
```

The Log window compiler messages will be of some help in identifying these errors as shown here for a missing semicolon:

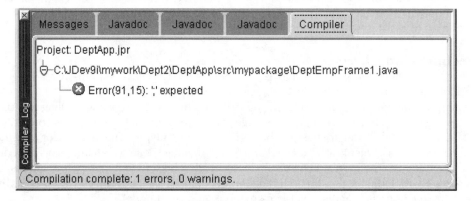

Double clicking the error in the Log window highlights the line of code in the Code Editor. In addition, as you are typing in the Code Editor, you will see syntax errors such as missing semicolons in the Structure window as follows:

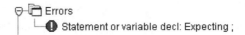

Double clicking the message in the Structure window will move the cursor to the problem line of code. If you have many missing semicolons or other punctuation, you may have to look above the problem line to see if the problem occurs earlier in the code. All of these Code Editor features allow you to check the syntax before incurring the overhead of compilation.

Other than mistakes due to a misunderstanding or misuse of the Java language, the errors mentioned will probably comprise 80 percent of the syntax errors that you experience. Since syntax errors must be corrected before you run the program, and since the debugger only works at runtime, this chapter will not discuss them further.

Correcting Data Condition and Logic Errors

The JDeveloper debugger assists in resolving runtime data condition and logic errors. This chapter focuses mainly on the debugging process that you can apply to these types of errors. One of the most pernicious errors for novice Java developers to watch out for results from the automatic casting of numeric datatypes. Be especially careful of strange rounding errors involving integer datatypes.

Another logic error is casting objects incorrectly. If an object is typed at a high level in the class hierarchy (for example, as an Object), it can be recast as anything under that level. Errors can occur when that object is cast to a type that does not match its use (for example, as a return value for a method). Using *typesafe methods*, which are checked for type upon compilation and avoid runtime type mismatch errors, and interfaces greatly reduces type mismatching problems. (Casting and interfaces are discussed further in Chapter 4.)

The best defense against logic errors is well-constructed, object-oriented code.

CAUTION
The compiler will not catch some logic errors that are a misuse of operators. For example, the expression "if (isValid = false)" will assign the value "false" to the boolean variable isValid instead of testing the value of isValid (as with "if (isValid == false)").

Correcting Resource Errors

Resource errors may be intermittent, and these are difficult problems to fix. If you can consistently reproduce the problem, the JDeveloper Profiler will help you to determine the point at which a program is failing. If you determine that there are no logic or data condition errors, you can then turn to external resources. Follow the process of elimination by substituting hardware or network resources and testing the problem. This should lead you to a solution. Sometimes such errors result from a recursive routine that is not terminating.

NOTE
The JDeveloper CodeCoach feature, described in Chapter 2, does not specifically address identifying and fixing bugs. However, CodeCoach does assist in writing more efficient code, which potentially uses fewer resources. Use of this tool could prevent resource errors from occurring.

Debugging Activities

The debugging process normally combines two interrelated activities: running and stepping through the code, and examining the values of variables, parameters, data, and array items. The process follows the steps and activities diagrammed in Figure 6-1. You normally test an application first in normal runtime mode to see if there are errors. If you find errors, you run the debugger and set up breakpoints to stop execution of the code. At those points you can stop the program execution and examine data values. When you are finished with those tasks, you exit the debugger.

Help with the Debugger

The JDeveloper help system topics that apply to debugging fall under the "Testing and Optimizing Application Code\Debugging in JDeveloper" node in the Contents page. Drill down through this node in the Contents page for applicable topics.

Do You Really Have to Run the Debugger?

The JDeveloper debugger is a powerful tool for finding and repairing defects in code that you create. As with many powerful features, there is a bit of complexity. You may not need to use the debugger for a problem that seems to be relatively simple. Instead, simple troubleshooting

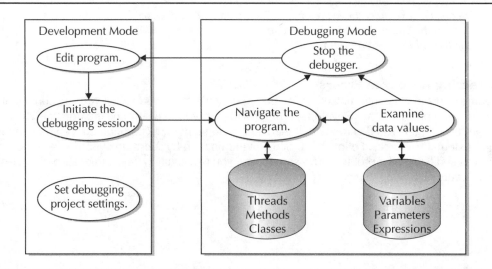

FIGURE 6-1. *A typical debugging session*

techniques may lead you to a solution without having to run the debugger. This section describes some of those techniques. They are your first line of defense in the battle against bugs. Several of the techniques address database connectivity because it is outside of normal Java work. Once you are certain that the database connection and BC4J interactions work, you can concentrate on debugging the application code.

Apply General Troubleshooting Techniques

The earlier section "Types of Program Errors" discusses common errors you would look for first. After looking for those errors, you can use the following techniques to troubleshoot the application:

- The first thing to do is to ensure that all projects have a current build. Click on each project node one at a time and click the Rebuild icon. Alternatively, you can select Rebuild Workspace from the right-click menu on a workspace node to build all projects in that workspace.

- Examine the Log window for compilation errors. The message text should indicate the line in which the error occurred. Double click the error message to navigate to the problem code. This should help you identify and fix code syntax problems.

- The curly bracket and parenthesis sets are highlighted, as mentioned in Chapter 2. If you place the cursor by one of a pair of symbols (such as the curly bracket), that symbol and its match will be highlighted. This allows you to check for properly formed code blocks and argument lists.

- For Java client programs (Java applications and applets), you can also double check that all properties and objects have been correctly defined by comparing the code with the properties and objects.

- For Java client applications, check that you have properly defined the hierarchy of objects by examining the Structure window nodes when the UI Editor is open. If something is out of place, you can select Cut from the right-click menu on that object. Then select the node that the object should appear under and select Paste from the right-click menu to position the object under that node.

Test and Edit the Connection

There are some tests that become part of the normal development process. For example, when you define a connection, you can test it to ensure that it accesses the database correctly. If you need to test it after the initial definition, use the following steps:

1. Select Edit from the right-click menu on a specific connections node (such as HR) in the Navigator window Connections node.

2. Select the Test tab and click the Test Connection button. A message will appear in the *Status* field to indicate the results of the test.

If there are errors, check and adjust the settings on the other pages of this dialog and retest the connection using the Test button. You may need to consult a database administrator to verify the proper host, port, and database (SID) name.

Test and Edit the BC4J View Object

Once you have defined view objects (as described in Part II of this book), you can test the query that each one represents using the following steps:

1. On the view object node under the package node in the BC4J project, select Edit <view object> from the right-click menu. The View Object dialog will open.

2. Click the Query tab and click the Test button. A message will appear at the top of the page indicating the state of the query.

If there are errors, modify the properties on the other pages so that the query is valid. You can click the Expert Node button to edit the query text if you need to test variations on the automatically generated query text. You need to repeat this test for each view object that does not work.

Test the BC4J Application Module

After defining a BC4J project, you can test its code using the Oracle Business Component Browser. Use the following steps:

1. Open the BC4J project node in the Navigation window and find the node that represents the application module. The application module is usually named with a suffix of "Module." For example, "DeptEmpModule."

2. On the application module node, select Test from the right-click menu. The Connect dialog will open. Verify the settings and click Connect. If another login dialog appears, enter the password and click OK. (If there is only one application module in the package, you can click the Run icon in the IDE toolbar to test the application module. This method bypasses the Connect dialog.)

3. The Oracle Business Component Browser window will appear. This window contains a navigator of view objects and a viewer. For testing purposes, you just need to double click a node for one of the view objects or select Show from the right-click menu on that node.

The view area will display an application that you can use to test the view object. The application contains a navigation bar that you can use to test the data-browsing features. If this application works, you can be certain that your business components are working. There are other features of this application that you can learn about by reading the help topic that appears when you select **Help | Contents**. Practices in Chapter 3 and Part II allow you to try out this browser.

Displaying Messages

A simple but effective technique that works in some situations is to temporarily add code to display a message while the program is running. The message can contain information about the method that is being run, and it can include variable values. This is usually useful only if you have a clear picture of the potential problem area and just need to quickly verify a value or ensure that the execution path reached a certain line of code. For other debugging situations, the debugger might be easier and more informative. The drawback with using messages is that you have to modify the code and strip out the messages when you are finished debugging.

There are two methods you can use when you want to display a message. Both can accomplish the main debugging objectives of program control and value checking.

NOTE
Some developers define a Boolean variable in the code and set it to "true" to turn on the messages. Each section of code that has a message tests the variable to see if the message should be displayed (for example, "if (debug) System.out.println ("message");"). When the developer is finished with the messages, she or he sets the Boolean variable to "false" so that messages will be suppressed. If the variable is defined as private, final, and static (for example, "public final static boolean debug = true"), the compiler will strip out the code that is not executed, which makes the compiled class file smaller.

Console Window

You can embed a call to this method in key positions in your code. For example, if you wanted to determine the value of an int variable called totalSalary, you would add the following line in a Java application or applet:

```
System.out.println("total salary = " + totalSalary);
```

This would display the text "total salary = 999" (if the variable value were 999) in the Log window. In a JSP file, you would use the following line:

```
<% out.println("This is a debugging message"); %>
```

This will print the statement in the HTML page that the JSP page generates. System.out.println in a JSP scriplet tag (<% %>) will print to the Java console on the server.

TIP
Left justify temporary print statements in your code so that they will be easier to find when you want to remove them.

NOTE
*The Project Settings dialog (**Project | Project Settings**) contains the nodes Configurations\Development\Compiler and Configurations\Development\Runner. These pages allow you to specify which messages appear in the Log window for files in that project during compile time and runtime, respectively.*

Message Dialog

For Java applications and applets, you can display a modal message dialog (message box) that contains text optionally concatenated with variable values. This allows you to stop and look at the dialog before the program continues. A message box is useful if you need to check the output on the screen in the middle of an operation. The console window technique described earlier does not provide this capability.

The code that you write calls a static (shared) method in JOptionPane, a class from the Swing library. JOptionPane offers a number of features, including specifying more than one button and providing a text input area that the user can fill in. It is an easy way to show a dialog box. For debugging message purposes, you only need its simplest format, shown in this example:

```
JOptionPane.showMessageDialog(this,
    "The debugging message. maxNum = " + maxNum);
```

This code displays the JOptionPane dialog and shows the value of a variable set before the dialog is called. The following shows the output of this code. This technique results in showing the same kind of message you would show using the console window technique, but this technique stops the processing and waits for the user to click OK. Since instantiating the JOptionPane class using the new keyword uses a bit of memory each time you display the dialog, it is better to use the syntax shown and directly call the static method from JOptionPane.

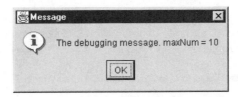

This technique is not applicable to JSP applications because JSP pages run on the server and do not use Swing components such as JOptionPane. For extra functionality, use the Dialog class as described in the sidebar "Using the Dialog Class."

Using the Dialog Class

Although JOptionPane will suffice for most debugging message requirements, you may need more functionality and additional components. The Dialog class demonstrated in the following steps displays a window with a customized dialog:

1. On any workspace node, select New from the right-click menu.

2. Double click "Project Containing a New Application" in the General\Projects category, and name the project and its directory "TestDialogJA."

3. Specify the package name as "testdialog," and click the Finish button on the Paths page. The New Application dialog will open.

4. Leave the defaults and click OK to create the application file and display the New Frame dialog.

5. Click OK to create the frame file.

6. If the frame file is not already open in the UI Editor, on the Frame1.java node, select UI Editor from the right-click menu. (The Document Bar may already contain a UI Editor session for Frame1.java.)

7. Add a JButton component to the frame in the UI Editor from the Swing page of the Component Palette. Select the button and change the *text* property to "Test Dialog" using the Property Inspector. Resize the button so that the text is completely visible.

8. Click Rebuild and Save All. Run the Application1.java file to check the design. (Specify the run target as Application1 if a dialog appears while running the file.) Close the runtime window.

While the practices in this book normally include clicking Rebuild to build the project, the Runtime node of the Project Settings is set by default to compile before running.

9. You will now create a dialog file. On the TestDialogJA project file node, select New from the right-click menu.

10. Double click Dialog in the Client Tier\Swing/AWTcategory to display the New Dialog dialog.

11. Name the dialog "TestDialog," and click OK to create the file.

12. Open the UI Editor for TestDialog.java if it is not already open. Change the *layout* property of "this" to "null" by clicking "this" in the Structure window and setting the *layout* property. Although you can place any component in this dialog panel, for this demonstration, just add a JTextField component from the Swing page of the Component Palette.

13. Switch to the frame file UI Editor. Click the Test Dialog button for the frame file, and click the Events tab in the Property Inspector.

14. Enter "TestDialogButton_clicked" in the *actionPerformed* event and press ENTER.

15. Control will switch to a method stub in the Code Editor. In a blank line between curly brackets, insert the following code:

```
TestDialog newDialog = new TestDialog();
newDialog.show();
```

16. Click Save All. Run the Application1.java file.

17. Click the Test Dialog button, and the dialog with the text field will display. Use the window closing buttons to close both windows.

This demonstrates how you can display a dialog window from an event such as a button press. Since the dialog can contain any component, you can build an input or selection area that will modify how the application works.

A variation on this technique is moving the instantiation (new) line to the class level (under `public class Frame1` in this example). This allows the dialog to be called from any method in that class. You can also instantiate the dialog with arguments (parent window, dialog title, and modal flag) as follows:

```
TestDialog newDialog = new TestDialog(this, "A test dialog", true);
```

If you set the *modal* property of the dialog's "this" window to "true," the window will be modal. (That is, it must be closed before focus can shift to the other window.)

The help system topic "Creating a Dialog Box" (called "dialog boxes creating" in the Index tab) contains more information about the Dialog class.

HTML Messages

For JSP applications and applet HTML startup files, you can embed simple text in the body section to show the HTML section that is being displayed. Simple message text embedded in the HTML body section can show that a particular tag was reached. You can also use hidden field values to show the parameter values that were passed to the page. (Consult your favorite HTML reference for details about hidden fields.) As a simple example, you might have a page containing the following HTML:

```
<HTML>
<BODY>
    <TABLE>

    . . .
    </TABLE>
after the table
</BODY>

</HTML>
```

The string "after the table" will be displayed if the HTML code successfully handles the HTML tags above it. You may not need to debug the HTML code if your HTML editor handles syntax errors automatically.

TIP
*To help identify problems in running applets, browsers usually offer a way to display messages from the client JVM. In Netscape, you can select **Communicator | Tools | Java Console** to show a window that will display messages about the session. In Internet Explorer, select **Tools | Internet Options** and click the "Java console enabled" checkbox in the Microsoft VM section of the Advanced tab. You can activate a similar window for the Java plug-in after you have started it in the browser by selecting Show Console from the right-click menu on the Java plug-in icon in the Windows task bar. Messages that you write to the console using System.out.println (for example, in a JSP application) will appear in this window.*

The JDeveloper Debugger

If you have determined that the alternative debugging techniques such as those just mentioned will not suffice, you will want to run a debugging session using the debugging mode. JDeveloper uses the Java 2 debugging API. It includes the ability to handle many JDK versions (version 1.2 and later), and to debug code on remote machines. Debugging is an essential activity that is worth the initial time investment to learn and set up. The more time you spend up front learning how to use the debugger, the easier it will be to respond to a problem program. The time to learn debugging is not when you encounter a problem in a high-pressure development situation.

Starting a Debugging Session

You start a debugging session from the IDE by clicking the Debug button, pressing SHIFT-F9, or selecting **Debug | Debug "*<project name>*"** from the menu (where "*<project name>*" is the name of the project, such as SortJA.jpr). The Debug "<project name>" button on the toolbar also starts a debugging session. You need to check the *Include Debug Information* checkbox on the Compiler page of the Project Settings dialog (**Project | Project Settings**). You also need to set the state of the "Set Start Debug Option" button in the debugging toolbar. The arrow beside this button displays a pulldown radio group that you can set to either Step Into (to stop at the first line of executable code), Step Over (to run through the code until reaching a method where tracing is enabled), or Run Until a Breakpoint Occurs (to run through code until the first breakpoint). The option setting is new as of release 9.0.3. The file compiles with special debugging information and runs in a modified JDeveloper window such as that shown in Figure 6-2.

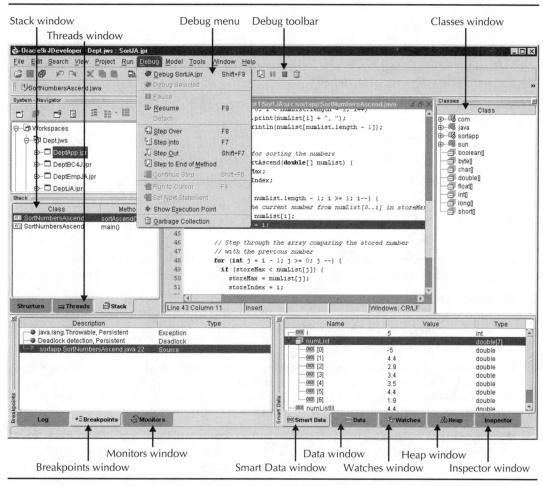

FIGURE 6-2. *JDeveloper running in debug mode*

NOTE
Another way to stop execution in the code is to start the debugger and click Pause to stop. The trick is to stop in the right place, but if the code execution is paused or stopped (such as when the program awaits user input), this is a reasonable technique to use.

A number of special debugging features appear when you run a file in debugging mode. Debugging menu options are enabled in the Debug menu.

Debug Windows

While in debugging mode, you can modify the default debugging session display using the **View | Debug Windows** submenu to display or hide the following windows:

- **Breakpoints** This window displays all breakpoints (program execution stopping points) that you have set or that are set by JDeveloper (such as exceptions and deadlocks). This window is viewable outside of debugging mode.

- **Threads** The Threads window shows all program execution lines. Since you can write multi-threaded programs in Java, you may need to examine the state of the current simultaneously executing threads.

- **Stack** This window shows the sequence of method calls that preceded the execution point (the *stack*).

- **Smart Data** This window shows variables, constants, and arguments that are used close to the execution point (the line of code that is being traced).

- **Data** The Data window displays values of all variables, constants, and arguments that are in scope for the current method.

- **Watches** You use this window to display the current values of the expressions you are watching.

- **Classes** This window displays the packages and classes that will be traced in the debug session. You can include or exclude tracing of specific packages using the right-click menu.

- **Heap** Use this window to examine the use of memory by objects and arrays in the program. This allows you to verify that an object is still in memory and to verify that garbage collection is occurring. The Memory Profiler described later contains more details about runtime memory.

- **Monitors** The Monitors window tracks the synchronization of data and activities between threads of execution. For example, you can use this window to determine which thread is waiting for another thread to complete. This kind of check is helpful in detecting deadlocks.

- **Inspector** This window is not available in the View menu, but is available as the Inspect option from the right-click menu after selecting a variable or expression (such as `storeMax * 100`) in the Code Editor, Watches window, Data window, or Smart Data window. You can open many Inspector windows and use each one to track a single variable or expression.

Some of these windows appear automatically in debug mode. As with other windows in the JDeveloper IDE, all can be anchored into the IDE frame as Figure 6-2 shows. You can place any window in any frame area in the IDE by dragging it over the frame using the draglines in the window title. If there is more than one window in a frame area, the windows will be selectable with tabs. You can drag each tab out of the frame to another frame or to a floating window.

Each window has a right-click menu with appropriate functions such as the following menu from the Breakpoints window:

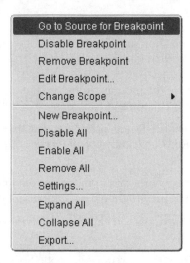

The right-click menus of most debug windows include a Settings item. This item displays the Preferences dialog page that manages the options for that window, such as the following dialog for the Breakpoints window:

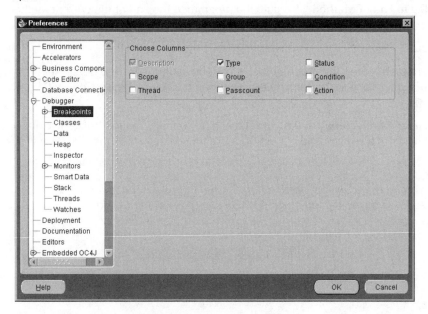

The Debug Toolbar Buttons

The buttons in the Debug tab toolbar shown next offer the main functions that you need when running a debug session. Many of these buttons are also in a toolbar that appears in the Log window when you run a program in debug mode.

The functions and the keyboard shortcuts (for the JDeveloper default key mapping) that you can alternatively use to activate them follow:

- **Debug <project>** Execute the program from the start to the first breakpoint or to the end of the program if no breakpoints are encountered (SHIFT-F9).

- **Set Start Debugging Option** Select an option for what happens when you start debugging (Step Into, Step Over, or Run Until a Breakpoint Occurs). This icon will change according to the option you select.

- **Resume** Continue a paused program from the current line of execution to the next breakpoint or to the end of the program if no subsequent breakpoints are defined (F9).

- **Step Over** Execute the next method call or instruction without tracing, and stop at the next executable line (F8).

- **Step Into** Execute the program and trace the code line by line (F7).

- **Step Out** Step out of the current method, and return to the next instruction of the calling method (SHIFT-F7).

- **Step to End of Method** Execute the program to the end of the current method or to the next breakpoint in the current method.

- **Pause** Temporarily stop the program as it executes.

- **Terminate** Stop the program that is in debugging mode. The debug settings, such as breakpoints and watches that you set during the debugging session, will be saved (CTRL-F2).

- **Garbage Collection** If the virtual machine supports manual triggering of garbage collection, force garbage collection and show the results in the Classes window.

NOTE
*The keyboard shortcuts (or "accelerators") listed in this section are those assigned by the default key map. You can select a different key map using the Accelerators page of the Preferences dialog (**Tools | Preferences**).*

The Debug Menu Items

Most Debug menu items are enabled only when you are in debug mode. The Debug menu options repeat the toolbar options and add the following functions:

- **Debug <selected file>** Start the debug session for the file selected in the Navigator window. If the selected file is the *default run target* (file that runs when the project is run), this option is the same as the Debug <project> option.

- **Detach** Stop the debugging session, but do not stop the running program. This is useful for remote debugging on an application server.

- **Continue Step** Resume tracing (into a step) after the debugger stops at an exception breakpoint (SHIFT-F8).

- **Run to Cursor** Run the program from its current execution point to the line of program code containing the cursor (F4).

- **Set Next Statement** Skip from the stopping point to the code at the location of the cursor, even if the cursor is before the stopping point. Code lines between the stopping point to the cursor location is not executed. This option is useful for backtracking to previously executed lines of code after you have changed data values.

- **Show Execution Point** Display the section of code that is currently running.

Some of the options in the toolbar and menu are also available in the right-click menu in the Code Editor.

Controlling Program Execution

One main debugging objective is to track and control the *execution point*—the section of code that is about to be executed. In a typical session, the debugger stops the program execution, highlights the execution point, and waits for you to resume the program. You use one of the debug actions (button, keyboard shortcut, or menu selection) to resume the program execution.

Debugging Actions

While the program is stopped, you can evaluate the stack and the order in which the program is executed to determine whether the program execution path is the problem. The Threads window and Stack window display this information. In the pause, you can also evaluate data values (as mentioned in the later section "Examining Program Data Values").

As you step through the code in this way, you are *tracing* its path. You can choose to skip tracing each line of code in a particular method that is called by stepping over the call. The method will still execute, but you will not stop in the method code. This is useful if you are certain that a method works and you do not want to take the time to look at it in detail. If you want to examine the method that is called next, you *step into* the method. If you start tracing in a method and determine that the rest of the code works, you can choose to *step out* of that method.

These are the main actions in a debugging session. There are other actions you can take in the debugger that are available from the right-click menus in the various debugger windows.

Other techniques such as stepping back, disabling tracing for classes that have not been loaded, and tracing into a class that has no source code file, are explained further in the help system node "Testing and Optimizing Application Code\Debugging in JDeveloper."

Breakpoints

A *breakpoint* is a defined pause point for the debugging session. It is the primary method that you use to control the program execution. When the debugger reaches a breakpoint, it stops and waits for an action.

JDeveloper supports the following breakpoint types:

- ■ **Source breakpoint**   This is set to pause at a particular line of code specified by the developer.

- ■ **Exception breakpoint**   This is set to pause when an exception for a particular exception class is thrown. An exception breakpoint is automatically set for `java.lang.Throwable`, but you may create exception breakpoints for other exception classes.

- ■ **Deadlock breakpoint**   This is automatically defined by JDeveloper to detect situations where one thread is waiting for another thread that is, in turn, waiting for it (a deadlock). This feature is only available for some JVMs. You can disable this deadlock using the Breakpoints window right-click menu, but you cannot define a deadlock breakpoint.

- ■ **Method breakpoint**   This occurs when a particular method is called. The method is defined in the Edit Breakpoint or Add Breakpoint dialog.

- ■ **Class breakpoint**   This occurs when any method in a particular class is called. The class name is entered in the Edit Breakpoint or Add Breakpoint dialog.

All breakpoint types except for the deadlock breakpoint may be created using the New Breakpoint dialog available from the right-click menu in the Breakpoints window. All breakpoint types may be edited, disabled, and enabled in the same menu.

Defining Breakpoints   Source breakpoints are marked with a red circle icon in the Code Editor's left margin so that you can easily identify the lines of code at which the execution will stop. The list of breakpoints appears in the Breakpoints window.

You can enable and disable or delete breakpoints using options in the right-click menu in this window. You can also delete or set a breakpoint in the Code Editor by clicking in the line and pressing F5 or by clicking the left margin on that line.

Breakpoint Groups   You can modify breakpoints as a group. A *breakpoint group* is a set of breakpoints that share the same name. You can enter or select the group name in the Definition tab of the Edit Breakpoint dialog (accessible from the right-click menu on the breakpoint in the Breakpoints window) as shown here:

The group name will then appear in the Breakpoints window as follows:

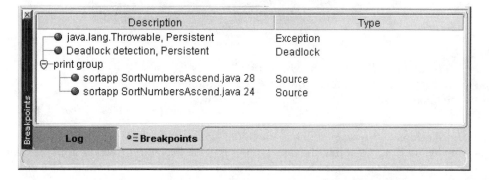

You can select Edit Group from the right-click menu on the group name node in the Breakpoints window to set conditions and actions for the entire set of breakpoints. You can also enable or disable the group using the Enable Group or Disable Group right-click menu options, respectively, in that window.

Conditions   You can define a breakpoint condition so that the program will stop at the breakpoint only if a variable value is within a certain range or a flag variable is set. You can also set a *pass count* that specifies that the execution will stop only after breakpoint is reached a certain number of times. For example, if the pass count is set to "3," the breakpoint will only stop execution the third time it is reached. This is an additional condition that is placed on the breakpoint that is added (using AND logic) to the other conditions that are defined.

You can set and define conditions for breakpoints on the Conditions tab of the Edit Breakpoint dialog shown next that appears when you select Edit Breakpoint from the right-click menu on the breakpoint listed in the Breakpoints window.

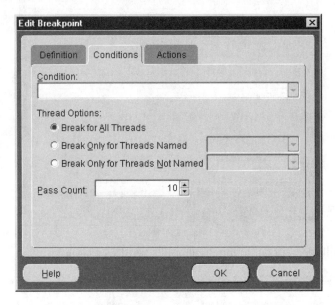

NOTE
The Edit Breakpoint dialog for an existing breakpoint is the same as the New Breakpoint dialog for a new breakpoint. Both are available from the right-click menu in the Breakpoints window.

Breakpoint Actions   You can define a number of actions to take place when a breakpoint occurs. The default action that this chapter assumes is "Halt Execution," which stops execution at the breakpoint line. You can also log the breakpoint occurrence, enable or disable a group of breakpoints, or issue a beep from the system's speaker.

All actions are set on the Actions tab of the Edit Breakpoints dialog described earlier. The following shows this dialog and how you would disable all the breakpoints in a group that you named "print group":

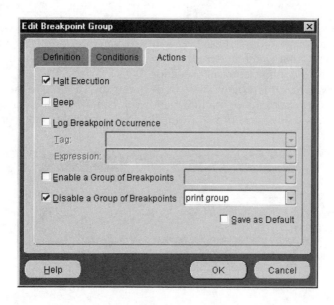

TIP
*The Breakpoints page of the Preferences dialog (**Tools** | **Preferences**)
allows you to set the columns that are displayed in the Breakpoints
window. A child page, Default Actions, lets you set the selections that
automatically appear in the Edit Breakpoint dialog. Setting defaults in
this way is useful if you want to have an action (such as a system
beep) occur for each breakpoint.*

Examining Program Data Values

The other main debugging objective is to examine the values of *expressions* that represent variables,
constants, and data structure values and the operators that act upon them. You may not use
method calls in a debugging expression. You also may not use local variables or static variables
that are unavailable (because of scope) to the code line you are executing. The following
windows described earlier allow you to examine expressions:

Data Window   As mentioned, this tracks variables, constants, and arguments that are close to
the execution point.

Smart Data Window   As mentioned, this tracks variables, constants, and arguments that are
close to the execution point.

Watches Window   This window shows the data values that are part of the expressions being tracked. A *watch* is an expression that contains program variables or other data elements and their operators. You set up a watch and monitor its value as the program executes. The watch displays the value for the context (current) execution.

You can add a watch as the program runs by selecting the variable in the Code Editor and selecting Watch (CTRL-F5) from the right-click menu. You can modify the watch expression as shown next by selecting Edit Watch (or Edit Expression) from the right-click menu in the Watches Window.

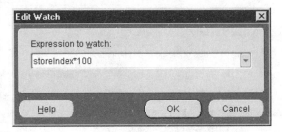

NOTE
You can delete a watch expression by highlighting it in the Watches window and selecting Remove Watch from the right-click menu.

Inspector Window   An inspector also allows you to examine data values just as with a watch. Display the Inspector window by selecting a variable in the Code Editor, Data window, Smart Data window, or Watches window and then selecting Inspect from the right-click menu. The expression is always evaluated within the current scope of execution. You can open more than one inspector at a time to track different expressions.

Modify Value Dialog   This dialog (shown next) displays the data state of a variable, constant, or argument within the context of the current program execution point.

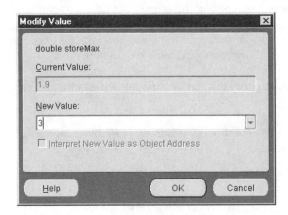

It is available by selecting the Modify Value option from the right-click menu on a variable in the Data window, Smart Data window, or Watches window. You can enter a new value in the

New Value field and click OK to set the value in the debugging session. This allows you to test a bug fix that would modify a value. The value type must match the type of the variable to which it is assigned. The change you make does not change your code. You can only alter primitive variables, strings, and reference pointers.

View Whole Value   If the value you are watching is too large for the cell in one of the data-related debug windows (such as the Data window or Smart Data window), you can show a multi-line window that contains the entire value by selecting View Whole Value from the right-click menu.

NOTE
You can modify the fields that appear when you expand a node in the data-related debug windows by selecting Edit Filters from the right-click menu. The Edit Filters dialog allows you to hide fields (such as value, offset, count, and hash) for selected classes. This can simplify the display so that you can concentrate on a particular set of fields.

Remote Debugging

Debugging an application that is running on a remote server (such as a JSP application or servlet) is a challenge because error and execution messages must be generated by the server instead of by the IDE. Although the basic approaches to debugging code are possible, such as adding calls to `System.out.println()` and logging this output to a file, these debugging methods do not always suffice, and you need to run the debugger on the server. When you run the debugger in the JDeveloper IDE, the program you are running (called a *debuggee process*) is attached to the debugger automatically. When you are running remotely on an application server, you start the program and then attach it to the debugger.

JDeveloper's support for remote debugging of server-side Java includes the features built into the local IDE debugger, such as controlled execution, breakpoints, watch expressions, and examination of variable values and properties during execution. Therefore, with JDeveloper, the same interface is used for both local and remote debugging.

More Information

Although the topic of remote debugging is beyond the scope of this book, most techniques mentioned in this chapter apply. The additional configuration steps and specifics on attaching and detaching remote processes are well documented in the JDeveloper help system. Start in the Contents tab node "Testing and Optimizing Application Code\Debugging in JDeveloper\ Debugging Remote Java Programs." In addition, Oracle's developer website, otn.oracle.com, contains white papers on remote debugging.

The Profiler

The Profiler is new to Oracle9*i* JDeveloper. This tool assists in debugging resource issues and in helping you make informed optimization decisions for your code. It collects and displays information that supplements the information that you can gather in the debugger. The Profiler tracks three main types of information: events, execution, and memory. Each profile type (or mode) has its own window and configuration settings. Although the Profiler is a single tool, the JDeveloper help system documentation uses the terms "Memory Profiler," "Events Profiler," and "Execution Profiler" to represent the three modes in which you can run the Profiler.

The following provides an overview of the general steps that you take to run this tool and provides a view of the different profiles. This will serve as an introduction to the technical details explained in the JDeveloper help system node "Testing and Optimizing Application Code\Profiling a Project" to which you can refer for further information.

NOTE
You can also use the Profiler to collect information about a remotely running program. In this environment, the local development machine is running the Profiler but not the program being profiled. Since the program being profiled and the Profiler are running on different machines, the Profiler and program do not compete for resources as they do when they are running on the same machine.

Running the Profiler

The steps for running the Profiler are similar for all three types of profiles and consist of the following activities:

■ **Setting Profiler options**   You need to configure the Profiler using the Project Settings dialog available by selecting Project Settings from the right-click menu on the project node in the Navigator window. Navigate to the Configurations\Development\Profiler node, and click the profile type that you want to set (Events, Execution, or Memory). Each has a separate page in the Project Settings dialog. For example, the following shows the settings for the Event Profiler:

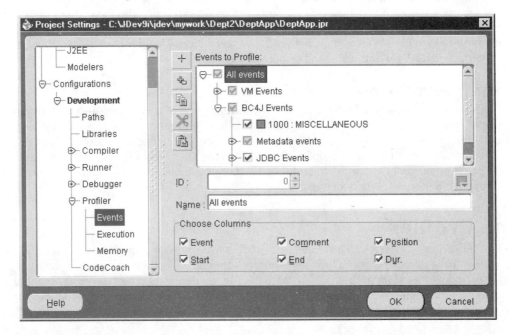

■ **Defining the Profiler class set** You have to declare which classes the Profiler will track (the *Profiler class set*). Navigate to the Profiler page of Project Settings as mentioned before, and list the packages and classes to include and exclude. This page also allows you to declare if you will be profiling remotely.

■ **Starting profiling** You start the Profiler using an option in the Run menu. For example, to run the Event Profiler, select the program in the Navigator window, and select **Run | Event Profile <project>**. This starts the program and displays the Profiler window.

■ **Examining results** When you reach a point in the program that you would like to examine, you click the Pause (yellow bars) button in the Profiler window. This refreshes the display in the Profiler to reflect the current state of the program. You can sort the table displays by clicking the column heading buttons. For the event and execution modes, you click the Clear button (eraser) to reset the display. Then click the Resume (green arrow) button to restart the program and collect more profile data. Click Pause again when you reach the end of the section of code that you are profiling. You can save the information collected into an HTML file by selecting Save to HTML from the right-click menu.

■ **Terminating the Profiler** When you are finished with the cycle of pausing, examining results, and resuming, you can close the Profiler window or select **Run | Terminate | <project>**. Closing the Profiler will also stop the program execution, but stopping the program will not close the Profiler.

Event Profiler

This profile allows you to view the timings of individual actions in your program and compare them with timings in the rest of the program. It helps you identify the exact area that is causing a slowdown in processing. As Figure 6-3 shows, each event includes timing information and a description that helps you identify the event.

You can set up your own events using the *Profiler API*, a package included with JDeveloper. Use this if there is an event that you want to profile but that is not included in the classes that your program uses. The API class is documented in the help node "Testing and Optimizing Application Code\Profiling a Project\Reference: Class ProfilerAPI."

Execution Profiler

This type of profile accumulates timing information about the current thread at regular intervals (defined in the Project Settings dialog). It allows you to identify the methods and threads that take the most time and therefore provide opportunities for tuning. Figure 6-4 shows the Execution Profiler window. Clicking a method line in the table on the left displays information about the method that calls it and about the methods that it calls.

Memory Profiler

The Memory Profiler helps you identify the cause of memory leaks. It also samples at an interval defined in the Project Settings dialog. A feature of this profile is that you can review a number of samples so that you can compare how memory was used at different times in the program execution. The Memory Profiler window is shown in Figure 6-5. The slider at the top of the window allows you to go back to a previous sampling and to compare how memory was used at different times.

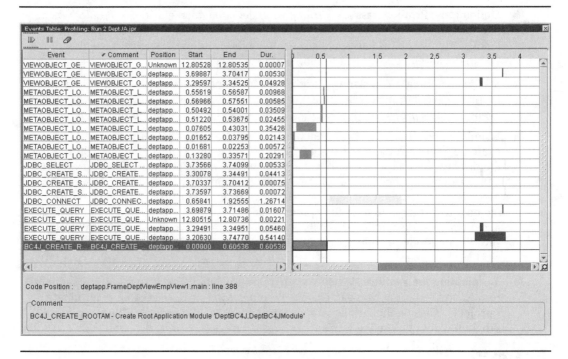

FIGURE 6-3. *Event Profiler window*

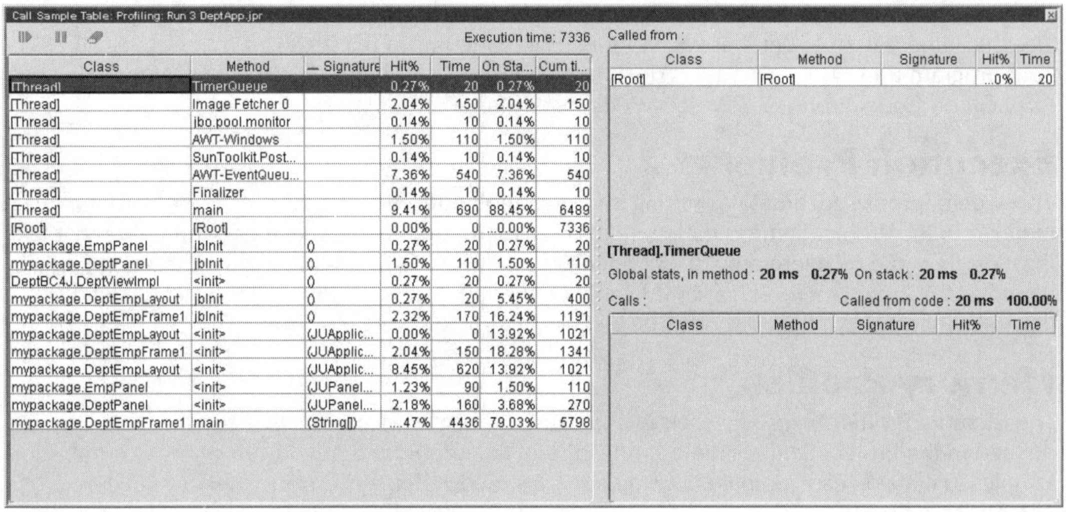

FIGURE 6-4. *Execution Profiler window*

Memory Sample Table: Profiling: Run 4 LocDeptJA.jpr

26/26

Class	Count	Size	No. Alloc	Sz Alloc	No. Freed	Sz Freed	Diff Alloc	Diff Sz
Totals :	34953	1,417,121	0	0	0	0	0	0
char[]	7724	485,224	0	0	0	0	0	0
java.lang.String	7554	181,296	0	0	0	0	0	0
int[]	533	111,840	0	0	0	0	0	0
java.util.Hashtable$Entry	3345	80,280	0	0	0	0	0	0
byte[]	1170	77,772	0	0	0	0	0	0
java.lang.Object[]	1401	54,396	0	0	0	0	0	0
java.util.Hashtable$Entry[]	234	36,628	0	0	0	0	0	0
oracle.xml.parser.v2.AttrDecl	592	33,152	0	0	0	0	0	0
java.util.HashMap$Entry	1160	27,840	0	0	0	0	0	0
long[]	1006	20,408	0	0	0	0	0	0
java.util.BitSet	1005	16,080	0	0	0	0	0	0
java.util.HashMap$Entry[]	263	13,076	0	0	0	0	0	0
java.util.Vector	543	13,032	0	0	0	0	0	0
java.util.HashMap	262	12,576	0	0	0	0	0	0
java.lang.String[]	543	12,548	0	0	0	0	0	0
java.util.jar.Attributes$Name	717	11,472	0	0	0	0	0	0
oracle.xml.parser.v2.CMLeaf	326	10,432	0	0	0	0	0	0
sun.java2d.loops.GraphicsPrimitiveProxy	309	8,652	0	0	0	0	0	0
java.util.Hashtable	212	8,480	0	0	0	0	0	0
javax.swing.JButton	20	7,860	0	0	0	0	0	0
oracle.xml.util.StringHashtable$Entry	241	6,748	0	0	0	0	0	0
com.sun.java.util.collections.HashMap$Entry[]	92	5,924	0	0	0	0	0	0
oracle.xml.parser.v2.ElementDecl	104	5,408	0	0	0	0	0	0
java.net.URL	85	4,760	0	0	0	0	0	0
oracle.xml.parser.v2.CMChoice	130	4,680	0	0	0	0	0	0
oracle.xml.parser.v2.CMNodeSeq	126	4,536	0	0	0	0	0	0
com.sun.java.util.collections.HashMap	92	4,416	0	0	0	0	0	0
byte[][]	9	4,296	0	0	0	0	0	0
java.lang.Integer	355	4,260	0	0	0	0	0	0

FIGURE 6-5. *Memory Profiler window*

NOTE
The Profiler button on the toolbar changes to reflect the last profile type that was run. For example, if you last ran the Execution Profiler, the button will run that profile for the selected project.

Hands-on Practice: Debug a Java Application

The best way to understand how the debugger works is to apply it to a task and to examine the activities required to find a problem. In this practice, you will walk through all of the major steps for carrying out the two essential debugging activities of controlling program execution and examining program data values. The practice follows these phases:

   I. Create a buggy application

  II. Prepare for the debugging session

 III. Control program execution

      ■ Run the debugger and step through the code

■ Disable and enable tracing of classes

IV. Examine Data Values

NOTE
Most debug functions may be called using the menu, right-click menu, toolbar, or keyboard shortcut, and this hands-on practice demonstrates a variety of methods. You can explore the other ways to call these functions (as mentioned in the sections before "The Debug Toolbar Buttons" and "The Debug Menu Items") to see which way is easiest for you.

I. Create a Buggy Application

Normally, you do not intentionally create buggy code. The sample application for this practice requires code with bugs to illustrate the debugging process and techniques. The application used in this practice processes a list of numbers entered as command-line parameters and sorts the numbers in ascending order. The results print in the Log window. A logic error in the program results in an incorrect sort, and the aim of the practice is to discover this error. Once the bug is found, a fix can be applied.

1. Create a project in an existing workspace by selecting the workspace node and selecting New Empty Project from the right-click menu.

2. Use "SortJA" for the directory and file name.

3. On the project node, select New Class from the right-click menu.

Additional Information: This opens the New Class dialog.

4. Enter "SortNumbersAscend" for the *Name* field and "sortapp" for the *Package* field. Leave the other defaults as shown in Figure 6-6, and click OK to create the file.

5. Click Save All.

6. Open the Code Editor for this class file, and edit it to match the following code. (This code is available on the authors' websites.)

```
package sortapp;

public class SortNumbersAscend {

  /**
   * main
   * @param args
   */
  public static void main(String[] args) {
    // Fill a list with the command line parameters
    int n = args.length;
    double[] numList = new double[n];
    for (int i = 0; i < n; i++) {
```

```
      numList[i] = Double.parseDouble(args[i]);
    }

    // display the numbers in the order they were entered
    System.out.println("The given set of numbers is: ");
    printNumList(numList);

    // sort the numbers in ascending order by calling a method
    sortAscend(numList);

    // Print the sorted list
    System.out.println("The numbers arranged in ascending order: ");
    printNumList(numList);
    }

    // The method for displaying the numbers in the message window
    static void printNumList(double[] numList) {
      for (int i = 0; i < numList.length - 1; i++)
        System.out.print(numList[i] + ", ");
      System.out.println(numList[numList.length - 1]);
    }

    // The method for sorting the numbers
    static void sortAscend(double[] numList) {
      double storeMax;
      int     storeIndex;

      for (int i = numList.length - 1; i >= 1; i--) {
        // store the current number from numList[0..i] in storeMax
        storeMax = numList[i];
        storeIndex = i;

        // Step through the array comparing the stored number
        // with the previous number
        for (int j = i - 1; j >= 0; j--) {
          if (storeMax < numList[j]) {
            storeMax = numList[j];
            storeIndex = i;
          }
        }
        // Swap the numbers if the current number is greater
        if (storeIndex != i) {
          numList[storeIndex] = numList[i];
          numList[i] = storeMax;
        }
      }
    }
  }
```

7. Click Save All.

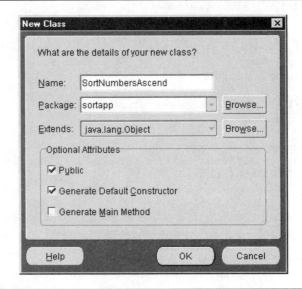

FIGURE 6-6. *New Class dialog*

What Just Happened?   You created a new workspace and project. You then added a Java class file with some buggy code that you can use for testing the debugger. The intended logic for this program follows:

1. Loop through the command-line parameter list of numbers, and build an array variable with one number in each array element.

2. Display the unsorted list in the Log window.

3. Sort the numbers using the sortAscend() method.

4. Display the sorted list.

The logic for the sortAscend() method follows:

1. Loop through the array that was passed from the main() method.

2. Store the value of the current element in storeMax and current index in storeIndex.

3. Loop through all numbers in the list before the current element. If storeMax is less than the number, swap the current element number with the number that is less than storeMax.

II. Prepare for the Debugging Session

The first stage in running the debugger is to prepare the project settings. You then compile your program to generate the symbolic debugging information required by the debugger.

1. On the SortJA project node, select Project Settings from the right-click menu.

2. Navigate to the Configurations\Development\Compiler page (as shown next), and ensure that there are check marks in *Include Debug Information* and *Show Warnings*.

   Additional Information: The *Include Debug Information* field specifies whether special debugging information will be compiled into the .class file. This information is required for debugging. The *Show Warnings* field indicates whether compilation error messages will appear in the Log window.

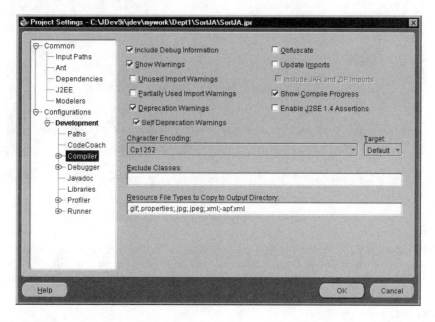

3. Navigate to the Configurations\Development\Runner\Options page, and be sure the *Make Project* checkbox is checked.

   Additional Information: This causes JDeveloper to automatically compile the code when you click Run or Debug. The alternative is to explicitly click Make before clicking Run or Debug.

4. Click the Runner node in the Project Settings dialog, and fill in the *Program Arguments* field with the following string of numbers, each separated by a blank space:

```
-5.0 4.4 2.9 3.4 3.5 4.4 1.9
```

The next illustration shows the Project Settings dialog with this string entered in the *Program Arguments* field.

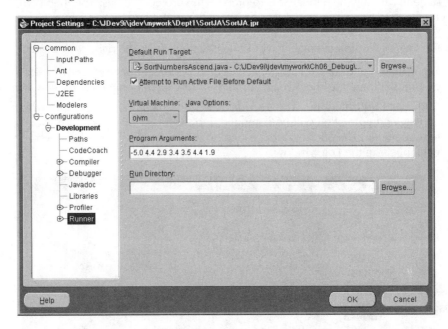

Additional Information: This string of numbers (the numbers to be sorted) will be passed to the application at runtime.

5. Click OK to close the Project Settings dialog. Click Save All.

What Just Happened? You set the project settings and command-line parameters to prepare for the debugging session. The debugger requires special instructions in the class file that are inserted when you set the project settings.

CAUTION
Remove the check on the "Include Debug Information" checkbox before generating the final production code so that the final code does not incur the slight overhead of the size of the extra debugging information. This checkbox is the same as using the "-g" switch when running the javac compiler from the command line.

III. Control Program Execution

Before starting the debugger, be certain that you have properly set the project settings as in the last phase. This phase will start the debugging session and illustrate how you track the program execution.

Run the Debugger and Step Through the Code

You can run the debugger by selecting Debug (using a menu item, button, or keyboard shortcut). The code will compile and run in debug mode using whichever Set Start Debugging Option you set (Step Into, Step Over, Run Until a Breakpoint Occurs). Step Into will stop at the first executable statement whether or not breakpoints were defined. Step Over will stop at the first executable method that is set to trace. Run Until Breakpoint Occurs will stop at the first breakpoint. Since this phase of the practice uses no breakpoints, the Step Into technique is used.

1. Select SortNumbersAscend.java in the Navigator, and select Set Start Debugging Option to Step Into on the option button in the toolbar. Click the Debug <project> button.

   Additional Information: If the code compiles successfully, the debugger will start and pause at the first executable line of code. The Smart Data, Data, and Watches tabs will be added in the Log window area. The current execution line will be indicated with an arrow in the left margin of the Code Editor.

   The debugger will add a Stack tab to the Structure window to display the method execution thread. It will also add a Breakpoints tab to the Log window to display the stopping points that you have set.

CAUTION
As mentioned, data will be shown in the Data tab only if the project property ""Include Debug Information" checkbox is checked in the Project Settings dialog.

2. Exit debug mode by clicking the Terminate button. This aborts the program without executing the rest of the code.

3. Click Debug <project> to restart the debugger. The red arrow indicating the execution point should point to the following line, which is the first executable line of code in the `main()` method:

   `int n = args.length;`

4. Click the cursor on the line of source code, making the first call to the method `printNumList(numlist)`.

5. Select **Debug | Run to Cursor**.

   Additional Information: This moves the execution to the location of the cursor. The Log window shows the output from the execution of the line of code prior to the call to the `printNumList()` method. This line causes the string "The given set of numbers is:" to be printed in the Log window.

6. Click the Step Over button in the toolbar.

   Additional Information: The Log window shows the numbers that were input as parameters as the output from the `printNumList()` method. This is because the Step Over command allows all of the code invoked by the call to execute to completion before pausing again.

7. Place the cursor on the line of code that makes the second call to the `printNumlist(numList)` method.

8. Press F4 (the same function as selecting **Debug | Run to Cursor**).

   Additional Information: You will see the output of the text string argument to the `println()` method—the text string "The numbers arranged in ascending order:".

9. Select **Debug | Step Into**.

   Additional Information: The execution point jumps to the first line of the `printNumList()` method.

10. Watch the Log window as you click the Step Into button on the debugging toolbar twice. Continue clicking the button four more times to watch the loop iterate.

11. Select **Debug | Step to End of Method**.

    Additional Information: The program executes the remaining iterations of the loop, and the execution point moves to the closing curly bracket of the `printNumList()` method.

12. Click the Terminate button to end the debugging session. If you look in the Log window, you will see that the output order of the numbers is the same as the input order. The sort function is not working, and this is the bug you need to fix.

Disable and Enable Tracing of Classes

In this application you have only one file, which you created and need to debug. However, when you have many source code files in your project and want to debug only one of these files, you will need to change the list of classes that the debugger will step into.

You can change the list of classes that will be traced at runtime or at design time. The following steps demonstrate both techniques:

1. Start the debugging session again by clicking the Debug button. Since the start option is set to Step Into, the debugger will stop at the first line of executable code.

2. If the Classes window is not displayed, select **View | Debug Windows | Classes**.

   Additional Information: The Classes window will appear as shown here with all classes loaded in this session.

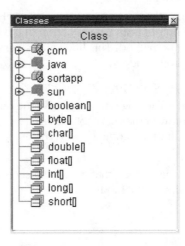

A gray icon for packages and classes indicates that they will be excluded from tracing. A colored package icon indicates a package that has classes that will be included in the tracing. For example, in the illustration before, the com and sortapp packages are included, and the java and sun classes are excluded.

3. On a node in the Classes window, select Tracing from the right-click menu.

   Additional Information: This displays the Tracing dialog, where you can enter class packages and classes to include or to exclude.

4. To test this feature, add ";sortapp.SortNumbersAscend" (including the leading semicolon) to the end of the *Tracing Classes and Packages to Exclude* field. Click OK.

TIP
You can use the Edit buttons in this dialog to construct the list of packages and classes. Using the dialogs from the Edit button will eliminate the problem of mistyping a name or punctuation, but may be a bit slower.

   Additional Information: The icon for SortNumbersAscend under the sortapp package node in the Classes window will turn gray. This action turns off tracing of the main application class file for demonstration purposes. If your project contained more than one file, you would use this technique to skip tracing in class files that were bug free. You need to restart the debugging session for the change in traced classes to take effect.

5. Click the Terminate button to end the debugging session.

6. Restart the debugging session by clicking Debug.

   Additional Information: The debugger will start the application, but will execute the application without stopping at any line of code.

NOTE
If you set breakpoints in an excluded class file, the debugger will still stop at those breakpoints.

7. On the SortJA project node in the Navigator, select Project Settings from the right-click menu. The Project Settings dialog will appear.

   Additional Information: Since the Classes window is only available while debugging, you cannot reset the exclusions list using the same method that you used to set it. The Project Settings dialog contains the same lists, and this dialog is available whether you are in design mode or debug mode.

8. Navigate to the Configurations\Development\Debugger node, and remove the ";sortapp.SortNumbersAscend" string from the *Tracing Classes and Packages to Exclude* field (including the leading semicolon). Click OK to dismiss the dialog.

9. Run the application again using the Debug button. The debugger will again stop at the first line of executable code. Click Terminate to stop the debugging session.

What Just Happened? You started the debugging session and practiced stepping into and stepping over code. You also viewed the messages that you can see in the Log window and tried two methods for disabling and enabling the tracing of specific classes and their child classes. Disabling tracing on a particular class or tree of classes will save your having to step out of or step over a set of code that you know to be problem free.

IV. Examine Data Values

Now that you know how to control the program execution, you can practice defining watches, setting breakpoints, and examining data element values. This will help you locate the problem area in the code.

1. Click Debug to start debugging. The execution point is in the first executable line of the `main()` method (`int n = args.length;`).

NOTE
If any of the steps in this section do not work, terminate the debugging session and start the debugging session again.

2. Click the Watches window (or the Watches tab if this window is merged with other windows). Since you have not defined any watches, the window will be blank.

3. Click Step Into twice to move the execution line to the `for` statement.

4. In the Code Editor, double click to select the variable word `numList` that appears in the line before the `for` statement:
   `double[] numList = new double[n];`

5. On the selected variable `numList`, select Watch from the right-click menu. This will display the Add Watch dialog, as shown here:

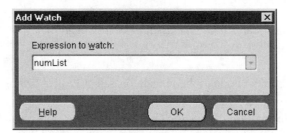

6. Click OK, and you will see the `numList` variable added to the Watches window as shown next.

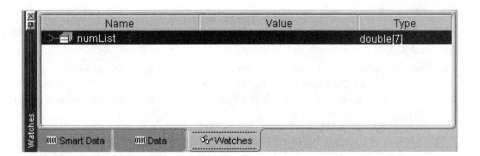

7. Click Step Into twice. Expand the numList node in the Watches window (using the + to the left of the word) to see that the array has been declared and the values of all elements in the array are set to "0" except for the first element.

8. Click Step Into twice more, and you will see that the value of the second element of the array has been filled in as the loop proceeds through the list of numbers.

   Additional Information: Since there are no errors until the sort method, you can skip all lines of code until the call to the sortAscend() method. You could just click the Step Over button until you reached that code, but there is a better way using a breakpoint.

   If you set a breakpoint on the line on which you want to stop, you can easily skip all lines of code before that. There are several ways to set a breakpoint:

   ■ Click the left border next to the line of code.

      Or:

   ■ On the line of code, select Toggle Breakpoint from the right-click menu.

      Or:

   ■ Press F5.

9. Create a breakpoint for the line that calls sortAscend() using one of the methods just listed. (You do not need to be in debug mode to set breakpoints.)

10. Click the Resume button to execute all lines until the breakpoint.

    Additional Information: The Watches window will show that values have been assigned to all elements of the numList array.

11. Click the Step Into button to trace the code in the sortAscend() method.

12. Place the cursor at the if statement immediately after the comment "Swap the numbers...". On that line, select Run to Cursor from the right-click menu.

    Additional Information: The execution point will transfer from the breakpoint to the if statement.

13. Click the Data window (as shown in the following illustration), and look at the values for the variables i, storeMax, and storeIndex. You can expand the numList node to see the individual elements in the array.

Additional Information: The sort routine correctly picked the largest number as 4.4 for the first iteration of the outer loop, but the array position of this number is not [6] and is the same as the value in i. This means that the exchange of values did not occur, as it should for a proper sort.

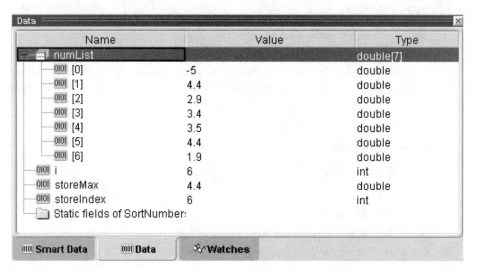

The watch for numList that was set earlier tracked the values of this variable, and these are displayed in both the Watches window and the Data window. All variables that appear in the current line of code are also displayed in the Data window, but since they have no watch defined, they are not shown in the Watches window.

TIP
You can examine the value of a variable by holding the mouse cursor over the variable name in the Code Editor. The value will be displayed in a tooltip next to the name, as shown here:

```
numList[storeIndex] = numList[i];
numList[i] = storeMax;
              numList[storeIndex] = 1.9
```

14. If you examine the code before the execution point, you can determine that the correct value is not being saved in the storeIndex variable. In the Code Editor, change the assignment of storeIndex in the j loop to "j" instead of "i" as follows:
storeIndex = j;
The file is still in debug mode while you are editing it.

15. Click Terminate to stop the program.

16. Click Run to run the program. Verify the results in the Log window, and ensure that the sort is correct.

What Just Happened?   You successfully debugged a logic error by setting up a watch and a breakpoint and examining data values during the program execution. This simple example showed the basic techniques that you could use to find and fix problems in your code. The sidebar "The Modify Value Dialog" demonstrates how you can change the values of variables during the debugging session. There are some other advanced features, as mentioned earlier, that you will want to explore once you have mastered these basics. The JDeveloper help system is the source for information about these techniques.

The Modify Value Dialog

You can use the Modify Value dialog to view and change values of variables. The following steps demonstrate how to work with this dialog using the example program in this practice:

1. Remove all breakpoints by selecting Remove All from the right-click menu in the Breakpoints window. The Breakpoints window usually appears as a tab in the Log window area. If the Breakpoints window is not displayed, select **View | Debug Windows | Breakpoints**.

2. Start a debugging session using Debug. The start option (on the Set Start Debugging Option button pulldown) should still be set to "Step Into."

3. In the `sortAscend()` method, click in the following line and select Run to Cursor from the right-click menu to run all code before that line:
```
if (storeMax < numList[j])
```

4. In the Data window, click the `storeMax` line and select Modify Value from the right-click menu to display the Modify Value dialog.

5. Enter "2" in the *New Value* field and click OK. The value "2" will replace the previous value of 1.9 and will display in the Data window. The program will then use the new number when that variable is next referenced.

6. Click Terminate to end the session.

CHAPTER
7

J2EE Architectures and Deployment Alternatives

You pays your money and you takes your choice.

—Punch (1846), X, 16

fter you create the application code and debug it, you need to install it into the production environment. The term *deployment* refers to this process of copying and installing the necessary application and configuration files. When you develop an application, you choose the user interface architecture long before you write the code. Therefore, you will know ahead of time what server will be assigned to the database, what the client platforms will consist of, and what use you will make of web servers. In the past, the architecture decision was often made with little guidance from the industry. This kind of decision is now a bit easier because Sun Microsystems has published best practices as part of the Java 2 Platform, Enterprise Edition (J2EE). Once you decide upon an architecture, you can develop the system and deploy it.

This chapter provides an overview of the architectures of two popular types of Java code. The first type of code, *Java client,* is a category that encompasses the Java application and applet styles. The second type is *JavaServer Pages (JSP) code,* which is a style of web-deployed code that displays HTML in the browser. The considerations for other styles of web-deployed code, such as servlets, are similar to JSP pages. Therefore, the discussions about JSP pages in this chapter will apply for the most part to servlets as well. The material in this chapter serves as a foundation for the chapters in Parts III and IV of this book, which provide details about how to develop Java client applications and JSP applications, respectively.

This chapter also gives an overview of the deployment process in JDeveloper. In addition, the hands-on practices at the end of the chapter show one way to deploy a Java application and one way to deploy a JSP application. The practices should help you understand the deployment process and the many variations for deploying applications. They will also familiarize you with some of the necessary terminology. As with other practices in this book, the material in the practices is not a repeat of the introductory material in the chapter. Therefore, since all systems need to be deployed, the authors recommend that you try the practices to help your understanding of the process.

Before discussing the specific styles of application development and deployment, it is necessary to briefly examine the features of J2EE.

A Summary of J2EE

J2EE is not a product. It is a combination of technologies and specifications that is available on the Sun Microsystems website. Many vendors including Oracle have seen the value of the direction that J2EE provides and have developed products that supplement or, at least, comply with the basic features provided by Sun. Two other Java 2 platforms offer some of the features of J2EE—Java 2 Platform, Micro Edition, and Java 2 Platform, Standard Edition. All specifications, guidelines, and Java language software included in these editions are available for browsing or download at the Sun Microsystems Java website (java.sun.com). The Sun website also includes free tutorials, quizzes, newsletters, and developer community forums that you can use to learn about the features of the Java 2 editions.

At the heart of all these editions is the Java language. At this writing, Java is available in version 1.4. Any version from 1.2 is considered "Java 2." The following sections describe the distinguishing features of the three editions.

J2ME

The *Java 2 Platform, Micro Edition* (J2ME) defines how applications are developed and deployed to devices such as cell phones, pagers, and personal digital assistants (PDAs). The keywords for J2ME are "small" and "light." J2ME supports client applications that have less than one megabyte (MB) of memory and/or a lightweight processor. Applications built with J2ME can be run on many platforms. More information about J2ME is at the Sun website java.sun.com/j2me/.

J2SE

Sun has also published *Java 2 Platform, Standard Edition* (J2SE), which consists of components such as the following:

- **Java language libraries** for writing and compiling Java applications and applet code in Java using Java Foundation Classes (JFC) Swing and Abstract Windowing Toolkit (AWT) controls.

- **Java Database Connectivity (JDBC)** classes that provide a standard API to any database with a JDBC driver. Connecting to an Oracle database using BC4J or Enterprise JavaBeans (EJB) relies on these classes.

- **Remote Method Invocation (RMI)**, which allows your program to call operations available in objects in a different program that is running under another Java Virtual Machine potentially on a separate machine.

J2EE

The J2EE environment provides a corporation-wide (enterprise) strategy for distributing application code into a multi-tier architecture. Code may reside in the database, in application servers, or on the client. A variety of products and communication protocols enable these options. J2EE has several major components: blueprints, specifications, software, and an application architecture model.

J2EE BluePrints

The *J2EE BluePrints* provide guidelines and best practices for working with a specific environment such as enterprise, wireless, high-performance, and web services. These BluePrints are available online at java.sun.com. They discuss the considerations and requirements of the specific environment. BluePrints make work within a particular environment easier by explaining the features and services that you need to use for effective deployments in each environment. BluePrints include *J2EE patterns* (such as Data Access Object and Front Controller) that describe a solution to a common design problem. One of the most pervasive of all J2EE patterns is *Model-View-Controller* (MVC).

Model-View-Controller (MVC)   MVC is a pattern that was inherited from the Smalltalk language. It defines a rigorous separation between these three components of an application:

- **Model**   This layer represents the data and values portion of the application.
- **View**   This layer represents the screen and user interface components.

■ **Controller** This layer represents the user interface events that occur as the user interacts with the interface (view).

The separation between layers allows the switching of one code layer without affecting the other layers. For example, if your application were built using the MVC pattern, you could switch the user interface from a Java application to a mobile cell phone interface and still use the underlying controller and model layers. This kind of flexibility is the key benefit of the MVC pattern.

The separation of layers also allows different developers to work on different parts of the application code. In addition, design work for data structures, interface screens, and processes affect the code in the model, view, and controller layers, respectively.

Another benefit of MVC is that testing of each layer can occur independently. Thus, the final code assembly requires only an integration test to ensure that the code works as a complete unit.

Specifications

The J2EE specifications describe all features of the platform and provide details about standards for security, transaction management, naming, APIs, interoperability, application assembly and deployment, application clients, and service provider interfaces.

Also part of J2EE are specifications for Java Servlet, JavaServer Pages technology, Enterprise JavaBean, JDBC, JavaMail, and other technologies. More information about J2EE is available on the Sun website java.sun.com/j2ee/.

Software

The software that comprises J2EE is primarily the Software Development Kit (SDK), formerly called the Java Development Kit (JDK). It contains development and runtime software for Java programming.

Application Architecture Model

J2EE provides a conceptual architecture model that is divided into multiple tiers, each of which is responsible for a specific function. Figure 7-1 depicts the architectural model. The model contains four logical tiers as follows:

■ **Client Tier** This tier, also called the *Client-Side Presentation Tier,* contains code and processes that run on the client machine and with which the user interacts. For example, this tier can contain a Java application that runs in a Java Virtual Machine (JVM) on the client and presents a user interface.

■ **Web Tier** This tier, also called *Server-Side Presentation Tier,* contains user interface code and processes that run on a common application server (J2EE server). For example, this tier can contain a JavaServer Pages application that constructs a user interface on the server and sends it to the browser on the client.

■ **Business Tier** This tier, also called the *Server Business Logic Tier,* contains data access code and, optionally, validation and business rule enforcement. This tier also resides on a J2EE (web) server. There is no user interface function housed on this tier.

■ **EIS Tier** The Enterprise Information System (EIS) Tier contains the persistent data storage mechanism—usually a relational database such as Oracle9i. The databases can be distributed across many servers, but all serve the function of an EIS server.

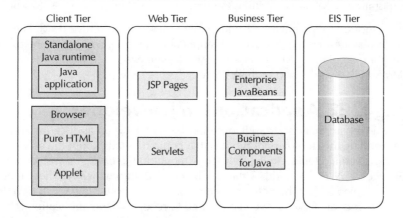

FIGURE 7-1. *J2EE application architecture model*

NOTE
The diagram in Figure 7-1 shows Business Components for Java
(BC4J) in the Business Tier. BC4J is a product of Oracle Corporation,
not Sun Microsystems as is EJB. BC4J can be deployed as EJBs, as
described in Chapter 16.

The J2EE tiers in Figure 7-1 show some examples of what the tier may contain. One
application style will use at most one part from each tier. Some application styles do not use
all four tiers. The discussions in this chapter of Java clients and JSP pages will use this diagram
as a basis for explaining the communications between tiers and the components used for each
application style.

Technologies introduced in the future should fit into one of these tiers. The reason that this
is a conceptual division of tiers is that a tier on the diagram does not necessarily represent a
physical machine. One or more machines could be allocated to each tier. Alternatively, tiers
can be combined on one machine.

JDeveloper and J2EE

JDeveloper provides rich support for all types of code that you can deploy into the J2EE tiers.
In addition, some specific features of JDeveloper categorize it as a J2EE development tool:

- The ability to create standard code that complies with the latest Enterprise JavaBean,
  servlet, and JSP standards.

- Wizard support to generate all deployment files required by the J2EE specifications.

- Full integration with Oracle9iAS Containers for J2EE (OC4J), a J2EE-compliant
  application server. This integration means that JDeveloper is integrated with Oracle9iAS
  because OC4J is part of Oracle9iAS.

- Incorporation of MVC as a coding standard for Java client as well as JSP applications.

- Wizard support to generate J2EE deployment files—Java Archive (JAR), Enterprise JavaBean Java Archive (EJB JAR), web application archive (WAR), or enterprise application archive (EAR). (WAR and EAR files are explained in the sidebar "EAR and WAR Files" at the end of this chapter.)

Deploying J2EE Applications in JDeveloper

You can deploy a web application from JDeveloper by setting up an application server connection, generating the deployment profiles that contain details about the server and the application, and selecting Deploy in the right-click menu. In the case of a web deployment (applet or JSP page), a WAR file and JAR file will be created automatically. These files will then be automatically copied across the network to the correct location in the OC4J or BEA WebLogic application server, and the server will be configured to recognize the application. The deployment process makes working with a J2EE server relatively simple. If your server is not OC4J or WebLogic, you can deploy to an appropriate JAR, EJB JAR, WAR, or EAR file. Since these are standard J2EE files, any server that is J2EE compliant will be able to use the archives.

The hands-on practices at the end of this chapter give you a feel for creating JAR, WAR, and EAR files in deployments created by JDeveloper. Chapter 16 briefly describes EJB JAR files.

Java Client Architectures

The term "Java client" refers to an application written in Java that is running in a JVM on the user's machine. There are two styles of Java client applications: Java applications and applets. Development techniques for Java applications and applets are discussed in Part III of this book.

NOTE
The terms "heavy client" and "rich client" have been applied to Oracle Forms running on the Web because the Java Virtual Machine runs on the client browser session. "Java client" is a bit different. Although you can run user interface code and BC4J code in the client browser's JVM, you can also run BC4J code in a JVM on an application server (not on the client). "Java client" encompasses that method of deployment as well.

Java Applications

The term "Java application" refers to a particular style of Java code. In Java terms, the code is really just an "application," but since that term is a common one in the IT world, it is usually preceded by the word "Java." A Java application runs on the client machine in a standalone JVM runtime process. The source code .java files are compiled into bytecode (.class) files and stored on the client machine, or on a local or wide area network server. No web server is required, and the runtime environment is located on the client machine outside of a browser. Therefore, a Java application runs using a typical client/server model.

Figure 7-2 shows one option for deploying a Java application into the J2EE tiers. As mentioned, other options exist for all of these styles of deployment. For example, the Java application could

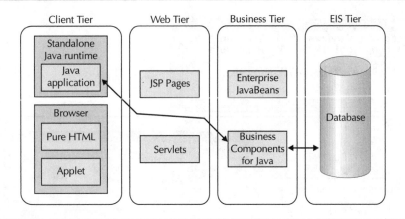

FIGURE 7-2. *Java application runtime architecture*

access data through EJBs instead of BC4J. (As mentioned in Chapter 16, BC4J can be also deployed as EJBs.) The arrowed lines between components represent the communication path. The Java application runs in a Java runtime (JVM) on the client presentation machine. The Java executables, application classes, and supporting libraries are all located on the Client Tier. The application communicates with BC4J business logic in the Business Tier. BC4J communicates with the database and sends data to the Client Tier.

The BC4J objects could also be located on the client machine, but this strategy does not allow them to be shared among users.

Calling Sequence

Java applications have a method called main() (as shown in Figure 7-3). This method is automatically executed when the class is run from the command line and usually calls a constructor. The constructor creates the first object, such as a frame. All requests for data flow from the application's frame through the BC4J layer.

To deploy a Java application, you install java.exe (the Java runtime JVM) and supporting Java libraries on the client machine. You also install the .class files for the application objects and set up the client's CLASSPATH so that the JVM can find these .class files. BC4J files are installed on the application server. To run the application, the user enters the following at the command line (or in a shortcut icon):

```
java deptemp.DeptEmpFrame
```

In this example, "DeptEmpFrame" is the compiled .class file inside the deptemp package (directory). This class contains a main() method that starts the application. The client machine would likely use a shortcut icon instead of requiring the user to type a command-line string.

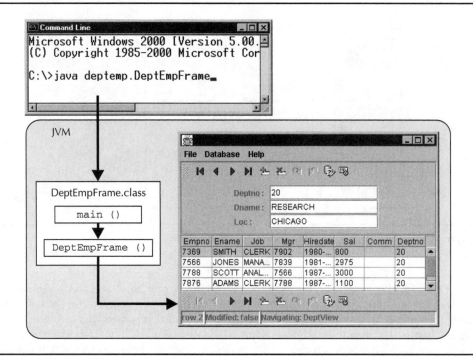

FIGURE 7-3.   *Java application calling sequence*

NOTE
Instructions for installing the JVM may be found in the install notes for the Java SDK. Additional information is available on the java.sun.com website (for example, at java.sun.com/getjava).

When to Use Java Applications

Use Java applications for intranet or small-department solutions with a small number of clients. As the number of clients grows, you will experience all of the same problems and resource drains as in client/server applications because, for each new client, a one-time Java runtime install and an application code install are required. If you do not want to worry about browser limitations and firewall restrictions and are able to easily manage local client installations, the Java application is the appropriate style.

In addition, if your application requires rich client controls that support rapid data entry and fast response from the user interface, a Java application might be indicated because it offers the rich GUI controls in the Swing library that are installed locally. A Java application also does not require a browser session as does an applet.

NOTE
The JDeveloper IDE runs as a Java application and provides a good example of the kinds of functionality you can build into Java applications.

Advantages of Java Applications

If you are accustomed to client/server deployments, Java applications provide you with an easy architecture in which to deploy Java code. The user interface responds to user events quickly because the code is running on the client machine. You gain all of the benefits of the Java language, such as object orientation and portability, without the need to learn to configure an application server.

GUI Controls   Java applications provide rich GUI possibilities. The available libraries of GUI controls, mainly Swing and AWT, provide all of the functionality of traditional windowed applications, but allow you the flexibility of modifying each aspect of the control.

Layout Managers   In addition to the AWT and Swing components, you can also use a Java feature called *layout managers* to manipulate components at runtime. A layout manager is an object that you define and attach to a container (such as a panel) using the *layout* property. It is responsible for resizing and repositioning the components inside that container when the user resizes the outer window. This is useful because you can deploy the Java application on diverse platforms and be assured that the layout manager will maintain your design regardless of differences in the hardware or JVM used for display. Chapter 20 discusses layout managers in detail.

Disadvantages of Java Applications

Java applications have no inherent disadvantages if they are used in environments that can benefit from their advantages and are not affected by the limitations of client/server environments.

Limitations of Client/Server Environments   Java applications run in either a pure client/server mode (where business logic is on the Client Tier) or in a variation on client/server mode (where business logic is on the application server, as in this example). Therefore, the characteristics of the client/server architecture must be taken into account when making the decision about whether to use the Java application style for deployment.

A significant problem is that runtime and application code must be maintained and installed on the client machine. WAN servers promise to ease this burden, but the reality is that they are often not responsive enough, so companies use LANs instead. The LAN solution for a large application is still not responsive enough and requires installation of the same code on more than one machine. This takes a lot of time and effort, as those who support client/server applications can attest. In addition, the client machine needs a large amount of resources because the application is running in its memory and using its disk space.

When the number of users grows, this architecture scales poorly. More users may require additional installations and further decentralization of the runtime code. Although the architecture makes no use of the benefits of web server technology for centralized installation and maintenance, the Java Web Start technology (described in the sidebar "About Java Web Start") greatly mitigates this effect.

Terminal Server Variation

Java applications can be run in a client's browser using terminal server technology (such as Citrix MetaFrame). The terminal server strategy is essentially a mainframe model. The client is a dumb terminal that presents a graphical version of the application that is actually running on the application server. Software installed on the client emulates the runtime display. The user can interact with the application through this emulator, but a JVM runs the Java application on the server. That JVM is the actual runtime session. The terminal server is just a Java application running on the application server that displays in the browser session.

Terminal server has all the advantages of Java applications and the additional advantage that it can be run from a centralized server location. The biggest disadvantage is that this solution requires extra software on both the client and server. Another disadvantage is increased resource use on the server, since it also uses a server session for each client session, which could be impractical for a large number of users.

About Java Web Start

The Sun Microsystems technology *Java Web Start* offers an alternative to other options for deploying Java applications. It is distributed with the Java runtime and SDK. Java Web Start relies on *Java Network Launching Protocol* (JNLP), a standard part of J2EE that uses an XML descriptor file on the server to specify details about how to start the application.

Once users install Java Web Start, they can download a Java application and its required support libraries by clicking a link in a web browser. This option provides Java applications with the ease of installation and code centralization that the applets strategy offers.

The client browser is required only to download the application. The JVM that runs the application is independent of the browser. Therefore, once the download is complete, the browser may be shut down, because the Java application will be running in a separate process, not within the browser process as is the case with applets. However, Java applications run using Java Web Start still execute in a restricted container that enforces the security model of the Java 2 platform just like applets.

JDeveloper supports deployment to the Java Web Start method. Select "Java Web Start (JNLP) Files" from the General\Deployment Descriptors category of the New gallery. There is also an item for "Java Web Start (JNLP) Files for JClient" if your project contains JClient objects. The Java Web Start Wizard will open. You need to have a JAR file containing all the application files before starting this wizard. The wizard steps through the creation of several XML files that are required for this alternative. The Java Web Start method will probably serve most of your purposes for client-side Java code. More information is available at the following Sun website:

http://java.sun.com/products/javawebstart/

Applets

Using applets is an alternative that leverages the strengths of web technology. When an applet is first run, the application files are copied ("downloaded") from the application server to the client machine and run within a browser session. In subsequent executions of the same version of the applet, the applet files that were copied to the client machine are run. Applets provide all of the functionality of a Java application, but allow you to maintain the application over the Web. As with Java applications, you are working entirely in a Java environment and can use JDeveloper to create the code.

Like Java applications, applets allow you to use the rich user interface components that are offered by Swing and AWT libraries. The applet differs from the Java application only in the way in which it is started (from a browser) and in the initial location of the code, which is an application web server. The steps in the applet startup and runtime processes are shown in Figure 7-4.

1. **The client browser requests an HTML startup file** from the web server through a standard URL. The HTML file may be static or dynamically generated from another application. It may or may not reside on the Web Tier, because the startup file is a normal HTML file. This HTML file contains a special applet tag such as the following:

```
<APPLET CODE = "dept.DeptEmp"
   CODEBASE = "/applet_code/"
   WIDTH = 250
   HEIGHT = 300
   ALIGN = middle >
</APPLET>
```

2. **The applet tag signals the browser to start an applet window** (within or outside of the browser window) for a JVM session and to load the application's .class file named by the *CODE* attribute. The applet tag's attribute *CODEBASE* specifies the location of the applet's .class files relative to the physical location of the HTML file. If the HTML file is in the same directory, the CODEBASE attribute is set to "." (the same directory). The CODE attribute

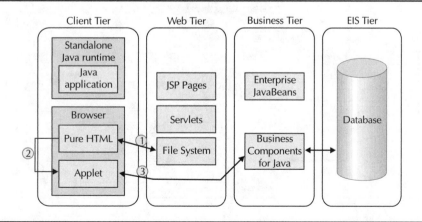

FIGURE 7-4. *Applet startup and runtime architecture*

finds a specific .class file in a directory listed in the CLASSPATH variable on the application server. The application's .class files and supporting libraries download from the application server and are presented in the applet window. The .class files are cached (in Java version 1.3 and later) on the client's hard drive for the next time the applet is run.

3. **The applet .class file runs in the browser's JVM.** This is the difference between applets and Java applications. The database communication occurs between the JVM and the Business Tier (BC4J components in this diagram) as with the Java application. As before, the applet could communicate to EJBs in the Business Tier.

Calling Sequence

The calling sequence starts with a URL in the browser to load an HTML file. The HTML file contains the applet tag that starts the applet window and downloads the class files if required. The applet JVM then runs the first class file and calls the init() method, which would present the user interface. Figure 7-5 depicts the calling sequence for an applet.

When to Use Applets

Also use applets within an organization. An applet gives you rich user interface controls without the overhead of maintaining a client/server environment. An intranet environment may also provide adequate bandwidth to provide a workable initial load time for large Java applets. Since an intranet system is a controlled environment, you will likely be operating behind the firewall, thus eliminating the security restrictions that are often applied to applets.

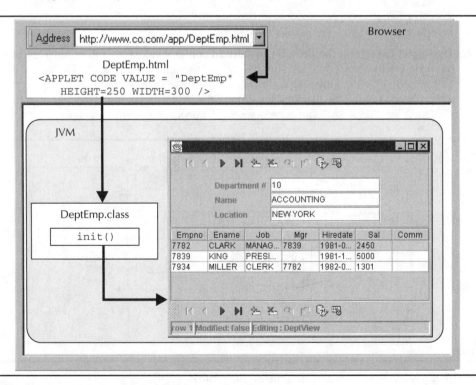

FIGURE 7-5.   *Applet calling sequence*

Advantages of Applets

For the most part, the same advantages that apply to Java applications apply equally to applets. An applet has the additional advantage of allowing you to use the web application server to store the code. As mentioned, Java Web Start technology diminishes this advantage because it allows Java applications to be installed from a server using a browser.

Disadvantages of Applets

Java applets require an initial download that can be lengthy. Once the application loads, the performance will generally be excellent. For e-commerce purposes, the load time for the applet is likely to be unreasonable.

In addition, the actions that the Java applet can perform on the client machine are restricted by the built-in security mechanisms of the browser, because the applet is executing inside a browser session. If those features are circumvented with security strategies such as signature files, Java applets can be written to perform tasks on the client machine such as reading from and writing to the file system. In many organizations, client machines reside behind a firewall that prohibits the downloading of Java applets.

Another disadvantage is that an applet uses an HTML browser to start the JVM. Some browser versions do not support Java at all. Other browsers do not support the Swing library libraries, which have more functionality than AWT libraries. AWT classes are fully supported in browsers, but require much more coding to connect to the data layer. The impact on applet technology is that you must ensure that your users can access and install the Swing library plugin offered by Sun Microsystems. This requires a one-time step to download and install the plugin.

JavaServer Pages Architecture

JSP pages are different in two basic ways from Java client applications:

- They do not require a JVM on the client.

- They output HTML (or other types of content) that is displayed in a browser.

JSP technology is an extension of servlet technology, so it is useful to briefly examine what a servlet is before discussing JSP pages. Development techniques for JSP pages are discussed in Part IV of this book.

A *servlet* is a Java class file that is stored and run on the application server and that extends the functionality of a server by providing extra services or application-specific logic. An *HTTP servlet* is a specific type of servlet that accepts requests from a client browser through an HTTP data stream (posted data or URL) and executes within a *container*—a service that can run code in a JVM. The *web container* runs servlets and JSP pages, and the *EJB container* runs EJBs. Each container runs the JVM and processes the target code in a specific way.

An HTTP servlet (or just "servlet" in a Java context) that is responsible for presenting a user interface can construct an HTML page by querying the database and outputting the HTML tags mixed with data from the query. The entire page is constructed dynamically by the program in a way similar to a common gateway interface (CGI) program.

The advantage of servlets over CGI programs is that they only require a new thread, not an entirely new process like CGI programs. This is a significant resource saver for the application server. In addition, unlike CGI output, servlets are cached, which provides performance benefits such as allowing the database connections to stay open. Servlets are coded entirely in Java and are therefore portable; they do not need a CGI language such as Perl.

JSP Technology Overview

JSP technology is a variation on servlet technology that mixes HTML and Java in the same source file. JSP pages have both dynamic and static elements, usually represented by the Java and HTML code, respectively. This allows developers to easily code the parts of the application that do not change. For example, the JSP code would include the `<html>` tag at the beginning and the `</html>` tag at the end of the page. It would also include all of the static links and boilerplate graphics and text.

A servlet has to generate these tags using a `println()` statement each time the program is run, whereas a JSP program represents the static tag exactly as it will be output. In reality, the JSP page is compiled into a servlet .java file. The clarity of the JSP code provides many developers with an advantage over the servlet style. In addition, because pure HTML code appears in the JSP page, you can use a visual HTML editor to work on the layout of the JSP page.

Here is an example of the default JSP code that JDeveloper creates when you select JSP Page from the New gallery's Web Tier\JavaServer Pages (JSP) category:

```
<%@ page contentType="text/html;charset=windows-1252"%>
<html>
<head>
<meta http-equiv="Content-Type" content="text/html; charset=windows-1252">
<title>
Hello World
</title>
</head>
<body>
<h2>
The current time is:
</h2>
<p>
<%= new java.util.Date() %></p>
</body>
</html>
```

This sample mixes standard HTML tags ("< >") and servlet tags ("<% %>"). The file extension .jsp indicates to the web server that the page requested is a JSP file. The web server passes the interpretation of the page to a *JSP container* (web container) program (also called a *JSP Translator*) that runs a JVM on the server. The JSP container creates a servlet file from the JSP code by adding `out.println()` statements for the HTML tags and adding print statements and other Java code for the JSP-specific servlet tags. The servlet is then run in the JVM, and the servlet output is sent to the browser as HTML.

Figure 7-6 shows the main elements of the JSP runtime architecture. The Web Tier runs the JSP container process and waits for a request from the browser.

When the request for a JSP page appears, the web server determines that the request is for the JSP container because the file name has a .jsp extension. The JSP container process (JVM) runs

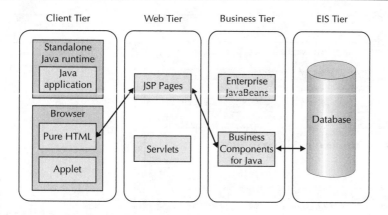

FIGURE 7-6.   *JSP architecture*

the application file and accesses the application code and libraries, as well as the BC4J code on the Business Tier. The BC4J files access the database. After the code is run and the HTML page constructed, the server sends the page back to the browser, and the browser displays it as it would any other HTML page.

The first time a JSP page is accessed, the server process creates a Java servlet file and compiles that file into bytecode in a .class file. For subsequent accesses, the .class file is cached on the server so that this compilation is not required unless the code is changed. The JSP container runs the .class file in its JVM session. The Java and .class files are generated dynamically from the JSP source code file. The BC4J layer sits on the application server and communicates with the database as in the other models. Figure 7-7 shows the various JSP code elements and the interaction with the browser. The dotted-line box represents a one-time compilation.

When to Use JSP Pages

Use JSP pages when your requirement is a simple, lightweight user interface client with no firewall limitations. JSP pages are best used to display data and interact with the user in an HTML environment. Use them anywhere you would use standard CGI-generated or static HTML pages. If you can restrict your application to the limitations of the HTML and JavaScript languages, JSP pages are a logical choice. Since this solution is more efficient on the server side than is a Java client application, you can support a large number of users, such as for an e-commerce application. If you are coding a heads-down, high-volume data entry application, JSP pages might not be as efficient from the user's standpoint as a rich client solution that uses Swing controls. Also, JSP pages are not the best alternative for executing extensive business logic because of the slight overhead they require to perform the JSP translation. Code on the Business Tier, such as BC4J or EJBs, is better suited to business logic.

Advantages of JSP Pages

The main advantage of the JSP method is that the output is standard HTML and is therefore compact and universally readable in any browser. HTML requires little from the client except a

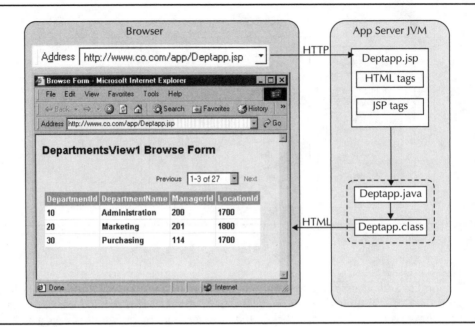

FIGURE 7-7. *JSP calling sequence*

compatible browser. There is no JVM running on the client, so there is no requirement for a set of Java runtime files or Java application files on the local machine.

The presentation look-and-feel of a page is embedded in HTML tags and *cascading style sheets* (an HTML facility for changing the appearance and formatting of common tags in a standardized way). Cascading style sheets are introduced in Appendix D. Since the HTML tags are directly embedded in the JSP source file, you can split the development work. A web graphics designer can use HTML to create the look-and-feel for a page, while the dynamic JSP-specific sections would be developed by a Java programmer. Merging the work is just a matter of embedding one into the other. JDeveloper provides the tools to create and test the JSP code. The web designer would work in another tool such as Microsoft FrontPage or Macromedia Dreamweaver.

Disadvantages of JSP Pages
The main advantage of JSP pages—that they output lightweight HTML—is also the main disadvantage. You do not use the feature-rich Swing (or AWT) controls to construct the user interface. The HTML language is not a programming language as such and has fewer features than the Swing controls for creating a user interface. In addition, simple functions such as scrolling down in a list of records, deleting a record, or changing the way information is sorted require a refresh of the page. You can embed JavaScript in the HTML page to enhance functionality if the users' browsers support JavaScript.

Additional Languages   Developing robust JSP applications requires that the developer (or at least someone on the development team) be skilled in Java, HTML, and JavaScript. For developers accustomed to using a single language for all coding, this will feel like a step backwards. Debugging is more difficult because the code is running on the server in the JSP container, although JDeveloper offers remote debugging features that assist in troubleshooting JSP applications.

The HTML limitation may not be important if you keep it in mind when deciding which technology to use for a certain application. Many HTML applications on the World Wide Web show reasonable complexity and suitability to their business functions.

Web Technology Complexity   Another disadvantage of JSP pages is in the added complexity of the JSP tags and the architecture. This extra complexity is not insurmountable and is made easier by J2EE servers and standards. On the development side, JDeveloper includes a number of wizards that help the developer quickly create basic data-aware JSP pages. The wizards help ease the learning curve that accompanies mastering the JSP tags. In addition, JDeveloper ships with the BC4J Data Tags Library (explored in Chapters 22–24), which provides a high-level approach to JSP tags. For example, one call to a single tag in this library, DataEdit, will build an entire edit form with a field for each attribute in a view object.

There is also added complexity in setting up the web server to support the servlet API and the JSP container.

Where Does OC4J Fit?

As mentioned, a container is a process running on a server that is set up to run a particular style of Java code in a JVM. For example, the JSP container is responsible for converting JSP code into a servlet, compiling the servlet, and running the servlet class file.

OC4J is a Java program that provides J2EE containers for Oracle9i Application Server (Oracle9iAS). A copy of OC4J is bundled with JDeveloper so that you can test code from within JDeveloper using a J2EE-compliant application server. This copy of OC4J is called the *Embedded OC4J Server*. You can also run the same copy of OC4J outside of JDeveloper as shown in the last practice in this chapter. The process of deploying to Oracle9iAS is the same as the process for deploying to OC4J.

Chapter 16 contains further discussion about OC4J and J2EE containers as well as practices for deploying BC4J to OC4J.

> **CAUTION**
> *Standalone OC4J is included with JDeveloper to help you test J2EE applications. Although it is a complete solution for testing and debugging code, it is not a production-quality application server. If you want to use OC4J in a production environment, you should use the copy included with Oracle9iAS. Other components of Oracle9iAS provide scalability and reliability features required by production deployments.*

Hands-on Practice: Deploy a Java Application

This practice demonstrates how to create a deployment profile and install a Java client application on a local machine. This practice deploys the Java application and its required libraries into a JAR file. The BC4J classes and other files are also copied into the same JAR file.
   This practice contains the following phases:

   I. Prepare a simple Java application

   II. Create a Java application JAR file

   ■   Create the deployment profile and JAR file

   ■   Examine the JAR file

   III. Install and test the JAR file

I. Prepare a Simple Java Application

This phase creates a Java application that you can use to test the deployment. It uses the JClient Form Wizard to generate a single table application. Refer to the hands-on practice in Chapter 1 if you need help with any of the steps.

   1. Open a BC4J project that contains a view object for the DEPARTMENTS table. This practice assumes that the name of this project is LocDeptBC4J.jpr. If your project has a different name, substitute your project name when appropriate.

   Additional Information: If you completed Phase II of the hands-on practice in Chapter 1, you can use the LocDeptBC4J.jpr project. If you do not have a BC4J project like this yet, create a workspace and a BC4J project (LocDeptBC4J) that contains BC4J objects for the DEPARTMENTS table. Phase II of the hands-on practice in Chapter 1 provides step-by-step instructions if you need help with this task.

   2. On the workspace node, select New Empty Project from the right-click menu. Name the directory and file "DeptJA." Click OK.

   3. On the project node, select New from the right-click menu. Double click the Form item in the Client Tier\Swing/JClient for BC4J node. The JClient Form Wizard will start.

   4. Click Next if the Welcome page appears. On the Form Types page, leave the defaults of "Single Table" and "Form" and click Next.

   5. Click Next to accept the default on the Form Layout page. On the Data Model page, click New to run the BC4J Client Data Model Definition Wizard.

   6. Accept all the defaults on the pages in this wizard, and click Finish on the Finish page. Click Next in the Data Model page.

   7. Click Next in the Panel View page after selecting DepartmentsView1. On the Attribute Selection page, all attributes should appear in the Selected Attributes pane. Click Next.

8. On the File Names page, change the *Package name* to "dept" and the *Form name* to "DeptForm." Change the *Master panel name* to "DeptPanel." Click Next and Finish.

9. Open the DeptForm.java file in the Code Editor. Find the call to `this.setSize()`, and change it to the following:

```
this.setSize(new Dimension(400,300));
```

This change will better size the outer window to the contents of the window. The new window size will be displayed in the UI Editor.

10. Run the DeptForm.java file. You should see something like the following:

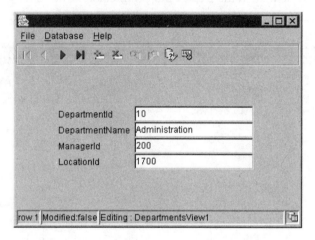

11. Navigate through the records to see that the database access works. Close the DeptForm window.

What Just Happened?   You created a one-table Java application that you will use for the deployment practice.

II. Create a Java Application JAR File

The next step in deploying the Java application is to create the JAR file that contains the required class files.

Since the main objective of the practices in this chapter is to introduce the concepts of deployment, this section uses the approach of deploying the BC4J project as part of the application's JAR file. This is called a BC4J *local mode* deployment and is fully viable in many situations. In production environments, you may choose to use *remote mode,* where the BC4J files are deployed on an application server to allow multiple users access to the same business logic layer. Chapter 16 discusses remote mode and provides examples of other options for deploying BC4J projects.

Create the Deployment Profile and JAR File

JDeveloper creates deployment files by default for some styles of projects such as JSP pages. There is no deployment file created for this project, so this section will create the deployment file.

1. On the DeptJA project node, select New from the right-click menu.

2. Double click the "Client JAR File - J2EE Client Module" item in the General\Deployment Profiles category.

3. In the Save Deployment Profile dialog, enter the *File name* as "DeptApp.deploy." It will be located, by default, in the DeptJA project directory. Click Save.

4. The Client JAR Deployment Profile Settings dialog will open, as shown here:

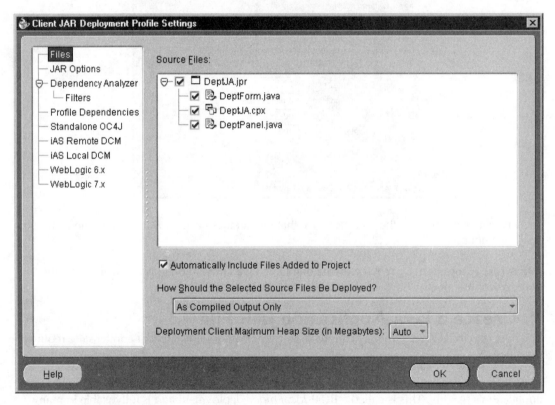

5. The default deployment profile settings are often sufficient for most deployments, but in this case, the profile needs to include all files that are required by this application. Therefore, you need to navigate to the Dependency Analyzer page in this dialog.

6. Check the checkboxes by the following nodes:
   JClient Runtime
   Oracle XMLParser v2
   JDeveloper Runtime
   BC4J Runtime
   Oracle JDBC
   Connection Manager
   BC4J Oracle Domains

   Additional Information: When you check a top-level node in this dialog, all files under the node are checked. The libraries you are selecting for this example are required to run the Java application and BC4J classes.

7. Leave the selection "Include All of Their Contents in the Output" selected. Navigate to the JAR Options page. Notice that the JAR file will be created in a subdirectory called "deploy" in the project directory (DeptJA).

8. Check the *Compress Archive* checkbox.

   Additional Information: This will reduce the size of the final JAR file (in this case, by about half), which will make copying the file faster. With smaller deployment file sets that do not contain all the base libraries, compression is not as important.

9. Click OK. The DeptApp.deploy file will be added to the project. You are now ready to create the JAR file.

10. On the DeptApp.deploy file node in the Navigator, select Deploy to JAR file from the right-click menu. You will see messages in the Log window that the dependency analysis is taking place and that the deployment process is creating the JAR file.

11. Click Save All when a message indicates that the deployment is finished.

Examine the JAR File
When learning how deployment works, it is instructive to examine the files that are contained in the JAR file.

1. Click the DeptJA project node and select **File | Open**. Click the Project button in the file dialog if the project directory is not open.

2. Uncheck the *Add to project...* checkbox so that the JAR file will not be added to the project, but will open in the Miscellaneous Files node of the Navigator so you can browse the file.

3. Navigate to the deploy subdirectory. Double click the DeptApp.jar file (not the DeptApp.jar folder). The file will appear in the Miscellaneous Files node and will open in a window such as the following:

Path	Date	Size	Compressed
C:\JDev9i\jdev\mywork\LocDeptWS\DeptJA\deploy\DeptApp.jar			
xdkjava_version_9.0.2.0.0_production	8/25/...	0	2
2.4.0.14	8/25/...	58	51
DeptJA.cpx	8/25/...	319	207
LocDeptBC4J.jpx	8/25/...	594	316
META-INF/MANIFEST.MF	8/25/...	64	66
META-INF/application-client.xml	8/25/...	302	206
TDGEngineApp$SymAction.class	8/25/...	1,195	634
TDGEngineApp$SymWindow.class	8/25/...	554	369
TDGEngineApp.class	8/25/...	6,598	3,115
com/sun/java/util/collections/AbstractCollection.class	8/25/...	2,678	1,386
com/sun/java/util/collections/AbstractList$Itr.class	8/25/...	1,735	914
com/sun/java/util/collections/AbstractList$ListItr.class	8/25/...	1,930	968
com/sun/java/util/collections/AbstractList.class	8/25/...	3,350	1,541
com/sun/java/util/collections/AbstractMap$1.class	8/25/...	977	470
com/sun/java/util/collections/AbstractMap$2.class	8/25/...	1,180	538
com/sun/java/util/collections/AbstractMap$3.class	8/25/...	986	473
com/sun/java/util/collections/AbstractMap$4.class	8/25/...	1,182	542
com/sun/java/util/collections/AbstractMap.class	8/25/...	3,703	1,719
com/sun/java/util/collections/AbstractSequentialList.class	8/25/...	1,810	854
com/sun/java/util/collections/AbstractSet.class	8/25/...	956	537
com/sun/java/util/collections/ArrayList.class	8/25/...	5,040	2,501
com/sun/java/util/collections/Arrays$ArrayList.class	8/25/...	884	486
com/sun/java/util/collections/Arrays.class	8/25/...	15,751	6,867
com/sun/java/util/collections/Collection.class	8/25/...	663	353
com/sun/java/util/collections/Collections$1.class	8/25/...	2,557	714
com/sun/java/util/collections/Collections$10.class	8/25/...	2,372	662
com/sun/java/util/collections/Collections$2.class	8/25/...	3,040	855

TIP
You can open any Zip or JAR file in JDeveloper by using this same technique even if you did not create the file in JDeveloper.

4. You will see more than 3600 files in this JAR file, including your application files, the BC4J project files, and all required library files.

Additional Information: The file size is more than 7MB compressed and would be more than 15MB uncompressed.

What Just Happened?   This phase created a deployment profile containing configuration information about the project. This deployment example creates a single JAR file containing the Java application classes, BC4J classes, and all supporting library files. This is a complete JAR file that only requires a Java runtime on the client. For production situations, the BC4J code could be installed on a centralized server so it could be shared. In addition, the client may already have installed the support libraries so they would not need to be included in the project's JAR file. If the support files were not required, the size of the JAR file would be greatly reduced.

III. Install and Test the JAR File

The last step in deployment is to copy the JAR file to the client machine. In this section, you will copy it to a new directory on your machine and test the installation. This will emulate the process of a new installation on a client machine. JDeveloper contains a copy of the Java runtime environment, so you already have a JVM available to you. If you were copying to another machine, that machine would need to have the Java SDK from Sun Microsystems (or another source) installed.

I. Start a command-line window by selecting **Start | Run** from the Windows start menu, entering "CMD" in the *Open* field, and clicking OK.

> **Additional Information:**   As mentioned, this practice assumes that you are running Windows 2000 or Windows NT. Adjust these instructions if your operating system is different.

2. Create a directory for test purposes and change to that directory:

```
mkdir TestJA

cd TestJA
```

3. Set your PATH environment variable so that the Java executables in the JDeveloper installation directory are available to the command-line window. All settings that you make to the PATH will apply only to the current command-line session. Use a command such as:

```
PATH=C:\JDev9i\jdk\bin
```

Substitute for "C:\JDev9i" the drive and directory into which you installed JDeveloper. This will override the list of directories currently in your PATH. Since you will only be performing Java calls in this window, you do not need the other directories.

4. Test the PATH by entering the following command:

```
java -version
```

5. You should see a message stating the version of Java. If not, check that the directory you entered in the PATH statement exists and contains the Java executable files.

6. Copy the DeptApp.jar file from the JDEV_HOME\ C:\JDev9i\jdev\mywork\LocDeptWS\DeptJA\deploy directory to the TestJA directory. Substitute applicable workspace and project directory names if appropriate to your installation. You may find it easier to use Windows Explorer to perform this task. The command line (if your JDEV_HOME were "C:\JDev9i") would be

```
copy C:\JDev9i\jdev\mywork\LocDeptWS\DeptJA\deploy\DeptApp.jar
```

7. Set the CLASSPATH variable for this command-line session by entering the following at the command line:

```
SET CLASSPATH=DeptApp.jar
```

> **Additional Information:**   If you had a CLASSPATH environment variable already set for your system, this command would overwrite it for this command-line session. As with

the PATH setting entered earlier, the SET CLASSPATH command only changes the CLASSPATH for this command-line session.

As mentioned in Chapter 4, the *CLASSPATH environment variable* specifies the names of directories as well as JAR and Zip files containing the classes that are required for an application at runtime. The Java engine reads this variable and locates classes within the directories and archive files by examining the subdirectories or package directory names in the archives.

8. Enter the following at the command line:

```
java dept.DeptForm
```

This should start the Java application that you developed earlier in this practice.

CAUTION
The Java runtime engine (java.exe) is case sensitive. Therefore, you need to enter the file and package names on the command line with the same case as you used to construct the application.

Additional Information: This command runs the Java Virtual Machine ("java.exe") whose directory you added to the execution path. This proves that you need no files other than those in the Java installation directory and in the JAR file. The "dept" prefix to DeptForm specifies the package in which the form file resides in the JAR file.

If you have problems with this command, check that the package statement at the beginning of the DeptForm and DeptPanel files is "dept." If not, use the package name in those files on the command line. If you get a message about a class that is not found, return to the deployment profile Dependency Analyzer page to check that you have included all required files.

TIP
The command line shown before disables the command-line window while the Java application is active. If you want to have control returned to the command-line window while the Java application is running, precede the command with "start." This will create a separate command-line session and run the command that follows it. Therefore, if you use the command "start /b java dept.DeptForm," a separate session will open, although you will not see the command-line window because of the "/b" parameter. The window from which you issued the command will have control returned to it immediately so you can enter other commands even if the Java runtime remains open.

What Just Happened?   In this section, you installed the JAR file and ran the Java application that it contains. Running the program required setting the executable PATH and the Java library CLASSPATH environment variables. The command line for entering the command was simple, but the setup commands are more than most users would want to type. You can create a Windows shortcut that executes the setup and runtime commands to make it easier for users. The sidebar "Creating a Java Application Shortcut" describes the method for defining a shortcut.

Creating a Java Application Shortcut

It is unreasonable to expect users to enter command-line commands. You can create a shortcut for your application that runs a batch file with the required commands so that the user can just double click the shortcut to start the application. The process of creating a batch file and shortcut for the Java application is no different from creating a shortcut for any other Windows command-line program.

1. You first need to create a batch file that will set the PATH and CLASSPATH and run the application within the same session.

2. Select **Start** | **Run** from the Windows Start menu. In the Open field, enter "notepad" and click OK. The notepad editor will open.

3. Type into the empty file the following:

```
@ECHO OFF
ECHO Starting the Departments application ...
PATH=C:\JDev9i\jdk\bin
SET CLASSPATH=DeptApp.jar
java dept.DeptForm
```

4. Save the file as "C:\TestJA\deptapp.bat".

5. Minimize all windows and right click the desktop. Select **New** | **Shortcut** and enter the following:

```
C:\TestJA\deptapp
```

6. Click Next and enter the name of your application (for example, "Browse Departments"). Click Finish.

7. Double click the new shortcut to test the application. The command-line window will open and display a message. The application will then start.

8. If you would like to hide the command-line window, select Properties from the right-click menu on the shortcut. Click the Shortcut tab and change the *Run* field to "Minimized." You can also change the icon associated with the shortcut in the Shortcut tab. Click OK.

Creating and Deploying Applets

Although the applet style of development is less common for new applications than JSP pages and Java applications, it is useful to briefly examine how applets are deployed. The concepts for deploying applets are similar to the concepts for deploying JSP applications, because both styles of code are run in a web environment from a browser.

Creating the Applet

You can create an applet file in the same way you create a Java application, by using the JClient Form Wizard accessed by double clicking the Form item in the New gallery Client Tier\Swing/JClient for BC4J category. Select Applet on the Form Types page, and the Java class will be built from the JApplet class instead of from the JFrame class (as is usual for a GUI Java application). You can run the applet class inside JDeveloper to test it, and you will see something like the following:

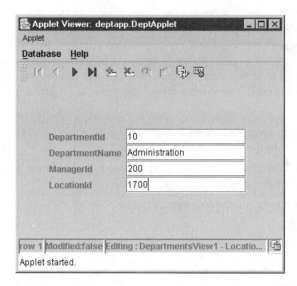

You can also create an applet class from scratch by extending the JApplet class and using the same development methods and components that you use for a Java application.

Creating the HTML File

You can create an HTML file that calls the applet using the Applet HTML File item in the New gallery's Client Tier\Swing/AWT category. This item starts the Applet HTML File Wizard, which creates the HTML file to start the applet. You can specify a template to use if you have created a template. The default file contains the `<applet>` tag that you could run from that HTML page or add to an existing HTML page.

NOTE
The CLASSPATH in the case of an applet is specified by code in the HTML file.

Deploying the Applet

The Applet HTML File Wizard contains a checkbox, *Create Deployment Profile for Applet,* that instructs the wizard to add a deployment file to your project. You can also add the deployment file using the New gallery's WAR File – J2EE Web Module item in the General\Deployment Profiles category. The deployment profile Settings dialog contains a page for Applet Options, where you specify details about the applet.

Since an applet runs in a web environment, you need to deploy the file to a server. If you have an OC4J server running and defined as an application server connection, you can deploy the files directly by selecting "Deploy to | <name of server>" from the right-click menu on the deployment file. This deployment process follows the same path as a JSP deployment. Setup of the OC4J server and deployment of a web application are described in more detail in the next hands-on practice. The deployment process creates the proper archive files for J2EE deployment and copies the files into the JDEV_HOME\j2ee\home\applications directory structure.

Running the Applet

The Log window displays messages about the deployment process. One of the messages indicates the root directory of the application that you can use to test the file. You can call the HTML file in your browser by using the URL supplied in the Log window. For example, if your workspace were called "LocDeptWS," your applet project were called "DeptAPP," and your applet HTML file were called "DeptApplet.html," you would call the HTML file in your browser using the following URL:

```
http://localhost:8888/LocDeptWS-DeptAPP-context-root/DeptApplet.html
```

If you see a gray box instead of the applet, it is possible that your browser does not support Swing classes. You can add the required support by downloading and installing the Swing plugin from the Sun Microsystems website at the following address:

```
http://java.sun.com/products/plugin/
```

This website also contains sample applets that you can use to test your browser's Swing library support.

Hands-on Practice: Deploy a JSP Application

This practice shows how to distribute JSP code that you create using the JDeveloper deployment wizards. The method described in this practice also deploys the BC4J files required by the JSP application. Chapter 16 provides practices for and information about how to deploy BC4J code in various ways.

JDeveloper contains support for deploying files directly to an OC4J server or to a WebLogic server. You can run the standalone OC4J included with JDeveloper in two main ways. When you want to use the JDeveloper IDE to test JSP pages, servlets, or applications that use EJBs, you run them within the Embedded OC4J Server. Practices in Chapters 1, 3, and 21–24 use this method. Alternatively, you can run these applications outside of JDeveloper using an OC4J (or other) server. This method allows you to access applications from outside of JDeveloper (even from across the network). This practice shows how to set up the standalone version of OC4J that is included with JDeveloper so that you can test your applications using the latter method.

This practice contains the following phases:

I. Set up OC4J

II. Create a JSP application

III. Deploy the JSP application

  ■ Create the application server connection

  ■ Define, test, and examine the deployment

NOTE
You do not need to use the steps in this practice for development work because the Embedded OC4J Server is automatically started when you run a JSP page from JDeveloper. This practice shows how to deploy the JSP page to a server outside of the JDeveloper IDE.

I. Set Up OC4J

For development and bugging purposes, you can rely on the JDeveloper Embedded OC4J Server. This server allows you to test JSPs in an OC4J environment without leaving the JDeveloper environment. To better emulate deployment to another server, this phase configures the Embedded OC4J Server to allow it to run outside of JDeveloper. This allows you to test the deployment files in a real server environment. If you have an OC4J server already set up with BC4J support, you can skip to Phase II of this practice.

NOTE
This practice assumes that you are working in an MS Windows environment. The steps will need to be altered appropriately for other operating systems.

   1. In a browser session, enter the following URL (location):

```
http://localhost:8888/
```

NOTE
You will receive an error that the page was not found. If you do reach a page, you already have an OC4J or other server running on the machine. Shut down the OC4J instance before proceeding.

   2. Start a command-line window by selecting **Start | Run** from the Windows start menu, entering "CMD" in the Open field, and clicking OK.

   3. In the command-line window, change directories to the directory in which you installed JDeveloper. For example, if you installed JDeveloper into "C:\JDev9i," enter the following on the command line:

```
cd \JDev9i
```

4. Enter the following on the command line to set the environment variables to point to the JDeveloper installation of Java:

```
jdev\bin\setvars -go
```

Additional Information: The `setvars.bat` batch file sets up a number of environment variables for this command-line session. If you had set variables for other installations of Java, this batch file would override them for the session. You need to rerun this batch file each time you open a command-line window if you need to run OC4J. The batch file ensures that the correct JDK will be used for the OC4J runtime. OC4J is already configured (in its applications.xml file) to read the BC4J base library classes.

5. Change directories as follows:

```
cd j2ee\home
```

You should see the name of the directory (JDEV_HOME\j2ee\home) in the command-line prompt. Enter the following command:

```
java -jar oc4j.jar -install
```

6. This runs a Java program that configures an administration user for the OC4J server. Supply a password for the admin user, and confirm the password when prompted. The OC4J server can now be started from the command line outside of JDeveloper.

Additional Information: You do not need to rerun the installation step again for the same installation of JDeveloper.

7. Start the OC4J server by entering the following at the command line:

```
start java -jar oc4j.jar
```

Additional Information: This command opens another command-line window (using the Windows `start` command) and starts the OC4J server. You will see a message indicating that the server is initialized, but no command-line prompt will appear in this window. Leave both command-line windows open.

8. Start your browser and connect to the following URL:

```
http://localhost:8888
```

The "localhost" portion of the URL points to your machine. The "8888" portion represents the port number to which the server listener is assigned.

9. You will see a page such as the following:

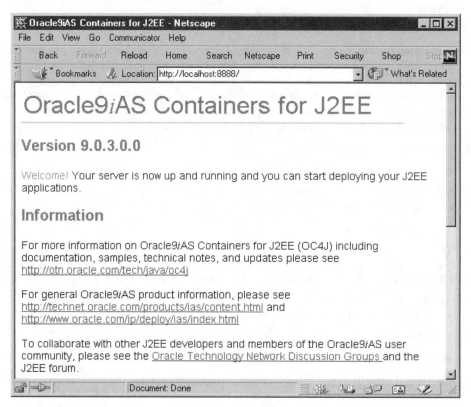

Additional Information: This page is the default connection page for the OC4J server. It is located in a file called index.html in the JDEV_HOME\j2ee\home\default-web-app directory. The index file contains links to a samples page for JSP pages and a samples page for servlets. These samples were developed by Sun Microsystems, and you can use them to test the server and capabilities of these styles of code. You can also view the source code from the links on the samples pages. A link on this page leads to the OC4J server documentation. All of these files are located in the JDEV_HOME\j2ee directory structure.

10. Leave the OC4J server running for now. When you need to stop it, activate the command-line window that you left running and that has a command-line prompt. Enter the following at the command line:

```
java -jar admin.jar ormi://localhost admin admin_pwd -shutdown
```

In this command, "admin_pwd" represents the password that you entered when setting up the OC4J server (step 6). The command-line window that showed the OC4J server initialization should close.

Additional Information: If the window does not close, switch to the OC4J initialization window, and press CTRL-C to stop the process and terminate the session. You can verify that the server has stopped by trying to connect to the welcome page.

What Just Happened? You installed the OC4J server outside of the JDeveloper IDE. This will allow you to test your deployment method and runtime environment. As mentioned, you do not need to go through these steps if you are just doing development and testing the code within JDeveloper. Also, if you have an existing OC4J server, you can use that instead of running through the process in this phase.

When you want to rerun the OC4J server, use the following steps:

1. Open a command line and navigate to the JDEV_HOME\j2ee\home directory.

2. Enter the command to set up the environment variables (`..\..\jdev\bin\setvars -go`).

3. Start the server with the command `start java -jar oc4j.jar`.

4. Test the server using the browser to connect to localhost:8888.

You can put these commands into a batch file that you run from the command line.

NOTE
You can check the version of OC4J by entering the following at the command line (after running setvars): "java -jar oc4j.jar -version". Be sure that the current directory is JDEV_HOME\j2ee\home.

II. Create a JSP Application

This phase uses the Data Page Wizard to create a browse page that you can deploy to the OC4J server. The first step in this phase is to locate or create a BC4J project that contains the DepartmentsView view object and a usage set up for that view object in the application module.

1. If you completed the application deployment earlier in this chapter, use the same workspace as you did in that practice so that the BC4J project will be available. You can then skip the next step.

2. Open a BC4J project that contains a view object for the DEPARTMENTS table. If you completed Phase II of the hands-on practice in Chapter 3, you can use the LocDeptBC4J.jpr project. If you do not have a project like this yet, create a workspace and a BC4J project (LocDeptBC4J) that contains BC4J objects for the DEPARTMENTS table. Phase II of the hands-on practice in Chapter 3 provides step-by-step instructions if you need help with this task.

3. Add an empty project to the workspace by selecting New Empty Project from the right-click menu on the workspace node. Name the project directory and file "LocJSP."

4. On the project node, select New from the right-click menu. Double click the Browse Form item in the Web Tier\ JSP For Business Components category.

5. In the Data Page Wizard, click Next if the Welcome page appears.

6. On the Data Definition page, click New to create a client data model if there is no data model in this project. Use all the defaults in the BC4J Client Data Model Definition Wizard and click Finish.

7. Select DepartmentsView1 on the Data Definition page, and click Next and Finish to create the JSP files.

8. Select DepartmentsView1_Browse.jsp and run the file. You should see something like the following:

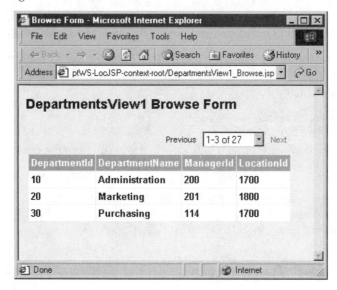

9. Scroll between the records to verify that the JSP page works.

10. Close the browser. Click Save All. Stop the Embedded OC4J Server by clicking Terminate from the right-click menu in the Run Manager tab (**View | Run Manager** displays this window).

What Just Happened?   You created a JSP application that you can use to test the deployment operation. Part of the deployment package will contain the BC4J files.

III. Deploy the JSP Application
Now that you have the OC4J server installed and running, you are ready to deploy the JSP application.

Create the Application Server Connection
The deployment features in JDeveloper require an application server connection. Like a database connection, an application server connection is a one-time setup step that you can use for all deployments to the same application server.

1. If you have stopped the OC4J server at the command line (not the Embedded OC4J Server), start it again using the technique described in the preceding phase of this practice.

2. Open the Connections node in the Navigator. On the Application Server node, select New Connection from the right-click menu.

3. Click Next if the Welcome page appears. In the Type page, enter the *Connection Name* as "LocalOC4J." Leave the *Connection Type* as "Standalone OC4J" and click Next.

4. Fill in the admin password, check the *Deploy Password* checkbox, and click Next.

5. Leave the defaults on the Connections page and click Next. The port number is not required because it is still the default of "8888."

Additional Information: Your machine name may show instead of "localhost" in the *URL* field. In the case of a local installation, it will not matter which name you use here.

6. Click Next. On the Test page, click Test Connection. If you do not receive the Success message, return to the previous pages and check your settings. When everything works, click Finish.

Define, Test, and Examine the Deployment

The Data Page Wizard creates a *deployment profile* that is used to define details about which project and library files will be copied to the server. The deployment profile is called `<project_name>_War.deploy`, where `<project_name>` is the current project. For this project, the file is called "LocJSP_jpr_War.deploy." You can examine its contents in the WAR Deployment Profile Settings dialog by selecting Settings from the right-click menu on the .deploy node as shown next:

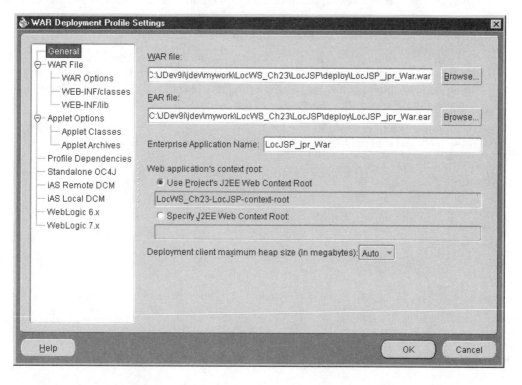

This section uses the deployment profile to copy files to the OC4J server.

1. On the LocJSP_jpr_War.deploy file node, select **Deploy to** | **LocalOC4J** from the right-click menu.

   Additional Information: The Log window will display messages about the progress of the deployment. One of the messages will provide the address that you can use to open the application in your browser.

2. Open your browser if it is not already open, and append the JSP file name to the address given in the Log window after a message such as "Use the following context root(s) to test your web application(s)." The full address will look something like this (all on one line):

```
http://localhost:8888/LocDeptWS-LocJSP-context-root/
    DepartmentsView1_Browse.jsp
```

NOTE
The port number may appear as "????" if the deployment process could not determine the port. Substitute your port number (usually "8888") for the "????" characters when you connect to the page in the browser.

3. The browser should display the JSP page. Open Windows Explorer, navigate to the JDEV_HOME\ j2ee\home\applications directory, and examine the files and directories.

   Additional Information: Figure 7-8 shows the files and directories created for the LocJSP project under the j2ee\home\applications directory.

   You will see a subdirectory named the same as your deployment profile (LocJSP_jpr_War) that contains a number of subdirectories and files. One of the subdirectories under LocJSP_jpr_War is a directory also called "LocJSP_jpr_War" that contains the JSP files and is designated as the *context-root* directory.

   The applications directory and its subdirectories contain a WAR file and an EAR file. These are standard J2EE files that are described in the sidebar "EAR and WAR Files."

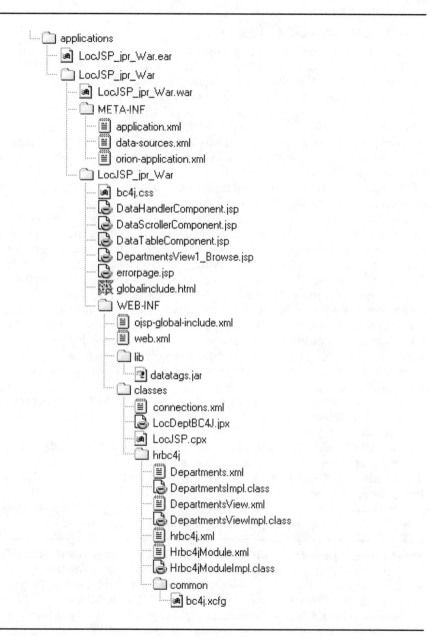

FIGURE 7-8.   *Files and directories created in a JSP deployment*

EAR and WAR Files

As part of the deployment process, JDeveloper creates J2EE standard *enterprise application archive* (EAR, also called "enterprise archive") and *web application archive* (WAR, also called "web archive") files. The *WAR* file contains all files required for the application's runtime. If the web application is a set of JSP pages, it will contain the JSP files in a root directory (that appears as a project subdirectory under the j2ee\home\applications directory). The WAR file also contains a number of files and directories inside a WEB-INF directory. These files are a combination of standard J2EE XML descriptor files (such as web.xml) and packages of BC4J files. The deployment process expands the WAR file into its component files and directories. A copy of the WAR file is kept in the project root directory.

The EAR file is used for standard J2EE deployments. It provides a single archive that contains all other archive and other files needed for an entire enterprise (many applications). The EAR file can contain one or more WAR files, JAR files, and EJB JAR files as well as several *deployment descriptor files* (files containing configuration information for a particular aspect of the server). One of these deployment descriptor files is *application.xml,* which provides the context-root virtual directory for one or more applications. You use this virtual directory to construct the URL for a JSP application. For example, the LocJSP project is contained within the LocDeptWS workspace. The connection URL for files in the application directory is http://host:port/ LocDeptWS-LocJSP-context-root/file.jsp, where "host: port" is the server name and JSP container port; file.jsp is the name of your JSP file; and LocDeptWS-LocJSP-context-root represents the context-root directory. For BC4J projects, application.xml contains a list of runtime files. Another configuration file in the EAR is *data-sources.xml,* which contains database connection information for the JDeveloper connections objects. The other deployment descriptor is *orion-application.xml*. This file provides application information to OC4J.

More information about deployment descriptors is in the JDeveloper online documentation node "Packaging and Deployment\Creating and Editing Deploying Files" in the help system Contents tab.

Both WAR and EAR files may be created in the New gallery's (**File | New**) General\Deployment Profiles node or from the right-click menu on a deployment profile (.deploy file). In addition, JDeveloper creates a default WAR and EAR when you select "Deploy to" from the right-click menu.

Java application and applet files contain .deploy file right-click menu options for JAR and EAR. The WAR file is not appropriate for a Java client deployment.

What Just Happened?   You deployed the JSP application to an external OC4J server. After the deployment profile is created, the process in JDeveloper of deploying to an external OC4J server is really only one step. The deployment process and OC4J handle compiling the JSP pages, copying the EAR file to the server, expanding the EAR and WAR files, and configuring the application in the OC4J environment. Deploying to a BEA WebLogic server is just as easy.

For other servers, such as Tomcat, you can copy the WAR created in JDeveloper to the webapps directory of the Tomcat server. When you stop and restart the Tomcat server, the application will be active. Some servers can accept EAR files (that contain the WAR files) for deployment. WAR and EAR files are created using the same right-click menu that you used when deploying to OC4J.

If the files you are using do not have a deployment profile, you can create one using the New gallery. Alternatively, you can select Create WAR Deployment Profile from the right-click menu on the web.xml (deployment descriptor) file that is copied into JSP projects.

NOTE
This practice has shown how to deploy JSP pages to OC4J. There are many other variations on deploying JSP pages to different servers. The JDeveloper online documentation contains extensive information about deployment files and which files are required for which servers and application types. It also describes the process of creating the required files in JDeveloper.

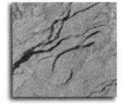

CHAPTER
8

The Class Modeler

I can't work without a model.

—Vincent Van Gogh (1853–1890),
The Complete Letters of Vincent Van Gogh, vol. 3, no. B19

s systems grew increasingly complex, a clear and concise way of representing them visually became more and more important. The Unified Modeling Language (UML) was developed by Grady Booch, Jim Rumbaugh, and Ivar Jacobson as a response to that need. In an attempt to create a single system for modeling and documenting information systems and business processes, the UML was created with an underlying object-oriented analysis and design philosophy. According to the Object Modeling Group's *OMG Unified Modeling Language Specification* (version 1.4), the UML is "a language for specifying, visualizing, constructing, and documenting the artifacts of software systems, as well as for business modeling and other non-software systems."

With the inclusion of part of the UML in JDeveloper, a question arises: Why is a modeling tool included in an application development product? The answer to this question is that JDeveloper is not simply a Java application development product. As mentioned in Chapter 1, JDeveloper is evolving into something much broader in scope. Model-driven design and development now have a proven track record of success. This is particularly true in the Oracle environment, where Designer set the standard by supporting all phases of the software development life cycle (SDLC). Since this was the case, why not simply expand Oracle Designer or at least use the familiar ERDs, function hierarchies, and module designers, and translate these into the Java environment? This could have been done.

However, JDeveloper includes a set of evolving modelers going in a new direction for Oracle, based on the UML rather than Designer-like ERD-based tools. Why was this shift necessary? First, there is a clear movement toward *object orientation.* Object extensions are creeping into relational databases, and programmers are leaning toward object-oriented programming languages. It seems to be the consensus of the IT community that an object-oriented (OO) way of looking at systems is superior to structural programming and data modeling approaches. The UML is the standard for object-oriented system design.

The UML is a collection of diagrams and standards that form a coherent framework for designing systems using object-oriented techniques. By switching its modeling standard to the UML in JDeveloper, Oracle accomplishes two goals. First, they adopt a rich, state-of-the-art, object-oriented standard for modeling the design of Oracle systems. It will take some time to determine how to best take advantage of this new conceptual foundation, but it provides much more flexibility going forward with JDeveloper. Second, the OO community already uses the UML for system design and programming. Therefore, by including the UML in JDeveloper, Oracle not only takes advantage of the experience of other products such as Rational Rose, but also delivers a product that is attractive to existing Java developers. This will be of great help to Java developers interested in writing applications that work with Oracle databases.

Out of the 12 UML diagrams, JDeveloper only includes modelers for class diagrams and activity diagrams. Discussion of the UML here will be limited to class diagrams. For a full discussion of UML and all of its diagrams, see the UML Documentation on the Object Management Group (OMG) website at www.omg.org.

Background

The UML is now the standard for object-oriented design and development. However, you must keep in mind that the UML was originally intended to support object-oriented programming (large C++ projects), and it fits best with that type of system.

This is not to say that the UML cannot be used for other purposes. A number of years ago, Oracle created the Object Database Designer (ODD) as part of Oracle Designer. Its function was to allow database designers to design and generate Oracle8 object extensions. In that situation, class diagrams (called "Type Models" in the tool) were used to support and generate database objects such as object types, nested tables, and VARRAYs. More recently, one of the authors has used UML class diagrams in conjunction with a business rules–based development approach to represent structural business rules and to generate relational structures. Other companies have used UML class diagrams to directly generate relational database tables, converting classes to relational tables and class associations to foreign key constraints.

Class diagrams have been used for purposes other than designing object-oriented programming classes. In particular, the UML Class Modeler in JDeveloper can be used to graphically represent BC4J entity objects and associations as well as Java classes and their associations.

Before launching into a discussion of the JDeveloper Class Modeler, it is important to understand some basic concepts about UML class diagrams, particularly as they relate to representing data structures. A more complete discussion of this topic can be found in *Oracle8 Design Using UML Object Modeling*, Dorsey and Hudicka (Oracle Press, 1999).

It is beyond the scope of this book to teach the complete syntax of UML class diagrams. However, a brief overview of class diagram syntax can be found in Appendix C. Keep in mind that the JDeveloper Class Modeler is not like the Oracle Designer Entity Relationship Diagrammer, where you can create a logical diagram that then translates into a physical model, and you can use the physical model to generate a SQL script that builds tables and columns. The JDeveloper Class Modeler actually generates code just as if you had created files in the System Navigator. If you have selected the *Automatically Generate Java* checkbox on the Model dialog, then when you create and modify classes in the diagrams, you are generating and modifying Java classes or BC4J entity objects and their associated Java classes and XML files.

The UML in Systems Development

The UML can be applied to two broad purposes. First, the UML can be used as a conceptual modeling language that allows database designers to represent their understanding of the design for a system. The process of translating these diagrams or UML documents into an actual system is the task for the IT professional.

Second, the UML can be used as a graphical front-end to generate code or other system elements. The tool's designers can explicitly define how each UML element will be translated into code and automatically generate code directly from the diagrams. This is how UML is used in the JDeveloper Class Modeler.

JDeveloper has six such translation mechanisms. One is based on a UML Activity Diagrammer that supports messaging and e-business integration. Its modeling and generation targets are Oracle Advanced Queuing (AQ) and Oracle Workflow with JMS access and XML message payloads.

This modeler goes beyond the scope of the book. The remaining five are associated with the Class Modeler and generate the following items:

- BC4J entity objects and associations

- Java classes or Java interfaces

- Physical tables in the database from BC4J entity objects and associations

- Enterprise JavaBeans (EJBs)

- Web Service

Some of these options will be discussed separately in later sections.

Objects within these contexts can have different meanings. In this book, BC4J entity objects and Java class support are both discussed in depth. Brief mention is made of table generation in Chapter 11.

JDeveloper Class Modeler Overview

The remainder of this chapter will discuss how to use the Class Modeler to create UML class diagrams. The sidebar "Techniques for Adding Elements to a Diagram" explains the four methods for adding items to your UML class diagrams.

Techniques for Adding Elements to a Diagram

Entity objects can be added to a class diagram using one of four methods:

- Drag the element directly from the Navigator onto a Class Modeler diagram. This is the simplest method.

- Create an entity object or class as you normally would in the Navigator using one of the BC4J wizards, and then select Add to Diagram from the right-click menu on the class diagram. Use the Add to Diagram dialog to expand the Business Components node and select the appropriate package. Expand the package node to select the desired element(s) from within the same project.

- Expand the Connections, Database, and Tables nodes, respectively, in the Navigator, and select and drag the desired tables onto the diagram. This will create BC4J entities.

- Use the Component Palette. Select the Entity Object icon, and click the diagram where you want it to appear.

TIP

In any of the Class Modeler Component Palette pages, you can "pin" the button icons so that you can create more than one element without reselecting the button icon. You can do this by holding the SHIFT *key while clicking the mouse button.*

Starting a Diagram

To create a class diagram, select a project node (.jpr) in the Navigator, and select New UML Diagram from the right-click menu. This opens the Class Model window and Component Palette. If the diagram is in a workspace with an existing BC4J components package, it creates a second package icon in the Navigator shown here to hold the Class Diagram file and all of the elements added to the diagram:

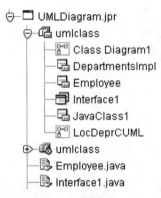

You can also open an existing diagram by selecting a project node and using **File | Open** or the "Open or create a file" icon to navigate to the desired diagram file. Objects can then be selected and dragged onto blank spaces in the diagram from several locations.

A sample class diagram session based on the LocDeptBC4J project created in the hands-on practice in Chapter 1 is shown in Figure 8-1.

Class Modeler Window Icons

There are five tiny icons (buttons) at the bottom of the diagram window as shown here:

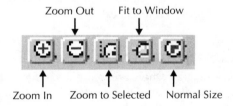

From left to right, the icon functionality is as follows:

■ **Zoom In (+ sign)**   Enlarges the view of the diagram

■ **Zoom Out (– sign)**   Allows you to see more of the diagram on the screen

■ **Zoom to Selected**   Fills the modeler window with the selected object

■ **Fit to Window**   Fits the entire diagram in the modeler window

■ **Normal Size**   Returns the diagram to its original size

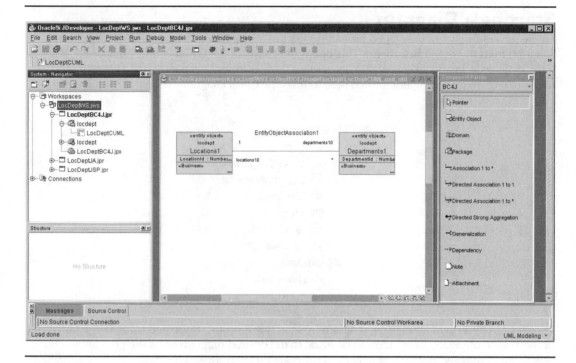

FIGURE 8-1. *Sample class diagram*

TIP
*You can change the visual attributes for all new elements in the diagram in the pages under the UML Diagram\Class Diagram node of the Preferences dialog (**Tools | Preferences**).*

Class Diagram Component Palettes

When you create a UML class diagram, there are four class modeler pages in the Component Palette for adding elements to the diagram. Once created in the diagram, all elements can be edited by double clicking on them.

BC4J Component Palette Page

The BC4J Component Palette page shown here is used to add entity objects, domains, and packages to the class diagram, along with the associations among these elements:

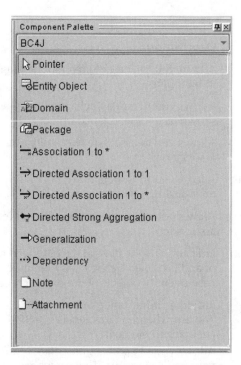

Table 8-1 lists the BC4J Component Palette elements with a brief description of their purpose and default colors. Note that all solid diagram elements and shapes are created using a default color. As mentioned in the preceding tip, these are fully customizable in the Preferences dialog (**Tools | Preferences**).

Diagram Element	Description
Pointer	Used to select items as in most applications.
Entity Object	Allows you to add an entity object to the diagram. Entity objects are shown in gray.

TABLE 8-1.   *Class Modeler BC4J Component Palette Page*

Diagram Element	Description
Domain	Allows you to add a domain to the diagram. Domains are shown in light pink.
Package	Allows you to add a package to the diagram. Packages are shown as a folder-shaped object in light orange.
Association 1 to *	Allows you to associate two entity objects with a one-to-many association.
Directed Association 1 to 1	Allows you to associate two entity objects with a one-to-one relationship.
Directed Association 1 to *	Allows you to associate two entity objects with a one-to-many association.
Directed Strong Aggregation	Indicates that the class at the other end of the association is a part of and is owned by the class identified by this association. In the case of entity objects, it denotes a cascade delete capability.
Generalization	Indicates inheritance between the connected elements. The arrowhead on the generalization line points toward the generalized element. Allows you to apply an inheritance structure between the connected elements. The arrowhead on the generalization line points toward the generalized element. Also referred to as "specialization," it depends which way you read the model. Manager and Salesperson are specializations of Employee and will inherit its attributes and behavior, while Employee is a generalization of Manager and Salesperson.
Dependency	Used to indicate that changes to one element will affect the dependent element. This has no effect on elements.
Note	Places a bright yellow area on the diagram to allow you to add any extra textual information to the diagram or elements on it. You can attach a note to any element on a diagram (see the Attachment icon next), but the attachment has no additional effect on the element concerned.
Attachment	Allows you to attach a note to another diagram element. Like the Note, this is for documentation purposes only.

TABLE 8-1. *Class Modeler BC4J Component Palette Page* (continued)

EJB Component Palette Page

The EJB Component Palette page is used to add beans and bean-related elements to a class diagram as well as to define the relationships between these elements, as shown here:

Table 8-2 lists the elements available on the EJB Component Palette. Note that relationships can only be created between Entity Beans.

Diagram Element	Description
Pointer	Used to select items as in most applications.
Session Bean	Opens the Enterprise JavaBean Wizard and places a representation (pink box) of the Session Bean on the diagram.

TABLE 8-2. *Class Modeler EJB Component Palette*

Diagram Element	Description
Entity Bean	Opens the Enterprise JavaBean Wizard and places a representation (green box) of the Entity Bean on the diagram.
Message Driven Bean	Opens the Enterprise JavaBean Wizard and places a representation (blue box) of the Message Driven Bean on the diagram.
Relationship 1 to *	Creates a one-to-many relationship between two Entity Beans.
Directed Relationship 1 to 1	Just as with Java classes, this creates a declaration of the second Entity Bean in the code of the first Entity Bean.
Directed Relationship 1 to *	Creates a collection on the "one" side.
Directed Strong Aggregation	Indicates that the class at the other end of the relationship is a part of and is owned by the Entity Bean identified by this relationship, and generates a collection.
EJB Ref	Used to connect any Bean to another Bean with a remote interface.
EJB Local Ref	Used to connect any Bean to another Bean with a local interface.
Dependency	Used to indicate that changes to one element will affect the dependent element. This has no effect on elements.
Note	Places a bright yellow area on the diagram to allow you to add any extra textual information to the diagram or elements on it. You can attach a note to any element on a diagram (see the Attachment icon next), but the attachment has no additional effect on the element concerned.
Attachment	Allows you to attach a note to another diagram element. Like the Note, this is for documentation purposes only.

TABLE 8-2. *Class Modeler EJB Component Palette Page* (continued)

Java Component Palette Page

The Java Component Palette page shown here is used to add Java classes, interfaces, and packages to the diagram along with the relationships between them:

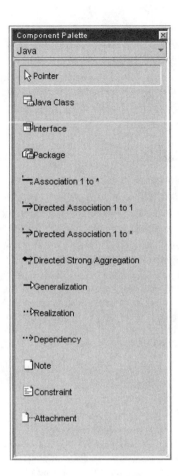

Table 8-3 lists the elements available on the Java Component Palette page.

Diagram Element	Description
Pointer	Used to select items as in most applications.
Java Class	Allows you to add a Java class to the diagram. Java classes are shown in pale yellow.
Interface	Allows you to add an interface to the diagram. Interfaces are shown in light bluish-purple.

TABLE 8-3. *Class Modeler Java Component Palette Page*

Diagram Element	Description
Package	Allows you to add a package to the diagram. Packages are shown as a folder-shaped elements in light orange.
Association 1 to *	Allows you to associate two classes or interfaces with a one-to-many relationship.
Directed Association 1 to 1	Allows you to associate two classes or interfaces with a one-to-one association.
Directed Association 1 to *	Allows you to associate two classes or interfaces with a one-to-many association.
Directed Strong Aggregation	Indicates that the class at the other end of the association is a part of and is owned by the class identified by this association.
Generalization	Indicates inheritance between the connected elements. The arrowhead on the generalization line points toward the generalized element. Allows you to apply an inheritance structure between the connected elements. The arrowhead on the generalization line points toward the generalized element. Also referred to as "specialization," it depends which way you read the model. Manager and Salesperson are specializations of Employee and will inherit its attributes and behavior, while Employee is a generalization of Manager and Salesperson.
Realization	Realization is used to implement relationships in the UML that specify that a modeled Java class implements a modeled Java interface.
Dependency	Used to indicate that changes to one modeled element will affect the dependent element. This has no effect on elements.
Note	Places a bright yellow area on the diagram to allow you to add any extra textual information to the diagram or elements on it. You can attach a note to any element on a diagram (see the Attachment icon at the end of this table), but the attachment has no additional effect on the element concerned.
Constraint	Allows you to add a restriction to a class or an association. Constraints are shown in gray with a turned-down corner. This has no effect on generated code.
Attachment	Allows you to attach a note or constraint to another diagram element. Like the Note, this is for documentation purposes only.

TABLE 8-3.   *Class Modeler Java Component Palette Page* (continued)

Web Service Component Palette Page
The Web service Component Palette page shown next can be used to add a web service element and dependency to a class diagram:

Table 8-4 lists the Web service Component Palette page elements. See Chapter 16 for more information about Web services.

Model Menu

You can make several categories of display modifications from the Model menu when working with class diagrams:

- **Align**, **Distribute**, or **Straighten Lines** options can be used to adjust the appearance of the model. The Straighten Lines option is particularly useful with complex models containing many objects and associations between them.

- **Bring to Front**, **Send to Back**, and **Minimize Pages** provide the standard Windows functionality for these operations. *Bring to Front* places the selected item in front of any other items on the diagram. *Send to Back* places the selected item in back of any

Diagram Element	Description
Pointer	Used to select items as in most applications.
Web Service	Opens the Web Services Publishing Wizard and places a web service (light blue) on the diagram.
Dependency	Used to indicate that changes to one diagrammed element will affect the dependent element.
Note	Places a bright yellow area on the diagram to allow you to add any extra textual information to the diagram or elements on it. You can attach a note to any element on a diagram (see the Attachment icon next), but the attachment has no additional effect on the element concerned.
Attachment	Allows you to attach a note to another diagram element. Like the Note, this is for documentation purposes only.

TABLE 8-4. *Class Modeler Web Service Component Palette Page*

other items on the diagram. *Minimize Pages* displays the diagram more compactly on the smallest number of pages.

■ The **Visual Properties** selection accesses the Visual Properties dialog, which allows you to specify certain visual display preferences for the diagram, enable the **Automatically Resize Shapes** feature (described in the section "Automatically Resize Shapes"), and set the diagram Grid Size. More information about the visual properties can be obtained by clicking the Help button on this dialog.

■ **Zoom** controls what portion of the diagram is visible on the screen at a given time.

■ **Node View** allows you to select between Iconic and Symbolic format for your diagram elements.

■ **Go to Source** is used to access the Java source code for the modeled Java classes and Java interfaces.

■ **Drill Down** and **Drill Up** functionality is used either for packages on a Class Diagram or for activities on Activity Diagrams.

■ **Publish Diagram** allows you to save your diagram as a JPEG (.jpg) or in Scalable Vector Graphics (.svg) format so that it can be used outside of JDeveloper in documents or web pages.

■ **Add to Diagram** allows you to access the Business Components, Library Elements, and Model Elements nodes of the Navigator to find the desired objects to add to your diagram.

■ **Show** gives you two options. **Show/Related Elements** adds elements that are connected by generalizations (one class extended by another) or implementation (a class implements an interface), and draws arrows from your existing Java classes in the diagram. **Show/ Implementation Files** creates a modeled Java class from the .java file that implements the entity object, for example, DepartmentsImpl.java.

■ **Generate** has a number of options. Diagrammed elements normally update or create code, so you would only need to access these items if the autogeneration feature is off.

   ■ **Java**   Generates the Java code for the Java classes or Java interfaces on the diagram.

   ■ **Java for Diagram**   Generates the Java code for all Java classes or Java interfaces on the diagram simultaneously.

   ■ **Automatically Generate Java**   When this option is checked, elements are automatically generated as soon as they are added to the diagram.

   ■ **Business Components**   Generates default business components for a selected entity object.

   ■ **Business Components for Diagram**   Generates default business components for all of the entity objects in the active diagram.

   ■ **Database Objects**   Generates the database object for the selected entity object in the active diagram.

- **Database Objects for Diagram**   Generates the database objects for all entity objects in the active diagram.

- **Web Service**   Generates a web service based on the currently selected class.

- **Stub/Skeleton**   Generates stub/skeleton code for the web service.

- **Sample Java Client**   Generates sample Java client code that uses the modeled web service.

- **E-Business Integration**   Used only for the Activity Modeler to visualize and generate the integration between e-business applications either within an intranet system or over the Internet.

- **Transform to Business Components**. (See "Using the Class Modeler as an Analysis Tool" section in this chapter for explanation.)

- **Publish Diagram**. (See the "Publishing a Diagram" section.)

Diagram Visual Properties

Within the JDeveloper Class Modeler, you can take advantage of the familiar visual editing behavior, such as snap to grid, of many drawing tools. To access this and other options, click any open space in the diagram, and select Visual Properties from the right-click menu. (A different version of Visual Properties is on the Model menu.) Select the appropriate diagram in the window, and you can modify the preferences for *Show Grid, Snap to Grid, Show Page Breaks,* and *Automatically Resize Shapes* using the checkboxes.

You can also modify the default visual property settings by selecting **Tools | Preferences**, expanding the UML Diagram and Class Diagram nodes in the Visual Preferences dialog, and changing the default preferences as desired.

Automatically Resize Shapes

If you activate the *Automatically Resize Shapes* property, depending upon what is displayed, the size of the class will automatically increase so that all sub-elements such as attributes are visible.

NOTE
When the Automatically Resize Shapes *feature is turned on, you cannot modify the vertical size of the class, but you can modify the horizontal size.*

Publishing a Diagram

You can export any diagram created in the Class Modeler to a .jpg file, a standard Internet graphics format. It also allows exporting to a .svg format, an XML Adobe Scalable Vector Graphics file that allows zooming and searching. To export a diagram, use the menu selection **Model | Publish Diagram**, or click a blank space in the diagram and select Publish Diagram from the right-click menu.

Importing a Diagram

You can import UML diagrams into JDeveloper by selecting "Diagrams from XMI Import" in the New gallery UML Diagram's category. The diagram must comply with certain standards as listed in the help system topic "Importing a UML Model Into JDeveloper" found in the "UML Modeling\ Modeling Java Classes\Importing a Class Model Using XMI" node of the Contents page.

Using the Class Modeler as an Analysis Tool

Java classes can effectively be used to do logical modeling. If you uncheck the *Generate Java* checkbox, no associated code will be created until you generate the class, so you can quickly and easily create classes and interfaces using the Component Palette and manipulate them within the model. Later, if you choose to implement the model, you can easily generate the Java classes.

Java classes can also be used to build BC4J entity objects in the Class Modeler. You can do this by creating a Java class and adding the appropriate entities and associations. When the logical model is correct, you can multi-select all of the objects for which you want to create corresponding elements in the BC4J layer. Each Java class will create a BC4J entity object. Each class attribute will create an entity object attribute. Select the desired objects on the diagram, and select Transform to Business Components from the right-click menu. You will have three alternatives:

- **Model Only** Creates the BC4J entity objects and associations, but does not place them on the diagram. They will appear in the Navigator.

- **Same Diagram** Creates the BC4J elements and presents them on the same diagram.

- **New Diagram** Creates the elements and places them by default on a new UML Class Diagram.

NOTE
The Model menu item "Transform to Business Components" is misleading since you are not changing the existing Java classes into BC4J components but actually are creating new entity objects and BC4J associations.

Class Modeler for BC4J

In previous hands-on practices in this book, you learned how to build a BC4J project using the wizards. As discussed in Chapter 3, a BC4J project is really composed of two different areas: entity objects and their associations, and views and view links. The JDeveloper Class Modeler only supports entity objects and associations. BC4J classes can be dragged from the Navigator to create a class diagram as shown next:

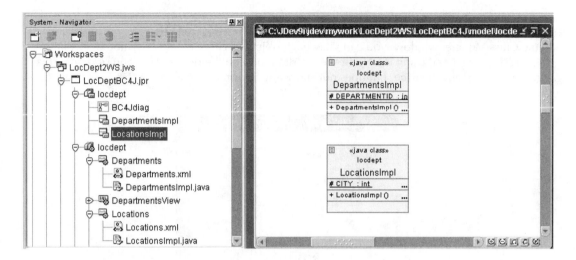

There must be a database connection for a diagram that includes BC4J elements. If you drag tables onto the diagram, they must come from the schema to which the diagram is connected. You can tell what connection your BC4J project is using by looking at the Structure window after clicking the .jpx file in the BC4J project. When you create a UML Class Diagram, it must be in a package.

To create a BC4J class diagram, you should first have a BC4J project. (See the hands-on practices in Chapters 1 and 3 for the detailed steps to create a BC4J project.) Since the diagram exists within a BC4J project, the only elements you will create are entity objects and associations.

When you create a BC4J entity object class in a diagram, JDeveloper automatically creates the associated BC4J entity object class file. Modifications to the diagram elements are also made to the BC4J elements. However, the BC4J Java classes for the BC4J entity object are not automatically created if you create the BC4J entity object from the Component Palette. If you use this method, in order to create the associated Java class, you must select **Generate | Business Components** from the right-click menu.

Creating a BC4J entity object on a diagram is the same as creating it from the Navigator using the Entity Object Wizard. Because the entity object on the diagram is simply a visualization of the entity object itself, modifications to the diagram elements instantly appear in the BC4J definition in the Navigator, and in its XML and Java code artifacts.

BC4J entity object classes associated with generated Java classes will be flagged with a rectangular icon in the upper-left corner of the class in the model window.

Class Modeler Window for BC4J Diagrams

In the Class Modeler window, you can view each object in either iconic or symbolic format by clicking the object and using the Node View radio group on the right-click menu. *Iconic* format is more aesthetically pleasing, but does not show any information except for the class name as shown here:

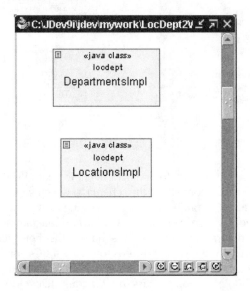

Symbolic format shown next includes the attributes, methods, keywords, and constraints associated with the class. An ellipsis (seen in the DepartmentsImpl object) indicates that there is more text that is not visible without expanding the object. What appears with the class can be manipulated using the Visual Properties window. Color and font preferences can also be set using the Visual Properties dialog. Just as in the BC4J Class Modeler, you can view objects in either iconic or symbolic format.

```
┌─────────────────────────────────────────────────────────┐
│ ▤                          «java class»                   │
│                              locdept                       │
│                         DepartmentsImpl                    │
├─────────────────────────────────────────────────────────┤
│ # DEPARTMENTID  : int                                     │
│ # DEPARTMENTNAME  : int                                   │
│                                                       ...  │
├─────────────────────────────────────────────────────────┤
│ + DepartmentsImpl ()                                      │
│ + createPrimaryKey (Number departmentId) : Key            │
│                                                       ...  │
├─────────────────────────────────────────────────────────┤
│                                                           │
│                                                           │
└─────────────────────────────────────────────────────────┘
```

```
┌─────────────────────────────────────────────────────────────────────────┐
│ ▤                              «java class»                                 │
│                                  locdept                                    │
│                               LocationsImpl                                 │
├───────────────────────────────────────────────────────────────────────────┤
│ # CITY  : int                                                              │
│ # COUNTRYID  : int                                                         │
│ # DEPARTMENTS  : int                                                       │
│ # LOCATIONID  : int                                                        │
│ # POSTALCODE  : int                                                        │
│ # STATEPROVINCE  : int                                                     │
│ # STREETADDRESS  : int                                                     │
│ - mDefinitionObject  : EntityDefImpl                                       │
├───────────────────────────────────────────────────────────────────────────┤
│ + LocationsImpl ()                                                         │
│ + createPrimaryKey (Number locationId) : Key                              │
│ + getCity () : String                                                      │
│ + getCountryId () : String                                                 │
│ + getDefinitionObject () : EntityDefImpl                                   │
│ + getDepartments () : RowIterator                                          │
│ + getLocationId () : Number                                                │
│ + getPostalCode () : String                                               │
│ + getStateProvince () : String                                            │
│ + getStreetAddress () : String                                            │
│ + setCity (String value) : void                                          │
│ + setCountryId (String value) : void                                      │
│ + setLocationId (Number value) : void                                     │
│ + setPostalCode (String value) : void                                     │
│ + setStateProvince (String value) : void                                  │
│ + setStreetAddress (String value) : void                                  │
│ # getAttrInvokeAccessor (int index, AttributeDefImpl attrDef) : Object    │
│ # setAttrInvokeAccessor (int index, Object value, AttributeDefImpl attrDef) : void │
├───────────────────────────────────────────────────────────────────────────┤
│                                                                           │
│                                                                           │
└───────────────────────────────────────────────────────────────────────────┘
```

It is possible to add BC4J Java classes to the diagram. Also, if you have a project with both BC4J components and other Java classes, these can be modeled on the same diagram. In some applications, you may choose to have Java classes and BC4J components in the same project.

Class Diagram Behavior

You can draw five main elements in a class model: Java class, Java interface, BC4J entity object, BC4J domain, and web service. In the following discussion we refer to these as "node elements." When you add a Java class or BC4J entity object to the diagram, the symbols shown here indicate visibility (private or public) or access specifiers (package or protected):

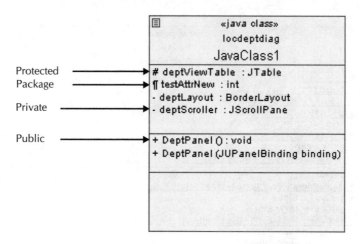

JDeveloper does not distinguish between diagrams that you create for class modeling or for BC4J modeling purposes. Thus, it allows you to create both Java classes and BC4J entity objects on the same diagram. While this is not a typical technique, it is possible to conceive of situations where a developer would want to do this. For example, you might want to create a BC4J entity object in a class diagram, and display the Java class that implements it (on the context menu, select Show Implementation Files). In this way you can view (and edit) the Java class that implements the BC4J entity object. You can even draw a dependency between the entity object and the implementation class if you want to.

BC4J Associations

BC4J associations (between BC4J entity objects) can be created in UML class diagrams in the same ways as adding BC4J modeled entity objects described earlier. As previously mentioned, selecting Add to Diagram from the entity object right-click menu is one method. If you add entity objects that are already associated with other entity objects to the diagram, the associations will *not* automatically be added.

If you create entity objects by dragging tables from the database when these are already associated because of existing foreign key constraints, the association that represents the foreign key constraint will automatically be copied onto the diagram. You can drag onto the diagram an existing association from the BC4J package that links two entity objects already on the diagram. You can also use any of the association type icons on the BC4J page of the Component Palette to connect two BC4J entity objects on the class diagram.

Once the association is represented on the diagram, you can double click it to open the Association dialog and specify or modify the association. If you create the associations between BC4J entity object classes using the Component Palette, JDeveloper creates a BC4J association between the two entity objects. The name of the association in the diagram is also the name of the BC4J association.

Association Roles

The association roles (words at the ends of the association line) are also the names of the accessors if you choose to expose them. Accessors are exposed by using a directed association element. You can modify which accessors are exposed (show the association as directed) by double clicking the association line in the diagram to access the Association Wizard. On the Association Properties page, you can use the *Expose Accessor* checkboxes to make the association directed.

Composition, Generalization, and Realization

You may choose to use *composition* rather than simple association to improve the readability of your diagram. It also enables you to implement cascade delete, which is not available otherwise.

Generalization, or its inverse, *specialization* (representing *inheritance* in standard class modeling), can be used between entity objects to model a specific type of subtyping. Employee and Customer are both specializations of Person, so you could create three entity objects—Person, Employee, and Customer—with the last two having generalization associations to Person. These three entity objects would be implemented as three tables with the attributes of Person (the generalization) being "inherited" into Employee and Customer (the specializations). If you are familiar with the process of transforming entity relationship subtype structures into a relational table design, you will recognize this process as *multiple table mapping,* where each supertype and subtype entity is transformed into an individual table, and the subtypes "inherit" the common attributes of the supertype.

JDeveloper will not allow you to place realizations between BC4J entity object classes.

Notes and Constraints

You can also use the Notes icon on any of the Component Palettes to add optional text to your diagrams. The Constraints icon can be used to attach constraints to other objects by using a dependency line. These are purely descriptive elements that have no impact on either the logical components or the physical implementation.

Hands-on Practice: Build a BC4J Class Diagram

This practice is based on the BC4J project created in Chapter 1.

This practice consists of the following phase with three sections:

I. Create the class diagram

- Create the BC4J project
- Create the UML diagram
- Add entity objects

I. Create the Class Diagram

You will create the diagram representing the association between Locations and Departments and add the entity objects to the diagram.

Create the BC4J Project

Use the following steps to create a Class diagram based on the Locations and Departments project you created in Chapter 1.

1. Create a new workspace by right clicking the Workspaces node in the Navigator and selecting New Workspace. Name both the directory and the file "UMLClassWS." Uncheck the *Add a New Empty Project* checkbox.

2. Click the UMLClassWS.jws node and select New Project from the right-click menu.

3. Select Project Containing New Business Components under "Items." Click OK. Click Next if the Business Components Project Wizard Welcome page is displayed.

4. Name both the directory and file "UMLBC4J." Click Next.

5. On the Paths page, enter "umlclass" in the *Default Package* field. Leave the other default settings. Click Next and Finish. Click Cancel to exit the Business Components Package Wizard.

   Additional Information: The reason for exiting the Business Components Package Wizard is that when you are creating a Class Diagram using existing database tables, the associations between the classes will not be shown on the diagram if the classes have already been added to the project.

6. Click Save All.

Create the UML Diagram

1. Click the UMLClassWS.jws node and select New Empty Project from the right-click menu.

2. In the New Project dialog, name both the directory and file "UMLDiagram." Click OK.

3. Click the UMLDiagram.jpr node and select New UML Diagram from the right-click menu.

4. Select Class Diagram from the General/UML Diagrams category. Click OK.

5. In the Create New Class Diagram dialog, if necessary, change the package name to "umldiagram" and the diagram name to "LocDeptCUML." Click OK. A blank diagram space and the Component Palette will be displayed.

6. Click Save All.

Add Entity Objects

You can now add entity objects to your diagram. The representation of an entity object in the Class Modeler is divided into compartments (Name, Attributes, and Operations) as shown in Figure 8-2. For this practice, you will use the existing tables in the HR schema for your class diagram.

I. Expand the Connections\Database\HR\HR\Tables node of the Navigator. Hold down the CTRL key, and click and drag the DEPARTMENTS and LOCATIONS tables onto the diagram. Leave the default setting on the Create From Tables dialog and click OK.

Additional Information: This method is just like using the high-level Business Components Project Wizard as in the Chapter 1 practice that creates a BC4J project for the first time. Note that the association between Locations and Departments is automatically added as shown here:

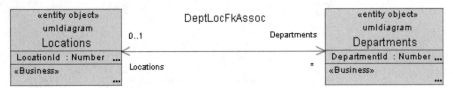

NOTE
If the model elements are not visible in the window, you may need to use the Zoom Out icon at the bottom of the modeler window and then reposition the entity objects.

CAUTION
If you drag the same tables into the same or another class diagram in the same project more than once, the association will not be re-created, and you will see an additional entity object with a number suffix in the Navigator.

Additional Information: The verb phrase for the resulting association between the two entity objects is the name of the association and is displayed on the association line in the Modeler. There is no logical directionality (arrow) on the association. Role names are the names of the accessor methods. Further details about the accessor methods can be found in Chapter 10.

Arrows appear on the line when the accessors are flagged as "exposed." BC4J entity objects appear as classes with an <<entity object>> stereotype. For details about UML class diagram syntax, see Appendix C.

The diagram can appear cluttered with more information visually displayed than is desired. For example, to suppress the display of operations, select a class (or CTRL-click to select multiple classes), and select Visual Properties from the right-click menu. In the Visual Properties dialog, uncheck Show Operations. Click OK.

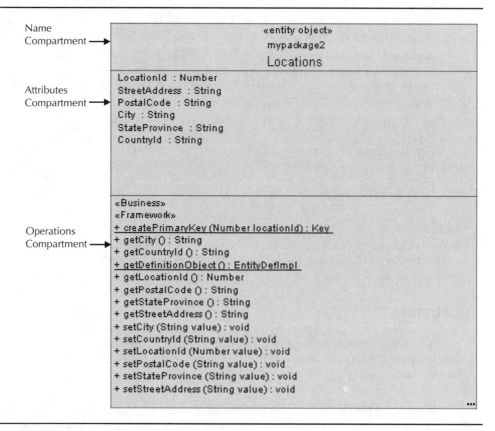

FIGURE 8-2. *Entity object representation in Class Modeler*

TIP
*You can also change what is shown with attributes and other visual properties using the Visual Properties dialog. The elements can be sized appropriately by manually adjusting the handles. When multiple objects are selected, you can also use **Model | Align** (or Align from the right-click menu) to access alignment and size adjustment. Vertical and horizontal distribution can also be managed from the right-click or Model menus.*

2. If necessary, adjust the association line by dragging the handles or by selecting the line and then selecting the Straighten Lines option from the right-click menu.

    Additional Information: If you select an attribute in the diagrammer, the location of the Java class from which the attribute is typed appears. You can change this by typing in another valid class. For example, the attribute "EmployeeId : Number" becomes "EmployeeId : oracle.jbo.domain.Number" when selected. This is also true for attributes in Java classes, Java interfaces, and BC4J domains.

TIP
Entity objects can be renamed in the Class Modeler by clicking the name field and typing in the new name. Most other names in the diagram can be changed in the same way.

What Just Happened?   You created a UML class diagram for a BC4J project and added Location and Department entity objects and their associations to it by dragging the tables from which the entity objects were built into the diagram. This is probably the most natural use of the Class Modeler, namely, starting with the database and directly creating BC4J entity objects by dragging in the database tables. This is a particularly useful technique for documentation of BC4J projects. You can also first create the BC4J entity objects and drag them onto the diagram.

Class Modeler for Java Elements

The Oracle9i JDeveloper Class Modeler is also a Java class modeler. In addition to modeling BC4J elements, it can also be used to create and manage Java classes, packages, and interfaces. When using the Class Modeler on BC4J objects, you can do various things in UML, some of which affect your code.

Java Code Generation

When you are working with the Class Modeler, it is important to decide whether you want the items you create in the diagram to automatically generate code. You may want to work with the diagram first before allowing the code to be generated. This option is controlled in the diagram right-click menu by selecting **Generate | Automatically Generate Java** and checking the *Automatically Generate Java* checkbox. For the hands-on practices in this chapter, assume that this checkbox is checked.

By judicious positioning of the diagram and the Code Editor, you can see how changes to either code or model are propagated between the two representations.

Java Classes

You can actually create a Java class on the diagram using the Class Modeler. However, this does not necessarily create the Java class unless the *Automatically Generate Java* checkbox is checked. It only creates a modeled representation of the Java class. Just as with the BC4J entity object class, it will appear under the package where the diagram resides. However, if you specify the UML diagram in the same package as the BC4J entity objects, a second representation of the package will be created when the entity object is created. To avoid confusion, you should specify a different package for the diagrams than is specified for the BC4J project.

> **NOTE**
> *In the Properties tabbed interface accessible by right-clicking a class in the Navigator, the "Namespace" field represents the diagram package.*

Assuming that the *Automatically Generate Java* checkbox is checked, any modifications to the class on the diagram will immediately be reflected in the model. When you generate a Java class from the Modeler, the class is created as a file in the appropriate package. Once the class is created, it can be manipulated like any other class by use of the Class Editor. Invoke the editor from a diagram by selecting the class and clicking Go To Source from the right-click menu. This loads the Java class file and invokes an editor window. From the Navigator, select the Java class source (<className>.java), and select Class Editor from the right-click menu.

You can manipulate the class-generated code in two ways. First, you can position the arrow in a blank area of the Java class on the diagram and double click or select Properties from the right-click menu. This will open a multi-tabbed property interface. You can use the context-sensitive Help button for additional information about the functionality on each tab. This same tabbed interface can also be accessed by selecting a .java file from the Navigator and selecting Properties from the right-click menu.

The second way to modify a Java class is by using the Class Editor. The Class Editor is accessed by right-clicking on a .java file in the Navigator and selecting Class Editor. The Class Editor contains a different set of tabs from the Properties interface that allows you to add, remove, or edit fields and methods as well as control which AWT or Swing events are fired. You can also import an existing event set using the Class Editor.

Creating a class in the Modeler defaults a number of properties that you might want control over initially. Creating them from the Navigator allows you to use the New Class dialog to specify the Name, Package, and other elements. To do this, select the package (either the model or the code package will do), and from the context menu click New. This invokes the New gallery. Select General/Simple Files in the Categories pane and Java Class in the Items pane as shown here:

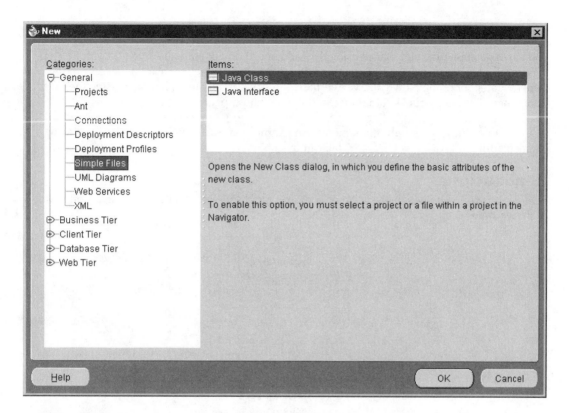

Once created this way, the class can easily be added to the diagram by clicking and dragging or by selecting Add to Diagram from the right-click menu in the diagram and selecting the desired class from the Model Elements node.

NOTE
If you select a class to add to the diagram that is already in the diagram, it will not be added. Each class can only be represented once in the diagram.

NOTE
Classes, packages, and interfaces found under the Model Elements node in the Navigator can be added to the diagram using the Add to Diagram dialog or by clicking and dragging elements onto the diagram.

If you add a class to a diagram that is an extension (subclass) of another class on that diagram, the generalization line connecting the two classes will automatically be added.

These different methods of adding and editing classes may be a bit confusing since there is some overlap of functionality. It is likely that later versions of JDeveloper will reorganize these different editing tools into a more intuitive user interface.

Interfaces

You can also create Java interfaces using the Modeler, then generate the Java as a second step. Interfaces can also be created by selecting **File | New**, then selecting Java Interface from the General category of the New gallery. Alternatively, you can create an interface using the Java Component Palette by clicking Interface and then a blank space in the diagram.

Existing Java classes on a diagram can be converted to interfaces by selecting Convert to Interface from the class's right-click menu. An example of this is included in the hands-on practice "Build a Java Class Diagram" later in this chapter.

Realizations

Realizations connect Java classes to interfaces and are displayed as a triangle with a dotted line as shown here:

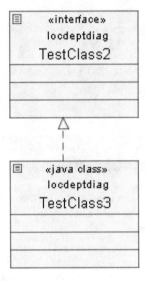

The triangle points to the interface. The effect on the code is that, in the associated Java class, the realization modifies the Java class so that it implements the interface.

NOTE
If you convert the Java interface to a class using the right-click menu in the diagram, the realization line will automatically change to a generalization. The underlying code will be modified to show that the first class extends the second class. Similarly, if you convert a Java class to an interface (using the right-click menu item), the generalization line will be changed to a realization line with the appropriate code modifications.

Packages

You can also create package symbols (¶) on the diagram using the BC4J or Java pages of the Component Palette. Packages in the Navigator are created immediately when the diagram element is created and do not need to be generated. BC4J packages are usually created when you create other objects such as workspaces, projects, and classes.

TIP

*You can change the way in which the Navigator is organized and displayed by selecting a project and selecting **Project | Show Categories** from the main JDeveloper menu or the Show Categories icon in the Navigator toolbar.*

Packages in the Diagram

As with other elements, packages can be added directly to the diagram by selecting Add to Diagram from the diagram right-click menu and selecting the desired package from the list. There is no node view for packages. However, you can change the colors and fonts by using the Visual Properties dialog.

When classes and packages are added to the diagram, the packages to which they belong are shown directly above the name of the class or package on the diagram. Java classes are displayed in the Navigator below the package in which they reside. Drawing a dependency arrow between the class and the package does not have any impact on the class or the package.

Dependency arrows can be drawn between a class and a package on a diagram to symbolize that the class "uses" a class that resides within that package.

TIP

You can use a number of diagramming operations that have no effect on your application but that can be used purely for documentation purposes to make the diagram clearer. If you are unsure of whether your diagram change has affected your code, before making the change, first Save All so that all model and BC4J elements are not in italics in the Navigator. Make the change to the diagram, and see if any elements in the Navigator other than the affected diagram elements appear in italics, indicating that they have been modified.

Packages in the Navigator

Packages are logical collections of elements that usually appear in the Navigator with their associated objects. For example, when you create a BC4J project, the BC4J elements appear within the BC4J package node. However, in an application project, typically you do not see the package. When you create a UML diagram in either a BC4J or application project, JDeveloper displays the name of the diagram under the node for the UML package in which the diagram resides. When BC4J elements are displayed in the Navigator, they are shown within a package with the special icon shown here:

UML Package vs. BC4J Package   If you build a UML class diagram in a project without BC4J components, the package will be shown in the Navigator with the UML package icon here:

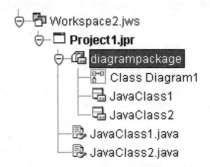

The *UML package* is used to organize the elements on a diagram. If you have BC4J components, you may have two package nodes referencing the same package name if you specified the same name when creating the diagram. These packages may also show the classes that belong to them. For example, in a BC4J project with a package "locdept," only a single BC4J package will be shown in the project. If a UML class diagram is created and placed in the same package, two package nodes will be displayed, one for the actual BC4J elements and another for the UML package as shown here:

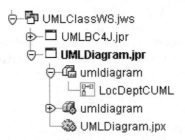

As you add BC4J elements to the diagram, the associated BC4J classes will be shown as associated sub-elements to the project package. Even if you remove the diagram elements, the classes will still appear in the Navigator under the regular (nondiagram) package node. You will see this package node within the project even if the diagram itself is deleted. This extra node will not affect your code and can be ignored.

A UI application project without a diagram will not contain a package node. If you create a UML class diagram, you will see a package node that contains the UML class diagram. As you add classes, those classes will appear under the corresponding package nodes. If you select a diagram element and select Remove from Diagram from the right-click menu, the item will only be deleted in the diagram, but will still appear under the project node and under the diagram package node in the Navigator.

You must select Delete from Model from the right-click menu to remove the element from the UML package node in the Navigator as well as from the diagram. When you select Delete from Model, the .java file will not be deleted in the Navigator. The Delete from Model option is not available for modeled packages. To remove a package from the Navigator, first delete all the nodes under that package, and then select the package and choose **File | Erase from Disk**. It is likely that later versions of JDeveloper will include a more intuitive way of removing elements from both the diagram and Navigator.

NOTE
The BC4J package represents some code in an XML file that you will deploy with the BC4J project. You can edit this file by selecting Edit from the right-click menu on the BC4J package node in the Navigator. This code is required by the BC4J project and will be deployed with the project element code. The UML package is an organizational concept and contains no code for deployment. You can edit its properties by selecting Properties from the right-click menu on the UML package node in the Navigator.

The Class Modeler section includes a tabbed Java Class dialog that is only available once a class has been placed in a UML class diagram. The Java Class dialog shown in Figure 8-3 is accessed by double clicking the class name under the package node in the project. This dialog allows you to modify the attributes, operations, realizations, and Javadoc associated with the class.

The tabs in this dialog are fairly self-explanatory. Each tab also includes a Help button to explain each of the options available. By examining the underlying code, you can view the results of any modifications made in the dialog.

Associations

Associations between classes will only affect the underlying code if they are *directed* (include the arrow). A simple (*nondirected*) association between Java classes has no effect on either class.

If you have a directed association between two classes, there will be a small modification to the class on the side opposite the arrowhead. This creates a field to store objects in the other class.

If the association on the side with the arrowhead has a cardinality of 0..1 or 1 (meaning that at most one object can be pointed to), then the field created is a simple field. If the cardinality is * or 1..*, an array variable is created.

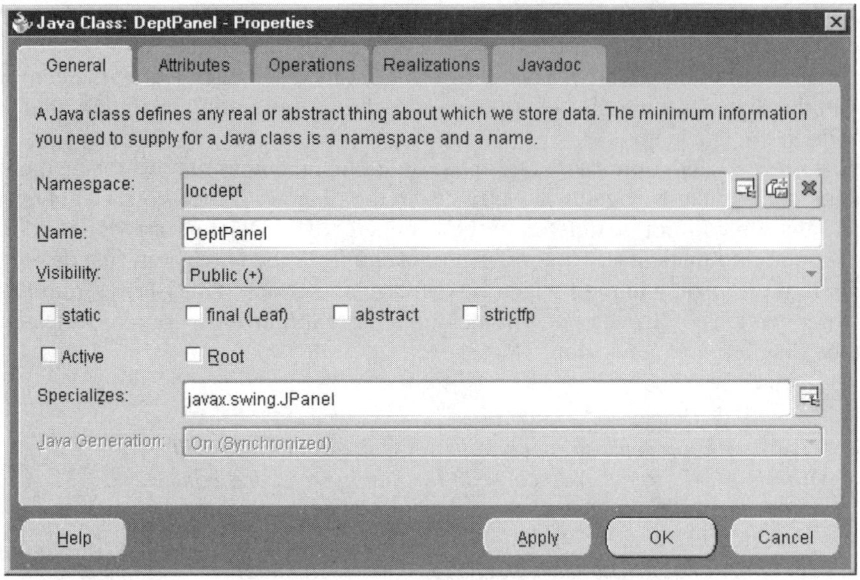

FIGURE 8-3. *Java Class dialog*

The name on the end of the association (association role) is used to specify the name of the field. Therefore, you must have a single-word role specified to have a directional association. If you make the association bidirectional (with arrows on both sides), then both classes will have stubs or fields to allow the objects to reference each other.

TIP
To add an elbow (equivalent to a dogleg in Designer) to a line in a diagram, hold down the SHIFT *key and click the line to be edited. Drag the line to the desired position. To remove the elbow, hold down the* SHIFT *key, and click the joint (extra point) of the elbow to be removed.*

Specialized Associations

Compositions (aggregations and strong aggregations) are treated in the same way as other associations. The composition symbol has no effect on the generated code.

Associations (directional or otherwise) when either object is connected to an interface, act (and generate code) exactly as if they were connected to regular Java classes.

A generalization between two Java classes will be implemented so that the specialized class extends the generalized class. The Class Modeler will not allow you to create a generalization from an interface, but will allow you to document that a Java class is a realization of (implements) an interface (as mentioned before) to a class.

Generalizations can be modeled between Java classes, between interfaces, and between modeled entity objects. Generalizations cannot be modeled between class and interfaces, classes/interfaces and entity objects.

Hands-on Practice: Build a Java Class Diagram

Using the Class Modeler to model Java classes and interfaces is very easy and intuitive. What, if any, impact the diagramming elements have on your code is not always so intuitive.

This hands-on practice contains a few simple steps. It is suggested that you draw various elements and look at the corresponding effects on your code on your own in order to become more familiar with this portion of the tool. Most of the usefulness of the Class Modeler will not be evident until you gain some familiarity with Java programming practices. When you acquire these skills, this mechanism for modeling and, to some extent, manipulating the code in your classes is quite useful.

This practice is based on the LocDeptJA project created in Chapter 3 and includes the following phases:

I. Create a class diagram

■ Add and modify classes

■ Add an attribute

II. Create an association between two classes

III. Add a generalization

IV. Change a generalization into an interface

This practice will help you become familiar with the common operations of the Class Modeler.

I. Create a Class Diagram

Use the following steps to create a class diagram.

Add and Modify Classes

At this point, you need to add classes to the diagram using the following steps:

1. Expand the LocDept2WS.jws node in the Navigator. Select the LocDeptJA.jpr node in the LocDeptWS workspace, and select New UML Diagram from the right-click menu.

2. In the New dialog, select Class Diagram from the UML Diagrams category. Click OK.

3. In the Create New Class Diagram dialog, enter "locdeptdiag" in the *Package* field, and type "LocDept2CUML" in the *Name* field. The CUML suffix indicates that this is a class UML diagram. Click OK.

CAUTION
Enter the diagram name carefully since you cannot rename a diagram.
You can only delete and re-create it.

4. Select all three of the Java classes (DeptPanel, LocDeptPanel, and LocPanel), and drag
them onto the diagram. Arrange the classes to look something like Figure 8-4.

TIP
*JDeveloper often places items at random locations far apart. Use the
Zoom Out button to find the diagram elements and reposition them.*

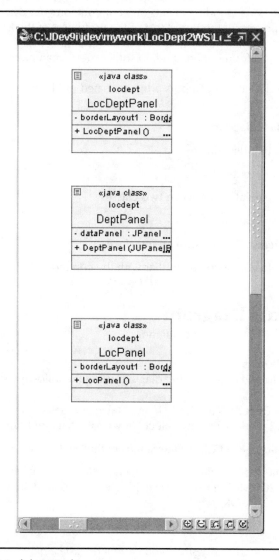

FIGURE 8-4. *Class Modeler window*

5. Double click the DeptPanel class on the diagram to access the Java Class dialog shown in Figure 8-5 to view the possible editing features. Click Cancel on the Java Class: DeptPanel – Properties window.

   Additional Information: This dialog is only available to classes that have been added to a diagram. It has similar functionality to the Class Editor, but this dialog has some additional features, such as allowing you to enter a default value for an attribute (called a "field" in the Class Editor) and entering Javadoc comments. You can make many significant modifications to your class using this dialog; however, because the DeptPanel class contains over 100 lines of code, if you are not familiar with Java programming, detecting the changed code may be tedious and may cause some unexpected side effects.

6. To create a class in your diagram, select Java Class from the Java page of the Component Palette, and click an empty space in the diagram. If the Component Palette is not visible, press CTRL-SHIFT-P to open it.

7. When you add the element, the name field is selected and editable. Change the name of the class to "TestClass1." You can access the name later by clicking it in the diagram.

   Additional Information: You can make in-place edits to most elements of the class on the diagram. The only element that cannot be modified this way is the stereotype. If you change the name of a class, the refactoring utility (also available in the Tools menu) will be activated.

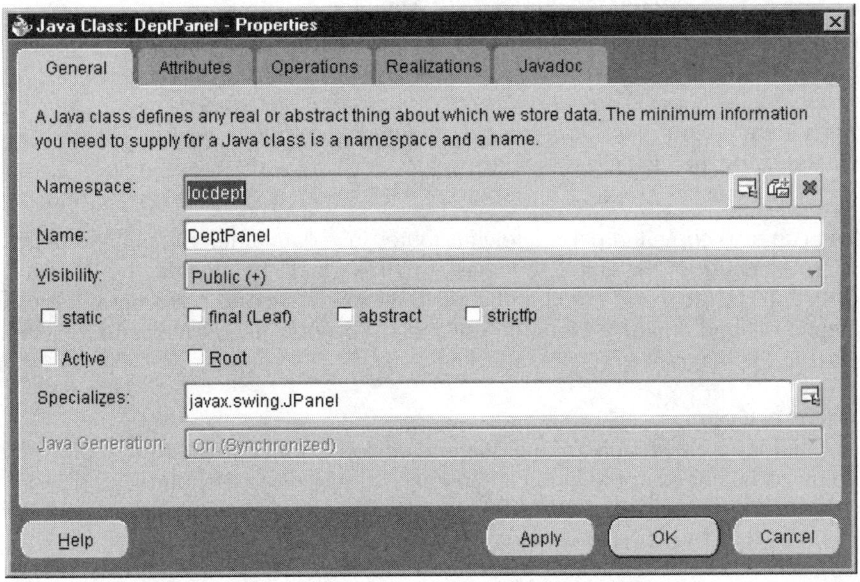

FIGURE 8-5. *Java Class dialog*

CAUTION
If you make changes to the diagram using in-place editing, there may be no validation.

You can drag and drop attributes from one class to another within the Modeler. You need to select the symbol next to the element and right click in order to drag it. If you hold down the CTRL key (after right clicking the symbol next to the element) while you drag and drop, the attribute will be copied (instead of moved) into the new class.

For simple structures, the drag feature moves the appropriate code around as you change the diagram. However, with complex classes containing a lot of underlying code, you should look carefully at the generated code after the drag and drop operation to be sure that it has been modified as expected.

Although operations can be moved or copied from one class to another on a diagram in the same way as attributes, only the signatures of the operations are actually copied or moved.

This functionality works best in an analysis or design environment before there is significant code in the classes.

NOTE
As mentioned, when you use in-place editing, there may be no validation of what is being entered. It is equivalent to typing in the corresponding Java code for these elements. Although you cannot create an entity object with the same name as another entity object, there is nothing to prevent you from assigning your class to a nonexistent package or linking attributes to nonexistent datatypes or domains. Therefore, in most cases, you should make modifications to Java classes using the Java Class dialog.

8. You can also copy and paste a few attributes (use dataPanel :JPanel and deptScroller :JScrollPane) from the DeptPanel class into TestClass1 by clicking the attributes using CTRL-C and CTRL-V and clicking the attributes area (second box from the top) in the DeptPanel and dragging them to TestClass1. You may need to expand the DeptPanel class in the diagram to see the attributes.

Add an Attribute

A number of dialogs are available for the diagram elements that allow you to modify the element without typing code. For example, you can add an attribute using the following steps:

1. Double click TestClass1 to access the Java Class dialog.

TIP
When double clicking items in the Modeler, always click in an area where there is no text so as not to activate the in-place editing accidentally. Double clicking in the upper-left corner always works.

2. Click the Attributes tab and click the New button to add a blank row in the *Name* multi-record field. Enter "testAttr" as shown in Figure 8-6. Click OK.

   Additional Information: If you click Apply, JDeveloper will generate the code but not close the window. If you close the window or click Cancel, your changes will be abandoned.

3. Open the Code Editor by selecting Go to Source from the TestClass1 right-click menu.

4. Find the line containing "testAttr" toward the beginning of the code listing. Use the **Search | Find** menu feature if you have trouble locating it. Examine the generated code.

5. Re-enter the Java Class dialog by double clicking TestClass1 on the diagram. On the Attributes tab, select testAttr in the *Name* multi-valued field display. Modify its name to "testAttrNew," and change its *Type* to "int" using the pulldown. Click Apply and OK. Click Save All and examine the changes in the Code Editor.

6. Save all.

What Just Happened?   In this phase, you created a class diagram and some Java classes. Diagramming Java classes is very useful for documentation of existing classes, but is of limited usefulness in application design, because only a small percentage of your code will be generated. Depending upon the type of application being built, you will either find the wizards and generated code extremely useful and timesaving, or you may be more comfortable writing the code by hand.

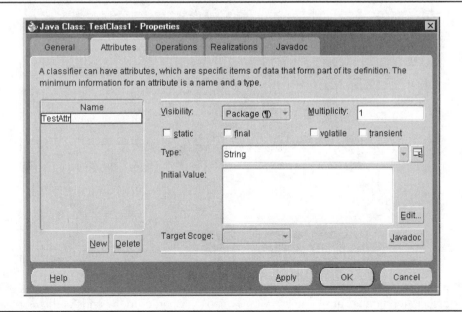

FIGURE 8-6.   *Java Class dialog Attributes tab*

II. Create an Association Between Two Classes

In this phase, you will explore the possibilities for creating associations in the Class Modeler.

1. Create a Java class and change its name to "TestClass2" using the in-place editing feature.

2. Select the "Association 1 to *" line from the Component Palette. Click TestClass1 and then TestClass2 to create the association line. (This is not a click and drag operation.)

   Additional Information: In the Component Palette, there are also directed associations with one side already flagged as Navigable. The first class you click will be the "1" side, and the second class will be the "*" (many) side. In addition to the 1 and *, JDeveloper adds a default name for the association and a role name on the TestClass2 side.

NOTE
If you look at the Java class for TestClass1 and TestClass2 in the Navigator, neither one is in italics after adding the association line, indicating that the underlying code was not modified.

3. Double click the association line to access the Java Association dialog. Click the Association Ends tab. Name the association ends "End1" and "End2," respectively, in the multi-valued *Name* field as shown here. Make both ends Navigable by selecting each one and checking the *Navigable* checkbox. Click OK.

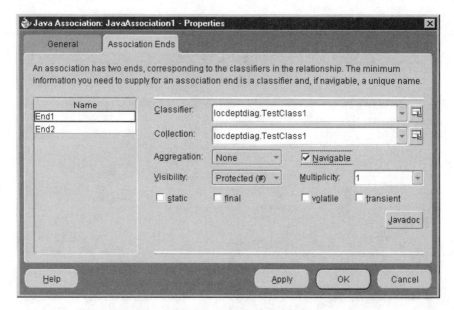

   Additional Information: Note that arrowheads have been added to both sides of the association line because you added *Navigable* properties to the ends of the association.

4. Click Save All.

   Additional Information: As described earlier, making both ends Navigable places fields in each of the classes. To learn what effect other association ends options have, click the Help button on the Association Ends tab of the Java Association dialog.

5. Examine the Java code for TestClass1 and TestClass2 by clicking each one and selecting Go to Source from the right-click menu. Find the fields added to each class. Hint: Look for the words "End1" or "End2" in the code. Notice that TestClass1 contains an array attribute, indicating that it can reference multiple objects created by TestClass2.

6. In the Class Modeler, double click the association line to access the Java Association dialog. On the Association Ends tab, change the *Aggregation* property to either "Aggregate (Weak)" or "Composite (Strong)" using the pulldown. Click OK and look for the change in the association symbol.

   Additional Information: Note that neither TestClass1 nor TestClass2 is italicized in the Navigator, which means that the code has not been affected.

7. Click Save All.

What Just Happened? In this phase, you added an association between two Java classes and examined the effect on the generated code. To support associations to multiple objects (the "many" side of an association), JDeveloper generates an array that requires a predefined cardinality as opposed to a vector with unlimited cardinality but marginally poorer performance.

TIP
If an array is generated, no value is entered. You must specify a value before your code will run. Even if you specify a value for the cardinality of the association end, it will not place that number as the array size.

III. Add a Generalization

Generalizations are used to model inheritance. They can be created between Java classes, between interfaces, or between entity objects. The Java code will show an extends *<class name>* statement in the class declaration when a generalization is present.

NOTE
Only one generalization relationship can be modeled from a Java class or entity object since multiple inheritance is not supported by Java.

1. Create "TestClass3" using the Java Class icon from the Java page of the Component Palette. Select TestClass3. Click Save All.

2. Select the Generalization arrow from the Component Palette. Click TestClass3 and then TestClass2.

   Additional Information: This will make TestClass3 a specialization of TestClass2. Note that the TestClass3 Java class in the Navigator has been modified by this operation.

The code defining TestClass3 (visible by selecting TestClass3 and Go to Source from the right-click menu) now reads

```
public class TestClass3 extends TestClass2
```

3. Click Save All.

What Just Happened?   In this phase, you created a generalization between two classes and examined the generated code. Generalization acts as expected by adding the extends keyword to the class declaration. Specifying generalizations in the Class Modeler rather than typing them directly into the code is not a huge timesaver, but may help in documentation.

NOTE
Removing the extends clause in the Code Editor does not delete the generalization on the diagram. Adding the extends clause to a class does not automatically create a diagram generalization line.

IV. Change a Generalization into an Interface
JDeveloper allows you to change generalizations into interfaces.

1. Click TestClass2 and select Convert to Interface from the right-click menu. Answer Yes to the confirmation dialog.

   Additional Information: Note that the Java code for TestClass2 and TestClass3 has been modified, as evidenced by their being italicized in the Navigator. The generated arrow has been changed to a realization arrow. TestClass3 has been modified so that it now implements the interface TestClass2. TestClass2 is labeled as an interface, but does not assume the default color of an interface.

2. Open the Code Editor for TestClass2 and TestClass3, either by double clicking the .java files in the Navigator, or by selecting Go to Source from the diagram element right-click menu. Observe the changes to the Java code.

What Just Happened?   In this phase, you changed a generalization class into an interface, which automatically changed the generalization into an implementation.

Using the UML Class Modeler for Database Design
Using UML class models for designing databases makes a great deal of sense. However, any UML modeling tool must overcome some significant challenges:

■   Object-oriented design tends to work with object IDs rather than primary keys as object identifiers. The physical implementation of a class into a table must determine what to use for the primary key. In general, primary keys are not included in object-oriented design. In fact, none of the physical elements of a relational database (tables, columns, indexes, tablespaces, or storage clauses) are explicitly part of the UML.

■ Generalization presents the same considerations that subtype/supertype structures do in ERDs, except that in object-oriented design, it is common to have a generalization tree with four or more levels. In products that translate UML diagrams into relational databases where each class is generated to a table, you risk a four-table join when querying a simple Employee record. Such an implementation strategy renders it virtually useless to employ generalization in the data model.

■ Composition and aggregation are association types in UML that have no direct correlates in ERDs.

How Can the UML Be Extended to Support the Elements Necessary for Physical Database Design?

None of the issues mentioned earlier has been adequately addressed in the current release of Oracle9i JDeveloper Class Modeler. Additionally, using UML class models in various places in the development lifecycle with appropriate versioning and project management is somewhat supported using SCM in the tool. You can version the diagram and class files using Oracle SCM. Oracle9i JDeveloper supports Oracle9i SCM, Rational ClearCase, and Concurrent Versions System (CVS). All UML model artifacts (diagrams and diagram elements) created in JDeveloper can be versioned using any of these supported technologies.

At this point in the maturity of the JDeveloper product, the Class Modeler cannot be used as an enterprise data modeling tool. For enterprise data modeling of large systems, Oracle Designer is still recommended. Its maturity and sophistication as a data modeling tool for Oracle databases far surpass any other product. However, Oracle's JDeveloper team is working to address these issues, and significant improvement in this area is likely to be included in an upcoming release.

Some useful features in the Class Modeler can assist you in designing and building applications. It is possible to generate tables or alter existing tables with the Class Modeler. For example, if you are building a system where the application requires a temporary table to store calculated values in a different application, you can create this table by making a BC4J entity object with the appropriate attributes corresponding to the column names.

You can generate tables, columns, and primary key constraints by selecting an entity object in the model window and selecting **Generate | Database Objects** from the right-click menu. Foreign key columns and foreign key constraints are not generated. You must create the foreign key columns manually since there is no automated way to do this in JDeveloper. In addition, there is neither a way to specify the tablespace to which the table is assigned nor to specify a storage clause, although you can use the Table Creation Wizard to create a table with tablespace and storage clauses.

The first thing that the table generator does is to drop the existing table (without a confirmation dialog). Any modifications made to the table before regenerating the prior table and all of its data will be dropped even if the operation does not require dropping the table, such as adding a column. The name of the generated table is the schema object property for the entity object and not the entity object name.

For creating a simple table or adding a column to an existing table where erasing all of the data is acceptable, this limited functionality in the JDeveloper Class Modeler is adequate.

PART
II

Business Components
for Java

CHAPTER
9

Introducing Business Components for Java

"Contrariwise," continued Tweedledee,
"if it was so, it might be, and if it were so,
it would be; but as it isn't, it ain't. That's logic!"

—Lewis Carroll [Charles Lutwidge Dodgson] (1832–1898),
Through the Looking Glass

 usiness Components for Java (BC4J) is a Java- and XML-based framework for developing business logic, including validation and default logic, queries, transaction handling, and data access. The BC4J layer of an application does not create a user interface at all. It is a pure encapsulation of business logic that communicates with a separate client application, which handles user interaction. Chapters 1 and 3 provided an overview of the range of features JDeveloper provides and the range of activities you can perform with it. In Part II, you will learn in depth about BC4J, one of JDeveloper's central features. Using BC4J is the simplest way to design data-aware applications with JDeveloper. However, Part II will not teach you everything you need to write a complete BC4J application. In addition to a collection of business components, BC4J applications involve client applications (sometimes called "clients" in Part II), which you will learn to create in Parts III and IV.

This chapter provides an overview of BC4J, describing the components and uses of BC4J. Chapter 10 explains how to create business components to represent database objects, object types, and constraints. Chapter 11 explains how to reverse the process and design business components in isolation from the database before creating database objects to provide a persistence layer. In Chapter 12, you will learn how to use BC4J to enforce business rules.

Chapter 13 explains how BC4J represents queries and relationships between query results and how it caches data. In it you will learn how to assemble the data your client needs while maintaining optimal performance. Chapter 14 explains how clients access the data and presents techniques for accessing data that will help you customize the client applications you will learn about in Parts III and IV. In Chapter 15, you will learn how to use the BC4J framework to customize transaction handling and scale your applications to effectively handle a large number of simultaneous transactions. In Chapter 16, you will learn more about deploying BC4J applications and the factors you should weigh in deciding how to deploy your business components.

NOTE
Many practices in Part II are sequential, but you can download starting files for any chapter's practice from the authors' websites mentioned in the front of the book.

This chapter includes a brief discussion of the advantages and disadvantages of using BC4J to enforce business logic and a quick tour of the different business components: entity objects, associations, view objects, view links, application modules, and domains. At the end of the chapter, a hands-on practice will demonstrate how to create and explore a simple business components application.

Why Use Business Components for Java?

Why create a new application layer to enforce business logic, rather than enforcing it in the user interface or in the database itself?

The advantage of BC4J over UI-enforced business logic is reusability. A single BC4J layer can provide the business logic for all of your company's needs. The business components can be used again and again, with multiple user interfaces. This saves you from having to rewrite business logic for every user interface.

The advantages of BC4J over database-enforced business logic are more complex. First, by maintaining a cache of data in memory, BC4J reduces the number of database trips required by your application, thus improving performance and scalability. Second, BC4J allows you to write your business logic in Java, saving you the trouble of integrating a Java GUI or JSP application with business logic written in PL/SQL code. Finally, moving business logic out of the database keeps the database from handling anything but data, which increases your application's modularity and the database's efficiency.

There are also advantages to implementing some business logic directly in the database. Business logic in the database is more robust. It will be enforced even in a SQL*Plus session. Business logic implemented in a BC4J layer will only be enforced in applications using that layer. This trade-off between robustness and performance is something you need to consider for your application. The most critical business logic should be implemented in the database or implemented redundantly in the database and a BC4J layer. The remainder of your business logic can be implemented in the BC4J layer alone.

Although you can write your own client code for BC4J, JDeveloper provides four ready-made architectures for business component clients:

- JClient, an architecture for creating Java GUIs (especially useful for intensive data-entry applications that require high interactivity) discussed in Part III of this book

- Thin JSP clients (useful for web-based applications for which a thin client is more important than very high interactivity, such as self-service applications and e-commerce applications) discussed in Part IV of this book

- XSQL clients, which generate XML for either flexible display with a style sheet or loose coupling between applications

- UIX, a framework-based architecture for developing web applications

XSQL clients and UIX are beyond the scope of this book.

BC4J also has the advantage of being "deployment-configuration independent." A single BC4J layer can be deployed as local Java classes or as an Enterprise JavaBean (EJB), with no rewriting of code necessary. Programmers using business components, unlike those creating Enterprise JavaBeans from scratch, do not need to design applications around their deployment architecture; they can concentrate on their business logic rather than on deployment requirements. You will learn more about maintaining tier independence in Chapter 14 and about how to deploy BC4J in various configurations in Chapter 16.

Whether deployed to a J2EE web module with JSP pages or as an EJB, business components are fully J2EE-compliant and, in fact, the BC4J framework automatically implements the J2EE BluePrints design patterns suggested by Sun Microsystems. You do not need to worry about these design patterns (Sun discusses them extensively on their website, java.sun.com); if you create a business components application, you will automatically be designing to them.

Entity Objects and Associations

An *entity object* usually represents a database table or database view, although it can also be used to represent EJB entity beans (for more information, see the sidebar "EJB Entity Facades"). It acts as a representation of the table or database view and handles all of the business rules for that

EJB Entity Facades

Until recently, BC4J entity objects could only be used to wrap database objects directly. In release 9.0.3, however, JDeveloper introduced the ability to use special types of entity objects, called EJB entity facades, as wrappers for EJB entity beans. In this configuration, the EJB entity beans handle data persistence; the entity facades handle business logic and (unlike standard entity objects) client binding.

Entity facades work a bit differently from standard entity objects, and if you use them, you will also use new forms of other business components (such as a new form of a view object called an EJB finder view object). A discussion of entity facades and related business components is beyond the scope of this book. For more information, see the on-line help.

Note that, although entity facades and related business components are fully J2EE compliant, standard business components are as well. You do not need to use entity facades unless you have a special reason to use EJB entity beans.

table or view including validation, defaulting, and anything else that happens when a row is created, deleted, or changed.

The power of BC4J is its interface with the database to be used in an application. A relational database consists of a set of tables, each of which contains columns. For example, consider the table DEPARTMENTS, with the following columns:

Column Name	SQL Datatype
DEPARTMENT_ID	NUMBER
DEPARTMENT_NAME	VARCHAR2
MANAGER_ID	NUMBER
LOCATION_ID	NUMBER

The BC4J layer represents the database table as an entity object. An entity object has *entity attributes*, which represent the table columns, although the mapping is not always perfectly one-to-one. (For more information, see Chapter 10.)

The types of the properties are Java classes that correspond to the SQL types of the columns. The entity object for this table might have the following entity attributes:

Attribute Name	Java Type
DepartmentId	oracle.jbo.domain.Number
DepartmentName	java.lang.String
ManagerId	oracle.jbo.domain.Number
LocationId	oracle.jbo.domain.Number

Java does not directly support SQL datatypes. However, each SQL datatype can be mapped to a Java type. Some of these Java types are classes in java.lang (such as java.lang.String), and others are in the package oracle.jbo.domain (which are discussed in the section "Domains").

An entity object has two parts: a Java class (such as DepartmentsImpl.java) and an XML file (such as Departments.xml). The Java class contains procedural code required to implement the entity object, while the XML file includes metadata describing the entity object, its attributes, and the table upon which it is based, as well as declarative code. These will be examined in more detail later in this chapter.

Associations

Just as tables are often related to one another, entity objects are often related to one another. Relationships between entity objects are represented by associations. You can think of an *association* as the representation of a foreign key relationship: it matches one or more attributes of a "source" entity object with one or more attributes of a "destination" entity object, just as a foreign key constraint matches one or more columns of a child table with one or more columns of a parent table. You can (but are not required to) base an association on a foreign key constraint in the database. The association is stored in an XML file.

You will learn how to define entity objects and associations in Chapters 10 and 11 and how to use them to implement business logic in Chapter 12.

View Objects and View Links

An entity object usually represents a table or view in the database. But you generally should not present all of the information stored in a database object in one application interface. Also, you may want data taken from more than one database object. SQL has queries so that you can select exactly the data that you need from one or more tables. This is also the reason why Business Components for Java has *view objects,* which correspond to SQL queries. A view object actually stores a SQL query.

Just as an entity object has entity attributes, a view object has *view attributes,* which correspond to columns of the query result. For example, consider the view object for the following query:

```
SELECT Departments.DEPARTMENT_ID,
   Departments.DEPARTMENT_NAME,
   Employees.EMPLOYEE_ID,
   Employees.FIRST_NAME,
   Employees.LAST_NAME
FROM DEPARTMENTS Departments, EMPLOYEES Employees
WHERE Departments.MANAGER_ID=Employees.EMPLOYEE_ID;
```

This view object would have the following view attributes:

Attribute Name	Java Type
DepartmentId	oracle.jbo.domain.Number
DepartmentName	java.lang.String
EmployeeId	oracle.jbo.domain.Number
FirstName	java.lang.String
LastName	java.lang.String

These view attributes can be, but do not need to be, associated with attributes from entity objects.

Like an entity object, a view object has two parts: a Java class (such as ManagerViewImpl.java) and an XML file (such as ManagerView.xml). The Java class handles the complex logic of your queries, controlling the client's access to the data. The XML file stores information about the query and its relationships to entity objects.

View Links

A *view link* represents a relationship between the query result sets of two view objects. It associates one or more attributes of one view object with one or more attributes of another. For example, you could create the following:

- A view object, DepartmentsView, containing the following query:

  ```
  SELECT Departments.DEPARTMENT_ID,
     Departments.DEPARTMENT_NAME
  FROM DEPARTMENTS Departments
  ```

- Another view object, EmployeesView, containing the following query:

  ```
  SELECT Employees.EMPLOYEE_ID,
     Employees.FIRST_NAME,
     Employees.LAST_NAME,
     Employees.DEPARTMENT_ID
  FROM EMPLOYEES Employees
  ```

- A view link, DeptEmpFkLink, that associated the DepartmentId attribute of EmployeesView with the DepartmentId attribute of DepartmentsView

DeptEmpFkLink represents a master-detail relationship between the query result sets of DepartmentsView and EmployeesView.

View links between view objects can be, but do not need to be, based on associations between underlying entity objects. A view link is represented in an XML file.

You will learn how to design view objects and view links in Chapter 13 and how to use them in client applications in Chapter 14.

Application Modules

An *application module* is a container for *view usages*, instances of view objects. It lists all of the view usages that your application requires and specifies the way in which they are related by view links. These relationships can be represented by a tree, called the application module's *data model*. For example, an application module might contain a usage of DepartmentsView, called DepartmentsView1, and a usage of EmployeesView, called EmployeesView1, linked by a usage of the view link EmpDeptFkLink called EmpDeptFkLink1. The application module would use the data model shown here:

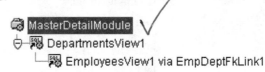

Using this model, the two view usages are tied together by a link representing a master-detail relationship between them. Through this application module, your client application could select a row in DepartmentsView1, and the BC4J framework would immediately synchronize EmployeesView1 so that it would only return employees from the selected department.

Alternatively, your application module could contain a usage of DepartmentsView and a usage of EmployeesView without using EmpDeptFkLink, as in the data model shown here:

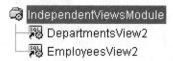

This module provides usages of the same two view objects, but the view usages are linked. Through this application module, your client application could select rows in DepartmentsView and EmployeesView usages independently.

You could even include two usages of EmployeesView in your application module: one linked with the view link and one at the top level, as in the data model shown here.

Through this application module, a client application could select rows in EmployeesView (through EmployeesView3) and have them automatically synchronized with DepartmentsView3 and could also select them (through EmployeesView4) independently. Data models will be discussed further in Chapter 13.

Client access to view objects always goes through the application module. Clients send a request to an application module to see a particular view usage, and the application module finds the view usage in its data model and passes it back to the client. Accessing application modules from clients will be discussed further in Chapter 14.

Application modules also handle transactions: starting a new one, setting locking options, and performing database posts, rollbacks, and commits. Transactions will be discussed further in Chapter 15.

Like an entity object or a view object, an application module has two parts: a Java class (such as MasterDetailModuleImpl.java) and an XML file (such as MasterDetailModule.xml). The Java class handles transaction logic and provides service methods clients can call to execute multiple operations in a batch. The XML file stores the data model.

Domains

Domains are special Java types used by BC4J as the types for many entity object and view object attributes. When entity objects were introduced earlier, you learned that the class that implements the Departments entity object has some entity attributes of type oracle.jbo.domain.Number. The entity attributes of an entity object Java class are objects, not primitive Java types such as int.

For database columns of SQL datatype VARCHAR2, there is an obvious Java class for the entity attributes—java.lang.String. For other SQL types (such as NUMBER or BLOB), Business Components for Java provides domains to wrap the SQL datatype. Some domains, like oracle.jbo.domain.Number, are basically object wrappers for scalar types. Others, like oracle.jbo.domain.BlobDomain, are more complicated classes that store extensive data.

JDeveloper will also automatically create a domain for you if you base an entity object on a table with an Oracle object type column in it. This domain represents the Oracle object type, giving you Java wrappers for each of the object type's fields and methods. Domains that represent Oracle object types will be discussed further in Chapter 10.

Finally, you may create your own domains. Suppose you have many database columns, possibly in different tables, that are all very similar. Not only are they of the same SQL type (for instance, VARCHAR2), but they all contain information in exactly the same form—for example, a URL.

You may have business logic that is simultaneously associated with multiple columns. For example, you may have validation logic that applies to any and all URLs—perhaps they must all begin with a protocol code, a colon, and two slashes. Rather than putting this logic in every entity object that contains one of these columns, you can create a URL domain that itself contains the validation code. Then you simply need to ensure that the appropriate entity attributes in the entity objects' Java classes are all instances of that domain rather than the type java.lang.String. Domains that enforce business logic will be discussed further in Chapter 12. Domain code is stored in Java and XML files.

Business Components, Java, and XML

As mentioned, entity objects, view objects, and application modules each have two parts: a Java class and an XML file. The Java class and the XML file have different purposes. BC4J is a framework, which means that much of its functionality is contained in a set of libraries. Business components Java classes extend (subclass) the base classes provided in those libraries to provide complex business logic, which requires the procedural power of Java to implement. If you need that sort of logic, you can easily write code to implement complex business rules inside your entity object Java classes, complex query logic in your view object classes, or complex transaction handling in your application module classes.

However, the base classes that make up the BC4J framework are preprogrammed to work with XML files. Some business logic is common and simple and can be handled with a line or two of declarative XML. Instead of writing a procedure to implement this sort of business logic, you can just declare that an entity attribute, for example, must obey a particular validation rule. The base entity object class (and by inheritance your custom Java class) can automatically read the XML file to enforce the rule. JDeveloper provides wizards that write and edit the XML files for you.

In addition, the BC4J framework, like many other frameworks, uses XML files to store static definitions such as the structure of a database table or a query. The base classes can discover the structure of particular business components by parsing the XML. This can have performance advantages. For example, an entity object does not need to query the database at runtime for structural information about the table it represents.

Hands-on Practice: Examine a Default BC4J Layer

In this practice, you will create and explore a default BC4J layer based on the HR schema. A *default BC4J layer* is one created entirely using the Business Components Package Wizard. It is basically a prototype. For enterprise applications, you should start with some wizard-generated components but design most of your business components by hand. In addition, a default BC4J layer does not contain any business logic. However, it provides examples of business components discussed in this chapter: entity objects, associations, view objects, view links, and an application module.

This practice steps you through the following phases:

I. **Create a BC4J layer**

- Create a workspace and empty project

- Create default business components for the HR Schema

II. **Explore a default entity object and a default association**

- Explore Departments

- Explore DepartmentsImpl.java

- Explore Departments.xml

- Explore EmpDeptFkAssoc

III. **Explore a default view object and a default view link**

- Explore DepartmentsView

- Explore DepartmentsViewImpl.java

- Explore DepartmentsView.xml

- Explore EmpDeptFkLink

IV. **Explore the default application module**

- Explore Defaultbc4jModule

- Explore Defaultbc4jModuleImpl.java

- Explore Defaultbc4jModule.xml

V. **Test the default Business Components**

- Open the Business Component Browser

- Test an independent usage of DepartmentsView

- Test two different usages of EmployeesView

- Test EmpDeptFkLink

I. Create a BC4J Layer

This phase creates a default BC4J project.

Create a Workspace and Empty Project

A new workspace and project for your business components can be created using the following steps:

1. On the Workspaces node in the Navigator, select New Workspace from the right-click menu. The New Workspace dialog opens.

2. Use "DefaultBusinessComponentsWS" as the name for both your workspace directory and your workspace file.

3. Click OK. The New Project dialog opens.

4. Use "DefaultBC4J" as the name for both your project directory and your project file.

Create Default Business Components for the HR Schema

Default business components can be created using the following steps:

1. On the DefaultBC4J.jpr project node in the Navigator, select New Business Components Package from the right-click menu. The Business Components Package Wizard opens.

2. If the Welcome page appears, click Next.

3. On the Name page, enter "defaultbc4j" as the package name. All of your business components will go into this package.

4. Ensure that "Entity Objects mapped to database schema objects" is selected, and click Next.
   Additional Information: The other two options allow you to create EJB Entity Facades and related business components. For more information, see the sidebar "EJB Entity Facades" earlier in this chapter.

5. On the Connection page, select HR from the *Connection Name* dropdown. Click Next.

6. On the Business Components page, use the right arrow to add DEPARTMENTS and EMPLOYEES to the *Selected* list. This will create an entity object from each of those tables and create associations from each of the foreign keys between them.

7. For this practice, leave the *View Objects and View Links* checkbox checked.
   Additional Information: This will create a default view object for each entity object and one view link for each association. As you will see later, default view objects and view links are not very useful for many real applications. (They correspond to SELECT * single-table queries and foreign-key–based master-detail relationships rather than the more complex queries and relationships that most applications need.) But they are useful for testing the functionality of the entity objects.

8. Also leave the *Application Module* checkbox checked, with the name "Defaultbc4jModule" filled in.
   Additional Information: This will create a default application module that contains the view objects in every possible combination, both independent and joined by view links. Again, the default application module would not be that useful for developing

a real application (it is generally too big and inefficient), but it is useful for testing a business components project. The page should look like the following illustration:

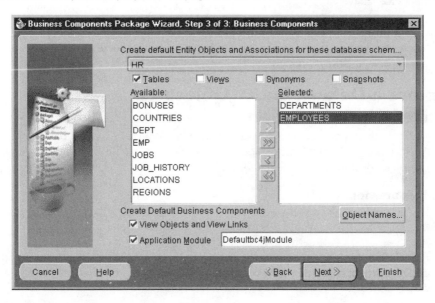

9. Click Next. The Summary page appears.

Additional Information: The Summary page lists connection information, the package name, and the primary business components (entity objects, view objects, and the application module) that the wizard will create, as shown next:

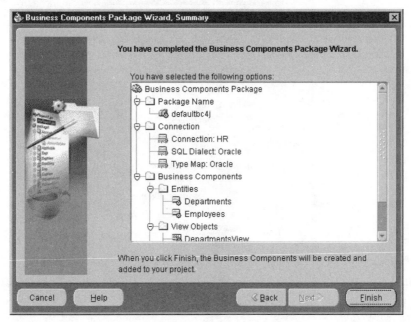

10. Click Finish.

11. Select **File** | **Save All**.

What Just Happened?   You created a BC4J layer. JDeveloper creates business components based on the choices you made in the wizard. The business components are under the defaultbc4j node in the Navigator, as shown in Figure 9-1.

II. Explore a Default Entity Object and a Default Association

This phase looks at the Departments entity object, which the wizard created based on the DEPARTMENTS table, and EmpDeptFkAssoc, the association which the wizard created based on the EmpDeptFk constraint from the database.

Explore Departments

You can view an entity object's entity attributes and their types using the Entity Object Wizard. This is a low-level wizard you would use to create or edit a non-default entity object.

1. In the System Navigator, expand the defaultbc4j node. On the Departments node, select Edit Departments from the right-click menu. A re-entrant version of the Entity Object Wizard appears.

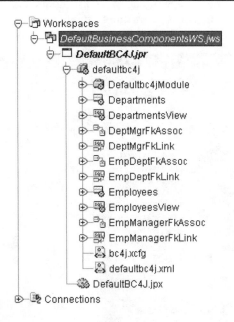

FIGURE 9-1.   *The default business components*

2. Select the Attributes node. You will see a list of the entity object's attributes, containing one attribute for each column in the DEPARTMENTS table, as shown here:

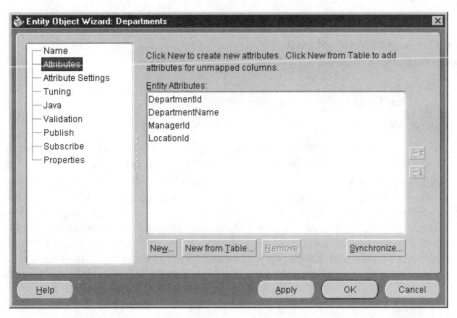

3. Select the Attribute Settings node. The first attribute, DepartmentId, will be listed in the *Select Attribute* field. Its Java type is Number.

4. Open the *Type* dropdown list to see the options for Java types of attributes, as shown here:

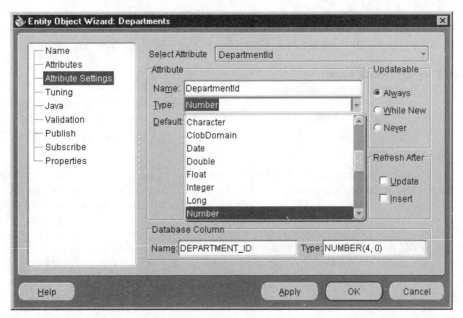

Additional Information: Of the types visible in the preceding illustration, ClobDomain, Date, and Number are all domains; the others are classes from the package java.lang.

5. Click Cancel to close the wizard without making any changes.

Explore DepartmentsImpl.java
Examine an entity object's Java source:

1. In the System Navigator, expand the Departments node. You will see the two entity object files: Departments.xml and DepartmentsImpl.java.

2. Double click DepartmentsImpl.java to open its source code.

3. Look in the Structure window for methods that start with "get" and "set." These are the methods that retrieve and change the values of each attribute.

   Additional Information: The Java class associated with each entity object has accessor methods that retrieve and change the values of each attribute. For example, the DepartmentsImpl class has methods `getManagerId()` and `setManagerId()` that retrieve and change the values of the ManagerId attribute. When an entity object Java class is instantiated, the resulting Java object represents one row of the database table. For example, if departmentsImpl1 is a particular DepartmentsImpl object, its getters would return values matching the values in a row of the DEPARTMENTS table as shown here:

Method Called	Value Returned
departmentsImpl1.getDepartmentId()	A Number domain holding the value 10
departmentsImpl1.getDepartmentName()	The String "Administration"
departmentsImpl1.getManagerId()	A Number holding the value 200
departmentsImpl1.getLocationId()	A Number holding the value 1700

In Chapter 12, you will learn how to change these methods to enforce business rules.

Explore Departments.xml
Examine an entity object's XML metadata:

1. Double click Departments.xml to open its source.

2. Find the <Attribute> tags. There is one for each attribute: DepartmentId, DepartmentName, ManagerId, and LocationId.

   Additional Information: The <Attribute> tags store metadata about the individual attributes, including the Java type of the attribute, the identity and SQL datatype of the column it maps to, and simple validation added with the Entity Object Wizard.

TIP
When an XML file is loaded into the Code Editor, you can expand the nodes of the Structure window to examine a summary of the structure of the file.

Explore EmpDeptFkAssoc

You can examine an association using the Association Wizard, a low-level wizard which you would use to edit or create a non-default association:

1. On the EmpDeptFkAssoc node in the Navigator, select Edit EmpDeptFkAssoc from the right-click menu. A re-entrant version of the Association Wizard appears.

2. Note that the source entity object (which contains the primary key) is Departments, and the destination entity object (which contains the foreign key) is Employees. The wizard page shows the primary key attribute under the source entity object node and the foreign key attribute under the destination entity object node.

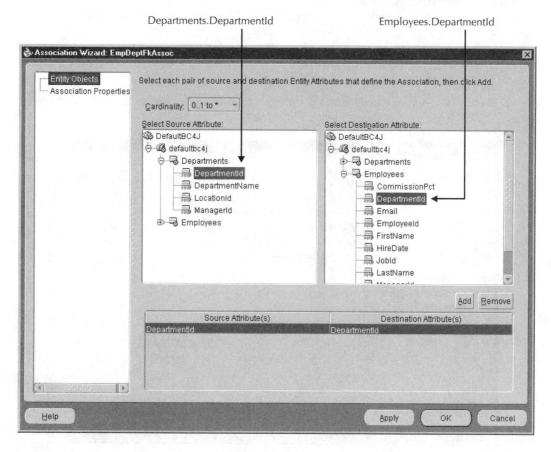

3. Click Cancel to close the wizard without making any changes.

What Just Happened? You looked at an entity object and an association. The entity object's Java file is where you would place procedures to enforce business rules; the XML file contains the metadata (such as datatypes) and declarative rules created using the Entity Object Wizard. The association links the entity object with another entity object, just as foreign key relationships link two tables.

III. Explore a Default View Object and a Default View Link

This phase examines DepartmentsView, the view object that the wizard created based on the Departments entity object, and EmpDeptFkLink, the view link that the wizard created between DepartmentsView and EmployeesView, another default view object.

Explore DepartmentsView

You can examine a view object's query and the entity objects on which it is based by using the View Object Wizard:

1. On the DepartmentsView node in the Navigator, select Edit DepartmentsView from the right-click menu. A re-entrant version of the View Object Wizard appears.

2. Note that this view object is based on the entity object Departments, as shown here in the *Selected* pane in the following illustration:

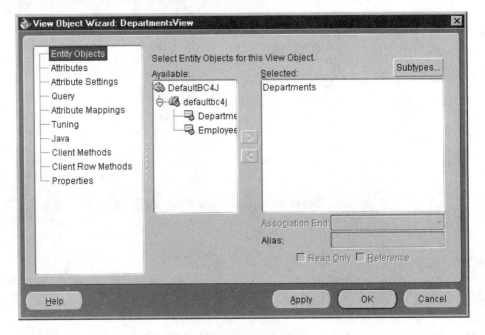

Additional Information: By using the arrow buttons, you could change this, and base DepartmentsView on either entity object, both, or neither.

3. Select the Query node to see the view object's query, as shown next.

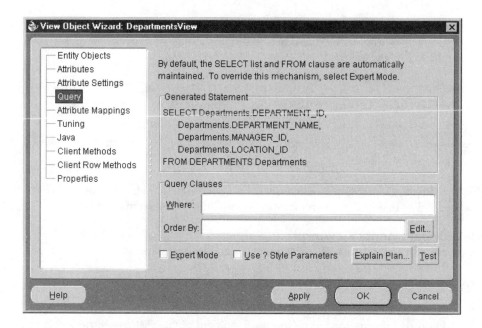

Additional Information: Default view objects such as DepartmentsView query every column in every row of the database table. When you create your own view objects, you probably will not want to do this. Instead, you will tailor your query to the application's data needs.

4. Click Cancel to close the View Object Wizard without making any changes.

Explore DepartmentsViewImpl.java

A view object's Java source can be examined using the following steps:

1. In the System Navigator, expand the DepartmentsView node. You will be able to see the two view object files: DepartmentsView.xml and DepartmentsViewImpl.java.

2. Double click DepartmentsViewImpl.java to open its source code.

3. Look in the Structure window or directly at the code and note that DepartmentsViewImpl extends ViewObjectImpl, but has no accessor methods.

Additional Information: Unlike the Java class for an entity object, a view object class does not have getters and setters for its attributes. An instantiation of a view object class does not correspond to a row, but instead to the entire results of the query. That instantiation has several methods, such as `first()`, `next()`, and `findByKey()`, inherited from ViewObjectImpl, which return objects called *view rows*. These do correspond to rows of returned data in a query, and they do have methods, `getAttribute()` and `setAttribute()`, which return and set values for the view attributes. For example, if DepartmentsViewImpl1 is a particular

DepartmentsViewImpl usage, `DepartmentsViewImpl1.first()` would return a view row with the ability to return the values of a row of the query as in the following table:

Method Called	Value Returned
`DepartmentsViewImpl1.first().getAttribute("DepartmentId")`	A Number holding the value 10
`DepartmentsViewImpl1.first()..getAttribute("DepartmentName")`	"Administration"
`DepartmentsViewImpl1.first().getAttribute("ManagerId")`	A Number holding the value 200
`DepartmentsViewImpl1.first().getAttribute("LocationId")`	A Number holding the value 1700

You can use the DepartmentsViewImpl class to override the methods inherited from ViewObjectImpl or to add your own methods to implement custom query logic.

Explore DepartmentsView.xml

A view object's XML file can be examined using the following steps:

1. Double click DepartmentsView.xml to open its source.

2. Find the <ViewObject> tag close to the top of the file.

   Additional Information: The top-level element of the XML file, <ViewObject>, has XML attributes that together specify the query. The SelectList XML attribute specifies the columns in the query's SELECT clause and the FromList XML attribute lists the tables in its FROM clause. If the query had a WHERE clause, it would be specified with a Where XML attribute.

3. Find the <EntityUsage> tag for the Departments entity.

   Additional Information: A view object's attributes can be, but do not need to be, associated with entity attributes. If at least some view attributes are associated with entity attributes, the view object's XML file will contain elements called <EntityUsage> that relate the view object to the entity objects.

4. Find the <ViewAttribute> tags.

   Additional Information: A view object's XML file contains a <ViewAttribute> element for every view attribute. These elements look a bit different depending upon whether the view attribute is associated with an entity attribute. Since all of the view attributes in DepartmentsView are based on entity attributes in Departments, all of its <ViewAttribute> tags contain references to the Departments entity and its attributes.

Explore EmpDeptFkLink

You can examine a view link using the View Link Wizard:

1. On the EmpDeptFkLink node in the Navigator, select Edit EmpDeptFkLink from the right-click menu. A re-entrant version of the View Link Wizard appears.

2. Note that the view link joins the DepartmentsView view object and the EmployeesView view object, as shown next.

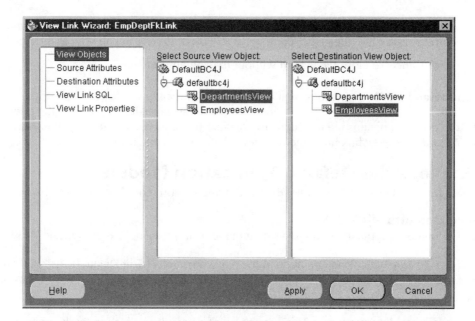

3. Click the View Link SQL node. In the Query Clauses box, you can see the WHERE clause that the view link will use to join Departments data to Employees data, shown next:

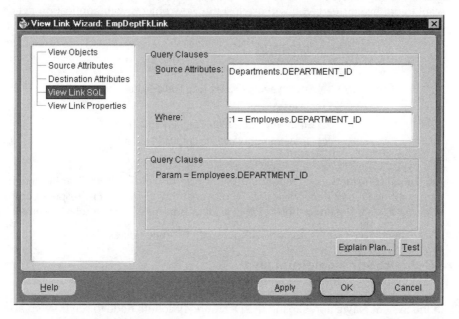

Additional Information: The parameter DepartmentsId from a row of the source view object will be substituted for :1 in the WHERE clause "WHERE :1=Employees.DEPARTMENT_ID" to limit the rows returned by a detail usage of EmployeesView. This definition is the reason why you will only be able to see employees for the selected department if you use this view link in your data model.

4. Click Cancel to close the wizard without making any changes.

What Just Happened? You looked at a view object and a view link. The view object's Java file is where you would place procedural logic that requires traversing the rows of the query's result. The XML file contains the metadata and declarative rules you create using the View Object Wizard. The view link links another view object to this one using a WHERE clause.

IV. Explore the Default Application Module

This phase looks at Defaultbc4jModule, the default application module created by the wizard.

Explore Defaultbc4jModule

You can examine an application module's data model using the Application Module Wizard:

1. On the Defaultbc4jModule node in the Navigator, select Edit Defaultbc4jModule from the right-click menu. A re-entrant version of the Application Module Wizard appears.

2. Examine the application module's data model.

   Additional Information: The data model of a default application module contains all possible view objects in all possible combinations: both independent and joined by view links. When you create your own application modules, you probably will not want to do this. Instead, you will use just the view objects your application needs, in just the combinations it needs. The following is the data model for Defaultbc4jModule:

   Additional Information: DepartmentsView1 and EmployeesView1 are independent usages of the DepartmentsView and EmployeesView view objects, respectively. The other usages are linked to those usages as details in master-detail relationships.

3. Click Cancel to close the wizard without making any changes.

Explore Defaultbc4jModuleImpl.java

An application module's Java source can be examined using the following steps:

1. In the System Navigator, expand the Defaultbc4jModule node to see the two application module files: Defaultbc4jModule.xml and Defaultbc4jModuleImpl.java.

2. Double-click Defaultbc4jModuleImpl.java to open its source code.

3. Use the Structure window to find the following methods, and double-click each to jump to the code for the method:

```
getDepartmentsView1()
getEmployeesView1()
getEmployeesView2()
getDepartmentsView2()
getEmployeesView3()
```

Additional Information: These methods return view object usages in the application module. You can call them from your client applications to access particular view object usages.

Explore Defaultbc4jModule.xml

An application module's XML file can be examined using the following steps:

1. Double click Defaultbc4jModule.xml to open its source.

2. Find the <ViewUsage> elements for each view object usage in the application module.

3. Find the <ViewLinkUsage> elements for each of the three times view links were used in the data model.

Additional Information: An application module's XML file contains the element <ViewLinkUsage> for each time a view link was used in creating the data model. The attributes SrcViewUsageName and DstViewUsageName specify the view usages that govern and are governed by the view link, respectively. A DstViewUsageName value of "defaultbc4j.Defaultbc4jModule.EmployeesView2" indicates that the detail view usage governed by the view link is EmployeesView2.

What Just Happened?   You looked at an application module. The application module's Java file is where procedural transaction logic can be implemented and where you can find methods that return the view object usages. The XML file contains the metadata and declarative rules that specify your data model.

V. Test the Default Business Components

Now that you have examined the business components, you can look at them in action. Business components do not have a user interface, so it is not really possible to see the business components working except through a user interface.

JDeveloper includes a user interface, the Oracle Business Component Browser, that can be run to test any application module. The browser will be used to test Defaultbc4jModule. Because Defaultbc4jModule contains all possible view objects in all possible combinations, testing Defaultbc4jModule is really a way of testing the entire business components project.

NOTE
As mentioned earlier, default application modules are not generally good for production-quality enterprise applications because they are too big. They contain usages of every view object, linked together in every possible combination, instead of just the data model the client needs. This leads to a needlessly large cache, which can degrade performance. However, they are excellent for testing all of your business components at once.

Open the Business Component Browser

The Business Component Browser can be opened to test an application module and its associated business components using the following steps:

1. On the Defaultbc4jModule node, select Test from the right-click menu. The Business Component Browser starts up, showing the Connect dialog.

2. The defaults in the Connect dialog are fine for the purposes of this practice, so click Connect. The main dialog of the Business Component Browser appears. In the left-hand pane, you can see the Defaultbc4jModule's data model, as shown next:

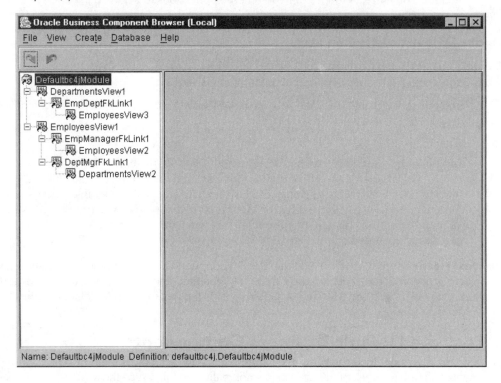

TIP
You can also click Run in the IDE toolbar after selecting the application module or BC4J project node in the Navigator. This method bypasses the Connect dialog.

Test an Independent Usage of DepartmentsView

You can scroll through the query results for an independent view object usage using the following steps:

1. Double click DepartmentsView1. In the right-hand pane, you can now see the data from DepartmentsView's query, one row at a time.

2. Click the blue right arrow to scroll forward to Department 30 as shown next:

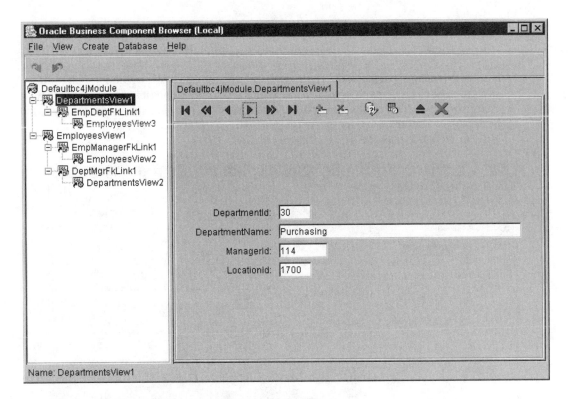

Test Two Different Usages of EmployeesView

You can contrast detail and independent usages of a view object using the following steps:

1. Be sure that department 30 is displayed. Double click EmployeesView3 in the left-hand pane. In the right-hand pane, you can now see data from EmployeesView's query, one row at a time.

2. Scroll forward through the data. Notice that all the employees listed have DepartmentId 30. This is because the business components framework uses EmpDeptFkLink to automatically synchronize EmployeesView2 with DepartmentsView. If the current row of DepartmentsView is 30, only employees with that department will show up in EmployeesView3.

3. Double click EmployeesView1. The same kind of single-row browser is displayed.

4. Scroll forward through the data. Notice that EmployeesView1 contains all of the employees, not just those with DepartmentId 30. That is because the EmployeesView1 usage, unlike the EmployeesView3 usage, is not governed by DepartmentsView1.

5. Click the red X in the browser toolbar to close each open window in turn.

TIP
If you want to pull a window out of the tester's frame, click the blue up arrow in the browser toolbar.

Test EmpDeptFkLink

You can view a split-screen display of joined view objects using the following steps:

1. Double click EmpDeptFkLink1. The right-hand pane is now split. In the top half, you can see rows from DepartmentsView1 one at a time, and in the bottom half, you can see a table of all rows currently showing in EmployeesView3. This is simply another way the Business Component Browser lets you view linked view objects. Selecting a view link lets you view both objects at once, as shown next:

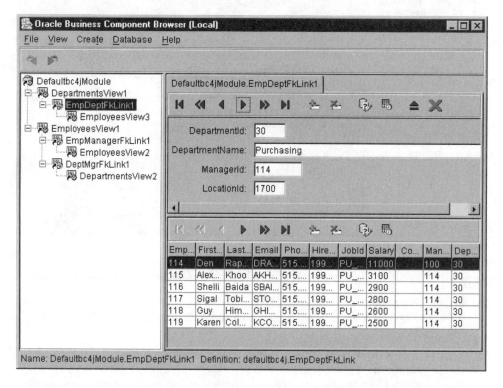

2. Scroll through the departments. The list of employees automatically changes.

3. Close the Business Component Browser.

What Just Happened?   You used the Business Component Browser to test your business components. You saw a display of all the view usages in your data model, two ways of displaying data in the Business Component Browser, and how view links synchronize detail view usages with their master view usage.

CHAPTER
10

Representing Data

It is a capital mistake to theorize before one has data.
—Sir Arthur Conan Doyle (1855–1930), *A Scandal in Bohemia*

 he first step in building a database application is representing the data itself. This chapter covers the use of entity objects as representations of units of data. Before you start this chapter, remember the following facts about entity objects from Chapter 9:

- An entity object is the representation of a database table or view.

- An entity object has one or more entity attributes that represent columns in the table or view.

- The Java types of the entity attributes are classes that correspond to the SQL types of the columns. Some entity attributes are mapped to particular Java classes called "domains."

- Associated with each entity object is a Java file with code logic and an XML file with the definition of the entity, including its attributes.

In this chapter, you will learn to edit entity objects like those created by the Business Components Package Wizard to delete entity attributes representing database columns you do not need, add transient entity attributes to represent calculated values, and represent PRIMARY KEY and NOT NULL constraints. You will also learn how to represent FOREIGN KEY constraints and other table relationships. In the hands-on practice, you will create, modify, and test business components to represent the HR schema.

You will not create new entity objects from scratch in this chapter. For most purposes, using the Business Components Package Wizard (as you did in Chapter 9) is sufficient for creating prototype entity objects for editing. If you want to create individual entity objects later, it is often best to use the Class Modeler. For information about doing this, see Chapter 11.

Entity Attributes

This section will discuss adding and deleting attributes from entity objects and changing those attributes' properties to add and remove constraints and affect their behavior.

Adding and Deleting Attributes

A one-to-one mapping between columns in a table and attributes in the corresponding entity object is most common. However, there are some exceptions. For example:

- The table may have columns that you know your business logic will never use. Entity attributes corresponding to these columns will just use up memory, so you may want to delete them.

- You may want to have *transient attributes*—attributes you calculate or set on a particular row that are needed for the duration of the transaction, but that are not stored in the database.

In these cases, you will need to add or delete attributes from an entity object. You might also want to add or delete attributes if your database table changes to include a new column or to drop an old one. The hands-on practice in this chapter will demonstrate how to add and delete attributes from an entity object.

Changing Datatypes

In Chapter 9, you learned that each database column (with its datatype) is mapped to an entity attribute (with Java type).

There are some restrictions on which Java types can correspond to particular SQL datatypes, but you have some flexibility as well. Table 10-1 lists some common mappings between Java types and SQL datatypes.

JDeveloper will select a default Java type appropriate to the database column datatype, but you can change it to any of the acceptable Java types listed in the table on the Attribute Settings page of the Entity Object Wizard, as shown in Figure 10-1.

You can also change the datatype to synchronize the entity object with the database if you have changed the column definition in the table.

SQL Datatypes	Acceptable Java Types
NUMBER	Number, Boolean, Integer, BigDecimal, String
TINYINT, SMALLINT, INTEGER, BIGINT, INT, REAL, DOUBLE, FLOAT, DECIMAL, NUMERIC, BIT	Number, String
VARCHAR2, NVARCHAR2, CHAR, VARCHAR, LONG	String, Char, Character
DATE, TIME, DATETIME	Date
TIMESTAMP	Date, Timestamp
RAW, LONG RAW	Raw
CLOB	ClobDomain
BLOB	BlobDomain
BFILE	BFileDomain
STRUCT	Object
ARRAY, VARRAY	Array
REF	Ref
ROWID	Object

TABLE 10-1. *Common Type Mappings*

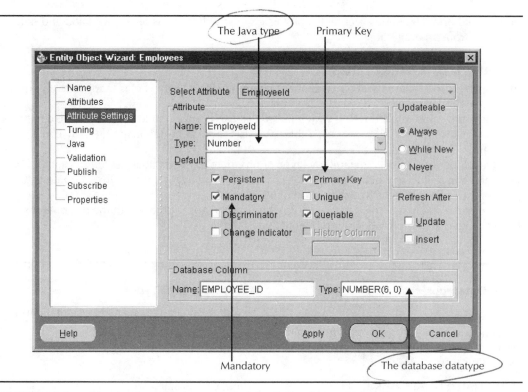

FIGURE 10-1. *The Attribute Settings page of the Entity Object Wizard*

NOTE
If you want to create BC4J objects that use a non-Oracle database, you will have to use a separate type map to associate datatypes with Java types—either JDeveloper's "Java" type map or a type map you create. You can find information about using BC4J with non-Oracle databases in the JDeveloper online help system.

Representing Column Constraints

Databases such as Oracle provide five constraints that can be applied to columns: PRIMARY KEY, NOT NULL, UNIQUE, FOREIGN KEY, and CHECK. As mentioned in the last chapter, foreign keys are represented by associations, and this is discussed later in this chapter. Check constraints, which typically provide for intercolumn validation and dependencies, are discussed in Chapter 12. Unique constraints are not used directly by BC4J, although BC4J can generate database tables with unique constraints, and this is discussed in Chapter 11. The constraints are represented in the XML for an attribute.

NOT NULL Constraints

When you create an entity object from a table, JDeveloper determines whether any of the columns in the table has a primary key or NOT NULL constraint. If either of these constraints has been defined, JDeveloper automatically generates the corresponding XML code.

The reason the BC4J framework allows you to represent NOT NULL constraints in entity objects is performance. Rather than posting data to the database every time your user changes a field value, the framework saves up changes until you request a post or commit. By representing the NOT NULL constraint in the entity objects, rather than just in the database, the framework can verify that the constraints are satisfied without making a round trip to the database.

PRIMARY KEY Constraints

The reason the BC4J framework represents the PRIMARY KEY constraint in entity objects is different. The framework uses the entity attributes tagged as parts of the primary key to look up particular instances of the entity object class. Without primary key attributes, the framework would have no way of distinguishing between different entity instances. If your table does not have a primary key, JDeveloper will create a RowId entity attribute, based on the pseudo-column ROW_ID, of type oracle.jbo.domain.RowId, and use it as a primary key.

CAUTION
If you want to use BC4J to access a non-Oracle database, you must ensure that all of your tables have primary keys.

Additional Constraints

You may also want to define constraints in an entity object that do not correspond to any database constraint, if any of the following conditions hold:

- You do not want to change your database tables, and you need a new constraint.

- You need a constraint but do not have permission to perform DDL operations to change the table.

- The constraint applies only to your applications; other applications using the same tables do not need it.

In addition, you might want to represent a column constraint that has been added to a database table since you created the corresponding entity object.

Use the following steps to represent a column constraint:

1. On the entity object node select Edit from the right-click menu.

2. Select the Attribute Settings node.

3. Choose an attribute from the *Select Attribute* dropdown.

4. To make the attribute NOT NULL, check the *Mandatory* checkbox.

5. To make the attribute part of a primary key, check the *Primary Key* checkbox. If you check this checkbox for multiple attributes, they will function as a multi-part key. Figure 10-1 shows an example of this dialog.

Synchronizing Entity Objects with the Database

In addition to manually adding and dropping attributes or constraints, you can use JDeveloper to automatically synchronize some or all of your entity objects with the database. On the BC4J package node in the Navigator, select Synchronize with Database from the right-click menu, and use the Synchronize with Database dialog to select and make any desired updates to the BC4J tier, as shown here:

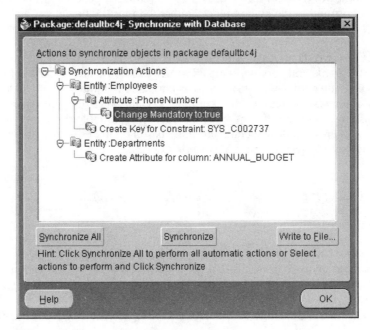

Representing Foreign Key Relationships

As mentioned in Chapter 9, foreign key relationships between tables are represented by associations between entity objects. Creating an association between two entity objects has the following possible effects:

- Creating XML elements for the associated entities
- Creating accessor methods in the associated Java classes
- Creating an XML file for the association

Each will be discussed separately.

Creating XML Elements for the Associated Entities   When you create an association, you can choose to *generate accessors* in either or both of the associated entities. If you generate accessors in an entity object, that entity object's XML file gets an XML accessor element. An XML accessor element contains both a unique accessor name and the name of the associated entity object. For example, when JDeveloper created the DeptMgrFkAssoc association between Employees and Departments, an XML accessor element called "Departments," with a reference to the entity object Departments, was added to Employees.xml.

NOTE
An XML accessor element is not the same as a Java accessor method, although as explained below, they are closely related.

If there are multiple associations between the same entity objects, each entity object may contain multiple XML accessor elements. For example, when JDeveloper created EmpDeptFkAssoc between Employees and Departments, an XML accessor element called "Departments1," also with a reference to the entity object Departments, was added to Employees.xml as well.

Creating Accessor Methods for the Associated Entities   This is where the name of the XML accessor element is most important. For each XML accessor element in an entity object's XML file, JDeveloper will generate accessor methods based on the XML accessor element's name. For example, EmployeesImpl will have the accessors `getDepartments()`, `getDepartments1()`, and `setDepartments1()`. The sidebar "Why is There no setDepartments() Method?" explains the reason that the `setDepartments()` method is missing.

Creating an XML file for the Association   Associations have their own XML files as well. These files contain the logical definition of the association, including elements that specify the entities linked at each end of the association, the XML accessor element names for those entities, and the master and detail attributes.

Creating an Association

The Business Components Package Wizard will automatically generate associations for each foreign key constraint in the database. However, you may want to create associations that do not correspond to foreign key constraints, or that correspond to newly added foreign key constraints.

Why Is There No setDepartments() Method?

The reason there is no `setDepartments()` method is that DeptMgrFkAssoc can associate many departments with an employee, and there is no way to simultaneously set a number of departments. If you look at the code, you will notice that `getDepartments()` and `getDepartments1()` have different return types: `getDepartments1()` returns a DepartmentsImpl (that is, an instance of the DepartmentsImpl class), as expected, but `getDepartments()` returns a `RowIterator`. This allows the program to manipulate any number of departments. You will learn more about associations that link single objects vs. associations that link multiple objects later in this chapter, and the RowIterator class is discussed in Chapter 12.

To create an association:

1. On the business components package node, select New Association from the right-click menu.

2. If the Welcome page appears, click Next.

3. On the Name page, enter the name (such as "DeptEmpFKAssoc") and package (for example, "hrbc4j") of the association and click Next.

4. On the Entity Objects page (shown next), select one of the master attributes under the entity corresponding to the master table (Departments) on the *Select Source Attribute* side and the corresponding detail attribute on the *Select Destination Attribute* side. Click Next.

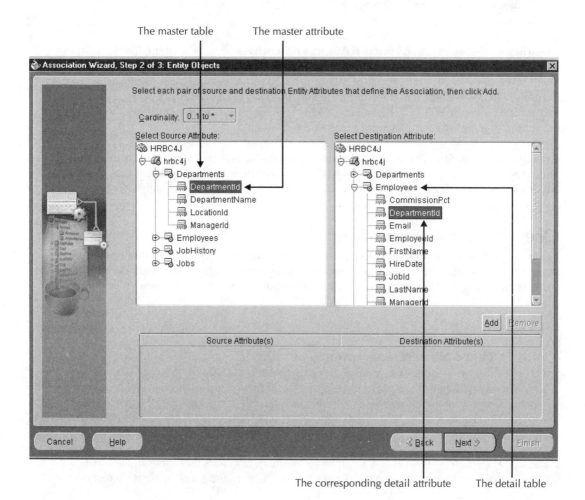

5. Click Add to add the master/detail attribute pair to the association.

6. Repeat steps 4 and 5 for each master/detail attribute pair in the foreign key relationship.

7. Click Next.

8. On the Association Properties page, enter accessor names (such as "EmployingDepartment" and "EmployeesInDepartment"). These will appear in the entity objects' XML files and will determine the names of the accessor methods in the Java class files. Click Finish.

Compositions

Consider two different sorts of foreign key relationships: relationships like the one between employees and the departments that employ them, and those like the one between line items in a purchase order and the order itself. Certainly, most employees are in a department, but an employee is not, strictly speaking, part of a department. Employees exist independently of their departments; a company could eliminate a department without necessarily eliminating its members. By contrast, a line item is part of a purchase order, rather than an independently existing thing. It makes no sense to delete an order without deleting all of its line items.

An association like the one between line items and purchase orders, where the detail is part of the master, is called a *composition*. You cannot delete a master in a composition without deleting all of its details.

If the Business Components Package Wizard detects that a database foreign key has ON DELETE CASCADE set, it will automatically create the corresponding association as a composition. You can also set an association to be a composition on the Association Properties page of the Association Wizard. You can either do this when you create the association, or you can re-enter the wizard by selecting Edit from the right-click menu on the association. On the Association Properties page, use the following steps:

1. Check the *Composition Association* checkbox. The *Implement Cascade Delete* checkbox will automatically be checked.

2. If you want to automatically delete details when someone tries to delete their master, leave *Implement Cascade Delete* checked. If you do not select this option, deleting a master that still has details will throw an exception.

One-to-One, One-to-Many, and Many-to-Many Relationships

The most common kind of relationship between tables is the one represented by a foreign key: a relationship where a row from the master table corresponds to any number of rows from the detail table. Each detail row, for its part, has at most one master row. This kind of relationship is a *one-to-many* relationship. For example, the relationship between departments and the employees in those departments is one-to-many as shown here:

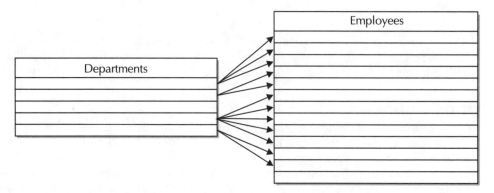

However, this is only one kind of relationship. Another is a *one-to-one* relationship, where there is a one-to-one correspondence between the rows of two tables. For example, you might have one table, DEPARTMENTS, containing basic information about departments, and another table, DEPARTMENTS_EXT, containing more information for each row as shown next:

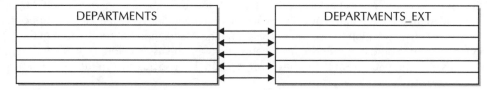

The most complex kind of table relationship is a *many-to-many* relationship, one where any number of rows from one table can be related to any number of rows from the detail table. Consider the JOBS table, which lists all of the jobs in the company, and the EMPLOYEES table. A relationship exists between employees and all the jobs they have held in the past.

This is not a one-to-one relationship, because an employee can have held any number of jobs. It is not a one-to-many relationship either, since either EMPLOYEES or JOBS could be considered the master. One possible relationship between the two tables is that a single employee may have held many jobs since joining the company. But another relationship is that every job has been held by a series of employees over the company's history. Each employee can correspond to many jobs, and each job can correspond to many employees, as shown here:

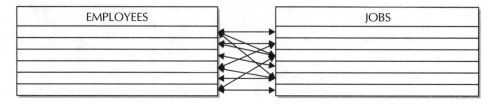

In addition to the standard one-to-many associations, JDeveloper lets you create one-to-one and many-to-many associations.

Creating One-to-One Associations

Creating a one-to-one association is straightforward. On the Entity Objects page of the Association Wizard, set the *Cardinality* field to "1 to 1".

When you make an association one-to-one, this change is noted in the association's XML file. In addition, it changes the Java files for the entity objects. As mentioned, an entity object's Java file can contain accessors (that is, getters and/or setters) for each associated entity object. In a one-to-many association, the master class has no setter but does have a getter that returns a RowIterator.

If you make an association one-to-one, both classes can have getter methods that return entity object classes, and both can have setter methods that take entity object classes as arguments. This makes one-to-one associations easier to work with.

Creating Many-to-Many Associations

Creating a many-to-many association is a bit more complex because it is not just a matter of associating a key from one table with a key from the other. Instead, many-to-many associations between two tables make use of a third table, called an intersection table.

An *intersection table* contains two foreign keys. One of them matches up with the primary key of one table, and the other matches up with the primary key of the other table as follows:

EMPLOYEES (Primary Key EMPLOYEE_ID)	JOB_HISTORY			JOBS (Primary Key JOB_ID)
	EMPLOYEE_ID	START_DATE	JOB_ID	
103	103	1993-01-04	SH_CLERK	SH_CLERK
104	103	1989-09-21	PU_CLERK	PU_CLERK
108	104	1996-02-17	PU_CLERK	ST_CLERK
114	108	1998-03-24	PU_CLERK	SA_REP
115	114	1999-01-01	ST_CLERK	
145	114	1999-12-07	PU_CLERK	
	115	1987-09-17	SH_CLERK	
	115	1999-01-01	ST_CLERK	
	145	1994-07-01	PU_CLERK	
	145	1998-03-01	SA_REP	

This creates two one-to-many relationships. For example, in the EMPLOYEES-JOBS case, there is a one-to-many relationship with EMPLOYEES as the master and JOB_HISTORY as the detail, and another one-to-many relationship with JOBS as the master and JOB_HISTORY as the detail.

You can think of these two one-to-many relationships as representing a single many-to-many relationship, which relates rows from EMPLOYEES and JOBS if they share a JOB_HISTORY detail as shown in the following illustration:

EMPLOYEES (Primary Key EMPLOYEE_ID)	JOBS (Primary Key JOB_ID)
103	SH_CLERK
104	PU_CLERK
108	ST_CLERK
114	SA_REP
115	
145	

The Business Components Package Wizard does not automatically create many-to-many associations for you, so if you want one, you will have to create it yourself. You can create a many-to-many association between two entities, so long as you have a third entity that represents the intersection table. You will create a many-to-many association in the hands-on practice later in this chapter.

The results of creating a many-to-many association differ from those of creating a one-to-many association or a one-to-one association in two ways:

- The association's XML file is different.

- Neither end's entity object class has a setter method corresponding to the association, and both ends' getter methods return RowIterators.

Representing Oracle Object Types

As mentioned in this chapter, BC4J automatically associates standard column types with Java classes—either standard Java classes (such as java.lang.String) or built-in domains (such as oracle.jbo.domain.Number). Some table columns, however, are of custom Oracle object types. As was mentioned in Chapter 9, Oracle object type columns are represented as custom domains.

When you create an entity object based on a table with an Oracle object type column, JDeveloper automatically creates a custom domain for you and maps the column to an entity attribute with that domain as its Java type. If you have object types embedded in object types, JDeveloper recursively creates custom domains for all of them.

CAUTION
BC4J does not support non-Oracle object types.

Using Custom Domains

A custom domain has both an XML file and a Java class file associated with it. Like an entity object, it has a number of attributes (one for each column in the Oracle object type), which are represented as <Attribute> tags in the XML file. The attribute also has getters and setters in the Java class. All attributes have Java types, which can be either standard Java classes or other domains.

However, a custom domain is much simpler than an entity object. All the features of tables that do not apply to Oracle object types are left out: Domains do not need (and cannot have) a primary key. They do not have column constraints. They are not the ends of associations (although they can be used to associate entities, just like any other entity attribute type).

Domains are not, however, used to represent Oracle object types that occur in object tables. If you create a table using CREATE TABLE <table> OF <object_type>, and you base an entity object on that table, the BC4J framework will not create a domain to represent the object type; instead, it will simply create entity attributes for each of the object type's columns.

You can delete attributes from domains, add transient attributes to them, or change attribute properties (except for PRIMARY KEY, which domains do not use), just as you can for entity objects.

Using Oracle Object Types

For example, consider an Oracle object type called ADDRESS_TYP, with the following definition:

```
CREATE TYPE ADDRESS_TYP AS OBJECT
   (STREET_ADDRESS VARCHAR2 (20),
    POSTAL_CODE VARCHAR2 (12),
    CITY VARCHAR2 (30),
    STATE_PROVINCE VARCHAR2(25),
    COUNTRY_ID VARCHAR2 (2));
```

You could create a table called CUSTOMERS that uses this object type as follows:

```
CREATE TABLE CUSTOMERS
   ( CUSTOMER_ID NUMBER(6),
     CUST_FIRST_NAME VARCHAR2(20),
     CUST_LAST_NAME VARCHAR2(20),
     CUST_ADDRESS ADDRESS_TYP );
```

If you create an entity object from the table, the entity object will have attributes called CustomerId, CustFirstName, CustLastName, and CustAddress, and you will automatically get a domain, AddressTyp, with attributes StreetAddress, PostalCode, City, StateProvince, and CountryId.

On the other hand, you can create a table called ADDRESSES as follows:

```
CREATE TABLE ADDRESSES
   OF ADDRESS_TYP;
```

If you then create an entity object from ADDRESSES, the entity object will have attributes called StreetAddress, PostalCode, City, StateProvince, and CountryId, and no domain will be created.

Hands-on Practice: Represent the HR Schema

In this practice, you will create entity objects and associations to represent the tables in the HR schema. The project you create will involve a transient attribute, a column constraint, and a many-to-many association.

This practice steps you through the following phases:

I. Create a workspace and empty project

II. Create default entity objects

III. Change the attributes

- Add a transient attribute

- Make an attribute mandatory

IV. Create a many-to-many association

    V. **Create default view objects and view links and a simple application module**

       ■ Create default view objects

       ■ Create a default view link

       ■ Create a simple application module

    VI. **Test the entity object layer**

       ■ Open the Business Component Browser

       ■ Test the mandatory attribute

       ■ Test transient and persistent attributes

       ■ Test the many-to-many view link

I. Create a Workspace and Empty Project

This phase creates a workspace and project for the BC4J objects.

1. On the Workspaces node in the Navigator, select New Workspace from the right-click menu. The New Workspace dialog opens.

2. Use "HRWS" as the name for both the workspace directory and the workspace file. Be sure to leave the directory and drive of the workspace intact.

3. Click OK. The New Project dialog opens.

4. Use "HRBC4J" as the name for both the project directory and the project file.

5. Click Save All.

What Just Happened?   You created an empty workspace and project for your BC4J layer.

II. Create Default Entity Objects

This phase creates default entity objects for the HR Schema.

1. On the HRBC4J.jpr project node, select New Business Components Package from the right-click menu. The Business Components Package Wizard opens.

2. If the Welcome page appears, click Next.

3. On the Package Name page, enter "hrbc4j". Leave the default radio group selection. Click Next.

4. On the Connection page, select HR from the *Connection Name* dropdown. Click Next.

5. On the Business Components page, select DEPARTMENTS, EMPLOYEES, JOBS, and JOB_HISTORY, and click the right-arrow button.

Additional Information: This will cause the wizard to create an entity object corresponding to each of those tables and associations for each of the foreign keys between the tables.

6. Uncheck the *View Objects and View Links* checkbox.

Additional Information: Later, you will add some attributes and create a many-to-many association, and you will need to base the view objects and view links on the changed entity objects and associations.

7. Click Next. The Summary page appears. If you want, inspect the summary. Click Finish to generate the objects.

8. Click Save All.

9. Expand the BC4J object nodes in the System Navigator and identify the objects that were created.

What Just Happened? You created entity objects for the BC4J layer. You did not create default view objects and view links or a default application module, because you will change the entity objects before you base view objects on them.

III. Change the Attributes
This phase modifies the Employees object to add a transient attribute and make an existing attribute mandatory.

Add a Transient Attribute
You need to add a transient attribute for yearly pay. As mentioned, in contrast to persistent attribute values, a transient attribute holds a value that is not stored in the database. Use the following steps to accomplish this task:

1. In the System Navigator, expand the hrbc4j package.

2. On the Employees entity node, select Edit Employees from the right-click menu.

3. Select the Attributes node.

4. Click New. The New Entity Attribute dialog appears.

5. Name this attribute "YearlyPay".

Additional Information: In Chapter 12, you will use this attribute to calculate an estimated yearly pay for an employee, based on that employee's monthly salary and commission. For now, it will be an uncalculated transient attribute.

6. Select Number from the dropdown list for the *Type* field.

7. Uncheck the *Persistent* checkbox. This makes the attribute non-persistent (transient). The dialog should look like this:

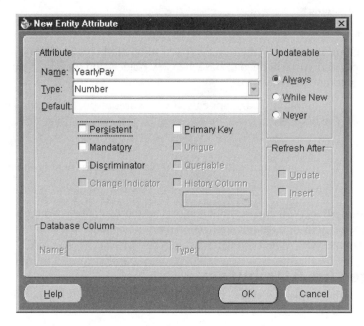

8. Click OK to close the dialog. YearlyPay will be added to the *Entity Attribute* list.

Make an Attribute Mandatory

You can make an attribute mandatory using the following steps:

I. Select the Attribute Settings node.

2. In the *Select Attribute* list, select PhoneNumber.

Additional Information: The PHONE_NUMBER column does not have a NOT NULL constraint in the database, so the Business Components Package Wizard did not automatically make PhoneNumber a mandatory attribute.

3. Check the *Mandatory* checkbox, as shown in the following illustration:

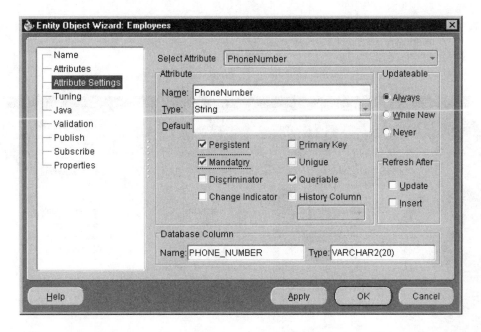

4. Click OK to close the wizard.

5. Click Save All.

What Just Happened?   The transient YearlyPay attribute you just added will be stored in the BC4J layer for as long as it is running, but will not be stored in the database. The mandatory PhoneNumber attribute will throw an exception if it is not populated.

IV. Create a Many-to-Many Association

This phase creates a many-to-many association between the Employees entity and the Jobs entity that links each employee with every job he or she has had in the past.

1. On the hrbc4j package node, select New Association from the right-click menu.

2. If the Welcome page appears, click Next.

3. On the Name page, enter "EmpPastJobsAssoc" for the association's name and click Next.

4. On the Entity Objects page, select "* to *" as the cardinality of the association.

5. In the *Select Source Attribute* tree, select EmployeeId under Employees.

6. In the *Select Intersection Attribute* tree, select EmployeeId under JobHistory.

7. Click the left-hand Add button to add the source/intersection attribute pair. The page should look as shown next:

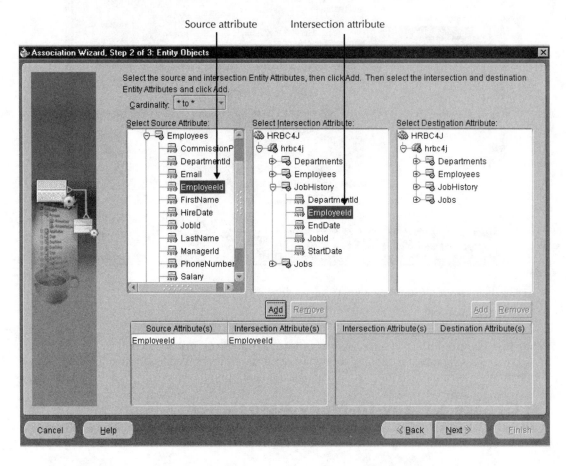

8. In the *Select Destination Attribute* tree, select JobId under Jobs.

9. In the *Select Intersection Attribute* tree, select JobId under JobHistory.

10. Click the right-hand Add button to add the destination/intersection attribute pair. The page should look as shown next:

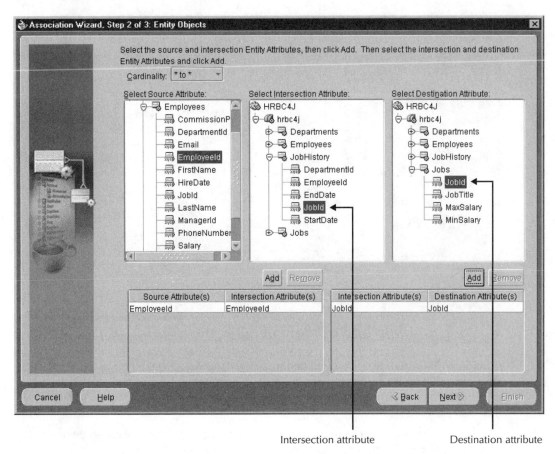

Intersection attribute   Destination attribute

11. Click Next.

12. On the Association Properties page, change the Source *Accessor Name* to "PastHolders" and the Destination *Accessor Name* to "PastJobs" as shown here:

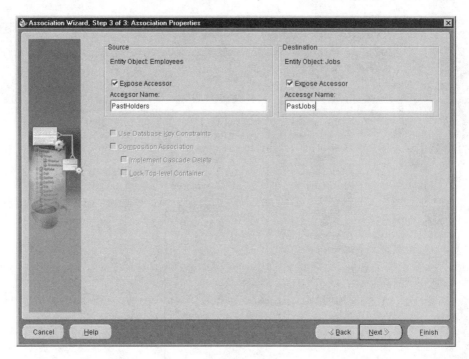

Additional Information: This will generate a getPastHolders() method in the JobsImpl Java class that returns everyone who has ever held a particular job, and a getPastJobs() method in the EmployeesImpl Java class that returns every job a particular employee has ever held.

You cannot make a many-to-many association into a composition, because there is no such thing as a single "master" row corresponding to a "detail" row.

13. Click Finish to generate the association.

14. Click Save All.

V. Create Default View Objects and View Links and a Simple Application Module

This phase creates view objects, a view link, and an application module for the entity objects and association you created. In the next phase, you use the Business Component Browser (tester) to test these BC4J objects. Because the Browser tests an application module and its contained view objects and view links, you have to create default view objects and links for the entity objects and associations you want to test. See the sidebar "Default View Objects and Testing" for more information.

Create Default View Objects

You can create default view objects for entity objects by using the following steps:

1. On the Jobs entity object node, select New Default View Object from the right-click menu. This creates a view object called JobsView.

2. Repeat step 1 for the Employees entity object.

3. Click Save All.

Create a Default View Link

You can create default view links for associations by using the following steps:

1. On the EmpPastJobsAssoc node, select New View Link from the right-click menu to open the View Link Wizard.

2. If the Welcome page appears, click Next.

3. On the Name page, enter "EmpPastJobsLink" in the *Name* field and click Next.

4. On the View Objects page, select EmployeesView as the source and JobsView as the destination.

5. Click Next to display the Source Attributes page.

Default View Objects and Testing

Chapter 9 mentioned a use for default application modules—they allow you to test all of your business components at once. Just as default application modules do not have much real-world use, default view objects do not either. They just select every attribute from an entity object's table (the equivalent of a SELECT * query in SQL). However, like default application modules (and like SELECT * queries), default view objects are useful for testing. Each one provides a direct window into the data and business logic represented by one entity object.

6. Select EmpPastJobsAssoc from the *Available Associations* list and click the arrow button. EmployeeId, the source attribute for the association, will appear on the *Selected Attributes* list as shown here:

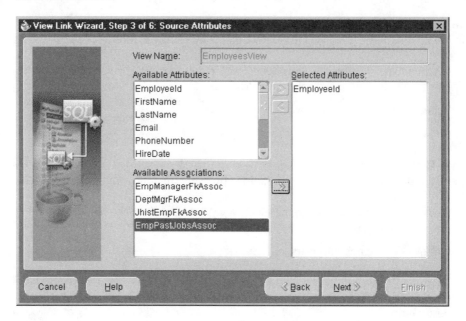

CAUTION
Do not select EmployeeId from the "Available Attributes" list. Even though the source attribute for EmpPastJobsAssoc is EmployeeId, you must select the association to base the view object on it. If you select EmployeeId, the wizard will have no way of knowing whether you want to use EmpPastJobsAssoc or EmpJobFkAssoc.

7. Click Next.

8. On the Destination Attributes page, verify that JobId is in the *Selected Attributes* list. If it is not, click Back, remove the EmployeeId attribute, add the association again, and click Next to try again.

9. If JobId is in the *Selected Attributes* list, click Next.

10. Leave the default settings on the View Link SQL page. Click Next.

11. On the View Link Properties page, check both *In View Object* checkboxes (for Source and Destination), as shown next.

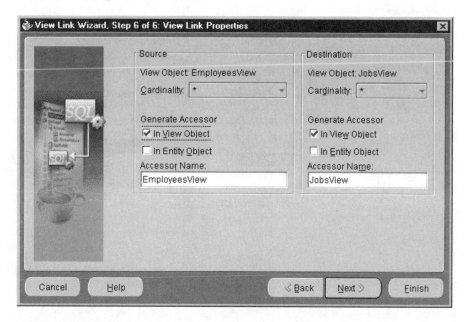

Additional Information: This allows you to use either EmployeesView or JobsView as the master view object.

12. Click Finish to create the view link. Click Save All.

Create a Simple Application Module

You can create a simple application module for testing using the following steps:

1. On the hrbc4j package node, select New Application Module from the right-click menu to open the Application Module Wizard.

2. If the Welcome page appears, click Next.

3. On the Name page, enter "EntityTestModule" in the *Name* field. Click Next.

4. On the Data Model page, select EmployeesView in the *Available View Objects* tree and click the right arrow button so that a usage called "EmployeesView1" appears on the *Data Model* tree as shown here:

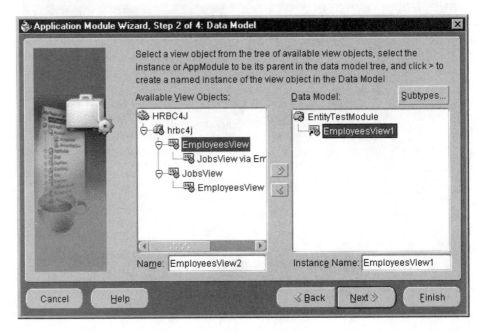

5. Repeat step 4 for JobsView (not "JobsView via EmpPastJobsLink"). Be sure to select Entity Test Module in the *Data Model* area before attempting the move.

6. Select EmployeesView1 in the *Data Model* tree. In the *Available View Objects* tree, select "JobsView via EmpPastJobsLink" and add a usage of it to the *Data Model* tree as shown here:

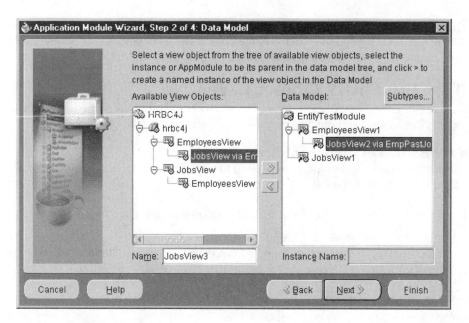

Additional Information: This creates a view object usage of JobsView governed by EmployeesView1.

7. Select JobsView1 in the *Data Model* tree.

8. In the *Available View Objects* tree, select "EmployeesView via EmpPastJobsLink" and include a usage of it in the *Data Model* tree.
Additional Information: This creates a view object usage of EmployeesView governed by JobsView1. Because EmpPastJobsLink is many-to-many, you may want to retrieve all jobs for a particular employee as well as all employees for a particular job.

9. Click Finish to create the application module.

10. Click Save All.

CAUTION
When working in the Data Model page of the Application Module Wizard, it is important to select the proper node in the "Data Model" tree before adding a view object usage from the "Available View Objects" tree. The wizard will warn you if you have not selected the proper node in the "Data Model" tree.

What Just Happened? You created view objects, a view link, and an application module that are sufficient to test the functionality of the entity objects and associations you created earlier. You will create customized view objects, view links, and application modules in Chapter 13.

VI. Test the Entity Object Layer

This phase uses the simple application module created in the previous phase to test the changed entity object, Employees, and the new many-to-many association, EmpPastJobsAssoc.

Open the Business Component Browser

The Business Component Browser can be opened to test an application module and its associated business components using the following steps:

1. On the EntityTestModule node, select Test from the right-click menu.

2. When the Oracle Business Component Browser – Connect dialog appears, click Connect. The main page of the Oracle Business Component Browser will appear, showing your data model for EntityTestModule on the left.

Test the Mandatory Attribute

You can test a mandatory attribute using the following steps:

1. In the Business Component Browser, in the right-click menu for EmployeesView1, select Show to display the first row of EmployeesView1 in the tester.

TIP
You can also double click the view object usage instead of selecting Show from the right-click menu to display the tester page.

2. Erase King's phone number.

3. Click the blue right-arrow to scroll to the next employee. You will get an error dialog, since the row now violates the mandatory constraint you added. Click OK to dismiss the dialog.

4. Add King's phone number ("515.123.4567") back in (or click the Rollback the Changes button in the top toolbar).

Test Transient and Persistent Attributes

You can observe the differences between transient and persistent attributes using the following steps:

CAUTION
In some builds of JDeveloper, default view objects will not expose transient entity attributes. If you cannot see the "YearlyPay" attribute in the Browser, exit the tester, double click EmployeesView in the System Navigator, and use the Attributes page to add the YearlyPay attribute to the "Selected Attributes" list. Reopen the Browser to continue with the practice.

1. Click the blue right-arrow to scroll to the next employee.

2. Fill in the YearlyPay attribute for employees 101 and 102. Estimate their yearly pay at 100000 each. (In Chapter 12, you will populate this field automatically.)

3. Use the blue arrows to look at employees 101 and 102 again. The BC4J framework retains the value of YearlyPay for both of these employees.

4. Scroll to employee 103. Give Hunold a raise by increasing his salary to 9500.

5. Click the green arrow icon in the top toolbar of the tester to commit your changes.

CAUTION
As mentioned in the Introduction of this book, you may have to disable the SECURE_EMPLOYEES trigger on the EMPLOYEES table if you are working after business hours.

6. Close the tester.

7. Reopen the tester and view EmployeesView1 as explained in "Open the Business Component Browser" section.

TIP
After selecting the application module node, you can click the Run button in the JDeveloper toolbar to run the tester without displaying the connection dialog.

8. Look at employees 101, 102, and 103. Note that the YearlyPay attribute values for Kochhar and De Haan are gone, but the change to Hunold's salary is still there.

   Additional Information: This is the difference between a transient attribute that is not stored in the database and a persistent attribute that is stored in a database column. Transient attributes are only maintained for as long as the BC4J layer is active.

Test the Many-to-Many View Link
The following steps show the many-to-many association by testing the master-detail view link for Employee to Job and the other master-detail view link for Job to Employee.

1. On the EmpPastJobsLink1 node, select Show from the right-click menu.

2. Scroll through the employees to view their past jobs. Note that some employees (like King) have had no jobs except their current job, and some (like Kuchar) have had more than one.

3. On the EmpPastJobsLink2 node, select Show from the right-click menu.

4. Scroll through the jobs and you will see the employees who have held them in the past.

5. Close the Business Component Browser.

What Just Happened?   You used the Business Component Browser and your simple view object layer to test the Employees entity object and the EmpPastJobsAssoc association. You saw the BC4J framework enforce the *Mandatory* attribute setting and saw both sides of a many-to-many association.

CHAPTER
11

Modeling Business Components and Generating Database Tables

First things first, but not necessarily in that order.
—John Flanagan and Andrew McCulloch, "Meglos," *Dr. Who*

I n Chapter 10, you learned how to use entity objects and associations to represent database tables and constraints. This is a natural activity for a programmer with a database orientation. For such a programmer, database objects are primary, and middle-tier objects are used to represent these database objects in an application.

However, some programmers, namely those with a UML modeling or J2EE orientation, will think of this approach as backwards. To these programmers, business entities (represented by objects such as Entity Beans in the middle tier) and the relationships between those entities come first. Database objects are just used to handle persistence for these middle-tier objects. Generally, these programmers do not want to design entity objects and associations to represent existing database tables. Instead, they want to design entity objects and associations from scratch and generate database tables and constraints to handle their persistence.

CAUTION
Although the JDeveloper table-generation features allow you to assign tablespaces and storage conditions, they are not a substitute for a full-featured database modeling tool such as Oracle Designer. In general, it is best to use JDeveloper to create only a few relatively small tables needed by a single application. Even then, you should consult closely with your data model architect to make sure you are not breaking rules of efficient database design.

JDeveloper's Class Modeler includes functionality to make it easy to design entity objects and associations without existing tables in the database. JDeveloper also lets you generate database tables and constraints from BC4J, and lets you keep BC4J and the database synchronized should either change later.

You learned about the Class Modeler and UML diagrams in general in Chapter 8. This chapter covers only one very specific use of the Class Modeler—creating entity objects and associations.

After examining the creation of entity objects and associations, this chapter discusses how to use those entity objects and associations to generate constraints in the database. In the hands-on practice, you will model an entity object and an association and use them to generate a new database table and several constraints.

The Class Modeler and BC4J

The Class Modeler is a tool that allows you to create a UML class diagram. UML syntax is explained in Appendix C. In all of the UML diagrams in this chapter, boxes represent entity objects, and lines between them represent associations. (There are two types of line symbols between entity objects that do not represent an association. For more information, see the sidebar "Generalizations and Dependencies.") For example, the following diagram represents the relationships between Employees and Departments:

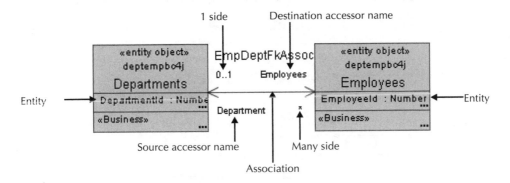

Starting a Class Model

As you learned in Chapter 8, you can create a new class model inside an empty project from the UML Diagrams section of the New gallery. You will see how this works in the hands-on practice.

If you have existing tables in your schema, you can create entity objects and associations for them and import them into your model by dragging them from the Connections\Database\<connection> node of the Navigator into your model. The Modeler automatically creates entity objects for the tables and associations based on the FOREIGN KEY constraints between any two selected tables. You will also try this out in the hands-on practice.

Modeling a New Entity Object

When you are working on a class diagram, the Component Palette includes an icon for entity objects, as shown in Figure 11-1.

Generalizations and Dependencies

When you work with the BC4J Component Palette in the Class Modeler, two of the options available are Generalization and Dependency.

The *generalization* relationship indicates that one business component is an extension of another. It is useful for those who want to customize the BC4J framework by making all entity objects extend a base entity object. It is also useful for those who want to further customize existing BC4J applications by creating new entity objects that extend the old entity objects, and substituting the new objects for the old ones throughout the application. Extending and substituting business components is beyond the scope of this book. For more information, see the JDeveloper online help.

The *dependency* relationship indicates that one business component depends on another. JDeveloper does not generate anything from this relationship. The dependency relationship only helps the person using the model understand the relationships between different entity objects. For more information about dependencies, see Appendix C.

The dependency and generalization icons are shown in Figure 11-1.

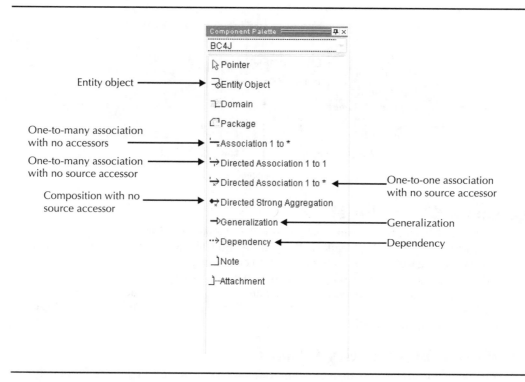

Entity object ⟶

One-to-many association
with no accessors ⟶

One-to-many association ⟶
with no source accessor

Composition with no ⟶
source accessor

⟵ One-to-one association
with no source accessor

⟵ Generalization

⟵ Dependency

FIGURE 11-1. *BC4J modeling icons*

Click the Entity Object icon, and then click on your diagram to create a new entity object. You can type the name of the entity object and a list of its attributes by typing directly in the Modeler. To make other modifications to the entity object, such as adding column constraints, double-click the entity object in the Modeler to open the Entity Object Wizard. You will create an entity object in the hands-on practice.

NOTE
Do not add foreign key attributes (that is, the destination attributes for planned associations) to entity objects. The Modeler will do this for you when you create the association.

Modeling New Associations

When you are working on a class diagram, the Component Palette contains four icons for associations, as shown in Figure 11-1. After you select an association icon, click first on the source entity object and then on the destination entity object to create the association. Destination attributes associated with the source entity object's primary key attributes will be added automatically.

You can change the name of an association, its cardinality (for example, to make a one-to-many association many-to-many), or the names of its accessors by selecting the appropriate label in the model and typing over it. For example, in the following illustration, the destination accessor name is being changed to "CurrentHolders":

After you create an association in the Modeler, you may need to double click it to open the Association Wizard for one of the following reasons:

- To set the source and destination attributes for the association, when the association should not be based on the source entity object's primary key

- To set the intersection table for a many-to-many association

- To generate a source accessor, if necessary

Generating Database Tables

You can generate database tables for your entire diagram by right-clicking outside any specific components (in the white space) and selecting **Generate | Database Objects for Diagram**. You can also generate a single database table by right clicking within an entity object and selecting **Generate | Database Objects**.

CAUTION
If you select a table to be generated, and it was already generated, JDeveloper will warn you that generating the table will overwrite the existing table, possibly resulting in the loss of database constraints and/or data. Triggers, views, and code using the table will have to be recompiled. If the table contains no data, and all of the constraints were generated from this BC4J layer, you can ignore this caution. However, because JDeveloper regenerates existing tables using DROP TABLE and CREATE TABLE rather than ALTER TABLE, you will lose existing data in the table, and any constraints not in the BC4J layer, by generating an existing table. If you need to alter a table with data in it, you should do so with SQL*Plus or another database tool.

The table names generated by the Class Modeler follow the naming conventions that the Business Components Project Wizard uses for deriving entity object names from table names. Recall that the Business Components Project Wizard replaces an underscore with capitalization of the next word. For example:

- A table named EMPLOYEE_BONUSES will correspond to an entity object named EmployeeBonuses.

- A table column named EMPLOYEE_ID will correspond to an entity attribute named EmployeeId.

When the Class Modeler generates tables for entity objects, it reverses this operation. For example:

■ An entity object named EmployeeBonuses will correspond to a table named EMPLOYEE_BONUSES.

■ An entity attribute named EmployeeId will correspond to a table column named EMPLOYEE_ID.

If you want to change these default names, edit your entity object before you generate the table. Change the name of the table on the Name page of the Entity Object Wizard, as shown next:

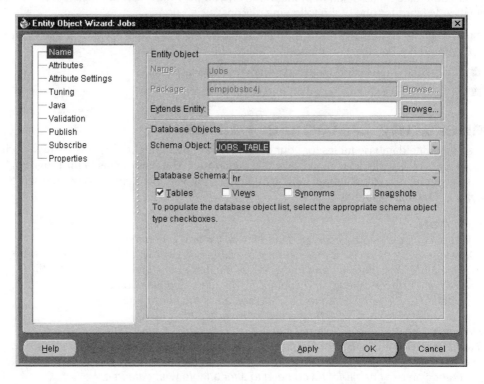

Change the name of a table column on the Attribute Settings page, as shown in the following illustration:

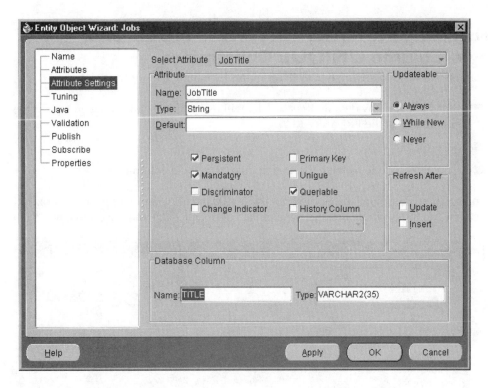

You can also use the Attribute Settings page to set the precision and scale of the generated columns. By default, the Modeler makes NUMBER columns as large as possible—that is, no specified precision or scale. It sets the size for VARCHAR2 columns to 255. However, you can override these default values on the Attribute Settings page as well.

Finally, you can use the Attribute Settings page to make an attribute transient. By default, a table column will be generated for every attribute—that is, the Modeler assumes that you want every attribute to be persistent. By changing an attribute to transient, you can prevent a table column from being generated for it.

Generating Table Constraints

You can generate common table constraints from business components. Some constraints, such as PRIMARY KEY, NOT NULL, and FOREIGN KEY, are easy to generate using wizards you are already familiar with. Others, such as CHECK, require the use of the Entity Constraint Wizard.

Generating PRIMARY KEY, NOT NULL, and Single-Column UNIQUE Constraints

You can generate the following types of constraints by editing the entity object:

- PRIMARY KEY (by default, the Modeler will make the first attribute you type in the sole component of the PRIMARY KEY)

- NOT NULL

- UNIQUE, so long as the constraint applies to a single column

You set these constraints using the *Primary Key, Mandatory,* and *Unique* checkboxes, respectively, on the Attribute Settings page of the Entity Object Wizard, as shown next:

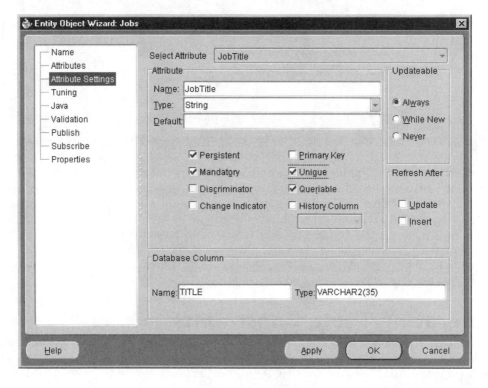

As discussed in Chapter 10, the BC4J layer uses *Primary Key* and *Mandatory* properties; the process of generation also enforces these rules at the database level. The BC4J layer, however, does not use the *Unique* property—selecting it affects the generated table only.

Set these constraints before you generate, or regenerate the table (by selecting **Generate | Database Objects** from the right-click menu on the entity object in the diagram).

Generating Foreign Key Constraints

By default, JDeveloper will automatically generate a FOREIGN KEY constraint for any association you create in the Modeler. This behavior is set by editing the association and selecting the Association Properties page in the Association Wizard, as shown here:

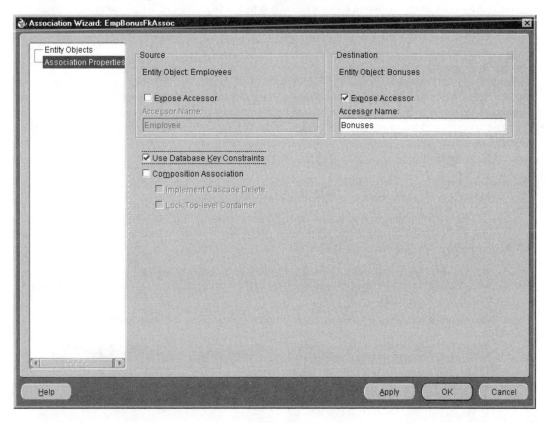

Use Database Key Constraints, which is selected by default, causes the association to generate a FOREIGN KEY constraint. *Implement Cascade Delete,* which is selected by default for compositions (and is only available for compositions), causes the generated FOREIGN KEY constraint to include the ON DELETE CASCADE clause.

NOTE
You cannot generate FOREIGN KEY constraints from a many-to-many association. You must create one-to-many associations from each end of the many-to-many association to the intersection entity, and generate foreign key constraints from the one-to-many associations.

Entity Constraints

You might need to generate database constraints other than those you can create using the Entity Object Wizard or Association Wizard. To do this, you must create an *entity constraint,* an attribute in an entity object's XML file that describes complex database constraints to generate. You must create an entity constraint to generate the following types of database constraints:

- UNIQUE constraints that are composed of more than one column
- CHECK constraints

You might also want to generate PRIMARY KEY, NOT NULL, FOREIGN KEY, or single-column UNIQUE constraints, but have more fine-grain control over them than the Entity Object Wizard and Association Wizard provide. For example, you might want to be able to choose a name for the constraint (as opposed to accepting BC4J's default name), or allow validation to be deferred until a COMMIT operation. You can also generate these table constraints by defining corresponding entity constraints, as follows:

1. On the entity object node in the Navigator, select New Entity Constraint from the right-click menu to open the Entity Constraint Wizard.

2. On the Name page, in the *Name* field, enter a name that BC4J will use to identify the entity constraint. In the *Constraint Name* field, identify the name to use for the database constraint. Click Next.

3. On the Attributes page, select the entity attributes that correspond to the columns to which this constraint applies and click Next. For a CHECK constraint, you do not need to specify attributes.

4. On the Properties page, shown next, select the type of constraint you want to create.

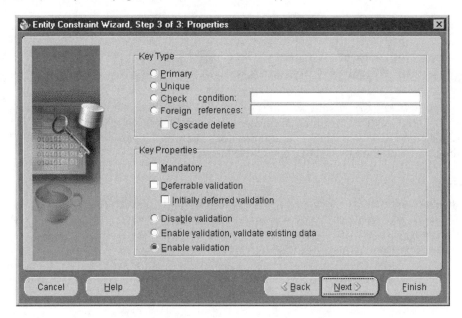

To create any constraint except NOT NULL, select the constraint type in the Key Type panel. To create a NOT NULL constraint, select the *Mandatory* checkbox in the Key Properties panel.

5. Still on the Properties page, select whether you want to allow the constraint check to occur only when a COMMIT is issued (the *Deferrable validation* checkbox) and, if so, whether you want it to be deferred by default (*Initially deferred validation* checkbox).

6. Still on the Properties page, select whether you want the constraint to start as disabled (*Disable validation*), to be enabled for both new and existing data (*Enable validation, validate existing data*), or to be enabled for new data but not checked against existing data (*Enable validation*).

7. Click Finish to create the constraint.

The constraint definition will appear in the entity object's XML file. In the case of PRIMARY KEY and NOT NULL constraints, the appropriate constraints will also be added to the entity object attribute properties. In the case of FOREIGN KEY constraints, an association will automatically be generated. Other constraints have no effect on the BC4J layer.

Set these constraints before you generate, or regenerate the table after you set them.

Hands-on Practice: Try Out Class Modeling and Database Generation

In this practice, you will create a model containing both entities and associations for existing tables and a new entity object and association. You then generate a table and several different kinds of constraints.

I. Create a workspace, project, and class model

II. Create entity objects and associations

- Create an entity object and association for an existing table

- Create the Bonuses entity object

- Create an association between Bonuses and Employees

III. Define constraints

- Prepare to generate NOT NULL constraints and rename a table column

- Prepare to generate a multi-column UNIQUE constraint

IV. Generate the table and constraints

V. Populate the BONUSES table

I. Create a Workspace, Project, and Class Model

In this phase, you will create a new workspace and empty project for your model and BC4J, and create an empty model that you will populate later.

1. Create a workspace named "ModelingWS," with a workspace directory also named "ModelingWS." Select *Add a New Empty Project*.

2. Name the project "BonusBC4J," and give it a project directory also named "BonusBC4J."

3. On the BonusBC4J.jpr node in the System Navigator, select New UML Diagram from the right-click menu.

4. On the Create New Class Diagram page, enter "bonusbc4j" in the *Package* field and "BonusBC4JCUML" in the *Name* field. Click OK.

5. Click Save All.

What Just Happened?   You created a workspace, project, and empty model for this hands-on practice. In the content pane, you should see a blank white page. This is your empty model.

II. Create Entity Objects and Associations

In this phase, you will create two entity objects, one from an existing table (EMPLOYEES) and one from scratch (from which you will generate a table called BONUSES). Then, you will create an association between them.

Create an Entity Object and Association for an Existing Table

Create an entity object and all the associations for which it is both the source and destination using the Modeler:

1. In the System Navigator, expand the Connections node.

2. Expand the Database node.

3. Expand the HR connection node and the HR schema node. The tree should look something like the following:

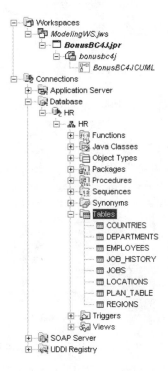

4. Expand the Tables node.

5. Drag the EMPLOYEES table onto the class diagram. The Create From Tables dialog is displayed.

6. Ensure that Business Components Entity Objects is selected and click OK.

   Additional Information: The Modeler creates an entity object, Employees, and an association, EmpManagerFkAssoc, representing the constraint EMP_MANAGER_FK, which is a FOREIGN KEY constraint between EMPLOYEES and itself, as shown next:

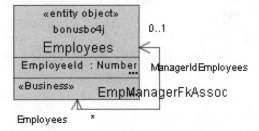

Create the Bonuses Entity Object

Create an entity object to represent employee bonuses using the following steps:

1. In the Component Palette, click the Entity Object icon, and click again on a blank space in the diagram.

Additional Information: The Modeler creates an entity object and allows you to type in its name.

2. Enter "Bonuses" as the entity object's name and press ENTER.

3. Click at the very top of the middle field to begin to type in attributes.

Additional Information: The Modeler creates a default first attribute, attr, of type String, as shown next. When you start typing, you will automatically override this choice.

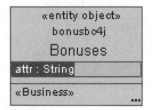

4. Enter "BonusId: Number" as the first attribute and press ENTER.

5. Enter the following attributes, pressing ENTER after each:

■ Year: Number

■ Quarter: Number

■ Amount: Number

6. Click outside the entity object to finish entering attributes.

Create an Association Between Bonuses and Employees

Create a one-to-many association between Employees and Bonuses, with accessors on both sides, by using the following steps:

1. In the Component Palette, click the "Directed Association 1 to *" icon.

Additional Information: This tells the Modeler that you want to create a one-to-many association with an accessor in the source object.

2. Click once on the Employees entity and once on the Bonuses entity in that order to add the association line.

Additional Information: The Modeler creates a one-to-many association, with Employees as the source and Bonuses as the destination. It also adds a destination attribute for the association, EmployeesEmployeeId, matching the name of the source attribute.

3. Using the technique of selecting the name and overtyping the default value, change the name of the association to "EmpBonusFkAssoc," the name of the source accessor to "Employee," and the name of the destination accessor to "Bonuses," as shown next:

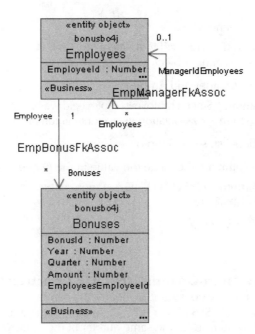

Additional Information: The source accessor name does not do anything yet, since there is no source accessor. However, JDeveloper will remember this name and use it for the accessor if you decide to create it later.

NOTE
If the names overlap, you can drag and drop them as appropriate.

What Just Happened?   You created an entity object based on the EMPLOYEES table, a new entity object to generate a BONUSES table, and a new association that will be used to generate a FOREIGN KEY constraint, all using the Class Modeler.

III. Define Constraints

In this phase, you will prepare Bonuses to generate NOT NULL constraints and a multi-column UNIQUE constraint.

Prepare to Generate NOT NULL Constraints and Rename a Table Column

This section adds mandatory flags to Year, Quarter, and Amount.

1. Double-click the Bonuses entity object in the model to open the Entity Object Wizard.

2. Select the Attribute Settings node.

   Additional Information: The first attribute you entered, BonusId, is already selected as the primary key.

3. In the *Select Attribute* list, select Year.

4. Check the *Mandatory* checkbox.

Additional Information: This will generate a NOT NULL constraint for Year when you create a table from this entity object.

5. Repeat steps 3–4 for Quarter and Amount.

Additional Information: Since EmployeesEmployeeId was created to be a foreign key attribute from a one-to-many association, JDeveloper automatically marked it as mandatory.

6. In the *Select Attribute* list, select EmployeesEmployeeId.

7. In the Database Column area, change the value in the *Name* field to "EMPLOYEE_ID."

Additional Information: EMPLOYEE_ID is a more natural name for the column than EMPLOYEES_EMPLOYEE_ID.

8. Click OK to close the wizard.

9. Click Save All.

Prepare to Generate a Multi-Column UNIQUE Constraint
In this section, you create an entity constraint to require the combination of BONUSES.YEAR, BONUSES.QUARTER, and BONUSES.EMPLOYEE_ID to be unique, that is, to prevent any employee from receiving two bonuses in the same quarter of the same year:

1. On the Bonuses entity object node in the Navigator, select New Entity Constraint from the right-click menu to open the Entity Constraint Wizard. Click Next if the Welcome page appears.

2. On the Name page, enter "BonusesUniqueKey" in the *Name* field and "BONUSES_UK" in the *Constraint Name* field.

Additional Information: BonusesUniqueKey is the name BC4J will use to identify the entity constraint. BONUSES_UK is the name of the database constraint that will be created later.

3. Click Next. On the Attributes page, select Year, Quarter, and EmployeesEmployeeId in the *Available* list, and add them to the *Selected* list. Click Next.

4. On the Properties page, select *Unique* and click Finish.

Additional Information: If you need to edit a constraint later, select the entity object in the System Navigator. Then, in the constraint's node in the Structure window, select Edit from the right-click menu.

What Just Happened? You prepared the business logic tier to generate the BONUSES.EMPLOYEE_ID column with the correct names, and to generate five additional database constraints:

- NOT NULL constraints for EMPLOYEE_ID, YEAR, QUARTER, and AMOUNT
- A UNIQUE constraint applying to EMPLOYEE_ID, YEAR, and QUARTER

You did not need to prepare to generate the PRIMARY KEY or FOREIGN KEY constraint. These constraints will be generated for you automatically.

IV. Generate the Table and Constraints

In this phase, you will generate the BONUSES table, the FOREIGN KEY constraint based on the EmpBonusFkAssoc association, the five constraints you specified in the last phase, and the PRIMARY KEY constraint the Modeler specified for you automatically.

1. On the Bonuses entity object in the diagram, select **Generate | Database Objects** from the right-click menu.

   Additional Information: This generates the BONUSES table and all the constraints.

2. In the Create Database Objects Summary dialog, click Show SQL.

   Additional Information: This displays the DDL statements used to generate the table and constraints.

3. Click OK and OK to close the dialogs.

4. On the Tables node under the HR database connection, select Refresh from the right-click menu and re-expand the Table node if necessary.

   Additional Information: The BONUSES table will appear in the tree.

What Just Happened?   You generated the BONUSES table and the seven table constraints.

V. Populate the BONUSES Table

In this phase, you will use the Business Component Browser to add some rows to the new BONUSES table.

1. On a blank space in the diagram, select **Generate | Business Components for Diagram** from the right-click menu.

   CAUTION
   Do not select Generate | Database Objects for Diagram, because this
   will delete all rows in the EMPLOYEES table.

   Additional Information: JDeveloper will create default view objects for each entity object in the diagram, default view links for each association, and a default application module for the entire diagram.

2. Expand the BC4J package node and click Bonusbc4jModule. (The BC4J package uses the package icon with the green circle.) The view object and view link usages will appear in the Structure window.

3. On the Bonusbc4jModule node in the Navigator, select Test from the right-click menu.

4. On the Connect page, click Connect.

5. When the main window of the Business Component Browser opens, double click EmpBonusFkLink1.

   Additional Information: The right pane divides into two frames: the top one represents rows of EMPLOYEES, and the bottom one represents the detail rows from BONUSES. You may have to enlarge the Browser or change the position of the separator to completely see both frames.

6. In the bottom pane, click the green plus sign to add a BONUSES row for King.

Additional Information: The EmployeesEmployeeId attribute is automatically populated by EmpBonusesFkLink.

7. Enter "100" in the *BonusId* field.

8. Enter "2000" in the *Year* field.

9. Enter "1" in the *Quarter* field.

10. Enter "25000" in the *Amount* field.

11. Scroll one Employees row to Employee 101, Neena Kochhar.

12. In the bottom pane, click the green plus sign to add a BONUSES row for Kochhar.

13. Enter the following values for the fields:

- ■ "101" for *BonusId*

- ■ "2000" for *Year*

- ■ "1" for *Quarter*

- ■ "10000" for *Amount*

14. Click the green plus sign again to add another BONUSES row for Kochhar.

15. Enter the following values for the fields:

- ■ "102" for *BonusId*

- ■ "2000" for *Year*

- ■ "1" for *Quarter*

- ■ "15000" for *Amount*

Additional Information: This violates the UNIQUE constraint; there are now two bonuses for Kochhar in the first quarter of the year 2000. However, since UNIQUE constraints are only validated at the database level, the BC4J layer does not detect this violation yet.

16. Press ENTER and try to save your changes by clicking the commit arrow (in the top toolbar).

Additional Information: The tester tries to post the changes to the database before committing, so you will get the following error message:

```
JBO-26041: Failed to post data to database during "Insert": SQL Statement " INSERT
INTO BONUSES(BONUS_ID,EMPLOYEE_ID,YEAR,QUARTER,AMOUNT) VALUES (:1,:2,:3,:4,:5)"
```

Detail 0 contains the database's error message:

```
ORA-00001: unique constraint (HR.BONUSES_UK) violated
```

17. Dismiss the error box, change Bonus 102's quarter to "2," and press ENTER.

18. Try again to save your changes. This time, the commit should be successful.

19. On the HR connection node, select SQL Worksheet from the right-click menu.

20. Enter and run the following SQL command:

```
SELECT * FROM BONUSES
```

21. Note that the data you entered in the Business Component Browser was saved in the database.

What Just Happened?   You created view objects, view links, and an application module to allow you to test your BC4J in the Business Component Browser. You then used the Browser to populate the BONUSES table and to see the UNIQUE constraint working, and verified that the BONUSES table had been created and populated. You also verified that the foreign key constraint was created between EMPLOYEES and BONUSES because as you scrolled the employees records, the bonus records were synchronized with the appropriate employee.

CHAPTER
12

Adding Business Rules

Let no act be done haphazardly, nor otherwise than
according to the finished rules that govern its kind.

—Marcus Aurelius (A.D. 121–180), *Meditations*

 n Chapters 9–11, you learned about entity objects simply as representations of data. Entity objects can also encapsulate the business rules pertaining to the data they represent. An entity object can enforce validation rules for attribute values, calculate default values of attributes, automatically calculate the values of transient attributes, and automatically react to data changes. This chapter explains using entity objects to capture business rules. In the hands-on practice, you will change the entity layer you created in Chapter 10 to enforce some business rules.

Overview of Entity Classes

Much of the business logic you will learn about in this chapter is implemented in Java classes. It was a simplification to say, as was said in Chapter 9, that an entity object is associated with one Java class. In fact, three Java classes can be associated with each entity object. The first, the entity object class, is a class you will learn about extensively in this chapter. This section contains an overview both of the entity object class and of the other two—entity definition classes and entity collection classes—but a detailed discussion of those other classes is beyond the scope of this book.

Entity Object Classes

You have already learned a lot about the *entity object class,* instances of which represent one row of a database table or view. Entity object classes have the same name as the entity object with an "Impl" suffix. For example, an entity object called "Departments" would have an implementation class called "DepartmentsImpl."

Entity object classes extend the class oracle.jbo.server.EntityImpl. EntityImpl has all the methods you need to read, insert, update, delete, and lock rows. In fact, strictly speaking, entity objects do not have to have entity object classes at all; they can simply use instances of EntityImpl to represent their rows. However, for most purposes, entity objects should have their own implementation classes, because creating these classes has two significant advantages:

Entity Object Classes Provide Getters and Setters for Each Attribute   Entity object classes, by default, provide typesafe accessors (getters and setters) for each attribute. For example, DepartmentsImpl will by default contain a method getDepartmentId(), which takes no arguments and returns a Number, and a method setDepartmentId(), which takes a Number as its argument. If you make a mistake with an attribute's name or Java type, you will get a compilation error that identifies the offending line. Either of the following lines of code will cause compile-time errors, the first because it assumes the DepartmentId attribute has the wrong type, and the second because it uses the wrong attribute name.

```
String myDeptId=myDepartmentsImpl.getDepartmentId();
Number myDeptId=myDepartmentsImpl.getDeptId();
```

You can still access attributes from EntityImpl directly, by using the methods
`EntityImpl.getAttribute()` and `EntityImpl.setAttribute()`, but these methods
are not typesafe. `EntityImpl.getAttribute()` takes a String (the attribute name) as an
argument and returns a java.lang.Object; `EntityImpl.setAttribute()` takes a String (the
attribute name) and an Object as arguments. If you make a typo in the attribute name, or forget
the Java type of your attributes, you will not get a compile-time error. Instead, your application
will throw an exception at runtime, requiring substantially more work to debug. Neither of the
following lines of code will cause compile-time errors (even though they make mistakes about
the type and name of the attribute); instead, they will likely cause crashes at runtime.

```
String myDeptId=(String)myEntityImpl.getAttribute("DepartmentId");
Number myDeptId=(Number)myEntityImpl.getAttribute("DeptId");
```

Entity Object Classes Allow You to Write Custom Business Logic   The accessors in entity
object classes have the advantage that you can edit their implementation. If you want to restrict
access to data, or validate changes, you can put custom Java code in the body of these methods
to enforce your requirements. If you want to trigger events whenever an attribute is changed, you
can write Java code to do that as well. As was stated in Chapter 9, you do not need Java code
for all business logic. If your requirements are simple, you may be able to implement them in
XML. However, you must implement more complex requirements in an entity object class.

Entity object classes can also override various methods in the EntityImpl class to implement other
sorts of business logic. For example, by overriding `EntityImpl.create()`, you can implement
defaulting logic or trigger events whenever a row is created.

Entity Definition Classes

An *entity definition class* is a class that represents an entire table, as opposed to a single
row. Entity definition classes have the same name as the entity object with a "DefImpl" suffix.
For example, an entity object called "Departments" would have definition class called
"DepartmentsDefImpl."

Entity definition classes extend oracle.jbo.server.EntityDefImpl. EntityDefImpl contains methods
that allow you to change the definition of the entity object itself—to add or remove entity attributes
or to change the properties of those attributes.

Just as entity objects can use instances of EntityImpl, rather than instances of an implementation
class, to represent their rows, they can use an instance of EntityDefImpl rather than an instance of
a definition class to represent the entire table. This is sufficient for most purposes. Unlike entity
object classes, which most users will want to generate for most entity objects, there are only two
real reasons to create an entity definition class:

- ◼ You want to override the method `EntityDefImpl.createDef()`, which is called
  as soon as the entity object is loaded into memory. By doing this, you can dynamically
  change the definition of the entity object without writing code in every application that
  uses it.

- ◼ You need a place to put a custom method that affects an entire table, as opposed
  to a single row (which should go in an entity object class) or all the rows returned
  by a particular query (which should go in a view object class).

In fact, not only will you probably not have to subclass EntityDefImpl, you may never have to call methods on it, unless you need to dynamically change the structure of an entity object.

Entity Collection Classes

Suppose an application just inserted a row into, or accessed a row from, the DEPARTMENTS table. When it did so, it instantiated a DepartmentsImpl object (or perhaps just an EntityImpl object). Chances are, however, that the application will need to access this row again in the near future, so rather than destroy the object, BC4J stores it in a cache called an *entity cache.* When the application changes the row, rather than immediately making a (time-consuming) round trip to the database, BC4J simply makes the change to the DepartmentsImpl object in the entity cache until the transaction is committed or the change is manually posted.

In general, an entity cache is implemented by an object of type oracle.jbo.server.EntityCache. However, should you need to change the behavior of the entity cache, you can generate an *entity collection class,* a class which extends EntityCache. Entity collection classes have the same name as the entity object with a "CollImpl" suffix. For example, an entity object called "Departments" would have definition class called "DepartmentsCollImpl."

Although this book will not discuss directly using the entity collection class, it will return to the entity cache in Chapter 13. You can also look at the Javadoc for more information on both entity definition classes and entity collection classes.

Generating Entity Object Classes

You choose whether to generate the various entity object classes on the Java page of the Entity Object Wizard:

1. On an entity object's node, select Edit from the right-click menu.

2. Select the Java node. The default setting is to generate the entity object class only, and to generate accessors in that class, as shown in Figure 12-1.

Validation Rules

You can add quite a bit of business logic to entity objects without writing a line of code. The BC4J framework supports a number of built-in XML *validation rules* that you can add to an entity attribute using the Entity Object Wizard. (You can also write your own validation rules; see the sidebar "Custom Validation Rules.") A validation rule is added to the entity object's XML file as a sub-element of the Attribute element. For example, a validation rule called the CompareValidator has been added to the Salary entity attribute represented next:

```
<Attribute
  Name="Salary"
  IsNotNull="true"
  Type="oracle.jbo.domain.Number"
  ...
  TableName="EMPLOYEES" >
<CompareValidationBean
  OnAttribute="Salary"
  OperandType="LITERAL"
```

```
    CompareType="GREATERTHAN"
    CompareValue="1000" >
  </CompareValidationBean>
</Attribute>
```

The CompareValidationBean element nested inside the Attribute element implements the CompareValidator rule.

Phase I of the hands-on practice in this chapter describes adding a validation rule.

The CompareValidator

A CompareValidator requires an attribute value to stand in some relation to a specified value. The relations available are as follows:

- Equals
- NotEquals
- LessThan
- GreaterThan
- LessOrEqualTo
- GreaterOrEqualTo

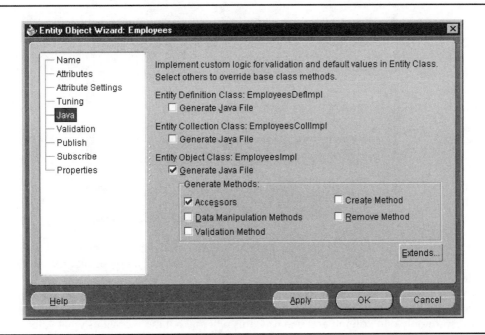

FIGURE 12-1. *Generating entity classes*

Custom Validation Rules

In addition to the XML validation rules provided with JDeveloper, you can write your own XML validation rules by creating a validation rule class and registering it with JDeveloper. Although writing a validation rule class requires writing Java, after such a class is written, it can be applied to entity attributes using the Entity Object Wizard just as the pre-built validation rules can. This option is especially valuable for large teams, where a small number of Java programmers can create sophisticated XML validation rules that other developers with little or no Java experience can use in their own entity objects.

Creating and registering validation rule classes is beyond the scope of this book. For more information, see the JDeveloper online help.

The simplest use of a CompareValidator is to require an attribute to stand in a relation to a particular literal value that you specify in the validation rule. For example, you can use a CompareValidator to require the value of the Salary attribute to be greater than 1000, as shown here:

It is also possible to use a CompareValidator to enforce a relation to a column from a query or a transient attribute. In addition to Literal Value, you can select Query Result or View Object Attribute from the *Compare With* dropdown.

If you choose Query Result, the attribute is compared with the value in the first column of the first row in the result set returned by the SQL query you enter. Of course, you can craft your query to return only one column and one row; this will make it more obvious what value will be used. The following illustration shows a single-row, single-column query used to enforce the rule that nobody can have a higher salary than the company president can.

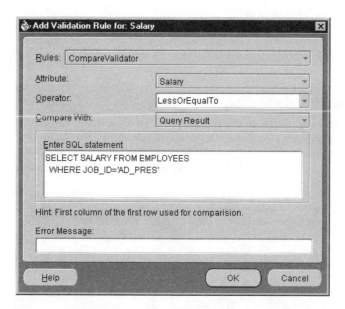

If you choose View Object Attribute, the value will be compared to the value of the selected view row attribute for the first view row. For example, you could require the first view row in EmployeesView to have the maximum salary for all the employees, as shown here:

Of course, if you use default view objects, you will have very little control over which view row is the first. For that reason, using a CompareValidator to compare an attribute to a view object attribute in a default view object is not very useful. Creating custom view objects will be discussed in Chapter 13.

The ListValidator

A ListValidator requires an attribute either to be in a list of possible values, or not to be in a list of excluded values. As with a CompareValidator, you can form your list from literal values, a query result, or a view attribute.

If you create your list from literal values, you simply type the list of values, one per line, as shown here:

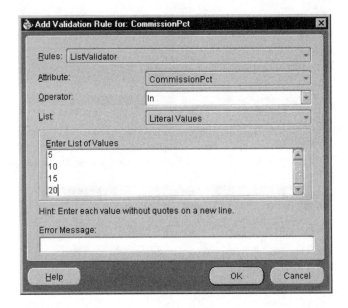

If you use a SQL query, the values for the list come from the first column, just as only the first column's value is used by a CompareValidator. However, unlike a CompareValidator, a ListValidator looks at all rows in the query result. For example, you can use the following SQL statement to require that the Employees JobId attribute match a JOB_ID in the JOBS table, as shown here:

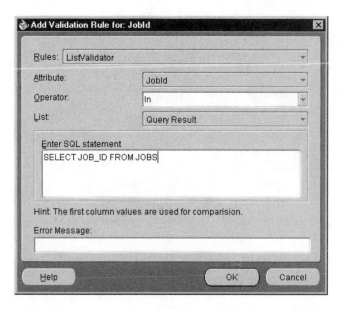

Using a ListValidator with a view attribute works the same way. The list is formed from the value of the view attribute in every row the view object returns. For example, you could select JobId from JobsView to have the same effect as the SQL statement earlier (with the added advantages that the BC4J framework would cache the query values for you and use any logic you added to the JobsView view object).

The RangeValidator

The RangeValidator requires the attribute to be either between two possible values or outside ("notBetween") a range of excluded values. Unlike a CompareValidator or a ListValidator,

a RangeValidator cannot use a query or view object to calculate the endpoints of the range—
they must be specified as literals, as shown here:

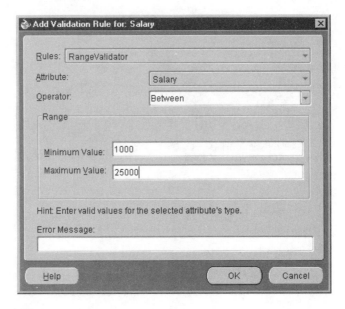

The MethodValidator

If none of the preceding validators provides the attribute validation you want, you can use the
MethodValidator to define it yourself. The MethodValidator calls a Java method in your entity
object class. The method must take a single argument of the same type as the attribute, it must
be public, and it must return a boolean value.

For example, consider the Email attribute of the Employees entity object. This attribute has
type String, but all the email addresses in the (fictitious) company the HR schema represents have
a particular form—eight or fewer alphabetic characters, all uppercase. You can create a method
like the following to return `true` if the email address has the correct format and `false` otherwise:

```
public boolean validateEmail(String value)
{
  /* Start out assuming the email is valid. */
  boolean isValid=true;
  int length=value.length();
  /* Emails longer than 8 are invalid. */
  if (length>8)
  {
    isValid=false;
  }
  else
  {
    /* Non-alphabetic and non-uppercase characters are invalid */
```

```
  for (int i=0; i<length; i++)
  {
    if (value.charAt(i)<'A' || value.charAt(i)>'Z')
    {
      isValid=false;
    }
  }
}
return isValid;
}
```

Then you can apply a MethodValidator to call the method, as shown here:

When Validation Fails

If a client tries to set a value for an attribute, and the value does not pass the requirements of a validation rule, one of two things happens:

- If the validation rule was a MethodValidator, the entity object class throws an oracle.jbo.ValidationException.

- If the validation rule was not a MethodValidator, the entity object class throws an oracle.jbo.AttrSetValException.

You can catch these exceptions in your client, and deal with them in whatever way you want. The exceptions contain error messages you can set when you create the validation rule. You will do this in the hands-on practice.

Adding Business Rules to Source Code

Validation rules are simple, declarative, and quick to use. However, for more complicated business rules, programs need to use Java. Using a MethodValidator on an attribute is one way to write business logic in Java. However, you can also write business logic directly in the setter of an entity attribute.

When JDeveloper generates an entity object class, it creates simple setters that do nothing but call a single method, setAttributeInternal(), as shown here:

```
public void setEmail(String value)
{
  setAttributeInternal(EMAIL, value);
}
```

setAttributeInternal() takes an int and an Object. The int corresponds to a particular entity attribute. (If you examine the source code for EmployeesImpl, you will find a constant, EMAIL, defined with a value of 3.) The Object corresponds to a value to set the attribute to.

The difference between setAttributeInternal() and setAttribute(), other than the fact that setAttributeInternal() accepts an integer instead of a String to identify the attribute, is that setAttribute() *calls* the setter method (if setter methods have been generated), but setAttributeInternal() simply checks the XML for validation rules and then sets the attribute's value.

In other words, if you call EntityImpl.setAttribute() or an entity object class's setter method, the first thing that will happen is that Java code in the setter will be executed. At some point, the setter method should call setAttributeInternal(). When that method is called, it will check for validation rules, and if none is found, or all of them are passed, it will set the value of the attribute. This process is illustrated in Figure 12-2.

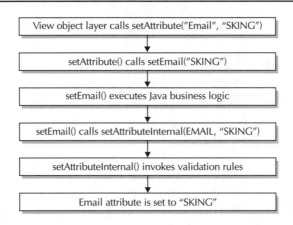

FIGURE 12-2. *Stages of validation*

The following is an example of some business logic written in a setter method. In this example, the `setEmail()` method, like `validateEmail()` in the earlier example, checks that only Strings of all uppercase letters, with length of at most eight, can be used for email addresses.

```
public void setEmail(String value) throws oracle.jbo.JboException
{
  boolean isValid=true;
  int length=value.length();
  if (length > 8)
  {
    isValid=false;
  }
  else
  {
    for (int i=0; i<length; i++)
    {
      if (value.charAt(i)<'A' || value.charAt(i)>'Z')
      {
        isValid=false;
      }
    }
  }
  /* If the email is valid, set the attribute. */
  if (isValid)
  {
    setAttributeInternal(EMAIL, value);
  }
  /* Otherwise, throw an exception. */
  else
  {
    throw new oracle.jbo.JboException(
     "An email address must be uppercase " +
     "and have at most 8 characters.");
  }
}
```

MethodValidators vs. Business Logic in Setters

The setter method just described implements exactly the same business logic as the MethodValidator presented earlier; both require email addresses to be made up of at most eight uppercase letters. There are some differences between MethodValidators and business logic added to a setter method, however:

MethodValidators and Setter Logic Are Called at Different Times   MethodValidators are called during the validation rule stage, during the execution of `setAttributeInternal()`. Setter logic either calls or does not call `setAttributeInternal()`. If you want your Java validation to come before all other validation, you can either make a MethodValidator your first validation rule or add validation to the setter method, but if you want it to come after some validation rules are invoked, you must use a MethodValidator.

Put another way, Java logic added to the setter is executed in the third box of Figure 12-2, before all validation rules. Logic in a MethodValidator is executed in the fifth box of Figure 12-2, among the validation rules.

MethodValidators Automatically Throw Exceptions   When a MethodValidator fails, it automatically throws a ValidationException. If you write validation code in a setter method, you have to throw an exception yourself. This can be an advantage, however, if you want finer-grained control over the exception thrown.

MethodValidators Are Represented in the XML File   Because validation rules are represented in the entity object's XML file, they can be manipulated at runtime using the EntityDefImpl class. EntityDefImpl provides a method, addVetoableChangeListener(), that lets you dynamically add validation rules (including MethodValidators) to attributes. This lets you decide, at runtime, which methods to use to validate a particular attribute. (Dynamically adding validation rules is beyond the scope of this book. Look at the Javadoc for EntityDefImpl for more information.)

MethodValidators Can Use the Same Method for Several Attributes   Imagine that Employees contained both a WorkPhone and a HomePhone attribute. You might want to use the same logic to validate each of them. You could add a MethodValidator to each attribute and have it call a validatePhone() method.

Setter Logic Can Be More than Just Validation   The MethodValidator, like all other validation rules, is intended to either allow or disallow setting an entity attribute to a particular value. You might, however, want other types of results when you set an attribute, such as automatically making a change to another attribute as well. (This will be discussed in more detail later in this chapter.) If you did this with a MethodValidator, the method would execute nonvalidation business logic as method side-effects. Clearly, this will make your code harder to understand and maintain. In general, if you want to add business logic that is not validation to the attribute setting process, you should add it to the setter rather than use a MethodValidator.

Setter Logic Matches Standard Java Practice   Many Java programmers are used to putting validation logic in JavaBeans' setters. Putting validation logic there will bring your application more in line with typical Java practice and may make it easier for others to understand and maintain.

Coding with Domains

In the Email validation examples earlier in this chapter, the attribute being validated was of type java.lang.String, so the business logic could use standard Java methods like String.length() and String.charAt(). However, if your business logic needs to access attributes with domain types, you must code to BC4J-specific APIs.

If you are using domains from the package oracle.jbo.domain, you have two options. The first option is to convert the domain to a standard Java type. You can then use methods and operators provided by Java itself. The following is a list of the conversion methods for the most common domains.

Domain	Conversion Methods
Number	int intValue(), long longValue(), short shortValue(), float floatValue(), double doubleValue(), byte byteValue(), java.math.BigDecimal bigDecimalValue(), java.math.BigInteger bigIntegerValue()
Date	java.lang.Date toDate()
Array	java.lang.Object[] getArray()
BFileDomain, BlobDomain, ClobDomain	byte[] toByteArray()

Alternatively, you can work directly with the domains, using methods provided in the domain classes. The following is a partial list of useful methods on common domains.

Domain	Methods
Number	add(), subtract(), multiply(), divide(), increment(), abs(), exp(), sin(), cos(), tan(), compareTo()
Date	addJulianDays(), addMonths(), round(), lastDayInMonth(), diffInMonths(), getCurrentDate()
BFileDomain	getInputStream(), getOutputStream(), closeOutputStream()
BlobDomain	getBinaryStream(), getBinaryOutputStream(), closeOutputStream(), getBytes(), getLength()
ClobDomain	getCharacterStream(), getCharacterOutputStream(), getSubstring(), getLength()

There are advantages to each of these alternatives:

- Standard Java classes and primitives will likely be more familiar to most Java programmers. By converting domains to standard Java types, you may make your code more readable and maintainable.

- The operators on Java primitives (such as double and int) are very efficient. If you are going to perform extensive manipulation of numeric types, it may be more efficient to convert the Number domain to a Java primitive.

- On the other hand, if you are only going to perform a few operations on a domain, calling the domain manipulation methods may be more efficient than first calling the method that converts the domain to a standard Java type, performing the operations, and then calling the constructor that converts the standard Java type back into a domain.

- If you are working with LOB types, you should not use the conversion methods, as large arrays of bytes are very expensive to work with. Use InputStreams and OutputStreams to copy the LOB into a file. For more information on file I/O in Java, see a beginning-to-intermediate Java text.

If your domains are based on Oracle object types, simply use the accessor methods that are created in the domains to retrieve and change values. For example, if the attribute Addr is of AddressTyp (described in Chapter 10), you can add validation logic that requires the address to be in the United States by changing the setAddr() method to the following:

```
public void setAddr(AddressTyp value)
{
  if (value.getCountryId().equals("US"))
    setAttributeInternal(ADDR, value);
  else
    throw new oracle.jbo.JboException(
      "Address must be in the United States.");
}
```

Adding Business Logic Using Domains

Validation rules and setter logic apply to one attribute of one entity object. If you apply a CompareValidator to the Salary attribute of Employees, or change the setter code of the PhoneNumber attribute of Employees, these changes will affect those attributes only. If you want to reuse the business logic for other attributes, you must add a separate CompareValidator with the same parameters or copy the setter code.

The MethodValidator provides one way to reuse validation code. If you write a validation method, you can apply MethodValidators that call it to several attributes. However, there is a limitation on this technique. If you place a MethodValidator on an attribute, the method called must be in the same entity object as the attribute; you cannot reuse method validation code in attributes of two different entity objects.

Recall the email validation that was mentioned before, requiring an email address to be made up of no more than eight capital letters. Although the HR schema only includes one column of email addresses, you might have email addresses in several tables. In this case, you would want to apply the same validation to all of these attributes.

You can apply the same validation logic to multiple attributes by creating a special domain to enforce it. By default (since the EMAIL column has SQL type VARCHAR2), the Email attribute is of type String. However, you can create a special domain that enforces your business logic and make Email of that type. You will create such a domain in the hands-on practice.

The Java class for a domain created to enforce business logic is a bit different from the Java class for a domain that represents an Oracle object type. A validation domain's class is based on another class, either another domain or a standard Java class. There are actually two types of validation domains: those based on the Number or Date domains, and those based on all other classes.

Domains based on the Number or Date domains extend oracle.jbo.domain.Number and oracle.jbo.domain.Date, and they inherit the methods for manipulation and conversion listed in the last section. Domains based on other Java classes, by contrast, do not extend those classes. Instead, they have a private field, mData, with a type matching the original class, and a public method, `getData()`, that returns mData cast to a java.lang.Object. (To work with the original class, you must cast it back.)

The validate() Method

All validation domains have a `validate()` method. This method is generated as an empty method, as follows:

```
protected void validate()
{
}
```

Whenever a new object of the domain's type is created, the BC4J framework calls this `validate()` method. By throwing an exception, you can block the instantiation of the domain. You can see an example of `validate()` code in the hands-on practice.

After you create a domain, it will appear in the *Type* list of the Attribute Settings page in the Entity Object Wizard for every entity object in your project, as shown here:

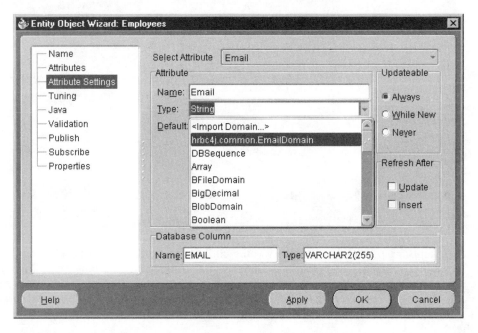

When you make an attribute correspond to a validation domain type, you must instantiate the domain before you can set the attribute value. You can do this by calling the domain's constructor, passing in an argument of the type the domain is based on. (BC4J JSP pages and JClient programs will do this automatically.) The validation logic you write will be enforced every time you even instantiate a possible value for the attribute. So, for example, `EmailDomain.validate()` is called as soon as an EmailDomain is created, before `EmployeesImpl.setEmail()` can be called. So, in the following example, `validate()` will be called during the execution of the first line. Any other validation will be performed during the execution of the second line.

```
PhoneDomain phone=new PhoneDomain("KINGSTON");
EmployeesImpl.setPhoneNumber(phone);
```

Because domains are validated before the setter method is called, domain-level validation takes place very early—before either setter method logic or validation rules are enforced.

Validation Domains and Column Constraints

On the Settings page of the Domain Wizard, you have a chance to specify whether a domain is mandatory, a primary key, or unique, just as you have these options on the Attribute Settings page of the Entity Object Wizard. The Settings page of the Domain Wizard is shown here:

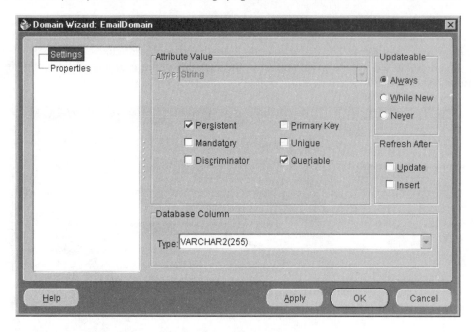

These constraints are passed down to every entity attribute of the domain type. Selecting Primary Key, for example, will make every attribute of the domain type part of a primary key. Therefore, you should not select this constraint if the domain will ever be used outside of a primary key. You can always leave the checkbox clear in the Domain Wizard, and select the constraint directly on an entity attribute if you want some uses of the domain to participate in primary keys but not others.

The *Persistent* checkbox is selected by default. If you leave this checkbox selected, no transient attribute can have the domain type. Again, you can always leave the checkbox clear in the Domain Wizard, and add it to individual entity attributes.

The validateEntity() Method

All of the examples of validation covered so far have been examples of *attribute-level* validation, that is, rules that apply to a specific entity attribute, such as Salary or Email. Some validation logic, however, does not apply to a single attribute, but rather, to multiple attributes in the same row.

For example, you might want to require both that no manager (that is, no employee whose job title ends in "MAN") have a salary less than 10,000 and that no other employee have a salary of 10,000 or greater. You cannot apply this logic in setter methods:

- You cannot implement this logic in the setter method for Salary alone, since it has to be applied when users enter or change an employee's JobId.

- You cannot implement this logic in the setter method for JobId alone, since it has to be applied when users enter or change an employee's Salary.

- You cannot implement this logic in both setter methods, since it will then be impossible to promote an employee to manager—if you try to promote him or her first, setJobId() will throw an exception because the salary is too low; if you try to give him or her a raise first, setSalary() will throw an exception because he or she is not yet a manager.

This kind of business rule requires *entity-level* validation, that is, a rule that applies to an entire row, rather than to a single attribute. You implement entity-level validation by overriding the method `EntityImpl.validateEntity()`.

`validateEntity()` is called whenever an instance of the entity object class loses currency—that is, whenever a client is done looking at a particular row. If `validateEntity()` throws an exception, the entity object instance will be prevented from losing currency. The Business Component Browser, or any other client, will meet an exception when it tries to scroll off the row. `validateEntity()` is also called when a client attempts to commit a transaction. The sidebar "What Is Entity Object Instance Currency, Really?" discusses what it is for an entity object instance to have or lose currency.

You can generate a stub to override `validateEntity()` by selecting the *Validation Method* checkbox on the Java page of the Entity Object Wizard, as shown in Figure 12-1. This will generate code like the following in the entity object's Java file:

```
protected void validateEntity()
{
  super.validateEntity();
}
```

What Is Entity Object Instance Currency, Really?

Entity objects do not maintain a pointer to a "current" row. What does it really mean to say an entity object instance "loses currency"?

As will be described in Chapter 14, view objects do maintain pointers to a current row. And as was mentioned in Chapter 9, a view object can be based on one or more entity objects. When a view object changes which view row is current, any entity object instance the old row was based on "loses currency" and triggers the `validateEntity()` method. You will learn more about the relationship between entity object instances and view rows in Chapter 14.

You should always keep the call to `super.validateEntity()`, so that your entity object class will continue to exhibit EntityImpl's default behavior in addition to your modifications. Put any business logic after that call. For example, the following code in EmployeesImpl would implement the manager-minimum-salary rule:

```
protected void validateEntity() throws oracle.jbo.JboException
{
  super.validateEntity();
  if (getJobId().endswith("MAN")
  {
    if (getSalary().intValue() < 10000)
    {
      throw new oracle.jbo.JboException(
        "Managers must have a salary of at least 10000.");
    }
  }
  else
  {
    if (getSalary.intValue() > 9999)
    {
      throw new oracle.jbo.Exception(
        "Non-managers cannot have a salary more than 9999.");
    }
  }
}
```

Just as with the `validate()` method in validation domains, `validateEntity()` needs to do something (throw an exception) only if the validation rule fails.

Hands-on Practice: Add Simple Validation to the HR Business Model

In this practice, you will add validation logic to the HRBC4J project in two ways: you will add a validation rule that enforces a minimum salary, and create a domain that enforces a format for phone numbers.

This practice builds on the results of the hands-on practice in Chapter 10. If you have not completed that practice, you can download the starting files for this practice from the authors' websites mentioned in the author information at the beginning of this book.

This practice steps you through the following phases:

  I. **Add a validation rule**

  II. **Enforce business logic at the domain level**

   ■ Generate a domain class

   ■ Add validation code to the domain class

   ■ Use the domain for an entity attribute type

III. Test the business logic

- Test the validation rule

- Test the validation domain

I. Add a Validation Rule

This phase uses the Entity Object Wizard to add a validation rule to the Salary attribute.

1. Open the HRWS workspace and expand the hrbc4j package node.

2. On the Employees node, select Edit Employees from the right-click menu. The Entity Object Wizard opens.

3. Select the Validation node.

4. Select Salary from the tree of *Declared Validation Rules.*

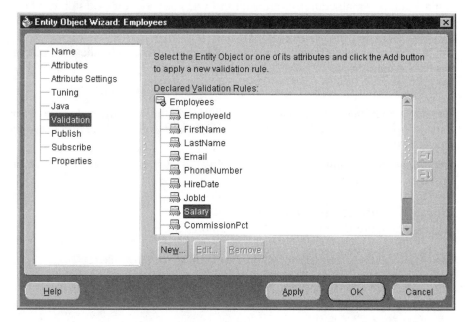

5. Click New to add a validation rule for Salary. The Add Validation Rule dialog opens.

6. Verify that CompareValidator is selected in the *Rules* dropdown list.

7. From the *Operator* dropdown list, select GreaterThan.

8. Enter "2000" in the *Enter Literal Value* area.

9. In the *Error Message* field, enter "Salary must be over 2000."

   Additional Information: This creates an error message for this use of the validation rule and adds it to a resource bundle file called EmployeesImplMsgBundle.java.

10. Click OK to close the dialog.

11. Click OK to close the wizard.

12. Build your project.

13. Save All.

What Just Happened?   You added a CompareValidator to the Salary attribute. The BC4J framework stored the validation information in the Employees.xml file.

II. Enforce Business Logic at the Domain Level

This stage creates a domain, EmailDomain, to enforce the rule that email addresses must be made up of at most 8 uppercase characters.

Generate a Domain Class

A validation domain for email addresses containing a `validate()` method stub can be generated using the following steps:

1. On the hrbc4j package node, select New Domain from the right-click menu. The Domain Wizard opens.

2. On the Name page, in the *Name* field, enter "EmailDomain." Click Next.

3. On the Settings page, verify that String is selected in the *Attribute Value Type* dropdown list and that VARCHAR2 is selected in the *Database Column Type* dropdown list. Click Finish.

   Additional Information: The wizard just created a validation domain, EmailDomain, based on the String type.

Add Validation Code to the Domain Class

You can add code to the `validate()` method to enforce the business rule:

1. Find the `validate()` method within the EmailDomain.java file.

2. Write the following code as the body of the method:

```
int length=mData.length();
if (length > 8)
{
  throw new oracle.jbo.JboException(
    "An email address must have at most 8 characters.");
}
else
{
  for (int i=0; i<length; i++)
  {
    if (mData.charAt(i)<'A' || mData.charAt(i)>'Z')
```

```
      {
        throw new oracle.jbo.JboException(
          "An email address must be uppercase.");
      }
    }
  }
```

3. Since this method now throws an exception, change the method signature to the following:

    ```
    protected void validate() throws oracle.jbo.JboException
    ```

Use the Domain for an Entity Attribute Type

Now you can use this domain instead of String as the Java type for any entity attribute to automatically enforce the business rule you added. You can use the domain as the type of the PhoneNumber attribute with the following steps:

1. On the Employees node, select Edit Employees from the right-click menu. The Entity Object Wizard opens.

2. Select the Attribute Settings node.

3. Select Email from the *Select Attribute* dropdown.

4. Select hrbc4j.common.EmailDomain for the attribute's type.

5. Click OK to close the wizard.

6. Build your project and Save All.

What Just Happened?   You created a domain, EmailDomain, that wraps a String. The `validate()` method of EmailDomain throws an exception if the String does not have the right format. You changed the Java type of Email from String to EmailDomain. Now, whenever Email is assigned, an exception will be thrown if the validation test fails. You could set the Java type of other entity attributes, in the same or another entity object, to use EmailDomain as well.

III. Test the Business Logic

Now that you have added this validation logic to the Employees entity object, you can use the Business Component Browser to test it.

Test the Validation Rule

You can see how the validation rule works by trying to set an employee's salary below 2000.

1. On the EntityTestModule node, select Test from the right-click menu.

2. On the Connect page, accept the defaults and click Connect.

3. When the main window opens, double-click EmployeesView in the data model to open it in the Business Component Browser.

4. Scroll forward to employee 104, Bruce Ernst.

5. Attempt to change Ernst's salary to "1500." As soon as you click on another field or try to scroll off of the row, you will get an exception dialog.

   Additional Information: The message you wrote in the CompareValidator validation that is attached to the Salary attribute will appear in the dialog. Validation is triggered when you navigate from that field to another field or from that record to another record.

6. Click OK to dismiss the dialog.

7. Press ESC to set Ernst's salary back to 6000.

Test the Validation Domain
You can see how the validation domain works by trying to set an employee's email address to each of two invalid formats. After that, test an acceptable form of the phone number to make sure that it is allowed by the domain's validation code.

1. Set Ernst's email address to "BRUCEERNST." As soon as you click on another field or try to scroll off of the row, you will get an exception.

2. Set Ernst's email address to "BERNST2." Again, as soon as you click on another field or try to scroll off of the row, you will get an exception.

3. Change the email address to "BLERNST." Note that this change is accepted.

4. Close the Business Component Browser.

What Just Happened? You tested the CompareValidator and the domain-level validation.

Adding Default Values to Entity Attributes

The examples of business logic discussed in the first part of this chapter are all triggered when an entity attribute is set or when an entity object instance loses currency. However, you might also want to write business logic that applies to new rows in the database (in other words, to new entity object instances) as soon as they are created.

The most common case where you would want such business logic is *defaulting,* that is, giving an entity attribute a default value as soon as a row is created. Just as with validation logic, there are two ways to implement defaulting logic: in XML, or in Java code for cases too complex to handle in the XML. The primary distinction is that static default values (where you specify one default value at design time that always applies to that attribute) can be handled in XML; dynamically calculated default values (where the attribute can have different initial values in different rows) must be added to Java code.

Static Default Values

The BC4J framework stores static default values as XML attributes. You can set static default values on the Attribute Settings page of the Entity Object Wizard, as shown here:

The attribute you want to set a default value for

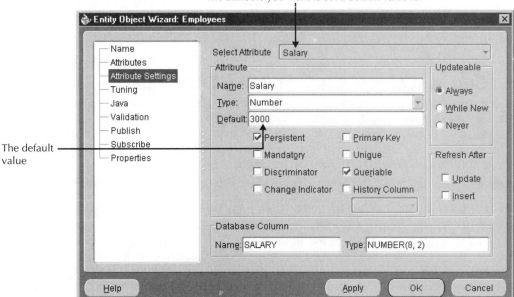

The default value

You can set static default values this way for any class with a String representation: String, as well as Number, Date, Boolean, and so on, and any validation domain based on one of these classes, but not, for example, BlobDomain, or a domain based on an Oracle object type. If you want to implement defaulting logic for these more complicated domains, you need to treat the default values as dynamic (even if they are really static), and use Java.

Dynamically Calculated Default Values

Some attributes should be automatically populated, but not necessarily with the same thing every time.

To dynamically assign default values, you must write Java code. You can do this by overriding the method `EntityImpl.create()`. `create()` will be called whenever a new entity object instance is created.

You can generate a stub to override `create()` by selecting the *Create Method* checkbox on the Java page of the Entity Object Wizard (see Figure 12-1). Just as the `validateEntity()` stub starts with a call to `super.validateEntity()`, the `create()` stub starts with a call to `super.create()`, which you should keep.

After the call to `super.create()`, you can add any logic you want to calculate and set defaults. For example, the following code would cause an employee's hire date to default to the date he or she was added to the database:

```
protected void create(AttributeList attributeList)
{
  super.create(attributeList);
  Date currDate=new Date(Date.getCurrentDate());
  setHireDate(currDate);
}
```

The SequenceImpl Class and the DBSequence Domain

One of the most common reasons to dynamically calculate a default value is to populate attributes in successive rows with a series of sequential numbers. The BC4J framework contains a class, oracle.jbo.server.SequenceImpl, that wraps Oracle database sequences for use in the Java universe.

The constructor for SequenceImpl requires that you pass in both the name of the sequence and a database transaction (so that the BC4J framework knows where the sequence is located). Fortunately, there is a method on EntityImpl, `getDBTransaction()`, that returns the current transaction. After calling `getDBTransaction()`, you can increment the sequence and extract the next value into a Number using `getSequenceNumber()`. You can find an example of this in the hands-on practice later in this chapter.

Instead of dynamically retrieving the attribute in Java, you can put a trigger in the database to update the attribute's table column. If you do this, you should make the attribute of type DBSequence. DBSequence maintains a temporary unique value in the BC4J cache until the data is posted.

The advantage of using DBSequence over coding with SequenceImpl is that it does not waste sequence numbers in transactions that are rolled back before they are posted to the database. However, using DBSequence only works if the database contains a trigger to populate the attribute; SequenceImpl populates the attribute at the Java level.

Calculated Transient Attributes

Business rules can also be used to calculate values for transient attributes. Recall that transient attributes exist only in the entity object; they do not correspond to any database column. The most common use of such transient attributes is to hold values calculated from other attributes.

Since the attribute is requested in the getter method, this is where it must be calculated the first time. Your code should test to make sure the attribute is not null (that is, that it has already been calculated), and if it is null, it should calculate it. It should both set the attribute to the calculated value and return that value. You can find an example of this in the hands-on practice.

In general, when you set the value of a calculated attribute, you should do so by using the method `EntityImpl.populateAttribute()`. `populateAttribute()` works exactly like `setAttributeInternal()`, with two exceptions. First, it bypasses all validation, including XML validation rules. Second, and importantly for calculated attributes, it does not mark the entity object instance as changed. See the sidebar, "Why Use populateAttribute()?" for more information.

Why Use populateAttribute()?

When you call `setAttributeInternal()`, the BC4J framework marks the entity object instance as changed. Later, when data is posted to the database, the framework will only attempt to post the rows it marked as changed; posting other rows would waste time. If you use `setAttribute()` or `setAttributeInternal()` to calculate transient attributes, every entity instance with a calculated attribute will be marked as changed, and therefore posted to the database. However, if the only change you have made to an instance is to calculate a transient attribute, there is generally no posting to be done. Your application will save network and database resources by using `populateAttribute()` so that the row is not posted.

You also need to make sure that the calculation stays up to date. A good way to do this is to put code that sets the transient attribute to null in the setter method of any attribute this attribute depends on. For example, if your calculation depends on JobId, you could add code to `setJobId()` to set the calculated attribute to null every time JobId is changed. The next time the transient attribute is requested, it will be recalculated (since it will be null). You can also find an example of this in the hands-on practice.

Traversing Associations

Sometimes business rules do not simply apply to a particular entity, but to relationships between entities. These relationships, as was discussed in Chapter 10, are implemented by associations, and using associations lets you implement cross-entity business rules.

Recall from Chapter 10 that creating an association creates accessors in the entity object classes at each end. Using these accessors from a particular entity object instance, you can access the related entity object instances at the other end.

Getting a Unique Associated Entity

The simplest kind of accessor occurs in the entity object at either side of a one-to-one association and at the "many" side of a one-to-many association. This accessor returns the associated entity instance at the other end. If myEmp is a particular entity instance, and `getJobs()` is the accessor associated with the association EmpJobFkAssoc, you can retrieve an employee's job (not simply his or her JOB_ID, but the complete associated row from JOBS) by calling `myEmp.getJobs()`. You could use this to discover or change details about the employee's job inside any business logic (setter method, `validateEntity()`, `create()`, etc.) in EmployeesImpl. You can find an example of retrieving a unique associated entity and using it inside a setter method in the hands-on practice later in this chapter.

Getting Many Associated Entities

The accessor on either side of a many-to-many association or the "one" side of a one-to-many association is a bit more complicated. It cannot simply return an associated entity instance, because there can be more than one associated entity instance. Instead, it returns an object of type oracle.jbo.RowIterator. You can think of a RowIterator as a collection of objects, called *row objects,* and a pointer to one particular row object, the "current" row object. This pointer can be moved around, and data can be extracted from the current row object.

A row object is actually any object that implements the interface oracle.jbo.Row. In fact, oracle.jbo.server.EntityImpl implements oracle.jbo.Row, so entity object instances are, in fact, row objects. Other things can be row objects too, but the RowIterators returned by associations accessor methods contain only entity object instances.

When a RowIterator is first created, its pointer starts at a slot before the first row object it contains. You can then call the method `RowIterator.next()`, which has the following two effects:

- It moves the pointer to the next row object in the RowIterator. (When the RowIterator is first created, this is the first row object.)

- It returns that row object.

`next()` is most useful when used in conjunction with the method `RowIterator.hasNext()`, which returns true if the RowIterator has at least one more row. Using `next()` and `hasNext()` together lets you write a loop that cycles through all the rows in the RowIterator, such as the following code:

```
while (myRowIterator.hasNext()
{
  Row currentRow = myRowIterator.next();
  // code that uses currentRow
}
```

Note that, as far as the Java language is concerned, `next()` simply returns a row object—an object of type oracle.jbo.Row. If you want to treat the object as belonging to a particular entity object class (for example, to call getters and setters on it), you must cast the Row to the appropriate class.

You can find an example of traversing an association, retrieving a RowIterator, and using that RowIterator in business logic in the hands-on practice.

Using Discriminator Columns

Occasionally, you may have a table that contains more than one type of row. For example, suppose that your company made a distinction between salaried, commissioned, and hourly employees, but you stored them both in the EMPLOYEES table. Suppose salaried employees have a monthly salary, commissioned employees have a monthly salary and commission, and hourly employees have an hourly rate. This table might look just like the HR schema's EMPLOYEES table except for having two more columns: EMP_TYPE, to distinguish salaried from hourly employees, and HOURLY_RATE, to specify the hourly rate for hourly employees.

You would probably want to implement different business logic for these different types of employees. For example, you would probably want YearlyPay to be one of the following values:

- 12 * Salary, for salaried employees

- 12 * Salary * (estimated sales) * CommissionPct / 100, for commissioned employees

- 40 * HourlyRate * 52, for hourly employees

A *discriminator column* is a column, like EMP_TYPE, that you can use to sort the rows of a table into two or more different types. You can create different entity objects for each of these types, each implementing different business logic, and create a main entity object for the entire table that automatically delegates to the appropriate sub-entities. You can base a view object on the main entity object, and the BC4J framework will automatically use the right business logic for each row.

To represent a table with a discriminator column, use the following steps:

1. Select Edit from the right-click menu of the entity representing the table.

2. Select the Attribute Settings node.

3. Select the attribute corresponding to the discriminator column from the *Select Attribute* dropdown list.

4. Check the *Discriminator* checkbox, as shown here:

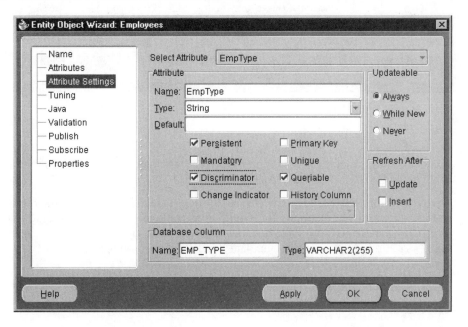

5. Click OK.

6. Next, you have to create each sub-entity. On the package node, select New Entity Object from the right-click menu.

7. If the Welcome page appears, click Next.

8. On the Name page, enter a name for your sub-entity in the *Name* field.

9. Click the Browse button beside the *Extends Entity* field, select your main entity object, and click OK. The wizard page should now look like this:

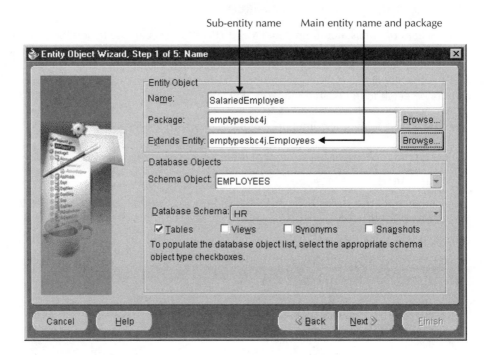

10. Click Next.

11. On the Attributes page, note that no attributes are listed. The reason for this is that, by default, the sub-entity simply inherits the business logic for all attributes for the main entity.

12. Using New from Table, add all the attributes whose default behavior you want to override in this sub-entity. For example, for the SalariedEmployees entity, you should add the YearlyPay and Salary attributes, because you will need to add specialized logic to `getYearlyPay()` (to initially calculate YearlyPay based on Salary) and to `setSalary()` (to reset YearlyPay when Salary changes).

13. Using New from Table, add the discriminator attribute.

14. Click Next.

15. On the Attribute Settings page, select the discriminator attribute in the *Select Attribute* list.

16. In the *Default* field, add the value of the discriminator column corresponding to this sub-entity. For example, for a sub-entity handling rows with an EmpType of "S," the page should look as follows:

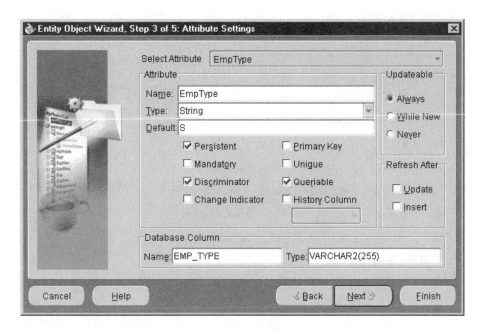

17. Click Finish to create the sub-entity.

18. Repeat steps 6–17 for each possible value of the discriminator attribute.

19. Use the Entity Object Wizard's Validation page, or edit the entity object class, for each sub-entity to add the business logic you want. For example, you would add specialized business logic to SalariedEmployeesImpl's `getYearlyPay()` and `setSalary()` methods.

20. Implement any business logic common to all sub-entities in the main entity object. For example, if you wanted to populate all employees' EmployeeId from the same database sequence, you would do this in the `create()` method for EmployeesImpl.

Hands-on Practice: Refine the HR Business Model

In this practice, you will continue to refine the business components project you created in Chapter 10. In addition to the minimum required salary and the required format for email addresses that you implemented in the previous hands-on practice, when you have completed this practice, the HRBC4J business components will automatically populate the EmployeeId attribute, calculate a value for YearlyPay, and enforce a requirement that managers make more money than their employees. It is this functional business model that you will use to design a view object layer and client in the next two chapters.

This practice requires that you have completed the preceding practice in this chapter. Alternatively, you can download the starting files for this practice from the authors' websites mentioned in the beginning of the book.

This practice steps you through the following phases:

I. Populate an attribute from a database sequence

- ■ Generate the create() method

- ■ Add defaulting code to the create() method

II. Calculate an attribute

- ■ Add calculation code to a getter method

- ■ Add reset code to setter methods

III. Add validation logic that traverses a one-to-many association

- ■ Traverse to the "one" end of the association

- ■ Traverse to the "many" end of the association

IV. Test the business logic

- ■ Test the attribute defaulting

- ■ Test the calculated attribute

- ■ Test the association-traversing validation code

I. Populate an Attribute from a Database Sequence

This phase populates the EmployeeId attribute with a dynamically calculated default value. The value is taken from a database sequence, EMPLOYEES_SEQ, using the SequenceImpl class.

Generate the create() Method

The first step in dynamically calculating a default attribute is to generate a stub for the `create()` method. You can generate the `create()` method stub using the following steps:

1. In the right-click menu for Employees, select Edit Employees.

2. Select the Java node.

3. Check the *Create Method* checkbox in the Generate Methods section.

4. Click OK to close the wizard and to generate a `create()` method stub in the EmployeesImpl.java class.

Add Defaulting Code to the create() Method

You can add code to retrieve a value from EMPLOYEES_SEQ and automatically populate EmployeeId using the following steps:

1. In the Navigator, expand the Employees node and open EmployeesImpl.java in the Code Editor.

2. Add the following line to the import block:

```
import oracle.jbo.server.SequenceImpl;
```

Additional Information: Importing SequenceImpl will allow you to refer to it without package qualification later. The import may be added in any order.

3. Find the `create()` method.

4. Change the `create()` method by adding code to get the next available sequence number for the Oracle sequence EMPLOYEES_SEQ. When you are done, the `create()` method should look like this:

```
protected void create(AttributeList attributeList)
{
  super.create(attributeList);
  SequenceImpl empSeq=new SequenceImpl("EMPLOYEES_SEQ", getDBTransaction());
  setEmployeeId(empSeq.getSequenceNumber());
}
```

Additional Information: Note that `super.create()` is still invoked first, and that `getDBTransaction()` is used to provide a DBTransaction for the SequenceImpl constructor.

5. Build your project and Save All.

What Just Happened? You added code to the `create()` method to automatically populate EmployeeId with the next number of the sequence. Since the `create()` method is called whenever a new row is created, new employees will have their EmployeeId default to a number picked from the database sequence.

II. Calculate an Attribute

This phase adds code to automatically calculate the value of the attribute YearlyPay, which you added to Employees in Chapter 10. When you have finished, YearlyPay will automatically be set to the estimated yearly pay for employees.

Add Calculation Code to a Getter Method

The first step is to change the `getYearlyPay()` method so that a value for YearlyPay is calculated the first time it is requested.

1. Find the `getYearlyPay()` method in the source code for EmployeesImpl.java.

2. Change the method's code so that it looks like this:

```
public Number getYearlyPay()
{
  /* Calculate YearlyPay if it is null and salary is
   * set. */
  if (
    getAttributeInternal(YEARLYPAY) == null &&
    getSalary() != null )
  {
    /* Base yearly salary is 12 times monthly salary. */
    int value = 12 * getSalary().intValue();
```

```
      if (getCommissionPct() != null)
      /* Estimate commission based on sales expectations of
       * five times salary. */
      {
        value += (int) (
          value * 5
          * getCommissionPct().doubleValue() / 100
        );
      }
      populateAttribute(YEARLYPAY, new Number(Value));
    }
    return (Number) getAttributeInternal(YEARLYPAY);
  }
```

Additional Information: Note the test at the beginning of the method. This keeps the getter from having to recalculate the value of YearlyPay every time the attribute is requested. The attribute is calculated once, before it is set to anything, and that value is used for each subsequent request, unless YearlyPay is set to null in the interim. It also keeps the getter from trying to calculate a value for YearlyPay before there's any value set for Salary.

Also note that YearlyPay is set using `populateAttribute()`.

Add Reset Code to Setter Methods

Since the value of YearlyPay is based on the values of Salary and CommissionPct, you need to make sure that YearlyPay is kept up to date whenever Salary or CommissionPct changes. You can do this by adding code to `setSalary()` and set `CommissionPct()` to reset YearlyPay to null.

I. Find the `setSalary()` method in the source code for EmployeesImpl.java.

2. Change the method's code so that it looks like this:

```
public void setSalary(Number value)
{
  setAttributeInternal(SALARY, value);
  populateAttribute(YEARLYPAY, null);
}
```

Additional Information: Note that, in the preceding code, you called `setAttributeInternal()` before resetting YearlyPay. The reason is that, if `setAttributeInternal()` fails (for example, if Salary had an XML validation rule that rejects the value), you would not want to update YearlyPay.

3. Find the `setCommissionPct()` method.

4. Change the method's code so that it looks like this:

```
public void setCommissionPct(Number value)
{
  setAttributeInternal(COMMISSIONPCT, value);
  populateAttribute(YEARLYPAY, null);
}
```

5. Build your project and Save All.

What Just Happened? You added code to `getYearlyPay()` to calculate the YearlyPay attribute. Then you added code to `setSalary()` and `setCommissionPct()` to ensure that YearlyPay is recalculated after Salary or CommissionPct are changed.

III. Add Validation Logic that Traverses a One-to-Many Association

This phase adds validation logic to ensure that no employee makes more than his or her manager does. The logic has to traverse the association EmpManagerFkAssoc in each direction: once to make sure no employee's salary is set higher than his or her manager's, and once to make sure no manager's salary is set lower than any of his or her employees'.

Traverse to the "One" End of the Association

First, you must add code to `setSalary()` that traverses EmpManagerFkAssoc from employees to their managers—that is, from the "many" end to the "one" end of the association. Since the "one" end is unique, this will involve retrieving a single entity.

1. In the source code for EmployeesImpl.java, find the `setSalary()` method.

2. Add this code before the `setAttributeInternal()` statement:

```
/* Start out assuming the employee's salary is low enough. */
boolean ok = true;
int mySal = value.intValue();
/* getManagerIdEmployees() is the accessor that returns
 * the manager. */
EmployeesImpl manager = getManagerIdEmployees();
/* If the employee has a manager, make sure the employee's
 * salary is the same or lower as the manager's. */
if (manager != null)
{
  if (manager.getSalary().intValue() < mySal)
  {
    ok = false;
  }
}
```

> **Additional Information:** The (`manager != null`) test is needed because `getManagerIdEmployees()` will return null for anyone (e.g., the company President) without a manager; you would risk a null pointer error if you did not eliminate those cases.

3. Embed the `setAttributeInternal()` call in the following if-else block:

```
if (ok)
{
  setAttributeInternal(SALARY, value);
}
```

```
else
{
  throw new oracle.jbo.JboException(
    "Managers' salaries cannot be lower than their employees'." );
}
```

4. Since this method now throws an exception, you should declare it. Change the method signature to:

```
public void setSalary(Number value) throws oracle.jbo.JboException
```

Traverse to the "Many" End of the Association

The code you just added to setSalary() ensures that an employee is not given a raise above his or her manager. However, to really enforce the business rule, you must also ensure that no manager is given a pay cut below any of his or her employees. This involves adding more code to setSalary() to traverse EmpManagerFkAssoc from managers to their employees, that is, from the "one" end to the "many" end of the association. Since the "many" end is not unique, this will involve retrieving a RowSet.

1. Add the following code to the body of setSalary(), right before the if-else block containing the setAttributeInternal() call:

```
/* getEmployees() is the accessor that returns all reporting
 * employees */
RowIterator reports = getEmployees();
/* current will hold each reporting employee as you cycle
 * through them */
EmployeesImpl current;
/* Cycle through the reporting employees. Make sure each
 * has a salary low enough. */
while (reports.hasNext())
{
  current = (EmployeesImpl) reports.next();
  if (current.getSalary().intValue() > mySal)
    ok = false;
}
```

Additional Information: This will still work if the employee is not a manager. In that case, the RowIterator will be empty, hasNext() will immediately be false, and ok will always stay true. Remember also that RowSet.next() returns a Row that must be cast to EmployeesImpl before you call its getSalary() method.

2. Build your project and Save All.

What Just Happened? You added business logic to a setter method that will throw an exception whenever a client tries to assign a salary that would violate the rule "An employee's salary cannot be higher than his or her manager's." This involved traversing an association in each direction: once to retrieve a unique entity instance (an employee's manager) and once to retrieve a RowSet (a manager's employees).

IV. Test the Business Logic

Now that you have added all this business logic to the Employees entity object, you can use the Business Component Browser to test it.

Test the Attribute Defaulting

You can see how attribute defaulting works by adding a new row.

1. Test EntityTestModule.

2. Double-click EmployeesView1.

3. Click the Add Row button (shown next) to create a row.

4. Note that the *EmployeeId* field is automatically populated with a new sequence number.

5. Click the Remove Row button (shown next) to remove the row.

Test the Calculated Attribute

You can see how your calculated attribute works by scrolling around and looking at its values on various rows. You will also test to make sure it stays in synch with Salary and CommissionPct.

1. Scroll forward to employee 104, Bruce Ernst.

2. Note that Ernst's YearlyPay is 72000, 12 times his Salary.

3. Change Ernst's salary to "7000". As soon as you click into another field or scroll off the row, Ernst's YearlyPay will change to 84000.

4. Give Ernst a CommissionPct of ".5". As soon as you click into another field or scroll off the row, Ernst's YearlyPay will change to 86100. This is because 0.5 percent of five times Ernst's yearly salary is 2100.

Test the Association-Traversing Validation Code

You can see how the setSalary() validation code works by trying to violate the rules: first, by setting a manager's salary too low, and then by setting an employee's salary too high.

1. Scroll forward to employee 145, John Russell.

2. Try to set Russell's salary to "25000". As soon as you click into another field or scroll off the row, you will get an exception.

    Additional Information: Russell reports to Steven King, the President, who has a salary of 24000. This change would violate the first part of the validation code you placed in `setSalary()`—you cannot set an employee's salary to be higher than his or her manager's.

3. Try to set Russell's salary to "9700." As soon as you click into another field or scroll off the row, you will get an exception.

   Additional Information: Employee 150, Peter Tucker, reports to Russell and has a salary of 10000. This change would violate the second part of the validation code—you cannot set a manager's salary to be lower than any of his or her reporting employees.

4. Set Russell's salary to "12000." Notice that the change is accepted.

   Additional Information: The error messages you got were not terribly informative. By writing more complex code (for example, keeping track of the EmployeeId and Salary of the reporting employee that caused the test to fail), you could have passed a String to the JboException's constructor that contained more useful information.

What Just Happened?   You tested each piece of business logic you added to the Employees entity object: the use of EMPLOYEE_SEQ to populate EmployeeId for new employees, the YearlyPay calculated attribute, and the validation code in `setSalary()` that traversed two different association directions.

Of course, you could add quite a bit more business logic to HRBC4J. The authors recommend you come up with more business rules and try to implement them.

CHAPTER
13

Working with Queries

All is waste and worthless, till
Arrives the selecting will,
And, out of slime and chaos, Wit
Draws the threads of fair and fit.

—Ralph Waldo Emerson (1803–1882), *Wealth*

hapters 9 and 11 explained how to represent and enforce rules on data in BC4J. In this chapter, you will learn how to expose that data to a client application. The BC4J framework does not allow client applications to access entity objects directly; instead, you select exactly what data you want clients to be able to access by exposing it in a view object. One view object should, in general, contain exactly the data your client will need in a single page.

Before you start this chapter, remember the following facts about view objects introduced in Chapter 9:

- A view object is the representation of a SQL query.

- A view object includes view attributes for every column in the query result set. The attribute types are Java classes that correspond to the SQL types of the columns.

- View attributes can be, but do not need to be, based on entity attributes.

- Associated with each view object is an XML file that contains tags representing the query, the view attributes, and any entity objects that contain entity attributes that the view attributes are based on.

- Also associated with each view object is a class that contains a number of methods that return view rows, which each represent one row of data from the query.

There are many more choices involved in initially constructing view objects than there are in constructing entity objects. In this chapter, you will learn about the structure of view objects (including the four kinds of attributes they can have) and how to determine which structure will be most effective and efficient for your purposes. Later in the chapter, you will learn about using view links and application modules to specify the relationships between your view objects.

This chapter has two hands-on practices. The first explores a number of different view object structures, and creates the simplest possible application module that lets you test their functionality. The second focuses on creating data models from those view objects by creating view links and application modules.

The Types of View Attributes

View attributes can, but do not need to, be based on entity attributes. They also can, but do not need to, map to query columns. These two choices yield four different kinds of view attributes: persistent, SQL-only, entity-derived, and transient.

Based on entity attributes

Corresponds to query columns	Yes	No
Yes	Persistent	SQL-only
No	Entity-derived	Transient

Persistent View Attributes   *Persistent* view attributes correspond to a query column and are based on a persistent entity attribute. The only reason you must use a persistent attribute is if you want to write changes to the database. You can only do this through persistent attributes, for they not only correspond to a database column (as opposed to a BC4J-only temporary value), but they also derive from an entity object that can make changes to the database.

There are several other advantages to using a persistent attribute. The most important is when two view objects share data. Instead of storing the data redundantly, they can maintain pointers to the same data in the entity object. For a complete discussion of reasons to use persistent attributes, see the section "The Advantages of Maintaining Data in Entity Objects" later in this chapter.

SQL-only View Attributes   *SQL-only* view attributes map to a query column but are not based on any entity attribute. The query retrieves data from the database, and the data is then stored directly in the view attribute.

You cannot use SQL-only attributes to update the database, only to retrieve data from it. If an attribute can be read-only, however, and the reasons described in the section "The Advantages of Maintaining Data in Entity Objects" do not apply, a SQL-only attribute can be more efficient than a persistent attribute, because it skips the step of storing the data in the entity object and maintaining a pointer to it.

A SQL-only attribute does not need to derive its value from a single database column. In fact, you can specify any SQL expression (so long as the SQL expression requires only tables in the FROM clause of the view object's query). The expression will be calculated in the database instead of in Java in the middle tier. This can be faster than calculating attributes in Java, but you can not use entity object synchronization.

> **CAUTION**
> *A Java-calculated attribute will immediately change as soon as relevant related attributes change in the cache. For example, the attribute YearlyPay is designed to change as soon as Salary or CommissionPct change. SQL-calculated attributes will not change until existing data is posted and the view object's query is reexecuted.*

Entity-Derived View Attributes   *Entity-derived* view attributes correspond to entity attributes, but they have no column in the SQL query. The entity attributes they map to must be transient. In the hands-on practices from Chapters 10 and 12, the view attribute YearlyPay in EmployeesView was an entity-derived attribute. It was based on the entity attribute YearlyPay in the entity object Employees.

Transient View Attributes   *Transient* view attributes correspond to neither entity attributes nor SQL query columns. Transient view attributes work just like entity-derived attributes do. They must be populated by hand or as calculated attributes. However, unlike entity-derived attributes, they do not correspond to transient entity attributes.

Caching

The most important difference between the types of view attributes is the way that they are cached. Caching, in data processing, is holding copies of data in memory. The primary benefit of caching in general is optimizing performance. BC4J's caching mechanisms optimize performance by holding the data in the middle tier, eliminating repeated trips to the database.

BC4J uses a two-level form of caching, maintaining caches for both entity objects and view rows. This two-level caching provides other benefits, as you can understand by examining the internal workings of the attribute types.

How Persistent View Attributes are Populated

When a usage of a view object with persistent attributes first executes its query, it sends the query to the database. The database returns a result, as shown in Figure 13-1.

The columns of the result are mapped to view attributes and to the entity attributes they are based on, as shown in Figure 13-2. The sidebar "How Does BC4J Know Which Columns Correspond to Which Attributes?" explains how this happens.

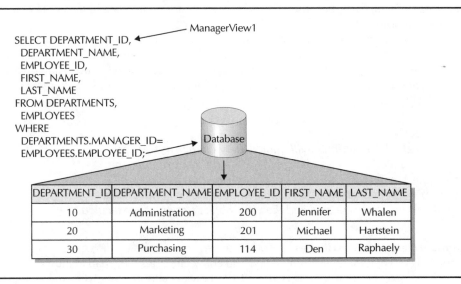

FIGURE 13-1.   *Executing a query and returning a result*

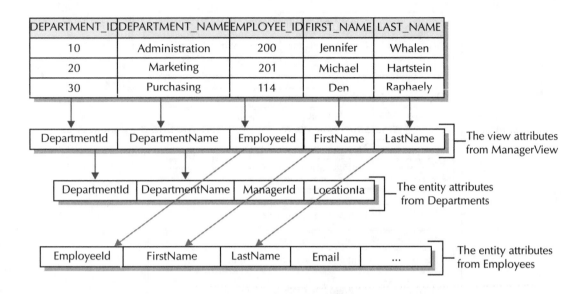

DEPARTMENT_ID	DEPARTMENT_NAME	EMPLOYEE_ID	FIRST_NAME	LAST_NAME
10	Administration	200	Jennifer	Whalen
20	Marketing	201	Michael	Hartstein
30	Purchasing	114	Den	Raphaely

DepartmentId	DepartmentName	EmployeeId	FirstName	LastName

The view attributes from ManagerView

DepartmentId	DepartmentName	ManagerId	LocationIa

The entity attributes from Departments

EmployeeId	FirstName	LastName	Email	...

The entity attributes from Employees

FIGURE 13-2. *Associating the result columns with view and entity attributes*

Next, instances of the entity object classes are created, and the attributes are populated with the appropriate result column data, and inserted into *entity caches*, as shown in Figure 13-3.

How Does BC4J Know Which Columns Correspond to Which Attributes?
The view object's XML file maintains mappings between query columns, view attributes, and entity attributes.

Typically, when you create a persistent view attribute from an entity attribute, JDeveloper creates a query column that corresponds to the entity attribute's table column. Since JDeveloper created the query column and the persistent view attribute based on your entity attribute selection, it can maintain the mappings between the query column, the view attribute, and the entity attribute automatically.

In certain cases, where you need more direct control over the view object's query, you will have to specify attribute mappings yourself. See the section "Expert Mode" for more information.

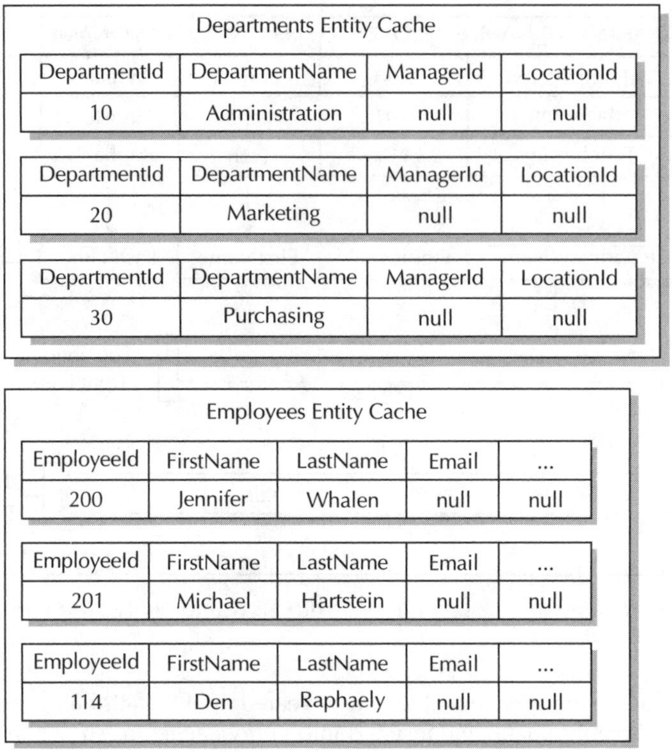

FIGURE 13-3. *Populating entity caches*

Finally, view rows are created, and the attributes are populated with pointers to the entity attributes in the entity cache. These view rows are inserted into the *view cache* for the usage of the view object, as shown in Figure 13-4.

In summary, there are two sorts of caches: entity caches and view caches. In the case of persistent attributes, entity caches hold the data in those attributes, and view caches hold pointers to that data.

How SQL-Only Attributes are Populated

SQL-only view attributes retrieve data from the database just as persistent view attributes do, as shown in Figure 13-1. After the data is retrieved, however, SQL-only view attributes are not added to any entity cache, unlike what is shown in Figure 13-3. Instead, when the view cache is created, the appropriate attribute is populated directly with the data, instead of a pointer to data in an entity cache, as shown in Figure 13-5.

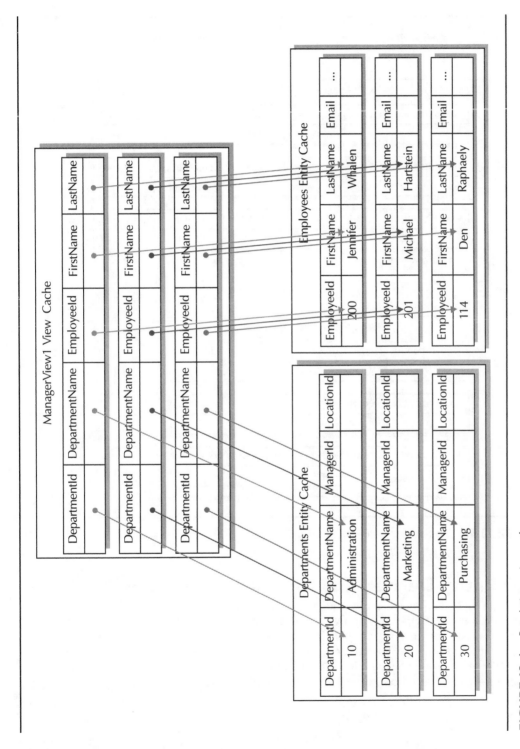

FIGURE 13-4. *Populating a view cache*

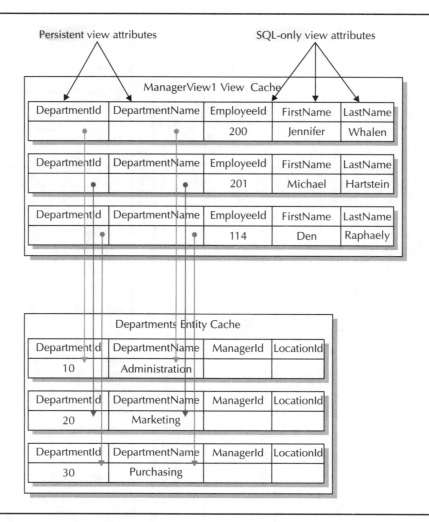

FIGURE 13-5. *Populating SQL-only attributes*

How Entity-Derived and Transient Attributes Are Set

The data for these attributes is set by your application. For example, you set the entity-derived attribute YearlyPay by adding code to getYearlyPay(), setSalary(), and setCommissionPct(). If the attribute is entity-derived, the view cache contains pointers to transient entity attributes, just as, for persistent view attributes, it contains pointers to persistent entity attributes (as was shown in Figure 13-4). If the attribute is transient, the view cache stores the data directly, just as it does for SQL-only view attributes.

The Advantages of Maintaining Data in Entity Objects

There are four main advantages to basing view objects on persistent and entity-derived view attributes, which store the data in entity caches.

Space-Saving Between View Usages   Multiple view objects can be based on the same entity attributes, and an application module can contain multiple usages of a single view object. By storing pointers to the same entity attribute instead of storing the data themselves, the view caches do not contain duplicate copies of memory-consuming data.

Space-Saving Within a View Object's Cache   A single query's result set may have several rows based on the same row of a table. Consider the following query:

```
SELECT EMPLOYEE_ID,
    LAST_NAME,
    JOB_ID,
    EMPLOYEES.DEPARTMENT_ID,
    DEPARTMENTS.DEPARTMENT_ID,
    DEPARTMENT_NAME
FROM EMPLOYEES, DEPARTMENTS
WHERE EMPLOYEES.DEPARTMENT_ID = DEPARTMENTS.DEPARTMENT_ID
```

Many rows returned by this query could contain data from the same row in DEPARTMENTS. For example, the following rows all reference department 90.

EMPLOYEE_ID	LAST_NAME	EMPLOYEES. DEPARTMENT_ID	DEPARTMENTS. DEPARTMENT_ID	DEPARTMENT_NAME
100	King	90	90	Executive
101	Kochhar	90	90	Executive
102	De Haan	90	90	Executive

There is no reason to store the values retrieved from the Departments table three times. The BC4J framework saves space by only adding a single entity object instance to the Departments cache, as shown in Figure 13-6.

Similarly, if a calculation only applies to one row of a database table, the calculated result can be stored in one row of the entity cache, instead of being stored in many rows of the view cache.

Synchronization   As was said earlier, multiple view objects can use the same attributes from the same entity. For example, both ManagerView and DeptEmpView use the entity object Employees, and both of them have view attributes mapped to the entity attribute LastName in Employees. If the value of the last name is changed, this change must be simultaneously reflected in usages of both ManagerView and DeptEmpView. The value of this persistent attribute is maintained in the entity cache for Employees, and the ManagerView's and DeptEmpView's LastName attributes contain pointers to Employees' LastName attribute. Consequently, making a change in ManagerView1

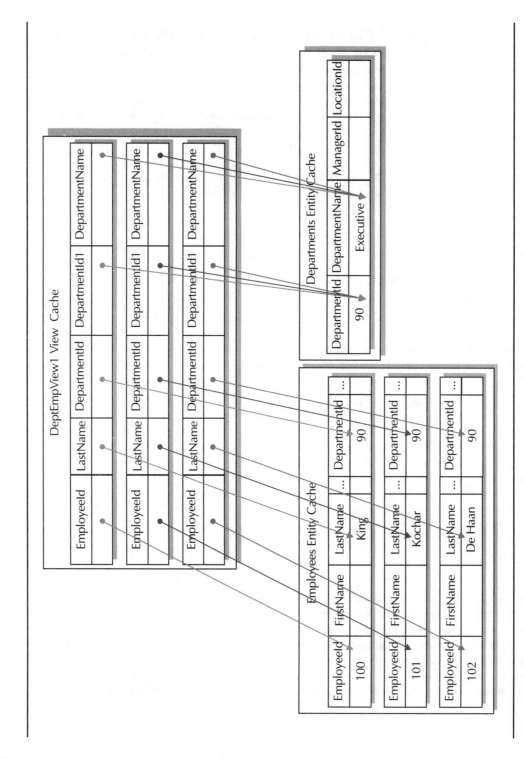

FIGURE 13-6. *Several view rows corresponding to one entity object instance*

really changes the data in Employees, a change that is immediately visible in DeptEmpView1, as shown in Figure 13-7.

This synchronization also applies to multiple usages of a single view object. For Example, changing LastName through DeptEmpView1 will be immediately visible in another usage called DeptEmpView2 because, and only because, the attribute is mapped to an entity attribute.

Use and Reuse of Business Logic View objects do all of their writing through entity objects. Consequently, any validation logic in your entity objects will get enforced for all persistent attributes. In addition, using persistent and entity-derived view attributes lets you take advantage of other business logic (such as defaulting for persistent attributes, or calculation for entity-derived attributes) in your entities.

Refining a View Object's Query

Once you select the attributes for a view object, the View Object Wizard creates a query to retrieve the persistent and SQL-only attributes. The SELECT clause is a list of all the database columns that correspond to the persistent and SQL-only columns. The FROM clause is a list of the tables that correspond to the entity objects on which the view object is based.

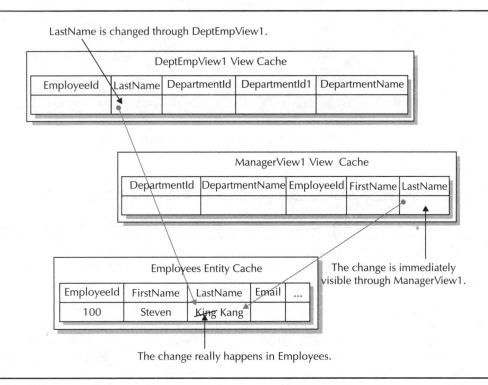

FIGURE 13-7. *View object synchronization*

If a view object is based on more than one table, the wizard also attempts to assemble a WHERE clause for you.

Changing the WHERE and ORDER BY Clauses

If you want, you can change the WHERE clause (including changing the WHERE clause to do an outer join), or add an ORDER BY clause, on the Query page of the View Object Wizard, as shown here:

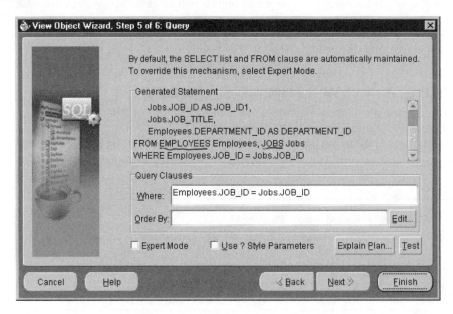

Do not type WHERE or ORDER BY in the fields; the wizard adds those for you.

Expert Mode

Expert mode allows you to create view objects based on any valid SQL query. Not only do you have control over the WHERE and ORDER BY clauses of the query (as you do in regular view objects), but you can also type in the entire query and specify the SELECT clause, the FROM clause, and even other clauses such as GROUP BY. Instead of storing the individual query clauses as attributes of the <ViewObject> XML tag, an expert-mode view object stores the entire query as a single XML attribute. There are two ways to use expert mode: with SQL-only view objects and with view objects based on entity objects.

SQL-only View Objects

Sometimes, you may have a view object with only SQL-only and transient attributes. If you will not need to make changes to the database and you do not need to take advantage of the synchronization or memory-saving features of entity objects, there is no reason to have any persistent or entity-derived attributes at all.

In this case, you can use a *SQL-only view object.* Not only do SQL-only view objects not use entity objects (which will save space and time if you do not need them), but they also allow you to use expert mode very easily.

When you create a SQL-only view object, JDeveloper will create attributes for each query column, using a convention much like the one the Entity Object Wizard uses for making entity attributes out of table columns:

- The first letter will be capitalized.

- Underscores will be removed, and the first letter after them will be capitalized.

- All other letters will be lowercase.

- Symbols not valid for Java identifiers (such as parentheses) will be removed.

For example, the query column COUNT(Emp.EMPLOYEE_ID) will map to a view attribute called "CountempemployeeId". By using a column alias, you can change the name of the attribute. For example, COUNT(Emp.EMPLOYEE_ID) AS NUM_REPORTS will map to a view attribute called "NumReports."

Expert Mode with View Objects Based on Entity Objects

Sometimes, you need the query flexibility of a SQL-only view object, but you want or need to use the entity-object layer (either because you want to write to the database, or to take advantage of the synchronization and space-saving that entity objects can provide). You can also use expert mode with view objects based on entity objects, although it is more complicated.

As was mentioned before, when you create a persistent view attribute from an entity attribute, JDeveloper maintains the mapping between the query column and the entity attribute automatically. When you use expert mode, however, you write the SQL query yourself. You have to specify the mappings between the query columns and the attributes yourself. Doing this incorrectly can cause problems. This should not be a problem for fairly simple queries. However, with complicated queries (for example, those involving multiple UNIONS or large numbers of columns or elements derived via functions or expressions), or when a query is repeatedly modified to add or delete columns or change their order, it is all too easy to get the mapping wrong, with harmful consequences.

For example, consider an expert-mode view object MgrReportsExpertView, based on a single entity object, Employees. The query of MgrReportsExpertView is as follows:

```
SELECT Mgr.EMPLOYEE_ID,
   Mgr.SALARY,
   COUNT(Emp.EMPLOYEE_ID) AS "NUM_REPORTS",
FROM EMPLOYEES Mgr, EMPLOYEES Emp
WHERE Emp.MANAGER_ID=Mgr.EMPLOYEE_ID
GROUP BY Mgr.EMPLOYEE_ID, Mgr.SALARY
```

EMPLOYEE_ID should map to a persistent view attribute based on Employees' EmployeeId attribute; SALARY should map to a persistent view attribute based on Employees' Salary attribute; and NUM_REPORTS should map to a SQL-only view attribute.

If you had accidentally mapped the NUM_REPORTS column to a persistent attribute based on CommissionPct, then when the view object executed its query and populated entity attributes (as in Figure 13-3), it would populate CommissionPct with the number of reporting employees. Since entity objects control changes to the database, and since CommissionPct maps to the database column COMMISSION_PCT, when changes were posted, the BC4J framework would attempt to overwrite the COMMISSION_PCT column of the database with the number of reporting employees. Generally, the BC4J framework can detect when a problem like this is happening, and you will get a RowInconsistentException instead of corrupted data. But you should still make sure you provide correct attribute mappings to avoid runtime errors.

Hands-on Practice:
Create View Objects for HR

In this practice, you will create a set of view objects to expose the data in HR to clients. This is the first step toward writing two batch clients: a career path lister and an accountant promotion client. The career path lister will provide a list of people currently holding every job at the company, along with a history of people who have previously held those jobs. The accountant promotion client will promote the accountants in a particular department to finance managers.

This practice builds on the results of the hands-on practice in Chapter 12. If you have not completed that practice, you can download the starting files for this practice from the authors' websites mentioned in the author information at the beginning of this book.

This practice steps you through the following phases:

   I. Remove the default view object layer

   II. Plan the view objects

   ■ Plan the view objects for the career path lister

   ■ Plan the view objects for the accountant promotion client

   III. Create a simple view object

   ■ Open the wizard and name the view object

   ■ Select an entity object

   ■ Select persistent attributes

   ■ Verify the query

   IV. Create a SQL-only view object

   ■ Open the wizard and name the view object

   ■ Make the view object SQL-only

   ■ Write the view object's query

   V. Create a view object based on two entity objects

   ■ Open the wizard and name the view object

   ■ Select entity objects

■ Select persistent and entity-derived attributes

■ Create a SQL-only attribute

■ Make attributes read-only

■ Verify the query

VI. Create view object based on an entity object using expert mode

■ Create the view object

■ Edit the query

■ Verify attribute mappings

VII. Test the view objects

■ Create and test a simple application module

■ Test a simple view object

■ Test a SQL-only view object

■ Test a view object based on multiple entity objects

■ Test an entity-based view object created with expert mode

I. Remove the Default View Object Layer

This phase removes the simple application module, simple view link, and default view objects that you created in Chapter 10.

1. If your HRWS workspace is not open, open it by selecting **File | Open**, and browse to mywork/HRWS.

2. Expand the hrbc4j package node if it is not already expanded.

3. In the right-click menu for EntityTestModule, select Delete EntityTestModule. When you are asked for confirmation, click Yes.

4. In the right-click-menu of EmpPastJobsLink, select Delete EmpPastJobsLink. Click Yes to confirm the deletion.

5. Delete the EmployeesView and JobsView.

6. Select **File | Save All**.

What Just Happened?   You deleted the application module, view links, and view objects you previously used to test the hrbc4j entity objects. Now that you are done testing the entity objects, you do not need these any more.

II. Plan the View Objects

This phase plans the view objects you need to create. The purpose of the view object layer is to collect and present the data that the BC4J clients need, so this design will be based on specifications for two client programs.

These client programs are simple command-line clients; you will learn how to create sophisticated Java GUI and JSP clients in Parts III and IV of this book. The simple clients will not be written until the next chapter, but you must know their design to know what view objects they will need.

Plan the View Objects for the Career Path Lister

Figure out precisely what the career path lister has to do to fulfill its functional requirements of showing how employees have advanced to a particular job:

1. Select a Job from the JOBS table.

   This will require the data returned by the following query:

   ```
   SELECT Jobs.JOB_ID, Jobs.JOB_TITLE
   FROM JOBS Jobs
   ```

   The data will be supplied by a view object called JobsView.

2. List the current holders of the job with their estimated yearly pay and the number of employees reporting to them.

   This will require the data returned by the following query:

   ```
   SELECT Employees.EMPLOYEE_ID, Employees.LAST_NAME,
      Employees.JOB_ID, COUNT(Reports.EMPLOYEE_ID) AS "NUM_REPORTS"
   FROM EMPLOYEES Employees, EMPLOYEES Reports
   WHERE Employees.EMPLOYEE_ID = Reports.MANAGER_ID (+)
   GROUP BY Employees.EMPLOYEE_ID, Employees.LAST_NAME,
      Employees.JOB_ID
   ```

   This data will be supplied by a view object called EmployeesView. EmployeesView will also have to contain an entity-derived attribute based on the transient attribute YearlyPay from Employees.

3. List the past holders of the job and their current job and estimated yearly pay.

   This will require the data returned by the following query:

   ```
   SELECT Employees.EMPLOYEE_ID, Employees.LAST_NAME, Employees.JOB_ID,
      Employees.DEPARTMENT_ID, Jobs.JOB_ID, Jobs.JOB_TITLE
   FROM EMPLOYEES Employees, JOBS Jobs
   WHERE Employees.JOB_ID = Jobs.JOB_ID
   ```

   The data will be supplied by a view object called EmpJobsView. EmpJobsView will also have to contain an entity-derived attribute based on the transient attribute YearlyPay from Employees.

   Additional Information: You may note that the preceding query selects JOB_ID from both EMPLOYEES and JOBS, even though the WHERE clause ensures that these values will be equal. You need to select EMPLOYEES.JOB_ID because, in the Accountant Promotion Client (see the next section), you are going to use this view object to change it. You need to select JOBS.JOB_ID because it is the primary key of JOBS. For every entity object a view object is based on, the primary key of that entity object must be selected as a persistent attribute. If your table does not have a primary key, you can use the RowId attribute JDeveloper will automatically create. (Non-Oracle tables must have a primary key.)

Plan the View Objects for the Accountant Promotion Client

Figure out precisely what the accountant promotion client has to do to fulfill its functional requirements of cycling through departments, printing out some information about each, and promoting all the accountants in the department:

1. Cycle through the departments.

   This will require the data returned by

   ```
   SELECT DEPARTMENT_ID, DEPARTMENT_NAME
   FROM DEPARTMENTS;
   ```

   This data will be supplied by a view object called DepartmentsView.

2. List each department's employees, their estimated yearly pay, and their current job.

   This will require, for each department, data returned by EmpJobsView.

3. For each of those employees, mention if he or she has had more than two previous jobs.

   This will require the data returned by JobsView.

4. Change all accountants in the department to finance managers.

   This will require data returned by EmpJobsView.

What Just Happened?   You examined your client's data needs to determine what view objects you will have to make. The view objects you must create are as follows:

- JobsView
- DepartmentsView
- EmpJobsView
- EmployeesView

Of course, it is not sufficient to plan the view objects the clients will need; before you create the clients, you will need to specify how these view objects are related to one another, using view links and application modules. You will plan the relationships in the next hands-on practice.

III. Create a Simple View Object

This phase creates a simple view object, JobsView. JobsView is based on a single entity object, Jobs.

Open the Wizard and Name the View Object

You can open the View Object wizard and name a view object using the following steps:

1. Locate and expand the hrbc4j package in your HRWS workspace.

2. In the right-click menu for the hrbc4j package, select New View Object to open the View Object Wizard.

3. On the Name page, name your view object "JobsView." Click Next.

Select an Entity Object

You can select a single entity object on which to base a view object using the following steps:

1. On the Entity Object page, select Jobs from the Available list and click the right-arrow button.

   Additional Information: Although JobsView is not going to be used to write to the database, you should base it on the Jobs entity object. There are two reasons for this: First, JobsView shares data with EmpJobsView, and it would be inefficient to store this data twice. Also, JobsView will be one end of EmpPastJobsLink, a bidirectional, many-to-many view link between jobs and employees who have previously held them. As will be explained in the next section, bidirectional, many-to-many view links must be based on associations, and the view objects they link must be based on the associated entity objects.

2. Select Read Only.

   Additional Information: The clients you will design do not need to change any data in the JOBS table. One way to do this would have been to not base the view object on the entity object Jobs, but to make it a SQL-only view object. However, as explained earlier, the View Object should be based on the entity object. But, you can still restrict clients to read-only access to Jobs data by only giving them access to view objects that use Jobs as read-only.

3. Click Next.

Select Persistent Attributes

You can select persistent attributes for a view object using the following steps:

1. On the Attributes page, select JobId and JobTitle from the Available list, and click the right arrow button.

   Additional Information: Because your clients do not need the MinSalary and MaxSalary attributes, you should not select them. Not retrieving extra data from the database saves time and memory, and not including potentially sensitive data in the view object layer hides it from clients.

2. Click Next.

Verify the Query

You can verify that a view object's query is what you wanted using the following steps:

1. Skip the Attribute Settings page by clicking Next again.

2. On the Query page, note that the query matches the one specified for JobsView in phase II earlier. Click Finish to generate the view object.

3. Select Save All.

What Just Happened?   You created a view object based on the Jobs entity object. The view object has two persistent attributes, JobId and JobTitle, based on the entity attributes in Jobs of the same names. Clients will be able to read JOBS.JOB_ID and JOBS.JOB_TITLE from the database, but because this view object is read-only, they will not be able to change them.

IV. Create a SQL-only View Object

This phase creates a SQL-only view object, DepartmentsView. DepartmentsView retrieves data from the DEPARTMENTS table, but does not use an entity object to cache this data. Instead, it maintains the data directly in the view cache.

Open the Wizard and Name the View Object

Create another view object in the hrbc4j package:

1. In the right-click menu for the hrbc4j package, select New View Object to open the View Object Wizard.

2. On the Name page, name the view object DepartmentsView.

Make the View Object SQL-Only

You can make a view object SQL-only using the following steps:

1. Skip the Entity Objects page.

    Additional Information: SQL-only view objects do not use any entity objects. Though you have an entity object, Departments, representing the DEPARTMENTS table, there is no reason for this view object to use it. The DepartmentsView will not share data with other view objects, does not need to update data, will not return multiple rows corresponding to a single table row, and (unlike JobsView) does not need to participate in a view link based on an association. Because of this, it can bypass the step of populating an entity cache, resulting in faster performance.

2. Skip the Attributes and Attribute Settings pages.

    Additional Information: When you write the view object's query, JDeveloper will create SQL-only attributes for each query result column. The only attributes you need to create yourself in a SQL-only view object are transient attributes.

Write the View Object's Query
You can write and test the query for a SQL-only view object using the following steps:

1. On the Query page, enter the following query in the Query Statement area:

   ```
   SELECT DEPARTMENT_ID, DEPARTMENT_NAME
   FROM DEPARTMENTS
   ```

   Leave the semicolon off your query. The Wizard will add it, and if you type it yourself, you will get an "Invalid Character" error.

   Additional Information: Note that, unlike with standard view objects, you have complete control over the SQL query of a SQL-only view object.

2. Click Test. The message "Query is valid." should appear in a dialog box.

3. Repeatedly click Next to scroll to the end of the wizard.

4. Click Finish to generate the view object.

5. Select Save All.

What Just Happened?   You created a SQL-only view object that returns data from the DEPARTMENTS table. The view object has two SQL-only attributes, DepartmentId and DepartmentName. Clients will be able to use this view object to read DEPARTMENTS.DEPARTMENT_ID and DEPARTMENTS.DEPARTMENT_NAME from the database, but because the attributes are SQL-only, they will not be able to change them.

V. Create a View Object Based on Two Entity Objects
This phase creates a view object, EmpJobsView, based on two entity objects, Employees and Jobs.

Open the Wizard and Name the View Object
Create a view object in the hrbc4j package and name it "EmpJobsView."

Select Entity Objects
You can select multiple entity objects on which to base a view object using the following steps:

1. On the Entity Object page, select Employees from the Available list, and click the right-arrow button.

2. Select Jobs from the Available list and click the arrow button.

3. Ensure that Read Only is selected for Jobs.

   Additional Information: Making the Jobs entity usage read-only keeps your clients from changing any data in the JOBS table.

4. Reference should also be selected for Jobs.

> **Additional Information:**   Consider a particular row of EmpJobsView, like the one shown next:

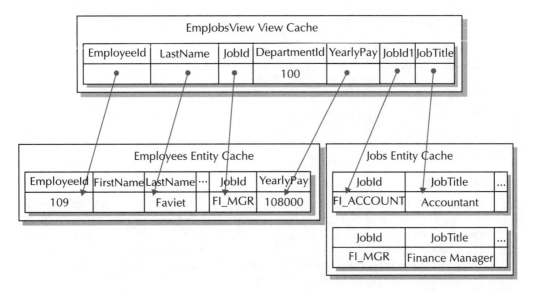

When you change a particular employee's JOB_ID from Accountant (FI_ACCOUNT) to Finance Manager (FI_MGR), you want the pointers to Departments to automatically change to reflect the new DepartmentId, rather than becoming unsynchronized.

Making Jobs a *reference entity object* instructs the BC4J framework to keep the Jobs row synchronized with the Employees row.

5. Ensure that Jobs, rather than PastJobs, is selected in the Association End dropdown list.

> **Additional Information:**   In the previous step, you ensured that the row from Jobs would be kept synchronized with the row from Employees. You want to make sure that the row from Jobs continues to be the one where JOBS.JOB_ID = EMPLOYEES.JOB_ID. That is, you want to maintain the relationship represented by EmpJobFkAssoc. Jobs is the accessor in EmpJobFkAssoc. PastJobs is the accessor from EmpPastJobsAssoc, which represents the wrong table relationship for the synchronization: if you selected that, the BC4J framework would instead try to make sure that the row from Jobs maintained the relationship JOBS.JOB_ID = JOB_HISTORY.JOB_ID AND JOB_HISTORY.EMPLOYEE_ID = EMPLOYEES.EMPLOYEE_ID.

6. Click Next.

Select Persistent and Entity-Derived Attributes

You can select persistent attributes from multiple entity objects using the same procedure as selecting persistent attributes from a single entity:

1. On the Attributes page, select the following attributes in the Available list.

   From under Employees:

   ■ EmployeeId

   ■ JobId

   ■ LastName

   From under Jobs:

   ■ JobId

   ■ JobTitle

   Additional Information: EmployeeId, JobId, and LastName are the only attributes from the EMPLOYEES table that should be persistent. JobId needs to be persistent because the client will change it, EmployeeId needs to be persistent because it is the primary key for the Employees entity, and LastName should be persistent to allow data sharing with the EmployeesView view object, which also uses it. The attributes from Jobs both need to be persistent to allow data-sharing with JobsView.

2. Click the right-arrow button.

3. Select the YearlyPay attribute from under Employees in the Available list.

4. Click the right-arrow button.

   Additional Information: This creates an entity-derived attribute, YearlyPay, in EmpJobsView, based on the transient attribute YearlyPay in Employees.

Create a SQL-only Attribute

You can create a SQL-only attribute for a view object using the following steps:

1. Click New to open the New View Attribute dialog.

   Additional Information: You use this dialog to create both SQL-only and transient view attributes.

2. Enter "DepartmentId" in the *Name* field.

3. Select Number from the *Type* dropdown.

4. Check the *Selected in Query* checkbox.

   Additional Information: By selecting this checkbox, you indicate that you want this attribute to be SQL-only. If you left the checkbox unselected, the attribute would be transient.

5. In the *Alias* field, enter "DEPARTMENT_ID."

6. In the *Expression* field, enter "Employees.DEPARTMENT_ID."

7. Check the *Queriable* checkbox.

> **Additional Information:**   Selecting the *Queriable* checkbox allows this attribute to participate in a view link. You need to do this since the attribute will be used in a view link that binds EmpJobsView to JobsView.

8. Click OK to close the dialog.

> **Additional Information:**   The expression you enter must come from a table corresponding to one of your entity objects (as it did in this case). To create SQL-only attributes that do not come from tables corresponding to entity objects, you need to create a SQL-only or Expert Mode view object.

9. Click Next.

Make Attributes Read-Only

You can make individual attributes read-only using the following steps:

1. On the Attribute Settings page, select EmployeeId from the dropdown list.

2. In the Updateable area, select *Never*.

3. Select LastName from the drop-down list.

4. In the Updateable area, select *Never*.

> **Additional Information:**   The only attribute your client will need to write to the database is JobId, to allow the client to change an employee's current job. JobId1 and JobTitle are already read-only because the Jobs entity object was selected as read-only. DepartmentId, although it is not read-only (and could have its value inside the view cache temporarily changed), cannot be used to write to the database because it is SQL-only, and YearlyPay does not correspond to any database column at all. Making EmployeeId and LastName never updateable will prevent clients from changing anything in the database but EMPLOYEES.JOB_ID.

Verify the Query

You can verify that a view object's query is what you wanted by using the following steps:

1. On the Query page, verify that this view object will return the data specified for DeptEmpView in phase II.

> **Additional Information:**   Note that YearlyPay is not in the query. Only persistent and SQL-only attributes come directly from the database, so only they correspond to query columns.

2. Click Finish.

3. Click Save All.

What Just Happened?   You created a view object with persistent and entity-derived attributes from two entity objects and a SQL-derived attribute. Clients will be able to use this view object to read EMPLOYEE_ID, LAST_NAME, JOB_ID, and DEPARTMENT_ID from the EMPLOYEES table; JOB_ID and JOB_TITLE from a synchronized row in the JOBS table; and YearlyPay from the Employees entity object's transient attribute. They will be able to change EMPLOYEES.JOB_ID, but nothing else.

VI. Create a View Object Based on an Entity Object Using Expert Mode

This phase creates a view object, EmployeesView, based on the entity object Employees (in order to share data with EmpJobsView). It will require an expert-mode query.

Create the View Object

1. In the hrbc4j package, create a view object named "EmployeesView."

2. Select Employees as the entity on which the view object is based.

3. Check *Read Only*.

4. Click Next.

   Additional Information: The query for EmployeesView has a FROM clause with two table usages in it. EmployeesView is based on two separate usages of the EMPLOYEES table, one of them taking the alias "Reports." However, the client will not be retrieving any persistent data from Reports. The only data it needs from Reports is COUNT(EMPLOYEE_ID), which will be a SQL-only attribute. Therefore, there is no reason to include a "Reports" entity usage.

5. On the Attributes page, select EmployeeId, LastName, JobId, and YearlyPay.

6. Skip the Attribute Settings page.

Edit the Query

You can edit the query for an expert-mode view object using the following steps:

1. On the Query page, check *Expert Mode*. The query will become editable.

2. The query should read:

```
SELECT Employees.EMPLOYEE_ID,
   Employees.LAST_NAME,
   Employees.JOB_ID
FROM EMPLOYEES Employees
```

   Change it so that it reads:

```
SELECT Employees.EMPLOYEE_ID, Employees.LAST_NAME,
   Employees.JOB_ID, COUNT(Reports.EMPLOYEE_ID) AS NUM_REPORTS
FROM EMPLOYEES Employees, EMPLOYEES Reports
WHERE Employees.EMPLOYEE_ID = Reports.MANAGER_ID (+)
GROUP BY Employees.EMPLOYEE_ID, Employees.LAST_NAME,
   Employees.JOB_ID
```

Additional Information: Expert mode allows the query to include a GROUP BY clause and a table usage (Reports) that does not correspond to an entity object usage.

Verify Attribute Mappings

You can verify attribute mappings for an expert-mode view object using the following steps:

1. On the Attribute Mappings page, verify that the query columns EMPLOYEE_ID, LAST_NAME, and JOB_ID correspond to persistent view attributes; that NUM_REPORTS corresponds to a SQL-only view attribute; and that YearlyPay corresponds to the transient attribute YearlyPay, as shown here:

This symbol means a view attribute is persistent.

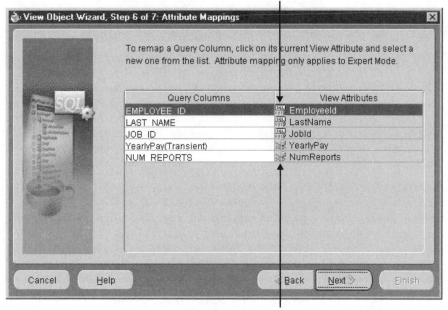

This symbol means a view attribute is SQL-only, entity derived, or transient.

Additional Information: Even though the YearlyPay view attribute is entity derived, it is labeled as "transient" on this page. The page does not distinguish between entity-derived and transient attributes, since neither map to query columns.

2. In the View Attributes column, click EmployeeId and open the dropdown list. Note that EmployeeId is based on an attribute from the Employees entity object, as shown here:

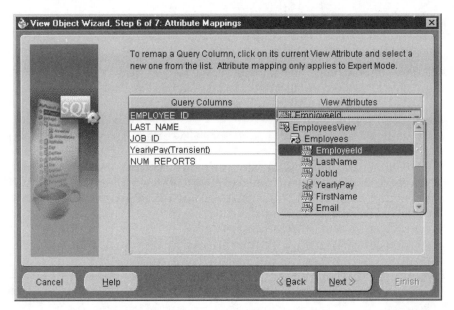

3. Repeat this for LastName and JobId.

   Additional Information: The View Object Wizard successfully identified those query columns as corresponding to the persistent attributes you selected. If it had misidentified the columns as corresponding to non-persistent attributes, or as corresponding to the wrong persistent attributes, you could correct the problem using the dropdown lists, either by changing the selection to another existing attribute, or by selecting "not mapped," which will create a SQL-only attribute corresponding to the column.

4. Click Next, then Finish, then Save All.

What Just Happened? You created an expert-mode view object based on the Employees entity. Clients will be able to use this view object to read EMPLOYEE_ID, LAST_NAME, JOB_ID, and COUNT(Reports.EMPLOYEE_ID) from the EMPLOYEES table, and YearlyPay from the Employees entity object's calculated attribute. Because all the attributes are SQL-only or read-only, this view object cannot be used to change any of them. The view object will use the Employees entity cache to store all of the data (except for COUNT(Reports.EMPLOYEE_ID)), and synchronize it with the data in EmpJobsView.

VII. Test the View Objects

This phase creates a simple application module and uses it to examine how the view objects work.

Create and Test a Simple Application Module

A simple application module can be created and opened in the Business Component Browser using the following steps:

1. In the right-click menu for the hrbc4j package, select New Application Module to open the Application Module Wizard.

2. On the Name page, name your application module "ViewTestModule."

3. On the Data Model page, select JobsView from the Available View Objects tree and click the right-arrow button.

4. Repeat step 3 for DepartmentsView, EmpJobsView, and EmployeesView.

5. Click Finish to create ViewTestModule.

6. In the Navigator, in the right-click menu for ViewTestModule, select Test. The Business Component Browser starts up, showing the Connect dialog.

7. The defaults in the Connect dialog are fine for now, so accept the defaults and click Connect.

8. Wait for the main window of the Business Component Browser to open, displaying ViewTestModule's data model in the left pane.

Test a Simple View Object

A simple view object, based on one entity object, can be tested using the following steps:

1. In the left pane of the Business Component Browser, double click JobsView1.

2. Note that only JobId and JobTitle, the attributes you selected, are visible. Further, the attributes are read-only. The tester can detect this and will not allow you to change them.

Test a SQL-only View Object

You can observe the properties of a SQL-only view object using the following steps:

1. In the left pane of the Business Component Browser, double click DepartmentsView1.

2. Note that the query attributes you selected are visible.

3. The first row should be Department 10, Administration. Change the DepartmentName attribute to "Customer Support."

   Additional Information: Although DepartmentName is a SQL-only attribute, you did not specify it as read-only, so you can change its value within the view cache.

4. Scroll forward to another department and back to 10. Note that the new value is maintained in the view cache.

5. Click the green arrow to commit the transaction.

6. Close the Business Component Browser.

7. Retest ViewTestModule.

8. Double click DepartmentsView1. Note that the name of Department 10 is again Administration.

Additional Information: Because DepartmentName was SQL-only, changes to it were not saved to the database, even when you committed the transaction.

Test a View Object Based on Multiple Entity Objects

You can observe the properties of a view object based on multiple entity objects using the following steps:

1. Double click EmpJobsView1.

2. Use the blue arrow buttons to find Employee 114, Raphaely.

3. Change the JobId field from PU_MAN to "AD_VP," and press ENTER.

4. Note that both JobId1 and JobTitle change appropriately.

Additional Information: The reason for this is that JobId1 and JobTitle come from Jobs, which is selected as a reference entity in EmpJobsView. If Jobs were not a reference entity, changing this view row's JobId would have no effect on its JobId1 or JobTitle.

Test an Entity-Based View Object Created with Expert Mode

The properties of an entity-based view object created with expert mode can be tested using the following steps:

1. Double click EmployeesView1.

2. The first row should be Employee 100, King. Note that NumReports has been calculated for King.

3. Use the blue arrow buttons to find Employee 114, Raphaely. Note that Raphaely's JobId is AD_VP, reflecting the change you made through EmpJobsView.

Additional Information: EmployeesView and EmpJobsView are different view objects, but they do not store separate copies of Raphaely's JobId. Instead, they have pointers to Raphaely's JobId in the entity object Employees. A change to JobId through one view object is immediately visible in the other. This is possible because JobId is persistent, instead of SQL-only, in both EmployeesView and JobsView. Without using the entity cache, you would not be able to take advantage of this synchronization.

4. Close the Business Component Browser.

What Just Happened?   You explored the view objects you have created. In particular, you observed the following:

- You cannot change attributes marked read-only.

- You can change attributes marked SQL-only in the view cache, but the changes will not be saved in the database.

- Rows from reference entity objects are kept synchronized.

- Changes made to a persistent attribute in one view usage are instantly visible through other view usages that have a persistent attribute based on the same entity attribute.

Representing Relationships Between Query Result Sets

As explained in Chapter 9, relationships that link query result sets are represented by view links that link view objects. A view link associates one or more attributes (persistent, SQL-only, entity-derived, or transient) in one view object (called the "source" view object) with one or more persistent or SQL-only attributes in another (the "destination" view object).

View Link SQL

When you create a view link, JDeveloper creates a parametrized SQL expression called the *view link SQL*, which represents the relationship between the view objects. The view link SQL contains a bind variable for each source attribute, and sets each bind variable equal to the SQL expression for the corresponding destination attribute.

For example, consider a view link EmpJobsLink, which associates the JobId attribute in DeptEmpView with the JobId attribute in JobsView. The SQL expression for the destination attribute is Jobs.JOB_ID, so JDeveloper creates an expression setting a bind variable (a stand-in for the source attribute) equal to Jobs.JOB_ID, as follows:

```
:1 = Jobs.JOB_ID
```

This expression is the view link SQL for EmpJobsLink.

NOTE
If the tables in the destination view object are aliased, the view link SQL will use those aliases. Since JobsView aliases JOBS to Jobs, EmpJobsLink uses the alias.

The BC4J framework uses the view link SQL to associate a row of the source view object with one or more rows of the destination view object. The source view attributes are passed into the bind variable, and the resulting SQL is added to the WHERE clause of the detail view object to return a more restricted set of rows. For example, consider a row of DeptEmpView that corresponds to the following row of DeptEmpView's query result:

EMPLOYEE_ID	LAST_NAME	JOB_ID	DEPARTMENT_ID	DEPARTMENT_NAME
106	Pataballa	IT_PROG	60	IT

The value of JOB_ID in this row is passed as a bind variable to EmpJobLink's SQL, yielding the following expression:

```
'IT_PROG' = Jobs.JOB_ID
```

When an application traverses the view link from the row of DeptEmpView containing Employee 106, this expression is appended to the WHERE clause of JobsView to return only the rows of JobsView with a JOB_ID of IT_PROG.

You can view and change view link SQL on the View Link SQL page of the View Link Wizard, as shown here:

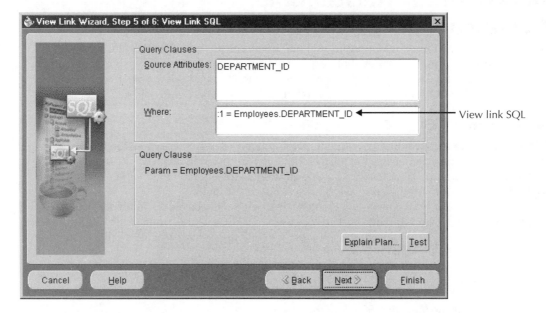

Changing the view link SQL has side effects, as described in the section "View Link Directionality and Cardinality."

Effects of Creating a View Link

In the most common cases (see the section "Bidirectional View Links" for exceptions), creating a view link between two view objects has the following possible effects:

- Creating an XML element for the source view object
- Creating an XML file for the view link

Each will be discussed separately.

Creating an XML Element for the Source View Object   When you create a view link, the source view object's XML file gets an XML accessor element. View link XML accessor elements are similar to association XML accessor elements. They contain both a unique accessor name and the name of the destination view object. For example, if you create a view link EmpJobLink between DeptEmpView and JobsView, an XML accessor element called "JobsView" with a reference to the entity object JobsView will be added to DeptEmpView.xml.

If there are multiple view links between the same view objects, the source view object may contain multiple XML accessor elements. For example, if you also create a view link called EmpPastJobsLink between DeptEmpView and JobsView, DeptEmpView will include an XML accessor element called "JobsView1," also with a reference to the view object JobsView.

The BC4J framework treats view link accessors as view attributes. For example, you can think of DeptEmpView having attributes called JobsView and JobsView1. These attributes will not appear in the View Object Wizard, but you can pass them to the `getAttribute()` method on the view object's view rows. `DeptEmpViewImpl.first().getAttribute("JobsView")` will return the associated view rows from JobsView.

Creating an XML File for the View Link   Like associations, view links have their own XML files. These files contain the logical definition of the view link, including elements that specify the view objects at each end of the view link, the XML accessor element names for the destination view object, and the source and destination attributes.

Entity Objects and View Link Accessors

Consider a view link that meets the following criterion. All the view link's source attributes are persistent and are associated with attributes from a single entity object. For example, in EmpJobLink, there was only one source attribute, JobId, which was associated with a single entity object, Employees.

In this case, a single entity instance—because it contains values for all the source attributes—completely determines a set of destination view rows, as shown in Figure 13-8.

In this case, in addition to being able to generate a view link accessor in the source view object, you have the option of generating one in the relevant entity object. Doing this adds an element to the entity object's XML file and a getter method (such as `getJobsView()`) to the entity object class.

You can only do this because all the source attributes (in this case, there is only one) come from a single entity object. If the view link had had JobId and DepartmentId as its source attributes, the accessor could not be exposed at the entity level, because JobId and DepartmentId come from different entity objects.

Exposing a view link at the entity level can be useful if you actually need to use query results, rather than simply sets of associated table rows, in your business logic. For example, your validation logic may require the data from a query involving joins or functions.

View Link Directionality and Cardinality

The previous section described the most commonly used view links, which are those that, from a single row of the source view object, return any number of rows from the destination view object—

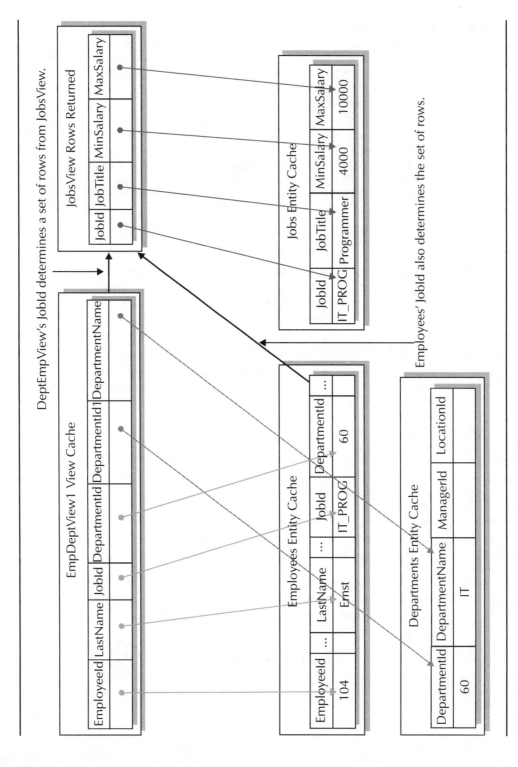

FIGURE 13-8. *An entity row determining a set of destination view rows*

a classic "parent-child" or "master-detail" relationship. View links can, however, work in more complex ways.

Bidirectional View Links

You might want to be able to use a view link in both directions, not only to access rows of the destination view object from a row of the source view object, but to access rows of the source view object from a row of the destination view object as well.

For example, you might want to have the option of using EmpJobsLink to access rows of DeptEmpView from rows of JobsView, such as the row corresponding to the following row of the following query result:

JOB_ID	JOB_TITLE	MIN_SALARY	MAX_SALARY
106	Pataballa	IT_PROG	60

You might want to use EmpJobsLink in such a way that you can traverse it from this row to access the rows of DeptEmpView with a JOB_ID of IT_PROG.

This is possible so long as both of the following conditions are satisfied:

■ You do not change the view link SQL generated by JDeveloper.

■ All of the source attributes are persistent or SQL-only.

The BC4J framework knows how to convert the source attribute (which maps to Employees.JOB_ID) and the view link SQL (:1=Jobs.JOB_ID) to the destination view attribute (which maps to Jobs.JOB_ID) and an inverse of the view link SQL (Employees.JOB_ID=:1), enabling you to use the view link as if you had created it in the other direction.

If you do not change the view link SQL, and none of the source attributes are entity derived or transient, you can make the view link bidirectional. This will add XML accessors to both the source and destination view objects, and include both accessor names in the view link's XML file.

One-to-One, One-to-Many, and Many-to-Many View Links

Like associations, view links have a cardinality. View link cardinality has a lot in common with association cardinality. The following properties should be familiar from the discussion of association cardinality in Chapter 10:

■ View links can be one-to-one, one-to-many, or many-to-many, just like associations.

■ A view link's cardinality affects the Java type of the view link accessor attributes, just as an association's cardinality affects the Java type returned by its accessor methods. The attribute corresponding to a "many" end of a view link is a RowIterator (just as the comparable accessor method for an association returns a RowIterator); the attribute corresponding to a "one" end is a Row. (This is different from the accessor for an association, which has an entity object class as its return type; you will learn how to use Rows in Chapter 14.)

However, there is a difference between view link cardinality and association cardinality. Associations represent table relationships, which are a far narrower class than relationships between query results. Table relationships are based on identifications between table columns, but view links can represent arbitrary relationships between query columns. A table relationship can only be many-to-many through the use of an intersection table, but a view link can be many-to-many with no intersection.

For example, consider a view link between DeptEmpView and JobsView, where DeptEmpView's Salary is the source attribute, and the view link SQL is as follows:

```
:1 > Jobs.MIN_SALARY AND :1 < Jobs.MAX_SALARY
```

This relationship is clearly many-to-many. Each row of DeptEmpView will correspond to many rows of JobsView (because each employee's salary is within the salary range of many jobs), and each row of JobsView will correspond to many rows of DeptEmpView (because each job's salary range encompasses the salaries of many employees). However, there is no intersection table—EMPLOYEES and JOBS are the only tables used.

Of course, this sort of relationship has a distinct disadvantage. It requires changing the view link SQL, and so cannot be used in a bidirectional view link. If you want to use a view link that is both many-to-many and bidirectional, you will have to use an intersection table.

You can use an intersection table by basing the view link on a many-to-many association. The view link SQL will be more complex than the view link SQL for a simple one-to-one or one-to-many view link. For example, the SQL for EmpPastJobsLink, based on EmpPastJobsAssoc (as you created in Chapter 10), would read

```
:1 = JobHistory.EMPLOYEE_ID AND JobHistory.JOB_ID = Jobs.JOB_ID
```

This SQL could be used to make a usage of JobsView a detail of a usage of DeptEmpView. However, because the BC4J framework generated this view link SQL, it can invert this SQL so that it can make a usage of DeptEmpView a detail of a usage of JobsView, as follows:

```
Employees.EMPLOYEE_ID = JobHistory.EMPLOYEE_ID AND JobHistory.JOB_ID = :1
```

Data Models

Once you have created the view objects that will select the data your client needs and have created the view links you need to link them, you can create an application module that represents your data model.

Recall the following from Chapter 9:

■ An application module contains the view usages your client needs for a single transaction. One view object can have several usages in a single application module.

- An application module specifies the way in which these view usages are related by view links.

- These relationships are represented by a tree, called the application module's data model.

- View usages represented by child nodes are details of the view usages represented by the parent nodes.

Detail View Usages

As explained earlier, you can use a view link accessor to get from a view row in one view object to all the corresponding rows in another view object. However, you can also associate master and detail rows by making a view usage a detail in a data model.

Detail view usages are automatically synchronized with their masters. For example, consider the data model illustrated here:

In this data model, the usage of JobsView, JobsView1, is a detail of the usage of DeptEmpView, DeptEmpView1.

Initially, JobsView1 will not contain any data in its cache. Making JobsView1 a detail means that when the current row of DeptEmpView1 is set, for example to a row with the JobId of 60, JobsView1 will retrieve only rows that have a value of 60 for their JobIds and put them into its cache. As soon as the current row of DeptEmpView1 changes, those rows will be hidden, and rows will be retrieved that have the new appropriate value for their JobIds. The old rows are maintained in the cache, so that when the current row of DeptEmpView1 returns to the row with the JobId of 60, they will not have to be retrieved again from the database.

When you create a row in a detail view usage, the destination attributes of the new row will automatically be populated to match the source attributes in the master's current row. For example, when the current row of DeptEmpView1 has a value of 60 for its JobId attribute, and you create a row in JobsView1, the JobId of the new row will be automatically set to 60.

Nested Application Modules

Sometimes, you will find that a number of your application modules share part of their data model. For example, you might find that, again and again, you are using an independent usage DeptEmpView with JobsView as its detail via EmpJobsLink. In this case, you can save time by creating an application module with just the often-reused portion of your data model, and nest usages of this application module into other application modules on the Application Modules page of the Application Module Wizard, as shown here:

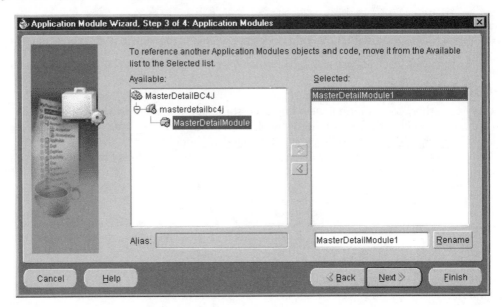

Your clients will be able to access the nested application module's view usages from within any application module you add it to.

Another reason to use nested application modules is the reuse of custom code. As you will learn in Chapter 14, you can add a custom method to an application module. By nesting that application module in many other application modules, the parents will all be able to access the method.

Polymorphic View Objects

Chapter 12 explained how to use discriminator columns and sub-entities to represent a table with two different kinds of rows, each with its own business logic. For a client to properly use these entity objects, however, it will have to be able to access a view object that knows which entity object to delegate to.

Such a view object is called a polymorphic view object. A *polymorphic* view object is based on an entity object with a discriminator column, and knows which sub-entity to delegate to.

To create a polymorphic view object:

1. Create a view object that uses the base entity object (it can also use other entity objects).

2. In the right-click menu for your view object, select Edit to re-open the View Object Wizard.

3. Select the Entity Objects tab.

4. Click the Subtypes button to open the Subtypes dialog.

5. Using the right-arrow button, add all of the sub-entities to the Selected list, as shown here:

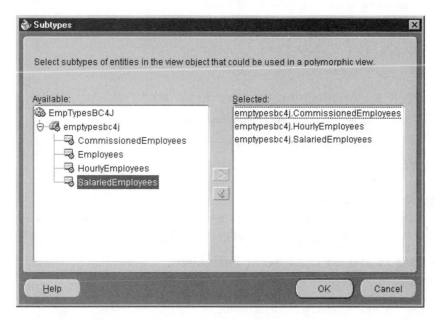

6. Click OK to close the dialog, and click OK again to close the wizard.

When your clients access a row from this view object, they will automatically use the business logic for the associated sub-entity.

Hands-on Practice: Create View Links and Application Modules for HR

In this practice, you will create a set of view links and two application modules to relate the view objects for your clients. When you are done with this practice, the hrbc4j BC4J layer will be almost ready for clients to use. You will make the last few enhancements in the next hands-on practice.

This practice requires that you have completed the preceding practice in this chapter. Alternatively, you can download the starting files for this chapter from the authors' websites mentioned in the beginning of the book.

This practice steps you through the following phases:

I. Plan the data models

■ Plan the data model for the career path lister

■ Plan the data model for the accountant promotion client

II. Create one-to-many view links

■ Create EmpJobLink

■ Create EmpDeptLink

III. Create a many-to-many, bidirectional view link

IV. Create and test CareerPathListerModule

- Create CareerPathListerModule

- Open the Business Component Browser

- Test a one-to-many view link

- Test a many-to-many, bidirectional view link

V. Create and test AccountantPromotionModule

- Create AccountantPromotionModule

- Test a master-detail-detail relationship

I. Plan the Data Models

This phase plans the view links and application modules you need to create. Each of the clients will use one application module, which will provide a data model tailored to that client's needs.

Plan the Data Model for the Career Path Lister

Recall what the career path lister will do:

1. Accept, as a parameter, a Job ID and display the Job title.

   This will require the data returned by an independent instance of JobsView, called "AllJobs."

2. List the current holders of the job with their estimated yearly pay and the number of employees reporting to them.

   This will require the data returned by EmployeesView, restricted to hold only the employees with a job that matches the current row of AllJobs. The restriction will be handled by a view link called EmpJobLink, with JobsView's JobId as the source attribute and EmployeesView's JobId as the destination attribute. The usage of EmployeesView will be called "CurrentHolders."

3. List the past holders of the job and their current job and estimated yearly pay.

   This will require the data returned by EmpJobsView, restricted to hold only the employees with a past job that matches the current row of AllJobs. This restriction will be handled by a view link based on EmpPastJobsAssoc, which will be called EmpPastJobsLink. The usage of EmpJobsView will be called "PastHolders."

In summary, the career path lister will require a data model as shown here:

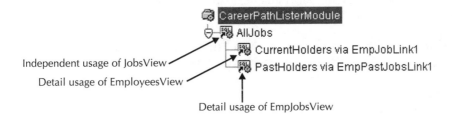

The client will access all this data through an application module called CareerPathListerModule.

Plan the Data Model for the Accountant Promotion Client

Recall what the accountant promotion client will do:

1. Cycle through the departments.

   This will require the data returned by an independent usage of DepartmentsView. This will be called "AllDepartments."

2. List each department's employees, their estimated yearly pay, and their current job.

   This will require data returned by EmpJobsView, restricted to hold only the employees with a department that matches the current row of AllDepartments. The restriction will be handled by a view link called EmpDeptLink. The usage of EmpJobsView will be called "DepartmentEmployees."

3. For each of those employees, mention if they have had more than two previous jobs.

   This will require the data returned by JobsView, restricted to hold only the jobs that match a past job of the current row of DepartmentEmployees. The restriction will be handled by EmpPastJobsLink. Note that this is the reverse of the way EmpPastJobsLink was used by the career path lister. The usage of JobsView will be called "PastJobs."

4. Change all accountants in the department to finance managers.

   This will use AllDepartments and DepartmentEmployees.

In summary, the Accountant Promotion client will require a data model like that shown here:

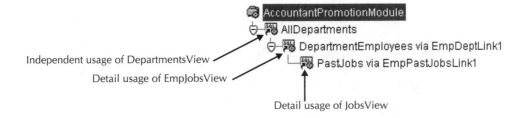

The client will access all this data through an application module called AccountantPromotionModule.

What Just Happened?   You examined your clients' data needs to determine what data models they require. The business components you must create are

- EmpJobLink

- EmpDeptLink

- EmpPastJobsLink

- AccountantPromotionModule

- CareerPathListerModule

II. Create One-to-Many View Links

This phase creates two one-to-many view links: EmpJobLink, which links EmployeesView to JobsView, and EmpDeptLink, which links EmployeesView to DepartmentsView.

Create EmpJobLink

You can create a one-to-many view link using the following steps:

1. In the right-click menu for the hrbc4j package, select New View Link to open the View Link Wizard.

2. On the Name page, name the view link "EmpJobLink."

3. On the View Objects page, select JobsView as the source and EmployeesView as the destination.

   Additional Information: If you are only going to use a view link in one direction, you should make the master view object the source and the detail view object the destination. In this case, EmpJobLink will only be used to make a usage of EmployeesView into a detail of a usage of JobsView, so JobsView should be the source and EmployeesView the destination.

   This will allow you to modify the view link SQL, should you need to at any time. Once the view link SQL is modified, you can only use the view link to make its destination a detail of its source, rather than the other way around.

4. On the Source Attributes page, select EmpJobFkAssoc and click the right-arrow button to add JobId to the *Selected Attributes* list.

   Additional Information: The *Available Associations* list contains all the associations that have a source entity object on which the source view object is based. When you select an association and click the right-arrow button, the source attributes of the association will be added to the *Selected Attributes* list. JobsView is based on Jobs, which is the source of EmpJobFkAssoc, using source attribute JobId.

   You could select JobId and click the right-arrow button, but selecting the association will automatically populate both the source and destination attributes. (See step 5.)

5. On the Destination Attributes page, make sure JobId is in the *Selected Attributes* list.

Additional Information: When you selected EmpJobFkAssoc, the wizard noted both the source and the destination attributes of the association and populated both *Selected Attributes* lists accordingly.

6. On the View Link SQL page, note the view link SQL in the *Where* field.

7. On the View Link Properties page, note the default properties of this view link, as shown next:

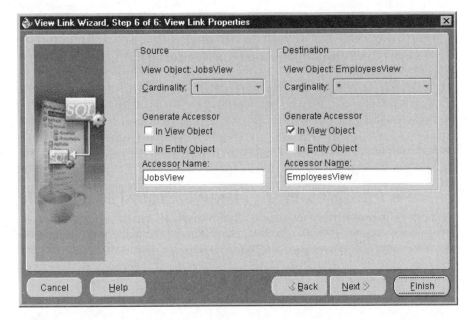

Additional Information: The view link is one-to-many, and there is a single accessor (in the source view object, JobsView) for the destination view object (EmployeesView). The accessor is currently named EmployeesView.

8. Change the accessor name to "CurrentHolders."

Additional Information: This will make it easier to recall exactly what this accessor does.

9. Click Finish to generate the view link.

Create EmpDeptLink

Create another one-to-many view link:

I. In the right-click menu for the hrbc4j package, select New View Link to open the View Link Wizard.

2. On the Name page, name the view link "EmpDeptLink."

3. On the View Objects page, select DepartmentsView as the source and EmpJobsView as the destination.

4. On the Source Attributes page, select DepartmentId and click the right-arrow button to add it to the *Selected Attributes* list.

   Additional Information: Unlike JobsView, DepartmentsView is not based on an entity object. For this reason, no associations appear on the Source Attributes page for EmpDeptLink. You must select the source attribute(s) for the view link yourself.

5. On the Destination Attributes page, select DepartmentId and click the right-arrow button to add it to the *Selected Attributes* list.

   Additional Information: Because you did not select an association on the Source Attributes page, the wizard cannot automatically populate the *Selected Attributes* column on the Destination Attributes page.

6. On the View Link Properties page, name the destination accessor "DepartmentEmployees."

7. Click Finish to generate the view link.

8. Select Save All.

What Just Happened? You created two one-to-many, unidirectional view links. You will use these view links when you construct the data models to be used by your client applications.

III. Create a Many-to-Many, Bidirectional View Link

This phase creates a many-to-many view link, EmpPastJobsLink, based on EmpPastJobsAssoc. EmpPastJobsLink will be used in both directions: to make a usage of EmpJobsView a detail of a usage of JobsView and to make a usage of JobsView a detail of a usage of EmpJobsView.

1. Create a view link named EmpPastJobsLink.

   Additional Information: In Chapter 10 you created a many-to-many, bidirectional view link, also called EmpPastJobsLink, also based on EmpPastJobsAssoc. You deleted it earlier in this chapter. This view link, however, is different. The old EmpPastJobsLink linked the default view objects for Employees and Jobs; the new EmpPastJobsLink links two new, custom view objects.

2. On the View Objects page, select EmpJobsView as the source and JobsView as the destination.

   Additional Information: Since this view link is going to be bidirectional, it does not matter which view object is the source and which the destination.

3. On the Source Attributes page, select EmpPastJobsAssoc and click the right-arrow button to add EmployeeId to the Selected Attributes list.

   Additional Information: When you created EmpJobLink, you only selected an association instead of an attribute for convenience. Selecting the association saved you a step on the Destination Attributes page. However, because EmpPastJobsLink is many-to-many, selecting EmpPastJobsAssoc instead of EmployeeId is vital.

When you select EmpPastJobsAssoc, the wizard will automatically populate both the source and destination attributes of the view link and will write view link SQL based on the association. The SQL will automatically access the intersection table used in this many-to-many relationship.

If, instead, you selected EmployeeId directly as the source attribute (and selected JobId directly as the destination attribute), the wizard would interpret this literally, and generate the following view link SQL:

```
:1 = Jobs.JOB_ID
```

Passing EmployeeId to this view link SQL would generate a WHERE clause that never matches any data.

7. On the Destination Attributes page, verify that the wizard has automatically selected JobId.

8. On the View Link SQL page, note the view link SQL.

    Additional Information: Contrast this query clause with the inadequate WHERE clause mentioned in step 6. You needed to base the view link on an association to have the wizard write this query clause for you; if you had edited the view link SQL yourself, it would prevent the view link from becoming bidirectional.

9. On the View Link Properties page, on the Source side of the page, under Generate Accessor, select *In View Object.*

    Additional Information: Selecting *Generate Accessor* does more than just create methods. It makes the view link bidirectional, allowing you to use it to bind the source to the destination as well as to bind the destination to the source.

10. Change the source accessor name from "EmpJobsView" to "PastHolders."

11. Change the destination accessor name from "JobsView1" to "PastJobs."

12. Click Finish to create the view link.

13. Click Save All.

What Just Happened? You created a many-to-many, bidirectional view link. You will use this view link once in each application module's data model: in AccountantPromotionModule, to make PastJobs a detail of DepartmentEmployees, and in CareerPathListerModule, to make PastHolders a detail of AllJobs.

IV. Create and Test CareerPathListerModule
This phase creates and tests CareerPathListerModule, which will be used by the career path lister client.

Create CareerPathListerModule
You can create an application module for the career path lister client using the following steps:

1. In the right-click menu for the hrbc4j package, select New Application Module to open the Application Module Wizard.

2. On the Name page, name the application module "CareerPathListerModule" and click Next.

3. On the Data Model page, in the *Available View Objects* tree, right under the hrbc4j package node, select JobsView.

4. In the *Name* field, enter AllJobs.

Additional Information: To add an independent usage of a view object to the data model, you must do the following:

- Make sure the application module is selected in the *Data Model* tree

- Select the view object in the *Available View Objects* tree, in the level directly under the package node

- Type the name of the usage in the *Name* field

as shown here:

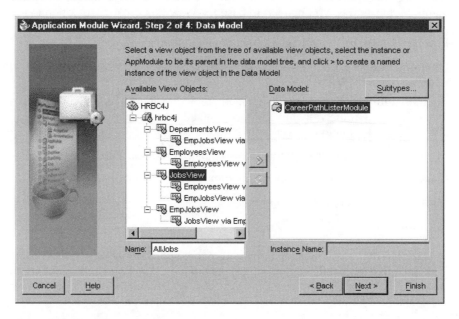

Then click the right-arrow button.

5. Click the right-arrow button to add an independent usage of JobsView to the data model.

6. In the *Available View Objects* tree, under the JobsView node, select EmployeesView via EmpJobLink.

7. In the *Data Model* tree, select the instance of JobsView (AllJobs) you just added.

8. In the *Name* field, enter "CurrentHolders."

Additional Information: To add a detail usage of a view object to the data model, you must do the following:

■ Select the master view object usage in the *Data Model* tree

■ Select the detail view object to in the *Available View Objects* tree, under the master view object, "via" the view link that links them

■ Type the name of the detail usage in the *Name* field

as shown here:

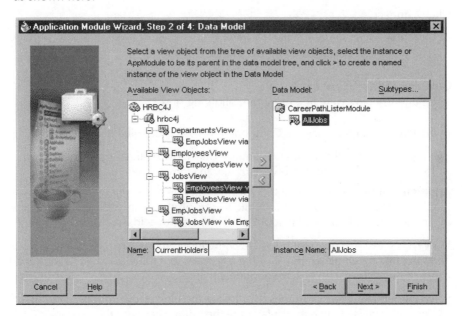

Then click the right-arrow button.

9. Click the right-arrow button to add an instance of EmployeesView, as a detail of AllJobs via EmpJobLink, to the data model.

10. In the *Available View Objects* tree, still under the JobsView node, select EmpJobsView via EmpPastJobsLink.

11. In the name field, enter PastHolders.

12. Click the right-arrow button to add an instance of EmployeesView, as a detail of AllJobs via EmpPastJobsLink, to the data model.

13. Make sure your data model looks like what is shown next, and click Finish.

Open the Business Component Browser

The Business Component Browser can be opened to test an application module and its associated business components using the following steps:

1. In the right-click menu for CareerPathListerModule, select Test. The Business Component Browser starts up, showing the Connect dialog.

2. Click Connect.

3. Wait for the main window of the Business Component Browser to open, displaying CareerPathListerModule's data model in the left pane.

Test a One-to-Many View Link

You can test a one-to-many view link using the following steps:

1. In the left pane of the Business Component Browser, double click EmpJobLink1.

2. The right pane will divide into two panels: one showing the data from one row of AllJobs and one showing the rows currently in CurrentHolders.

   Additional Information: Note that this information displayed by JobsView and EmployeesView linked by EmpJobLink is very similar to the information displayed by EmpJobsView. Both display JobId, JobTitle, EmployeeId, LastName, and YearlyPay.

   However, they have different uses. The view link is more useful for selecting jobs first and then finding all the employees that have that job; the view object's joined query gives all this information at once about each employee.

3. Scroll through the rows of AllJobs by clicking the blue arrow buttons. Note that the rows of CurrentHolders change to display only the employees with the appropriate JobId.

   Additional Information: CurrentHolders has its query restricted by EmpJobLink's view link SQL.

Test a Many-to-Many, Bidirectional View Link

You can test one direction of a many-to-many, bidirectional view link using the following steps:

1. Using the blue arrow buttons, scroll through the jobs to ST_CLERK ("Stock Clerk").

2. In the left pane of the Business Component Browser, double click PastHolders.

3. The right pane will show the data from one row of PastHolders.

4. Scroll through the rows of PastHolders. Note that only two rows, the former stock clerks, are included.

   Additional Information: PastHolders has its query restricted by EmpPastJobsLink's view link SQL.

5. Close the Business Component Browser.

What Just Happened?   You created and explored CareerPathListerModule. In particular, you observed a one-to-many view link and one direction of a many-to-many, bidirectional view link.

V. Create and Test AccountantPromotionModule

This phase creates and tests AccountantPromotionModule, which will be used by the accountant promotion client.

Create AccountantPromotionModule

You can create an application module for the accountant promotion client using the following steps:

1. In the right-click menu for the hrbc4j package, select New Application Module to open the Application Module Wizard.

2. On the Name page, name the application module "AccountantPromotionModule."

3. On the Data Model page, select DepartmentsView from the *Available View Objects* tree, name the usage "AllDepartments," and click the right-arrow button to add an independent usage of DepartmentsView to the data model.

4. In the *Data Model* tree, select AllDepartments.

5. In the *Available View Objects* tree, select EmpJobsView via EmpDeptLink and name the usage "DepartmentEmployees."

6. Click the right-arrow button to add a usage of EmpJobsView, a detail of AllDepartments via EmpDeptLink, to the data model.

7. In the *Data Model* tree, select DepartmentEmployees.

8. In the *Available View Objects* tree, select JobsView via EmpPastJobsLink and name the usage "PastJobs."

9. Click the right-arrow button to add a usage of JobsView, a detail of DepartmentEmployees (which is itself a detail of AllDepartments) via EmpPastJobsLink.

   Additional Information: In CareerPathListerModule, you used EmpPastJobsLink to make a usage of JobsView a detail of a usage of EmpJobsView—that is, to make the destination of a view link the detail of its source, which is the standard direction of view link binding. In this application module, you are using EmpPastJobsLink to make a usage of EmpJobsView a detail of a usage of JobsView—that is, to make the source of the view link a detail of its destination. You can do this because EmpPastJobsLink is bidirectional.

10. Make sure your data model looks like that shown next, and click Finish.

11. Select Save All.

Test a Master-Detail-Detail Relationship

You can examine the effect of a data model with multiple-nested view objects using the following steps:

1. Test AccountantPromotionModule with the Business Component Browser.

2. In the left pane of the Business Component Browser, double click AllDepartments.

3. Scroll forward to department 80.

4. In the left pane of the Business Component Browser, double click DepartmentEmployees.

5. Scroll through the employees. Note that only employees in department 80 are displayed.

6. Scroll to Employee 145, Russell.

7. In the left pane of the Business Component Browser, double click PastJobs.

8. Scroll through the Jobs. Note that there are only two jobs displayed, PU_CLERK and SA_REP.

   Additional Information: There are two things to notice here.

   The first is that you have just used EmpPastJobsLink to retrieve all the past jobs of a particular employee. In phase IV, you used it to retrieve all the past holders of a particular job.

   The second is that AccountantPromotionModule, unlike CareerPathListerModule, has a data model with more than two layers. In addition to making view usages details of independent view usages, you can link them to view usages that are themselves details in a master-detail relationship. Selecting a result set for such a deeply nested view usage is a two-step process: First, you must select a particular row from the independent view usage. This will restrict the result set for its detail view usage. Then, you must select a particular row from that restricted result set. Only then will there be a determinate result set in the deeply nested view usage.

   This is what the accountant promotion client will do. First, it will cycle through the departments. For each department, it will cycle through that department's employees. Then, for each employee, it will retrieve information about that employee's past jobs.

9. Close the Business Component Browser.

What Just Happened?   You created and explored AccountantPromotionModule. In particular, you observed a multi-level master-detail-detail relationship and the operation of a second direction of a bidirectional view link.

CHAPTER
14

Working with Queries
at Runtime

The Analytical Engine has no pretensions to originate anything.
It can do whatever we know how to order it to perform.

—Ada Byron King, Countess of Lovelace (1815–1852),
Notes on L.F. Menabrea's "Sketch of the Analytical Engine
Invented by Charles Babbage, Esq."

 BC4J layer just encapsulates data and business logic. By itself, it does not do anything; it only acts in response to requests from clients. In Chapters 9 through 13, you did not write any clients yourself. You used the Business Component Browser as a client.

JDeveloper provides several client architectures for you to use. Two of these, introduced in Chapter 1, will be covered in more detail in Part III (Java applications and applets) and Part IV (JSP pages) of this book.

Sometimes, instead of using the functionality provided by JClient and BC4J JSP pages, you need to write code directly to the BC4J API. You might do this for two reasons:

■ You need clients that do not use the JClient or BC4J JSP architectures. For example, you can use the BC4J client API to write *batch clients,* clients with no user interface that automatically perform a large number of operations. You will create two simple batch clients in the hands-on practice in this chapter.

■ You need to extend the functionality of JClient and BC4J JSP applications. JClient and BC4J JSP use the BC4J client API to automatically perform many common tasks. By coding to the API yourself, you can customize those applications to perform more specialized tasks.

This chapter discusses coding directly to the BC4J API. You will learn how to perform functions that the Business Component Browser performs: accessing an application module and view usages, and using those view usages to retrieve, update, and insert data. In the hands-on practices in this chapter, you will create batch clients for CareerPathListerModule and AccountantPromotionModule that perform the tasks for which those application modules were designed.

Overview of View Classes

All client interaction with business components takes place through the Java classes that implement application modules and view objects. View objects can be associated with two classes: the view object class and the view row class.

View Object Classes

The *view object class* was introduced in Chapter 9. It represents the SQL query and its results. View object classes have the same name as the view object with an "Impl" suffix. For example, a view object called "DepartmentsView" would have a view object class called "DepartmentsViewImpl."

View object classes extend the class oracle.jbo.server.ViewObjectImpl. ViewObjectImpl has all the methods needed to execute a query, change a query at runtime, navigate through the results of a query, and create rows in the view cache. This can have the effect of creating rows in one or more tables, as described in the later section "Creating and Deleting Rows." In fact, view objects do not have to use view object classes at all; they can just use instances of ViewObjectImpl to represent their query and the query's results—just as entity objects can use EntityImpl to represent their rows.

The reason you might want to extend ViewObjectImpl is to implement *service methods,* custom methods stored in the BC4J layer that clients can call, that simultaneously affect multiple rows of a query's results. Service methods are discussed at greater length later in this chapter.

As mentioned in Chapter 13, application modules can contain multiple view usages of the same view object. These usages are instances of the view object class.

View Row Classes

The *view row class* represents a particular row in a query result—one of the "rows" that appears in the view cache introduced in Chapter 13. View row classes have the same name as the view object itself, with a "RowImpl" suffix. For example, a view object called "DepartmentsView" would have a view row class called "DepartmentsViewRowImpl."

View row classes extend oracle.jbo.server.ViewRowImpl. ViewRowImpl offers methods to read and update the attribute values in a row, to remove existing rows, and to retrieve entity rows on which the view rows are based.

Just as view objects can use instances of ViewObjectImpl rather than instances of a view object class to represent a query and its results, they can use instances of ViewRowImpl rather than instances of a view row class to represent individual rows. There are two main reasons to use a view row class:

- Like entity object classes, view row classes can provide typesafe getters and setters for their attributes. ViewRowImpl provides only the non-typesafe methods `getAttribute()` and `setAttribute()`.

- You can use view row classes to implement service methods that affect a single row of a query's result.

Although view row classes are not generated by default, their typesafe getters and setters are very useful. You will generate and use view row classes in the hands-on practice later in this chapter.

Generating the View Classes

Just as you choose whether to generate entity classes on the Java page of the Entity Object Wizard, you choose whether to generate the view classes on the Java page of the View Object Wizard. The default setting is to generate the view object class only, as shown next:

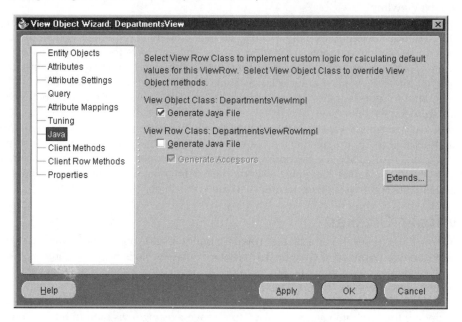

If you generate the view row class, the default is to generate typesafe accessors.

The Application Module Class

Application modules have only one class associated with them. This class, the application module class, is the client's point of entry to the view usages and to the transaction information of the business components. Application module classes have the same name as the application module itself with an "Impl" suffix. For example, the application module AccountantPromotionModule would have an application module class called "AccountantPromotionModuleImpl."

As with all other BC4J component classes, application module classes are optional. They extend oracle.jbo.server.ApplicationModuleImpl. An application module can use an instance of that class directly rather than an instance of its own class. Application module classes are most useful for implementing service methods that are transaction-wide, affecting more than one view usage.

You can choose whether to generate an application module class on the Java page of the Application Module Wizard. By default, the *Generate Java File(s)* checkbox is checked so that JDeveloper will generate the class as shown next:

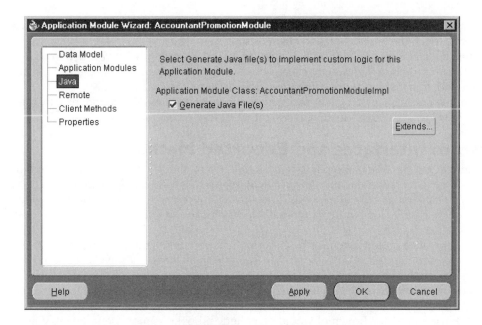

Interfaces, Implementation Classes, and Exported Methods

Clients will use the view object and application module classes. However, those classes should never be mentioned directly in client code, so that applications can maintain independence from a specific deployment configuration.

One of the advantages of the BC4J framework is that it allows you to easily deploy the same business logic in multiple configurations. For example, you could deploy a BC4J layer and client code to the same place, or deploy the BC4J layer to a separate application server as an Enterprise JavaBean (EJB). You will learn more about BC4J deployment in Chapter 16, but it is important to understand how to maintain independence from deployment configurations before you develop your client.

The package oracle.jbo.server, and anything that extends a class from that package, is part of the BC4J layer. If a client calls any class from the BC4J layer, the client will work when the BC4J layer is deployed locally but will fail if you deploy your BC4J layer as an EJB, because the client will not be able to find the classes that it calls. If you code your client to these classes, you will permanently lock yourself into one mode of deployment.

Instead, your client should make use of a set of deployment configuration-independent interfaces. These interfaces are in the oracle.jbo package, which you will deploy with both the client and the BC4J layer. The interfaces in oracle.jbo are all implemented by classes in oracle.jbo.server, for example:

- oracle.jbo.server.ViewObjectImpl implements oracle.jbo.ViewObject.

- oracle.jbo.server.ViewRowImpl implements oracle.jbo.Row.

- oracle.jbo.server.ApplicationModuleImpl implements oracle.jbo.ApplicationModule.

If a client calls methods on an interface when the BC4J layer is local, the method is automatically executed through the implementation class, as shown in Figure 14-1.

When a client calls methods on the same interface, and the BC4J layer is deployed as an EJB, the BC4J framework uses lightweight client-side classes. These classes also implement the interfaces in oracle.jbo, to handle network communication, as shown in Figure 14-2.

From the perspective of a client program, the local and EJB BC4J cases are exactly the same. The client makes a call to an interface, and the BC4J framework handles the rest.

Custom Interfaces and Exported Methods

The interfaces in the oracle.jbo package expose those methods in the base implementation classes—ApplicationModuleImpl, ViewObjectImpl, and ViewRowImpl—that clients are allowed to use. You can add additional methods on your application module, view object, or view row classes, such as service methods or typesafe accessors, to this list by adding them to custom interfaces.

You generate a custom interface by choosing one or more methods in your class to *export*, or to expose on that interface. You will export methods from all three kinds of classes in the hands-on practice later in this chapter.

A custom interface has the same name as the class on which it is based, minus the Impl, and it is in the common subpackage of the class's package. For example, a custom interface based on hrbc4j.DepartmentsViewRowImpl would be called "hrbc4j.common.DepartmentsViewRow." The "common" subpackage contains the custom classes (such as custom domains) and interfaces that clients need to use. Unlike the business components package itself, the common subpackage is always directly accessible to the client. In local mode, calls to the custom interfaces are directly executed by the classes on which they are based, as shown in Figure 14-3.

When the BC4J layer is deployed as an EJB, lightweight classes automatically generated by JDeveloper handle communication with the EJB behind the scenes, as shown in Figure 14-4.

Again, the local BC4J and EJB BC4J cases look exactly the same to your client. The client just calls a method on hrbc4j.common.DepartmentsViewRow, and the BC4J framework handles the rest.

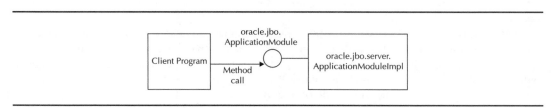

FIGURE 14-1. *Executing a method on local BC4J code*

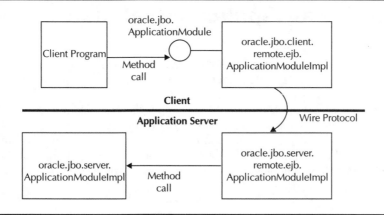

FIGURE 14-2. *Executing a method on BC4J code deployed as an EJB*

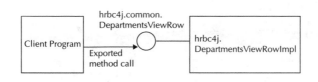

FIGURE 14-3. *Executing a method on local custom BC4J*

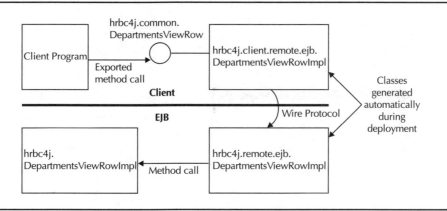

FIGURE 14-4. *Executing a method on custom BC4J deployed as an EJB*

Instantiating an Application Module and View Usages

The first task that any BC4J client must accomplish is getting access to an application module and the view usages that will handle its data access. Although, like all classes, application module and view object classes have constructors (for example, the `ApplicationModuleImpl()` constructor creates objects of type ApplicationModuleImpl), clients should not use these constructors, because that requires direct reference to the classes rather than to the interfaces, which will lock the client into local mode. Instead, clients should use deployment configuration-independent methods provided by the BC4J framework to instantiate an application module and view usages.

The first tasks your client will need to perform are covered by the following methods:

Task	Method
Instantiate the primary application module	`createRootApplicationModule()`
Retrieve any nested application modules	`findApplicationModule()`
Retrieve view usages	`findViewObject()`

These methods are described next.

The createRootApplicationModule() Method

You will create an application module instance using the `createRootApplicationModule()` method in the hands-on practice later in this chapter. This method has a return type of oracle.jbo.ApplicationModule, providing deployment configuration-independent access to an application module. `createRootApplicationModule()` takes two String objects for arguments. The first contains the application module's package, followed by a period and then the name of the application module. The second contains the name of a configuration. Configurations will be discussed in detail in Chapter 16, but for now, the only configurations you will need to work with are named after the application module with a "Local" suffix.

If you have exported a service method on your application module, you need to cast it to the custom interface before you can call those methods.

JClient and BC4J JSP applications will automatically instantiate an ApplicationModule for you. You will instantiate one in the hands-on practice in this chapter.

The findApplicationModule() Method

If your application module contains nested application modules, you can retrieve them using the method `ApplicationModule.findApplicationModule()`. For example, suppose AccountantPromotionModule contained a nested application module usage called ListAccountantsModule1. After instantiating AccountantPromotionModule (as discussed in the previous section), you could retrieve ListAccountantsModule1 with the following code:

```
ApplicationModule listModule =
    acctPromModule.findApplicationModule("ListAccountantsModule1");
```

The findViewObject() Method

Once you have an application module instance, you can retrieve any view usage in that application module's data model using the `ApplicationModule.findViewObject()` method. You will use `findViewObject()` to retrieve view usages in the hands-on practice in this chapter.

Navigating Through Result Sets

Once you retrieve a view usage, you can use it to retrieve specific rows of data.

TIP
ViewObject has a method, `executeQuery()`, that will issue the SELECT statement associated with the view object and populate the entity and view caches. However, you do not need to explicitly call `executeQuery()` before navigating through view usage rows. If you call a row navigation method on a view usage that has not had its query executed, the BC4J framework will call `executeQuery()` automatically. Later in this chapter, you will see some uses for calling `executeQuery()` explicitly.

Stepping Through a Query's Result Set

The ViewObject interface extends the RowIterator interface first described in Chapter 12. Because of this, it contains methods called `next()` and `hasNext()` that allow you to step forward through the query. Like other RowIterators, a ViewObject is a collection of objects of type oracle.jbo.Row, and a pointer to one particular Row (that is, one particular instance of the Row interface), the "current" Row. This pointer can be moved around, and data can be extracted from the current Row.

As with other RowIterators, a ViewObject's pointer starts at a slot before the first Row it contains. Because of this, when a ViewObject is first created, calling `next()` moves the pointer to the first Row of the query result and returns that Row. You will use `next()` to navigate through a view usage's result set in the hands-on practice in this chapter.

first(), last(), and previous()

The ViewObject interface also contains methods that let you quickly jump to the first, last, or previous row of a query's result set as in the following example:

```
/* Jump to the first Row */
Row firstRow = allDepts.first();

/* Jump to the last Row */
Row lastRow = allDepts.last();

/* Because last() was just called, the pointer is now on the
   last row, so the following steps backwards through the
   result set */
while (allDepts.hasPrevious())
{
  Row currRow = allDepts.previous();
}
```

Row Keys

A *key* is a set of attributes that allow you to quickly retrieve one or more rows in a view usage's result set that match all or part of it. A view object based on one or more entity objects automatically has a key made up of all the attributes based on primary key attributes in those entity objects. In addition, you can assign attributes in a SQL-only view object, or additional attributes in an entity-based view object, to be part of the view object's key.

For example, EmpJobsView's key is made up of EmployeeId and JobId1, based on the primary key attributes (Employees.EmployeeId and Jobs.JobId) of the entity objects upon which it is based. At runtime, you can create a key object containing a value for one or both of these attributes, and then use this key object to retrieve an array containing some or all of the rows that match the appropriate values.

Creating a Key

Before you create a key, you must create an array of objects that corresponds to it. Each object in the array should correspond to one of the view object's key attributes, in the order in which those attributes appear in the view object. For example, the array of objects should contain a value for EmployeeId and a value for JobId1, in that order. The following code creates an array for a key with EmployeeId 102 and JobId1 AD_VP:

```
Object[] empJobKeyValues = new Object[]
{
  new Number(102),
  "AD_VP"
};
```

To create a partial key, for example, to create a key that will find all rows corresponding to JobId "AD_VP," the array should still have objects for each key attribute but with "null" used for the attributes you are not interested in. The following code creates such an array:

```
Object[] empJobPartialKeyValues = new Object[]
{
  null,
  "AD_VP"
};
```

After you create and load the object array, pass it to the Key() constructor to create a key, as in the following two examples:

```
/* Create a Key with EmployeeId 102 and JobId AD_VP */
Key empJobKey = new Key(empJobKeyValues);

/* Create a Key with no EmployeeId and JobId AD_VP */
Key empJobPartialKey = new Key(empJobPartialKeyValues);
```

If you already have a row, you can also retrieve its key using getKey(), as follows:

```
Key empJobKey = departmentEmps.current().getKey();
```

This can be useful if you want to remember the location of a row for retrieval later.

Retrieving Rows

After you create a key, use the method `ViewObject.findByKey()` to retrieve an array containing matching rows. `findByKey()` takes two arguments: the key and a maximum number of rows to return (or –1 if you want to return all the rows—but make sure your array is big enough to hold them). For example, the following code returns the single row with EmployeeId 102 and JobId AD_VP:

```
Row[] fullKeyRows = departmentEmps.findByKey(empJobKey, 1);
Row foundRow = fullKeyRows[0];
```

The following code returns an array containing the first 10 rows with JobId AD_VP:

```
Row[] partialKeyRows = departmentEmps.findByKey(empJobPartialKey, 10);
```

If fewer than ten rows match the key, the extra elements of partialKeyRows will be null. If no rows match the key, the array will be empty.

Changing the Current Row Pointer

Calling `findByKey()` only returns Row objects. It does not change the current row pointer in the view usage. If you want to set the current row pointer, pass one of the Rows to `ViewObject.setCurrentRow()` as follows:

```
departmentEmps.setCurrentRow(partialKeyRows[0]);
```

Hands-on Practice: Create Simple Batch Clients

In this practice, you begin to create a pair of batch clients, AccountantPromotionClient and CareerPathLister. When you are done with this practice, the clients will each perform their first step, as described in Chapter 13: AccountantPromotionClient will cycle through departments, and CareerPathLister will find a job using a key. You will continue writing the clients in the next hands-on practice.

This practice builds on the results of the hands-on practice in Chapter 13. If you have not completed that practice, you can download the starting files for this practice from the authors' websites mentioned in the author information at the beginning of this book.

This practice includes the following phases:

I. Create view row classes and interfaces

- ■ Create view row classes
- ■ Export view row accessors

II. Create a project for AccountantPromotionClient

- ■ Create an application project
- ■ Add a dependency on the BC4J layer

III. Add code to begin AccountantPromotionClient

- ■ Retrieve the application module and view usage

- ■ Cycle through the departments

- ■ Test the application

IV. Create a project for CareerPathLister

V. Add code to CareerPathLister

- ■ Retrieve the application module and view usage

- ■ Find a job by its key

- ■ Test the application

I. Create View Row Classes and Interfaces

In this phase, you will create view row classes and interfaces so that your clients can use typesafe accessors.

Create View Row Classes

This section creates view row classes for each view object. These classes contain the typesafe accessors for the clients to use.

1. If your HRWS workspace is not open, open it by selecting **File** | **Open** and browsing to JDEV_HOME\mywork\HRWS.

2. Expand the hrbc4j package node if it is not already expanded.

3. On the DepartmentsView node, select Edit DepartmentsView from the right-click menu. The View Object Wizard opens.

4. Select the Java node.

5. Under View Row Class, select *Generate Java File*. *Generate Accessors* will automatically be selected.

6. Click OK.

   Additional Information: JDeveloper creates a DepartmentsViewRowImpl class (DepartmentsViewRowImpl.java) and places it under the DepartmentsView node in the Navigator.

7. Repeat steps 3–6 for EmpJobsView, EmployeesView, and JobsView.

8. Click Save All.

Export View Row Accessors

This section exports the view row accessors to custom interfaces, so that clients can call them in a deployment configuration-independent manner.

1. On the DepartmentsView node, select Edit DepartmentsView from the right-click menu. The View Object Wizard opens.

2. Select the Client Row Methods node.

3. Notice that the *Available* list has getters for every view attribute and setters for every view attribute that is not read-only.

4. Click the >> button to add all of these to the *Selected* list.

5. Click OK.

    Additional Information: JDeveloper creates a DepartmentsViewRow interface and places it under the DepartmentsView node in the Navigator.

6. Repeat steps 1–5 for EmpJobsView, EmployeesView, and JobsView.

7. Click Rebuild and Save All.

What Just Happened?   You created view row implementation classes and the following deployment configuration-independent view row interfaces:

- EmpJobsViewRow

- DepartmentsViewRow

- EmployeesViewRow

- JobsViewRow

You can now cast Row objects to these interfaces in your clients and call accessors on them.

II. Create a Project for AccountantPromotionClient

In this phase, you will create a project that will contain AccountantPromotionClient and then ensure that it has the right classpath.

Create an Application Project

This section creates a project to contain AccountantPromotionClient.

1. On the HRWS.jws node, select New Project from the right-click menu.

2. Select Project Containing a New Application, and click OK to open the Application Project Wizard. Click Next if the Welcome page appears.

3. On the Location page, change the project directory name to "AccountantPromotionJA," and change the project file name to "AccountantPromotionJA.jpr." Click Next.

4. On the Paths page, name the default package "accountantpromotionja." Click Next.

5. On the Libraries page, add BC4J Oracle Domains to the *Selected Libraries* list.

    Additional Information: Since your client will be working with domains, it will need this library on its classpath. Moving the library to the Selected Libraries list will add the library to the classpath for this project. If you create a BC4J JSP or JClient application, or any other of JDeveloper's standard client application types, JDeveloper will add the library for you automatically.

6. Add Connection Manager to the *Selected Libraries* list.

   Additional Information: Since your client will run in local mode, it will need the Connection Manager on its classpath to handle JDBC connections. If you were running in EJB mode, your client would still need the Connection Manager to handle the connection to the business components EJB. Again, if you create a BC4J JSP or JClient application, JDeveloper handles this for you.

7. Add BC4J Runtime and Oracle JDBC to the *Selected Libraries* list.

   Additional Information: Your client only needs these libraries because it is running in local mode. If the client were communicating with an EJB, it would use the much smaller BC4J EJB Client library. Again, if you create a BC4J JSP or JClient application, JDeveloper handles this for you.

8. Click Finish. Doing so will create the project and open the New Application dialog.

9. Name the application "AccountantPromotionClient."

10. Uncheck *Add Default Frame*.

    Additional Information: Since this is a batch client that has console output without a GUI window, you do not need a frame.

11. Click OK.

Add a Dependency on the BC4J Layer
This section adds a dependency on the BC4J layer to the project's properties:

1. On the AccountantPromotionJA.jpr node in the Navigator, select Project Settings from the right-click menu.

2. Select the Dependencies node.

3. Check the checkbox next to *HRBC4J.jpr*.

   Additional Information: This ensures that HRBC4J.jpr will be compiled and added to AccountantPromotionJA's classpath whenever you compile or run the client. It also ensures that HRBC4J.jpr is deployed with the client when you deploy in Chapter 16.

4. Click OK to close the Project Settings dialog.

5. Click Save All.

What Just Happened?   You created a project, with a simple application file, for AccountantPromotionClient. You also added required libraries and the BC4J layer to the project's classpath by adding libraries to the project properties.

III. Add Code to Begin AccountantPromotionClient
In this phase you will write code to retrieve the application module and a view usage for AccountantPromotionClient and cycle through the departments.

Retrieve the Application Module and View Usage

This section instantiates an application module and finds the AllDepartments usage in its data model:

1. From the Navigator, open AccountantPromotionClient.java in the Code Editor.

2. Add the following lines right after the package statement:

```
import oracle.jbo.*;
import oracle.jbo.domain.*;
```

   Additional Information: This allows you to use the BC4J framework's deployment configuration-independent interfaces—ApplicationModule, ViewObject, and Row—and to use domains such as oracle.jbo.domain.Number.

3. Add the following line after the lines you just added:

```
import oracle.jbo.client.Configuration;
```

   Additional Information: The BC4J framework contains a class, oracle.jbo.client.Configuration, that is always present with the client (even if the BC4J layer is deployed as an EJB). This class contains the static method (that is, a method you can call on the class directly, without instantiating it) createRootApplicationModule(), which you will use to instantiate your application module.

4. Add the following line after the last line you entered:

```
import hrbc4j.common.*;
```

   Additional Information: This allows you to use the custom interfaces you created in Phase II.

5. Add the following code to the main() method under the line "new AccountantPromotionClient();":

```
ApplicationModule acctPromModule =
  Configuration.createRootApplicationModule(
    "hrbc4j.AccountantPromotionModule",
    "AccountantPromotionModuleLocal"
  );
```

   Additional Information: createRootApplicationModule() instantiates the application module named in its first argument (with its package) in a configuration, specified as the second argument. Configurations are discussed in detail in Chapter 16, but for now, the only configurations you will need to work with are named after the application module with a "Local" suffix.

6. Add the following code after the lines you just added:

```
ViewObject allDepts =
  acctPromModule.findViewObject("AllDepartments");
```

Additional Information: `findViewObject()` takes the name of a view usage in the data model and returns that view usage.

7. Rebuild your project. Click Save All.

Cycle Through the Departments
The following cycles through the result set of AllDepartments using the following steps:

1. Add the following code right after the code you just added:

```
while (allDepts.hasNext())
{
  DepartmentsViewRow currDept = (DepartmentsViewRow) allDepts.next();
  System.out.println("Now accessing department " +
    currDept.getDepartmentId() + ": " +
    currDept.getDepartmentName() + "."
  );
}
```

Additional Information: This "while" loop scrolls through allDepts. Casting the row to DepartmentsViewRow allows you to use the typesafe accessors such as `getDepartmentId()`. The loop stops when allDepts runs out of rows.

2. Click Rebuild and Save All.

Test the Application
Test the AccountantPromotionClient application using these steps:

1. Right click AccountantPromotionClient.java and select Run AccountantPromotionClient.java.

2. Note the output in the message view. The first few lines should read

```
Now accessing department 10:  Administration.
Now accessing department 20:  Marketing.
Now accessing department 30:  Purchasing.
```

What Just Happened? You wrote code for AccountantPromotionClient to access the application module and its DepartmentsView usage, AllDepartments, and to use AllDepartments to cycle through the departments and retrieve information about each department. This is the beginning of a client that you will deploy as a command-line client in Chapter 16.

IV. Create a Project for CareerPathLister
Create a project for CareerPathLister, just as you created one for AccountantPromotionClient.

1. On the HRWS.jws node, select New Project from the right-click menu. Then select Project Containing a New Application, and click OK to open the Application Project Wizard.

2. Click Next if the Welcome page appears. On the Location page, change the project directory name to "CareerPathListerJA," and change the project file name to "CareerPathListerJA.jpr." Click Next.

3. On the Paths page, name the default package "careerpathlisterja." Click Next.

4. On the Libraries page, add the following libraries to the Selected Libraries list:

   - ■ BC4J Oracle Domains

   - ■ BC4J Runtime

   - ■ Connection Manager

   - ■ Oracle JDBC

   This is the same set of libraries you added to the last project.

5. Click Finish to create the project and open the New Application dialog.

6. Name the application "CareerPathLister."

7. Uncheck *Add Default Frame.*

8. Click OK.

9. Edit the project settings of CareerPathLister, just as you did for AccountantPromotionJA, and add a dependency on the HRBC4J project.

10. Save all.

What Just Happened?   You created a project, with a simple application file, for AccountantPromotionClient. You also added required libraries and the BC4J layer to the project's classpath.

V. Add Code to CareerPathLister

In this phase, you write code to retrieve the application module and a view object usage for CareerPathLister and to find a job by its key.

Retrieve the Application Module and View Usage

This section adds code to instantiate an application module and to find the AllJobs usage in its data model:

1. In the Navigator, double click CareerPathLister.java to open it in the Code Editor.

2. Add the following lines right after the package statement:

```
import oracle.jbo.*;
import oracle.jbo.domain.*;
import oracle.jbo.client.Configuration;
import hrbc4j.common.*;
```

These are the same imports that you added in the previous application.

3. Add the following code to the `main()` method after "new CareerPathLister();":

```
ApplicationModule careerModule =
  Configuration.createRootApplicationModule(
    "hrbc4j.CareerPathListerModule",
    "CareerPathListerModuleLocal"
  );
ViewObject allJobs = careerModule.findViewObject("AllJobs");
```

Additional Information: This creates an instance of CareerPathListerModule and finds the AllJobs view usage in its data model.

4. Rebuild your project to test the code and directives you have written so far.

Find a Job by Its Key

You can find a view row by its key using the following steps:

1. Right after the code you just added in the `main()` method, add the following code:

```
if (args.length==0)
{
  System.out.println("This program requires a Job ID as a parameter.");
  System.exit(0);
}
String requestedJobId = args[0];
```

Additional Information: This code validates that the user entered a parameter on the command line. The career path lister application will receive a Job ID value as a command-line parameter and use it to create the key for JobsView.

2. After that code, add the following:

```
Object[] jobKeyValues = new Object[]
{
  requestedJobId
};
Key jobKey = new Key(jobKeyValues);
```

Additional Information: Because JobsView only has one key attribute, JobId, you can create a key object for it as the only entry in the jobKeyValues array.

3. After that code, add the following:

```
Row[] foundJobs = allJobs.findByKey(jobKey, 1);
JobsViewRow requestedJob = (JobsViewRow) foundJobs[0];
allJobs.setCurrentRow(requestedJob);
```

Additional Information: This code calls findByKey() to retrieve an array of rows that match jobKey. Because jobKey is a complete key, retrieving an array of length one is sufficient.

4. After that code, add the following:

```
String jobTitle = requestedJob.getJobTitle();
System.out.println("Found job " +
    requestedJobId + ": " +
    jobTitle + "."
  );
```

Additional Information: This code calls the typesafe accessor getJobTitle() to return the title associated with the job ID.

5. Click Rebuild and Save All.

Test the Application

Set up the command-line argument for CareerPathLister and run the client:

1. On the CareerPathLister.jpr node, select Project Settings from the right-click menu. The Project Settings dialog opens.

2. Under Configurations\Development, select the Runner node.

3. In the *Program Arguments* field, enter "IT_PROG" as shown here:

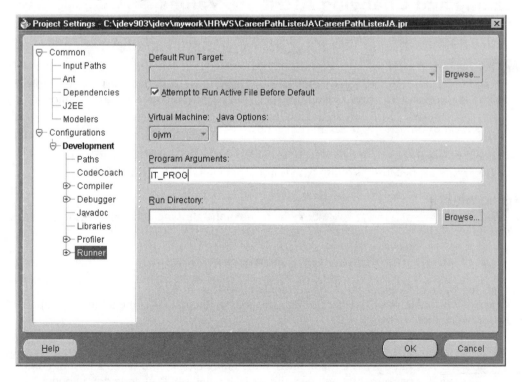

Additional Information: After you deploy your projects in Chapter 16, you will pass a JOB_ID (such as IT_PROG) to your batch client as a command-line argument. For testing in JDeveloper, you pass command-line arguments to your program using this field.

4. Click OK to close the dialog.

5. On the CareerPathLister.java node, select Run CareerPathLister.java from the right-click menu.

6. Note the output in the message view. The output should look like the following:

```
Found job IT_PROG: Programmer.
```

What Just Happened?   You wrote code for CareerPathLister to access the application module and its JobsView usage, AllJobs, and to find a row in AllJobs using a Key. Like the AccountantPromotionClient created earlier, this is the beginning of an application you will deploy as a command-line application in Chapter 16.

Manipulating Data

You can use ViewObject, Row, and custom row classes to retrieve and modify the data in your tables.

Reading and Changing Attribute Values

Just like the EntityImpl class, the Row interface has getAttribute() and setAttribute() methods that you can use to retrieve and set values for the attributes of a particular row.

getAttribute()

The method getAttribute() takes the name of the attribute as its argument. For example, if currEmp is a Row from a usage of EmpJobsView, you might use code such as the following:

```
Number currEmployeeId = (Number) currEmp.getAttribute("EmployeeId");
```

This code retrieves the value of EmployeeId in currEmp. You have to cast the value of getAttribute(), because its return type is just java.lang.Object.

setAttribute()

The method setAttribute() takes both the name of the attribute and a value as its argument. Here is an example:

```
currEmp.setAttribute("EmployeeId", new Number(954));
```

This sets the value of EmployeeId in the current EmpJobsRow to 954.

The exact behavior of setAttribute() depends on the nature of the attribute you pass into it following these rules:

■ If the attribute is persistent, setAttribute() will call the attribute's setter in the entity object. The value will be maintained in the entity cache, and when a post or commit operation is performed, it will be written to the database. Post and commit operations are discussed in Chapter 15.

■ If the attribute is entity-derived, setAttribute() will call the attribute's setter in the entity object. The value will be maintained in the entity cache, but the database is not affected.

- If the attribute is SQL-only or transient, `setAttribute()` will change the value of the attribute in the view cache. Since the attribute is not based on an entity object, the database is not affected.

- If an attribute is read-only, `setAttribute()` on that attribute will throw an exception. This prevents client programs from changing data you do not want changed.

If you have generated a view row class, exported its getters and setters, and cast the Row to the custom view row interface, you can call the getters and setters instead of `getAttribute()` and `setAttribute()`, as in the following example:

```
EmpJobsViewRow castEmp = (EmpJobsViewRow) currEmp;
Number currEmployeeId = castEmp.getEmployeeId();
castEmp.setEmployeeId(new Number(954));
```

Using the getters and setters has the following two advantages:

- Like the entity object accessors, view row getters and setters are typesafe. If you pass the wrong datatype into them, or misspell the attribute name, you will get an easily debugged compile-time error instead of a runtime exception.

- Setters are not generated for read-only attributes. If you accidentally call a setter for a read-only attribute, you will get a compile-time error instead of a runtime exception.

Creating and Deleting Rows

The ViewObject interface contains three methods that let you insert and delete rows from the view cache: `createRow()`, `insertRow()`, and `removeCurrentRow()`.

If the view object is based on one or more entity objects, the relevant entity rows will be created or marked for deletion. When a commit operation is called, these rows will be added to or deleted from the database.

`createRow()` returns a new Row, and `insertRow()` inserts that Row into the view cache right before the current row, as in the following example:

```
Row newEmp = departmentEmps.createRow();
departmentEmps.insertRow(newEmp);
```

`removeCurrentRow()` does not return anything or change the current row pointer; you will have to execute `next()` to get the next, undeleted, row. Here is an example that deletes a row and sets the current row pointer to the next row:

```
departmentEmps.deleteCurrentRow();
Row nextEmp = departmentEmps.next();
```

Until you navigate off of the row, the current row pointer points to null.

You can also delete a row by calling remove() directly on the Row object. The row deleted in this way does not need to be current. The following example deletes a Row called badEmp:

```
badEmp.remove();
```

NOTE
Remember that creating and deleting rows in this way does not affect the database until you issue a commit or post statement.

Traversing View Links

As mentioned in Chapter 13, a view link implements a relationship between two view usages and can be used to restrict one view usage's query based on the current row of the other.

There are two ways to return the results of a restricted query through a view link: through the data model and through view link accessors.

Traversing a View Link Through the Data Model

Consider CareerPathListerModule, the application module used in the practices, which contains both a usage of JobsView (called AllJobs) and a usage of EmployeesView (called CurrentHolders) that is a detail of AllJobs via EmpJobLink. Suppose you have retrieved both AllJobs and CurrentHolders using `findViewObject()`. If you change the current row of AllJobs, the result set of CurrentHolders will immediately change to contain only those rows of EmployeesView that are details of that row of AllJobs. You can cycle through the detail rows for the current job just by cycling through all of the rows currently in CurrentHolders. You will do this in the hands-on practice in this chapter.

Traversing a View Link Through an Accessor

Recall that EmpJobsLink includes a generated accessor for EmployeesView, called CurrentHolders. This means that EmployeesView has an attribute, CurrentHolders, that can be passed into the `getAttribute()` method.

The behavior of view link accessors is similar to the behavior of association accessors; that is, what they return depends upon their cardinality. Because EmployeesView is the "many" end of a one-to-many association, its accessor returns a RowIterator. An accessor for the view object at the "one" end of an association returns a single Row.

As discussed in Chapter 12, RowIterators have a `next()` method that returns Rows, just as ViewObjects do. So you can cycle through the rows in a RowIterator just as you can through the rows in a ViewObject.

You will traverse a view-link accessor and cycle through the resulting RowIterator in the hands-on practice later in this chapter.

The Data Model vs. Accessors

There is one major difference between the RowIterator returned by a view link accessor and the ViewObject bound by that view link in the data model: the detail ViewObject is dynamically synchronized with the master ViewObject.

If, after you retrieve CurrentHolders, you change the current row of AllJobs again, the result set of CurrentHolders will immediately change. You can use the same loop to cycle through the rows of EmployeesView that are details of the new current row of AllJobs. The current row pointer for CurrentHolders is also reset to the slot before the first row every time you change the AllJobs current row pointer.

By contrast, a RowIterator returned by an accessor will not change after it is created. It will remain restricted by whatever row was used to create it.

Whether you should use the data model or an accessor to traverse a view link depends upon on which of these options you want. If you want to create a dynamically changing set of rows that stays synchronized with a master query, you should use the data model. If you want to retrieve the detail rows for a particular master row, and keep working with those rows even if the master view usage's current row pointer changes, you should use the view link accessor. For example, suppose you want the sales staff to be able to select a particular customer and open that customer's orders in another window. You want them to be able to keep that customer's orders open while they continue to browse through the customers list. In this case, you would use the view link accessor, rather than the data model, to retrieve the customer's orders.

There is one additional reason to use a view link accessor instead of the data model. You may want to create a service method inside a view row or view object class that traverses a view link. You can call an accessor to do this. You will create a view row method that traverses a view link in the hands-on practice in this chapter.

Changing a View Usage's WHERE Clause at Runtime

Sometimes, you need to further restrict the rows returned by a view usage at runtime. View links provide one way to do this, as explained in Chapter 13. By selecting a row in the master view usage, you can pass the source attribute as the parameter of the view link SQL and add the resulting condition to the detail view usage's WHERE clause. However, there are several other ways to change a view usage's WHERE clause at runtime that do not involve joining it to another query.

Using setWhereClause()

If you want to completely replace a view usage's WHERE clause, you can call the method `ViewObject.setWhereClause()`. After you call `setWhereClause()`, you need to call `executeQuery()` to refresh the view usage's result set to reflect the new restriction. This will also reset the current row pointer to the slot before the first row. You will use `setWhereClause()` in the hands-on practice. For more information about how `executeQuery()` works, see the sidebar, "executeQuery() and Updated Data."

---

executeQuery() and Updated Data

When you call `executeQuery()`, your entity cache may contain data (such as changed attributes, new rows, or row deletions) that has not been posted yet. `executeQuery()` will not overwrite those changes; the entity cache will keep those attributes and rows that have been created, deleted, or changed since the last database post, merging them with any additional data retrieved from the database.

Parameterized WHERE Clauses

Instead of changing an entire WHERE clause, you might just want to be able to substitute particular values into it. For example, suppose you need a view object that provides a list of all employees making a certain amount of money, but you want to be able to change that amount of money for specific usages at runtime. You can do this in the View Object Wizard by providing a parameterized WHERE clause in the *Where* field as shown here:

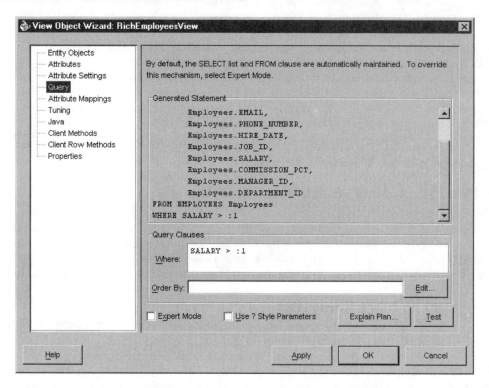

The parameter ":1" stands in for the attribute you will set at runtime. You can have WHERE clauses with multiple bind parameters named ":1," ":2," ":3," and so on.

If your view object has a parameterized WHERE clause, you can fill in the parameters at runtime by calling `ViewObject.setWhereClauseParam()`. This method takes two arguments: the index of the parameter (0 for the first parameter, 1 for the second, and so on) and the value of the parameter. For example, the following code changes the WHERE clause of a view usage called RichEmployees to "SALARY > 3000":

```
ViewObject richEmployees = appMod.findViewObject("RichEmployees");
richEmployees.setWhereClauseParam(0, new Number(3000));
```

Alternatively, you can set all WHERE clause parameters at once by calling `setWhereClauseParams()`, which takes an array of Objects instead of a single Object.

After you call `setWhereClauseParam()` or `setWhereClauseParams()`, you will need to call `executeQuery()` to refresh the view usage's result set and reflect the new restriction.

`setWhereClauseParam()` and `setWhereClauseParams()` are both more efficient than `setWhereClause()`. Therefore, if you just need to change individual values in your WHERE clause, instead of changing the WHERE clause's entire structure, you should use a parameterized WHERE clause rather than calling `setWhereClause()`. Of course, you need to define the view object to use parameters as described.

Abstract View Objects

Generally, view links are only used to restrict view usage queries when that restriction takes the form of another query's result set. However, it is possible to use a view link for another kind of query restriction. This involves linking the view object usage to a usage of an abstract view object.

An *abstract view object* is a view object with only transient attributes. It was a simplification in Chapter 9 to say that a view object represents a SQL query. The vast majority of view objects do represent SQL queries, but strictly speaking, only the persistent and SQL-only attributes of a view object have any connection to a query. By creating an abstract view object, you can eliminate a query entirely.

The most common use of this idea is to restrict the data in a usage of another view object using a WHERE clause. For example, suppose you have a company with departments in three locations: the United States, Germany, and Japan. You also have plans to expand to the United Kingdom, but you do not have departments in the United Kingdom yet. Suppose your company has a DEPARTMENTS table like the following:

DEPARTMENT_ID	DEPARTMENT_NAME	LOCATION
10	Administration	US
20	Marketing	US
30	Purchasing	US
40	Human Resources	DE
50	Shipping	DE
60	IT	JP
70	Public Relations	US
80	Sales	JP

Because your company has only three locations, you might not have bothered to create a LOCATIONS table. However, you might want to create a view object, DepartmentsView, which can be used to list all the departments in any one of the three locations.

You could do this by defining DepartmentsView with a WHERE clause containing a bind variable, "LOCATION = :1", and setting this parameter at runtime. However, this is not the conceptually cleanest option. Conceptually, you want a detail usage of DepartmentsView, that is, a usage governed by another choice.

You can represent this in your data model by creating an abstract view object, making the usage of DepartmentsView a detail of the usage of the abstract view object, and inserting the data into the abstract usage at runtime.

Using an Abstract View Object

To use an abstract view object, follow steps such as in this example:

1. Create a view object containing only transient attributes (for example, LocationId) that are queriable. As explained in Chapter 13, attributes must be queriable to participate in view links. Leave its query blank. In the preceding example, you could create a view object called "LocationsView" with a single transient attribute, "LocationId."

2. Create a view link between the new view object and the one you want to restrict, and use the view link to link usages of the view objects in an application module's data model, as shown here:

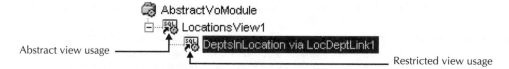

Abstract view usage ──────── ↑ DeptsInLocation via LocDeptLink1
                                                                   Restricted view usage

3. From the client, populate the abstract view usage. You can do this in two ways:

   ■ The simplest option is to insert a single row into the abstract view usage (master) to restrict the rows in the data view object (detail). When you need to navigate to another set of detail rows, change the master row's transient attributes to restrict the detail view usage's WHERE clause. For example, the following code restricts DeptsInLocation's result set to LocationId "US, " then to "JP, " and then to "UK" (which will cause the detail to have no rows, because there are no departments in the UK), and adds a department with LocationId "UK."

```
ViewObject locs = AbstractVoModule.findViewObject("Locations");
ViewObject depts = AbstractVoModule.findViewObject("DeptsInLocation");
Row loc = locs.createRow();
locs.insertRow(loc);
locs.setCurrentRow(loc);
loc.setAttribute("LocationId", "US");
loc.setAttribute("LocationId", "JP");
loc.setAttribute("LocationId", "UK");
Row ukDept = depts.createRow();
depts.insertRow(ukDept);
```

   ■ If the client needs more interactivity (for example, you want to display all the possible selections and let the user pick one by hand), create multiple rows in the view usage as shown next:

```
ViewObject locs = abstractVOModule.findViewObject("Locations");
Row usRow = locs.createRow();
usRow.setAttribute("LocationId", "US");
```

```
locs.insertRow(usRow);
Row deRow = locs.createRow();
deRow.setAttribute("LocationId", "DE");
locs.insertRow(deRow);
Row jpRow = locs.createRow();
deRow.setAttribute("LocationId", "JP");
locs.insertRow(jpRow);
Row ukRow = locs.createRow();
ukRow.setAttribute("LocationId", "UK");
locs.insertRow(ukRow);
```

After you have created these rows in the Locations usage, you can navigate between them (for example, using findByKey()) to restrict the rows returned by the DeptsInLocation view usage.

Hands-on Practice:
Traverse View Links and Change Data

In this practice, you continue work on the batch clients that you created in the preceding practice, making them perform the rest of the steps described in Chapter 13. The accountant promotion client will cycle through each department's employees, flagging those with more than two past jobs, and will then promote all the accountants in each department. The career path lister client will cycle through the current and past holders of each job. At the end of the practice, you will have created and exported service methods at the view row, view object, and application module level, traversed view links through both the data model and view link accessors, and changed a view object's WHERE clause at runtime.

This practice requires that you have completed the preceding practice in this chapter. Alternatively, you can download the starting files for this chapter from the authors' websites mentioned in the beginning of the book.

This practice guides you through the following steps:

I. Create and export service methods

- ■ Create a row-level service method

- ■ Create a view object–level service method

- ■ Export the row-level service method

- ■ Export the view object–level service method

II. Refine AccountantPromotionClient

- ■ Retrieve the other view usages

- ■ Cycle through each department's employees

- ■ Flag employees with many past jobs

- ■ Write code to promote the accountants in the department

- ■ Test AccountantPromotionClient

III. Refine CareerPathLister

- Retrieve the other view usages

- Cycle through the current and past holders of the job

- Test CareerPathLister

IV. Create a silent accountant promotion client

- Create an application module–level service method

- Export the application module–level service method

- Create a client to call the service method

I. Create and Export Service Methods

In this phase, you will add service methods at the view object– and view row–levels for your clients to use and export them to custom interfaces. You will create an application module–level service method in Phase IV.

Create a Row-Level Service Method

This section creates a service method to determine if a given employee has held at least two jobs before the current one.

1. Open EmpJobsViewRowImpl.java, under the EmpJobsView node, in the Code Editor.

   Additional Information: You are going to create a method that determines whether a particular employee has had at least two past jobs. Since this applies to a particular employee (that is, one row of EmpJobsView), this method should go on EmpJobsViewRowImpl instead of EmpJobsViewImpl.

2. Add the following method to EmpJobsViewRowImpl.java to return true if the employee has had more than two jobs in the past:

   ```
   public boolean manyJobs()
   {
     oracle.jbo.RowIterator pastJobs = getPastJobs();
     if (pastJobs.getRowCount() >= 2)
     {
       return true;
     }
     return false;
   }
   ```

   Additional Information: getPastJobs() is the accessor method for the view link EmpPastJobsLink, so it returns all the jobs this employee has had in the past. getRowCount() is a method you can call from both RowIterator and ViewObject—it returns the total number of rows in the RowIterator or the ViewObject's result set.

3. Make the file to check for syntax errors.

Create a View Object–Level Service Method

This section creates a service method that applies to the entire result set of a query.

1. Open EmpJobsViewImpl.java in the Code Editor.

Additional Information: You will now create a method that promotes every employee in the query's result set. Because this applies to the entire result set, instead of a particular row, it should be in the view object class.

2. Add the following method:

```
public void promoteAll()
{
  while (hasNext())
  {
    EmpJobsViewRowImpl currRow =    (EmpJobsViewRowImpl) next();
    String currJob = currRow.getJobId();
    String newJob = nextJob(currJob);
    currRow.setJobId(newJob);
  }
}
```

Additional Information: You could have put this code in the client, but because it is useful for more general purposes than just promoting accountants, you can put it in the view object and reuse it among many different clients.

Note the casting of next() to EmpJobsViewRowImpl. Casting something to a view row class (or any other implementation class) in the client would break deployment configuration-independence. Because this method is in the BC4J layer, which will have access to the implementation classes in any deployment configuration, you can make this cast without breaking deployment configuration-independence.

This method contains a call to nextJob(), a method you will write next.

3. Add the following method:

```
private String nextJob(String thisJob) {
   if (thisJob.equals("AD_VP")) return "AD_PRES";
   if (thisJob.equals("AC_MGR")) return "AD_VP";
   if (thisJob.equals("AC_ACCOUNT")) return "AC_MGR";
   if (thisJob.equals("FI_MGR")) return "AD_VP";
   if (thisJob.equals("FI_ACCOUNT")) return "FI_MGR";
   /* You could go on, but this is more than sufficient for this practice */
   return thisJob;
}
```

Additional Information: This is just a utility method to help promoteAll(). It returns the "next job up" in a typical career path.

4. Rebuild the project. Click Save All.

Export the Row-Level Service Method

This section exports the row-level service method to the EmpJobsViewRow interface:

1. On the EmpJobsView node in the navigator, select Edit EmpJobsView from the right-click menu to open the View Object Wizard.

2. Select the Client Row Methods page in the View Object Wizard.

3. Select the manyJobs() method you created, and move it to the right using the > button.

   Additional Information: nextJob() is not included in the list because it is private. Only public methods can be exported.

4. Click Apply. Do not close the wizard yet.

   Additional Information: JDeveloper adds manyJobs() to the EmpJobsViewRow interface. You can now call this method from the client without breaking deployment configuration-independence.

Export the View Object–Level Service Method

This section creates a deployment configuration-independent custom view object interface.

1. Still in the View Object Wizard, select the Client Methods tab.

   Additional Information: The Client Row Methods tab is for row-level methods; the Client Methods tab is for view object–level methods.

2. Select the promoteAll() method and move it to the right using the > button.

3. Click OK.

   Additional Information: JDeveloper creates the EmpJobsView interface under the EmpJobsView node in the Navigator. This interface contains promoteAll(). You can use this interface from the client without breaking deployment configuration independence.

4. Rebuild the project.

5. Click Save All.

What Just Happened? You created a single-row service method for EmpJobsView that returns true if the employee has had at least two previous jobs. Then you created a service method that applies to an entire result set for EmpJobsView, promoting every employee in the result set. Finally, you exported the single-row method to a custom view row interface you created in the previous hands-on practice, and you exported the view object–level method to a new custom view object interface.

When you use findViewObject() to retrieve a usage of EmpJobsView, you can cast the returned ViewObject to EmpJobsView and call the custom view object–level method (promoteAll()) on it. Similarly, when you cast a Row to EmpJobsViewRow, you can call the custom row-level method (manyJobs()) on it.

II. Refine AccountantPromotionClient

In this phase, you will write more code for AccountantPromotionClient, the Java application created in an earlier hands-on practice in this chapter. This application cycles through the employees in each department, retrieves information about them, and promotes all accountants in each department.

Retrieve the Other View Usages

Your client already retrieves the usage of DepartmentsView from AccountantPromotionModule.
Retrieve the other usages using the following steps:

1. Open AccountantPromotionClient.java to open it in a source editor.

2. Find the following line of code:

```
ViewObject allDepts =
   acctPromModule.findViewObject("AllDepartments");
```

3. Add the following code after that line:

```
EmpJobsView departmentEmps =
   (EmpJobsView) acctPromModule.findViewObject("DepartmentEmployees");
ViewObject pastJobs = acctPromModule.findViewObject("PastJobs");
```

   Additional Information: By casting to the custom interface you created in Phase I
   (EmpJobsView), you will be able to call the service method (promoteAll()) you
   exported.

4. Rebuild your project. Click Save All.

Cycle Through Each Department's Employees

This section traverses DeptEmpLink through the data model, cycles through the restricted result
set, and prints information.

1. Find the loop that cycles through the departments. It starts with this line:

```
while (allDepts.hasNext())
```

2. Embed the following WHILE loop before the closing curly bracket at the end of the
   WHILE loop you just found:

```
while (departmentEmps.hasNext())
{
  EmpJobsViewRow currEmp = (EmpJobsViewRow) departmentEmps.next();
  System.out.println("  Employee " +
    currEmp.getEmployeeId() + ": " +
    currEmp.getLastName() + " makes about $" +
    currEmp.getYearlyPay() + " as a(n) " +
    currEmp.getJobTitle() + "."
  );
}
```

   Additional Information: Since EmpJobsView is bound to DepartmentsView in the data
   model, this loop will only cycle through the rows of EmpJobsView corresponding to the
   current row of DepartmentsView.

3. Rebuild your project. Click Save All.

Flag Employees with Many Past Jobs

This section calls the custom row method to flag employees with at least two previous jobs.

I. Insert the following code right after the `System.out.println()` statement you just added, still inside the inner WHILE loop:

```
if (currEmp.manyJobs())
{
   System.out.println("    This employee has had more than two jobs.");
}
```

Additional Information: You can only call the `manyJobs()` method because your currEmp is an instance of the custom interface.

Write Code to Promote the Accountants in the Department

This section creates code to promote all the accountants in the department by further restricting the EmployeesView usage and calling `promoteAll()`.

I. In AccountantPromotionClient.java, right after the end of the `while (departmentEmps.hasNext())` loop, add the following code:

```
departmentEmps.setWhereClause("Employees.JOB_ID = 'FI_ACCOUNT'");
departmentEmps.executeQuery();
```

Additional Information: This code restricts the query in this usage of EmpJobView to the accountants and reexecutes the query to reflect the new results.

This code uses `setWhereClause()` to restrict the query. Because you use the same view object, EmpJobsView, without a WHERE clause elsewhere, you could not use a bind variable to accomplish this.

Alternatively, you could have created a separate view object to use instead of EmpJobsView here, with a bind variable in its WHERE clause. Then you could have used the more efficient `setWhereClauseParam()` instead of `setWhereClause()`.

2. Right after that line, add the following:

```
System.out.println("    Promoting all accountants in the department.");
departmentEmps.promoteAll();
departmentEmps.setWhereClause(null);
```

Additional Information: You can only call the exported method `promoteAll()` because your departmentEmps is an instance of the custom view object interface.

After promoting all the accountants, you must set the WHERE clause back to null so that the next iteration of the `while (allDepts.hasNext())` loop can use departmentEmps to flag all employees, rather than just the accountants, with more than two past jobs.

3. Rebuild the project and click Save All.

Test AccountantPromotionClient

This section runs AccountantPromotionClient.

1. Right click AccountantPromotionClient.java and select
   Run AccountantPromotionClient.java.

2. Note the output in the Log window. The first few lines should read something
   like the following:

```
Now accessing department 10:  Administration
   Employee 200: Whalen makes about $52800 as a(n) Administration Assistant.
   Promoting all accountants in the department.
Now accessing department 20:  Marketing
   Employee 167: Banda makes about $74772 as a(n) Sales Representative.
   Employee 201: Hartstein makes about $156000 as a(n) Marketing Manager
   Employee 202: Goyal makes about $72000 as a(n) Marketing Representative
Promoting all accountants in the department.
```

   Additional Information: Each department has similar output statements. After you run
   the accountant promotion client, if you check your database, you will notice that the
   accountants are not promoted. This is because the changes were made in the entity
   cache only; your program does not currently commit data to the database. You will
   change the client to commit data in Chapter 15.

What Just Happened?   You wrote code for AccountantPromotionClient to perform the following
functions for each department: print information about each employee, restrict the view of employees
to the accountants, and then promote all the accountants. Then you ran the client to test it.

III. Refine CareerPathLister

In this phase, you will write more code for CareerPathLister, the Java application you created in
the first hands-on practice of this chapter. The code you will add cycles through the current and
past holders of each job.

Retrieve the Other View Usages

Your client already retrieves the usage of DepartmentsView from CareerPathListerModule.
The following steps add code to retrieve the other usages:

1. Open CareerPathLister.java in the source editor.

2. Find the following line:

```
ViewObject allJobs = careerListerModule.findViewObject("AllJobs");
```

3. Add the following code right after that line:

```
ViewObject currHolders =
  careerModule.findViewObject("CurrentHolders");
ViewObject pastHolders = careerModule.findViewObject("PastHolders");
```

Additional Information: In the data model for CareerPathListerModule, the EmployeesView usage CurrentHolders is bound to allJobs via EmpJobLink, so it contains only the current holders of the currently selected job. The EmpJobsView usage PastHolders is bound to allJobs via EmpPastJobsLink, so it contains the past holders of the currently selected job.

4. Rebuild your project. Click Save All.

Cycle Through the Current and Past Holders of the Job
This section writes code to traverse the view links through the data model, cycle through the restricted result sets, and print information.

1. Find the following statement in CareerPathLister.java:

```
System.out.println("Found job " +
  requestedJobId + ": " +
  jobTitle + "."
);
```

2. After the statement, add the following:

```
System.out.println(
  "The following employees currently have the job title " +
  jobTitle + ":"
);
while (currHolders.hasNext())
{
  EmployeesViewRow currEmp = (EmployeesViewRow) currHolders.next();
  System.out.println(
    currEmp.getLastName() + ", who makes about $" +
    currEmp.getYearlyPay() +" and has " +
    currEmp.getNumReports() + " direct reports."
  );
}
```

Additional Information: This code cycles through the CurrentHolders view usage, which is restricted by the master AllJobs view usage via EmpJobsLink, and displays information about each row.

3. After the code you just added, insert

```
System.out.println(
  "The following employees previously had the job title " +
  jobTitle + ":"
);
while (pastHolders.hasNext())
{
  EmpJobsViewRow currPastHolder = (EmpJobsViewRow) pastHolders.next();
  System.out.println(
    currPastHolder.getLastName() + ", who now makes about $" +
    currPastHolder.getYearlyPay() + " as a(n) " +
```

```
        currPastHolder.getJobTitle() + "."
    );
}
```

Additional Information: This code cycles through the PastHolders view usage, which is restricted by the master AllJobs view usage via EmpPastJobsLink, and displays information about each row.

4. Rebuild the project and Click Save All.

Test CareerPathLister
This section runs CareerPathLister to test it.

1. On the CareerPathLister.java node, select Run CareerPathLister.java from the right-click menu.

2. Note the output in the Log window. The output should read something like the following:

```
Found job IT_PROG: Programmer
The following employees currently have the job title Programmer:
Hunold, who makes about $108000 and has 3 direct reports.
Ernst, who makes about $72000 and has 0 direct reports.
Austion, who makes about $57600 and has 0 direct reports.
...
The following employees previously had the title of Programmer:
De Haan, who makes about $204000 as a(n) Administration Vice President.
```

What Just Happened?   You refined CareerPathLister, writing code to traverse both view links through the data model and print information about the current and past holders of each job. Then you ran the client program to test it.

IV. Create a Silent Accountant Promotion Client
In this phase, you create a client much like AccountantPromotionClient, with the following two differences:

- ■ This client will promote individuals with Job ID AC_ACCOUNT instead of FI_ACCOUNT.

- ■ More importantly, this client will be "silent." All the processing will be done in an application module–level service method as opposed to in the view object–level service method. This is called "silent" because there is no interactivity with the client and no information displayed.

Create an Application Module–Level Service Method
This section creates a single service method to cycle through departments and promote every employee with Job ID AC_ACCOUNT.

1. In the Navigator, expand AccountantPromotionModule in the HRBC4J project, and open AccountantPromotionModuleImpl.java in the Code Editor.

2. Add the following method to AccountantPromotionModule:

```
public void promoteAccountants()
{
  DepartmentsViewImpl allDepts = getAllDepartments();
  EmpJobsViewImpl departmentEmps = getDepartmentEmployees();
}
```

Additional Information: An application module class has methods like `getAllDepartments()` and `getDepartmentEmployees()` that return view object classes for each of its view object usages. Because of this, when you are on the server side, you can use these typesafe methods instead of `findViewObject()`, which is not typesafe.

3. Add the following code in `promoteAccountants()` right after the code you just added:

```
departmentEmps.setWhereClause("Employees.JOB_ID = 'AC_ACCOUNT'");
while (allDepts.hasNext())
{
  allDepts.next();
  departmentEmps.promoteAll();
}
```

Additional Information: Since the view object classes implement the ViewObject interface and custom view object interfaces, all methods available on the interfaces (such as `next()` and `promoteAll()`) are available on the classes directly.

4. Click Rebuild and Save All.

Export the Application Module–Level Service Method
Use the following steps to export the `promoteAccountants()` method.

1. On the AccountantPromotionModule node in the Navigator, select Edit AccountPromotionModule from the right-click menu.

2. Select the Client Methods page.

3. Move `promoteAccountants()` to the Selected pane and click OK.

Additional Information: This creates an AccountantPromotionModule interface.

4. Click Save All.

Create a Client to Call the Service Method
Create a very simple application that calls the service method and prints a "Success" message:

1. On the HRWS.jws node, select New Project from the right-click menu. Select Project Containing a New Application, and click OK to open the Application Project Wizard. Click Next if the Welcome page appears.

2. On the Location page, change the project directory name to "SilentAccountantPromotionClientJA," and change the project file name to "SilentAccountantPromotionClientJA.jpr." Click Next.

3. On the Paths page, name the default package "silentaccountantpromotionclientja." Click Next.

4. On the Libraries page, add the following libraries to the Selected Libraries list:

   ■ BC4J Oracle Domains

   ■ BC4J Runtime

   ■ Connection Manager

   ■ Oracle JDBC

5. Click Finish to create the project and open the New Application dialog.

6. Name the application "SilentAccountantPromotionClient."

7. Uncheck *Add Default Frame.*

8. Click OK.

9. Edit the project settings of SilentAccountantPromotionClientJA, just as you did for AccountantPromotionJA, and add a dependency on HRBC4J.

10. Open SilentAccountantPromotionClient.java in the Code Editor, and add the following after the package statement:

    ```
    import oracle.jbo.client.Configuration;
    import hrbc4j.common.AccountantPromotionModule;
    ```

    Additional Information: Since all of the processing is occurring in the BC4J layer, the client only needs access to Configuration (to access the application module) and to AccountantPromotionModule (to call the service method).

11. Add the following code to the body of the `main()` method after "new `SilentAccountantPromotionClient();`":

    ```
    AccountantPromotionModule accPromModule =
      (AccountantPromotionModule)
      Configuration.createRootApplicationModule(
        "AccountantPromotionModule",
        "AccountantPromotionModuleLocal");
    accPromModule.promoteAccountants();
    System.out.println("Success!");
    ```

12. Click Rebuild and Save All.

What Just Happened? You created a "silent" version of the accountant promotion client. Instead of accessing individual view usages, this version of the client leaves all processing to a service method in the application module.

In a deployed project, with the client and the BC4J layer possibly on different machines, the strategy of processing in the application module can reduce network traffic. However, this strategy comes at the cost of far less interactivity on the part of the client. For example, in the silent version, the client could not print information about each department, since that would require accessing a usage of DepartmentsView directly.

Changing the Data Model at Runtime

Sometimes, instead of just restricting a view usage's query, you want to alter the entire structure of your data model at runtime to accomplish one of the following tasks:

- Add new usages of predesigned view objects to the data model.

- Create a new view object based on a user-defined query and add a usage of that view object to the data model.

- Change the master-detail relationships between view usages.

There are limitations to the entirely new view objects and view links you can create at runtime, although these limitations do not apply to usages of predefined view objects and view links you add to the data model. The limitations follow:

- You cannot create view objects based on multiple entity objects.

- You cannot create view objects based on entity objects with expert-mode queries.

- You cannot create view objects with transient or entity-derived attributes.

- You can only create unidirectional view links.

Adding a Usage of a Predefined View Object to the Data Model

Suppose you have a number of view objects that you know your application may need to use, but you do not know which ones it will need until runtime. You could just add usages for all of them to the application module's data model at design time, but if there are many possible view objects, this could bloat your application module.

An alternative is to create the view objects at design time but not to add usages to the data model until runtime. You can do this with the method `ApplicationModule.createViewObject()`. `createViewObject()` takes the following two arguments:

- The view usage name

- The package-qualified view object name

For example, the following code would create a usage of the EmployeesView view object:

```
String viewUsageName = "EmployeesView1";
String viewObjectName = "hrbc4j.EmployeesView";
ViewObject emps = dynamicModule.createViewObject(viewUsageName, viewObjectName);
```

This code would create a usage of EmployeesView. It would add a usage of the new view object to dynamicModule's data model at the top level (you could then link it, as you will see later) and return the usage as emps.

Creating a SQL-Only View Object

You can create a SQL-only view object at runtime using `ApplicationModule.createViewObjectFromQueryStmt()`. This method both creates a new view object and adds a usage of it to the application module's data model. You pass two Strings into `createViewObjectFromQueryStmt()`. The first is a name for the view usage to be added to the data model. The second is a string containing the complete SQL query. For example, the following code would create a dynamic SQL-only view object and add a usage called "RunTimeQueryResults" to the data model:

```
String viewUsageName="RunTimeQueryResults";

String query="SELECT EMPLOYEES.EMPLOYEE_ID, EMPLOYEES.LAST_NAME, " +
  "DEPARTMENTS.DEPARTMENT_ID, DEPARTMENTS.DEPARTMENT_NAME " +
  "FROM DEPARTMENTS, EMPLOYEES " +
  "WHERE EMPLOYEES.DEPARTMENT_ID = DEPARTMENTS.DEPARTMENT_ID";

ViewObject empsDepts =
  dynamicModule.createViewObjectFromQueryStmt(
    viewUsageName,
    query);
```

This code would create a view object with attributes EmployeeId, LastName, DepartmentId, and DepartmentName, based on that query. It would add a usage of the new view object to dynamicModule's data model at the top level (you could then link it, as you will see later) and return the usage as empsDepts.

Creating a View Object Based on an Entity Object

You can create a view object based on an entity object at runtime, provided that the view object is based on only one entity object, contains only persistent attributes, and does not use an expert mode query.

Create such a view object, and add a usage of it to the data model using the method `ApplicationModule.createViewObjectFromQueryClauses()`. This method takes six arguments:

- The name of the view usage to be added to the data model.
- The package-qualified entity object name. For example, if your BC4J is in a package called "hrbc4j" and your entity object is called "Employees," this string would be "hrbc4j.Employees."
- The list of columns to select from the table.
- The table to select the columns from. This should be the table on which your entity object is based.

- The WHERE clause (without the "WHERE" keyword, just as you would enter it in the View Object Wizard).

- The ORDER BY clause (without the "ORDER BY" keyword, just as you would enter it in the View Object Wizard).

For example, the following code would create a view object based on the Countries entity object:

```
String viewUsageName = "DynamicEntityBasedUsage";
String entityObjectName = "bc4j.Countries";
String selectClause = "COUNTRY_ID, COUNTRY_NAME";
String fromClause = "COUNTRIES";
String whereClause = null;
String orderByClause = "COUNTRY_ID";

ViewObject newVO = dynamicModule.createViewObjectFromQueryClauses(
  viewUsageName, entityObjectName, selectClause,
  fromClause, whereClause, orderByClause);
```

Like the other two methods you have seen, `createViewObjectFromQueryClauses()` both adds a usage to the application module's data model at the top level and returns the usage.

Linking View Usages at Runtime

There are two reasons you might want to link a view usage at runtime:

- You might not know the query restrictions at design time.

- You might have added the view usage to the data model at runtime, which always places it at the top level of the application module data model, and you might not want it there.

You can link view usages that have a predefined view link. You can also link view usages that have no view link predefined.

Linking View Usages with a Predefined View Link

If you have a predefined view link between the view objects, you can use it to link usages of those view objects at runtime by calling `ApplicationModule.createViewLink()`. This method takes four arguments:

- A unique name for the view link usage to be added to the data model

- The package-qualified view link name

- The master view usage (not a name, but a ViewObject instance)

- The detail view usage (again, a ViewObject)

For example, suppose the data model contains a usage of EmployeesView called SomeEmployees, and a usage of JobsView called SomeJobs. It also contains a view link, EmpPastJobsLink, that joins EmployeesView and JobsView. You can make SomeJobs a detail of SomeEmployees in the data model, via EmpPastJobsLink2, using the following code:

```
ViewObject master = dynamicModule.findViewObject("SomeEmployees");
ViewObject detail = dynamicModule.findViewObject("SomeJobs");
String viewLinkName = "hrbc4j.EmpPastJobsLink";
String viewLinkUsage = "EmpPastJobsLink2";

dynamicModule.createViewLink(
   viewLinkUsage, viewLinkName, master, detail);
```

Linking View Usages with No Predefined View Link

Linking view usages without a predefined view link between the view objects is more complicated than using a predefined view link, but it may be necessary. For example, if one or both of the view objects is created dynamically with `createViewObjectFromQueryStmt()` or `createViewObjectFromQueryClauses()`, it is not possible to define a view link between them in advance.

In this case, the first step in linking one view usage to another at runtime is to create lists of the source and destination attributes. These lists are arrays of objects called AttributeDefs. You can create AttributeDefs using a method called `ViewObject.findAttributeDef()`. This method takes the name of the view attribute as an argument. For example, the following code creates arrays of AttributeDefs to make SomeEmployees a detail of AllDepartments:

```
ViewObject source = dynamicModule.findViewObject("AllDepartments");
ViewObject dest = dynamicModule.findViewObject("SomeEmployees");

/* Create an array containing DepartmentsView.DepartmentId,
   the source attribute */
AttributeDef[] sourceAttrs = new AttributeDef[1];
sourceAttrs[0] = source.findAttributeDef("DepartmentId");

/* Create an array containing EmployeesView.DepartmentId,
   the destination attribute */
AttributeDef[] destAttrs = new AttributeDef[1];
destAttrs[0] = dest.findAttributeDef("DepartmentId");
```

After you create these attribute lists, you can call `ApplicationModule.createViewLinkBetweenViewObjects()` to link the view usages. `createViewLinkBetweenViewObjects()` takes seven arguments:

- A name for the view link usage that will link the view objects

- An accessor name for the destination view object

- The source view usage (the ViewObject, not the usage name)

- The source view attribute list

- The destination view usage (the ViewObject, not the usage name)

- The destination view attribute list

- The view link SQL, or null if you want to let the BC4J framework generate default view link SQL (which is just like the default view link SQL generated by the View Link Wizard) for you

For example, the following code makes SomeEmployees a detail of AllDepartments, using standard view link SQL:

```
ViewLink empJobLink = dynamicModule.createViewLinkBetweenViewObjects(
  "DynamicViewLinkUsage", source, sourceAttrs,
  dest, destinationAttrs,
  null);
```

Dynamically created view links are always one-to-many and unidirectional.

Secondary Row Set Iterators

As discussed earlier, a view usage contains not only a set of Rows, but a pointer to a "current" row that changes when you call the navigation methods next(), first(), last(), previous(), or setCurrentRow(). One such pointer is enough for most purposes, but if you want to keep two or more separate pointers to "current" rows, you can create *secondary row set iterators,* which are extra pointers for your view usage. For example, you might want one user to be able to browse the same result set in multiple separate windows, not keeping the current rows synchronized; you can use a secondary row set iterator for each new window.

A secondary row set iterator is an object that implements the interface RowSetIterator. Like ViewObject, RowSetIterator has next(), first(), last(), previous(), and setCurrentRow() methods. These methods move the current row pointer of the secondary row set iterator around the view usage's result set, just as the same methods on ViewObject move the view usage's primary current row pointer around its result set. Also, next(), first(), last(), and previous() return the Row the pointer moves to, just as they do for ViewObject.

For example, the following code creates a secondary row set iterator for EmpJobsView and uses it to navigate around EmpJobsView's result set independently of EmpJobsView's primary current row pointer:

```
ViewObject empJobsView = appMod.findViewObject("EmpJobsView");

/* Pass a unique name into createRowSetIterator() to get a
   secondary row set iterator */
RowSetIterator secondIterator =
  createRowSetIterator("EmpJobsSecondaryIterator");

while (secondIterator.hasNext())
{
  Row currRow = secondIterator.next();
```

```
    /* code that uses currRow */
}

Row firstRow = empJobsView.next();
```

At the end of the loop, the secondary iterator is pointing to the last row. The current row pointer for empJobsView, however, is still pointing to the slot before the first row.

Optimizing Query Caching

Chapter 13 introduced two ways to make use of BC4J's caching mechanisms to optimize your program's use of resources, as follows:

- Using the entity cache, when view usage queries share data with one another or return multiple rows corresponding to one row of a table

- Turning off entity caching by making a view object SQL-only, when entity caching will not improve a view object's use of resources, and you do not need to use the view object to write to the database

This section explains two more ways to customize caching behavior to get the best performance out of a BC4J layer.

Forward-Only Mode

In some circumstances, you may know in advance that you will only navigate through a result set using the next() method. The most common case of this is a predominately non-interactive application that prints a report. The report will go through the rows returned by the query, in order, with no need to ever go back.

In this case, there is no reason to maintain a cache of the view usage's rows. Your application can just retrieve the first row from the database (or the entity cache if it is already populated) and, when it is ready to move on, discard that row and retrieve the next row. Because the application will never return to a previous row, it does not need to save a copy of it.

A view usage that uses no view cache is said to be in *forward-only mode*. View usages in forward-only mode cannot call first(), previous(), or findByKey() (these methods will throw exceptions), so you should never use forward-only mode unless you are sure that the view usage will not need to scroll backwards through rows. In exchange for accepting these limitations, your application will save a significant amount of memory by never maintaining more than one view row in memory at a time.

When you put a view usage into forward-only mode, any currently existing view cache is discarded, and the view usage starts maintaining only one row in memory at a time. The following is an example of placing a view usage in forward-only mode and then turning view caching back on:

```
deptView.setForwardOnly(true);
deptView.setForwardOnly(false);
```

If you have a usage of a SQL-only view object with forward-only mode, there is no data caching at either the view- or entity-object level. This is restrictive, providing no ability to write, no synchronization, and no ability to move backwards in the query result set, but it has a smaller memory footprint and higher speed than any other option.

You may want to try adding a call to `deptView.setForwardOnly(true)` to AccountantPromotionClient, right after deptView is declared. It will make the client run more efficiently.

Ranges

Many applications—for example, search engines—display only a small subset of a result set at a time. For example, a JSP application might display only the first ten results of a search and have a "Next" link to display the next ten results.

If an application will only display ten rows at a time, it should not retrieve hundreds or thousands of rows from the database at once. It is likely that the user will never see most of those rows before exiting the application. You can restrict the number of rows your view usage retrieves at one time by using ranges. A *range* is a window into the result set of a query. The view cache only stores rows to the end of the range. This way, you can retrieve a small subset of rows at a time.

You can make a view usage use a range by passing a number of rows to the method `ViewObject.setRangeSize()`, as shown here:

```
currHolders.setRangeSize(10);
```

When you set a range size of some number *n,* the range of the view usage will be set to the first *n* rows of the view usage's result set, and those rows will be retrieved into the view usage's cache. You can quickly navigate around the range using `getRowAtRangeIndex()`, and you can call `setCurrentRow()` to set the current row pointer to them. For example, the following code sets the current row pointer to the fifth row in the range:

```
currHolders.setCurrentRow(empJobsView.getRowAtRangeIndex(4));
```

When you want to retrieve a different range of rows, you can call the method `ViewObject.scrollRange()` to move the range forward or backward. For example, the following code will scroll the range forward 20 rows, and then backward by 10 rows:

```
currHolders.scrollRange(20);
currHolders.scrollRange(-10);
```

After the first line is called, the view cache will contain 30 rows: the 10 it retrieved originally, plus the 20 it advances by. The range will contain the last 10 of those 30. The second line scrolls the range backwards to contain the 10 middle rows in the view cache.

If you want to stop working with ranges, you can pass –1 to `setRangeSize()`, as follows:

```
currHolders.setRangeSize(-1);
```

CHAPTER
15

Managing Multiple
Transactions

What's mine is mine and what's yours is yours.

—One of the four kinds of people, according to the *Midrash Avot*

 database needs to be able to handle numerous transactions, allowing multiple users to have their own, consistent view of the data without interfering with the views of other users. In the same way, a BC4J layer needs to be able to handle many simultaneous users, keeping separate caches, connections, and database transactions for them and specifying when their changes are posted, committed, or rolled back. This chapter explains how to use BC4J to manage the data in a single transaction, to maintain consistency across transactions, and to handle large numbers of simultaneous transactions while maintaining performance and stability. In the hands-on practice, you will experiment with different ways to handle row locking and will modify one of the batch clients created in the Chapter 14 hands-on practice to commit changes and customize the commit cycle.

The Transaction and DBTransaction Interfaces

Everything about a single transaction, including its view and entity caches, its database connection, and when it should be committed and rolled back, is handled by an object of type oracle.jbo.server.DBTransactionImpl.

A new DBTransactionImpl (that is, a new instance of the DBTransactionImpl class) is created as soon as a root application module is instantiated, and it lasts for the lifetime of the application module. Unlike an RDBMS transaction or a standard EJB transaction, a BC4J DBTransactionImpl survives commit and rollback operations. Because of this, one DBTransactionImpl can correspond to multiple database transactions over the course of its lifetime.

A root application module and all nested application modules share a DBTransactionImpl. Because of this, changes from within one nested application module are immediately visible in all others, and changes in different nested application modules will all be committed or rolled back simultaneously.

For most applications, you do not use the DBTransactionImpl class directly. Instead, you access these objects through two interfaces implemented by DBTransactionImpl: oracle.jbo.Transaction and oracle.jbo.server.DBTransaction.

The Transaction Interface

oracle.jbo.Transaction is a tier-independent interface, accessible by both your clients and the BC4J layer. You can obtain a Transaction by calling `ApplicationModule.getTransaction()`. For example, the following code obtains the Transaction for the application module acctPromModule:

```
Transaction acctPromTrans = acctPromModule.getTransaction();
```

Since a root application module and all nested application modules share a DBTransactionImpl, it does not matter whether you call `getTransaction()` from the root application module or from a nested application module; either method call will retrieve the same object.

The DBTransaction Interface

oracle.jbo.server.DBTransaction is a server side–only interface. Your client applications should not use this interface directly, because that would break deployment configuration-independence; they should use Transaction only.

DBTransaction extends Transaction. That is, all the methods you can call on Transaction, you can call on DBTransaction as well. DBTransaction also exposes other methods, such as methods that create JDBC commands or that directly manipulate the entity cache, but using those methods is beyond the scope of this book.

The most important difference between DBTransaction and Transaction is the way in which they are obtained. You can obtain a DBTransaction through `EntityImpl.getDBTransaction()`. For example, you could write the following code inside an entity object class such as DepartmentsImpl:

```
DBTransaction currentTrans = getDBTransaction();
```

This is useful when you need to perform transaction operations as part of an entity object's business logic, rather than from the client or an application module. For example, you might want to roll back changes as soon as the validation logic in an entity object's `validateEntity()` method (discussed in Chapter 12) catches an error.

Committing and Rolling Back Changes

Once you have a Transaction, you can commit your changes by calling `Transaction.commit()` or roll them back by calling `Transaction.rollback()`.

`commit()` posts all of your pending changes to the database and then sends a COMMIT command. You will call `commit()` in the hands-on practice in this chapter.

`rollback()` sends a ROLLBACK command to the database and clears the entity and view caches (so that they no longer contain changes that have been discarded in the database).

If you do not include a call to `commit()` or `rollback()`, the transaction will terminate (and the database will automatically perform a ROLLBACK) when the client finishes its execution, just as your transaction will be terminated and rolled back if you exit from SQL*Plus without committing.

The Commit Cycle

When you call `Transaction.commit()`, you initiate a chain of events called the *commit cycle*. The commit cycle commits your changes to the database, but it also performs other processing.

First, the BC4J framework posts all of the changes in the entity caches to the database. By default, the BC4J framework uses INSERT, UPDATE, and DELETE operations to post changes to the database. However, you can change this behavior (for example, to use a stored procedure to perform database updates) by overriding `EntityImpl.doDML()`. You can generate a stub for doDML() in your entity object class by checking the *Data Manipulation Methods* checkbox on the Java page of the Entity Object Wizard, as shown here:

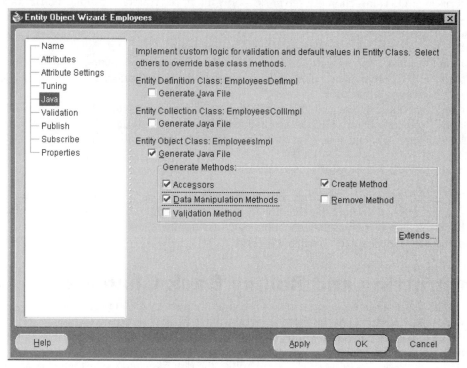

See the Javadoc for more information about overriding doDML().

Second, the BC4J framework calls beforeCommit() on all view object usages and on entity object instances that are new, marked for deletion, or changed. ViewObjectImpl and EntityImpl already have beforeCommit() methods, which perform processing such as making sure that entity instances satisfy their validation requirements. You can override these methods in your entity object or view object classes if you want to implement your own behavior in entity or view objects before a commit operation. You will override beforeCommit() in an entity object class in the hands-on practice later in for this chapter.

Third, the BC4J framework sends a COMMIT command to the database.

Fourth, the BC4J framework calls afterCommit() on all the view object and entity object instances that were new, marked for deletion, or changed. Like beforeCommit(), ViewObjectImpl and EntityImpl already have afterCommit() methods, which you can override in your entity object or view object classes to implement your own behavior after a commit operation.

By default, the commit cycle stops here. The entity and view caches are maintained after a commit so that queries do not need to be re-executed. However, if you want to make sure that changes made in transactions committed by other users are picked up immediately, you can call Transaction.setClearCacheOnCommit() to empty the entity and view caches after every commit, as shown here:

```
acctPromTrans.setClearCacheOnCommit(true);
acctPromTrans.commit();
acctPromTrans.setClearCacheOnCommit(false);
```

In this example, because of the call to `setClearCacheOnCommit(true)`, the cache is cleared after the `commit()` method call. Because of the call to `setClearCacheOnCommit(false)`, future `commit()` method calls will not clear the cache.

The Rollback Cycle

Calling `Transaction.rollback()` or terminating a BC4J application initiates a chain of events called the *rollback cycle.* Much like the commit cycle, the rollback cycle performs processing as well as rolling back your changes.

First, the BC4J framework calls `beforeRollback()` on all view object usages and on entity object instances that are new, marked for deletion, or changed. Just like `beforeCommit()`, you can override this method to implement your own behavior.

Second, the BC4J framework sends a ROLLBACK command to the database.

By default, the BC4J framework empties all entity and view caches after a `rollback()`. You can change this behavior by calling `setClearCacheOnRollback()`, as shown here:

```
acctPromTrans.setClearCacheOnRollback(false);
acctPromTrans.rollback();
acctPromTrans.setClearCacheOnRollback(true);
```

In this example, because of the call to `setClearCacheOnRollback(false)`, the cache is not cleared after the `rollback()` method call. Because of the call to `setClearCacheOnRollback(true)`, future `rollback()` method calls will again clear the cache.

If the caches are not cleared, they will be reverted. That is, all changes will be undone, new rows will be discarded, and rows marked for deletion will be unmarked. Clearing the cache on rollback, by forcing query re-execution, just assures that changes committed by other transactions will be visible immediately.

Locking

Locking is an RDBMS feature that prevents users in different transactions from causing data conflicts. When a lock is acquired on a row, it prevents other transactions from changing that row. Locks persist until the RDBMS transaction ends.

Pessimistic Locking

By default, BC4J uses *pessimistic locking,* which means it attempts to lock a row as soon as one of its attributes is changed (via a call to `setAttribute()`, as described in Chapter 12). This is the safest locking mode, because with pessimistic locking, two transactions will never make inconsistent changes to the same row. Suppose Transaction1 and Transaction2 are two transactions using pessimistic locking, both of which try to change the same piece of data, as follows:

1. In Transaction1, the application calls `DepartmentsImpl.setDepartmentName("IT")` on a particular row. Transaction1 immediately acquires a lock on that row.

2. In Transaction2, the application calls `DepartmentsImpl.setDepartmentName` (`"Internal Support"`) on the same row. Transaction2 tries to acquire a lock on the row and receives an oracle.jbo.AlreadyLockedException.

Optimistic Locking

Pessimistic locking can tie up rows for long periods. If one user changes data and then waits a long time before committing or rolling back, no other users will be able to change that data at all. Optimistic locking can be more efficient than pessimistic locking. Instead of locking a row as soon as it is changed, under *optimistic locking,* BC4J waits until a changed row is posted before attempting to acquire a lock. Optimistic locking can allow the entity caches in two transactions to diverge substantially. An exception is not thrown until the conflicting transactions attempt to post their changes to the database. Suppose Transaction3 and Transaction4 are two transactions using optimistic locking, both of which try to change a piece of data in the same row, as follows:

1. In Transaction3, the application calls `DepartmentsImpl.setDepartmentName` (`"IT"`) on a particular row. Transaction1 does not immediately acquire a lock on that row.

2. In Transaction4, the application calls `DepartmentsImpl.setDepartmentName` (`"Internal Support"`) on the same row. Transaction3 and Transaction4 now have differing entity caches.

3. In Transaction4, the application calls `commit()`. As part of the commit cycle, the changed row is posted to the database. Before the update can be executed, Transaction4 acquires a lock on that row (although the lock expires almost immediately, when the COMMIT command is sent to the database).

4. In Transaction3, the application calls `commit()`. As part of the commit cycle, BC4J tries to post the changed row to the database. Right before posting, it attempts to acquire a lock on that row. BC4J recognizes that the row has been changed outside of the transaction, and that updating the row would overwrite another transaction's changes, so it throws an oracle.jbo.RowInconsistentException.

You can write your application to catch a RowInconsistentException and, for example, alert users and show them the updated data. You can set a Transaction to use optimistic locking mode by calling `Transaction.setLockingMode()`, passing in the static constant Transaction.LOCK_OPTIMISTIC, as shown here:

```
acctPromTrans.setLockingMode(Transaction.LOCK_OPTIMISTIC);
acctPromTrans.setLockingMode(Transaction.LOCK_PESSIMISTIC);
```

The first line sets the locking mode to optimistic; the second sets it back to pessimistic.

Explicitly Locking Rows

Whatever locking mode you use, you can lock a row at any time by calling `EntityImpl.lock()` on the corresponding entity object instance. For example, the following code, inside DepartmentsImpl, locks rows of DEPARTMENTS as soon as DepartmentName is changed, even if the locking mode is optimistic:

```
void setDepartmentName(String value) {
   lock();
   setAttributeInternal(DEPARTMENT_NAME, value);
}
```

Change Indicators

As explained before, whenever a Transaction attempts to acquire a lock, the BC4J framework checks whether the row has been changed outside of the transaction. If so, it throws an oracle.jbo.RowInconsistentException.

By default, the framework checks for row changes as follows:

1. When the entity cache is first populated, or whenever commit() is called, the framework saves an as-is copy of the data currently in the row. This copy is maintained even if the value in the cache is later changed.

2. When the transaction attempts to acquire a lock, every attribute in the copy is compared with the corresponding table column. If any of these comparisons fail, the framework throws the RowInconsistentException.

If you are attempting to acquire locks for many rows, and each row has a large number of columns, this can be an expensive operation. You can make the process more efficient by using a *change indicator,* which is an attribute (such as a timestamp) or a set of attributes that correspond to table columns you know will change every time any value in the row changes.

When you use a change indicator, the framework only performs the comparison for attributes in the change indicator, instead of for every entity attribute. You set an attribute to be part of a change indicator by checking the *Change Indicator* checkbox on the Attribute Settings page of the Entity Object Wizard, as shown here:

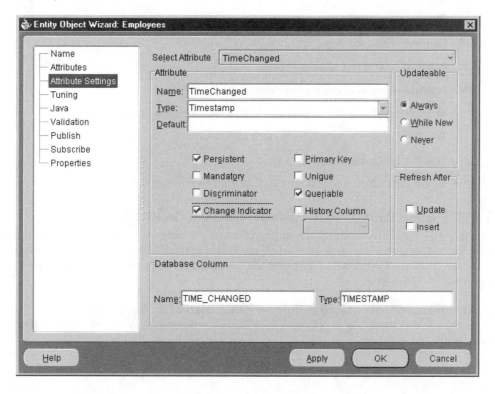

Hands-on Practice: Commit Changes and Customize the Commit Cycle

In this practice, you use the Business Component Browser to observe the different behaviors of pessimistic and optimistic locking. Then you modify AccountantPromotionClient, one of the batch clients you created in Chapter 13, to use optimistic locking, attempt to commit its changes, and use the commit cycle to provide information about the status of the commit process.

NOTE
The HR schema contains a trigger and a constraint that do not allow an employee to change jobs twice in the same day. You may encounter problems running this tutorial if someone has changed the employees' jobs in your database on the same day.

This practice builds on the results of the hands-on practices in Chapter 14. If you have not completed those practices, you can download the starting files for this practice from the authors' websites mentioned in the author information section at the beginning of this book.

This practice guides you through the following steps:

    I. Test pessimistic and optimistic locking

        ■ Test AccountantPromotionModule in pessimistic locking mode

        ■ Test AccountantPromotionModule in optimistic locking mode

    II. Use optimistic locking

    III. Attempt to commit changes

    IV. Provide reports on the commit operation

        ■ Report before attempting to commit each changed row

        ■ Report before rolling back each changed row

    V. Test the batch client

    VI. Modify the promoteAccountants() method to commit data

I. Test Pessimistic and Optimistic Locking

In Phase II, you will modify AccountantPromotionClient to use optimistic locking. But the difference between the two locking modes will be more clearly visible in the Business Component Browser. This phase uses the Business Component Browser to test AccountantPromotionModule in both pessimistic and optimistic locking mode.

Test AccountantPromotionModule in Pessimistic Locking Mode

In this section, you use the Business Component Browser to test AccountantPromotionModule in pessimistic locking mode:

1. Test AccountantPromotionModule by selecting Test from the right-click menu and connecting to the Business Component Browser.

2. Repeat step 1 to open a second instance of the browser.
   Additional Information: Different clients (including different instances of the browser) use different application module instances, and therefore separate transactions.

3. In each instance of the browser, double click DepartmentEmployees.

4. In the first instance of the browser, change Whalen's JobId to "AD_VP."

5. In the second instance of the browser, attempt to change Whalen's JobId to "MK_MAN."

6. Note the error message.
   Additional Information: As explained before, the default locking mode is pessimistic. Therefore, the first instance of the browser locked the row of Employees as soon as it changed a value.

7. Close both instances of the browser.

Test AccountantPromotionModule in Optimistic Locking Mode

In this section, you use the Business Component Browser to test AccountantPromotionModule in optimistic locking mode:

1. Open two instances of the Business Component Browser.

2. In the first instance of the browser, select Properties from AccountantPromotionModule's right-click menu to open the Business Component Application Module Properties dialog.

3. Double click the value of Transaction.LockMode to make it editable, as shown here:

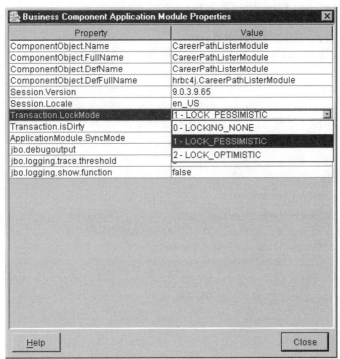

Property	Value
ComponentObject.Name	CareerPathListerModule
ComponentObject.FullName	CareerPathListerModule
ComponentObject.DefName	CareerPathListerModule
ComponentObject.DefFullName	hrbc4j.CareerPathListerModule
Session.Version	9.0.3.9.65
Session.Locale	en_US
Transaction.LockMode	1 - LOCK_PESSIMISTIC
Transaction.isDirty	0 - LOCKING_NONE
ApplicationModule.SyncMode	1 - LOCK_PESSIMISTIC
jbo.debugoutput	2 - LOCK_OPTIMISTIC
jbo.logging.trace.threshold	
jbo.logging.show.function	false

Business Component Application Module Properties

Help   Close

4. Select LOCK_OPTIMISTIC and close the dialog.

   Additional Information: Changing this value causes the browser to call `SetLockingMode()`.

5. Repeat steps 2–4 for the second instance of the browser.

6. In each instance of the browser, double click DepartmentEmployees.

7. In the first instance of the browser, change Whalen's JobId to "AD_VP."

8. In the second instance of the browser, change Whalen's JobId to "MK_MAN."

   Additional Information: Since the browser is using optimistic locking mode, the first instance did not lock the row when it changed the value of JobId.

9. In the second instance of the browser, click the Commit button.

10. In the first instance of the browser, click the Commit button.

11. Note the error message.

    Additional Information: Since the second instance of the browser committed, the first instance will encounter inconsistent data when it attempts to post.

12. Close both instances.

What Just Happened?   You saw the differences between pessimistic and optimistic locking modes. Pessimistic locking mode locks the row as soon as it is changed, so data conflicts favor the first client to change data. Optimistic locking mode does not lock the row until the commit cycle, so data conflicts favor the first client to commit the data.

II. Use Optimistic Locking

This phase modifies AccountantPromotionClient to use optimistic locking.

1. Open the HRWS workspace if it is not already open. If you have not completed both hands-on practices in Chapter 14, return to those practices and complete the steps. Alternatively, you can download a copy of the starting files from the authors' websites mentioned in the beginning of the book.

2. In the AccountantPromotionJA.jpr project, open AccountantPromotionClient.java in the Code Editor.

3. Find the following command:

```
ApplicationModule acctPromModule =
  Configuration.createRootApplicationModule(
    "hrbc4j.AccountantPromotionModule",
    "AccountantPromotionModuleLocal"
  );
```

4. Right after that command, insert the line

```
Transaction acctPromTrans = acctPromModule.getTransaction();
```

Additional Information: This returns the application module's BC4J Transaction. You will use this transaction both to set the locking mode and to attempt the commit operation.

5. Right after the command you just inserted, insert the following line:

```
acctPromTrans.setLockingMode(ApplicationModule.LOCK_OPTIMISTIC);
```

Additional Information: This sets AccountantPromotionClient's Transaction to use optimistic locking mode, which will not attempt to obtain a lock until data is posted to the database.

6. Build your project and click Save All.

What Just Happened?   You retrieved a transaction and set its locking mode to optimistic. In the case of batch clients, such as AccountantPromotionClient, the difference between optimistic and pessimistic locking modes is not very important. Batch clients have no user "think time." Because of this, they do not typically hold transactions open for very long, and the chance of conflicts with other transactions is low. However, you would use this procedure to set the locking mode in any client application program.

III. Attempt to Commit Changes

This phase modifies AccountantPromotionClient so that it attempts to commit the changes it has made before terminating and performs a rollback if the commit operation fails to acquire the locks it needs.

1. Add the following code to the end of AccountantPromotionClient's `main()` method:

```
try
{
  System.out.println("Attempting to commit changes.");
  acctPromTrans.commit();
  System.out.println("Commit successful.");
}
```

Additional Information: This code attempts to commit your changes to the database and displays console messages before and after the attempt.

2. Add the following code right after that block:

```
catch (RowInconsistentException e)
{
  System.out.println("Data conflict detected. Rolling back.");
  acctPromTrans.rollback();
}
```

Additional Information: As mentioned earlier, in a batch client, attempts to acquire locks are unlikely to fail. However, if they do fail, since AccountantPromotionClient is using optimistic locking, they will fail during the commit cycle. (If AccountantPromotionClient were using pessimistic locking, the locking attempts would fail during `setAttribute()` calls.)

When an attempt to acquire a lock fails, the BC4J framework throws a RowInconsistentException. The block you just added handles that exception by rolling back the transaction.

3. Click Rebuild and Save All.

What Just Happened?   You wrote code that will attempt to commit AccountantPromotionClient's changes to the database and added an exception handler for the case where the commit operation fails.

IV. Provide Reports on the Commit Operation

This phase overrides the beforeCommit() and beforeRollback() methods in EntityImpl to print the changes being committed or rolled back.

Report Before Attempting to Commit Each Row

This section overrides EntityImpl.beforeCommit() to perform operations on each entity instance before committing its data.

1. In the HRBC4J.jpr project node, expand the hrbc4j package node. Under the Employees entity object node, open EmployeesImpl.java in the Code Editor.

   Additional Information: Entity objects (such as EmployeesImpl) handle writing data to the database. Even though AccountantPromotionClient uses EmpJobsViewRow, the data posting in the commit cycle happens at the entity object level.

2. Add the following line to the import block:

```
import oracle.jbo.server.TransactionEvent;
```

   Additional Information: TransactionEvents are arguments that are passed to beforeCommit(), afterCommit(), and beforeRollback(). Working with TransactionEvents directly is beyond the scope of this book. For the vast majority of applications, you just need to be aware that a TransactionEvent will be sent as an argument to these methods, and that you should pass it on to the superclass method.

3. Add the following method inside the EmployeesImpl class (for example, after the EmployeesImpl() constructor code block):

```
public void beforeCommit(TransactionEvent e)
{
  System.out.println(
    "About to commit changes to employee " +
    getEmployeeId()
  );
  super.beforeCommit(e);
}
```

   Additional Information: This code prints a message before trying to commit each row.

Note the call to `super.beforeCommit()`. This call is important to make sure the default framework behavior is executed as well.

4. Click Rebuild and Save All.

Report Before Rolling Back Each Changed Row
The code added in this section uses `EntityImpl.beforeRollback()` to perform operations on each entity instance before rolling back its data.

1. Add the following method to the EmployeesImpl class:

```
public void beforeRollback(TransactionEvent e)
{
  System.out.println(
    "Discarding changes to employee " +
    getEmployeeId()
  );
  super.beforeRollback(e);
}
```

2. Click Rebuild and Save All.

What Just Happened?   You added logic to the EmployeeImpl class that will print a message whenever a changed row is about to be committed or rolled back.

NOTE
Unlike all the other calls to `System.out.println()` you have added to the application, these calls happen in the BC4J layer instead of in the client. As long as you run this application in JDeveloper or in local mode, this difference will not matter, because the BC4J and the client application are running in the same process and so will output to the same console. However, if you deploy the BC4J as an EJB or web service (as demonstrated in Chapter 16), the messages from the BC4J layer will be printed to the server's console.

V. Test the Batch Client
This phase runs AccountantPromotionClient to test the `commit()` and `beforeCommit()` operations.

NOTE
The client you will run in this phase commits changes to the EMPLOYEES table in the HR sample schema. To restore the employee records, follow the procedure in the upcoming "What Just Happened?"

1. Navigate to the HR connection under Connections\Database. On the HR node, select SQL Worksheet from the right-click menu.

2. Enter the following SQL statement and click the Execute button. This will display job IDs that are affected by the promotion routine:

```
SELECT *
FROM EMPLOYEES
WHERE JOB_ID IN('FI_ACCOUNT', 'FI_MGR')
```

3. Select Run AccountantPromotionClient.java from AccountantPromotionClient.java's right-click menu.

4. Note the output in the Log window. The last few lines of the output should be similar to those shown here:

```
Attempting to commit changes.
About to commit changes to employee 109
About to commit changes to employee 110
About to commit changes to employee 111
About to commit changes to employee 112
About to commit changes to employee 113
Commit successful.
Process exited with exit code 0.
```

5. Run the same query you ran before in SQL Worksheet to verify that the employees with the 'FI_ACCOUNT' have all been promoted to the 'FI_MGR' job.

What Just Happened?   You tested the batch client and observed both that the information in `beforeCommit()` was printed to the Log window and that the changes were committed to the database. Since there were no problems with row inconsistency, this did not test the rollback code.

To restore the JOB_ID values in the EMPLOYEES table, run the following statement in the SQL Worksheet:

```
ALTER TRIGGER UPDATE_JOB_HISTORY DISABLE;
UPDATE EMPLOYEES
  SET JOB_ID = 'FI_ACCOUNT'
  WHERE EMPLOYEE_ID BETWEEN 109 AND 113;
ALTER TRIGGER UPDATE_JOB_HISTORY ENABLE;
```

The trigger is disabled to avoid an INSERT error. The trigger inserts a record into JOB_HISTORY for each UPDATE statement. The way that the trigger is written, multiple updates to the same EMPLOYEES record are not allowed unless the START_DATE changes. The examples in this practice do not change the START_DATE, so the trigger must be disabled when the employee JOB_ID values are restored.

VI. Modify the promoteAccountants() Method to Commit Data

This phase modifies the `promoteAccountants()` method so that SilentAccountantPromotionClient will also commit changes to the database.

CAUTION
After you modify the method, do not run
SilentAccountantPromotionClient. You will need to have the data
unchanged for Chapter 16's hands-on practice. If you do accidentally
run the client application, see the end of the Chapter 16 hands-on
practice for instructions on restoring the schema.

1. In the System Navigator, under the hrbc4j package and the AccountantPromotionModule node, double click AccountantPromotionModuleImpl.java to open it in the Source viewer.

2. Find the `promoteAccountants()` method.

3. Add the following code to the end of the method:

```
Transaction acctPromTrans = getTransaction();
try
{
  System.out.println("Attempting to commit changes.");
  acctPromTrans.commit();
  System.out.println("Commit successful.");
}
catch (RowInconsistentException e)
{
  System.out.println("Data conflict detected. Rolling back.");
  acctPromTrans.rollback();
}
```

What Just Happened?   You added the same logic to `promoteAccountants()` (in the BC4J layer) as you added to the client in Phase III.

Application Module Pooling

The caches maintained in a Transaction can be an expensive resource. When large numbers of clients connect to a BC4J layer simultaneously, maintaining all of this data in memory could tax the capabilities of the server machine on which BC4J is running, which could lead to performance or stability problems.

An *application module pool* is a resource manager that helps maintain scalability by determining which caches need to be maintained in memory, which can be temporarily swapped to the database (for more information, see the sidebar "Where the Swapped Caches are Stored"), and which can be discarded entirely. There is one application module pool for each application module type. For example, there is an application module pool for AccountantPromotionModule and another application module pool for CareerPathListerModule.

Using an application module pool properly will allow you to create a highly scalable application. Using it improperly may result in an application that degrades rapidly in performance or stability as the number of users increases.

Where the Swapped Caches Are Stored
By default, the application module pool swaps application modules to the database table PS_TXN. You can also swap to disk by passing a value of "file" for the property jbo.passivationstore to the Java virtual machine that runs your BC4J. You will learn more about passing properties to the Java virtual machine later in this chapter and in Chapter 16.

You can think of an application module pool as a collection of root-level application modules (of a particular type), each with its own Transaction and caches. When a client program is accessing an application module, that application module is said to be *checked out* of the pool. When the client program stops accessing the application module (even temporarily), the application module should be checked back into the pool.

You can check application modules back into the pool in three different *release modes:* Stateless, Reserved, and Stateful. *Stateless* release mode discards the application module state when you check it in, *Stateful* mode uses the database to help manage application module state, and *Reserved* mode forces the application module state to be retained by the pool.

Creating an Application Module Pool and a SessionCookie

There are two ways to create an application module pool. First, an application module pool is implicitly created for you the first time a client application calls `Configuration.createRootApplicationModule()`.

You can also create an application module pool explicitly. This has the advantage of giving you a handle on the application module pool, which you need if you are planning to use Stateful or Reserved release mode, as described later.

The first step in creating an application module pool explicitly is to obtain the singleton instance of the class oracle.jbo.common.ampool.PoolMgr. This class is available from both the client and BC4J layers. You can obtain the singleton instance by calling the static method `PoolMgr.getInstance()`, as shown here:

```
import oracle.jbo.common.ampool.*;
...
PoolMgr poolMgr = PoolMgr.getInstance();
```

After you have an instance of PoolMgr, you can use `PoolMgr.findPool()` to find the application module pool if another client has already created it or to create it if it does not exist. `findPool()` takes the following four arguments:

- **The name of the pool** Pools created implicitly (by `Configuration.createRootApplicationModule()`) use the package-qualified name of the application module, for example, "hrbc4j.AccountantPromotionModule."

- **The name of the package**   This is the BC4J package that contains the application module, for example, "hrbc4j."

- **The name of the configuration**   This is a name like the one you would pass to `Configuration.createRootApplicationModule()`, for example, "AccountantPromotionModuleLocal."

- **An object of type java.util.Properties**   For most purposes, you can pass in a value of null.

The following code would find or create an application module pool for AccountantPromotionModule:

```
ApplicationPool acctPromPool = poolMgr.findPool(
  "hrbc4j.AccountantPromotionModule",
  "hrbc4j",
  "AccountantPromotionModuleLocal",
  null);
```

To use an application module pool that you have created or found explicitly, you need to create a SessionCookie. SessionCookies are not to be confused with browser cookies— although the BC4J JSP client architecture uses browser cookies when it creates session cookies. *SessionCookies* are objects of type oracle.jbo.common.ampool.SessionCookie, which store uniquely identifying information about the client that creates them. You create a SessionCookie by calling `ApplicationPool.createSessionCookie()`, which takes the following three arguments:

- **An application module ID**   This is a string that identifies the application module instance that you want to retrieve. This is important if one client application needs two application module instances from the pool. The client would keep track of the application module instances by creating two separate SessionCookies, with different application module IDs. If one instance of the client will only use one instance of the application module, the value of this string is not important.

- **A session ID**   This is a string that uniquely identifies this client application. This can be any string you want, so long as you are sure that no two clients will use the same string. Good possibilities for this string are a timestamp taken when the client was instantiated, or, for web applications, the client's IP address.

- **An object of type java.lang.Properties**   For most purposes, this can be null.

The following code would create a SessionCookie, `acctPromCookie`, for access to acctPromPool:

```
String timeStamp = (new java.util.Date()).toString();
SessionCookie acctPromCookie = acctPromPool.createSessionCookie(
  "acctPromModule1",
  timeStamp,
  null
);
```

Checking Application Modules Into and Out of the Pool

While a client is actually working on data (reading it from the database or cache, or making changes), the cache needs to be maintained in memory. As explained before, an application module instance that a client application is currently working on is described as "checked out."

You should keep application modules checked out for as little time as possible. This will allow the application module pool to manage memory resources. For example, in a web application, you should check application modules back into the pool for the user's "think time."

You can check an application module out of the pool for the first time in two ways. The first is to call `Configuration.createRootApplicationModule()`, as you did in the Chapter 14 hands-on practice. You can also call `SessionCookie.useApplicationModule ()` as shown here:

```
ApplicationModule acctPromModule =
   acctPromCookie.useApplicationModule();
```

When a client application requests an application module for the first time, the application module pool tries to find an application module instance, already created but marked as available for use, for it to check out. If the pool finds an available instance, the instance is *recycled* (that is, its caches are cleared), it is checked out, and `createRootApplicationModule()` or `useApplicationModule()` returns it, as shown in Figure 15-1. Reusing application modules in this way has the two following advantages:

■ It reduces the total number of application module instances, saving memory.

■ It reduces creation of application module instances, saving processing overhead.

If the pool does not find an available instance, a new one is created, checked out, and returned to the client, as shown in Figure 15-2.

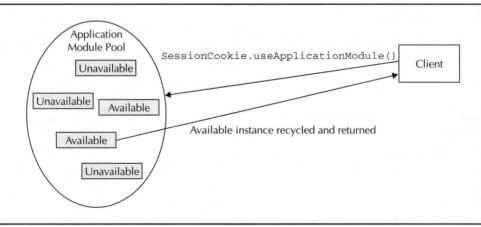

FIGURE 15-1. *useApplicationModule()* *finds an instance marked for recycling*

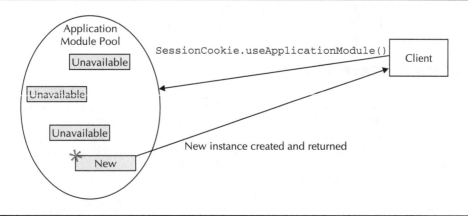

FIGURE 15-2. *useApplicationModule()* does not find an instance marked for recycling

By default, the pool starts out containing no application module instances, so the first few clients will always trigger the application module pool to create new application module instances, until some have been marked for recycling. If you want to avoid this overhead, you can start the application module pool with a certain number of application modules in it by passing a value for the property jbo.ampool.initpoolsize to the Java virtual machine that runs your BC4J. For testing your BC4J in JDeveloper, you can set this value in the Runner page of the Project Settings dialog for your client application, by adding a value to the *Java Options* field for passing "-Djbo.ampool.initpoolsize" as a Java option, as shown here:

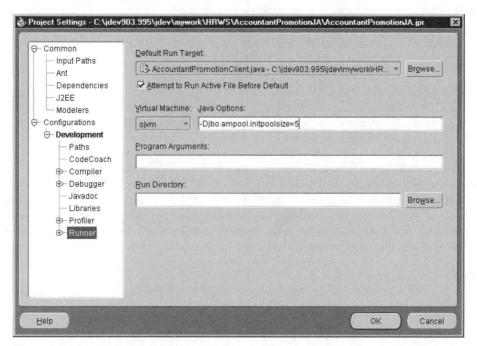

Chapter 16 will explain how to set this property in deployed projects using Configurations.

As soon as your client application stops working on an application module, you should check it back into the pool, using Stateless, Reserved, or Stateful release mode.

Stateless Release Mode

When you check in an application module instance in Stateless release mode, the instance is immediately marked as available for recycling. The next time a client tries to create a new application module instance, the pool will instead recycle and return this instance.

You should release an application module in Stateless mode when you are really finished with it, for example, right before the client application terminates. Once an application module is released in Stateless mode, its cache cannot be retrieved.

If you are not working with the application module pool explicitly, you can only check in application modules in Stateless mode. You can do this by using the static method `Configuration.releaseRootApplicationModule()`. Pass the application module and the value `false` into the method, as shown here:

```
Configuration.releaseRootApplicationModule(acctPromModule, false);
```

Passing in a value of `true` actually destroys the application module instance instead of checking it into the pool.

If you are working with the application module pool explicitly, you can check an application module into the pool in Stateless mode by calling `SessionCookie.releaseApplicationModule()`. This method takes two arguments. For Stateless release mode, you should pass `true` as the first argument, and `false` as the second. The next time you call `SessionCookie.useApplicationModule()`, the method will return a new or freshly recycled instance, as shown in Figure 15-1 and Figure 15-2. For example, the following code releases an application module instance in Stateless mode and then accesses a new application module instance:

```
acctPromCookie.releaseApplicationModule(true, false);
acctPromModule = acctPromCookie.useApplicationModule();
```

Reserved Release Mode

When you check in an application module instance in Reserved release mode, the instance will never be marked as available for recycling. This will reduce your application's scalability, because using Reserved release mode in all your clients will rapidly lead to a very large application module pool. However, you may want to use Reserved release mode if you need to be absolutely sure that your application module will be available immediately when you request it again.

You can check an application module into the pool in Reserved mode by calling `SessionCookie.releaseApplicationModule()` with `false` as both arguments. The next time you call `SessionCookie.useApplicationModule()`, it will return the same application module instance. For example, the following code releases an application module instance in Reserved mode and then checks it out again:

```
acctPromCookie.releaseApplicationModule(false, false);
acctPromModule = acctPromCookie.useApplicationModule();
```

Stateful Release Mode

For most purposes, Stateful mode is preferable to Reserved mode. It allows you to maintain your caches and transaction state, even for many clients, while keeping the application module pool to a reasonable size.

When you first release an application module in Stateful mode, it is not marked as available for recycling. The application module pool holds on to it until the pool grows to a certain number of application module instances, called the *recycle threshold,* as shown in Figure 15-3. Before this point, the application module is treated as if it were in Reserved mode. That is, the client that released it can immediately retrieve it by requesting it again.

The recycle threshold defaults to 10, but you can change it by passing a value for jbo.recyclethreshold to the Java virtual machine that runs your BC4J. As with jbo.ampool.initpoolsize, you can set jbo.recyclethreshold in the *Java Options* field of the Project Settings dialog for testing inside JDeveloper. For example, in the following illustration, both the pool's initial size and the recycle threshold are being changed:

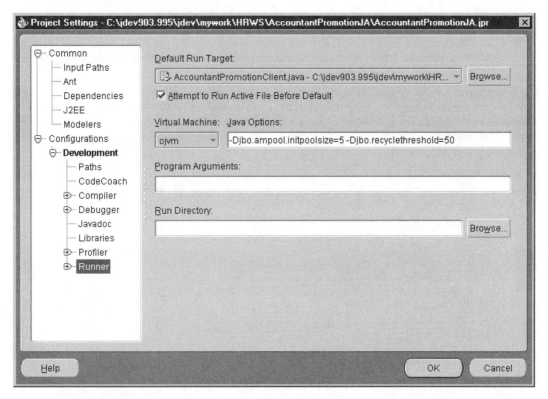

Chapter 16 explains how to use Configurations to set the recycle threshold, like all the properties mentioned in this chapter, for deployed business components.

Once the recycle threshold is reached, the pool starts recycling Stateful application modules, starting with the one that has been released the longest. Before a Stateful application module's cache is emptied, a redo log of the transaction's changes, along with a primary key based on the

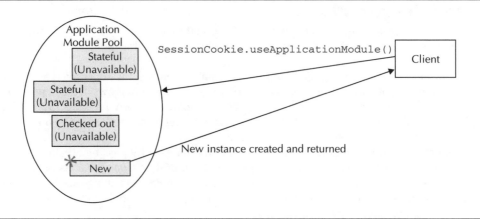

FIGURE 15-3. *Stateful release mode, before the recycle threshold is reached*

SessionCookie, is saved (for details, see the sidebar "Where the Swapped Caches Are Stored" earlier in this chapter), as shown in Figure 15-4.

When the client that released the application module requests it back, the pool finds the record in the database corresponding to the session ID, creates a new application module (or recycles an available one), repopulates it from the database record, and delivers the application module to the client, as shown in Figure 15-5. From the client's perspective, it is as if it had gotten the old application module back.

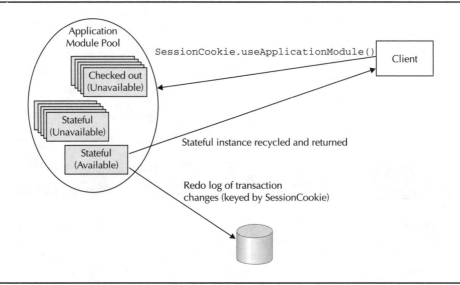

FIGURE 15-4. *A Stateful application module is recycled*

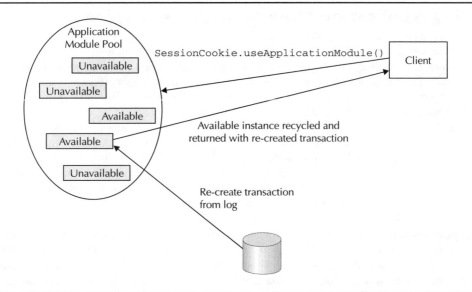

FIGURE 15-5. *A client requests a Stateful application module that has been recycled*

Setting your recycle threshold properly is necessary for the best possible performance and scalability. On the one hand, the recycle threshold should be low enough that the server is never in danger of running out of memory and having to continuously swap to disk. On the other, because writing an application module's state to the database and retrieving the state into a new application module is time-consuming, the recycle threshold should be high enough that Stateful application modules are rarely recycled. Generally, you should set your recycle threshold as high as is safe for your server without extensive use of virtual memory. Start with a fairly low number (such as 10), and monitor your memory consumption, raising the threshold when possible.

TIP
"10" is an extremely low value for the recycle threshold. It is a safe number to start testing with, but most applications will be optimized at a substantially higher number.

You can check an application module into the pool in Stateful mode by calling `SessionCookie.releaseApplicationModule()` with `true` as both values. The next time you call `SessionCookie.useApplicationModule()`, you will request the instance back, and the method will return the same instance (if it has not been recycled yet) or an instance re-created from the database table. For example, the following code releases an application module in Stateful mode and then retrieves either the same application module or a duplicate:

```
acctPromCookie.releaseApplicationModule(true, true);
acctPromModule = acctPromCookie.useApplicationModule();
```

Letting Application Module Instances Expire

Suppose that your application module pool briefly experiences a flurry of activity. Many application module instances are created, far beyond the number that are usually in use.

If this number exceeds the recycle threshold, or the application modules are released in Stateless mode, the instances will gradually be recycled as more clients request them. However, the pool still might be much bigger than necessary. It may be very unlikely that all the instances will simultaneously be needed at any time in the near future.

To save memory, you can allow surplus application module instances to expire. By setting the following properties (all of which can be set in the same ways as jbo.ampool.initpoolsize or jbo.recyclethreshold, in the Project Settings dialog or by using Configurations), you can determine how the application module pool discards old instances. Figuring out the best values for these properties requires experimentation. Start with the defaults and observe when and how often your application uses large amounts of processing time or memory.

jbo.ampool.minavailablesize   As explained earlier, creating application module instances requires processing overhead. For this reason, you should, whenever possible, have a few instances in the pool that are available for recycling. The pool will never allow all of the available instances to expire, no matter how old they get. The jbo.ampool.minavailablesize property defines this minimum number of available instances to keep indefinitely. The default value for this property is "5," meaning that the pool will keep five available instances before looking for ones to discard.

jbo.ampool.maxinactiveage   If there are more available instances on hand than jbo.ampool.minavailablesize specifies, the pool will start looking for old instances to discard. An "old" instance is one that has not been checked out for an amount of time specified (in milliseconds) by jbo.ampool.maxinactiveage. The default value for this property is "600000," meaning that the pool will let an instance remain inactive for ten minutes before considering it old.

jbo.ampool.maxavailablesize   Sometimes the number of available instances gets so large that it can become a danger to memory stability or can threaten to require extensive disk swapping. In this case, the pool should remove available instances immediately, without waiting for them to get old. The jbo.ampool.maxavailablesize specifies the threshold for this, that is, the maximum number of available instances to allow before removing instances that are not yet old. The default value for this property is "25," meaning that the pool will immediately start discarding available instances if the number grows above 25.

Connection Pooling

Just as multiple clients can share application module instances in an application module pool, multiple application module instances can share database connections in a connection pool.

For example, suppose you have an application module pool containing many instances of AccountantPromotionModule. Those instances all need to connect to the database using the information stored in the HR connection.

Since all your application modules need connections with exactly the same information, they can share a limited number of connections. When an application module is created, it can request a connection from the connection pool instead of opening a new database connection. When an application module times out or is recycled, its connection is not destroyed, but rather is checked back into the pool for another application module to use.

Although some technologies use the term "connection pooling" to refer to sharing connections among client programs, in BC4J, the term "connection pooling" refers exclusively to sharing connections among application modules. If you use application module pooling, you will automatically share connections among client programs, even if you do not use connection pooling. Because of this, the overhead of maintaining a connection pool usually outweighs the advantages of connection pooling. For this reason, BC4J does not use connection pooling by default. You can enable connection pooling by passing the value "true" for the property jbo.doconnection pooling. This property is set the same way as the previously mentioned properties (in the Project Settings dialog or by using Configurations).

Just like the application module pool, by default, the connection pool initially contains no instances, so the first few application modules will always need to create new connections until some have been returned for reuse. If you want to avoid this overhead, you can start the connection pool with a certain number of connections in it by passing a value for the property jbo.initpoolsize (not to be confused with jbo.ampool.initpoolsize, which determines the initial size of the application module pool) to the Java virtual machine that runs your BC4J. This property is also set the same way as the previously mentioned properties (in the Project Settings dialog or by using Configurations).

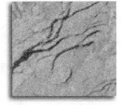

CHAPTER
16

Deploying Business
Components

Fly, my pretties! Fly! Fly!

—Noel Langley, Florence Ryerson, and Edgar Allan Wolfe,
The Wizard of Oz (screenplay)

 hapters 9 through 15 discussed BC4J almost exclusively within the context of the JDeveloper environment. In those chapters, you accessed application modules through the Business Component Browser and through clients running inside JDeveloper, but did not examine how a BC4J layer and its client can run and communicate in a production environment. This chapter explains the various configurations in which you can deploy BC4J applications and how to deploy in those configurations.

Before you start this chapter, remember the following facts from Chapter 7 about deployment and Java 2 Platform, Enterprise Edition (J2EE):

- J2EE is a set of standards provided by Sun for organizing enterprise-level applications.

- J2EE applications are divided into one or more of four tiers: the Client Tier, the Web Tier, the Business Tier, and the EIS (Enterprise Information System) Tier.

- The *Client Tier* contains Java applications and applets that run on the end user's machine.

- The *Web Tier* contains user interface code and processes that run on a server, such as JSP pages.

- The *Business Tier* enforces business rules. In JDeveloper, BC4J is the easiest way to create a Business Tier, and it is the one this book will cover.

- The *EIS Tier* handles persistent data storage.

- The four tiers are purely logical divisions—they need not run on separate machines.

- Java clients reside in the Client Tier and provide a rich user interface, especially appropriate for intranet or small-department solutions.

- JSP clients reside in the Web Tier and provide a lightweight user interface, especially appropriate for e-commerce and self-service applications to be delivered over the Web.

In this chapter, you will see how the logical tiers explained in Chapter 7 can be mapped to physical and software processes. In the hands-on practice, you will deploy the BC4J applications you created in Chapters 10 through 15 in three different configurations.

J2EE Containers

As explained in Chapter 7, a deployed BC4J application will usually make at least some use of an Application Server that is J2EE compliant. A J2EE-compliant Application Server is one that includes two separate *containers,* or services, for Java applications: the web container and the EJB container.

The *web container* executes code in the Web Tier: JSP pages and servlets, and any component classes they need to help generate a UI. However, as explained later in this chapter, the web container can also be used to execute the Business Tier.

When the *EJB container* is used, it executes code in the Business Tier. The components that run in the EJB container are *Enterprise JavaBeans (EJBs)*, which are Java components that multiple applications can access remotely. An EJB has an interface, called its *remote* interface, which exposes some of its methods. The servlets and JSPs in the web container (and any other application written in Java with access to the network) can find EJBs through a lookup service, the Java Naming Directory Interface (JNDI), and call the methods on the remote interface through a protocol, Remote Method Invocation (RMI).

JDeveloper provides completely automated deployment to two J2EE-compliant Application Servers: BEA's WebLogic server and Oracle9i Application Server (Oracle9iAS), as well as the standalone OC4J that comes with JDeveloper. JDeveloper also provides partial automation for deployment to the open-source JBoss Application Server. You can deploy applications from JDeveloper into any other J2EE-compliant Application Server, but you will have to do a fair amount of manual work to configure any server but WebLogic, Oracle9iAS, and JBoss.

Deployment Configurations for Java Clients

As you saw in Chapter 7, you can deploy BC4J with a Java client, that is, a UI that runs in a JVM on a user's machine. BC4J applications with Java clients have three J2EE tiers: The Client Tier (containing the application or applet), the Business Tier (containing the BC4J), and the EIS Tier (the database).

There are two ways to map the Java client architecture to a physical implementation. In *local mode*, the Client Tier and Business Tier run in the same JVM on the user's machine. In *remote mode*, the Client Tier runs on the user's machine, and the Business Tier resides in the EJB container of an Application Server.

Java Clients in Local Mode

Local mode deployment is shown in Figure 16-1. This mode is the most like the "thick client" configuration used by client-server programmers.

With a Java client in local mode, the only use of the network (other than downloading the application) is to communicate with the database over JDBC.

You deployed a BC4J application with a Java client in local mode in one of the hands-on practices for Chapter 7. In that practice the Java client was built with the JClient architecture, which automates a large part of the pre-deployment process. In this chapter's hands-on practice, you will deploy the career path lister application in local mode. Because you wrote the career path lister client by hand, you will get a closer look at the pre-deployment process.

Java Clients in Remote Mode

A BC4J application with a Java client in remote mode is shown in Figure 16-2. In this mode, the Client Tier runs in a JVM on the user's machine, but the Business Tier runs in an Application Server's EJB container, with the application module deployed as an EJB that implements Sun's "session facade" design pattern.

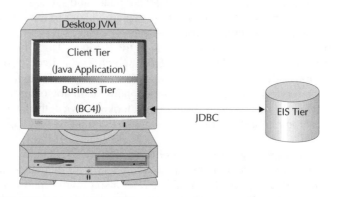

FIGURE 16-1. *A BC4J application with a Java client in local mode*

With a Java client in remote mode, the network is used in two ways: the client communicates with the BC4J layer using JNDI and RMI, and the BC4J layer communicates with the database over the JDBC protocol.

You will deploy a BC4J application with a Java client in remote mode in the hands-on practice at the end of this chapter.

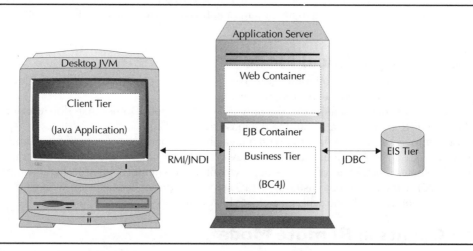

FIGURE 16-2. *A BC4J application with a Java client in remote mode*

Java Clients: Local Mode vs. Remote Mode

As mentioned in Chapter 7, Java clients provide a rich and responsive user interface, but at the cost of requiring application code to be installed and run on many individual machines. Once you have decided to use the Java client style, you can use the following considerations to decide whether to deploy it in local or remote mode.

Advantages and Disadvantages of Local Mode for Java Clients

Local mode is much faster than remote mode because the only network activity in local mode is JDBC. However, local mode deployment best highlights the main disadvantage of Java clients. The entire application (both Client and Business Tier) must be deployed to many separate machines. In addition, local mode places a large memory and processing load on client machines, which need to execute both the Client Tier that generates a user interface and the Business Tier that enforces business rules and caches data.

Advantages and Disadvantages of Remote Mode for Java Clients

Remote mode can, to a certain extent, mitigate the main disadvantage of Java clients. While the Client Tier must be deployed to many separate machines, the Business Tier can stay on a centralized server. This does not usually reduce the size of code deployed on client machines, because the libraries that allow clients to use RMI and JNDI are often as large as the Business Tier. But so long as the Business Tier's deployment configuration–independent interfaces are kept constant, remote mode allows you to change the business logic without needing to redeploy to client machines. In addition, remote mode places a much smaller memory and processing load on client machines than does local mode, because client machines do not have to enforce business rules or cache data.

However, remote mode is substantially slower than local mode, because RMI can have considerable overhead. Remote mode is best used only when the disadvantages of local mode are especially serious considerations; that is, when the client machines you plan to deploy to would be placed under strain if they had to execute your BC4J code or when you anticipate changing your Business Tier much more frequently than you change your Client Tier.

Deployment Configurations for JSP Clients

As you saw in Chapter 7, you can also deploy BC4J with a JSP client, that is, with a client providing a UI that runs on an Application Server. BC4J applications with Java clients make use of four J2EE tiers: The Client Tier (which does nothing but render HTML and possibly execute JavaScript), the Web Tier (containing the application or applet), the Business Tier (containing the BC4J code), and the EIS Tier (the database).

There are two ways to map the JSP architecture to a physical implementation. In *web module mode,* the Web Tier and Business Tier both run in the web container of an Application Server. In *remote mode,* the Web Tier runs in the web container, and the Business Tier resides in the EJB container.

JSP Clients in Web Module Mode

Web module mode deployment is shown in Figure 16-3.

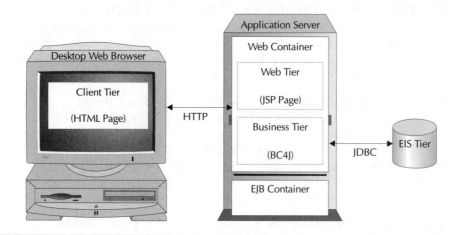

FIGURE 16-3. *A BC4J application with a JSP client in web module mode*

With a JSP client in web module mode, there are two uses of the network: HTTP communication between the user and the web container, and JDBC connection between the web container and the database.

You deployed a JSP client in web module mode in one of the hands-on practices in Chapter 7.

JSP Clients in Remote Mode

A JSP client running in remote mode is shown in Figure 16-4. In remote mode, the Web Tier runs in the web container, and the Business Tier runs in the EJB container with the application module deployed as a session facade.

Generally, a JSP client in remote mode uses the network for two purposes: HTTP communication between the user and the J2EE container, and JDBC connection between the J2EE container and the database. However, it must also use the RMI protocol, although (assuming the web and EJB containers are in the same Application Server) the protocol is only used to communicate between two processes in the same machine, as shown in Figure 16-4.

Deploying JSP clients in remote mode is rare. This book will not show an example of a JSP client deployed in remote mode, although the basic procedure is very similar to that for a Java client in remote mode.

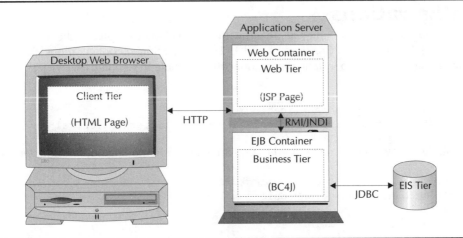

FIGURE 16-4. *A BC4J application with a JSP client in remote mode*

JSP Clients: Web Module Mode vs. Remote Mode

Chapter 7 explained that JSP clients are compact and require no processing on the client machine except that needed to render HTML (and possibly execute JavaScript). They are readable from any web browser, but at the cost of a less interactive user interface than Java clients provide. Once you have decided to use the JSP client style, you can consider the following pros and cons in order to decide whether to deploy the JSP client in web module mode or remote mode.

Advantages and Disadvantages of Web Module Mode for JSP Clients

For the vast majority of applications, web module mode is preferable to remote mode for JSPs. Web module mode is much faster than remote mode, because it avoids RMI and JNDI overhead. It has no disadvantages, unless you have a specific need to use EJBs, as described next.

Advantages and Disadvantages of Remote Mode for JSP Clients

The only reason to deploy a JSP client in remote mode is to use the EJB architecture by having your application module deployed as a session facade. You may need to use EJB security features or have an organization-wide requirement to use the EJB architecture. If you are not required to use EJBs, remote mode has no advantages for JSP clients. Since remote mode is much slower than web module mode, deploying JSP clients in remote mode is not recommended for most users.

Configurations

A *configuration* is a set of properties deployed with a BC4J client that tell the client how to access and configure the BC4J layer. Chapters 14 and 15 briefly mentioned configurations. Recall the following command, used to instantiate an application module in Chapter 14:

```
ApplicationModule careerModule =
    Configuration.createRootApplicationModule(
      "hrbc4j.CareerPathListerModule", "CareerPathListerModuleLocal");
```

Also recall the following command, used to find an application module pool in Chapter 15:

```
ApplicationPool acctPromPool = poolMgr.findPool(
    "hrbc4j.AccountantPromotionModule",
    "hrbc4j",
    "AccountantPromotionModuleLocal",
    null);
```

As was mentioned in Chapters 14 and 15, the strings "CareerPathListerModuleLocal" and "AccountantPromotionModuleLocal" are the names of configurations.

The configuration named after the application module, with a "Local" suffix, is a configuration automatically created by JDeveloper when you first create an application module. When a client tries to create an application module with this configuration, it assumes the application module is deployed in local or web module mode. The client also uses the default values for the BC4J runtime properties, such as those described in Chapter 15 that control pooling functionality (for example, jbo.recyclethreshold).

Creating and Editing Configurations

As was just mentioned, the default "Local" configuration is created automatically as soon as you create an application module. Similar default configurations for remote deployment are created as soon as you create a profile to deploy to an EJB container. For example, when you create a profile to deploy CareerPathListerModule to the EJB container for OC4J, JDeveloper will create both a configuration called "CareerPathListerModuleBM9iAS," for use with OC4J in external mode, and one called "CareerPathListerModuleBM9iASEmbedded," for use with OC4J in embedded mode. These default configurations, like the default "Local" configuration, will use default values for the BC4J runtime properties, although they will tell the client to look for (and where to look for) the remotely deployed BC4J layer.

If you do not want to use these default runtime properties, you can edit one of the configurations JDeveloper creates. In addition, you may want to create a new configuration if, for example, you want multiple configurations (specifying different runtime properties) for the same deployed BC4J layer.

The Configuration Manager

You can edit or create configurations by choosing Configurations from an application module's right-click menu. This opens the Configuration Manager, where you can choose either to edit an existing configuration or to create a new configuration, as shown here:

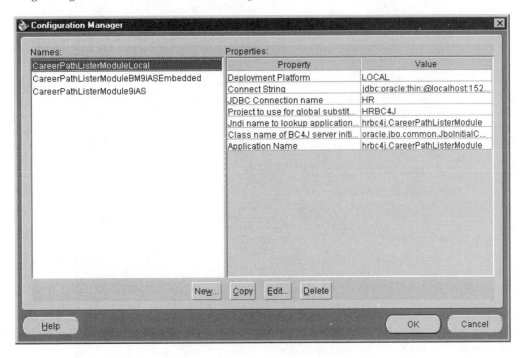

Clicking Copy makes a copy of the selected configuration, with the same platform, for you to edit. This is generally easier than creating a new configuration from scratch.

After you click Edit, the Business Component Configuration editor opens. This editor has three tabs: Application Module, Pooling and Scalability, and Properties. Generally, you will not need to edit the information on the Application Module tab or the Properties tab, but you can use the Pooling and Scalability tab to set the BC4J runtime properties introduced in Chapter 15, as shown here:

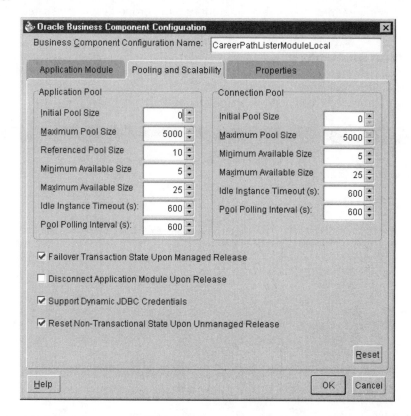

The *Referenced Pool Size* field sets the recycle threshold, and the *Idle Instance Timeout* field sets the maximum inactive age. All the other fields on the Application Pool side set the properties of the same name, as described in Chapter 15.

Using a Configuration to Instantiate an Application Module

Once you have a configuration, you can use it to instantiate an application module directly or to find an application module pool. This has already been shown using the default "Local" configuration (in Chapters 14 and 15, and in the introduction to the "Configurations" section in this chapter).

You can use exactly the same technique to instantiate application modules and pools in other configurations. Simply use the appropriate configuration name, as in the following code:

```
/* Instantiate an application module that you have
 * deployed to OC4J as a session facade */
ApplicationModule careerModule =
  Configuration.createRootApplicationModule(
    "hrbc4j.CareerPathListerModule",
    "CareerPathListerModule9iAS");

/* Find a pool of instances of an application module
 * that you have deployed to OC4J as a session facade. */
ApplicationPool acctPromPool = poolMgr.findPool(
  "hrbc4j.AccountantPromotionModule",
  "hrbc4j",
  "AccountantPromotionModule9iAS",
  null);
```

Changing the name of the configuration like this is all you have to do to switch deployment modes. To create a client that needs no code changes at all, see the sidebar, "Switching Deployment Modes Without Changing Code."

Switching Deployment Modes Without Changing Code

If you want to make your code completely deployment independent, you can parameterize which configuration to use. For example, in AccountantPromotionClient.java, you could use the following code to instantiate the application module:

```
String mode = args[0];
String config;

if (mode = "Local" || mode = "WebModule") {
  config = "AccountantPromotionModuleLocal";
}
if (mode = "Remote") {
  config = "AccountantPromotionModule9iAS";
}
ApplicationModule acctPromMod =
  Configuration.createRootApplicationModule(
    "hrbc4j.AccountantPromotionModule", config);
```

This will allow you to specify the mode as a command-line argument to the client.

The BC4J Client-Side Architecture

In Chapter 14, you learned that the BC4J framework makes use of a set of deployment configuration–independent interfaces, such as ApplicationModule, ViewObject, and Row, in the oracle.jbo package. In addition, you saw that you can create custom interfaces for application modules, view objects, and view rows that expose accessors and custom methods. These interfaces can be accessed with simple Java calls because they are always present in the same JVM or container as the client, even in remote mode, as discussed in Chapter 14.

For the BC4J framework to handle network communication automatically, allowing you to write regular method calls and ignore the complexities of JNDI and RMI, it needs to have some BC4J classes and interfaces in the same tier as the client. In local mode, of course, this is the complete set of BC4J classes, including the oracle.jbo.server classes and your custom classes, as well as the deployment configuration–independent interfaces and a few other classes, such as oracle.jbo.client.Configuration, the domains in oracle.jbo.domain, and the application module pooling classes in oracle.jbo.common.ampool.

In remote mode, you still need the deployment configuration–independent interfaces (and the configuration, domain, pooling, and other utility classes). You do not need the oracle.jbo.server classes or your custom implementation classes, but you do need lightweight, client-side classes that handle network communication—both framework classes such as oracle.jbo.client.remote.ejb.ApplicationModuleImpl and classes that JDeveloper creates for your custom interfaces when you deploy in remote mode, such as hrbc4j.client.remote.ejb.DepartmentsViewRowImpl, as discussed in Chapter 14.

The reason remote mode involves a much smaller load on the client machine is that these lightweight classes are much less computationally intensive than the full, server-side implementation classes.

When you use JDeveloper to deploy a client that uses BC4J JSP or JClient technologies, JDeveloper will automatically ensure that the right classes are deployed with your client. When you create a client by hand, you will have to add these classes to the client libraries yourself. You will do that in the hands-on practice in this chapter.

Service Session Facades

Using the BC4J client-side architecture makes developing EJB applications much easier, because it handles network communication for you. However, some experienced EJB programmers may not wish to use the client-side architecture for one of the following reasons:

- They are comfortable with EJB programming and prefer to have direct control over RMI communication.

- Client overhead is extremely important to them. Although the BC4J client-side architecture is lightweight, they may want to eliminate it from their client entirely.

- They want complete control over what their clients can do. They may not, for example, want their clients to be able to call methods like getAttribute(), setAttribute(), or next(), but only to call custom methods that they design to be exposed.

If you are willing to give up the conveniences offered by the BC4J client-side architecture, you can deploy BC4J as a service session facade. A *service session facade* is a generic EJB that exposes particular methods on its remote interface and delegates those methods to an application module as shown in Figure 16-5.

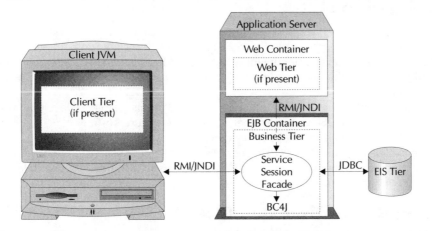

FIGURE 16-5. *Clients communicating with a service session facade*

You cannot access a service session facade using a
`Configuration.createRootApplicationModule()` or
`SessionCookie.useApplicationModule()`, because both Configuration and
SessionCookie are part of the BC4J client-side architecture. You have to access it the
way you would any generic EJB, by creating a hash table containing the EJB environment
variables, setting up an initial context from that hash table, looking up an EJB home in the
initial context, and using a `create()` method to create an instance of the EJB. You can
access any methods you exported from your application module, because JDeveloper
automatically adds them to the EJB's remote interface.

> **NOTE**
> *If the preceding procedure makes no sense to you, do not worry. The
> service session facade deployment option is provided for experienced
> EJB programmers. You can get the same functionality (plus a bit more,
> as explained later) by using the BC4J client-side architecture.*

For similar reasons, you cannot use JDeveloper's client technologies, such as JClient, BC4J
JSP, or the Business Component Browser, with service session facades. These technologies rely
on the BC4J client-side architecture.

Using a service session facade has another limitation, although for certain purposes it may be
an advantage, because of the extra degree of control it affords. Clients cannot use service session
facades to get direct access to view objects or view rows. All a client can do with a retrieved service
session facade is call exported methods on an application module. Because of this, service session
facades are not appropriate for clients that need a high level of interactivity. They are intended
for clients that need to send a small number of requests to the BC4J layer, which will process
those requests and return the results.

The hands-on practice in this chapter contains a hint about how you could deploy a BC4J
layer as a service session facade.

Web Services

A *web service* is a business service (such as an exported application module-level service method) available via the *Simple Object Access Protocol* (SOAP), a lightweight protocol based on HTTP. Web services are published via a document written in the *Web Services Description Language* (WSDL), which describes the available methods and their parameters. Any client with access to the Web can call a web service by using SOAP.

In addition to the other deployment modes mentioned in this chapter, JDeveloper can deploy BC4J as a web service to a J2EE web container, as shown in Figure 16-6.

To publish BC4J as a web service, you have two choices: you can require clients to locate and parse the WSDL, or you can have JDeveloper generate a client-side stub that will allow clients to call methods on the web service as if they were local Java code. You will deploy BC4J as a web service in the hands-on practice.

Advantages and Disadvantages of Deploying BC4J as a Web Service

Deploying BC4J as a web service has many advantages for a specific kind of application. It is the way to maintain the highest degree of openness about clients, since any sort of client can access a web service:

- A Java client

- A JSP

- Another web service

- A non-Java application that can understand SOAP and WSDL or that can pass a call to a client-side Java stub

Like Java clients in remote mode, the Business Tier can be updated at any time by redeploying to the Application Server, although changing the API may break client code. SOAP, like HTTP, is

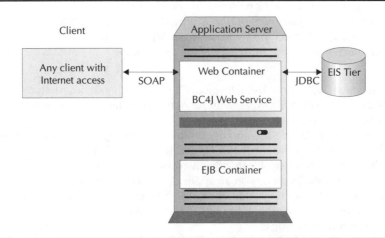

FIGURE 16-6. *BC4J deployed as a web service*

a lightweight protocol, so overhead is almost as low as it would be for a JSP client in local mode. As with service session facades, web services do not need to use any BC4J-specific client-side architecture.

However, deploying BC4J as a web service is simply inappropriate for many applications. Although SOAP is lightweight, using it does involve use of the network, so web service clients are generally not as fast as Java clients in local mode. Most importantly, as with service session facades, web services do not provide fine-grained access to the BC4J layer. Clients will only be able to call exported application module-level service methods. Finally, you cannot use JDeveloper client technologies such as JClient or BC4J JSP to access BC4J deployed as web services.

In general, deploying a BC4J layer as a web service is ideal when the developer has no idea what sorts of clients may access them and wants to provide a specific set of methods on the Web. The most common cases of this are genuine "business services," methods that a company (such as a company that provides stock information) wants to make accessible to subscribers (such as companies that display stock information to end users) for use in their own programs.

Hands-on Practice: Deploy a BC4J Application

In this practice, you deploy the CareerPathLister application and its BC4J layer in local mode and in remote mode. Then you publish AccountantPromotionModule as a web service and access it through SilentAccountantPromotionClient.

This practice builds on the results of the hands-on practices in Chapter 14 and, for the web services phase, Chapter 15. If you have not completed those practices, you can download the starting files for this practice from the authors' websites mentioned in the author information at the beginning of this book.

I. Deploy CareerPathLister and its BC4J layer in local mode

- Deploy CareerPathLister to the file system

- Run CareerPathLister in local mode

II. Deploy CareerPathListerModule as a session facade

- Deploy the BC4J Layer to OC4J

- Test CareerPathListerModule in remote mode

III. Deploy CareerPathLister in remote mode

- Modify CareerPathLister to use a remote configuration

- Deploy CareerPathLister to the file system

- Run CareerPathLister in remote mode

IV. Create and use a web service

- Publish AccountantPromotionModule as a web service

- Create client-side Java stubs

- Create a client that invokes the web service

- Deploy the client to the file system and run it

I. Deploy CareerPathLister and Its BC4J Layer in Local Mode

In this phase, you will deploy the CareerPathLister application in local mode and run it from the command line.

Deploy CareerPathLister to the File System

This section deploys CareerPathLister as a JAR in local mode.

1. Open the HRWS workspace.

2. On CareerPathListerJA.jpr, select New from the right-click menu.

3. Select JAR file – Simple Archive from the General\Deployment Profiles category and click OK.

4. In the Save Deployment Profile dialog, enter "CareerPathListerLocal.deploy" in the *File Name* field and click Save. The JAR Deployment Profile Settings dialog will open.

   Additional Information: This is not the name of the JAR you will deploy to. It is the name of the *deployment profile,* a file that will store your deployment information.

5. Select the JAR Options node in the tree.

6. Click the Browse button by the *JAR file* field.

7. Create an empty folder (using the Create new subdirectory button), for example, "C:\deployments\CareerPathListerLocal."

TIP
The deployment process will create directories. For example, you can enter the file name "C:\deployments\CareerPathListerLocal\ CareerPathListerLocal.jar" in the "JAR file" field. If the directory does not yet exist, it will be created when the deployment process creates the JAR file.

8. In the *File Name* field, enter "CareerPathListerLocal.jar," and click Open to return to the Deployment Profile Settings dialog.

9. Select the Dependency Analyzer node in the tree.

10. Select each of the top-level nodes in the *Which libraries are involved in dependency analysis?* pane as shown here:

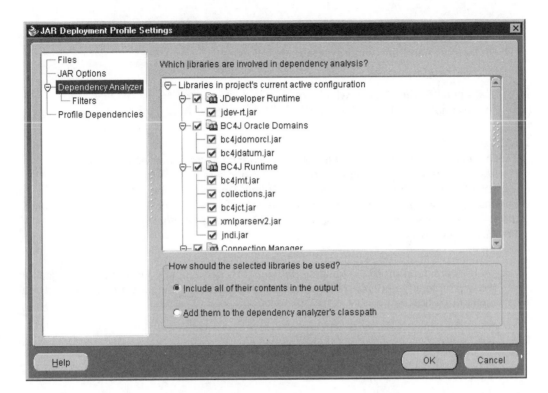

The children will automatically be selected.

11. Click OK to close the dialog, and create the "CareerPathListerLocal.deploy" file in the CareerPathListerJA.jpr project.

12. On the CareerPathListerLocal.deploy node, select Deploy To JAR File from the right-click menu.

13. Monitor the progress of the deployment in the Log window. You will see a message indicating when deployment to the JAR file is complete.

Run CareerPathLister in Local Mode
This section runs CareerPathLister in local mode from the command prompt.

NOTE
These directions are for a Windows 2000 operating system. If you are using another operating system, use the appropriate technique to set the system path and run a command-line program.

1. In the Start menu, select Run and enter "CMD".

2. In the command-line window, enter the following:

   ```
   PATH=JDEV_HOME\jdk\bin
   ```

   Substitute the directory in which you installed JDeveloper
   (for example, "C:\JDev9i" for "JDEV_HOME").

NOTE
*This method sets the environment for only this command-line session.
If you need to repeat this command in more than one session, create
a batch (.bat) file with the PATH command. When you start the new
command-line window, enter the name of the batch file to modify
the PATH for that session. This preserves the PATH setting for other
Windows sessions.*

3. At the command prompt, change to the directory containing your deployed application.
   For example, if you deployed the application to C:\deployments\CareerPathListerLocal,
   enter the following:

   ```
   C:
   cd \deployments\CareerPathListerLocal
   ```

4. Enter the dir command to ensure your file was successfully deployed as
   CareerPathListerLocal.jar.

5. Check to be sure that java.exe is available using the following:

   ```
   java -version
   ```

   Additional Information: This will display the version of Java if the PATH is set correctly.

6. Enter the following on one line:

   ```
   java -cp CareerPathListerLocal.jar
     careerpathlisterja.CareerPathLister IT_PROG
   ```

   Additional Information: The "–cp" option tells the JVM to include all classes in the JAR
   file in the classpath. "careerpathlisterja.CareerPathLister" is the package-qualified name
   of the class that needs to be executed.

   CareerPathLister will print its output directly to the console. The output should be
   something like this:

   ```
   Found job IT_PROG: Programmer
   The following employees currently have the job title Programmer:
   Hunold, who makes about $108000 and has 3 direct reports.
   Ernst, who makes about $72000 and has 0 direct reports.
   Austion, who makes about $57600 and has 0 direct reports.
   ...
   The following employees previously had the title of Programmer:
   De Haan, who makes about $204000 as a(n) Administration Vice President.
   ```

If you were using libraries already deployed with another application, you would add that application's JAR file to the classpath. For example, if you deployed AccountantPromotionClient.jar, intending to use CareerPathListerLocal.jar's libraries, you would enter the following on one line:

```
java -cp "CareerPathListerLocal.jar;AccountantPromotionClient.jar"
    accountantpromotionclientja.AccountantPromotionClient
```

What Just Happened?   You created a deployment profile to deploy the client, the BC4J, and the libraries needed to run BC4J applications in local mode. Then you deployed the application to the file system as a JAR file and ran it in local mode from the command line. This is the method you would use to create a standalone JAR file that you could run on any machine that has the Java runtime installed.

You may have noticed that the deployment JAR file is rather large (over 10MB) for a very small executable class file. The reason for the size is that this JAR file includes all the supporting libraries. Normally, you would want to share the supporting libraries.

II. Deploy CareerPathListerModule as a Session Facade

In this phase, you will deploy the HRBC4J project to the EJB container of OC4J, with CareerPathListerModule exposed as a session facade. This will allow you to deploy and execute the CareerPathLister application in remote mode.

Deploy the BC4J Layer to OC4J

This section deploys CareerPathListerModule as a session facade to the EJB container of OC4J.

1. If you have not set up OC4J or created a connection to it as described in Phase I of the hands-on practice "Deploy a JSP Application" in Chapter 7, do so now.

2. If OC4J is not running, restart it.

   Additional Information: After setting up OC4J as described in Chapter 7, you can start it by opening a command-line window and navigating to the JDEV_HOME\j2ee\home directory. Enter the command to set up the environment variables (..\..\jdev\bin\ setvars –go) and the command to start the server (start java –jar oc4j.jar).

3. Open the HRBC4J.jpr node. On the HRBC4J.jpx node, select Create Business Component Deployment Profiles from the right-click menu to open the Business Components Deployment Wizard.

   Additional Information: You only need to use this wizard if you want to run an application in remote mode. To run an application in local mode, just deploy your business components with your client, as in the previous phase and in Chapter 7's practices.

4. Click Next if the Welcome page appears. On the Profiles page, add "EJB Session Beans" to the *Selected* list. Click Next.

5. On the EJB Session Beans page, add "Session Facade (BMT)" to the *Selected* list.

   Additional Information: Note that you have four options: you can choose to deploy as a session facade or a service session facade, and independently, you can choose whether to use bean-managed transactions (BMT) or container-managed transactions (CMT). *Container-managed transactions* require that the client manage the EJB transaction, which is distinct from the RDBMS transaction or the BC4J Transaction. *Bean-managed transactions* allow the session facade to manage the EJB transaction automatically. If you are not an EJB developer interested in controlling the EJB transaction from the client, you should always use BMT.

6. Ensure that the LocalOC4J connection is selected in the *Server Connection* dropdown list. Click Next.

7. On the AppModules page, select CareerPathListerModule and move it to the *Selected* list.

   Additional Information: The entire hrbc4j package will be deployed to the EJB container, but you can select here which application modules to publish as EJB Session Beans. Clients can access only the application modules you publish.

8. Click Finish to close the wizard.

   Additional Information: JDeveloper creates a profile (called HRBC4Jejb.bcdeploy) to deploy the BC4J layer to OC4J and expose CareerPathListerModule as an EJB; a remote-mode configuration (called CareerPathListerModule9iAS) for CareerPathListerModule; and a new project, HRBC4JBeanManagedClient.jpr, containing the lightweight client-side classes that handle RMI communication with the BC4J EJB.

9. In the Navigator, expand the HRBC4JEjb.bcdeploy node.

10. On the HRBC4Jcommon.deploy node, select Settings from the right-click menu.

11. Select the JAR Options node in the tree.

12. Click the Browse button next to the *JAR file* field.

13. Browse to or create an empty folder on your disk, for example, "C:\deployments\ CareerPathListerRemote."

14. Click OK to close the file selection dialog, and click OK again to close the wizard.

    Additional Information: Previously, when you deployed and ran the project in local mode, you were working with the entire HRBC4J project. This deployment profile, generated when you created the HRBC4JEjb.deploy deployment profile, includes only the XML files and the interfaces and classes in the hrbc4j.common package, that is, tier-independent interfaces and custom domains. These are the only classes your client will need. However, you have to make sure they are available to the client. By changing the location of the JAR file to the place you will deploy the client, you will make it easy to access them later.

15. On the HRBC4JEjb.bcdeploy node in the Navigator, select Deploy from the right-click menu. This will create the JAR file in the directory you specified in the deployment profile dialog.

16. Monitor the progress of the deployment in the Log window. Wait until a message indicates that the deployment is finished.

    Additional Information: You will now have an EJB JAR file in the directory you specified in the deployment profile dialog.

17. On the HRBC4JBeanManagedClient.jpr node, click Rebuild, and click Save All.

Additional Information: When you created the deployment profile, JDeveloper automatically created the lightweight client-side classes (in the HRBC4JBeanManagedClient project) that handle RMI communication with the BC4J EJB. Before you can access the BC4J layer in remote mode, you must compile these classes.

Test CareerPathListerModule in Remote Mode

Use the Business Component Browser to make sure your EJB was deployed properly:

1. On the CareerPathListerModule node (under the hrbc4j package node), select Test from the right-click menu.

When the Connect page opens, select CareerPathListerModule9iAS from the Business Component Configuration Name dropdown, as shown next:

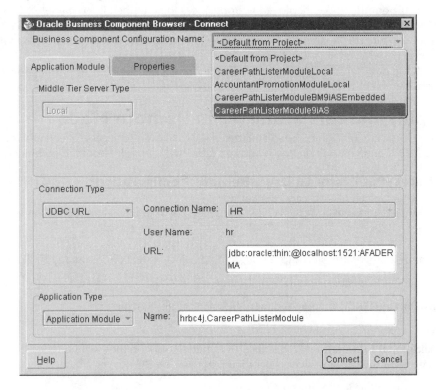

Additional Information: In previous chapters, you kept the <Default from Project> selection. Note that there are multiple choices in this dropdown as follows:

■ **<Default from Project>** This uses a configuration just like the "Local" configurations that JDeveloper creates for you when you create an application module.

- ■ **Configurations with a "Local" suffix** Initially, there's no difference between the "Local" configurations and <Default from Project>. However, if you edit the "Local" configurations, they can diverge from the default.

- ■ **CareerPathListerModuleBM9iASEmbedded** This was also created for you when you created the deployment profile. It uses OC4J running in embedded mode.

- ■ **CareerPathListerModule9iAS** This was created for you when you created the deployment profile. This is the configuration clients should use to connect to your BC4J in remote mode, and this is what you want to test here.

2. Click Connect.

3. When the main window of the browser opens, explore the application module to make sure the EJB is working. Close the browser when you finish.

What Just Happened? You deployed your business logic to the EJB container of OC4J, exposing CareerPathListerModule as a session facade, and tested the bean with the Business Component Browser. This bean is the one that the CareerPathLister client will access in remote mode in Phase III.

Although the browser was running inside JDeveloper, it accessed OC4J running in external mode, just as the client will.

III. Deploy CareerPathLister in Remote Mode

In this phase, you will modify the CareerPathLister client to allow it to access CareerPathListerModule in remote mode. Then you will deploy it and run it, in remote mode, from the command line.

Modify CareerPathLister to Use a Remote Configuration

This section changes the libraries and the call to `Configuration.createRootApplicationModule()` so that CareerPathLister will run in remote mode:

1. On the CareerPathListerJA.jpr node, select Project Settings from the right-click menu.

2. Select the Dependencies node in the tree.

3. Expand the HRBC4J node and then the HRBC4JEjb.bcdeploy node.

4. Uncheck *HRBC4J* and check *HRBC4JCommon.deploy*.

   Additional Information: This ensures that the common files will be redeployed whenever the client project is deployed, in case the BC4J layer changes.

5. Select *HRBC4JBeanManagedClient.jpr*.

   Additional Information: This project, generated in Phase II, contains the lightweight client-side classes. Checking the checkbox ensures the project will be included in the client JAR.

6. Select the Libraries node in the Project Settings tree.

7. Remove the BC4J Runtime library from the Selected Libraries list.

Additional Information: In remote mode, the client does not need access to the server-side framework classes in the BC4J Runtime library.

8. Add the following libraries to the Selected Libraries list:

   ■ BC4J Oracle9iAS Client

   ■ J2EE

   ■ Oracle XML Parser v2

   Additional Information: BC4J Oracle9iAS Client contains the lightweight framework classes (such as oracle.jbo.client.remote.ejb.ApplicationModuleImpl, as shown in Figure 14-2). J2EE helps the client create an RMI connection to OC4J. Oracle XML Parser v2 allows the client to read the BC4J XML files. It is included in BC4J Runtime, but you removed that library in step 7.

9. Click OK to close the Project Settings dialog.

10. Edit the CareerPathLister.java file in CareerPathListerJA.jpr.

11. Find the following code in the `main()` method (toward the beginning of the file):

```
Configuration.createRootApplicationModule(
    "hrbc4j.CareerPathListerModule",
    "CareerPathListerModuleLocal"
);
```

12. Change it to the following:

```
Configuration.createRootApplicationModule(
    "hrbc4j.CareerPathListerModule",
    "CareerPathListerModule9iAS"
);
```

13. Click Rebuild and Save All.

Deploy CareerPathLister to the File System
This section deploys CareerPathLister as a JAR in remote mode.

1. On the CareerPathListerJA.jpr node, select New from the right-click menu.

2. In the New dialog, in the Categories list, select the Deployment Profiles folder under General.

3. In the Items list, select JAR file – Simple Archive and click OK.

4. In the Save Deployment Profile dialog, enter "CareerPathListerRemote.deploy" in the *File name* field and click Save. The JAR Deployment Profile Settings dialog will open.

5. Select the JAR Options node in the tree.

6. Click the Browse button next to the *JAR file* field.

7. Browse to the folder you used for the HRBC4JCommon.deploy profile, for example, C:\deployments\CareerPathListerRemote.

8. In the *File name* field, enter "CareerPathListerRemote.jar" and click Open to return to the Deployment Profile Settings dialog.

9. Select the Dependency Analyzer node in the tree, and again select each of the nodes in the "Which libraries are involved in the dependency analysis?" tree.

10. Click OK to close the dialog.

11. On the CareerPathListerRemote.deploy node, select Deploy To JAR File from the right-click menu.

12. Monitor the progress of the deployment in the Log window. Wait until a finish message appears.

13. Click Save All.

Run CareerPathLister in Remote Mode

This section runs CareerPathLister in remote mode from the command prompt.

1. Open a command-line window if one is not already open, and reinitialize the PATH. Change to the directory containing your deployed application, for example, C:\ deployments\CareerPathListerRemote.

2. Enter the following on one line:

```
java -cp "HRBC4JEjbCommon.jar;CareerPathListerRemote.jar"
    careerpathlisterja.CareerPathLister IT_PROG
```

The output should be the same as in Phase I.

What Just Happened?   You removed the BC4J layer from the client and replaced it with the necessary client-side architecture. Then, after a small code change, you redeployed the client and tested it in remote mode.

IV. Create and Use a Web Service

This phase publishes AccountantPromotionModule as a web service to the standalone installation of OC4J, and creates a WSDL file and client-side Java stubs for clients to use.

Publish AccountantPromotionModule as a Web Service

This section creates a web service class and deploys it to OC4J. It also generates a WSDL file for the web service.

1. On the HRBC4J.jpr node, select Project Settings from the right-click menu.

2. In the Project Settings dialog, under Common, select the J2EE node.

3. Change the *J2EE Web Context Root* field to "HRBC4J," and click OK to close the dialog.

    Additional Information: When you deploy an application to a web container, the context root becomes part of any URL used to access it. A shorter context root than the default will be easier to remember and communicate to users.

4. On the AccountantPromotionModule node under the hrbc4j package, select Generate Web Service Class from the right-click menu.

   Additional Information: This generates a server-side class called "AccountantPromotionModuleWS," which wraps AccountantPromotionModule for publication. AccountantPromotionModuleWS exposes to users of the service the method `promoteAccountants()` (added in Chapter 14's practice).

5. On the HRBC4J.jpr node, select New from the right-click menu.

6. In the New dialog, select the Web Services node under the General category.

7. Select Java Web Service and click OK to open the Web Service Publishing Wizard. Click Next if the Welcome page appears.

8. On the Web Service Class, Name and Platform page, select "hrbc4j.AccountantPromotionModuleWS" in the *Select the class* pulldown.

   Additional Information: The *Web Service Name* field will automatically change to match the class name.

   You cannot publish business components directly, but you can publish the web service class that wraps an application module.

9. Click Next.

10. On the Expose Methods page, check the checkbox next to the `promoteAccountants()` method and click Next. This indicates that you want to expose the `promoteAccountants()` method.

11. On the File Locations page, note that the target namespace is http://hrbc4j/ AccountantPromotionModuleWS.wsdl. Edit it so that it is unique to you—for example: http://<*your_org*>/<*your_name*>/hrbc4j/AccountantPromotionModuleWS.wsdl

   Additional Information: This is not a URL you need to be concerned with, except that it must be unique. It is important that you use a unique URL, so that your web service will not conflict with others'.

12. Click Finish.

   Additional Information: The Log window will display the results of the web service generation. This will generate a WSDL file called "AccountantPromotionModuleWS.wsdl" and a deployment profile called "WebServices.deploy."

13. Verify that your local OC4J is still running. On the WebServices.deploy node, select Deploy To > LocalOC4J from the right-click menu.

14. Monitor the progress of the deployment in the Log window. Notice that one of the last messages contains the URL of the context root directory for this web service.

15. Click Save All.

Create Client-Side Java Stubs

This section creates client-side Java stubs for your web service. This will allow you to use the web service without knowing WSDL.

1. On the HRWS.jws node, select New Empty Project from the right-click menu.

2. Name the project directory and project "WebServiceClientJA" and click OK.

3. On the WebServiceClientJA.jpr node, select New from the right-click menu.

4. Select the Web Services node, and double click Web Service Stub/Skeleton to open the Web Service Stub/Skeleton Wizard. Click Next if the Welcome page appears.

5. On the Select Web Service Description page, in the *Enter the URL* field, enter the location of the deployed WSDL file. Replace "my-host" with the hostname or IP address of your computer as shown in the Deployment tab of the Log window. If your computer is called localhost, enter
   http://localhost:8888/HRBC4J/hrbc4j.AccountantPromotionModuleWS?WSDL

   Additional Information: This is the URL of the deployed WSDL file. Note that the context root (HRBC4J) appears in the form of a virtual directory.

6. Change the default package to "webserviceclientja" and click Next.

7. Click Finish to generate the stubs.

   Additional Information: This generates a Java class called AccountantPromotionModuleWSStub, containing a public method called `promoteAccountants()` that uses SOAP to call `AccountantPromotionModule.promoteAccountants()`. If you wanted, you could compile this class and distribute it to customers as an easy way to call your web service.

Create a Client That Invokes the Web Service

This section creates a simple client that uses the stubs to invoke a web service.

1. On the WebServiceClientJA.jpr node, select New Class from the right-click menu.

2. Name the class "WebServiceClient."

3. Check the *Generate Main Method* checkbox.
   Additional Information: This will make the client runnable.

4. Click OK.

5. Edit WebServiceClient.java in a source editor.

6. Change the package to "webserviceclientja." Click OK.

7. Add the following code to the `main()` method before its closing curly bracket:

```
AccountantPromotionModuleWSStub stub =
  new AccountantPromotionModuleWSStub();
stub.promoteAccountants();
```

8. Modify the main method declaration so that it reads

```
public static void main(String[] args) throws java.lang.Exception
```

Additional Information: Any one of a number of exceptions can be thrown by the web service process. java.lang.Exception covers them all.

9. Click Rebuild and Save All.

Deploy the Client to the File System and Run It

This section deploys the client to a JAR file and runs it from the command line.

You do not need to add any libraries to the project. The only library the project needs is Oracle SOAP, which was automatically added when you created the web service Java stubs.

NOTE
The client you will run in this phase commits changes to the EMPLOYEES table in the HR sample schema. To restore the employee record, follow the procedure at the end of this practice.

1. On the WebServiceClientJA.jpr node, select New from the right-click menu.

2. In the New dialog, select the Deployment Profiles folder in the Categories list.

3. In the Items list, select JAR file – Simple Archive and click OK.

4. In the Save Deployment Profile dialog, enter "WebServiceClient.deploy" in the *File Name* field and click Save. The JAR Deployment Profile Settings dialog will open.

5. Select the JAR Options node in the tree.

6. Click the Browse button next to the *JAR file* field.

7. Browse to or create an empty folder on your disk, for example, C:\deployments\ WebServiceClient.

8. Change the *File name* field to "WebServiceClient.jar," and click Open to return to the Deployment Profile Settings dialog.

9. In the *Main Class* field, enter "webserviceclientja.WebServiceClient."

10. Select the Dependency Analyzer node in the tree, and check the checkbox for the Oracle SOAP node. You do not need to check the checkbox for JDeveloper Runtime because you will not run this in JDeveloper.

11. Click OK to close the dialog.

12. On the WebServiceClient.deploy node, select Deploy To JAR File from the right-click menu.

13. Monitor the progress of the deployment in the Log window.

14. Click Save All.

15. Navigate to the HR connection under Connections\Database. On the HR node, select SQL Worksheet from the right-click menu.

16. Enter the following SQL statement and click the Execute button. This will display job IDs that are affected by the promotion routine:

```
SELECT *
FROM EMPLOYEES
WHERE JOB_ID IN('AC_ACCOUNT', 'AC_MGR')
```

Additional Information: There is one employee (ID 206) who is assigned the "AC_ACCOUNT" job.

17. In the command-line window, change to the directory containing your deployed application, for example, C:\deployments\WebServiceClient. Enter "DIR" to view the files in the directory.

18. Enter the following at the command line:

```
java -jar WebServiceClient.jar
```

You will not see any output in the command-line window.

19. Run the same query you ran before in SQL Worksheet to verify that employee 206 is now assigned a Job ID of "AC_MGR."

What Just Happened?   You created, deployed, and tested a web service based on AccountantPromotionModule and created, deployed, and called a client that used it.

To restore the JOB_ID value in the EMPLOYEES table, run the following statement in the SQL Worksheet:

```
UPDATE employees
SET job_id = 'AC_ACCOUNT'
WHERE employee_id = 206;
```

PART

III

Java Client
Applications

PART

III

Java Client
Applications

CHAPTER
17

Java Client Overview

May my application so close
To so endless a repetition
Not make me tired and morose
And resentful of man's condition.

—Robert Frost (1874–1963), *In Time of Cloudburst*

 ava client applications are applications running in a Java Virtual Machine (JVM) on the Client Tier. The user interface portion is usually written using Sun's Swing components. In the past, AWT (Abstract Windowing Toolkit) components were often used as well. The term *Java client* (as used in this book and often in industry publications) refers to two different types of deployments: Java applications and Java applets (as introduced in Chapter 7).

Java applications are standalone programs that run within the Java Virtual Machine on the client. They are deployed like any other client/server environment. *Applets* are similar to Java applications in construction but are run in a JVM in a browser. Only a small amount of code needs to be changed in order to convert an application to an applet or vice versa. For example, applets start from an `init()` method and are subclassed from the JApplet class, whereas Java applications start from a `main()` method and are subclassed from window classes such as JFrame. The main difference between applications and applets is that applets are deployed to an application server, so when users command the applet to be run, it is loaded and run within the browser. Although once popular, applets represent an infrequently used architecture, having been supplanted in web development by the JSP architecture.

As of this writing, it is impossible to match the data-entry performance or graphical quality of the user interface that can be achieved in a Java application or applet using a JSP application or any similar web development environment. For core internal applications where a high-performance user interface is required, there are still situations where you need rich user-interface components available to Java client applications rather than the limited controls available in HTML environments (created by JSP pages).

Java applications and applets allow developers to build applications that are as fully featured as any C++ application. When you write Java applications or applets, your code uses the Java language primarily, as opposed to JSP pages, which use a combination of tag languages and Java. Chapter 7 contains more detailed information about Java and how it is used in JSP pages.

The chapters in this part of the book deal with Java applications, but the same considerations apply to applets. This chapter provides an overview of the architecture decisions and discusses container components such as JPanels and JFrames. Chapter 7 discusses the architectures of Java client applications within the J2EE strategies. Chapter 18 discusses the user interface Swing components. Chapter 19 covers the strategy behind menu and toolbar design, and shows how these structures are supported in Java applications. The uses and functions of each of the possible layout managers are discussed in Chapter 20.

The rule of thumb when working with any Java IDE is to try to reduce the amount of hand coding. Of course, expert Java programmers may produce code just as fast as a generator. However, generated code is consistent, predictable, and error free. Although it is not possible to create an enterprise-class application using only the wizards and existing components, these features give you a big head start and greatly minimize the supplemental code that you have to write. If you are careful about how elaborate your GUI becomes, the amount of code you need to write will be very small. The details that Java requires to make the code work, such as imports and constructors, can all be handled by the code generators and Property Inspector.

One of the key features that the JDeveloper IDE offers is quick access to commonly used Java components. A Java *component* corresponds to what other languages or environments (such as Windows) call a "control," and the words "component" and "control" are often used interchangeably. Components (which technically are JavaBeans) are used to create Java client applications, not servlets or JSP applications. Typically, a component represents a visual object, but the term can be extended to cover nonvisual data control objects. The IDE allows you to drop components into your project, set most properties, and define events, all without writing code. This method of designing a user interface is very similar to that used in the Forms Developer environment, though JDeveloper creates 3GL code and Forms is a 4GL tool. The code that is generated from these actions in JDeveloper is ready to run, error free, and can be edited using the Code Editor.

The Component Palette of the JDeveloper IDE offers the ability to create components and generate code. The available pages of the Component Palette are dependent upon which type of file is open in the Code Editor. Chapter 2 introduces this editor. The hands-on practice in this chapter includes examples of how to work with these components to create a simple data-aware Java application. With this knowledge, you will be better able to explore the other components and understand where to get information about developing Java client applications.

Java Applications and Applets in JDeveloper

When you build Java applications and applets using JDeveloper, your work is organized within workspaces and projects just as with all other JDeveloper development. The first step in application development is to build or add the BC4J project or projects that will support your program. These BC4J projects must be open in the same workspace as your application. Next you build the user interface portion of the program. This will usually reside in its own project or projects within the same workspace as the BC4J project.

The organization of directories has changed significantly from JDeveloper 3.2. The following example helps to illustrate the organization in Oracle9i JDeveloper. Assume that you are building a simple application with a BC4J project and a single-user interface project in the same workspace. The workspace is stored in "workspace_directory01" under "test_applications," and the projects are stored in their own project subdirectories under "workspace_directory01."

Deployment is based on the packages associated with the various objects in your program. Packages also help organize your work in the development directories. In the preceding example, the BC4J project is associated with a package called "bc4jpackage," and the UI project is associated with the package "uipackage." If you navigate to the operating system, the directory structure will be as shown here:

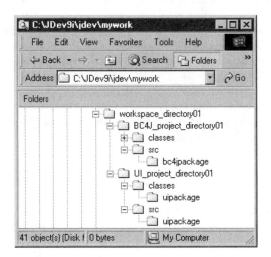

By default, subdirectories called "src" and "classes" are automatically added to each project subdirectory. The "src" directory stores the source code for your classes, and the "classes" directory stores the compiled code. These directory names will become familiar to developers and should not be changed, although JDeveloper supports changing the names used for these directories when you create the project or in the project settings. Notice how the package name is used for subdirectories under the src and classes directories. It is in these package subdirectories that your files will be stored.

JDeveloper does not require that you place the project directories under the workspace directory, but using this structure provides an easy way to delete (or back up) an entire program by just deleting (or backing up) the workspace directory and all of its subcomponents.

This chapter discusses some of the basic concepts associated with building Java client applications. As mentioned, there is little difference in the development process between a Java application and an applet. In both cases, you are writing the user interface program completely in Java. The difference is mainly in the deployment, the starting method, and the parent class. The applet also has an HTML page or link that is used to run the application. More information about deployment can be found in Chapter 7. Some programs that you write may not be suitable as applets because your deployment environment may place a security limitation on what applet code is allowed to do. Performance of applets is only a problem for the initial download. Once the download occurs, applets start up as quickly as Java applications. In addition, the download can be eliminated if the applet code is installed on the client.

Building Java applications and applets requires careful planning. You need to decide how your program is to be structured before you start building it. It is a bad idea to just start building the application and then allow it to "evolve." You have many alternatives in structuring your application. Many of these decisions are very difficult to change later in the project. The next section will discuss some of these decisions.

Java Client Architecture Decisions

This section describes the decisions that have to be made when building a Java application or applet. These decisions can be quite hard to change after the development process is well under way.

Should You Build a Java Application or Applet?

Are you going to build your program as a Java application or as an applet? If you are going to deploy it as an applet, you may want to limit the size of your program. You may want to break it up into several smaller programs to limit the size of each portion.

Security considerations may influence your decision. Many programs may be difficult to deploy as applets. If your program needs to perform operations that are usually considered unsafe in a browser (for example, create/delete/read hard disk files, or write files to the local hard disk), you will have to set up extra security files to give your applet the ability to override the security controls inherent in your browser. This adds a level of complexity to your deployment that many may find challenging.

How Many Independent Programs Will You Use?

One of the temptations when writing programs in Java is to write very complex, graphics-intensive programs just because it is possible. For developers who have been restricted for years as to what they could build in a 4GL environment, this new capability can be very tempting. The dream of building a "super program" that can support a major portion of a complex system can be realized. But this new capability can lead to programs that are so large that they suffer from poor performance and are difficult to maintain.

There is no restriction on the number of physical programs that make up the construction of a Java application. One advantage of a 3GL environment is that you can partition your code any way you like.

Very large programs take longer to load and may consume enough memory resources that the program runs slowly. It is easier to manage a few programs of moderate size than one giant program. Large programs should be partitioned into manageable chunks.

Breaking Java Applications into Separate Classes

Notice that when you build a master-detail Java application using the JClient Form Wizard (such as in the Chapter 1 practice), the tool generates four classes that are nested inside each other. You can break your program into classes any way that you like. In building this Java application by hand, it would be logical to combine the first two classes into a container class, but it is recommended that you keep the master and detail classes separate. Using one class for each table is a good way to organize your code.

How Many Directories, Workspaces, and Projects Will You Create?

You have a lot of flexibility in how you manage your program within JDeveloper. Workspaces and projects are merely logical folders where you place your work. You can place many programs in the same workspace or split a single program across multiple workspaces. You can build reusable components that can be used by several programs, and you can store your work in multiple folders/directories in the operating system.

JDeveloper is well suited to manage up to a few dozen classes in a single project and can support several projects in the same workspace. However, the product supports neither logical groups of classes within the project nor logical groups of projects in the workspace. So, for very large programs, the developer will be able to significantly improve the readability and manageability of the code by partitioning the code into several projects, and perhaps even several workspaces. Oracle9i JDeveloper allows you to have multiple workspaces open at the same time, and this feature allows you to work on many logically distinct application areas at the same time.

What Is the BC4J and Data Validation Strategy?

As discussed in Chapter 1 and Part II, there are several possible strategies for BC4J usage. The main architecture-level BC4J-related decision to be made is where the data validation will take place.

Data validation can be supported in many places in a Java application. The selection of the validation location is the same kind of decision that had to be made in a 4GL environment. In a 4GL environment, a decision must be made about whether the validation would take place in the database or in the application. In a Java application, data validation can be accomplished in one of three places: in a database, within BC4J entity objects, or in the user interface portion of the application.

In addition, data validation can take place in the BC4J view objects, but that does not make much sense and is only recommended when there is a specific validation requirement for a particular user-interface screen.

What Type of Container Layout Should Be Used?

Laying out the containers (frames, panes, and panels) in your Java application or applet is something that should be accomplished before you get very far into your application. It is quite easy to change your mind about the container structuring at any time during development if you are a skilled Java developer. If you want to rely on the JDeveloper wizards to lay out your containers for you and to make sure that they are bound to BC4J correctly, then it is much easier to think through the structure before doing much development. See Chapter 18 for a discussion of containers and Swing components.

How Many Packages Will You Create and How Will You Name Them?

Packages govern the deployment, internal .jar file structure, and the work area subdirectory names for your program. They are also the logical internal storage area names for your program. The point here is that the package names are used in many places. Changing package names after development can be quite difficult. Similarly, going from a single-package structure to a multiple-package structure after significant development has been done is difficult to implement.

Changing the default package name in a JDeveloper project (in the project settings dialog) will only change the package for future objects. Anything already created will belong to the original package.

Other Issues

In addition to trying to figure out what code to use, it is also often difficult to determine where to put the code. The scope and visibility of Swing components does not always lead to an obvious conclusion about where to place the appropriate code.

As in any new product, the first time you try to do something it will take some time to figure it out and get it to work. With JDeveloper and Swing components, you will quickly need to go beyond JDeveloper's default behavior. Because the possibilities are virtually limitless, you will be figuring out many more little tricks than would have been needed in a product like Oracle Forms. Two of the authors estimated that to be an efficient developer in Forms, you would need about 1000 tips and techniques at your fingertips. With years of experience, it is possible to keep this number of tricks in memory. Even if the exact code syntax needs to be looked up, it is usually easily found.

To be an excellent Java programmer, the number of techniques required on a day-to-day basis is probably closer to 10,000 and therefore not manageable in one developer's head. Even after years of experience, you will still be constantly finding new things that you need to do and others that you have forgotten. Too much information must be absorbed.

There is usually no unique way to accomplish a task in Java, and often there are a number of equally good ways to do something. Even the way in which a basic application is built with enclosing frames and panels is not unique. The JDeveloper wizards have evolved over time, making significant modifications to the way in which generated applications are constructed.

JClient Architecture

To create Java applications and applets, you use *Swing components*, UI Java classes supplied by Sun. Swing components are explained more completely in Chapter 18. In Part II, you learned about BC4J architecture to support interaction with the database. The JClient technology is used with Java client applications such as Java applications and applets. The JClient architecture is the glue that connects the Swing components to the BC4J objects. It is a thin layer used to set up and manage communication between the Swing components and the underlying BC4J data sources.

In the 2.0 version of JDeveloper, in addition to using standard Swing components with BC4J, Oracle wrote extensions to many of the Swing classes called Data Aware Controls (DACs) that were built on Sun's InfoBus architecture, which was the standard at the time. The InfoBus architecture is no longer considered a viable standard. As mentioned in Chapter 7, Sun's Model-View-Controller (MVC) architecture is an important strategy for separating the user interface from the model and behavior aspects of an application. The JClient architecture represents the model tier of MVC. It couples to the Swing components' *model* or *document* properties (depending upon the context) in the JDeveloper Property Inspector.

The DAC extensions to the Swing components were written to allow users to quickly build Java applications and applets by facilitating interaction of the Swing components with the BC4J layer. The new JClient architecture provided in Oracle9i JDeveloper refines this interface, allowing developers to use any Swing component and couple it to the BC4J layer. JClient can also be used to support AWT controls. Since Swing controls have almost completely replaced the older AWT controls, this book will focus only on Swing controls.

The issue of connecting standard Java components to database objects is one that requires much thought and effort. The traditional solution is to write code that connects to the database and retrieves and updates values based upon settings in user interface objects such as text fields and checkboxes. Oracle has solved this using the JClient architecture. JClient sets up a code layer that performs the *binding* of Java user interface components (JavaBeans such as JTextField and JCheckBox) to BC4J objects. This allows developers to easily bind the interface elements to data; for example, to connect a text field to a BC4J attribute (that represents a column in a table), the only thing required is a property setting on the text field's property list.

Recall that in BC4J, you specify an application module that is a collection of view-object and view-link usages. This application module logically defines how the view objects and view links will be visible to the application. All interaction with the user interface portion of the application to BC4J is accomplished by using this application module. Before the user interface project can have access to the application module, you need to register the application module with the UI project through the creation of the client data model. This links the UI project to a particular application module. Once this link has been established, Swing panels and frames can be bound to view-object usages in the application module, and UI Swing components such as text fields can be bound to view-object attributes. A diagrammatic representation of JClient architecture for a form based on EmployeesView is shown in Figure 17-1.

In addition to the JDeveloper help system, some additional sources of information about JClient can be found on the Internet at:

- otn.oracle.com/products/jdev/htdocs/JClient/forms_Client.html

- otn.oracle.com/products/jdev/htdocs/jclientsod/JavaClientSOD.html

Developing a Client Data Model

JClient (as well as JSP pages built with the BC4J Data Tags Library) requires a client data model to connect to BC4J. The *client data model* is a definition stored in an XML file that describes the BC4J application module to which the application will connect. You create the BC4J client data model through the wizards by adding a data model to the user interface project using the Business Components Client Data Model item in the Client Tier\Swing/JClient for BC4J category of the New gallery. The wizard creates an XML file (with a .cpx extension) that is used by the wizards to determine which tables and columns to display, and is used by the Oracle libraries to interface with the BC4J layer.

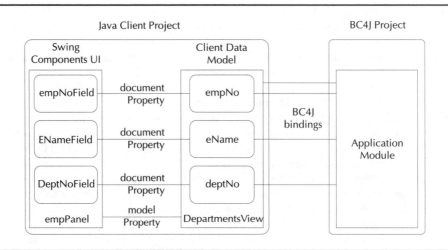

FIGURE 17-1. *Panel components and data-binding layers*

You can have only one BC4J client data model file per project, but you can have more than one client data model defined within that file. JDeveloper names the file using the project name concatenated with ".cpx" (for example, "LocDeptJA.cpx").

NOTE
It is not necessary to have a client data model definition before you run wizards that require a client data model such as the JClient Form Wizard. Those wizards contain a link (via a New button) to start the BC4J Client Data Model Definition Wizard, so you can create the client data model on the fly during the wizard session.

Binding Swing Components to BC4J

As depicted in Figure 17-1, the *model* property is used for BC4J binding of a container (such as a JPanel or naviagtion bar) to a view usage. The binding of components such as text fields uses the property *document*. After clicking the button labeled "…" next to the *model* property in the Property Inspector for a JClient panel, you will see the JClient property editors. You can select an editor from the pulldown list. Some components have more than one JClient property editor, since they support more than one type of binding to the middle tier. You can edit the current value by clicking the "…" button.

Binding Panels

As you create frames and add supporting panels, you usually bind the parent panels for each of your program areas to the BC4J data model. As mentioned earlier, you must first specify a BC4J application module for your UI project.

Once the application module is specified, you can bind your containers to BC4J. In the high-level wizards, this is done as you generate the program. You can bind any of the types of containers mentioned in Chapter 18 with the exception of JFrames and JInternalFrames. Once you bind a container, its nested containers are automatically bound.

The JDeveloper wizards bind the top-level JPanel container in the project. Then in each additional class, they pass that binding as a parameter when instantiating the data-bound classes (such as DepartmentsPanel and LocationsPanel in the earlier example). This is not a bad idea. Because the wizard-generated application is partitioned across classes, if each class were not individually bound, code that refers to BC4J objects would have to be prefaced with a class name where the original bound container is declared. If your entire application is bound in a single, top-level class, you do not have to do this.

The original binding of the top panel is accomplished by the code shown next. First, the panel binding is declared and associated with the application module in the `main()` method as follows:

```
JUPanelBinding panelBinding = new JUPanelBinding("UI.Bc4jpackageModule", null);
    panelBinding.setApplication(app);
```

Declare the panel binding in the JFrame class as shown here:

```
private JUPanelBinding panelBinding = new JUPanelBinding
    ("UI.Bc4jpackageModule", null);
```

Since the panel binding is passed by value, it did not need to be specified again here. When the class is instantiated, the panel binding is passed as shown in the following code:

```
DepartmentsView1Form frame = new DepartmentsView1Form(panelBinding);
```

All classes are handled with a similar mechanism.

Further discussion of JClient architecture is beyond the scope of this book. As an example of JClient advanced features, there is an excellent white paper available in the JDeveloper "How To" section of OTN (otn.oracle.com) called "Using a Custom Subclass of a JClient Control Binding." This paper discusses how to write your own custom JClient control binding to add specific functionality that does not exist in the default JClient code.

Hands-on Practice: Create a Basic JClient Java Application

This hands-on practice familiarizes you with some of the basic components used in many Java applications and applets, and how they are bound to BC4J through the client data model. It provides some practice in using both the JDeveloper wizards and UI Editor to create a simple JClient Java application. Chapter 3 contains a more complete Java application that is bound to BC4J objects should you require further practice in the concepts.

This practice assumes that you have completed Phase II of the hands-on practices in Chapter 1 and have created and tested the BC4J code. Return to Chapter 1 and complete that phase if you have not already done so.

The two phases for this practice are as follows:

   I. Create the panel class

   II. Add interface components

I. Create the Panel Class

This phase creates a UI application project and adds a Java class file that is bound to the BC4J application module. BC4J objects are bound to Swing controls by including a JPanel component in the frame and binding the panel to a BC4J view usage defined in the client data model. Extra properties then become available to the Swing components so they may be tied to the BC4J application module.

   1. Right click the LocDeptWS.jws node in the Navigator, and select New Empty Project from the right-click menu.

   2. Enter "DeptJA" in both the *Directory Name* and *File Name* fields in the New Project dialog.

   3. Add an Empty Panel file from the Client Tier\Swing/JClient for BC4J category in the New gallery (**File | New**). The JClient Empty Panel Wizard will open. Click Next if the Welcome page appears.

Additional Information: The Empty Panel Wizard creates a data-bound JPanel class file. A Panel item in the same category also subclasses JPanel and automatically creates components linked to a specific view usage. This practice shows you how to build that file from scratch using the Empty Panel item in the New gallery. In addition, a Panel item is in the New gallery's Client Tier\Swing/AWT category. This item also creates a subclass of JPanel, but the subclass created has no data binding features.

4. On the Data Model page, select New to open the BC4J Client Data Model Definition Wizard. Click Next if the Welcome page appears.

5. In this wizard, you can create the data model for the BC4J application module from the Chapter 1 practice. Click Next on the Definition and Definition Name pages. Click Finish to complete the client data model definition. Control will pass back to the JClient Empty Panel Wizard, and the Data Model page will be automatically filled in as shown here:

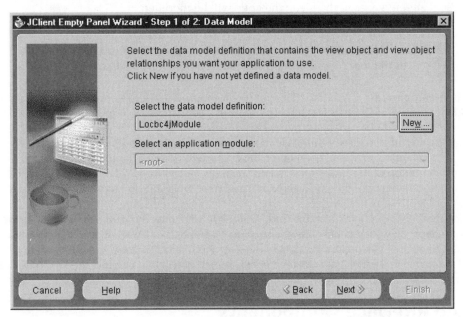

6. Click Next on the Data Model page. In the File names page, change the *Package name* to "deptapp," and check the *Generate a runnable panel* checkbox. Click Next and Finish to create the panel file.

Additional Information: You may need to expand the width of the dialog window if the checkbox is not visible. Checking the checkbox causes the wizard to add a `main()` method and related code that allows you to run this file directly without using a frame application to call it.

7. Click Save All.

   Additional Information: The file will be named something like "PanelLocdeptModule.java."

8. Select the panel file in the Navigator, and select **Tools | Refactor | Rename Class**. In the Rename Class dialog, fill in the new name as "deptapp.DeptPanel" and click OK.

   Additional Information: The .java file extension will be added automatically. You may receive a confirmation dialog about an *Update Imports* property in the project settings. Click Yes if this dialog appears.

   If the Rename Class option is disabled, click something else in the Navigator, select PanelLocdeptModule.java again, and select **Tools | Refactor | Rename Class**.

9. Click OK on the final Rename Class dialog and click Close. The file will be renamed, and all references to the file in the code will be modified.

10. Click Rebuild DeptJA to verify that the code was correctly modified.

   Additional Information: If you had used **File | Rename** to rename the file, the references in other files to this file would not be properly updated.

What Just Happened?   You created a project to house the user interface application code and added a Java class file that is bound to the BC4J application module in the workspace. The project contains the DeptPanel.java panel class file as well as the DeptJA.cpx client data model XML file. It is useful to pause at this stage to explore the files that you just created.

Open the DeptJA.cpx file in the Code Editor. You will notice a standard XML-format that contains a definition of the project name and specifics for the BC4J session, including the application module name, the package name, and the configuration name. Close the Code Editor window for DeptJA.cpx.

Open the DeptPanel.java file in the Code Editor if it is not already open. You will notice that the class declaration shows the panel class as a subclass ("extends") of JPanel. It also implements the interface JClientPanel that defines the data binding for this JPanel. The `setPanelBinding()` method defined in this panel class creates a panel binding object that provides the link to BC4J and that can be passed as a parameter to other panels.

II. Add Interface Components

This phase demonstrates how to add components and bind them to a specific BC4J view usage and view attributes.

1. If the DeptPanel.java file is not open in the UI Editor, open it now. Add two label fields using the JLabel icon on the Component Palette's Swing page. Select the JLabel icon and click on "this" in the Structure window. Do this twice—once for each label.

CAUTION
If the background color for the panel object appears the same as the UI Editor background, the following layout steps may be difficult. To fix that problem, select the panel in the UI Editor. In the Property Inspector, change the "background" property to "Color.lightGray."

2. Change the JLabel1 *text* property to "Dept#" and the JLabel2 *text* property to "Name."

3. Drag the labels to the center area of the screen. Place the labels as shown here:

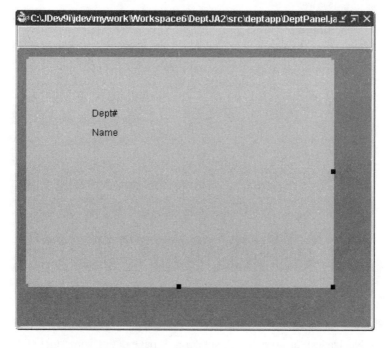

4. Add two text fields next to each label using the JTextField icon on the Swing page of the Component Palette. Use the alignment tools at the top of the UI Editor window to line up the labels and text fields.

5. Change the *name* property on the top field to "idTextField" and on the bottom field to "nameTextField."

6. Select the idTextField and select "JClient Attribute Binding" from the *document* pulldown in the Property Inspector. The following document dialog will open:

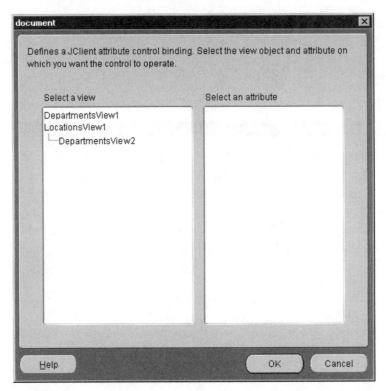

7. Select DepartmentsView1 and the DepartmentId attribute. Click OK.

8. Repeat steps 6 and 7 for the nameTextField and select the DepartmentName attribute.

9. Add a JUNavigationBar from the JClient controls page of the Component Palette by clicking the icon and clicking the panel in the UI Editor (so that the default size of the navigation bar is maintained). Position it to be centered at the top of the panel, above the fields.

10. The data binding for the navigation bar is accomplished using the *model* property. Click JClient View Binding in the pulldown for *model* in the Property Inspector for that component and select DepartmentsView1. Click OK to accept the model selection. Notice that you need not select an attribute, because the navigation bar works on the view usage level.

11. Click Rebuild DeptJA.jpr and click Run.

12. When you run this application, you should see something like the following. The buttons in the toolbar will allow you to navigate among the Department records, add and delete rows, commit and rollback, and find rows using query by example. All this functionality is built into the navigation bar object.

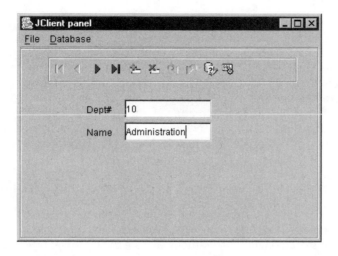

NOTE
If you are using the Oracle look-and-feel option for the JDeveloper IDE, you will notice that the design-time version of this panel looks different. The runtime takes its look-and-feel assignment from the runtime environment (Windows). You can explicitly set the look-and-feel in the `main()` *method as explained in Chapter 18.*

What Just Happened?   You used the JDeveloper wizards and UI Editor to create a simple Java application showing department numbers and names. Binding a Swing container or component to the BC4J layer is just a matter of setting up a panel class that implements the JClientBinding interface and assigning properties to view-object and attribute-level Swing components. All of this is possible because of the client data model in the .cpx file.

If you want to continue working on this form, you can add more fields to represent the other attributes in DepartmentsView1. You can also add a status bar (JUStatusBar in the JClient controls page of the Component Palette) that is attached to the view usage level and that displays various messages about the record scrolling and commit status.

As mentioned, for more experience with Swing components and binding, step through the Java application practices in Chapters 3 and 18.

Getting the Right Information

What is the critical success factor for building Java applications and applets quickly and efficiently using JDeveloper? Information, information, information. You can find tips and techniques from a wide variety of sources. In trying to manipulate a specific component in a certain way, the best way may be found only in one of many sources or may need to be gleaned from a combination of sources.

It would take many hundreds of pages to describe in detail all the components included for use in JDeveloper, along with their methods and properties. In addition, these components are the more common of the thousands of components available. Although Chapter 18 provides short hints about the components installed in the JDeveloper IDE, describing all of them goes far beyond the scope of this book. The good news is that many components are fully documented in a reference form within the JDeveloper help system. Browse under the Reference node in the Contents page, or look for the library in the Index page. You will also find some examples and techniques in the same help system.

In addition, many reference books on the market provide details of the Swing components and show even more examples of their use. The sidebar "Java and Swing Tutorials" describes some of these reference sources. For more information about the Oracle components, look for examples and descriptions on the Oracle Technet website (otn.oracle.com). Appendix B provides a list of resources for many subjects in this book including Java applications and applets. Another source of information is the Web. The best advice is to do both of the following:

- **Build a Java library**   You should not scrimp on the book budget in this area. Collect a library of Java reference books.

- **Use the Internet**   There are many useful websites, and more spring up all the time. Use your favorite search engine to find them. Be sure to take advantage of the tutorials on the Java website (java.sun.com) as mentioned in the sidebar "Java and Swing Tutorials."

CAUTION
Always be skeptical of what you read. Many white papers from scholarly sources are out of date or inaccurate.

Java and Swing Tutorials

As of this writing, the Sun Microsystems website (java.sun.com) contains several tutorials that may provide the details that you need to become more familiar with the components in the Swing and AWT categories. These tutorials are also available in printed format in the following reference books:

- *The Java Tutorial, Third Edition,* Mary Campione and Kathy Walrath. Addison-Wesley, 2000.

- *The Java Tutorial, Continued: The Rest of the JDK,* Campione, Walrath, Huml, et al. Addison-Wesley, 1998.

- *The JFC Swing Tutorial,* Walrath and Campione. Addison-Wesley, 1999.

These are just a few examples of the available books that describe the Sun components in depth.

CHAPTER
18

User Interface
Components

Progressively, continuously, and almost simultaneously, religious and scientific concepts are ridding themselves of their coarse and local components, reaching higher and higher levels of abstraction and purity.

—René Dubos (1901–1982), "On Being Human"

hapter 17 included an overview of the Java client architecture and development methods, container management, and the Swing components. This chapter provides some details about the visual Swing components that you place in your programs and shows you how to use them. There are dozens of visual Swing components available to the programmer. Developers accustomed to a product such as Forms Developer (that has fewer than 20 Swing-like components) will quickly get a sense of how much more flexibility is available in Java. Beyond the dizzying array of components, each Java component has much greater flexibility than its correlate in Forms or similar products. Each component also has many methods and events that are available to it. Each component also supports many different listeners and events so that the component can be used to trigger other program behavior.

This chapter lists and briefly describes the Java client components that are installed in JDeveloper so that you can get a sense of the wide range of functionality that they offer. When you decide to use one of these components, you can obtain more information from the JDeveloper online help system. The chapter then provides some detail about how to work with Swing components in JDeveloper and how to use the Swing and JClient container components.

A hands-on practice in this chapter shows how to create a tabbed application including basic labels and fields, a table, and a tree structure. This practice provides examples of how you can use many of the UI components included with JDeveloper. Another practice demonstrates how to create a Component Palette page, how to add components to the page, as well as how to reorder components within the preinstalled pages.

NOTE
You can add, rearrange, or remove any of the components or component pages installed with JDeveloper.

The Component Palette

The Component Palette for Java client component is normally located under the menu bar in the JDeveloper window when the UI Editor is open. A pulldown allows you to select from a number of pages:

- AWT
- Code Snippets
- JClient controls
- Swing
- Swing Containers

The following sections describe and show what each page contains by default to give you a feel for some of the controls. Remember that you are not bound by the components installed by default. You can add or remove pages in the Component Palette and add, remove, or move components as described in the hands-on practice later in this chapter.

The Component Palette offers controls that are appropriate to the file that you are editing in the UI Editor. This chapter describes only the Component Palette pages that appear when a Java application or applet is active in the UI Editor.

TIP

You can place a large number of objects on a single page and use the page's navigation arrows to access the components. However, the most developer-friendly interfaces usually do not require scrolling. Therefore, you should limit yourself to the number of components that may be viewed without scrolling when the window is maximized.

AWT

The components on the AWT (Abstract Windowing Toolkit) page shown here are JavaBeans distributed as part of the Java SDK from Sun Microsystems. The JavaBeans use the underlying operating system–specific controls to display the user interface components.

NOTE
As mentioned, the Component Palette normally appears in a horizontal form just under the menu bar. As shown in examples in this chapter, you can also display the Component Palette in a vertical format and dock it to a side of the IDE window. This technique is described in Chapter 2. Also, although this chapter shows the names of the components for illustration purposes, you can choose to hide the names by selecting Icon View from the right-click menu on the Component Palette.

Although they are easy to use, AWT components are less flexible than their Swing component counterparts. Therefore, it is recommended that you use Swing components instead to help ensure better consistency across platforms.

Table 18-1 lists the default components on the AWT page and a brief description of each.

Component	Description
Button	A standard push button that you can label with text or an icon or both. The hands-on practice in Chapter 19 works with buttons on a toolbar.
Checkbox	A box that toggles between checked and unchecked. The value changes from "true" to "false" when a checkbox is unchecked. You can set the *icon* property to use a graphic other than the check mark.
CheckboxGroup	This component does not have a visual representation. It is a container for Checkbox components.
Choice	A pulldown list that presents multiple values for the user to select from. You can allow the user to enter a value by setting the *editable* property to "True."
Label	This is a text label to which you can also attach an icon. Normally, you use this for field prompts.
List	A control that presents a list of text strings without a scrollbar. The AWT control supplies a scrollbar, while the Swing version does not.
MenuBar	A component to which you add menus and menu items. The menu bar appears under the title bar of a window and offers a pulldown menu system. Chapter 19 provides a hands-on practice for menus. Unlike the Swing versions, the AWT control is not available for applets.
PopupMenu	This component defines a menu that appears when the user right clicks a component. Chapter 19 also contains a practice for popup menus.

TABLE 18-1. *AWT Components*

Component	Description
Panel	This component does not have a visual representation, although you can set properties to visually display the border. This is a panel into which you place other objects. This control is responsible for layout manager functionality (as described in Chapter 20).
Scrollbar	A vertical or horizontal bar with a button that moves the display or manipulates a value.
ScrollPane	This pane allows you to define horizontal and vertical scrollbars. The user moves the scrollbars to access objects in the pane that are outside the pane's borders.
TextArea	A text editing area that shows text strings ending in newline characters. No scrollbar is on this control, but you can place it in a JScrollPane container if the user will need to scroll.
TextField	A single-row text editing area. Many of the hands-on practices in this book use the Swing version of this control.

TABLE 18-1. *AWT Components* (continued)

For more details about the AWT components available in JDeveloper, see the help topic "About AWT JavaBeans" by entering "About AWT JavaBeans" in the Search tab.

Code Snippets

As mentioned in Chapter 2, you can create a reusable *code snippet* (a small amount of code that you may want to use over and over in your projects), and store it on the Code Snippets Component Palette.

Although Code Snippets is one of the Component Palette pages, most code snippets are nonvisual, and you cannot add them in the UI Editor. You must use the Code Editor. Snippets can be grouped and added to the Component Palette in a separate page containing the snippet group or added individually to an existing page. The Configure Component Palette dialog accessed by selecting **Tools | Configure Palette** from the menu adds snippets to the Component Palette. Clicking a snippet inserts text in the Code Editor.

As an example, you can add code from the hands-on practice in Chapter 3 to the Code Snippets page. This snippet could then be reused to set the column widths on forms that include a Departments view object. You can do this by right clicking anywhere on the Code Snippets Component Palette and selecting Add Component. You then enter the name and code for your snippet in the Add Code Snippet dialog as shown in Figure 18-1.

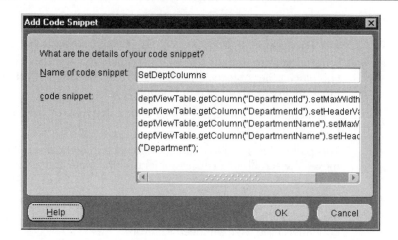

FIGURE 18-1. *Add Code Snippet dialog*

The Code Snippets page of the Component Palette is shown here with the added SetDeptColumns snippet.

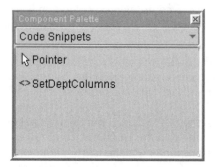

JClient Controls

JDeveloper includes a set of controls to supplement the standard Swing components, as shown next:

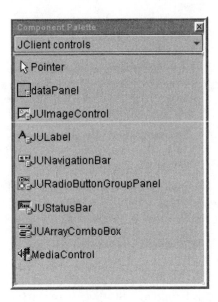

These controls implement the JClient facility discussed in Chapter 17 and allow normal Swing components to be bound to BC4J objects. These controls are accessible in the UI Editor by selecting JClient Controls on the Component Palette pulldown.

You can select from the components shown in Table 18-2.

Component	Description
dataPanel	A container that serves the same purpose as a JPanel but that can be used to hold data controls in your project. It offers the BC4J binding capability. Existing data panels can be reused within the same project.
JUImage	A display control that binds to a BC4J view object to support LONG RAW, RAW BLOB datatypes, and *inter*Media IMAGE types. JUImage uses the JClient attribute *model* property settings to display the BC4J attribute values.

TABLE 18-2. *JClient Controls*

Component	Description
JULabel	A non-editable field, similar to JLabel, that binds to a BC4J attribute to retrieve data. JULabel uses the JClient data model settings to display the BC4J attribute values. This is useful if you want to display data in a non-editable form.
JUNavigationBar	A toolbar that can be bound to a view-object usage, to control items in the same panel, or to a JUPanel to control items in child panels.
JURadioButtonGroupPanel	Another panel control used in combination with the LOV binding to bind BC4J view attribute values for a set of radio buttons. User-friendly attribute values can be displayed rather than less meaningful values using the LOV model editor. The button selection made by the user causes the LOV binding to update the attribute value.
JUStatusBar	A container that displays the status of data items in a panel that is bound to a BC4J view usage. The JUStatusBar uses the JClient view model to control BC4J view-object interactions.
JUArrayComboBox	A pulldown that presents values from one BC4J view attribute. This allows you to define a control bound to a BC4J attribute of type Oracle.jbo.domain.array.
MediaControl	A display object that is bound to a BC4J attribute for multimedia data. MediaControl uses the JClient attribute model settings to display the BC4J attributes. (This control may be called "OrdMediaControl," depending upon your version of JDeveloper.)

TABLE 18-2. *JClient Controls* (continued)

More specific information about the functionality of each of these components can be found by searching for "JClient controls" in the help system Search tab and examining the topic "About JClient-Specific Controls."

Swing

The Swing components in the Swing page of the Component Palette (shown next) are part of the Java Foundation Classes library in the Sun Java SDK:

The Swing component class names usually start with the letter "J" and are contained in the javax.swing package. They are an extension of the AWT controls described before, but Swing components offer a more complete set of properties.

The items in the Swing page of the Component Palette are described in Table 18-3.

For specific information about each of these components, see the help topic "About Swing JavaBeans Components" by searching for "Swing" in the Index tab.

Component	Description and Example
JButton	A standard push button that you can label with text or an icon or both. The hands-on practice in Chapter 19 works with buttons on a toolbar.
JCheckBox	A box that toggles between checked and unchecked. The value changes from "true" to "false" when a checkbox is unchecked. You can set the *icon* property to use a graphic other than the check mark.
JComboBox	A pulldown list that presents multiple values for the user to select from. You can allow the user to enter a value by setting the *editable* property to "True." This control is also called a "poplist" (as in Forms Developer) or a "popup menu" (although there is a different control with the same name that displays a right-click menu). The term that refers to this control with the least confusion and that is generally accepted by Java experts is "combobox."
JEditorPane	A box that can display text formatted in HTML or RTF. It can be used for formatted displays such as that in a help system.
JLabel	This is a text label to which you can also attach an icon. Normally, you use this for field prompts.
JList	A control that presents a list of text strings without a scrollbar. Use the JScrollPane container if you need a scrollbar for this control.
JPasswordField	The same type of control as JTextField, except that this one hides the input by displaying an asterisk character (*) for each character typed.
JProgressBar	A container that graphically displays the completion percentage for a process.
JRadioButton	A single selection button that will be part of a set of buttons in a radio group (ButtonGroup class). Only one button in the group may be selected.
JScrollBar	A vertical or horizontal bar with a button that moves the display or manipulates a value.
JSeparator	This component is used in menus to separate menu items with a horizontal line. It can also be used as a horizontal or vertical straight line or as a spacer in toolbars.
JSlider	A control that is visually and functionally similar to the scrollbar. This control is used more often to change values than is the scrollbar.
JTable	A spreadsheet-like (grid) display of data. The user can modify column widths at runtime.

TABLE 18-3. *Swing Components*

Component	Description and Example
JTextArea	Another text box that shows text strings ending in newline characters. There is no scrollbar on this component, but you can place it in a JScrollPane container if the user will need to scroll.
JTextField	A single-row text editing area. Many of the hands-on practices in this book use this control.
JTextPane	A subclass of JEditorPane that allows you to edit formatted text and embed images and other components within that text. (JEditorPane only allows images within HTML or RTF text.) This means that you can embed other frames or window components as in a Multiple Document Interface (MDI) window.
JTree	Use this to display hierarchical data in a form that emulates the Windows Explorer. A hands-on practice in this chapter includes techniques for working with this component.
JToggleButton	This component looks like a JButton control, but when pressed, it sets a state to "True" until pressed again (similar to the way checkboxes work).

TABLE 18-3. *Swing Components* (continued)

TIP

If you are using Swing classes, you can change the look-and-feel (general appearance) of the runtime. There are four possible styles: Metal, CDE/Motif, Oracle, and Windows". Metal" is the default and has a cross-platform appearance. "CDE/Motif" and "Windows" emulate the general user interface of those operating systems. You can change to CDE/Motif using the following code at the beginning of the main() *method (before any constructors) in any Java application file that uses Swing controls:*

```
try {
    UIManager.setLookAndFeel(new
       com.sun.java.swing.plaf.motif.MotifLookAndFeel());
}
catch (Exception exemp){
  exemp.printStackTrace();
}
```

Substitute "windows.WindowsLookAndFeel" for "motif.Motif LookAndFeel" if you want the runtime to emulate Windows. Use "metal.MetalLookAndFeel" if you want to specify the Metal look, but this is the default. You can right click in the UI Designer and select the look of that window during design time.

Swing Containers

This page of the Component Palette (shown next) also contains Swing components that are used as *containers,* or boxes into which other components are placed:

Technically, many Swing controls are containers because they are subclassed from the java.awt.Container class. For example, JButtons and JTextField are both subclassed from Container, although you do not use them as receptacles for other components. The components on this page are more commonly used to hold other components.

Table 18-4 lists the Swing Containers and a brief description of each.

For specific information about the container components, see the help topic "About Containers" by searching for "Swing containers" in the Search tab.

Component	Description
JMenuBar	A component to which you add menus and menu items. The menu bar appears under the title bar of a window and offers a pulldown menu system. Chapter 19 provides a hands-on practice for menus.
JPanel	This component does not have a visual representation, although you can set properties to visually display the border. JPanel is the main container that is used in many places in the application. It acts as a generic container to hold other objects. It is used in the JTabbedFrame to represent each of the tabs. This control is also responsible for layout manager functionality (as described in Chapter 20).

TABLE 18-4. *Swing Containers*

Component	Description
JPopupMenu	This component defines a menu that appears when the user right clicks a component. Chapter 19 also contains a practice for popup menus.
JScrollPane	This pane allows you to define horizontal and vertical scrollbars. The user moves the scrollbars to access objects in the pane that are outside the pane's borders, for example, multi-record data items. Another example is a window that may need scrolling, such as a large navigation tree. The JViewport view displays the data specified in the data model.
JSplitPane	This container provides the user with two work areas and a movable bar that the user can move to manipulate the width of the panes. The panes can contain other components and can be split either horizontally or vertically. It is a highly useful component, although uncommon in 4GL design tools.
JTabbedPane	This component offers a standard tab folder interface with multiple pages. You can define the edge that the tabs appear on, and use any Container component for the pages. A hands-on practice in this chapter shows how this control works.
JToolBar	This pane provides a container for buttons and other components. The toolbar is floatable, so the user can drag it out of the window into its own window. You can define the toolbar with a horizontal or vertical orientation. Chapter 19 contains a hands-on practice for creating a toolbar.

TABLE 18-3. *Swing Containers* (continued)

Working with Swing Components in JDeveloper

Swing components are Java program units written to conform to a specific (JavaBean) protocol. Swing components are added to a project to control the layout and visibility of your data. All Swing components have three aspects to their use as described in the J2EE *Model-View-Controller* (MVC) architecture:

- **Model** How the component accesses data
- **View** The component's look-and-feel
- **Controller** The component's response to events

The client data model as described more fully in Chapter 17 is an implementation of the MVC Model layer. Most Swing components are visual in nature, which provides the View layer. The event code you write for each component corresponds to the Controller layer.

Using Swing Components

It is as simple to use Swing components in Oracle9*i* JDeveloper as it is to use any control in a 4GL product. The JDeveloper environment is slightly different in that objects can be added in three ways. They can be placed into the Structure window in a tree structure, dropped directly into the UI Editor, or added in the code. Getting the components on the screen and coupling them to BC4J is very straightforward. With practice, you can quickly be as productive at adding components as in any 4GL tool such as Oracle Forms Developer.

Trying to control the objects you have created reveals both the blessing and the curse of using Java. Java is almost limitlessly flexible. You can do just about anything you want; however, almost anything you might want to do other than dropping a Swing component into your application and setting properties in the Property Inspector requires a good deal of work to figure out how to achieve the desired result.

Even a simple-sounding task such as making a field wider, adding a double-click event, or changing the color of a field in a specific context may be a frustrating experience if you do not have some guidance. Using the right layout manager may help. It may take you a few tries until you find the right clue in the right Java book or find the answer to your question on an Internet list server to solve some of the problems you may encounter.

Adding Swing Components to a Program

Swing components are the most often used Java UI components. Therefore, the major focus in this chapter will be on Swing components. The JClient architecture that guides the JClient controls is introduced in Chapter 17.

Adding Swing components to a program is very simple. You can add many components at once by using the high-level wizards in JDeveloper or one at a time by using the UI Editor. Of course, you can also add them by editing the code itself.

If the component you want to add is in the Component Palette (while the UI Editor is open), you can select it and click either on the UI Editor where you want the component to appear or in the Structure window in the desired position. It is usually easier to add components to the Structure window and then to adjust their position in the UI Editor. It is important to have each component in its correct logical place. Sometimes it is hard to position an object in the correct place (usually in a particular JPanel) by using the UI Editor, because a layout manager imposes a particular behavior.

When you add a Swing component using the Component Palette, JDeveloper writes code into your program. For example, when you add a button (JButton) using the UI Editor, the wizard first adds a line of code that declares the button as shown here:

```
private JButton jButton1 = new JButton();
```

Next, in the `jbInit()` method of the code, the wizard will typically set one or more properties of the component. In this case it only sets a single property as shown next:

```
jButton1.setText("jButton1");
```

Finally, it adds the component to the container in the position in a logical place as shown here:

```
dataPanel.add(jButton1, BorderLayout.CENTER);
```

In addition, it adds the appropriate import statements so that the proper class files are available. In this example, JDeveloper adds the following code:

```
import javax.swing.JButton;
```

If you rename the component or modify properties, the code will be updated to reflect the change.

Categories of Swing Components

Swing components are usually written very flexibly so that virtually any aspect of the component can be changed to meet your requirements. The various types of Swing components can be loosely grouped as follows:

- **Container**   Windows, frames, panes, and panels. Components that act as areas on the screen and into which you place visual objects such as fields and labels.

- **Data**   Text fields, checkboxes, tables, trees, charts that display data.

- **Action**   Buttons, sliders, free-standing scrollbars, and so on. Components that control other components, generate actions, generate a value, or respond to events.

- **Static**   Labels and graphic items that are not data related.

- **Nonvisual**   Timers and similar components that are not displayed.

- **Dialog**   Help messages, modal alert boxes, and similar components.

Using most of these components is pretty straightforward. Containers are a bit more complex and require a bit of explanation.

Container Objects

Container objects are typically the first Swing components you add to a user interface application. They act as the windows and canvases on which to place other objects. As discussed in Chapter 17, you need to bind container components to BC4J so that the data components within the containers will be able to access data.

Most of the common Swing containers are described in the "Swing Containers" section earlier in this chapter (JPanel, JTabbedPane, JScrollPane, and JSplitPane). Other common containers follow.

JFrame	This is the main container frame for the program. It appears as a window on the screen. There is usually only a single JFrame in a program.
JInternalFrame	This appears as a window in the user interface. It is used to support Multiple Document Interface (MDI).
JDesktopPane	This is an enclosing panel to support the JInternalFrame windows.

Laying out the frames and panels for an application is an important step. This is similar to understanding the layout of the frames in Oracle Report Builder, except that rather than having only a single type of frame, you now have many to choose from.

NOTE
Containers are often nested. Chapter 20 discusses nested containers and the container hierarchy.

Container Layout Guidelines

Laying out panels and frames is a critical and challenging step in the UI design of a program. Those with Oracle Report Builder experience will find that it is similar to using frames in the Reports Layout Model.

Creating frames, panels, and panes can be accomplished in the three following ways:

- **Use the wizards.** This is typically where you start your development. Until you are comfortable with the code that wizards generate, this is the easiest way to create working code that you can modify to meet your specific needs.

- **Use the JDeveloper UI Editor and Property Inspector.** This is the method you will most often use to add containers. The code generated by the UI Editor and Property Inspector is quite robust.

- **Write code manually in the Code Editor.** You can use the UI Editor or Structure window to add frames more quickly, easily, and reliably than in the Code Editor. However, if you are more comfortable and efficient with typing your own code, you have that option in JDeveloper.

What Containers Should Be Used Where?

This question is not as complex as you might think. If you look closely at the generated layout, you will see that the container structure in Java is very logical.

JFrame and JPanel For a Java application, you always start with a JFrame as the outside container (the window). Then you access its contentPane and place a JPanel directly inside it. This is just like the primary window and the main content canvas in Oracle Forms. The JPanel acts as your main container to partition the screen into different areas. You may add other containers for specific purposes. For all containers, you need to make decisions about the layout manager (as described in Chapter 20).

JScrollPane The next most common type of container is the JScrollPane. This is a special container used whenever you want a scrollbar to traverse large quantities of data or images that will not fit on the available screen size. There is also a Swing component that is a scrollbar, but usually it is more convenient to use the JScrollPane and take advantage of its default behavior. The JDeveloper wizards create a scrollbar to scroll through a set of records just by placing a JTable (providing a multi-record display) inside a JScrollPane (which provides the scrollbar).

JTabbedPane   To make a tab container, you create a JTabbedPane in your program and then add a JPanel for each tab page. Each tab page in the tab container is a JPanel.

JSplitPane   A JSplitPane contains exactly two JPanels that share the area defined for the JSplitPane. JSplitPanes can divide a given area in either the horizontal or vertical direction.

JDesktopPane   If you want to have multiple independent or floating windows in your program, you can add a parent container called a JDesktopPane and then add child JInternalFrame containers for each window you wish to display.

Container Layout Example
The following is a simple example of how the JClient Form Wizard in JDeveloper builds the frame and panel containers for a standard master-detail application. This discussion is based on the structure of what is generated in the Chapter 1 Java application hands-on practice. An examination of the four classes that the wizard generates reveals the container structure described here.

The Frame Class   The first class generated by the wizard is the program-level container class represented by the diagram shown here:

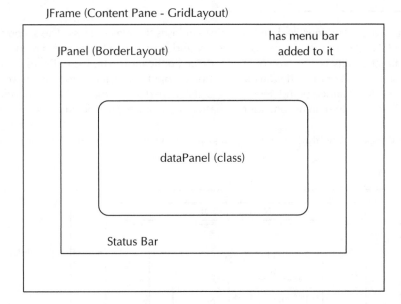

JFrame (Content Pane - GridLayout)

JPanel (BorderLayout)

has menu bar added to it

dataPanel (class)

Status Bar

This class is the outside container, so it is a JFrame (with a GridLayout layout manager) as is expected. Inside the JFrame is a menu bar. Also inside the JFrame is a JPanel with a BorderLayout layout manager that encloses all of the remaining user interface components. Layout managers and BC4J bindings are designed to work with panels, so this container is required. Finally, inside the main JPanel is the data panel, which is just an instance of the panel class (described next) and has the purpose of controlling the layout for the remaining components.

The Panel Class   The second class extends a JPanel and has a border layout as shown here:

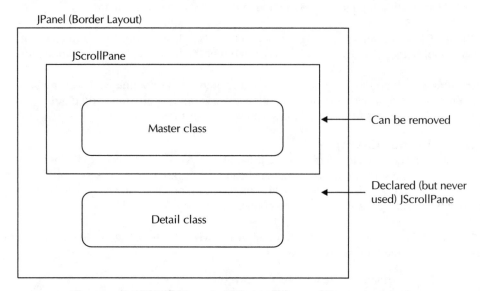

There are two JScrollPanes declared. The first encloses the master class. The second is declared but never used. Neither of these panes is necessary and neither can be removed manually without affecting the functionality of this type of master-detail application. The JScrollPanes are built by the wizards for use in some of the other layout options. Within the master JScrollPane is an instance of the master class. An instance of the detail class is also added to the main JPanel. This effectively divides the JPanel into two areas: one for the master class, one for the detail class.

The Master Class   The third generated class is the master class for the Locations area as shown here:

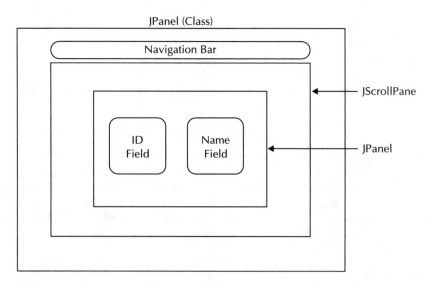

The master class is a JPanel with a BorderLayout layout manager. Inside this panel are a navigation bar and a JScrollPane. Inside the JScrollPane is a JPanel that holds the data fields.

The Detail Class   The fourth class in the application is also a JPanel as shown here:

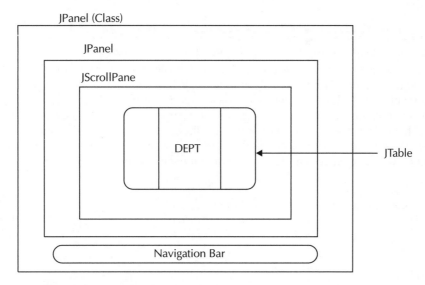

This class is a JPanel used for the Departments area (the detail in the master-detail). Just like the Locations class, it contains a navigation bar. Inside the class is another JPanel. Inside that is a JScrollPane to hold the JTable (which provides the multi-column, multi-row grid display of the Departments information).

Modifying Swing Components

Most common properties of a Swing component can be modified using the Property Inspector. What you are really doing when you make changes to the Property Inspector is modifying your program code. For example, if you access the properties of a button and change the *border* property of the button to be a raised bevel border, you will find the following line added to your code:

```
jButton1.setBorder(BorderFactory.createBevelBorder(BevelBorder.RAISED));
```

The following imports are also added to support the added code:

```
import javax.swing.BorderFactory;
import javax.swing.border.BevelBorder;
```

You can also directly modify the component by calling the appropriate method. You can see a list of the methods available for each component by using the JDeveloper feature, Code Insight. To activate this feature, type the name of the component followed by a "." After a short pause, a list will appear containing the available methods, classes, and constants. For a simple button, there are hundreds of items in the list. You can also activate Code Insight by pressing CTRL-SPACEBAR after typing the "." Code Insight is also available for packages and attributes.

Component objects can be manipulated without restriction at runtime. In addition, objects are created at runtime without restriction. For example, if you took the code for adding a button and executed it in an event somewhere in your code, the button would be created dynamically even though it was not "physically" represented in the UI Editor.

Binding a Swing Component to BC4J

Different Swing components bind differently to BC4J. The *model* property is used for BC4J binding to view-level objects such as panels. For attribute-level objects such as JTextField, the Swing-named *document* property is used for binding. While editing the component in a JClient panel (panel with a panel binding) and selecting the *model* property in the Property Inspector, you will see the different JClient property editors. You can select an editor from the list. Some components have more than one JClient property editor, since they support more than one type of binding to the middle tier. You can edit the current value, by clicking the "…" button. The following code will be created after setting the *document* property:

```
mLocationId.setDocument
(JUTextFieldBinding.createAttributeBinding(
panelBinding,    //referencing the panelBinding for the Application Module
mLocationId,
"LocationsView1",
null,
"LocationsView1Iter",
"LocationId"));
```

setDocument is the Swing component's method to set the data source of the field. JUTextFieldBinding is an Oracle-supplied class that allows you to pass the binding information to the JTextField. For information about the individual parameters, search the JDeveloper help system for "JUTextFieldBinding."

In summary, binding Swing components available to BC4J in JDeveloper is done by simply filling in a property on the Property Inspector. You will have little reason to manipulate the binding other than through the Property Inspector properties of document or model. You can inspect the underlying binding code to see how Java handles the binding.

Defining Events

Swing components are JavaBean classes that include the ability to fire events. An example of an event is the action performed when the user clicks the button. Events allow you to execute code based on user interaction with your application. Events can be anything from the trivial detecting that a button has been pressed, to more complex events such as detecting that a component has been moved.

Events require two types of code as follows:

- **An event listener** to detect the event and to call an event handler
- **A method** (event handler) with code that executes when the listener determines that the event has occurred

Events are most easily created using the Property Inspector. After clicking the object in the UI Editor, the Property Inspector will show a Properties tab with properties applicable to that component and an Events tab, shown in Figure 18-2, with a list of events offered by that component.

FIGURE 18-2. *Events tab*

You select the event in the Events tab and click the "…" button for that event. A dialog such as the one shown here for the actionPerformed event will appear where you can rename the method stub where you will put your code:

When you click OK, the dialog will create both the listener and the code stub for you, and place the cursor in the code stub so you can add the event code. You cannot add the code directly in the Property Inspector. However, you can type the name of the code stub into the event field in the Property Inspector and press ENTER. The Property Inspector will create the code stub and pass the focus to the Code Editor. The event dialog will not appear in this case.

The hands-on practice later in this chapter shows how to build a button with a button-pressed event.

Hands-on Practice: Create a Tabbed User Interface Application

Tabbed user interfaces are very familiar to most developers and users. This practice will create an application that gives you practice in using some of the most common Swing components in a simple multi-tabbed application.

This practice includes the following phases:

I. Create the BC4J project

II. Create the Java application project

III. Create a three-tab user interface

■ Create the main panel and three tabs

■ Create labels and fields on Tab 1

- Create a table on Tab 2
- Modify the column width
- Add a tree structure on Tab 3

If you need help or more detailed explanations for any of the basic steps, refer to the hands-on practice in Chapter 1.

I. Create the BC4J Project

In this phase, you select the business components that will be used in the Java application that you will create in Phase II.

1. On the Workspaces node in the Navigator, select New Workspace from the right-click menu.

2. Change the *Directory Name* and the *File Name* fields to "DeptEmpWS." Uncheck the *Add a New Empty Project* checkbox, and click OK to create the workspace file.

3. On the DeptEmpWS node, select New Project from the right-click menu. Select Project Containing New Business Components and click OK.

4. Click Next if the Welcome page of the Project Containing New Business Components Wizard appears. Fill in the *Directory Name* and *File Name* as "DeptEmpBC4J" and click Next.

5. On the Paths page, fill in the *Default Package* as "deptempbc4j." Leave the other default settings.

6. Click Next and Finish to create the project. The Business Components Package Wizard will be displayed.

7. Click Next if the Welcome page appears. On the Package Name page of the Business Components Package Wizard, ensure that "deptempbc4j" is shown in the *Package Name* field and that the "Entity Objects mapped to database schema objects" radio button is selected. Click Next to display the Connection page.

8. Be sure the HR connection is selected in the *Connection Name* field and click Next.

9. On the Business Components page, select DEPARTMENTS and EMPLOYEES, and move them to the *Selected* pane by using the right-arrow button. Click Finish. The wizard will create default BC4J objects in the new project.

10. Rebuild and save the project.

What Just Happened?   You created a default BC4J project containing department and employee objects using the wizards. The BC4J project includes the package and module needed for the application project to be created in the next phase.

II. Create the Java Application Project

The application you use for this practice can be relatively basic, but it needs some specific elements. The following abbreviated steps will create a minimal application that you can use as a basis. You will use the JClient Form Wizard to create an application based on the business components you defined before.

1. Create an empty project in the DeptEmpWS.jws workspace. Change the *Directory Name* and the *File Name* fields to "DeptEmpJA."

2. On the DeptEmpJA.jpr node in the Navigator, select New from the right-click menu. In the New gallery, select Swing/JClient for BC4J from the Client Tier node and Empty Form from the Items list. Click OK to open the JClient Empty Form Wizard.

3. Click Next if the Welcome page appears. On the Data Model page, click New to create a Client Data Model called "DeptEmpModel." Complete the BC4J Client Data Model Definition Wizard.

4. Ensure that "DeptEmpModel" appears as the data model definition on the Data Model page of the JClient Empty Form Wizard. Click Next to display the Form name panel.

5. Change the *Package name* field to "deptempapp" on the Form Name page. Change the *Form name* to "DeptEmpForm" as shown here:

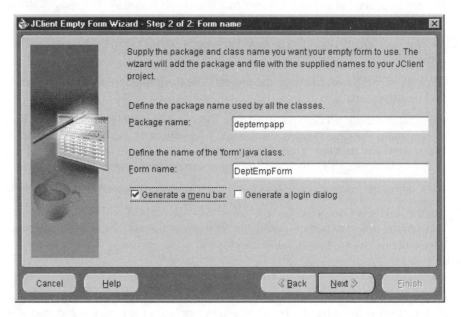

6. Click Next and Finish. You will now see the DeptEmpForm.java file added to the Navigator, and the UI Editor will open to show the user interface shown in Figure 18-3.

7. Click Save All.

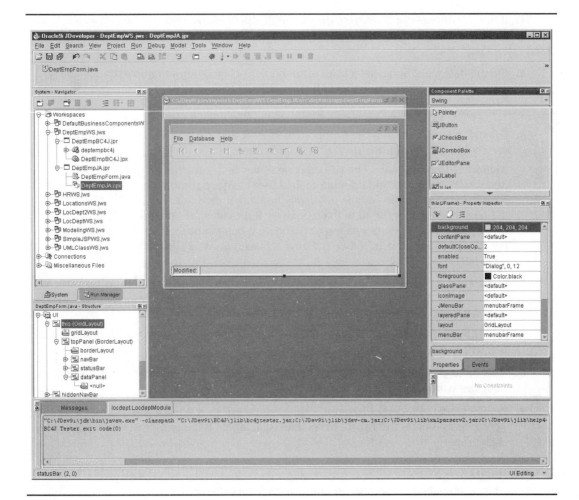

FIGURE 18-3. *UI Editor for DeptEmpForm*

What Just Happened?   You created a simple Java application and form using the JDeveloper wizard that will serve as the basis for adding more user interface components in the following phases. This application already has the JClient data binding available so that components created in the panel will be able to bind to the BC4J objects.

III. Create a Three-Tab User Interface

In this phase, you will add three tabs to display the data in the form you just created.

Create the Main Panel and Three Tabs

This section adds a tab container and three tab pages.

I. If the UI Editor is not displayed, on the DeptEmpForm.java node in the Navigator, select UI Editor from the right-click menu. In the Structure window, expand the UI, "this," and topPanel nodes.

2. On the dataPanel node, select Cut from the right-click menu to remove the dataPanel. This will leave you a space to add a JTabbedPane component.

3. Select Swing Containers from the Component Palette pulldown.

4. Select JTabbedPane from the Component Palette, and click topPanel in the Structure window to add the tabbed pane to the application.

Additional Information: The tabbed pane serves as a container for multiple panels and is perfectly suited for a standard multi-tabbed user interface common to many applications. Tabs in Java are handled a little differently from other products. The JTabbedPane serves as the outside container for all of the tab pages. It provides the tab "buttons" and the logic for navigating between tab pages, only showing one tab page at time. The actual tab pages are regular JPanels. When a JPanel is placed inside a JTabbedPane, it appears as a tab page.

5. In the Property Inspector, change the *name* property to "mainTab" and press ENTER. You will see mainTab under topPanel in the Structure window. In the Property Inspector, ensure that the *constraints* property is set to "Center."

Additional Information: This main tab will serve as the container for the multiple tabs you will create for this application.

6. Select JPanel from the Swing Containers Component Palette, and click mainTab in the Structure window to add the first tab.

7. On the JPanel1 Property Inspector, change the *name* property to "tab1," and change the *constraints* property to "Tab 1" to set the visual label on the tab. Press ENTER after setting each property.

CAUTION
As of this writing, the "constraints" property for a JPanel does not appear in all of the look-and-feel options. If you do not see the "constraints" property, switch to the Windows look-and-feel.

8. Repeat steps 6 and 7 twice to create tab2 and tab3 (using *constraints* of "Tab 2" and "Tab 3," respectively).

9. Click Save All. The Structure window should look like Figure 18-4.

10. Run the DeptEmpForm.java file to make sure that everything is working. The application should look like the following:

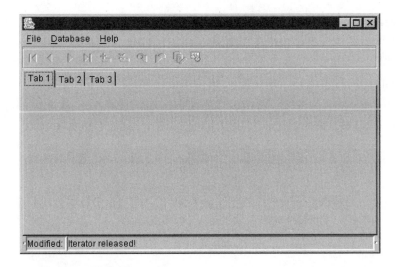

Create Labels and Fields on Tab 1

Use these steps to create a basic user interface showing labeled fields.

    1. On the Property Inspector for tab1, change the *layout* property to "null."

FIGURE 18-4.   *Structure window for tabbed application*

2. Change to the Swing page in the Component Palette using the pulldown. Select JLabel and click tab1 in the Structure window.

3. Select JTextField on the Component Palette, and click tab1 in the Structure window.

4. Repeat steps 2 and 3 to add another label and text field to tab1.

5. Use the UI Editor to drag and drop and to resize the labels and text fields until it looks something like this:

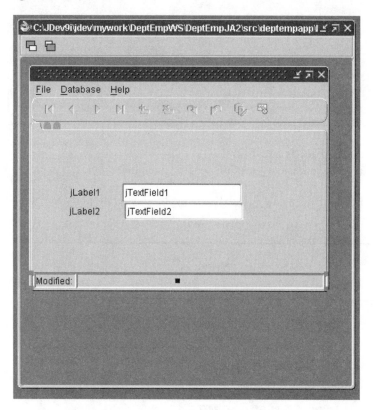

6. Select jLabel1, and SHIFT click jLabel2. Click the Align Center icon in the UI Editor window to line up the labels.

7. Select the two text fields, and click the Align Center icon to align the fields.

8. Select JTextField1 in the Structure window. Select JClient Attribute Binding from the *document* property pulldown.

9. Select DepartmentsView1 in the left pane of the document window and DepartmentId in the right pane as shown next. Click OK.

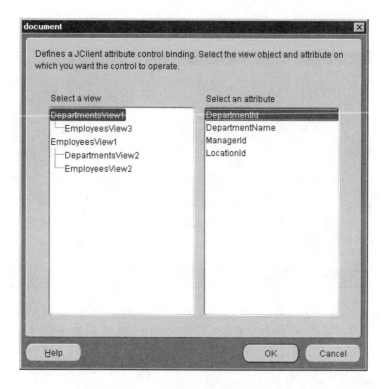

10. Enter "departmentIdField" in the *name* property field. Press ENTER.

11. Select the JLabel1 node in the Structure window. Change the *name* property to "departmentIdLabel" and the *text* property to "ID."

12. Select JTextField2 in the Structure window. Select JClient Attribute Binding from the *document* property pulldown.

13. Select DepartmentsView1 in the left pane of the document window and DepartmentName in the right pane. Click OK.

14. Enter "departmentNameField" in the *name* property. Press ENTER.

15. Select the JLabel2 node in the Structure window. Change the *name* property to "departmentNameLabel" and the *text* property to "Name."

16. In the Structure window, select the navBar node. Select "JClient View Binding" in the *model* property to display the model dialog.

17. Select "DepartmentsView1" and click OK. This associates the navigation bar control at the top of the form with the DepartmentsView1 view usage, which will allow you to scroll through records in the form.

18. Click Save All.

19. Select DeptEmpForm.java and Run. You should see something like this:

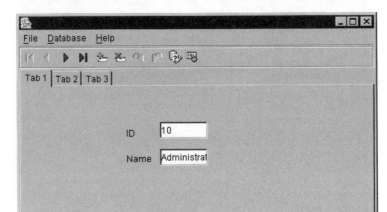

20. Try the navigation bar buttons to ensure that you can scroll through records in the DEPARTMENTS table. Note that the *Name* field is too small for some of the data.

21. Close the window and return to the UI Editor. Adjust the Name window using the center drag handle on the right side of the *Name* field to make it long enough so that the department names will not be truncated.

22. Click Save All and run DeptEmpForm.java again to see that the changes were made successfully.

Additional Information: The Departments information appears because you have correctly bound the Swing components to the BC4J objects using the *document* and *model* properties.

Create a Table on Tab 2

These steps demonstrate how to create a table UI control to show data in a multi-column, multi-row form.

1. To view tab2 in the UI Editor, you need to temporarily reorder the tabs. If necessary, expand the UI, "this," topPanel, and mainTab nodes in the Structure window. Select the Tab 2 tab in the UI Editor, and click the Bring to Front icon on the UI Editor toolbar.

2. Select JScrollPane from the Swing Containers page, and click tab2 in the Structure window to add a scrollable panel for your table.

3. Select jScrollPane1 in the Structure window. Change the name to "tableScrollPane."

4. Select the JTable icon from the Swing page, and click tableScrollPane in the Structure window. You will see the jTable1 component added under tableScrollPane in the Structure window.

Additional Information: The table may appear as a tiny area (black square) on the top left corner of Tab 2. If this happens, click the visible handle and drag the table out to the desired size.

TIP
When working with multi-tabbed or paneled applications in the UI Editor, to ensure that you are placing components correctly, it is usually better to click the Component Palette icon and then the appropriate node in the Structure window.

5. Change the *name* property to "empTable."

6. Select "JClientAttribute list binding" from the *model* property pulldown. Select EmployeesView3 (the detail table for Departments View1) from the "Select a view" pane.

7. Move all attributes but FirstName and LastName from the "Selected attributes" pane to the Available Attributes pane by using the left-arrow button as shown here. Click OK.

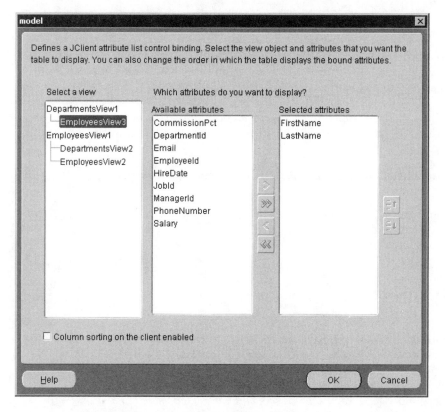

8. To update the column titles, expand the DeptEmpBC4J.jpr and deptempbc4j nodes in the Navigator window and select EmployeesView.

9. In the Structure window FirstName node, select Edit FirstName from the right-click menu. In the Attribute Wizard, click Control Hints and enter "First Name" in the *Label Text* field. Click OK.

   Additional Information: JDeveloper uses control hints to determine how BC4J objects are displayed. More information about control hints can be found in Chapter 23.

10. In the Structure window LastName node, select Edit LastName from the right-click menu. In the Attribute Wizard, click Control Hints and enter "Last Name" in the *Label Text* field. Click OK.

11. Click on the UI Editor to access the Structure window again. To reorder the tabs, select tab1 in the Structure window, and click the Bring to Front icon in the UI Editor toolbar.

12. Click Save All.

13. Select DeptEmpForm.java and click Run to verify that everything is working. The table display on Tab 2 will change depending upon what Department is selected on Tab 1. (Department 50 has many entries for Tab 2.)

14. Close the application.

Modify the Column Width

At this point, you need to adjust the column widths. Since there is no JTable property to handle this, you will need to modify the code to create an object pointer to the appropriate column, and manipulate the width properties.

1. Click the DeptEmpForm.java code editor button in the document window to display the Code Editor. Add the following import statement to the beginning list:

   ```
   import javax.swing.table.*;
   ```

   Additional Information: Without this package, the emptable.getColumn call will not compile.

2. In the Structure window, double click setPanelBinding(JUPanelBinding) to navigate to that method in the Code Editor. Scroll to the jbInit() call, and add the following code after that method:

   ```
   TableColumn firstNameColumn = empTable.getColumn("First Name");
   firstNameColumn.setMinWidth(100);
   firstNameColumn.setMaxWidth(100);
   ```

TIP
The first line of code where you are referencing the First Name column must be spelled exactly as it is in the BC4J Control Hint – Label Text specification. You can ensure that this is correct by double clicking the EmployeesViewRowImplMsgBundle.java file for EmployeesView in the deptempbc4j package and copying and pasting the value of the "FirstName_LABEL" into the code ("First Name" in this case, with a space between the words).

3. Select DeptEmpForm.java and click Run. Tab 2 should look something like the following. Note that what is displayed on Tab 2 depends upon what is selected in Tab 1. The navigation bar at the top of the form allows you to scroll through DEPARTMENTS records, so the child employee records will change on Tab 2 when you use the scroll buttons.

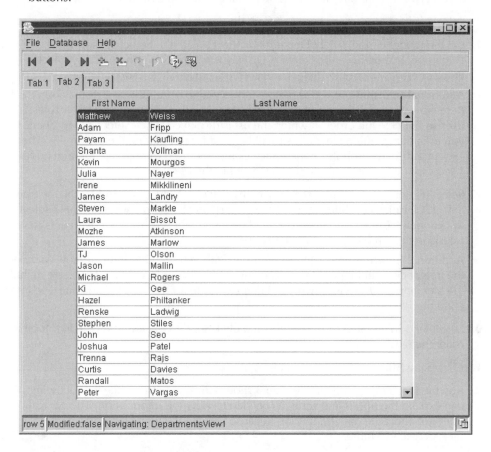

Add a Tree Structure on Tab 3

The following steps demonstrate how to add a tree structure to the third tab of the UI.

1. Select the DeptEmpForm.java UI Editor button in the Document Bar. Expand the UI, "this," topPanel, and mainTab nodes, if necessary.

2. Select tab3 in the Structure window, and click Bring to Front in the UI Editor toolbar.

3. Select JScrollPane from the Swing Containers page. Click tab3 in the Structure window to add the scroll pane.

4. Select JScrollPane1 in the Structure window. Change the *name* to "treeScrollPane."

5. From the Swing page of the Component Palette, add a JTree component to the treeScrollPane in the Structure window.

6. Select jTree1 in the Structure window. Change the *name* property to "deptEmpTree."

7. Select "JClient Node type binding" from the *model* pulldown.

8. On the model dialog, select DepartmentsView1 from the Select A View pane, and select DepartmentName from the Select A Display Attribute pane. In this case, select EmployeesView from the "Select an accessor" pane. Click "Add new rule."

Additional Information: This dialog allows you to set up the tree display. On the Edit Rule tab, you select the list of nodes to be displayed in the tree. The Show rules tab is used to indicate the order in which the list is displayed. The "Select a view" pane allows you to indicate which view object will be used for populating the tree nodes. The "Select a display attribute" pane indicates the rule used to populate the tree nodes. "Accessor definition" links to the next level in the tree.

9. Select deptempbc4j.EmployeesView in the Select A View pane and LastName from the Select A Display Attribute pane. Leave the default "Select an accessor" field selection set to "<none>." Click "Add new rule" and OK. You will see "root: DepartmentsView1 + (2 rules)"on the JTree object in the UI Editor.

Additional Information: On the "Edit rule" tab, you need to indicate how each level of the tree nodes will be populated. The number indicates how many levels are included in the hierarchy. In this case, two were defined—one for the parent node and one for the child branch.

10. Select tab3 in the Structure window, and click Send to Back in the UI Editor toolbar to order the tabs correctly.

11. Click Save All.

12. Run the DeptEmpForm.java file. Tab 3 should look something like the following. You can expand the nodes and scroll as needed to view the information. The navigation bar does not affect the data on this tab because you are viewing all records in the DEPARTMENTS table.

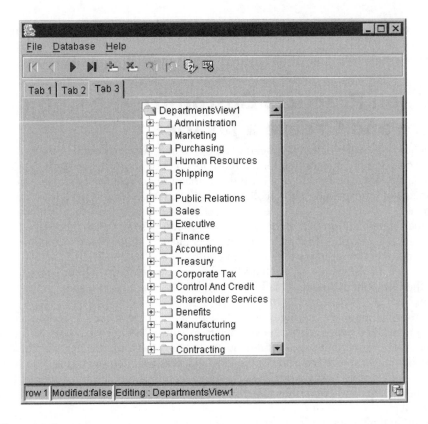

13. Close the form.

NOTE
*Set the "rootVisible" property of the tree control to "False" if you want
to hide the top node that shows the view usage name.*

What Just Happened?   In this phase, you added a tree structure to Tab 3 to display the
departments information in another format. Because of the way the binding is made, you can
control the structure and order of the parent and child tree nodes as well as the number of tree
levels in the hierarchy.

You created a form with three tabs. Each tab displayed the information in a different format:

■ Labels and fields

■ Table

■ Tree structure

These UI components are typical of the types of user interfaces you will use in creating applications with JDeveloper.

Study this example carefully before trying to branch out to other components.

Hands-on Practice: Customize the Component Palette and Create a JavaBean

In this practice, you will create a JavaBean component and library to contain the JavaBean. A *JavaBean* is one or more classes that form a reusable component. All objects on the Component Palette are JavaBeans. The benefit of a JavaBean is that it offers reusability and enables you to take advantage of introspection, which allows a tool like JDeveloper to get a list of its properties. Another benefit is that it has a visual design aspect, so JDeveloper and other design tools can show a visual representation of the component. Once you design, create, and debug the bean, you can leverage that work by using it over and over again. The JavaBean hides the complexity of its code and offers an interface that you can control.

This practice also steps you through adding the component to an "Other" page that you create for the Component Palette. Finally, you will build a simple application to test the new component.

You can add components to pages of the Component Palette as well as reorder components within the preinstalled pages. You can even delete existing pages. For example, you could remove the AWT component page. While you are learning the tool, it is probably best to keep the preinstalled pages intact and add components that you need to new pages. You will be able to find components more easily when they are referenced in examples and documentation. After you learn the product and components better, you will be better able to customize the pages to match your style.

For ordering the components on the page, you can either choose a logical organization or an alphabetical organization (which requires you to know the names of the items). By default, the product ships with the components arranged alphabetically from left to right. You should probably stay with this configuration. This will make it easier for developers coming from other environments to find the components for which they are looking.

This practice consists of the following phases:

I. Create and deploy a JavaBean

■ Create the JavaBean

■ Deploy the JavaBean

II. Create a library for the JavaBean

III. Add a Component Palette page and a custom JavaBean

■ Create a Component Palette page

■ Add a custom JavaBean to the page

IV. Test the custom component

I. Create and Deploy a JavaBean

The easiest way to manage your custom JavaBeans is to store them in a separate workspace and project. This way you are able to keep them in an isolated area, and deploy them as necessary in your projects. Although this practice creates a JavaBean that might not be used in a real production application, it will familiarize you with the steps required to create and add your own customized Beans for reuse in your JDeveloper projects.

Create the JavaBean

This section creates a JavaBean by extending an existing component.

1. On the Workspaces node in the Navigator, select New Workspace from the right-click menu.

2. Change the *Directory Name* and the *File Name* to "CustomBeansWS." Leave the *Add a New Empty Project* checkbox checked. Click OK.

3. In the New Project dialog, change the *Directory Name* and the *File Name* to "CustomJOption." Click OK to create the project.

4. On the CustomJOption.jpr project node, select New from the right-click menu. Select JavaBeans from the Client Tier category and Bean from the Items list. Click OK to display the New Bean dialog shown here:

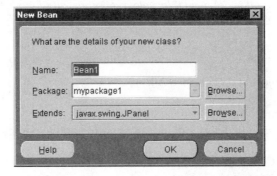

5. Enter "DemoJOptionBean" in the *Name* field and "custombeans" in the *Package* field.

6. Click the *Extends* field pulldown and select java.lang.Object. Click OK.

7. Click Save All.

8. If the file is not open in the Code Editor, double click DemoJOptionBean.java to open the Code Editor.

9. Add the following import statements just below the first line of code declaring the package for the class:
   import javax.swing.*;
   import javax.swing.JOptionPane;

10. Replace the default public `DemoJOptionBean()` constructor with the following code:

```
public DemoJOptionBean(JPanel inPanel)
{
  JOptionPane.showMessageDialog(
      inPanel,
      "This is a modal dialog box",
      "Sample Information Dialog",
      JOptionPane.INFORMATION_MESSAGE);
}
```

This code shows a message dialog (alert or message box) with a default message and title within a specific panel referenced by the input argument, `inPanel`.

11. Click Rebuild and Save All.

12. Select **File | Import**. Select Existing Sources and click OK.

13. Click Next if the Welcome page of the Import Existing Sources Wizard appears. Click Add and navigate to the following file: JDEV_HOME\jdev\multi\system\templates\images\generic.gif.

14. Check the *Copy Files to Project Directory* checkbox.

NOTE
You may have different .gif files, depending upon your version of JDeveloper. If generic.gif is not available, select another .gif file to represent the added component.

15. Click Next and Finish. You will see the .gif file added to the project in the Navigator.

16. Rebuild the project and click Save All.

Deploy the JavaBean
The following steps are used to define a deployment profile and to deploy your bean.

1. Right click the CustomJOption.jpr node in the Navigator window and select New.

2. Select General\Deployment Profiles\Client JAR File – J2EE Client Module. Click OK.

3. In the Save Deployment Profile – Client JAR File – J2EE Client Module dialog, change the *File name* to "demojar.deploy." Click Save.

4. Accept the default settings in the Client JAR Deployment Profile Settings dialog, and click OK to generate the deployment profile.

5. Click Save All. The Navigator should look like the following:

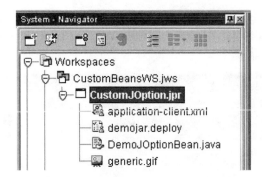

6. Select the demojar.deploy node in the Navigator, and select "Deploy to JAR file" from the right-click menu. You should see a message such as "Deployment finished" in the Log window.

What Just Happened?   You created a new JavaBean that can be an instantiatable (as opposed to static) class and deployed it to a JAR file. In the next phase, you will reference this JAR as a library in order to allow the bean to be reused.

II. Create a Library for the JavaBean

You need to make the new JavaBean available to JDeveloper by including it in a library. A *library* is a name for one or more JAR and/or Zip files that contain code required to run an application. You can add libraries to a project in two ways. The first way is to add the library to the default project settings (**Project | Default Project Settings**) so that every project created from that moment on will be able to use the library. You can also add the library to the settings for a specific project (after selecting the project, select **Project | Project Settings**) so that only that project will use the library.

  This phase creates the library and adds it to the default project settings area so that any new project will be set up to use it. This demonstrates how to add libraries to all future projects. When you or a JDeveloper wizard adds a library to a project, the files in the library are added to the CLASSPATH when running the project. When you deploy the project, the libraries attached to the project can be added through the Dependencies node of the Project Settings dialog (as shown in Chapter 16). Since this particular library will not be used for development after this practice, a later phase will remove it from the default project settings.

1. Select **Project | Default Project Settings** from the menu.

2. In the Project Settings dialog, if needed, expand the Configurations and Development nodes and select Libraries.

3. In the lower-right corner, click New to create a library.

4. In the New Library dialog, change the *Library Name* to "CustomJOptionBeans."

5. Click the Edit button to the right of the *Class Path* field. Then click Add Entry in the Edit Class Path dialog.

6. In the Select Path Entry dialog, navigate to CustomBeansWS, then to CustomJOption, deploy, and demojar.jar. Click Select and OK. The New Library dialog should look like this:

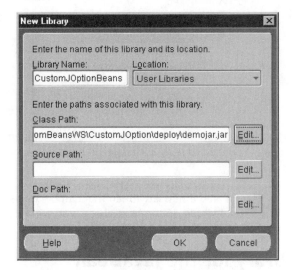

7. Click OK to close the New Library dialog. You will see the new library listed in the Selected Libraries pane. Click OK to close the Project Settings dialog.

What Just Happened?   In this phase, you created a library to reference the JAR file containing the JavaBean from Phase I. Since you made the modifications to the default project setting, this will affect all future projects. A later phase will reverse this setting.

III. Add a Component Palette Page and a Custom JavaBean

In this phase, you will add the custom bean you created in Phase I to a new Component Palette page and will learn how to add predefined and user-defined components to the palette.

Create a Component Palette Page

You can easily create pages to hold additional components using the steps such as the following:

1. Open the UI Editor by selecting any .java file in the Navigator and selecting UI Editor from the right-click menu. In this case, you can use the DemoJOptionBean.java file created in Phase I.

2. To create a Component Palette page, place the cursor in a blank area of the Component Palette, and select Add Page from the right-click menu.

3. On the New Palette Page dialog, enter "Other" in the *Page Name* field. Leave "java" as the *Page Type.* Click OK.

4. You will now see "Other" in the Component Palette pulldown and a blank area to its right for adding components.

Additional Information: You can also accomplish this task by selecting Properties from the right-click menu on a Component Palette blank area to open the Configure Component Palette dialog. You will use this dialog later in the practice to add components.

Add a Custom JavaBean to the Page

The following steps will add the DemoJOptionPane component to the Other page you just created. The only information needed to add a component to a tab is its name, a library location, and the icon file name. The DemoJOptionBean is located in the CustomJOptionBeans library.

1. To add the component, select "Other" in the component pulldown. Right click in the blank area to the right, and select Add Component to open the Add JavaBeans dialog, as shown in Figure 18-5.

2. Using the Library pulldown, select CustomJOptionBeans.

3. Expand the custombeans node. Select DemoJOptionBean.

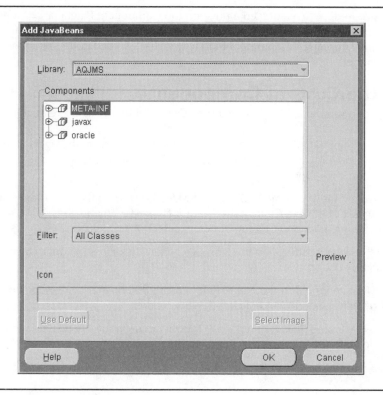

FIGURE 18-5. *Add JavaBeans dialog*

4. To use the generic.gif icon, click the Select Image button. Then navigate to JDEV_HOME\jdev\mywork\CustomBeansWS\CustomJOption\src\generic.gif. Click Open to select the icon. The path will be shown in the *Icon* field, and the icon will be displayed under "Preview." Click OK to dismiss the Add JavaBeans dialog.

5. Click Yes in the Confirm JavaBean Installation dialog and OK to confirm. You will see the generic icon on your Other Component Palette page as shown here:

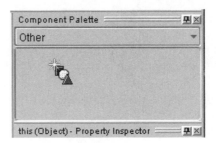

Hold the mouse cursor over the icon, and you will see the name of the class that the icon represents.

What Just Happened?   You created a page on the Component Palette and added the DemoJOptionBean component to it. This component will be available for use in the UI Editor for any Java class file. Dropping this component to a class file will add code to add the component to the frame or panel.

IV. Test the Custom Component
This phase creates a sample application that uses DemoJOptionBean to create a message dialog.

I. In the CustomBeansWS workspace, select New Project from the right-click menu. Select Project Containing a New Application from the General\Projects category in the New gallery and click Open.

2. Click Next if the Welcome page appears. Use "TestOptionPane" for the directory and file names. Click Next. Change the *Default Package* name to "beantest," and leave the default Source Path and Output Directory selections. Click Next.

3. Leave the default settings on the Libraries page. Click Finish to open the New Application dialog.

4. Enter "TestOptionJA" in the *Name* field. Ensure that beantest is the package. Leave the other default selections and click OK.

5. In the New Frame dialog, enter "TestOptionFrame" in the *Name* field, and accept the other default settings. Click OK to create the files.

6. Click Save All.

7. Select TestOptionFrame.java in the Navigation window, and select UI Editor from the right-click menu.

8. Select the "this" node in the Structure window. Change the *layout* property to "BorderLayout."

9. From the Swing Containers page of the Component Palette, click the JPanel icon and then click the "this" node in the Structure window.

10. Using the jPanel1 Property Inspector, change properties as shown here:
     name property to "mainPanel"
     layout property to "BorderLayout"
     constraints property to "Center"

11. From the Swing page of the Component Palette, select the JButton icon and click in the center of the frame. The button will fill the panel.

12. Change the following JButton properties:
     name to "testButton"
     text to "Test"
     constraints to "South"

13. Click Save All.

     The UI Editor should look something like the following:

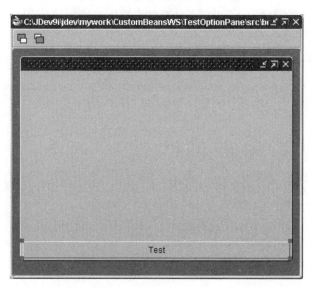

14. Select the DemoJOptionBean component that you created earlier from the Other page of the Component Palette, and add it to the UI node in the Structure window.

Additional Information: Notice that the bean is added under the Other node at the bottom of the Structure window. The UI Editor window will go blank because the new component has no visual design aspect.

15. In the Property Inspector for the demoJOptionBean1 object, change the name to "demoOptionBean."

16. Click testButton under mainPanel in the Structure window, and click the Events tab of the Property Inspector. Click the *actionPerformed* field and then click on the ellipsis (…) button to open the actionPerformed dialog.

17. Leave the default name and click OK. The Code Editor will open and display a code stub for the event method.

18. Find the line of code that instantiates the DemoJOptionBean:

```
private DemoJOptionBean demoOptionBean = new DemoJOptionBean();
```

Additional Information: This line was added when you dropped the component into the Structure window.

Cut this line of code, and paste it between the curly brackets after this line of code at the end of the file:

```
private void testButton_actionPerformed(ActionEvent e)
```

19. Modify the line of code in the new position to look like the following. (Note that you will be deleting the word "private" and adding a parameter to the constructor call.)

```
DemoJOptionBean demoOptionPane = new DemoJOptionBean(mainPanel);
```

TIP
When you make changes to the JavaBean source code, you need to rebuild the JAR file, but do not need to redo the Component Palette additions.

20. Rebuild the project and click Save All.

Additional Information: Navigate to the top of the file, and look for the import statement for DemoJOptionBean. This line was also automatically added when you dropped the component into the Structure window.

21. Run the TestOptionJA.java application and click the Test button to try the dialog. The dialog window title will be "Sample Information Dialog," and the message will appear in the dialog as shown next:

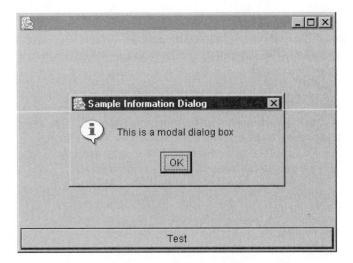

22. Click OK and close the window.

Additional Information: The reason that the Java application found the new component is that you included its library in the project settings information. On the TestOptionPane.jpr node, select Project Settings and check that the Selected Libraries pane in the Libraries page contains the CustomJOptionBeans library that you added to the default project settings. All new projects will include that library as well so that your new component will be available.

NOTE
The code that JDeveloper writes for you in this case is minimal if you do not modify properties in creating the JavaBean. However, by using this framework, you can pass parameters to your custom class and return reusable custom components of almost any complexity.

23. This practice showed how to add a library to all new projects. Since this demonstration JavaBean is not required in future work, you can remove it from the default project settings by selecting **Project | Default Project Settings** to display the Project Settings dialog.

24. Select the Libraries node in the navigator. Select CustomJOptionBeans and click the left-arrow button to remove it from the selected list. Click OK. New projects will not include this in their Selected Libraries list.

NOTE
*If you also want to restore the Component Palette to its default,
display the Other page of the Component Palette, and select Remove
Page from the right-click menu.*

What Just Happened?   You created a small test application and tested adding and running
the new component. You may want to try some other variations, such as using ERROR_MESSAGE
instead of INFORMATION_MESSAGE. This will change the dialog's icon. You can also try other
methods, such as showConfirmDialog, showInputDialog, or showOptionDialog. Study this
example carefully before trying to branch out to other components.

CHAPTER
19

Menus and Toolbars

Man is a tool-using animal....
Without tools he is nothing, with tools he is all.

—Thomas Carlyle (1751–1881), *Sartor Resartus*

very user of client/server applications is familiar with the traditional design elements
of menus and toolbars. Both provide easy-to-use and well-understood user interfaces
for many application functions. Menus enable users to execute the standard tasks in
an application. Toolbars enable users to execute the most commonly used tasks in
the menu. Providing these two elements to your users gives them the tools to perform
their work most efficiently. Menus and toolbars in Java applications and applets work exactly like
their counterparts in the client/server world.

This chapter explains some general considerations for designing menus and toolbars for Java
applications and applets (which this book refers to as "Java client applications"). The best way to
describe how to create menus and toolbars in JDeveloper is to step through examples. The
hands-on practices at the end of the chapter supply such examples.

NOTE
*While the design considerations in this chapter apply to any style of
development, the techniques describe the use of menu and toolbar
components from the Swing and AWT libraries. Designing menus and
toolbars for a JSP light-client application has similar design concerns,
but the controls that you use are different in appearance and in
development. This chapter emphasizes Swing components, which
most developers prefer because of their superior functionality.*

Design Considerations

An integral part of any user-interface design is determining how the user will perform the actions
required to complete a task. For example, when designing an online transaction processing
application, you have to decide how the user will add, search, modify, delete, and save data.
The first decision you must make is whether you will use menus and toolbars at all. If you do
not use them, you have to decide how to supply the functionality that they normally provide.
The deployment method that you select for an application will, to a large extent, help you with
this decision.

In a client/server application, menus and toolbars are natural features that users easily
understand and expect to see. Since applets on the Web emulate the controls that users are
accustomed to, menus and toolbars have a fairly standard appearance. If the application is
deployed through servlets, JavaServer Pages (JSP) applications, or other HTML interfaces, menus
and toolbars may appear, but can take on many different formats.

The role of menus in an HTML environment is played by textual links, graphical links, or
navigation bars. The role of toolbars is played by buttons or icons on the page. Pulldown menus
sometimes appear in HTML applications through the use of JavaScript (because HTML does not
support the standard menu look-and-feel). The functions that menus and toolbars deliver are
integrated into design elements of the website, and that design is often unique to each site.

Once you have decided that the application requires menus and toolbars, you need to design
the layout and organization and determine which functions you want to provide. There are some
general factors to consider and guidelines to follow when creating this design.

TIP
Refer to Sun Microsystems' website for more design information about menus and toolbars. You can connect to http://java.sun.com/products/ jlf/ed1/dg/higm.htm or search for "design menus and toolbars" in the java.sun.com website.

What Do You Put on a Menu?

When structuring a menu system, it is important to emulate standard menu items that users are accustomed to in most Windows applications. This will lessen the learning curve that the user interface may require and speed up user acceptance of your application. Menu design should take into consideration the organization of elements that your users expect. For example, if your menu structure contains File, Edit, View, Window, and Help menus, users will quickly understand where to look for a particular function because these menus are commonly used in Windows applications. While most Windows client/server applications interact with files, your applications will more commonly interact with a database, so you may have to stretch the meaning of the item names in some cases. A standard menu structure follows:

File Menu   This menu usually contains Open, New, Save, Close, and Exit items among others. You can provide those same items in data-aware Java applications, even though the concept of file interaction does not usually apply. An Open item could select a table or application to browse; a Close item could clear current data from the form; and Save could commit the changed data.

Edit Menu   Menu items may add or remove records or otherwise manipulate data. For example, you can include an item to copy an existing record or to fill the current record with default values. Another common item to include on the Edit menu is one for Options that allows users to modify personal preferences such as colors, fonts, and backgrounds. Options may also include how default values are filled in and what is shown when the user opens the application—for example, a find window or an automatic query of all records.

View Menu   Items on this menu may navigate to a particular section or record. The View menu can also contain items for Find, Sort, and Filter to modify how a set of records is displayed. You can also allow users to display or hide a toolbar using a check mark menu item.

Application-Specific Menus   These menus, which should be placed to the left of the Window menu, will provide functionality that is specific to the application. It is best to keep the number of other menus to a minimum so that the user is not overwhelmed with choices. As a rule of thumb, a maximum of ten pulldowns (main menu headings), each with a maximum of 15 selections, will give users up to 150 choices. This should be plenty for a standard application. If the items are logically arranged, users will be able to find a function easily without having to browse the menus frequently.

Selections in other menus might include functions such as navigating to other applications, stepping the user through a difficult task, or using wizards to enter data.

Window Menu   The items on this menu can be used to arrange the various open windows and allow navigation between them.

Help Menu   Items perform the expected calls to the help system or Help About dialog.

Other Menu Features

Menus offer other design features. You can take advantage of all of these in JDeveloper, but some may require extra coding.

Nested Menus

Menus can contain nested submenus, as shown in an example of the JDeveloper IDE menu in Figure 19-1. In other words, when you select a menu item from a pulldown, another side menu opens for the actual selection. In this example, when you select Refactor from the Tools menu, a submenu containing three choices opens.

Design Suggestion   Although you can create menus to virtually any level of depth, a good rule of thumb is to limit yourself to three levels, as in Figure 19-1. Using more than three levels requires some extra dexterity from your user and can lead to frustration if the user cannot easily select a menu item.

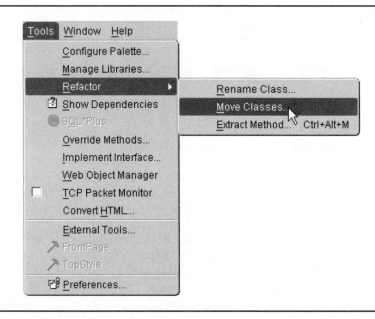

FIGURE 19-1.   *Multi-level menu*

Popup Menus

You can define *popup menus* that appear when the user clicks the right mouse button. Popup menus are not attached to the top of the window, but normally appear at the mouse cursor location when the secondary mouse button (right button for right-handed mouse users) is clicked on an object. They are also called *context menus* or *right-click menus* because they appear based on the context or location of the mouse cursor. Popup menus are usually customized for the object that was clicked and allow quick access to functions that apply only to that object. For example, right clicking a text item could display a menu for Cut, Copy, and Paste to manipulate the text in the item. Right clicking a panel in a data form might display a menu that allows users to add or remove records and save or undo changes. Users find right-click (more properly called "alternate-button click" to accommodate left mouse users) menus a fast way to get to a particular menu item. They require less mouse movement than using a pulldown menu to access the required functions. An example of a popup menu is shown to the right.

Design Suggestion   It takes some training to make users aware of and accustomed to the functionality on popup menus. However, if your application requires repetitive actions to access or input data, popup menus may help. Examine the possible ways that your application will be used when determining what items to include on popup menus, and customize them for the most commonly used menu items that a user would require when working with a particular object. Popup menu items are usually items that also appear on the main application menu.

    Design the popup menu as simply as possible. For example, nested submenus within a popup menu make the popup menu difficult to use. Popup menus often contain fewer items than a normal pulldown menu, and you may want to set a limit of six or eight items (plus separators).

NOTE

As mentioned in the Introduction, this book calls context or popup menus "right-click menus."

Check Mark and Radio Group Items

Menu items can appear as normal items or with check marks or radio buttons. A *check mark menu item* represents a single state of a toggle, such as displaying or hiding a toolbar. For example, you might have a View menu that contains a check mark menu item (Toolbar) that displays the component toolbar. If the menu item is checked, the toolbar is displayed. If users select the item when it is checked, the check mark vanishes and the toolbar is hidden.

    Radio group menu items offer more than one option and display the selected option with a round bullet icon. If you create a group of items, only one of the group items will be "checked" at once. The menu item functionality will take care of the visual display, but you need to write code to handle what happens when the user makes a selection.

    For example, you might have a main menu item called Sort that is a submenu. When a user selects the item, a nested menu appears with a radio group of items for the columns that will be sorted (such as Name, Hire Date, Salary, and so on). When the user selects one of this group, the radio button next to the item will appear filled in, and the code you write would re-sort the display based upon that column.

Design Suggestion   Other than the View menu suggestions just mentioned, check and radio group menu items are not frequently used. It is more common to provide the functionality that they offer using an options dialog.

Mnemonics and Accelerators

Mnemonics are quick access keys that help users select a menu or menu item without using the mouse. Pulldown menus are typically activated using the ALT key combined with the first letter in the menu text. For example, to activate the File pulldown, the user would press ALT-F. In this example, "F" would be underlined to indicate to the user that this was the key to press with the ALT key. The user accesses a menu item within the pulldown using the underscored letter. For

example, the Exit item in the File menu would be activated when the user pressed the X key. The letter used as the mnemonic must appear in the menu item's text property. An example of the underlined letters that indicate mnemonics is shown to the left.

An *accelerator key* is a shortcut to the functionality that is offered in the menu. The user can press this key combination to run the same code that the menu item activates. This saves the user from having to interact with the menu. Mnemonics and accelerators are

similar, but accelerators do not display the menu selection and are usually a CTRL key combination instead of the mnemonic's ALT key combination. The accelerator key combination appears next to the menu item, as shown here for the Save function.

> **NOTE**
> *The Swing class JMenuBar uses a property called "accelerator" to supply the functionality of an accelerator. If you use the AWT class MenuBar, the property name is "shortcut."*

Design Suggestion   When you make the decision about which mnemonics and accelerators to include, a good rule of thumb is that you should provide mnemonics for every menu selection so that a user without a mouse can successfully navigate within your application. It is important to respect the standards supported by existing applications. For example, you should provide the commonly known accelerators such as CTRL-S for Save. Examine common Windows programs to get a feeling for the common accelerators. In addition, you should avoid reassigning commonly used accelerators such as CTRL-X, CTRL-C, and CTRL-V that usually represent the functions Cut, Copy, and Paste, respectively.

It is important to think about accelerators and mnemonics because they allow users an alternative to using the mouse to access application functions. This is particularly critical for users who, because of a visual or other disability, are unable to use a mouse.

Disabling and Enabling Items

Many modern applications disable menu options that are not applicable to a certain mode. For example, if you have not made any changes to data on a form, the Save option is not required and therefore should be disabled. When a change is made to the data, the item would be enabled.

Design Suggestion   Well-designed applications enable and disable menu items at the appropriate time, and this feature is the ultimate in user friendliness. However, disabling options requires a bit of code, and you have to weigh the benefits of this friendliness against the extra time and effort involved in coding and debugging. Depending upon your target audience's tolerance and the frequency with which a function may be accessed, issuing a dialog to indicate that a function is not available in a certain mode will serve the purpose and not cause undue user frustration.

Menu Item Icons
You can associate a .gif file with a menu or menu item. You can display the menu text with the graphic.

Design Suggestion   Although this technique allows you to associate a visual clue with the text, it is unclear whether menu icons assist the user in more quickly identifying a menu item. The extra space that the graphic requires is probably not worth the benefit in most situations.

Separators
A *separator* is a thin horizontal line that is not user-selectable and contains no functionality.

Design Suggestion   Arrange the menu so that the items are grouped by similar functionality, and add a separator between groups. For example, an Edit menu may contain, among others, functions for Cut, Copy, and Paste. Those functions are logically similar and may be grouped using separators before the first and after the last item. The menu objects for this example would be Separator, Cut, Copy, Paste, Separator. Another use for separators is to visually group a set of radio group menu items.

Tooltips
Menu items can have tooltip text associated with them. This text pops up when the user rests the mouse over the item, as the following shows:

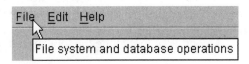

Design Suggestion   Menu tooltips are useful only if menus or menu items are hard to understand. Since you should strive for intuitive wording in your applications, you should not need this feature for most menu items.

NOTE
You will not see accelerators, mnemonics, or icons in the Menu Editor. If you define them in the properties or code, they will appear only at runtime.

What Do You Put on the Toolbar?

Think of the toolbar as a subset of the menu. All functions on the toolbar should also be available in the menu. Therefore, it is best to design the menu first and repeat frequently used menu selections in the toolbar. Examples of commonly used items for a transaction processing system would be Save and Undo. Users need to interact with data frequently, and saving and undoing changes are often-performed tasks. You may have to validate your designation of commonly used functions with a user trial of your application.

Toolbars are usually iconic in nature. In other words, the user selects a toolbar button by identifying an iconic picture located in a panel. This saves space and clutter on the screen over the alternative of identifying the buttons with text labels. Toolbar buttons are also a standard size as opposed to text buttons that are usually sized to their labels. Although there is a bit of a learning curve for users to understand what the pictures represent, it is faster for users to find a picture in the toolbar than a word once that learning curve is overcome.

Other Toolbar Features

Many features of menus are also available for toolbars. However, the design considerations are different for toolbars and menus, as follows:

- **Icons**   While you may not choose to use icons on menu items, you would usually use them on toolbar buttons.

- **Mnemonics and accelerators**   If you follow the guideline that toolbar items are derived from menu items, the menu items will fulfill the need that mnemonics and accelerators serve. Therefore, you do not need mnemonics and accelerators for toolbars.

- **Tooltips**   While you do not use tooltips for menu items, you normally supply tooltips for an iconic toolbar button so that the user can get a hint about the function that the button performs.

- **Enabling and disabling items**   You might want to go through the same process as you do with menus to determine how you will handle enabling and disabling items. Since toolbar buttons duplicate functionality on the menu, you can extend the code you write to disable and enable a menu item to include the toolbar button with the same functionality.

You also need to consider multiple toolbars and toolbar arrangements when designing toolbars.

Multiple Toolbars

After you decide what to put in the toolbar, you need to determine how many toolbars to supply. Sometimes, there are more items to put in a toolbar than there is horizontal space in the window. Also, there may be logical, task-oriented groupings of buttons that you might want to represent.

The solution for these issues is to supply more than one toolbar. Each user may work with your application in a different way, and you can account for this by allowing the user to select which toolbar is displayed using an options dialog.

Design Suggestion   Use multiple toolbars if you have many functions that need to be represented or if you think some users might want to have control over the groups of buttons that are displayed. If the latter is the case, you have to write code to enable users to specify which toolbars are displayed.

Toolbar Arrangements

Although toolbars normally appear on the top of the window just under the menu, you can also build toolbars in a vertical orientation to leave more vertical space for user-interface objects.

You can also define the toolbar as part of a separate window or as a panel that the user can "undock" from the main window so that it floats outside the main window. This gives the user the option to shrink the main window but still have all elements visible without scrolling. The toolbar buttons will be easily available in this arrangement.

Design Suggestion   Horizontal toolbars are a standard and expected interface object. Vertical toolbars are a personal preference that you might want to let the user determine. Floating toolbars are also something that you can supply to the user. Some styles of applications such as drawing programs undock the toolbars to provide more drawing space, but database applications usually appear with the toolbar initially docked to the main window.

Summary of User Access Methods

When you design your menu and toolbar, you have to consider the functions that the users need to access. You also need to plan the method that will provide each of these in the application. The following are the main methods available to application designers:

- Toolbar button
- Menu item (main menu)
- Accelerator key
- Popup menu item

For example, the Cut function is usually available in the Edit menu as well as in the popup menu for items that support data editing. In addition, the design could provide for a toolbar button that offers users the choice of clicking the button for the Cut function. As in most applications, the accelerator CTRL-X would be mapped to the same function.

There is an additional method that you can offer to particular users—the command line. While this is not the normal method for applets, there may be some functions that you would allow the user to perform from a command-line prompt (such as opening or converting a file).

Menus and Toolbars in JDeveloper

JDeveloper supports the creation of Java client applications that include all of the menu and toolbar functionality described earlier. Therefore, you have wide scope when designing the features that you want to include. Some features are easier to implement because JDeveloper writes the code for you. For example, to attach an icon to a button, you just fill in the *icon* property of the button object with the .gif file name, and the setIcon() code will be created. Setting the mnemonic and accelerator for a menu item can be accomplished using properties, as the hands-on practices at the end of this chapter demonstrate. Runtime behavior such as disabling and enabling menu items and buttons requires writing custom code. For example, to enable the Save menu item, you would add the following code to the application:

```
saveMenuItem.setEnabled(false);
```

You can automatically generate default menus and toolbars using the wizards. For example, the New Frame dialog that is called from the New Application dialog contains checkboxes for a menu and toolbar, as Figure 19-2 shows. When you check those checkboxes, the New Frame dialog creates a default menu that contains a File menu with an Exit item. The toolbar contains buttons for file open, file close, and help. Both structures contain no code (other than a generic call to exit the application) and are only outlines of what you would use for a real application. Therefore, you need to add code and buttons and modify the contents after the dialog is finished. Other wizards, such as the JClient Form Wizard, also automatically generate a full menu and toolbar. (The JClient Form Wizard is available in the New gallery's Client Tier\Swing/JClient for BC4J category.) In this case, the code for the buttons and menu items is also generated and completely functional.

There are other JDeveloper features for menu objects and toolbar objects that are worth exploring. The hands-on practices at the end of this chapter give you some of the steps to complete when creating menus and toolbars.

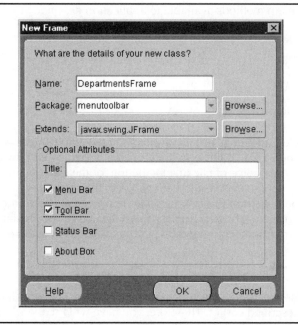

FIGURE 19-2. *Specifying a menu and toolbar in the New Frame dialog*

Menu Objects

The object for a menu system that appears on the top of a window is called a *menu bar* (implemented using a Swing component such as JMenuBar). This is the root object that you drag into an application from the JDeveloper Component Palette. A menu bar is a container that holds two kinds of objects: menus and menu items (implemented by components such as JMenu and JMenuItem, respectively). Menus correspond to the headings that you click for a pulldown or submenu (nested menu or menu within a menu). Menu items are the items in the pulldown menu. In the case of multi-level menu systems, submenus look similar to menu items, but include a right arrow to indicate that they display other menu items. For example, in Figure 19-1, the Tools menu contains a selection for Refactor, which is actually a menu because it contains selections such as Rename Class and Move Classes. Therefore, you can say that menus may contain other menus and menu items.

The Menu Editor

The easiest way to lay out a menu is with the Menu Editor feature of the UI Editor. You access this window using the following steps:

 1. In the Navigator, select UI Editor from the right-click menu on the frame Java file.

    Additional Information: This displays the UI Editor with GUI components (if any) in the Java file.

 2. If a menu exists, expand the Menu node in the Structure window, and click the menu node to switch the display to the Menu Editor as shown in Figure 19-3.

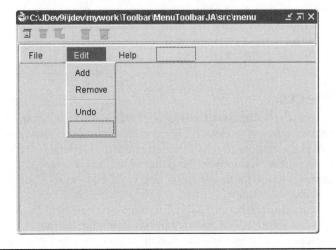

FIGURE 19-3. *Menu Editor*

3. If you want to add a menu, click the Menu node in the Structure window. Select the JMenuBar component from the Swing Containers page of the Component Palette, and drop this component onto the Menu node in the Structure window.

Additional Information: You can switch back to the UI Editor by clicking any component in the UI node of the Structure window.

NOTE
The JDeveloper Menu Editor contains toolbar buttons such as Insert MenuItem, Insert Separator, and Insert Submenu that you can use to manipulate menus and menu items. You may find that the toolbar buttons speed up your work in the Menu Editor.

The right-click menu for Menu Editor objects contains functions that you use to create the menu structure. After creating the menu structure, you write code that will be activated when a menu item is selected. The right-click menu options allow you to create or delete an item or separator and create a submenu (nested menu). The right-click menu also has selections to convert a normal menu item to a checkable menu item and to disable or enable a menu item. The latter just toggles the *enabled* property from "True" to "False." You can also toggle this property at runtime using the `setEnabled()` method.

You fill in the menu item label in the editor and press ENTER to register the label. This will move the cursor to a blank item where you can type the next text label. The code and properties areas will update as you make changes to the design area. To edit the text for an existing item, double click the item in the Menu Editor.

TIP
You can drag and drop menu items, separators, and submenus within the Menu Editor to rearrange their order. Dropping on top of an item will arrange the dragged item above that item. Selecting a right-click menu option to add an item or separator will add the item or separator above the selected item.

Toolbar Objects

Toolbars are made up of a set of buttons inside a container called a *toolbar.* The toolbar has special properties that allow users to detach the container from the main window. You can use the *floatable* property of the toolbar to specify whether users can detach the toolbar. Since the toolbar is a container, you can manipulate the group of buttons by manipulating the toolbar. For example, if you want to hide the toolbar buttons, you write code to hide the toolbar. All buttons inside the toolbar will also be hidden.

You lay out the toolbar using the UI Editor. The sequence consists of dropping a toolbar container object in the application and adding buttons inside the toolbar.

Buttons require event code to execute the desired action. You can attach icons to buttons so that they have a picture on top. You can also fill in the *text* property with a text string that will appear on top of the button. (AWT objects use the *label* property for the button text.) Normally, toolbar buttons use icons as decoration, but not text labels. Therefore, you need to remove the value of the *text* property (or the `setText()` call in the source code) so that there will be no text label.

A hands-on practice in this chapter steps through the process of creating a toolbar with buttons.

TIP

As mentioned, you can reorder objects on the Menu Editor by dragging and dropping. You can reorder buttons in a toolbar in the same way, using drag and drop. You can also reorder buttons and menu items by cutting them from the Structure window (CTRL-X) and pasting them (CTRL-V) on top of another object node in the Structure window. The pasted object will be placed on the top or on the bottom of the list of objects beneath the target object.

NOTE

The order of objects in the Structure window represents the order in which the objects will be rendered in the application. This ordering scheme is referred to in Java as the "z-order" and is described in a sidebar in Chapter 20 called "A Word About Z-Order."

Using a Navigation Bar

A quick way to create a toolbar that has record and database manipulation buttons is to use a navigation bar. The JClient controls Component Palette page contains a JUNavigationBar class that you attach to a client data model. This navigation bar provides Next, Previous, First, Last, Add, Delete, Save, Undo, Find, and Query functions for the data model. You do not have to write any customized code to make the navigation bar buttons work. A hands-on practice in this chapter contains examples of how to create a navigation bar.

Hands-on Practice: Prepare a Sample Application

The practices that follow require a sample data form Java application as a starting point. You can download this starting application from the authors' websites and skip this practice. Alternatively, you can use the following steps to create this application.

You will use the JClient Form Wizard to create a database interface form for the Departments table.

1. In the Navigator, find an existing workspace that contains an HR BC4J project (such as the one created in Chapter 1). Alternatively, you can use the Project Containing New

Business Components item in the New gallery to create a default BC4J project for the DEPARTMENTS table. After you have a BC4J project, select New Empty Project from the right-click menu on that workspace node. The New Project dialog will start.

2. Specify the name of the directory as "MenuToolbarJA." Name the project "MenuToolbarJA." Click OK to create the project.

3. Click Save All.

4. Select New from the right-click menu on the new project node. Double click Form from the Client Tier\Swing/JClient for BC4J category. The JClient Form Wizard will start. Click Next if the Welcome page appears to display the Form Types page.

5. Click Next to accept the defaults on this page (single table with a form), and click Next to accept the defaults on the Form Layout page (a single column with labels to the left). The Data Model page will appear.

6. Click the New button to define a data model. The BC4J Client Data Model Definition Wizard will start. Click Next if the Welcome page appears to display the Definition page.

7. Select the HR project and application module from the pulldowns if they are not already selected and click Next to display the Definition Name page.

8. Click Next to display the Finish page. Click Finish to create the data model and return to the JClient Form Wizard.

9. Click Next to display the Panel View page. Select DepartmentsView1 and click Next to display the Attribute Selection page.

10. The default selections on this page are usable, so click Next to display the File Names page. Enter the following names:
    Package name as "menutoolbar"
    Form name as "DepartmentsForm"
    Master panel name as "DepartmentsPanel"
    Generate a menu bar unchecked

11. Click Next and Finish to exit the wizard and create the files.

12. Open DepartmentsForm in the Code Editor and search for the following line of code:

```
this.setSize(new Dimension(800, 600);
```

13. Change "800, 600" to "400, 300" so that the window will appear smaller when it is run.

14. Click Save All. Click Run to run the DepartmentsForm file. The application will look something like the following:

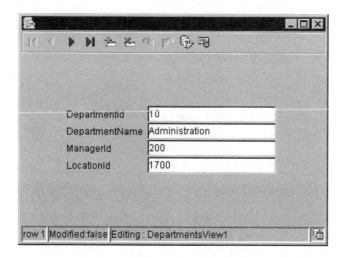

15. Close the window.

What Just Happened?   You used the wizard to create a data form Java application that accesses the Departments table. The wizard also helped you create a client data model that defined the application model for the BC4J project in the same workspace. This data form is fully functional for all data manipulation. However, the form has no menu.

To run this form, you run DepartmentsForm, which is a subclass of JFrame, a Java window. DepartmentsForm calls DepartmentsPanel, which contains the UI elements such as labels and text fields. The next practice will add a menu to the window class (DepartmentsForm.java).

Hands-on Practice: Build a Menu

This practice builds a menu system for the sample application created in the previous practice. Adding a menu to an existing application consists of the following main phases:

    I. Lay out the menu elements

   II. Set the menu element properties

  III. Write the menu item code

As mentioned earlier, there is a preparation step where you design the structure that your menu will use. The menu you will build in this practice uses the structure shown in Figure 19-4.

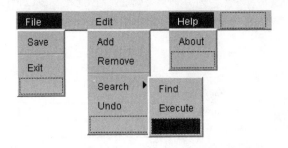

FIGURE 19-4. *Sample menu structure*

NOTE
This practice is written as a demonstration of the menu editing facilities in JDeveloper. It assumes that you are creating a menu system from scratch. Since the items on this menu are the same as those created by the JClient Form Wizard, you could also just rearrange the generated items.

I. Lay Out the Menu Elements

The first phase defines the structure of the menu and adds menu elements to the JFrame (window) class, DepartmentsForm.java. At this point, you do not need to worry about all of the properties or names of the elements. Use the following steps to lay out a menu bar:

1. Open the UI Editor for DepartmentsForm.java if it is not already open. Click the Menu node in the Structure window. The UI Editor will change to a Menu Editor blank window.

2. In the Swing Containers Component Palette page, click JMenuBar, and click the Menu node in the Structure window to add the menu to the application. The Structure window will display the new menu bar as shown here:

3. Change the *name* property to "mainMenuBar" in the Property Inspector.

Additional Information: At this point, you will see nothing in the UI Editor other than a dotted rectangle that you will use to enter a menu item.

NOTE
You can change between the UI Editor and Menu Editor by clicking the appropriate node in the Structure window (UI and Menu, respectively).

4. To add the first menu item, click the dotted rectangle in the upper-left corner of the Menu Editor and enter "File." Press ENTER after typing the text. The text is written into the *text* property of the menu element. The Menu Editor window will look like this:

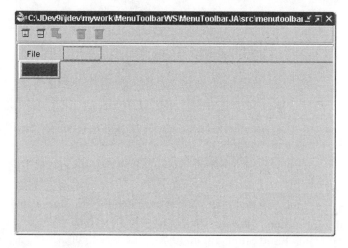

Additional Information: When you add a menu, the Menu Editor opens a new menu to the right and a new item below. Each time you add a menu item, the Menu Editor opens a blank item below it. New menu elements are shown with a dotted or selected box. Clicking a new element allows you to type text.

CAUTION
*If new (dotted rectangle) items do not appear when you enter the "File" label, try the operation using the Windows look-and-feel (**Tools | Preferences**, Environment page, set the "Look and Feel" field to "Windows," click OK, and reload JDeveloper).*

5. Click the box to the right of the File menu, and type "Edit" for the text. Press ENTER. This adds another menu (top-level) element. Add another menu element for "Help." Your menu will look like this:

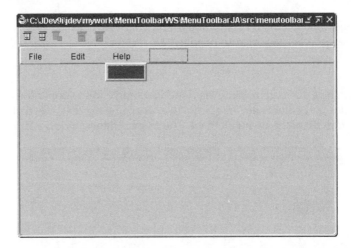

6. Click the File menu and click the box under it. Type the label as "Save" and press ENTER. Click the box under Save and type "Exit" and press ENTER.

7. Select "Exit" and click Insert Separator in the Menu Editor toolbar. This adds a separator above the Exit item.

8. Add items under the Edit and Help menus to match the structure shown in Figure 19-4.

Additional Information: For the submenu on Search, select "Search" and click Insert Submenu in the Menu Editor toolbar. This converts Search to a submenu and opens an edit box to the right. Enter "Find" for the menu item and "Execute" for another menu item in this submenu. The resulting Edit menu is shown to the right.

9. Click Save All.

NOTE
You can also select menu editing actions such as Insert Submenu from the right-click menu.

What Just Happened?   You just added a menu bar component to the application and used the Menu Editor to define the menus and menu items that will be displayed. Since the menu bar attaches to the window title bar, you do not have to worry about the layout in the frame.

NOTE

If your design included check menu items, you would use the Make Checkable toolbar button to convert the item to a check menu item.

II. Set the Menu Element Properties

Now that the menu structure is laid out, you need to modify the properties. The primary property that you need to change is the *name* property. Other properties to modify are *mnemonic* and *accelerator*. Changing properties requires visiting the Property Inspector for each item. Use the following steps to accomplish this:

1. Click the JMenu1 (top) icon under mainMenuBar in the Structure window. Change the *name* property to "fileMenu" in the Property Inspector and press ENTER.

2. Change the name of the first menu item under fileMenu to "saveMenuItem."

3. Repeat steps 1 and 2 for all menus and items using the same pattern. You do not need to rename the separators. The Structure window should appear as follows:

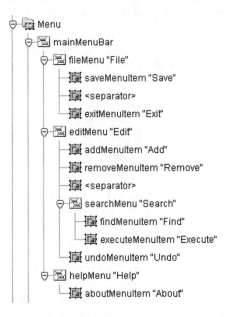

4. Add mnemonics for each menu item by assigning the *mnemonic* property using the following table:

Menu or Menu Item	*mnemonic* Property
File	F
Save	S
Exit	X

Menu or Menu Item	*mnemonic* Property
Edit	E
Add	A
Remove	R
Search	S
Find	F
Execute	X
Undo	U
Help	H
About	A

Additional Information: A mnemonic is a letter or character that users can press to activate the menu item. The rule is that you need to select a mnemonic letter that is part of the string in the *text* property. Letters may be repeated as above if the items that they represent are in different menus.

For example, you can set the File menu to pull down when the user presses ALT-F by assigning the *mnemonic* property as "F." This assignment will place an underscore on the matching letter during runtime as the following shows:

4. Click the Save menu item. Assign the *accelerator* property in the Property Inspector by selecting "KeyStroke" from the pulldown. This opens a dialog where you select the modifier and key for the accelerator. In this case, select "CTRL_MASK" (the CTRL key) as the modifier and "VK_S" (the "s" key) as the key. Click OK to close the dialog. Click Save All.

Additional Information: Recall that accelerators are shortcut keys that allow the user to access the function of a menu item without activating the menu. In this case, the key combination of CTRL-S will activate the function for the Save menu item. Although you will not see the shortcut key indicated in the editor, when you run the file the shortcut key appears next to the menu item during runtime, as the following shows:

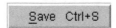

What Just Happened?   You changed the names of the menus and menu items to comply with a naming convention (mentioned in Chapter 5) that requires a suffix to denote the type of each object. You also added mnemonics and an accelerator to assist users in accessing the menus and menu item functions.

III. Write the Menu Item Code

You do not need to write code to display menu elements because this function is performed by the control. However, you do have to write the event code that each menu item executes when it is selected.

Attaching code to a component is a three-step process:

1. Write a listener for the object that will wait for an event to occur on the object.

2. Identify the type of event the user will activate (such as mouse click, keypress, and focus-gained), and write a method for that event inside the listener definition. A generic event for menu items and button clicks is the *actionPerformed* event; this event occurs when the default action for the item occurs (for example, a button click or menu item selection). The event method calls another method defined in the class file.

3. Write the method that is called by the event method.

   For example, the Save menu item event will use a listener defined by the following code:

```
saveMenuItem.addActionListener(new ActionListener()
{
    public void actionPerformed(ActionEvent e) {
        saveMenuItem_actionPerformed(e);
    }
  }
);
```

   This code creates a listener for the Save menu item that calls the `saveMenuItem_actionPerformed()` method when the *actionPerformed* event occurs; in this case, the action performed event corresponds to the user selecting the Save menu item. The `saveMenuItem_actionPerformed()` method contains the code that executes the commit action on the navigation bar as follows:

```
private void saveMenuItem_actionPerformed(ActionEvent e)
{
    // calls an action on the navigation bar
    hiddenNavBar.doAction(JUNavigationBar.BUTTON_COMMIT);
}
```

Event Code

This section adds code to handle the events that occur when a menu item is selected. JDeveloper assists in creating the listener, its event method, and the method that the event method calls, as the following steps demonstrate:

1. Invoke the UI Editor to display the menu for the DepartmentsForm.java file if it is not already displayed.

TIP
At any point, if the UI Editor and Structure window are out of sync, click in the UI Editor, and then click in the Structure window. When you click the UI Editor again, the Structure window should refresh.

   2. Click the icon for saveMenuItem in the Structure window. Click the Events tab in the Inspector.

   Additional Information: In the Events tab are event names (in the properties column) and the associated called method names (in the property values column). The method names do not appear until you define the event in the Property Inspector. You can specify the method name that you want the event to call in your code by filling out the value column for an event. The default name is a concatenation of the object name and the event name. For example, the saveMenuItem event for actionPerformed defaults to "saveMenuItem_actionPerformed."

   3. Click the *actionPerformed* event and click the "..." button to display the actionPerformed dialog.

   4. Leave the default name and click OK. The Code Editor will open to a method stub for `saveMenuitem_actionPerformed()` that was just added.

   Additional Information: JDeveloper also creates code to define the listener. Take a moment to search from the top of the file for "saveMenuItem_actionPerformed." The first occurrence of this string is in a section of code that sets properties for the Save item.

NOTE
If you change the name you assign to an existing event in the Property Inspector, the code for the method and listener will be modified automatically.

   5. In the `saveMenuItem_actionPerformed()` method stub at the bottom of the file, add a line between the { } and enter the following code (all on one line):

```
hiddenNavBar.doAction(JUNavigationBar.BUTTON_COMMIT);
```

   Additional Information: The JClient Form Wizard added a navigation bar object into the frame file (DepartmentsForm.java). This navigation bar (`hiddenNavBar`) is bound to the DepartmentsView view object and provides data manipulation functions such as `INSERT`, `DELETE`, `COMMIT`, and `ROLLBACK`. You can take advantage of these functions by calling a method, `doAction()`, that performs the same action as a specific button on the navigation bar (in this case the commit button). Calling pre-built data aware code is much easier than writing code from scratch code.

   6. Return to the Menu Editor by clicking the DepartmentsForm.java UI Editor tab in the toolbar area.

   7. Repeat steps 2–6 for the other menu items using the actionPerformed method code listed here:

Item	Method Code
exitMenuItem	`_popupTransactionDialog();` `System.exit(0);`
addMenuItem	`hiddenNavBar.doAction(` `JUNavigationBar.BUTTON_INSERT);`
removeMenuItem	`hiddenNavBar.doAction(` `JUNavigationBar.BUTTON_DELETE);`
findMenuItem	`hiddenNavBar.doAction(` `JUNavigationBar.BUTTON_FIND);`
executeMenuItem	`hiddenNavBar.doAction(` `JUNavigationBar.BUTTON_EXECUTE);`
undoMenuItem	`hiddenNavBar.doAction(` `JUNavigationBar.BUTTON_ROLLBACK);`

aboutMenuItem	`JOptionPane.showMessageDialog(this,`
	  `"Department browse and edit window",`
	  `"Department Browse",`
	`JOptionPane.INFORMATION_MESSAGE);`

TIP
*You can bypass the event dialog by entering the event method name
in the Property Inspector's event field instead of clicking the "..."
button.*

    Additional Information: The About menu item calls JOptionPane to display a modal
dialog. The Exit item calls the transaction dialog created by the JClient Form Wizard that asks
the user if uncommitted changes should be saved. If there are no uncommitted changes, the
dialog does not appear. The other menu items call button actions on the navigation bar.

  8. Click Rebuild and Save All in the toolbar.

  9. Run the DepartmentsForm file and test all menu items.

TIP
*In addition to the Help About dialog, you might want to build an
entire help system for your application. JDeveloper includes support
for creating your own help files. Details about the Oracle Help for
Java feature are contained in the help system Contents node
"Developing Help With Oracle Help for Java."*

What Just Happened?   You wrote event-handler code for each menu item in the layout. Most
of the items call code that emulates a button click on a hidden navigation bar.

The menu bar appears at the top of the frame in the UI Editor as shown here:

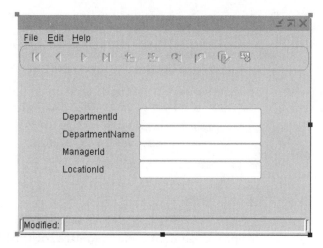

If you are interested in adding code that enables and disables menu items, generate an application using the JClient Form Wizard and specify that the wizard create a menu. The code in the _updateButtonStates() and menuItemsUpdate() methods that are generated will give you an idea about how to implement enabling and disabling menu options.

Hands-on Practice: Build a Popup Menu

The method for creating a popup menu (shown in Figure 19-5) is similar to the method for creating a regular menu. It uses the sample application from the preceding practice as a starting point. As before, you can also use the application available in the sample files on the authors' websites.

Although completing the previous practice is not a requirement, this practice abbreviates many steps that were explained in that practice. If you need further explanation for a particular step in this practice, refer to the preceding practice. There are two main phases in creating a popup menu:

I. Lay out the elements

II. Write the menu code

■ Display the popup menu

■ Handle an event for each menu item

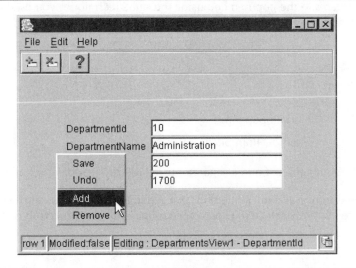

FIGURE 19-5. *Popup menu*

I. Lay Out the Elements

The first phase uses the UI Editor to place the objects on the frame. Be sure that the workspace for the previous practice or the sample application created in the "Hands-on Practice: Prepare a Sample Application" section is open.

1. Open the UI Editor for DepartmentsForm.java if it is not already open.

2. Drop a JPopupMenu component from the Swing Containers page of the Component Palette onto the Menu node of the Structure window. The Structure window will display the following:

3. Rename the popup menu to "mainPopupMenu" using the *name* property in the Property Inspector. Change the *label* property to "mainPopupMenu."

4. Add four items to the popup menu using the same techniques you used in the previous practice, and change the *name* properties as in the following table:

Item	name
Save	savePopupItem
Undo	undoPopupItem
Add	addPopupItem
Remove	removePopupItem

5. Select the Add item and add a separator using the Insert Separator toolbar button.

Additional Information: Remember that separators and menu items will be added above the currently selected item. You can drag and drop objects to rearrange them in the Menu Editor.

TIP
When adding items to a menu, pressing ENTER *after entering the name will add an item below and move focus to the new item. All you need to do is start typing the new text at that point.*

6. Click Save All.

What Just Happened? You added the popup menu to the application frame. It appears in the Menu node of the Structure window but, unlike menu bars, will not be displayed until you write code to perform that action. In this phase, you also used the Menu Editor to lay out the menu items in a single menu. Unlike a menu bar, a popup menu does not have top level menus that display a pulldown with items. The remaining task is to write some code.

II. Write the Menu Code

You need to write event-handling code for displaying the popup and for performing a function when a menu item is selected. As with the main menu, JDeveloper helps you create the code for both purposes.

Display the Popup Menu

While a pulldown menu is usually displayed at the top of the window, a popup menu usually appears when the user clicks the right mouse button. (You can display a popup menu on a button click or other event as well.) Therefore, in this example, you need an event handler to display the popup menu on a mouse click. This handler consists of a listener on a panel in the application that calls a custom method. The following steps create this code:

1. Open the UI Editor for the DepartmentsForm.java file if it is not already open.

2. Expand the UI node in the Structure window and the "this" node under it. Click the first panel in the list (for example, topPanel).

3. Click the Events tab in the Property Inspector and click the "…" button on the *mouseReleased* event to display the mouseReleased dialog.

4. Notice that the event name is "topPanel_mouseReleased." This name is fine for this example, so click OK. The Code Editor will open, and a blank method stub will appear for the name you just entered.

5. Add a blank line between the curly brackets and enter the following in the blank line:

```
if (e.isPopupTrigger()) {
  mainPopupMenu.show(this, e.getX(), e.getY());
}
```

Additional Information: This code shows the popup object inside the main frame object ("this"). You can programmatically attach the popup menu to other objects in the same way. The code also shows the popup menu at the mouse cursor's location (x and y positions) when the right mouse button was clicked.

JDeveloper also adds a listener, `topPanel.addMouseListener(new MouseAdapter()`, that calls this new method. You do not need to modify the listener code.

6. Click Save All. You may want to run the DepartmentsForm file to check the popup menu display. Right-clicking anywhere in the main window will display the popup menu. The menu items will not yet be functional because you have not written the code.

Handle an Event for Each Menu Item

The code to handle events for each popup menu item works the same way as it does with a pulldown menu. The code you create for a popup menu item consists of a new listener that calls a wizard-generated method used by the main menu. This section uses the same methods created for the menu bar in the preceding practice. Most of those methods call functionality on the hidden navigation bar generated by the JClient Form Wizard. If you want to use functionality that is not on the navigation bar, you can write your own code instead of calling existing methods.

1. In the UI Editor for DepartmentsForm.java, click savePopupItem in the Structure window. In the Events tab of the Property Inspector, enter "saveMenuItem_actionPerformed" for the *actionPerformed* event and press ENTER.

Additional Information: The focus will shift to the Code Editor and navigate to the existing method. If you did not complete the preceding practice, the method will be blank. If this is the case, return to the previous practice and fill in the code listed for the saveMenuItem. Notice that you did not need to display or interact with the event dialog because you typed an event name in the Property Inspector. The ENTER key completes the entry process and causes the Code Editor to be displayed. JDeveloper also creates a listener for the popup menu item to call the event handler method.

2. Repeat step 1 for each item in the following list:

Item	Event Method
undoPopupItem	undoMenuItem_actionPerformed
addPopupItem	addMenuItem_actionPerformed
removePopupItem	removeMenuItem_actionPerformed

3. Click Save All.

4. Compile the project and run it. Try all functions using the popup menu.

What Just Happened?   You wrote the code for the main event handler that pops up the menu when the right mouse button is clicked. You also wrote code to execute the appropriate function from the navigation bar as in the previous practice. If you have new items that do not use existing code, the steps are the same except that you have to write the code into the code stub that the Property Inspector creates.

Hands-on Practice: Build a Toolbar

A toolbar is usually created as an extension of a menu, and it contains the most commonly used menu items. This practice demonstrates how to develop a toolbar that calls some of the same methods called by the menu. Although the toolbar only contains three buttons, you can use the same techniques to add more buttons. This practice will show how you can build a toolbar from scratch should you find that the navigation bar does not meet your needs. For example, you may want to add buttons of your own or to replace the navigation bar's native query-by-example find utility with one of your own.

This practice uses the sample data form application that is built in the earlier "Hands-on Practice: Prepare a Sample Application" section. You may also use the application that resulted from either of the preceding practices in this chapter, but it is not a requirement that you complete those practices.

This practice uses phases that are similar to those in the menu practice as follows:

I. Lay out the toolbar elements

- ■ Add the toolbar
- ■ Import the image files
- ■ Create image icon objects
- ■ Add the buttons

II. Set the button properties

III. Write the button code

At the end of this practice, you will have created a toolbar that looks like the one shown here under the menu:

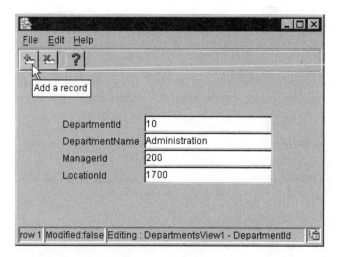

I. Lay Out the Toolbar Elements

As with the menu, the toolbar will be contained in the form file built from JFrame (the window). In this phase, you will drop a toolbar onto a panel that is assigned a BorderLayout manager. This layout allows you to fix the toolbar to the top of the parent container. (Chapter 20 describes layout managers in detail.)

Add the Toolbar

The first step is to add the toolbar container and buttons to the frame.

1. Open the UI Editor for the DepartmentsForm.java file if it is not already open.

2. Expand the UI node in the Structure window and the "this" node under it. The Structure window will look something like the following:

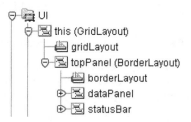

3. Drop a JToolbar component from the Swing Containers page of the Component Palette on top of the panel (in this example, topPanel) under the "this" node in the Structure window.

4. Change the following properties for the toolbar:
   name to "mainToolBar"
   constraints to "North"

   Additional Information: Although you will see the object in the Structure window, it will not be prominent in the editor. The toolbar will grow when you drop buttons into it later.

5. Be sure that the *constraints* property of dataPanel (under topPanel in the Structure window) is set to "Center" and the statusBar *constraints* property is set to "South." Change these if needed.

Import the Image Files

You have to load the icon files that you will be using for the toolbar images into the project. This practice uses .gif files already available in the JDeveloper directories but you can use the same techniques to import your own image files, if needed.

1. Click the project node and select **File | Import**.

2. Select Existing Sources and click OK to display the Import Existing Sources Wizard. Click Next if the Welcome page appears.

3. Click Add and navigate to the JDEV_HOME\BC4J\redist\ bc4j\webapp\images directory.

   Additional Information: If the specified directory does not exist, open the images directory under the webapp.war directory (actually an archive file that looks like a directory in the JDeveloper file dialog) in the JDEV_HOME\BC4J\redist directory.

NOTE
If the files or directories mentioned do not exist in your installation, search for similar files in the JDeveloper directories using Windows Explorer.

4. Select the files addnew.gif, deleterec.gif, and help.gif (using CTRL click to group select them).

5. Click Open to add the files to the *Refine Files to Be Added* pane.

6. Check the checkbox Copy Files to the Project Directory and click Browse. Navigate to the menutoolbar package directory under src and click Select. The directory, JDEV_HOME\jdev\mywork\MenuToolbarWS\MenuToolbarJA\src\menutoolbar, will appear in the text field.

7. Click Next and Finish. The files will be copied to the menutoolbar directory and will be displayed in the Navigator as shown here:

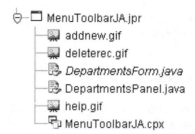

Additional Information: When the project is built, the .gif files will be copied to the classes\menutoolbar directory so that they will be available to the compiled Java files at runtime.

NOTE
The icon files will be packaged with your other code files for distribution, and they will be easier to find if they are contained in the same directory. In addition, if the files are in the project directory, the code that the Property Inspector creates when you set the icon file properties will not include the path, which will make the code more portable.

8. Select one of the graphics files in the Navigator and check that the file name displayed in the JDeveloper IDE status bar includes the src\menutoolbar directory.

9. Click Save All.

Create Image Icon Objects

You will use the Swing JButton class to create buttons in this form. The JButton class contains an *icon* property that allows you to create an iconic button by defining an image file as the icon. The setIcon() method for a button object requires the parameter of an *image icon*, an object that is linked to an image file. Therefore, you need to programmatically create image icon objects for the graphics files to make the icons available to the button properties. This section adds the appropriate code to create the image icon objects.

1. Open the Code Editor for the DepartmentsForm.java file and find the following line that defines the class:

```
public class DepartmentsForm extends JFrame  {
```

2. There are a number of object declarations under this line. Add the following declarations directly under the class declaration line (after the opening curly bracket):

```
// button icons
private ImageIcon imageAdd = new ImageIcon(
  DepartmentsForm.class.getResource("addnew.gif"));
private ImageIcon imageDelete = new ImageIcon(
  DepartmentsForm.class.getResource("deleterec.gif"));
private ImageIcon imageHelp = new ImageIcon(
  DepartmentsForm.class.getResource("help.gif"));
```

Additional Information: This code creates image icon objects that can be assigned to the *icon* properties of the buttons.

Add the Buttons
You are now ready to add the buttons.

1. Return to the UI Editor window by clicking the appropriate file name in the Document Bar. Expand the UI node until you see mainToolbar. Shift click the JButton component in the Swing page of the Component Palette. The button will *pin* (appear outlined) so that you can draw more than one button without reselecting the component.

2. Click the mainToolBar node in the Structure window. A button will be added as shown in this excerpt from the UI Editor:

3. Click the mainToolBar node twice more to create two more buttons.

4. Click the Pointer (arrow) icon in the Component Palette to unpin the button tool.

What Just Happened? You added a toolbar component to the layout and placed buttons in it. You also prepared the project for the assignment of icon images by adding image files to the project and creating image icon objects in the code.

II. Set the Button Properties
You now need to set the button properties to refine the definitions.

1. Select the buttons as a group by clicking the top button in the Structure window and CTRL clicking the other button.

2. When the buttons are selected, apply the following properties' values to the group. Click ENTER after setting each property.
   maximumSize to "25,25"
   minimumSize to "25,25"
   preferredSize to "25,25"
   text to blank (no value)

3. Click the top button in the list in the Structure window to ungroup the buttons. Change the following properties:
   name to "addButton"
   icon to "imageAdd"
   toolTipText to "Add a record"

NOTE
The button image may not show correctly in the UI Editor. This will be corrected when you rebuild or run the project.

4. Repeat step 3 to set the properties for the second button as follows:
   name to "deleteButton"
   icon to "imageDelete"
   toolTipText to "Delete this record"

5. Repeat step 3 to set the properties for the third button as follows:
   name to "helpButton"
   icon to "imageHelp"
   toolTipText to "Help about"

CAUTION
If you have a problem assigning the icon property, double check the location of the image files and the image icon object code as described in the earlier sections.

Additional Information: You can use a number of different properties to assign various icons to a button for different purposes. The *icon, pressedIcon, disabledIcon, disabledSelectedIcon, rolloverIcon,* and *rolloverSelectedIcon* properties define which icon appears on the button in different situations. For example, if you define a different icon for the rolloverIcon property, the icon will change if the user holds the mouse cursor over the button. For brevity, this practice only assigns an icon file to the *icon* property.

6. Click the JSeparator icon in the Swing page of the Component Palette, and drop it between the second and third buttons in the UI Editor. The right-hand button will move to the right. The separator serves the same purpose in the toolbar as it does in the menu— to create logical groupings of functions.

7. Click the separator and set the following properties:
   maximumSize to "10,25"
   orientation to "VERTICAL"

8. Click Rebuild and Save All. The image files will be copied into the classes\menutoolbar directory and the UI Editor will now display the correct icons as shown in this excerpt from the UI Editor window:

9. Click Save All and Run. The form will run and look something like the following. (The buttons you added will not yet be functional.)

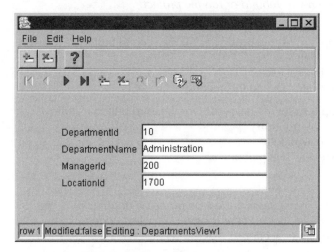

10. Notice that there are now two toolbars. The navigation bar in the DepartmentsPanel.java file and the toolbar you just created. Close the running form file. Open DepartmentsPanel in the Code Editor and find the code that adds the navBar object to the panel (add(navBar, BorderLayout.NORTH);). Comment this line of code so that it appears as follows:

```
// add(navBar, BorderLayout.NORTH);
```

11. Run the form file to confirm that the navigation bar is not displayed.

What Just Happened?   This phase set the button properties for size and icon. You used the object grouping feature to apply common property values to a group of objects. You also used the button pinning feature to drop multiple copies of the same component. In addition, you added a separator to define a logical grouping of buttons.

The sidebar "Moving Objects Around" provides some techniques for repositioning objects.

Moving Objects Around

At this point, it is a good idea to take a few minutes to practice moving buttons around. The techniques you try here on toolbar buttons can be used with any visual object. Start this practice with the UI Editor. You can drag and drop buttons or the separator within the toolbar to reorder them. You can also drag them outside the toolbar, and they will reposition themselves in the Structure window nodes. Try this out, but be sure you restore the layout.

Another method for reordering objects is to cut and paste them in the Structure window. Whenever you paste an object on another object such as a pane, the pasted object will take a position either on the top or on the bottom of other objects inside that pane. Try cutting the delete button by selecting it in the Structure window and pressing CTRL-X. Paste it on top of the toolbar node by clicking that node and pressing CTRL-C. Try this on other buttons, but be sure to restore the layout when you are done.

III. Write the Button Code

The last step is to add the code to handle the button events. You use the same steps here as in the menu practices. The code calls the same methods as the menu items call.

1. Open the DepartmentsForm.java file in the UI Editor if it is not already open. Select the addButton object. In the Property Inspector, click the Events tab and enter "addMenuItem_actionPerformed" in the *actionPerformed* event on the Events tab.

2. Press ENTER, and the focus will shift to the existing code in the Code Editor.

   Additional Information: If you did not complete the earlier menu practice, this method will have no code. Fill out the method body with the code contained in the menu practice. JDeveloper also creates the listener code for the toolbar button that calls this method.

3. Repeat steps 1 and 2 for the deleteButton and use the event name "removeMenuItem_actionPerformed".

4. Repeat steps 1 and 2 for the helpButton and use the event name "aboutMenuItem_actionPerformed".

5. Click Save All. Run the application.

6. Click the Help About button to test the code. Hold the mouse cursor above each button to see the tool tips. Try the add and remove buttons. The sidebar "Vertical and Floating Toolbars" contains details about toolbar features.

7. Exit the application.

What Just Happened?   You added and tested the code that will be executed when the buttons are clicked. This code is similar to the code that you wrote for the menu practice. Once you have the code for the menu, creating the toolbar is just a matter of layout and some property settings.

Vertical and Floating Toolbars

At runtime, try clicking a nonbutton part of the toolbar and dragging the toolbar to the right or left side of the window. The toolbar outline will change to a vertical orientation, and when you release the mouse button, the toolbar will stick to the side of the window, as the following shows:

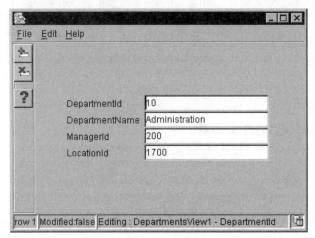

You can resize the outer window if you need to provide more room for the toolbar. You can also drag the toolbar out of the window, as in the following:

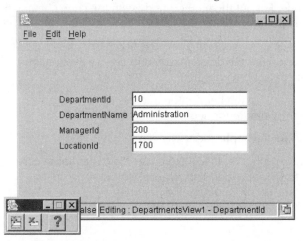

This creates a separate floating toolbar window that acts in the same way as the windows in JDeveloper's Oracle Business Component Browser. Clicking the window close icon in the upper-right corner of the floating toolbar anchors it again inside the window. The toolbar component provides this functionality. You can disable floating by setting the *floatable* property of the toolbar to "False."

CHAPTER
20

Layout Managers

Mad world! mad kings!
mad composition!

— William Shakespeare (1564–1616), *King John (II, i, 561)*

ne of the strengths of the Java language is the capability of applications built with Java to be deployed to diverse operating systems and platforms. In fact, the principle of platform independence is one upon which the language was built. One manifestation of this principle is in the area of user interface design. When applications are deployed on different platforms, the windows and the objects within them are not always the same size. In addition, users may resize the windows in an application to match their preferences.

Developers grapple with this task in many programming languages and often have to develop customized solutions. Java offers a feature—the ability to use layout managers—that directly addresses the layout problems that occur when displaying applications on different platforms. A *layout manager* is a class that you instantiate and attach to a container (such as a JPanel object). This class determines how objects within the container are positioned and sized at runtime both initially and when the container is resized.

NOTE
Layout managers are available only for Java application and applet styles of development because they are implemented only in the Abstract Windowing Toolkit (AWT) and Swing class libraries. Most developers prefer to use Swing libraries because they are more full featured and platform independent. Therefore, this chapter concentrates on the Swing class use of layout managers.

You can take advantage of the layout manager features in a Java application or applet by associating the layout manager with a container and by setting a few properties. The layout manager handles the calculations and functions necessary to perform the positioning and sizing manipulations. A number of layout managers are supplied by Java and available in JDeveloper. In addition, you can add layout managers to JDeveloper that you or a third party create. To work effectively with this feature, you need to be aware of what is available and how each of the managers works.

This chapter explains the concepts of layout managers and the details about each layout manager that JDeveloper provides. It also provides some hands-on practices to show you how to apply some of the more commonly used layout managers.

Layout Manager Concepts

A layout manager (or "layout" for short) is a separate object that exists within the context of a *container*. A container is an object that can hold other objects (usually interface objects). The container's layout manager determines how objects inside the container will be placed and sized both in design time and at runtime. In Java, there are three main levels in what is called the *Containment Hierarchy*:

■ **Top-level container**   A top-level container is an object that supplies the visual root for all objects in a Java application or applet. It appears in a separate window and houses all other components and containers. The top-level containers are classes such as JFrame, JApplet, and JDialog. The "this" container in the JDeveloper Structure window represents the current object for a Java application. For example, if your base class is JPanel, "this" represents the JPanel object. "this" is a Java keyword.

■ **Panel**   This level is an intermediate container, such as a JPanel, that is not visible (although you can make it visible by assigning a border object as described later in the "Panel Borders" sidebar). Toolbars, scroll panels, and tab panels include borders and are visible. Panels contain other components or containers (such as panels). It is common practice to embed panels within panels to more easily and precisely manage portions of the frame or dialog. JDeveloper also allows you to create a panel class that you can execute if it contains a `main()` method. However, the discussion here focuses on the panel component that is used to contain other components.

■ **Atomic components**   These are objects such as buttons and text fields that cannot contain other objects. If a component cannot contain another object, it is an atomic component; otherwise, it is a container.

NOTE
In most layouts, each area of the layout manager (or cell in the case of GridBagLayout) can contain only one component. That component may be a panel that contains other components and may use a different layout manager from its parent container.

Laying Out a User Interface

The standard procedure in JDeveloper for creating a user interface layout consists of the following steps:

I. **Create a top-level container.**   This is a container such as a frame or applet that acts as the outermost container for all other components and containers. While a top-level container can have a layout manager, it has some restrictions, so it is best also to create an intermediate container.

Panel Borders

Normally panels are not visible unless they have a *border object* associated with them. A *border object* supplies a visual aspect to the panel. The examples in this chapter that use a panel also assign a border so that you can see the panel's sides. In previous versions of JDeveloper, you had to write code to create a border object. In Oracle9i JDeveloper, a property editor dialog associated with panels makes assigning the border easier. Select Swing Border from the *border* property pulldown (or click the "..." button in the property value field) to display this dialog. You can use this dialog to select from various styles of borders such as BevelBorder, EmptyBorder, EtchedBorder, and TitledBorder.

TIP
You can make a container resize automatically to its contents using the pack() *method. The following example could be used in a constructor method so that the frame will compress to surround its contents when it is initialized:*

```
try {
   jbInit();
   pack();
}
```

2. **Create an intermediate container (panel).**   This will house all other containers and components. JDeveloper creates this intermediate container when you use the New Frame dialog to create a frame. The following illustration shows how an intermediate container panel (mainPanel) would appear in the Structure window:

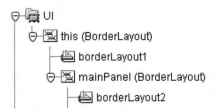

3. **Assign a layout manager and set layout manager properties.**   These tasks are described further in the next sections.

4. **Add components.**   When you drop components from the Component Palette into a container in the Structure window or UI Editor, JDeveloper creates the code to call the add() method on the panel. This takes arguments of the component name and a constraint that is specific to a layout. For example, the code JDeveloper creates for adding a button (jButton1) to a panel (jPanel2) with a FlowLayout or GridLayout (which have no constraints property to assign) would be the following:

```
jPanel2.add(jButton1, null);
```

For a panel that is assigned as BorderLayout, the code would be the following:

```
jPanel2.add(jButton1, BorderLayout.SOUTH);
```

NOTE
For some layout managers, such as GridBagLayout, you might add components to a container with a null layout and then assign the layout manager after aligning the components. For other layout managers, such as BorderLayout, you can assign the layout manager and then add the components. Both techniques are demonstrated in the hands-on practice in this chapter.

5. **Set the component constraints.** The *constraints* property appears on the Property Inspector window for each component. This property (assigned for a particular object by the code shown in the previous step) manages where the component will appear in the container. The *constraints* property takes different values depending upon the selected layout manager.

6. **Set component properties.** Other properties of the component, such as *preferredSize,* manage the behavior and display of the component. With some layouts, you can drag and draw out a component (such as a button) into the UI Editor. This will set the size and placement properties for you. If you just drop the component onto the Structure window, you will have to set the properties afterward.

Once you have completed the layout tasks, you can write extra code for handling events.

Assigning a Layout Manager

When you set the *layout* property for a container component (such as jPanel1), the code that is created adds a layout manager to the container. If *layout* is not set, it will have a value of the *default layout* for that container enclosed in "< >" (for example, "<FlowLayout>"). These markers indicate that a default layout manager is in effect, and you can see this in the Structure window under the panel, as the example here shows:

The default layout manager is only a placeholder to indicate the style of layout that the object will use by default. This default layout has no properties to manipulate. You will need to assign an actual layout manager to the container if you need to change layout manager properties.

Setting Layout Manager Properties

Since it is an object, a layout manager has properties. When you click the layout object in the Structure window, the Property Inspector will show the layout properties, as shown in the following example:

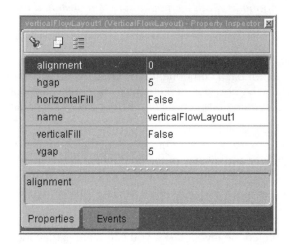

Some layout managers use gap properties to define how much space (in pixels) will appear between components that are inside the container. There are horizontal gap (*hgap*) and vertical gap (*vgap*) properties. Some layout managers have a property, *alignment,* to specify whether the components within the container will be left justified, centered, or right justified. The value for this property is an integer (0, 1, and 2, respectively).

TIP
To verify that the layout manager is working properly, you can check the effect of resizing the window at runtime. You may want to test your application on different resolutions, different browsers (if it is an applet), and different operating systems (such as Macintosh and Windows).

UI Editor Tools

To assist with layout, the UI Editor toolbar performs some of the common operations for the layout manager of the selected container. For example, if you use a null layout manager (no layout manager), the UI Editor toolbar contains buttons for alignment such as Align Left, Align Right, Align Top, and Align Bottom. Many layout managers offer Bring to Front and Send to Back buttons that change the *z-order* (layering and ordering of components explained in the sidebar "A Word About Z-Order").

A Word About Z-Order

Z-order defines the order in which components are layered, which is important if components overlap and you need to define which one overlays another. Overlapping components is not the normal situation, but z-order is also used as the *tab order*, the sequence of navigation for components on the form. For example, a form might contain three items and a button. When the user tabs from the first item, the cursor will pass to the second item. From that item the cursor will pass to the next item in the tab order.

The z-order represents the order in which the objects are drawn in the UI. Normally, you want the tab order to be "top to bottom and left to right." Keeping the tab order in your applications in line with this guideline will help users as they work with the application. The upper-left corner of the item determines whether it is before (above or to the left of) or after (below or to the right of) another item.

The first item that the cursor moves to when the form starts will be the first item listed under the first container in the Structure window. You can move objects around in the Structure window using the right-click menu in the UI Editor, for "Bring to Front" or "Send to Back." These options also appear in the UI Editor toolbar for most layout managers. The menu items and toolbar buttons will move objects around in the Structure window list. You can also cut and paste in the Structure window.

Another way to alter the tab order is by changing the alignment of objects in the form. You can also alter the tab order by setting the *nextFocusableComponent* property as the name of the object that will receive navigation when the user presses TAB. You can effectively remove an item from the tab order in this way. If you do not want the user to click in the item, set the *enabled* property to "False."

Some of the toolbar items are also displayed in the right-click menu on a component in the UI Editor. In addition to Undo, Redo, Cut, Copy, Paste, and other standard operations, the toolbar offers the same z-order items Bring to Front and Send to Back.

Layout Managers in JDeveloper

Most work with the layout managers is accomplished in the JDeveloper UI Editor and the Structure window. Table 20-1 contains a list of layout managers supplied by JDeveloper and indicates whether they are referenced from the standard Java Foundation Classes (JFCs), have been modified to work with the JDeveloper UI Editor, or are specific to JDeveloper.

Each layout manager is described in this chapter. It is possible to add layout managers from other sources to this set, and it is also possible to create your own layout managers. The JDeveloper help system contains information about how to add to this set, but the group in Table 20-1 should suffice for most purposes.

NOTE
The null layout manager is not really a layout manager, but the absence of a layout manager. It is described later in this chapter.

Layout Manager	Source
BorderLayout	Standard
BoxLayout2	Modified version of the JFC BoxLayout
CardLayout	Standard
FlowLayout	Standard
GridBagLayout	Standard
GridLayout	Standard
null layout	Standard
OverlayLayout2	Modified version of the JFC OverlayLayout
PaneLayout	Specific to JDeveloper
VerticalFlowLayout	Specific to JDeveloper (a modified version of the JFC FlowLayout)
XYLayout	Specific to JDeveloper but deprecated

TABLE 20-1. *JDeveloper Layout Managers and Their Sources*

Overview of the Layout Managers

The following discussion provides some details about the layout managers that JDeveloper offers. The information in this chapter will get you started; but, as you progress with your Java work, you will want to refer to other Java books for further examples and explanations.

The layouts are explained in alphabetical order. A table at the end of this section summarizes the key uses for each layout. The hands-on practices at the end this chapter further explain some commonly used layout managers. In addition, the "Other Resources" section at the end of the book contains references to online sources of Swing class information such as layout managers.

Although panels are used in some examples as components within the container, you can place any component type in a container. Panels are used in the examples as generic objects with no implied functionality.

NOTE
It is important to understand how layout managers behave and the easiest way to come to this understanding is to look at examples. The examples in this chapter demonstrate a layout manager by setting the layout of the JPanel object that is inside the frame container. The frame container layout manager is left at its default setting (BorderLayout). The JPanel object is assigned to the center area of the parent container. Since the panel is the only container under the frame, it fills the frame. Therefore, when you resize the window (frame) at runtime, you are essentially resizing the inner JPanel container that manages the layout.

BorderLayout

The BorderLayout manager divides the container into five areas that are named geographically: North, South, East, West, and Center, as shown in Figure 20-1. Each area may contain only one object. If you need to place more than one component in a container, use a panel as the single object and add components to it. BorderLayout takes care of sizing the components within each area.

If the user resizes the window so that it is shorter, the Center, East, and West areas will shorten, as shown here:

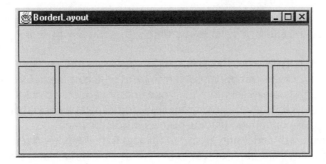

Expanding the height will expand the Center, East, and West areas in the same way. If the user narrows the window, the Center, North, and South areas will narrow. Expanding the width will expand the same areas. Components inside the areas will resize accordingly.

The heights of the North and South areas and the widths of the East and West areas are fixed based upon the size of the components. If the user moves the sides of the window inside the limits that those areas define, some areas will be hidden.

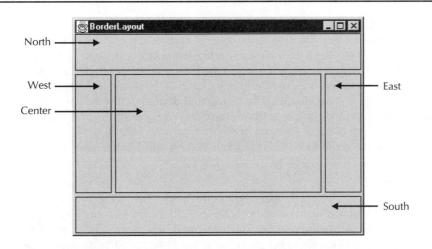

FIGURE 20-1. *BorderLayout sample*

Layout Properties

The BorderLayout manager has the following two properties:

- **vgap**   The amount of vertical space between areas. This applies to the space between the North, South, and Center areas.

- **hgap**   The amount of horizontal space between areas. This applies to the space between the East, Center, and West areas.

Both properties are measured in *pixels* (picture elements that correspond to dots on the screen). You will be able to see the effect of a change in these values in the UI Editor.

Component Constraints and Properties

The *constraints* property of the component determines in which of the five areas the component will be placed. Although you can set more than one component constraint to the same area, only one component will be visible at any given moment. You can get around this limitation by using a panel as the single component and placing objects inside the panel.

The heights of the North and South areas are managed by the *preferredSize* property of their contents. Thus, if you place a toolbar object in the North area and a status bar object in the South area, the heights of those areas will be determined by the heights of the objects. If the object height needs to be expanded, reset the second number in the *preferredSize* property of the component. This property is assigned a pair of numbers that indicates the width and height. For example, if the property value is "50, 50" and you need a 100-pixel height, change the value to "50, 100." The first number sets the width; BorderLayout ignores this number because it determines the width based upon the outer container's size.

Similarly, the widths of the East and West areas are managed by the *preferredSize* property of their contents. The height number in the *preferredSize* value is ignored for East and West areas. The Center area ignores the *preferredSize* property completely.

Uses for BorderLayout

BorderLayout is useful for any situation where one or more edges of the window contain objects and the edges need to be resized automatically when the window resizes. Normally, you would combine this layout with others, as described in the later section "Multiple Layouts."

This layout style is commonly used for placing toolbars or button areas and status bars. Since these objects are normally fixed to the extreme top and bottom of the window, the BorderLayout manager would be set on the first panel under the frame. It is not necessary to use the East and West areas if you are not placing anything in them.

A hands-on practice at the end of this chapter steps through creating an example of this layout.

BoxLayout2

The BoxLayout2 manager (an Oracle extension of the BoxLayout manager) arranges components within it in a vertical or horizontal layout. A container with the BoxLayout2 layout can be defined through the *axis* property as either vertical or horizontal. If it is set to horizontal (components arranged on the X axis), all components placed in the container will be arranged side by side and fill the horizontal space. By default (before setting component properties), each component receives an equal amount of horizontal space and completely fills the vertical space. The manager only

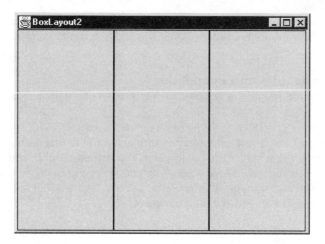

FIGURE 20-2. *BoxLayout2 sample*

allows a single row for each container and will not wrap if the container is resized. Figure 20-2 shows this arrangement using three panels inside a container managed by the BoxLayout2 manager.

At runtime, resizing either width or height will resize the components so they still fill the horizontal and vertical space, as shown here:

If you specify that the layout is vertical (components arranged on the Y axis), the components will be stacked top to bottom to fill the vertical space. By default (before setting component properties), each component receives the same amount of vertical space and completely fills the horizontal space. Resizing the outer container preserves this layout, and the components fill the available horizontal and vertical space.

With both arrangements, it is possible to alter the sizes of the components and maintain the stacking effect that this layout offers. This is described in the "Component Constraints and Properties" section.

Layout Properties

There is only one property on the layout—*axis*. You set this to "X_AXIS" to specify a horizontal (row) arrangement of components or to "Y_AXIS" to specify a vertical (column) arrangement of components.

Component Constraints and Properties

The component *constraints* property is not used by the BoxLayout2 manager. A number of properties affect the layout:

- **maximumSize**   For a vertical (column) arrangement, the first number (width) of this property affects the width of the component. The second number affects the height. If both are set to the default (32767 for a panel object), the component will take up as much space as the layout manager can provide. Set the first number to less than the maximum to make the component narrower.

- **minimumSize**   The layout respects this property, and the component will not resize under the minimum.

- **preferredSize**   This works with the *maximumSize* property to allow you to size the component less than the maximum. For a vertical (column) arrangement, the layout manager uses the largest width value in this property to size all components. If a component has a maximum or minimum size that conflicts, the preferred size will be ignored.

- **alignmentX**   This property is set to "0" to left align the component in its space (for a vertical arrangement). A value of "0.5" indicates a center alignment, and a value of "1" indicates a right-justified alignment. The value is ignored for a horizontal (column) arrangement.

- **alignmentY**   This property is set to "0" to top align the component in its space (for a horizontal arrangement). A value of "0.5" indicates a center alignment, and a value of "1" indicates a bottom-justified alignment. The value is ignored for a vertical (row) arrangement.

The alignment properties can lead to some interesting variations because the alignments are based on the positions of the other components in the container. It takes some experimenting and observation to effectively use different alignments for different components.

Uses for BoxLayout2

Unlike other layout managers, BoxLayout2 can preserve the component alignment and size. Therefore, it is useful in situations where you want to have components stack together in rows or columns and do not want the wrapping effect offered by FlowLayout and VerticalFlowLayout. By default, there is no gap between components, and this is a good layout manager to use if that is required. You can, however, define a gap using a separator if you need to use this layout manager and a gap is important. The sidebar "Using a Separator" explains this technique.

Using a Separator

Some layout managers do not have a gap property, but you can emulate this effect using the JSeparator component on the Swing Component Palette page. For example, with the BoxLayout2 application shown in this section, you can drop the JSeparator onto the outer JPanel object in the Structure window. Then reposition it so it falls between the components you want to separate. You can change the *maximumSize* and *preferredSize* properties as needed.

The following is an example of two separators that have been added to the sample BoxLayout2 application:

The separators were dropped into the Structure window and reordered using the UI Editor's right-click menu options **Z-Order | Bring to Front** and **Z-Order | Send to Back**. The *maximumSize* properties were set to "0, 32767." The "0" height passes control of this dimension to the *preferredSize* property. The *preferredSize* properties were set to "5, 0" to provide a five-pixel vertical gap. The separator can be hidden if needed by setting the *background* and *foreground* color properties to match the frame (usually "Light Gray").

CardLayout

The CardLayout manager allows you to place components on top of one another. Only one component is visible at any given time, but you can use the show() method of the layout manager to display it (for example, cardLayout1.show(jPanel1, jPanel4);). Each component in a container with this layout fills the entire container. The name "CardLayout" evokes a stack of cards, where one card is piled upon another and only one is showing. (The same metaphor is sometimes used to describe the UI for wireless devices.)

For example, you might have an interface such as the one in Figure 20-3. This example has two panels—one for the top and one for the bottom of the display. The top panel contains a combo box, and the bottom panel is assigned the CardLayout manager and contains two more panels. One of these panels contains a button, and the other contains a text field. The application displays one panel or another based on code executed when the combo box element is selected.

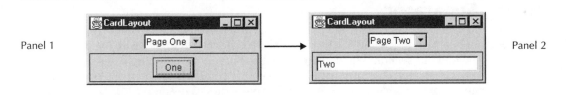

FIGURE 20-3. *CardLayout sample*

Layout Properties
CardLayout has the following gap properties:

- **hgap** The distance in pixels between the left and right sides of the container and the component within the container

- **vgap** The distance in pixels between the top and bottom of the container and the component within the container

Component Constraints and Properties
The component *constraints* property is not used by this layout manager. There are no component properties that affect the layout manager.

Uses for CardLayout
CardLayout is similar to the functionality of a tab control. The Swing tab component (JTabbedPane) is easier to use because it is a single component instead of several components that are required for this layout. However, if you need to control the display with a component other than the tab interface (such as with a push button, radio button, or combo box), this layout manager will provide the correct functionality.

FlowLayout
The FlowLayout manager arranges components inside it in a row. If the row is filled and there are more components to display, the layout starts another row, as Figure 20-4 shows. This layout manager works in the same way as the word-wrap feature in word processors. Rows span the entire width of the container and are as high as the highest component on a particular row. The contents are centered on the row by default, but they can be right or left justified as well.

The actions that this layout offers are similar to the BoxLayout2 manager with a horizontal (X_AXIS) axis setting. This layout offers the wrapping feature that BoxLayout2 does not. FlowLayout does not restrict the container from being sized smaller than the minimum size of the components.

When the user resizes the container, the layout wraps the components as required so they will fit in the horizontal space, as shown here:

Layout Properties

FlowLayout offers the following properties other than *name*:

- **alignment**   This property is set to "1" by default, which indicates that the components are centered within the horizontal space. A value of "0" indicates that the components will be left justified in the space, and "2" means a right justification.

- **hgap**   This property sets the amount of space in pixels between components that are on the same line.

- **vgap**   This property sets the amount of vertical space in pixels between a row and the row underneath it. The row height is the same as the tallest component in that row.

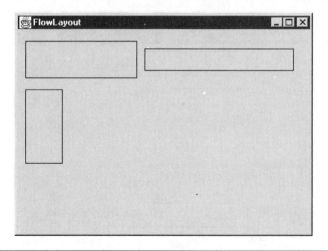

FIGURE 20-4.   *FlowLayout sample*

Component Constraints and Properties

The component *constraints* property is not used by this layout manager. The component's *preferredSize* property determines the row height and the width that the components use for their display. The row is sized on its height dimension based on the highest component (the one with the largest value in the second number in the *preferredSize* property). The row's width is based on the width of the container.

Uses for FlowLayout

Panels created with classes such as JPanel use this layout as the default. As mentioned, you cannot assign properties to a default layout manager, so a normal step in development is to explicitly assign a layout manager (such as FlowLayout) to containers that you want to manipulate. FlowLayout is particularly useful for a row of buttons that you want to have wrap to another line if the window width is narrowed.

A hands-on practice at the end of this chapter steps through creating an example of this layout.

GridBagLayout

The GridBagLayout manager creates grid cells to contain components. Like the GridLayout (discussed in the "GridLayout" section), each cell may be assigned only one component. Unlike the GridLayout, containers using the GridBagLayout allow the cells to be different sizes and the components within the cells to span several cells or to be less than the area of a single cell. Unlike FlowLayout and VerticalFlowLayout, this layout uses the preferred heights and widths of components to determine the cell height and width. For example, the height of a row of components is determined by the largest preferred size of components in that row.

Figure 20-5 shows a complex layout with a number of components demonstrating the cell and component size concepts. When the user resizes this container, the contents shift and resize according to the values of the component *constraints* property.

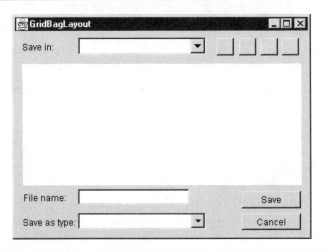

FIGURE 20-5. *GridBagLayout sample*

The layout manager object does not include any properties to modify its behavior. However, it offers a high level of control through the *constraints* property of the components within the container. With this level of control comes complexity, and the GridBagLayout is the most complex of the layout managers to set up. However, because of its flexibility, GridBagLayout is the most commonly used layout manager.

Working with GridBagLayout

As you might expect with a complex layout manager such as GridBagLayout, there are many ways to manipulate it.

Using Drag Handles   When you add a component to the container managed by this layout, a cell is created. The cell borders are visible in the UI Editor, although they will not be visible at runtime. You can turn the grid display on and off using the right-click menu option Show Grid. When you select the component in the Structure window or UI Editor, a set of drag handles will appear both on the cell and on the component inside the cell, as shown here:

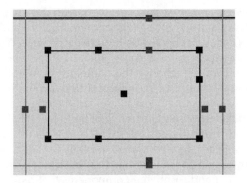

You can resize the cell and the component separately using these drag handles. Initially, both the cell and component are the same size, but you can resize the cell using the blue handles and resize the component using the black handles. You can also drag the component around within the cell to change its position. When you are first learning about this layout manager, this often ends up being an exercise in frustration because you get unexpected and unwanted results as the new object size affects other components. This is clearly not the best way for beginners to work with a GridBagLayout.

Using the Constraints Dialog   Instead of dragging and positioning components as just described, you can set the constraints values for each component through the Constraints dialog (available in the Property Inspector's *constraints* property). You can also just write code that sets the values. In any case, you have to be fairly certain of the exact values and how they will affect the interaction with other components. This is definitely more scientific than the first method, and you have to be fairly accurate in estimating how large an area (for example, 100 pixels) will be in the layout. Therefore, this method can generate a lot of manual calculation and take some time.

TIP
In addition to using the Constraints dialog, you can select Constraints window from the right-click menu on a component (or in the View menu) to display a floating (or dockable) window that contains the same settings as the Constraints dialog. The benefit of this window is that it is not modal, and you can change values and click the Apply button to check the result in the UI Editor without having to close the window.

Using the UI Editor Toolbar   In addition to the Bring to Front and Move to Back items in the UI Editor toolbar, a container with the GridBagLayout manager attached to it offers toolbar selections for weight, fill, anchor, padding, and inset properties (described in the "Component Constraints and Properties" section). The weight, fill, and anchor items are pulldown buttons that provide a number of values for the specific property.

Converting from null Layout   The best way to work with this layout is not to work with this layout initially—you set the container to be another layout before adding components. The null layout is a good choice because it imposes no rules on its contents. You can lay out components freely using the UI Editor and its alignment tools (such as Align Top and Align Left). When everything looks the way you want it, change the container from null layout to GridBagLayout. The tool will set the constraints values based on the existing layout. You will need to adjust some of the values, but adjusting values is much less work than the other methods. In this way, you will be able to take advantage of the power and flexibility of both the UI Editor and the GridBagLayout.

When using this method, carefully consider which objects really require the benefits of GridBagLayout and which objects could be placed in other layouts. The idea is to reduce the complexity of constraints by placing as many objects as possible in simpler layouts and leaving the GridBagLayout manager to handle only the components that require its features.

For example, a typical application uses a toolbar and status line. The BorderLayout is perfectly suited for managing these types of components, so the top-level container should be defined with a BorderLayout. You would assign the *constraints* property of the toolbar to be "North" and the status bar to be "South." You could then place a panel in the layout and define its *constraints* property as "Center." The new panel could be set up initially as a null layout container and converted to GridBagLayout after the other objects were positioned.

NOTE
As with all editors and wizards in JDeveloper, setting or modifying "constraints" attributes in the Property Inspector dialogs modifies code that you can manipulate in the Code Editor.

Layout Properties
There are no layout properties for the GridBagLayout manager.

Component Constraints and Properties
The component constraints, as described earlier, are the heart of this layout manager. The component size properties (minimum, maximum, and preferred) are used to set default initial sizes and are used when the layout manager does not specify a dimension. It is useful to examine each value

briefly. The JDeveloper help system and the Java Tutorial (online at java.sun.com) contain further descriptions and examples. The Constraints window appears if you select Constraints window from the right-click menu on a component.

You can also display a Constraints dialog as shown in Figure 20-6 by clicking the "..." button in the "constraints" property of the Property Inspector. This dialog appears initially inside the Property Inspector window, but you can drag it outside that window and resize it. The Property Inspector Constraints dialog does not allow you to apply changes without dismissing the dialog. The right-click menu Constraints window allows you to apply changes without closing the property editor window.

As with other properties in Java that manage size, the unit of measurement is the pixel. The main areas of this dialog and their values follow. Each description includes the actual name of the property behind the value in the dialog.

Grid Position   These values manipulate the grid cell around the component:

- **X**   The *gridx* property specifies in which column the upper-left corner of the component appears. A value of "0" indicates the first column, and "1" indicates the next column.

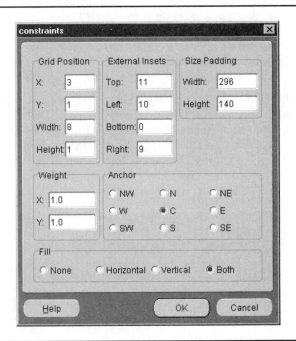

FIGURE 20-6.   *GridBagLayout constraints editor*

- **Y**   The *gridy* property specifies in which row the upper-left corner of the component appears. A value of "0" indicates the first row, and "1" indicates the next row.

- **Width**   The *gridwidth* property specifies how many columns the component spans. The default is "1."

- **Height**   The *gridheight* property specifies how many rows the component spans. The default is "1."

Here is an example showing part of the layout of a frame. The upper-left corner of the combo box (poplist) component appears in cell "1, 0" and spans two columns and one row. Therefore, the values of X, Y, Width, and Height are "1, 0, 2, 1."

TIP
Dragging the component to a new position in the UI Editor will also modify the "gridx" and "gridy" values. It is best to drag the component by its upper-left corner and to watch the IDE status bar and the gray outlines for visual feedback.

External Inserts   This area of the constraints dialog specifies four values that are used in a single property called *inset*. The values specify the number of pixels that act as a margin between the cell border and the component (external to the component). Each value specifies a component side: Top, Left, Bottom, and Right. The following is part of a frame layout. The text item has a blank space between the cell borders and three of its sides. The bottom of the component rests on the cell border, but other sides are inset, which creates the blank spaces. The Top, Left, Bottom, and Right values for this example are "11, 10, 0, 9."

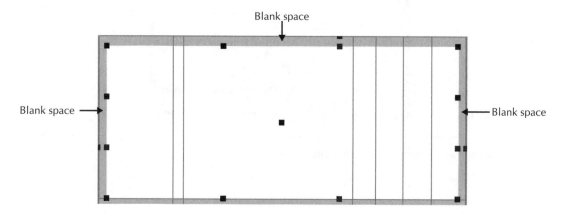

TIP

You can modify the insets in the UI Editor by moving the blue reshape handles. As before, watch the status bar for additional information.

Size Padding   The padding properties, *ipadx* and *ipady* (for Width and Height, respectively), define an amount of space in pixels that is added to the minimum size of the component. Therefore, a component may end up wider than its minimum height if you have defined a padding width. A padding width of "0" indicates that the component property sizes will be used. You can set the values to be negative, which will make the component smaller than its minimum size.

TIP

You can modify the "ipadx" and "ipady" values in the UI Editor by moving the black reshape handles. Be sure to check the status bar for information during this operation.

Weight   When a user resizes a container, there may be extra space into which components can expand. The weight properties (*weightx* and *weighty* for the X and Y values in this dialog, respectively) specify a rule by which the expansion occurs. The value (between "0" and "1" with decimals allowed) represents a percentage of the extra space that the component will take.

For example, there are three buttons in a row. The first and second have an X (width) weighting of "0.2," and the third has an X weighting of "0.6." If the container is widened, the first two buttons will widen by 20 percent of the additional space, and the third button will widen by 60 percent of the additional space.

Components in the same row will be allocated extra width based on their X weight property. If all components in a particular row use a weighting of "1," they will all receive the same amount of extra width. If all components in the row have a weighting of "0," none will be resized. The concepts apply similarly to the Y weighting and the heights of the components.

For example, the following frame contains three equal-sized fields that have X weightings of "0.2," "0.2," and "0.6." As the user widens the container, the fields widen according to their relevant weighting. If the container were widened by 100 pixels, the first two components would widen by 20 pixels each, and the third component would widen by 60 pixels.

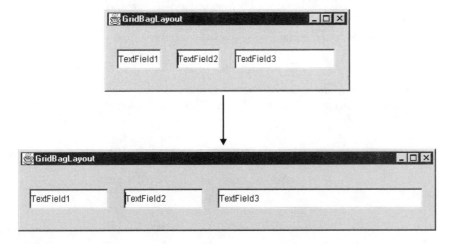

Anchor   This is actually a single property (*anchor*) with one of the following values: NW, N, NE, W, C, E, SW, S, or SE. The value specifies the coordinate area where the component appears inside the cell. For example, the following shows part of a frame in the UI Editor. The field inside the cell is set to an anchor of "W." Changing the value to "E" makes the component move to the right side of the cell. Anchors are preserved at runtime.

Fill   This is also a single property (*fill*) with one of the following values: None, Horizontal, Vertical, or Both. If the value is "Horizontal," the component fills the width of the cells it is assigned to (less the inset X value). If the value is "Vertical," the component fills the height of the cells it is assigned to (less the inset Y value).

If it is "Both," the component's width and height expand to fill the cells it is assigned to. If the container resizes and the cells resize, the component will resize accordingly. A value of "None" means that the component will be sized using only its size properties. The following is part of a layout that uses horizontal fill on the field and a left and right inset of "10":

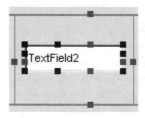

NOTE
The fill properties will take precedence over the component size and padding. Therefore, if you set a fill of "Horizontal," the component will fill the width of its cells, and the padding space will be disregarded.

TIP
When making changes to the properties in the Constraints window, you can check the results of a change in the UI Editor by clicking the Apply button.

Component Menu

You can quickly set some values for constraints in the UI Editor using the right-click menu on components. This menu is particularly useful for applying changes to many objects at the same time, because you can group the objects (using CTRL click) and affect them all with one menu selection.

The following are items or submenus in this menu. Unless noted, all act upon components that are selected before displaying the menu. The submenus offer items that are described here.

- ■ **Constraints Window** This item displays the Constraints window for the selected component. Initially, the window will appear at the bottom of the Property Inspector window, but you can drag it out of that window using the double-line handles at the top of the window. If more than one component is selected, the values that the components have in common will be displayed, and the other values will be blank. Any value that you enter in this dialog will be applied to the selected components. This is a powerful tool but one that you must be cautious with because you could easily set values that you did not intend to set. The best practice is to check what is selected before using this menu item. Be sure to click the Apply button if you want a changed setting to take effect.

- ■ **Weight** The Weight Horizontal and Weight Vertical items of this submenu set the *weightx* and *weighty* values, respectively, to "1" (the maximum weight). The horizontal weight determines the amount of extra space the component will be allocated relative to other components in the same grid row. The vertical weight determines the amount of extra space relative to other components in the same grid column. Weight is discussed further in the earlier section, "Weight." The Weight Both menu item sets both vertical and horizontal weights to "1." The Weight None menu item sets both *weightx* and *weighty* values to "0," which gives them no percentage of the extra space created if the container is resized.

- ■ **Fill** The Fill Horizontal and Fill Vertical items of this submenu set the *fill* property to "Horizontal" or "Vertical," respectively. A horizontal fill means that the component will fill the cell width but not the height. A vertical fill means that the component will fill the cell height but not the width. The Fill Both sets the *fill* property to "Both." When you apply the Fill None item to a component, it means that the size will be set not by the *fill* property but by the component size properties (such as *minimumSize*).

- ■ **Anchor** This submenu contains items for all anchor settings mentioned before.

- ■ **Remove Padding** This item sets the values of the selected component's *ipadx* and *ipady* properties to the default value of zero. Since the padding adds to the value in the *minimumSize* property, a zero padding means that only the *minimumSize* will define the smallest dimensions of the component.

- ■ **Remove Insets** This item sets the Top, Bottom, Left, and Right inset properties to "0." This removes the space between the component and the cell borders.

- ■ **Show Grid** This check menu item displays or hides the cell border lines in the UI Editor. The grid will not show at runtime regardless of this setting. This does not depend on which components are selected.

NOTE
The constraints property for GridBagLayout components is actually an object with properties of its own, such as anchor and fill. For consistency and because the constraints object shows in the Property Inspector as a property, you can think of it as a single property when working in the UI Editor.

Uses for GridBagLayout

Use the GridBagLayout when complex layout is required and you cannot find any other way to place the objects. In many cases, you can accomplish the desired layout using the other layout managers by themselves or in combination. (See "Multiple Layouts" later in this chapter for an example.) However, if you get stuck and cannot find a way to implement a specific design, you can turn to the GridBagLayout manager. The JDeveloper wizards use this layout manager for containers in data forms and panels. Once you master the interactions of its attributes, this layout manager will give you much flexibility in the user interface design.

A hands-on practice at the end of this chapter steps through creating an example of this layout and provides more details about property and constraint settings.

GridLayout

The GridLayout manager creates a set of layout areas that consists of rows and columns of equal-sized cells. Each cell can contain one component, and that component fills the entire cell. Figure 20-7 shows a grid with three rows and three columns. This grid contains properties defining a two-pixel horizontal and vertical gap. When the user resizes the container, the cells automatically resize and retain their equal size, as in the following:

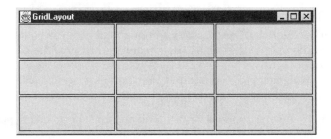

When you define this container, you specify the number of rows and columns. As you add components to the container, the layout manager arranges them into equal-sized cells based on the maximum number of rows or columns specified.

Layout Properties

The GridLayout manager object uses the following properties to define its behavior:

- **columns** This sets the maximum number of columns that will appear in the grid.

- **hgap** This property specifies the number of pixels between columns.

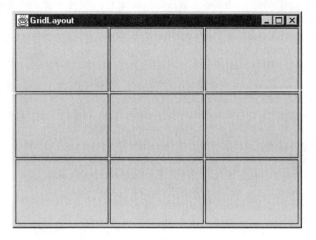

FIGURE 20-7. *GridLayout sample*

- **rows** This sets the maximum number of rows that will appear in the grid.

- **vgap** This property sets the number of pixels that will appear between each row.

If there are more cells than the maximum (the number of rows times the number of columns), the layout manager will add columns but retain the maximum number of rows. All cells will still be of equal size.

Component Constraints and Properties
No component constraints or other properties are used. The sizes of the cells are taken purely from a calculation of the available space divided by the number of cells (less any defined gaps).

Uses for GridLayout
This layout is perfect for an application that requires same-sized cells that will resize when the container resizes. Examples are a calendar, toolbar, and number pad.

null Layout
Technically, the null layout manager is not really a layout manager, but represents the assignment of "null" to the *layout* property for a container. This assignment means that there is no layout manager associated with the container. JDeveloper contains features that manage a container that is assigned this way, so this chapter treats the null layout assignment in the same way that it does true layout managers.

The null layout manager does not impose any sizing or placement logic. It therefore allows you to place components anywhere in the container. Components can be any size. When the container is resized, the components will not move or resize. This makes it easy to lay out components, because you will not have to work against the rules that a layout manager imposes. You can create any layout possible, but that layout will be static when the application is run. Figure 20-8 shows an application with components inside a null layout container.

CAUTION
Since null is not really a layout manager, there are no behavior changes imposed when a user resizes the container, and objects may be partially or completely hidden. Different resolutions may resize the window automatically, and this may cause the container's components to be hidden. If this effect is possible in your application, a true layout manager that imposes layout logic is a better choice than the null layout. In most cases, it is better to include the behavior of a true layout manager, so you will convert the null layout to a true layout manager before deploying the application.

Layout Properties
The null layout does not create an actual Java object, so there are no properties for this layout.

NOTE
The UI Editor displays a grid of dots when you draw or move a component inside a null layout manager. These dots assist you when you need to line up components.

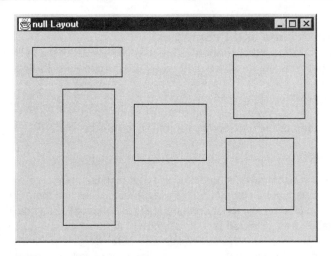

FIGURE 20-8. *null layout sample*

Component Constraints and Properties

You can place any number of components within a container that is assigned the null layout. Each component's *constraints* property is made up of four numbers: X position, Y position, width, and height. For example, a *constraints* property value of "270, 140, 75, 100" specifies that the component appears 270 pixels to the right and 140 pixels down from the upper-left corner of the container and is 75 pixels wide and 100 pixels high. You can change the numbers manually or drag and drop in the UI Editor to resize and reposition the component. Other component properties do not affect the *constraints* property assignment.

Component Menu

Despite the limitations mentioned, the null layout does provide powerful design-time alignment tools that are available on the component menu for a component (along with the usual menu selections). You can use the "Bring to Front" and "Send to Back" items on the UI Editor's right-click menu (and toolbar) to move components in the same way as the other layout managers. There are other tools for aligning grouped components. You can group components by selecting a component and holding the CTRL key while you select another component. Once you have selected a group of components, you can select from the following submenus of the right-click menu:

- **Align**   This submenu provides items for lining up the components with the first selected component's left side, horizontal center, or right side. The submenu also contains items to line up components with the first selected component's top, vertical center, or bottom.

- **Size and Space**   The menu selections in this submenu allow you to assign the same height or width to selected components. It also allows you to lay out the selected components with the same horizontal or vertical gap between each. These items are enabled only if you select more than two components.

NOTE
The XYLayout described later contains the same characteristics as the null layout, but it is JDeveloper specific and is included only for backwards compatibility. In fact it is a deprecated feature. New applications should use the null layout because the null "layout" is a standard Java layout concept.

Uses for null Layout

Other than the layout technique mentioned for GridBagLayout container design, this layout is useful mostly for prototyping or for applications that do not require resizing and repositioning. A dialog or window that you do not allow the user to resize and a simulation of an existing paper form are other possible candidates. However, you also have to take into consideration that resizing may occur due to another platform, operating system, or screen resolution.

TIP
Regardless of which layout manager you select, you can prevent the user from resizing the window by setting the "resizable" property on the "this" frame to "False."

OverlayLayout2

The OverlayLayout2 manager (an Oracle extension of the OverlayLayout manager) allows components to be placed on top of other components. Like CardLayout, all components in the container will be placed on top of other components in the same container. Unlike CardLayout, however, OverlayLayout2 allows the components to be smaller than the container, which means that more than one component may be seen at the same time.

The alignment properties of the component define how the overlap occurs. Figure 20-9 shows an example of a container that is defined with an OverlayLayout2 manager. When the user resizes the container, the components resize in a relative way and retain their overlap.

Layout Properties

OverlayLayout2 has no properties.

Component Constraints and Properties

The *constraints* property of the component is not used for this layout. The layout manager uses the size properties (*minimumSize*, *preferredSize*, and *maximumSize*) to determine how large to make the area that holds the component. The layout will respect the minimum size and not allow the outer container to resize so that the component would be smaller than that value. The layout uses the *alignmentX* and *alignmentY* properties to position the component relative to the other components within the container. These properties use the values "0" (for left or top), "0.5" (for center), and "1" (for right or bottom) to set the alignments.

In the example shown in Figure 20-9, the following property values are set on the two components of this panel:

Property	Large Panel	Small Panel
AlignmentX	0.5	0.5
AlignmentY	0.0	0.5
MaximumSize	300, 200	200, 50
MinimumSize	100, 100	10, 10
PreferredSize	10, 10	10, 10

The order in the Structure window determines which component will be visible on top. In this example, the small panel appears before the large panel in the Structure window list. You can change the order using the right-click menu's Z-Order options in the UI Editor. If you set the *opaque* property to "False" for any or all components, the entire border of the underlying component will be displayed.

Uses for OverlayLayout2

Although this layout is rarely used, there are some situations where you need to place all components on top of all other components in the same container and view them all at once. For example, you may need to attach a scrollbar to a component and have that scrollbar appear on top of the component. This layout would help in this situation. It would also help if you had

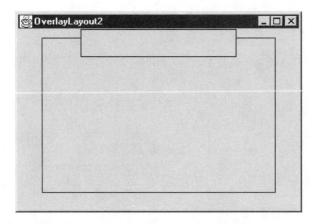

FIGURE 20-9. *OverlayLayout2 sample*

separate graphical elements that needed to be overlaid. For example, you might have an image that you want to use as a watermark (behind items and labels on the screen). This layout would allow you to place the image in back of the other objects.

PaneLayout

The PaneLayout manager allows you to place multiple components in the container and size them proportionally to each other. The logical areas that are created are called *panes,* and the component inside a pane fills the pane completely. The first pane you lay out (by dropping a component into the container) becomes the "root," and all other panes are specified in relationship to that pane. Figure 20-10 shows a container with a PaneLayout manager and four components inside the container. A gap of two pixels has been defined to better show the components within the container.

When the user resizes the container, the layout maintains the placement of one component to another and resizes the components proportionally based on their properties, as shown next:

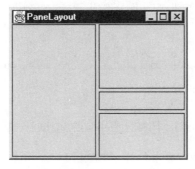

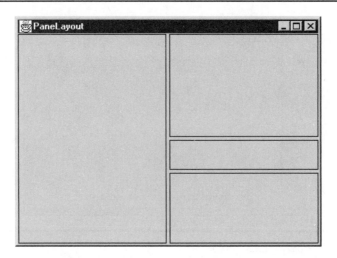

FIGURE 20-10. *PaneLayout sample*

The steps for adding components to an empty container with this layout follow:

1. Add a component. It will fill the entire container. This component becomes the root component.

2. Add another component. It will split the container with the root component.

3. Open the PaneConstraints dialog for this component in the Property Inspector (from the *constraints* property of the new object). Set the position relative to the previous component and specify the percentage.

4. Repeat steps 2 and 3 for each additional component.

The order in which you add components matters because each time you add a component, it splits the last component. The position and size of the new component are set in relation to the last component.

Layout Properties
The only property offered by PaneLayout is *gap,* which specifies the number of pixels between components.

Component Constraints and Properties
You specify the *constraints* property using a dialog that contains the following fields:

■ **Name** This is the name of the component upon which you are setting the constraint.

- **Splits** This is the name of the component that you have just split by adding this component. Think of the "splits" component as the parent object that was already added before the component you are working on.

- **Position** You can specify where you want this component to appear in the new pane (Top, Bottom, Left, or Right). If you select "Top," for example, the new component will take over the top part of the area formerly used by the "splits" component and the splits component will be positioned under it.

- **Proportion** This is a number between 0 and 1. A value of "0.5" indicates that 50 percent of the space in the pane will be taken by the new component.

Uses for PaneLayout

An important use for this layout is in a split panel that allows the user to dynamically resize the panes. Otherwise, you can use this layout anytime you need the "diminishing boxes" effect, where each additional component splits the one before it, and the relative proportions of those panels are maintained when the user resizes the container.

Instead of the PaneLayout manager, you could use the Swing component JSplitPane. JSplitPane provides the same functionality of additional panes and also allows the user to dynamically resize the panes. In addition, JSplitPane offers many more properties that you can use to modify the panes.

VerticalFlowLayout

The VerticalFlowLayout works in the same way as the FlowLayout except that it arranges components in a column. If there is not enough space in the column, the layout wraps the other components to the next column. Figure 20-11 shows an example of this layout.

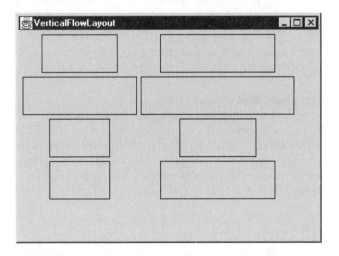

FIGURE 20-11. *VerticalFlowLayout*

When the user resizes the container to make it shorter, the components reposition themselves, as shown here:

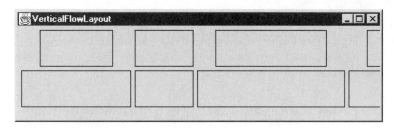

In this example, the user would also widen the window so the components on the right would be visible.

Layout Properties
The VerticalFlowLayout offers the following properties:

- **alignment** This is set to "0" by default, which indicates that the components are aligned at the top of the container. A value of "1" indicates that the components will be centered vertically. A value of "2" means that the components will be bottom justified.

- **hgap** This sets the amount of space in pixels between columns of components.

- **horizontalFill** This is set to "True" by default, indicating that the components will expand to the width of the container. Set this to "False" if you want to set the width using the *preferredSize* property.

- **verticalFill** This is set to "False" by default, which indicates that extra space at the bottom of the last component will be left intact. Setting this to "True" indicates that if there is empty space after the last component, the last component will expand to fill the space.

- **vgap** This sets the amount of vertical space in pixels between a component and the component underneath it.

Component Constraints and Properties
VerticalFlowLayout does not use the component *constraints* property. The component's *preferredSize* property is used to determine the row height and the width. Be sure that the layout manager *horizontalFill* is set to "False" if you want to change the width of the component.

The row is sized on its height dimension based on the highest component (the one with the largest value in the second number in the *preferredSize* property). The row's width is based on the width of the container.

CAUTION
You will not be able to change the first number (the width) of the "preferredSize" property if the layout's "horizontalFill" property is set to "True."

Uses for VerticalFlowLayout

This layout has the same kind of uses as FlowLayout, except that it applies to applications where you need a column layout style with wrapping. Vertical button bars are a good use for this layout.

XYLayout

The XYLayout is so similar to the null layout mentioned before that there is no need to explain or demonstrate the details of this layout, and you can refer to the discussion of the null layout for an explanation of features and behaviors. The main differences between null layout and XYLayout follow:

■ **XYLayout is a real class.** The null layout is merely an assignment of "null" to the *layout* property. The assignment of "XYLayout" to the *layout* property creates a layout object that has properties.

■ **XYLayout is specific to JDeveloper.** The null layout is a standard Java option and, therefore, has more universal support.

The only difference is that null does not allow for the user to set a width and height for the layout. This turns out to be a moot point, however, since you can get the same effect by manipulating the size properties (*minimumSize, maximumSize,* and *preferredSize*) of the parent container. All of the same options are available in the UI Editor.

Layout Properties

The null layout manager provides properties for *height* and *width.* You can emulate these properties for the null layout using the outer container's *minimumSize, maximumSize,* and *preferredSize* properties. However, the surrounding container may automatically set the sizes. For example, if the surrounding container were managed by BorderLayout, setting these properties would have no effect because the surrounding container would impose a size.

Uses for XYLayout

Since the XYLayout is specific to JDeveloper and the only benefit is the additional properties of the layout manager object, it is better to use the standard Java null layout when the behavior of the XYLayout is required. Both XYLayout and null layout are useful for initial layouts of components in the UI Editor because you can take advantage of the UI Editor's mouse drag-and-drop support.

CAUTION
Since the XYLayout does not impose any resizing logic, it is best to change the container to another layout manager before deploying to take advantage of automatic sizing and positioning features.

Layout Manager Usage

Table 20-2 summarizes the main uses for each layout manager so that you can select the right layout for a specific container.

Layout Manager	Usage
BorderLayout	Used to place components in five areas. It is particularly useful for a status bar and toolbars.
BoxLayout2	Used to cleanly align components in a row or column without wrapping.
CardLayout	Used to change the contents of an area. Components take the entire space, and you write code to display one component at a time.
FlowLayout	Used to align components in a row, with the ability to wrap to the next row if required. Useful for button bars.
GridBagLayout	Used when complex layouts are required. Useful in situations where you cannot use another layout manager.
GridLayout	Used whenever cells of the same size are required. An example is a calendar object.
null	Used for prototypes and applications where automatic resizing and placement is not required. Rarely used in production environments because it does not manage anything.
OverlayLayout2	Used to place components on top of one another and allow all of the multiple components to be visible. Rarely used.
PaneLayout	Used to define panes for layout that need to keep their proportional size and placement when the container is resized. This is rarely used because the Swing components provide the same features with more flexibility.
VerticalFlowLayout	Used to align components in a column with the ability to wrap to the next row if required. Like FlowLayout, it is useful for button bars.
XYLayout	Used for backwards compatibility with previous releases of JDeveloper in the same way as the null layout. Its use is not recommended because it is JDeveloper specific.

TABLE 20-2. *Uses of JDeveloper Layout Managers*

Multiple Layouts

When you are designing an application, one of the key considerations is how to best use the layout managers. Keep in mind that one layout manager may not suffice for a particular application. It is common practice to nest containers that have different layouts and to take advantage of the strengths of each layout manager. To get an idea of the possibilities, it is useful to look at an example. A master-detail application could contain instances of different layout managers. The running form is shown here:

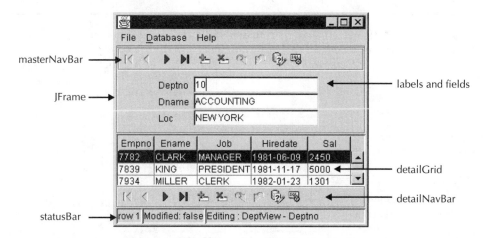

The JFrame area is the overall frame class file that is represented by the "this" node in the Structure window.

Figure 20-12 is a diagrammatic representation of the frames and major objects with a designation of the assigned constraints and layouts where applicable. Most of the objects in this diagram are containers (created from the JPanel object). The interplay of objects is best described by describing the contents of this application as follows:

- The JFrame container is assigned a BorderLayout object by default. Actually, there is another panel that is used as the overall container for the objects. This pane (called "layoutPanel" in this example) is a normal JPanel object that is also assigned a BorderLayout manager. While it may seem redundant to add a panel that fills the window entirely and acts as an additional layer, this is a standard technique. The problem is that the layout manager for a top-level container such as a frame or window is limited in behavior. The solution is to add this extra panel and to assign a layout manager to it.

- Inside layoutPanel is a status bar assigned to the South area. The BorderLayout ensures that the status bar always appears at the bottom of the frame, that the status bar height will be maintained, and that the status bar width will resize as the window width is resized. The formPanel object is assigned to the Center area, and there are no other objects directly within the contentPane container. Therefore, the formPanel fills the rest of the frame, and its height and width are resized as required when the outer window is resized. The East, West, and North regions of the layout manager are not used.

- The formPanel is assigned a GridLayout manager. It contains two equal-sized panels (specified as two rows) for the master and detail views (called "masterTable" and "detailTable," respectively). The *columns* property of the layout manager is set to "1" so that the two panels will be stacked vertically. The layout manager ensures that the panels are always the same size regardless of the size of the window.

- The masterTable panel uses a BorderLayout manager and contains a navigation bar (masterNavBar) assigned to the North area of the layout and a panel (masterPanel) assigned to the Center area of the layout. If the window is resized, the cells in the grid will

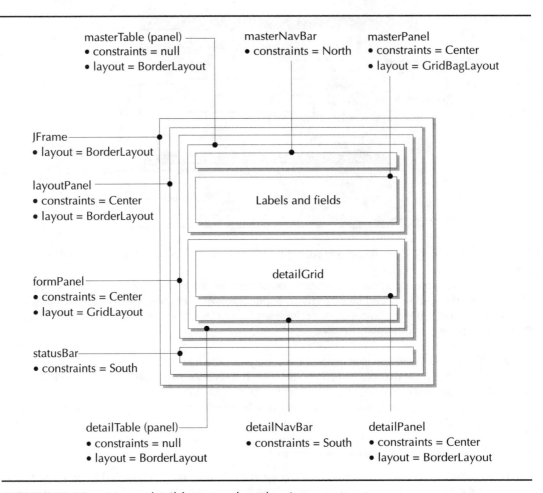

FIGURE 20-12. *Master-detail form panels and major components*

resize, causing the BorderLayout areas to resize according to the BorderLayout rules. The navigation bar will retain its height and allow its width to resize. The masterPanel area will resize along its height and width because it is assigned to the Center area.

■ The masterPanel is assigned a GridBagLayout manager that contains the labels and text fields for the DEPARTMENTS table. The GridBagLayout causes its contents to retain their relative positions and centering within the panel if the window is resized.

■ The detailTable panel uses a BorderLayout manager and contains a navigation bar (detailNavBar) assigned to the South area of the layout and a panel (detailPanel) assigned to the Center area of the layout. As the detailTable's cell area is resized, it imposes the BorderLayout rules on the contents so that the navigation bar retains its height, and the panel resizes on both height and width dimensions. The detailPanel's component, detailGrid, represents the grid display of EMPLOYEES table fields.

This application demonstrates a number of principles. The first is that you can nest containers created by the JPanel class. The second is that you can assign different layout managers to different containers depending on the behavior that you want their contents to adopt. The last principle is that the layout managers offer an easy way to achieve complex functionality that would otherwise require many lines of code to implement.

Hands-on Practice: Work with Layouts

This practice creates applications that contain three layout managers—BorderLayout, FlowLayout, and GridBagLayout. Each practice creates a separate application and frame to run it. There is no database connection required, as the objective is to practice a user interface feature.

After setting up a sample application, this practice shows how to do the following:

I. Use the BorderLayout manager

- Add the components
- Resize the side panels
- Try some variations

II. Use the FlowLayout manager

- Add the components
- Change the component sizes
- Try some variations

III. Use the GridBagLayout manager

- Add the components
- Align and size the components and convert the layout
- Set the constraints property

Hands-on Practice Sample Application

The practices in this chapter use a basic application that contains an empty frame as a starting point. Each phase uses a new application as its starting point. You can download a starting application for all of these exercises from the authors' websites. However, it may be faster to use the following steps to create a starting application for a particular phase. The application file names are different for each phase as described in these following steps.

1. In an existing workspace, create an empty project (on the workspace node select New Empty Project from the right-click menu).

2. Specify the name of the directory as "LayoutJA." Call the project "LayoutJA." Click OK.

   Additional Information: You only need one project for all practices in this chapter, so you may skip steps 1 and 2 if you have already created the project.

3. With the LayoutJA project selected, select New from the right-click menu and double click Application (in the Client Tier\Swing/AWT category). Specify the name as the name of the layout style (for example, "BorderLayoutApp") and the package as "layoutapp." Specify a new empty frame, and click OK to display the New Frame dialog.

4. Use the layout style as the basis for the *Title* for the BorderLayout and FlowLayout applications (for example, "BorderLayout"). For the GridBagLayout, use "Save As" for the title. For all three applications use the layout as the *Name* of the frame (for example, "BorderLayoutFrame"). Click OK.

5. Check the Document Bar to see if the frame class is already loaded into a UI Editor session. If the frame file is not already loaded, on the frame class, select UI Editor from the right-click menu. Maximize the UI Editor window.

6. Click Save All.

What Just Happened?   These steps created a rich-client Java application file that displays a Frame object. You can start the application file and verify that it displays correctly. You will add objects in the frame file to demonstrate layout manager features.

Repeat steps 3 through 6 to create a new application for each new layout practice.

I. Use the BorderLayout Manager

This practice steps through creating a layout using the BorderLayout manager. You can place any component inside the areas of this layout manager, but this practice will lay out panels to illustrate the technique. Since panels are normally not visible, you will also assign a border for the panels so you can see them.

Add the Components

The following steps start with the application created in the "Hands-on Practice Sample Application" section:

1. If the frame is not visible in the UI Editor, select UI Editor from the right-click menu. Click the "this" node in the Structure window. If the Structure window does not display the objects in the UI Editor, click the UI Editor window.

2. Change the *layout* property in the Property Inspector to "BorderLayout."

   Additional Information: The default layout manager for an application frame is "null," which signifies no layout manager. By applying an actual layout manager, you can take advantage of the behavior that it offers. In this example, the BorderLayout will size the panel that you will add next to fill the frame.

3. Click the JPanel component icon in the Swing Containers page of the Component Palette to select the panel component. Click the "this" node in the Structure window to add the container inside the main ("this") window.

4. Set the *layout manager* property of this panel (jPanel1) to "BorderLayout." Be sure that the *constraints* property is set to "Center" so that the panel will fill the "this" frame.

   Additional Information: This creates a layout manager object for this container that you can manipulate. The display of the Structure window will change to the following:

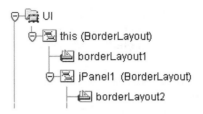

5. Click the JPanel component in the Swing Containers page of the Component Palette. Click the jPanel1 node in the Structure window.

   Additional Information: This adds a panel under the jPanel1 object. The layout manager assigns a constraints value of "Center" to this panel so that it fills the parent container.

6. Click jPanel2 to select it, and drag the center drag handle to the South area. Try dragging it to other areas. Check the Property Inspector *constraints* property after dragging to ensure that the assignment is correct.

   Additional Information: Watch the lower left status bar of the JDeveloper IDE window as you drag. It will show the location of the cursor (that is, in which area the component will be placed if you release the mouse button). The idea with this step is to give you practice in repositioning components within the areas of the BorderLayout manager.

7. Click the jPanel2 object and apply a border by selecting Swing Border in the Property Inspector's *border* property. A dialog will open where you can select "EtchedBorder" (and click the "LOWERED" radio button). Click OK to apply the border.

8. Click jPanel2 in the Structure window and press CTRL-C (to copy). Click jPanel1 (the parent) and press CTRL-V (to paste).

   Additional Information: This shows how you can copy objects using the Structure window. You have to be careful that the proper parent object is selected before you paste.

9. Repeat the copy procedure until you have five panels as child containers under jPanel1 as shown here:

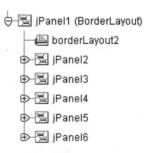

NOTE
If your arrangement looks different, delete the misplaced panels and be sure that you select jPanel1 before pasting.

10. Using the Property Inspector, change the *name* property of jPanel1 to "mainPanel."

11. Check the *constraints* property for each panel in the Property Inspector to make sure that you have a panel in each of the areas. As you are checking, change the other panel names to "northPanel," "southPanel," "centerPanel," "westPanel," and "eastPanel" to match each area.

12. Change the *border* property of northPanel to "BevelBorder" and "RAISED" so that you can see the effect of a different border.

13. Click Save All.

Resize the Side Panels

Panels are laid out in a BorderLayout with default sizes. You can change these most easily in the Property Inspector.

1. Click westPanel and CTRL click eastPanel to group the two panels. Set the *preferredSize* property to "50, 14."

2. Click the northPanel and CTRL click southPanel to group the panels. Set the *preferredSize* property to "14, 50." The UI Editor should appear as follows:

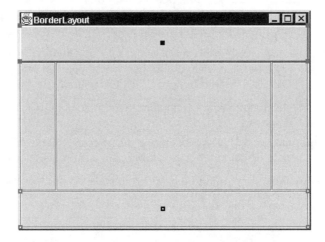

3. Click Save All. Select BorderLayoutFrame.java and rebuild it. On the BorderLayoutApp.java node, select Run from the right-click menu to run the application. Select the BorderLayoutApp file if a dialog appears for the target application.

4. Try resizing the frame's height and width to test the effect of the BorderLayout manager. You will notice the following behavior:

   ■ The North and South panels resize only their widths.

   ■ The East and West panels resize only their heights.

   ■ The Center panel resizes both its height and width.

5. Close the window using the window close button in the top-right corner of the window.

Try Some Variations
You can set properties of the layout manager to add gaps between components.

1. Click the layout object under mainPanel in the UI Editor. Set the following properties:

    ■ *hgap* to "5"

    ■ *vgap* to "5"

    The layout will show the gaps between components.

2. Rebuild and run BorderLayoutApp. Try resizing the window to check the effect on the gaps.

What Just Happened?   You specified a BorderLayout manager for a panel and added other panels inside it. You also made the panels visible by adding border objects and resized the areas by adjusting properties of the components assigned to them.

> **NOTE**
> *In a BorderLayout container, an area can display only one object at a time. You can, however, make that object a container such as a panel, which contains other objects. The container would require a layout manager of its own that is appropriate to its contents. Figure 20-12 shows how containers with different layout managers can be nested in this way.*

II. Use the FlowLayout Manager
This practice steps through the use of the FlowLayout manager using a simple frame and panels inside the frame.

Add the Components
The first set of steps adds the components to the frame.

1. Before starting, create another application (called "FlowLayoutApp") and an empty frame (called "FlowLayoutFrame") inside a new project. The earlier section "Hands-on Practice Sample Application" will help you prepare this application.

2. On the FlowLayoutFrame.java file, select UI Editor from the right-click menu .

3. Change the layout manager for "this" to BorderLayout.

4. Add a JPanel component under "this" by selecting the JPanel button in the Swing Containers page of the Component Palette and dropping it on the "this" node in the Structure window.

5. Change the name of the new panel (called jPanel1 by default) to "mainPanel" using the Property Inspector *name* property.

6. Set the *layout* for mainPanel from the default to "FlowLayout" and the *constraints* property to "Center." This creates the layout manager for this panel.

TIP
If you change the layout manager to "FlowLayout" and the value remains set to "<default>" or "<FlowLayout>," change the value to another layout manager such as "BorderLayout" and then to "FlowLayout."

7. Click the JPanel component in the Swing Containers page of the Component Palette. Click the mainPanel node in the Structure window to add a panel under mainPanel.

8. Click the new panel in the Structure window, and you will see it selected in the editor.

9. Change the *preferredSize* property to "150, 50." Press ENTER. Although there is no border yet, you will see the corners of the new panel resize in the UI Editor.

10. Click jPanel1 and select "Swing Border" in the *border* property of the Property Inspector. Change the *border* property to "EtchedBorder" and select "LOWERED." Click OK to dismiss the border editor. The border allows you to see the panel.

11. Select jPanel1 in the Structure window and copy it (CTRL-C). Select mainPanel and paste (CTRL-V) to add this panel. The editor will show the new panel. The border is copied with the panel.

12. Look at the panels in the UI Editor. The panels appear side by side because the layout manager's rules place new objects in the same row.

13. Click Save All. Click Rebuild <project> and run the FlowLayoutApp file.

14. Resize the window so the right side of the frame is on top of the rightmost panel. The layout manager will wrap the panel to the next row. This is an effect that this layout manager provides.

15. Try resizing the window so that the bottom side of the frame is on top of the bottom panel. The layout manager does not resize the components to account for this action. Therefore, the bottom component will not be fully visible.

16. Close the application and add another panel under mainPanel using the copy and paste method. The new panel will wrap to the next line, as shown here:

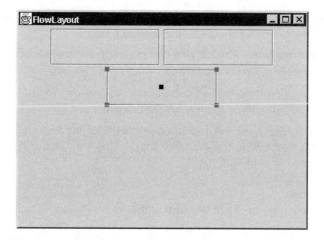

Additional Information: So far, all components have appeared in the center of the layout because the outer panel's *constraints* property specifies a center alignment.

17. Click Save All and Rebuild <project>. Run the FlowLayoutApp file. You see the same effects as before when you resize the window. If you increase the width of the window sufficiently, the second row's panel moves up to the first row.

Change the Component Sizes
The next set of steps uses the Property Inspector to change the component sizes.

1. Click the second panel in the UI Editor and change its *preferredSize* to "50, 100." The first component moves down so that all components are vertically centered. This is another effect of the layout manager.

2. Click the third panel and change its *preferredSize* property to "250, 20." The designer should appear as follows:

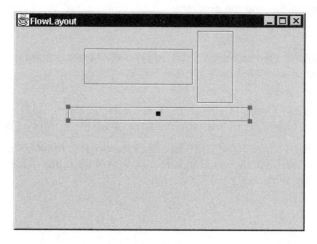

3. Click Save All and Rebuild <project>. Run the application file. Move the right side in to the left until the tall panel moves to the second row.

   Additional Information: The top row component will move up because the first row is now shorter. Rows in this layout manager are sized to the height of the tallest component.

4. Move the right side out so that all components appear on the first row. The row height will resize to accommodate the highest component.

5. Move the right side, trying to keep all components on the first row. The components will always be centered within the available space. This is another function of this layout manager. Close the application.

Try Some Variations

You can try a few things to test more of the capabilities of this layout.

1. Click the flowLayout1 node under main Panel in the Structure window. If you do not have a flowLayout1 node, follow the instructions in the preceding tip.

   Additional Information: The layout manager properties appear in the Property Inspector. The *alignment* property is set to "1" by default. This indicates that the components will be centered within the width of the row.

2. Change *alignment* to "2." This right justifies the components within the container. Run the application if you want to see how changing the window size changes the layout.

3. Change the *alignment* to "0." This left justifies the components.

4. Change the *hgap* property to "10." The effect is to increase the horizontal space between the left side of one and the right side of the next component. Increase the *vgap* property to "10."

   Additional Information: You can see that this property increases the vertical space between the bottom of one component and the top of a component under it. The UI Editor displays the change immediately so that you can check the visual effect of the change without running the program.

NOTE
After you change a property value, be sure to press ENTER *or click the mouse in another property to apply the new value.*

5. Click Save All and Rebuild <project>. Run the application file. The gaps and alignments are preserved regardless of how you resize or move the window. Close the application.

6. Click the second panel in the UI Editor. Click the Bring to Front button in the UI Editor toolbar. The panel will move to the left and you will see it first in the list under mainPanel in the Structure window.

Additional Information: This shows that the order of the components in the Structure window will determine the layout within the container. You can also cut and paste objects in the Structure window to reorder them. Drag and drop within the Structure window is not supported.

What Just Happened?   You defined a FlowLayout manager and added panels to it. You also resized the components and set the alignment and gap properties to experience the effects of the layout manager's placement logic.

III. Use the GridBagLayout Manager

This practice demonstrates how to work with the GridBagLayout manager by building a simple application with components and a design similar to the Save As file dialog that is common to many programs. Usually, the Save As dialog is not resizable, but for the purposes of demonstration, you will create a window that is resizable (although it will have no functionality). This phase shows how to create and position components using the null layout and how to convert the null layout to the GridBagLayout manager when all components are positioned.

Add the Components

The following steps start with the application created in the "Hands-on Practice Sample Application" section. The first section of this practice places objects on the frame in their approximate positions. The exact positions and sizes are set in the next phase.

1. Display the UI Editor for the frame file.

2. Change the JFrame ("this") window's *layout* property to "BorderLayout."

3. Add a JPanel object from the Swing Containers page of the Component Palette. Check that the panel's *constraints* property is set to "Center." Change the jPanel1 object's *layout* property to "null."

    Additional Information: This gives you a full-frame container (jPanel1) that will allow you to place and size objects in any way that you want.

4. Create the following objects using the layout in Figure 20-13 as a guide to placement. All components are from the Swing page of the Component Palette. Do not worry at this stage about exact placement or sizing.

UI Object	Component
Combo box	JComboBox
Four buttons	JButton
Multiline text area	JTextPane
Text field	JTextField
Combo box	JComboBox
Two buttons	JButton
Three labels	JLabel

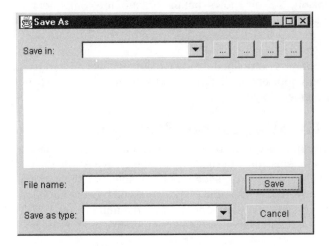

FIGURE 20-13. *Save As dialog layout using Swing components*

NOTE
You can hold the SHIFT *key when you click a component in the Component Palette to pin the button. This allows you to add more than one of the same object to the UI Editor without having to reselect the component's button. Click the Select (arrow) button to unpin the button.*

   5. Change the *text* property of the labels to match the text in the sample.

   6. Change the *text* property of the text pane and text field to blank (no text).

   7. Change the *text* property of the buttons in the bottom of the screen to match the sample. Do not worry about the icons in the buttons on the top of the screen. This is not a functional demo.

   8. Click Save All.

Align and Size the Components and Convert the Layout

When converting a layout to the GridBagLayout, it is important that objects line up as much as possible. The reason is that the conversion process calculates grid cells for the components, and if a component is slightly out of alignment with another component, two rows or columns will be created even if one would suffice. If the objects are aligned, the conversion process will use fewer cells, which makes the layout easier to manipulate.

   1. Carefully size the leftmost button on the top of the screen by setting the last two numbers in its *bounds* property to "23," for example, "238, 7, 23, 23." Press ENTER.

      Additional Information: This explicitly sets the button's height and width to 23 pixels.

2. Select the rightmost button and CTRL click the other buttons at the top of the frame from right to left to select them as a group. Be sure to select the leftmost button last because this button will be used as the pattern to set the group.

3. Select the following from the right-click menu on a button in this order:

■ **Size and Space | Same Size Horizontal**

■ **Size and Space | Same Size Vertical**

■ **Align | Align Top**

■ **Size and Space | Even Space Horizontal**

Additional Information: This step aligns and spaces the buttons. It also accomplishes the same height and width operation that the explicit *bounds* setting accomplished in step 1. This method allows you to set the sizes as a group and can be more efficient because it takes less time than setting the *bounds* property for each component.

4. Set the last number in the *bounds* property of the top combo box (the height) to "23."

5. Select the bottom combo box and CTRL click the text field and top combo box (to group the three components), and on the top combo box, click the Same Size Vertical button in the UI Editor toolbar. This copies the height value in the *bounds* property of the top combo box ("23") to the other controls.

6. Select all objects in the first row (the label, combo box, and four buttons) and click Align Middle in the toolbar. This lines up all objects on the top of the screen.

7. Select both buttons at the bottom of the frame, and select the following from the UI Editor toolbar:

■ Same Size Horizontal

■ Same Size Vertical

■ Align Left

8. Select the text field and combo box on the bottom of the frame, and click the same three toolbar buttons.

9. Select all labels (select the "Save as type" label first), and select the following from the right-click menu:

■ Same Size Horizontal

■ Align Left

10. Click Save All.

11. Rebuild and run the SaveAsApp.java file. When you resize the window, no resizing or repositioning occurs because the container is managed by the null layout, which imposes no resizing behavior.

Additional Information: Before proceeding, be sure that you used the alignment tools in the previous section to line up and size the components. The better aligned the components are, the fewer cells you will create when you convert to GridBagLayout.

12. Be sure that the *constraints* property of jPanel1 is "Center," which will ensure that both horizontal and vertical sizes will be affected when the window is resized.

13. Set the *layout* property of jPanel1 to "GridBagLayout." If the components resized or repositioned, you may want to revert to the null layout and use the alignment menu items again on those components.

14. Click Save All.

15. Rebuild and run the application, and notice the difference in behavior when you resize the window.

Set the Constraints Property

Now that the layout is a GridBagLayout, you can set the *constraints* properties of the components to fine-tune the behavior. This is an application that you can use to experiment with the constraints settings.

1. Select a component in the UI Designer, and you will see the grid borders of the cells that were created when you converted to GridBagLayout, as in the following illustration:

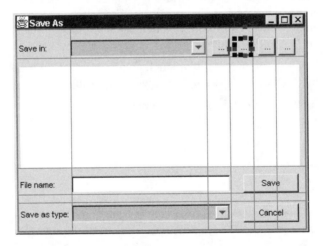

Additional Information: The following instructions refer to this setup, and you may need to adjust the steps if your grid is slightly different. In this section the effect of the properties is more important than the exact layout.

2. The button in the upper-right corner may not be spaced evenly with the other buttons. On that button, select Constraints window from the right-click menu.

Additional Information: The Constraints window will usually appear in the same frame as the Property Inspector, but it may appear outside that frame as a separate window. Resize this window so that you can see most of it. If you scroll to the bottom, you will see an Apply button.

NOTE

The Constraints window is available from the right-click menu on all components, but constraints only apply to components inside containers that use the BorderLayout, GridBagLayout, PaneLayout, and XYLayout.

3. Change the *External Insets – Left* value to a smaller number. Remember that negative numbers are allowed. Click the Apply button and check the layout.

   Additional Information: You may have to scroll the Constraints window to see the Apply button.

4. Adjust the number and check the effect until the spacing of the top buttons is even.

   Additional Information: The insets modify the space between the edge of the cell and the component.

5. When you run this application, the combo boxes resize in a horizontal direction but not in a vertical direction when you resize the window. Run the application to verify this effect. Close the application.

6. To see the effect of the *Fill* property, change the value of this property to "Both" for the bottom combo box. You also need to change the *Weight – Y* property to "1.0" so that the fill will be activated.

7. Click Apply. Run the application to verify that the bottom combo box resizes vertically as well as horizontally. Close the application.

8. Reset the *Fill* property to "Horizontal" and the *Weight – Y* property to "0." Click Apply.

9. Click the right-hand button at the top of the frame, and click the "…" button in the *constraints* property of the Property Inspector.

   Additional Information: This displays the Constraints dialog that allows you to change and apply changes. You can also use the Constraints window, where you click OK to close the window and apply the changes. Neither of these windows works on grouped components.

10. The horizontal and vertical weights should be set to "0." Verify that the buttons in the top of the frame have the same setting.

11. Click Cancel and run the application. When you resize the window, the buttons do not resize because they have no weighting. Close the application.

12. Group the buttons on the top of the frame together. Change the horizontal weighting of the group of buttons by selecting **Weight** | **Weight Horizontal** from the right-click menu. With the buttons grouped, select **Fill** | **Fill Horizontal** from the right-click menu.

   Additional Information: These operations set the horizontal fill so that the buttons will resize horizontally when the window is resized. The weighting settings are required so that the fill will take effect.

13. Rebuild, run, and watch the effects on the buttons of resizing the window. The buttons will resize horizontally when the window is resized. Close the application.

14. Click the bottom combo box and display the Constraints window. Change the *Grid Position – Width* property to one more than the current setting. (For example, if it is "2," change it to "3.") Click Apply and watch the effect on the component.

Additional Information: Setting the width property determines how many cells the component will span horizontally. The *Grid Position – Height* property works the same way for the component's height in one or more cells.

15. The easiest way to move a component to another cell is to adjust the X and Y positions. Note the setting for the *Grid Position – X* property and change it to "0." Click Apply and watch the effect.

Additional Information: The component will move horizontally to the leftmost cell (the "0" column). The X position sets the column in which the component will appear. The *Grid Position – Y* property works in the same way for the component's row assignment. Since a component may span cells, these two properties indicate the position of the top-left corner of the component.

16. Click the text field at the bottom of the frame in the UI Editor and display the Constraints window.

17. Change all insets to "0" if they are not set that way and click Apply. If the *Anchor* property is set to "C," you will see the component reposition to the center of the cell. Set the *Anchor* property to "N" and click Apply. You will see the component attach to the top (North) border of the cell, as in the following:

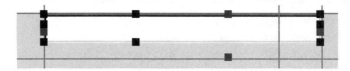

18. Set the anchor to "S" and apply the change. You will see the component reposition to the bottom (South).

19. Verify that the *fill* property is set to "Horizontal," and select an anchor of "W." Click Apply.

Additional Information: The component will not move horizontally because the fill property indicates that the component fills the horizontal space within the cell. Therefore, it is already attached to the left border of the cell, which is what the anchor of "W" would accomplish. This shows the interaction between the *fill* property and the *anchor* property.

20. In the Constraints window for the same text field, set the *Size Padding – Height* to "0" and click Apply. The height will change if the padding was more than zero.

21. Change the *Size Padding – Width* to "0" and click Apply. If the setting is "0," set it to "4" and apply the change. Then set it to "0" and apply the change.

Additional Information: The width will not change relative to the cell because the *fill* property is set to "Horizontal," which means that the component fills the width of the cell regardless of sizes or other properties.

22. Change the *Fill* to "None" and click Apply. The component width will change (and may become very narrow) because it is no longer set to fill the width of the cells to which it is assigned.

23. Modify the *Size Padding – Width* to 20 more than the current value (for example, "100" if the current setting is "80") and click Apply.

Additional Information: You should see the padding increase the component width because the *fill* property is no longer set and allows the padding to take effect. This demonstrates the interaction between the fill and padding properties.

What Just Happened? You added components to a frame and set their properties. You then converted the null layout to the GridBagLayout manager. The GridBagLayout is influenced mostly by the *constraints* values. For proper understanding of the power of this layout, you might want to take some time to further explore other constraint properties such as Grid (X, Y, Width, and Height). Watch how the settings interact with one another and how they affect the runtime behavior.

NOTE
This layout uses complex logic to determine the interaction and precedence of components. However, while initially learning to use this layout, use common sense to determine how the interactions will occur. For example, common sense would dictate that if the fill property is set to horizontal, the component's size properties will be ignored because the component must "fill" the cell's horizontal space. Using this approach will help you quickly come to an understanding of the logic used by this component and be able to better predict the effect of a change in properties.

PART
IV

JavaServer Pages
Applications

CHAPTER
21

JSP Development

EVERY man spins a web of light circles
And hangs this web in the sky
Or finds it hanging, already hung for him,
Written as a path for him to travel.

—Carl Sandburg (1878–1967), *Webs (Good Morning, America)*

 s with many innovations in the Java community, the concept of JavaServer Pages (JSP) technology gained ground quickly. It caught the most attention as an easy method for using the Java language to quickly develop and deploy lightweight client applications. Providing HTML output from a serious programming language is an old concept that has taken many forms recently. JSP pages are attractive in the same way as Perl and the PL/SQL Web Toolkit—they offer the powerful combination of development using a full-featured programming language (Java in the case of JSP technology) with presentation using HTML in the browser. This combination, along with ease of development, provided many Java developers with a compelling reason to move to this expansion of the Java servlet concept.

JDeveloper (in its 9.0.3 release) supports the JSP 1.2 specification. The chapters in this part of the book build upon the introduction to JSP architecture in Chapter 7. They discuss what you need to know to get started building basic JSP 1.2 applications using JDeveloper. This chapter describes how to create and modify JSP pages in JDeveloper. It is aimed at those who need an introduction to JSP coding and to how to create JSP pages in JDeveloper. If you have a background in JSP development, you can skip to the section "Custom Tag Libraries" or skim the material up to that point.

Chapter 22 focuses on how to develop JSP pages using the BC4J Data Tags Library—a set of JSP tags included with JDeveloper that access BC4J objects and make database operations easier for the JSP developer. Chapter 23 discusses more techniques for using the BC4J Data Tags Library to create JSP pages in JDeveloper. Chapter 24 further examines the BC4J Data Tags Library and provides a closer look at and practice with some of the lower-level tags.

The necessary background for the technical discussions in the next four chapters is the description of the architecture, advantages, and disadvantages of the JSP technology presented in Chapter 7. You also need a basic understanding of BC4J as described in Chapter 9 (and detailed in the other chapters of Part II in this book). JSP is a technology created by Sun Microsystems, and the java.sun.com/products/jsp/ website offers introductory material as well as language reference guides. In addition, many books on the market discuss JSP technology, and you will want to refer to one or more for additional material. You can also search in the JDeveloper product area on the Oracle technology website (otn.oracle.com) for white papers, how-tos, sample code, and documentation that serve as valuable reference material.

The practices in this chapter step you through the process of creating and modifying basic, nondata-aware JSP pages. They give you experience with JSP coding and how it is accomplished in JDeveloper.

TIP
The JDeveloper help system contains a wealth of information about JSP pages. Examine the folders and topics under the help Contents node "Developing Web Applications."

Basic JSP Tags

A *JSP tag* is a piece of code that encapsulates a repeatable process and serves as a small program within the JSP page. The purpose of a JSP tag is to reduce redundant coding, increase code legibility, and provide features that can be applied to multiple JSP pages with minimal alteration. JSP tags use a tag syntax similar to other tag languages such as HTML. As with other tag languages, JSP tags are bracketed by "< >" symbols, and many have *attributes* that supply information to the tag and customize its behavior for a particular requirement. The mechanics and syntax of JSP tags are a bit different from those of other languages and need a more detailed description. Therefore, the following discussion presents details about standard JSP tags and examines how they are processed to the servlet and HTML page.

Two kinds of files have a .jsp extension, and both can be created in JDeveloper. The kinds of files are as follows:

■ **JSP page**   A JSP page contains HTML and JSP tags and uses JSP tag syntax. The examples in this book concentrate on this type of file.

■ **JSP 1.2 document**   A JSP 1.2 document is an XML file with a .jsp extension. The code in this document mixes XML tags and normal JSP and HTML tags.

Processing of Standard Tags

Working effectively with JSP pages requires an understanding of how the code you write is processed. How the code is processed (compiled into a servlet and rendered in HTML) depends on the type of tag. All JSP tags can be categorized as one of the following types:

■ Scripting elements

■ Directives

■ Actions

NOTE
The main reference for native JSP tags is the "JavaServer Pages Specification" available online at java.sun.com.

Scripting Elements

Scripting elements are tags that the JSP container converts to Java code in the servlet that it generates from the JSP file. There are three kinds of scripting elements: expressions, scriptlets, and declarations. In addition, you can add different kinds of comments to a JSP file. Their descriptions follow.

Expressions   Expressions produce values that are output directly in the HTML page. The expression takes the following form:

```
<%= expression %>
```

The expression will be embedded inside a print statement in the servlet and can be as simple as a hard-coded value or mathematical expression such as the following:

```
<%= 450 %>
<%= 50*6 %>
```

More often, the expression will be the return value from a Java method call or a variable value such as the following:

```
<%= new java.util.Date() %>
<%= salAmount %>
```

Scriptlets   *Scriptlets* are snippets of standard Java code that you want the JSP container to insert into the servlet. Scriptlets are designated using the delimiters "<% %>", as in the following syntax:

```
<% Java code; %>
```

The JSP container pulls the code from inside the tag delimiters and embeds it as is into the Java servlet when the JSP page is translated. Unlike expressions that are just values, scriptlets must be syntactically correct and must be combined into complete Java code statements. Syntax problems in the Java code will be caught when the servlet is compiled. IDEs such as JDeveloper will provide compile error messages for the Java code inside scriptlet tags.

You use scriptlets if you want to do something that JSP tags do not offer. One reason to use scriptlets is to incorporate constructs such as loops or conditional tests. For example, the following scriptlets conditionally test for a value and present an <h2> title if the value matches; if the value does not match, a scriptlet formats an HTML table with an error message. (The variable value is hard-coded in this code example. Normally, it would be loaded dynamically in the code.)

```
<%
   int salAmount = 3000;
   if (salAmount > 0) {
%>
<h2>The salary is positive.</h2>
<%
   }
   else  {
%>
<table border=1>
  <tr align=center>
    <td><b>Warning!</b></td>
  </tr>
  <tr align=center>
    <td>Salary is negative or zero.<br>
        Contact your Financial Advisor.
    </td>
  </tr>
</table>
<%
```

```
}
%>
```

The preceding code displays the following if the salAmount is positive:

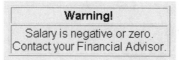

The salary is positive.

It will display the following if salAmount is zero or negative:

Warning!
Salary is negative or zero. Contact your Financial Advisor.

The scriptlet code is contained in the sections surrounded by "<% %>" delimiters.

NOTE
The preceding code example may be a bit difficult to read at first because of the mixture of Java code and HTML tags. At this writing, a standard in progress at Sun Microsystems, called "JavaServer Pages Standard Tag Library" (JSTL), promises to ease this confusion by providing iteration ("forEach") and conditional evaluation ("if" and "choose") tags, among other functions. JSTL is currently packaged as part of the Java Web Services Developer Pack and, as with all JSP efforts, is well documented on the java.sun.com website.

Sometimes expressions and scriptlets can be used for the same purpose. The following two tags will each display the same amount in the HTML page:

```
<%= salAmount %>
<% out.println(salAmount); %>
```

Scriptlets are best used where there is a unique logic requirement for a JSP page. They do not promote the idea of reusable code because they are written specifically for a single JSP page. If you use a large scriptlet in more than one JSP page, you should consider embedding the logic in a class that you call from a scriptlet or in a custom JSP tag.

CAUTION
When embedding Java logic constructs (such as "if" and "for") in a scriptlet, be sure to enclose the code that follows the keyword within block delimiters ("{ }"), as shown in the "if...else" construct in the preceding code example, because the JSP container may generate code under the "if" statement. If you were to have only one line of code under "if," you could normally avoid using the block symbols. However, if the JSP container were to generate an additional line under yours, the resulting logic would be incorrect.

Declarations   The JSP container inserts expressions and scriptlets into the `_jspService()` method of the servlet. This is the method that starts automatically when the JSP page is run. If you want to insert code outside this method, you can use a *declaration*, which is delimited by "`<%!` `%>`" symbols. As with the scriptlet, you need to use valid Java code. Declarations do not cause any output in the browser. They are intended to generate Java code inside the class file but outside of the `_jspService()` method.

Declarations are particularly useful if you need to declare a servlet-specific method that you will call more than once in scriptlets or expressions. For example, the following would create code for a method in the servlet class that is outside of the `_jspService()` method:

```
<%!
  public static double calcRaise(int salary) {
    return(salary * 1.3);
  }
%>
```

This method could be called from any expression or scriptlet inside the JSP page.

You can also declare class variables (that are outside of any method) in this same way. By combining scriptlets and declarations, you can add almost any type of code to the servlet class file.

Types of Comments   A Java comment inside scriptlet tags will appear in the Java servlet file. For example, the scriptlet "`<% // this is a comment %>`" will be written as "`// this is a comment`" into the Java code. (You can also use the multi-line Java comment, delimited by "`/*`" and "`*/`", in this same way within a scriptlet.)

The JSP file can contain a JSP comment (also called a *page comment*) that is not copied into the servlet file. It is used only for documentation in the JSP file. This comment uses the delimiters "`<%-- --%>`".

Although it is not a JSP tag, you can embed HTML comments using the normal HTML form "`<!-- -->`". These will appear as is in the browser's View Source window. The JSP container prints all HTML (including HTML comments) using a call to `out.write()`.

TIP
You can dynamically generate an HTML comment by embedding an expression within the comment using the format "`<!-- static comment <%= expression %> static -->`".

Scripting Elements in the Servlet   When the JSP container creates the Java servlet from the JSP file, it transforms the JSP tags into pure Java. Different types of scripting elements appear differently in the servlet. For example, consider the following code, an excerpt from a JSP page called DemoTag.jsp. (The line numbers do not appear in the JSP page.)

```
01: <!-- Salary display -->
02: <%-- scriptlets --%>
03: <%
04:   int salAmount = 3000;
05:   if (salAmount > 0) {
06: %>
```

```
07: <h2>The salary is positive.</h2>
08: <br>
09: <%
10:    out.write("The new salary is " + calcRaise(salAmount));
11: %>
12: <%
13:    }
14:    else {
15: %>
16: <h1>The salary is
17: <%-- expression --%>
18: <%= salAmount %>
19: </h1>
20:    <%
21:    }
22:    %>
23:
24: <br>
25: <%// expression %>
26: <%= "Salary is " + salAmount %>
27:
28: <%-- declaration --%>
29: <%!
30:    public static double calcRaise(int salary) {
31:       return(salary * 1.3);
32:    }
33: %>
```

The JSP container will convert this JSP code to Java code in a servlet file called DemoTag.java. It will also compile the Java file into a .class file.

NOTE
The servlet code listing is simplified somewhat for understanding. The sidebar "Details About the JSP-Generated Servlet" provides extra information about the servlet file that is created by the JSP container.

The JSP page excerpt corresponds to the following lines in the Java servlet. The line numbers refer to the lines in the JSP file that was the source for the code. The "\n" symbol creates a new line in the HTML page. Notice that lines 2 and 17 do not appear in the servlet because they are page comments that do not create code outside of the JSP page.

```
01: out.write("<!-- Salary display -->\n");
04:    int salAmount = 3000;
05:    if (salAmount > 0) {
07-08:    out.write("<h2>The salary is positive.</h2>\n<br>\n");
10:       out.write("The new salary is " + calcRaise(salAmount));
13:    }
14:    else {
16:       out.write("<h1>The salary is \n");
```

```
18:    out.print( salAmount );
19:    out.write("\n</h1>\n");
21:  }
24:    out.write("<br>");
25:    // expression
25:    out.write("\n");
26:    out.print ( "Salary is " + salAmount );
27: out.write("\n");
30: public static double calcRaise(int salary) {
31:  return(salary * 1.3);
32: }
```

Lines 01–27 are written into the _jspService() method. Lines 30–32 appear in the servlet before the _jspService() method because the JSP lines that created them were written inside a declaration tag. The code uses both out.print() and out.write() to output text into the HTML that is displayed in the browser. Both methods are equivalent.

This converted code reflects the following rules for the different types of JSP code:

- Scriptlets are written as Java code into the _jspService() method.

- Expressions are embedded into out.write() Java statements.

- Declarations are written as Java code outside the _jspService() method.

- Page comments are not copied into the servlet file.

If you view the source on the HTML page that this JSP produces, the following will be shown:

```
<!-- Salary display -->
<h2>The salary is positive.</h2>
<br>
The new salary is 3900.0
<br>
Salary is 3000
```

Neither page comments ("<%-- --%>") nor Java comments ("<%// %>") are displayed in the HTML page or in the View Source window.

Directives

The *directive* tag allows you to affect the structure of the Java servlet that is generated from the JSP file. A directive appears in the format "<%@ *directive_name* %>" where "*directive_name*" is page, include, or taglib.

page   The page directive allows you to specify file-level commands such as the imported classes or the page content type. Here are some examples:

```
<%@ page contentType="text/html;charset=windows-1252" %>
<%@ page import="java.util.*, oracle.jbo.*" errorPage="errorpage.jsp" %>
```

Details About the JSP-Generated Servlet

The servlet code shown in this section is accurate, but it is simplified for easier understanding. The JSP container creates some additional code elements in the servlet around the Java code shown in these examples. Some of the details of the actual code created follow.

The HTML code that will be created as is from the JSP source file to the browser is loaded into a `char` array called `text` in a private class called `__jsp_StaticText()` in the servlet file. (Notice the two underscores in the prefix of that class name.) One element in the `char` array is loaded for each section of HTML code in the JSP page. A section of HTML code is the code that appears between scriptlets, expressions, or other JSP code. In the JSP code example before, lines 07–08 would be one HTML section, and line 16 would be another section. The array element is printed using the `out.write()` method, for example, "`out.write(__jsp_StaticText.text[1]);`".

The servlet code also contains comments such as the following before each line of code that is inserted from a scriptlet:

```
/*@lineinfo:user-code*//*@lineinfo:16^1*/
```

This comment documents the line number of the scriptlet in the JSP code. Similar comments (without the line numbers) document the code that was generated to call `out.write()`.

The first page directive specifies to the servlet the type of content—in this case, HTML ("text/html"). This generates the following servlet line in the `_jspService()` method:

```
response.setContentType( "text/html;charset=windows-1252");
```

The second line specifies the addition of the following to the servlet import section:

```
import java.util.*;
import oracle.jbo.*;
```

It also designates which file will be displayed if an error occurs. The errorPage attribute adds the page name to the assignment of the pageContext variable in the servlet's `_jspService()` method, as shown here:

```
PageContext pageContext = JspFactory.getDefaultFactory().getPageContext( this,
    request, response, "errorpage.jsp", true, JspWriter.DEFAULT_BUFFER, true);
```

include The include directive inserts the text from another file (for example, a JSP or an HTML page) into the generated .java file. This is useful for a design element that will be shared by many pages. The following example inserts the output of a JSP file:

```
<%@ include file="TimeInfo.jsp" flush="true" %>
```

The TimeInfo.jsp file consists of the following:

```
<!-- Current Time is here -->
<br>The current time is: <%= new java.util.Date() %></p>
```

The JSP container inserts the entire file into the main JSP page before the page is translated into a servlet. The tags and text within the included file are treated in the same way as other tags and text in the main JSP page.

The code from the included file (in this case, a JSP page) is embedded into the servlet that is generated from the JSP page and therefore does not need to be compiled as a separate file. The included file is not run along with the main JSP page and does not need to be present at runtime. The source code to be included must be present when the JSP is compiled.

If the included file changes, the JSP page must be recompiled to incorporate the changes. If the included source file is not available when the JSP page is compiled, you will receive a compile error.

Another way to include a page inside another page is by using the <jsp:include /> tag. This is technically an action tag (discussed next), but it accomplishes a similar task to the include directive even though the mechanism is different.

taglib The taglib directive specifies the name (alias) and location of the tag library descriptor (.tld) file that contains the mapping of tag names to the Java classes that implement the tags. The uri (uniform resource identifier) attribute identifies the location of the tag library definition. The prefix attribute provides an alias for the tag library that will be used in action tags. An example follows:

```
<%@ taglib  uri="/webapp/DataTags.tld"  prefix="jbo" %>
```

There is no corresponding code generated in the servlet for the taglib directive. However, the JSP container looks in the tag library identified in this tag for information about the class names of the action tags that are used in the JSP page. For example, the JSP page might have a call such as the following:

```
<jbo:DataTable datasource="Locbc4jModule.LocationsView1" />
```

The JSP container looks in the tag library definition file identified by the prefix "jbo" specified in the taglib directive for a reference to the class and path that represents the DataTable tag (in this case, the DataGridTag.class). It then generates code in the _jspService() method to instantiate the class (the DataTable tag in the JSP page) and pass it parameters based on the attributes of the tag. The DataTable tag generates some other code related to this object.

Actions

Actions allow you to specify a component from a tag library or a standard tag. Actions may display output in the HTML page or may just write code into the servlet without showing output. The syntax for an action includes the tag prefix and the name of the action component as follows:

```
<prefix:action_name  attribute=value />
```

The action name is the tag name and the tag has attributes with values. It is mapped to a Java class in the tag library as mentioned before and as shown in this example used earlier in this chapter:

```
<jbo:DataTable datasource="Locbc4jModule.LocationsView1" />
```

Much of the work you do in JDeveloper with BC4J JSP pages uses action tags such as this for the BC4J components.

Other Standard Action Tags   JSP pages support a set of standard action tags. There are no extra libraries to specify in the code to access these tags although the JSP container needs to have CLASSPATH information that points to the core JSP JAR files. Table 21-1 provides a brief summary of the standard action tags. All of the standard tags are documented in the Sun Microsystems "JavaServer Pages 1.2 Specification" file, available at java.sun.com. Standard tags use a prefix of "jsp," which is automatically known by the JSP container and needs no taglib directive. You will notice that some tags in Table 21-1 support applet and bean plugins.

Tag	Description and Example

`<jsp:fallback>`	The fallback action must appear inside a plugin action tag (described later). It defines what will happen if the plugin fails to load. The following example loads the CalcErrorLoad.html page if the CalcSalary applet cannot be started:
	
	`<jsp:plugin type=applet code="CalcSalary.class" >`
	`  <jsp:fallback>`
	`    http://www.download.com/CalcLoadError.html`
	`  </jsp:fallback>`
	`</jsp:plugin>`

`<jsp:forward>`	The forward action passes a request to another JSP page, servlet, or HTML file. The target location may be an expression that is dynamically loaded by other actions or Java code. The request may include parameters and values. A simple example follows: `<jsp:forward  page="EmpCalc.jsp" />`

TABLE 21-1.   *Standard JSP Action Tags*

Tag	Description and Example
`<jsp:getProperty>`	The getProperty tag returns the value of a bean property. The bean must be used before this tag (for example, using a useBean action) so that it has been instantiated. In the following example, the *value* property of the item called "newItem" will be printed on the page: `<jsp:getProperty name="newItem" property="value" />`

`<jsp:include>`	This tag embeds a file inside the JSP page at runtime. It is similar to the include directive, but the included file (JSP or HTML) does not need to be available when the main JSP page is compiled. However, it does need to be available when the main JSP page is run. If the included file is a JSP page, it needs to be compiled for the main JSP page to run correctly. But if the included JSP page is not compiled, compilation will occur when the main JSP page is run. For example:
	
	`<jsp:include page="TimeInfo.jsp" flush="true" />`
	
	This tag can specify a page dynamically if you embed an expression in the page attribute. This kind of functionality is not possible with the include directive. For example, you assign the page file name to a variable includePage based upon some condition. The include tag would appear as follows:
	
	`<jsp:include page="<%= includePage %>" flush="true" />`

`<jsp:param>`	The param action specifies a name/value pair that is embedded in (and must appear within) the fallback, include, and params tags. The params tag description contains an example of the param action.

`<jsp:params>`	The params action, like the fallback action, can only occur inside of a plugin action tag. It surrounds the <jsp:param> actions inside a plugin block. For example:
	
	`<jsp:plugin type=applet code="CalcSalary.class" >`
	`  <jsp:params>`
	`    <jsp:param name="id" value="101" />`
	`    <jsp:param name="name" value="Tiger" />`
	`  </jsp:params>`
	`</jsp:plugin>`

TABLE 21-1. *Standard JSP Action Tags (continued)*

Tag	Description and Example
`<jsp:plugin>`	The plugin tag runs an applet or bean that may require a browser extension (plugin). The JSP engine returns an HTML tag ("embed" for Internet Explorer or "object" for Netscape). A number of attributes specify the plugin name, the type (bean or applet), the size of the display window, the directory that contains the plugin, and so on. A short example follows:

```
<jsp:plugin  type="applet"
   code="ShowSalary.class"  codebase="/devices/"
   name="MainSalaryDisplay"  align="bottom"
   height=400  width=600>
</jsp:plugin>
```

Tag	Description and Example
`<jsp:setProperty>`	The setProperty tag, like the getProperty tag, works with beans. It assigns the property of an existing bean object. The object must be instantiated before you call the setProperty tag. The following example sets the *value* property of the newItem object to "Harry":

```
<jsp:setProperty  name="newItem"  property="value"
   value="Harry" />.
```

Tag	Description and Example
`<jsp:useBean>`	The useBean tag allows you to embed a Web Bean inside the JSP file. A *Web Bean* is a Java class that outputs HTML. You can pass attributes to this bean to alter its functionality and define its use. Here is an example:

```
<jsp:useBean  id="mainToolbar"  scope="page"
    class="oracle.jdeveloper.jsp.wb.Toolbar">
</jsp:useBean>.
```

TABLE 21-1. *Standard JSP Action Tags (continued)*

Beginning and Ending an Action Tag   As with all well-formed tag languages, you need to provide an ending tag for each starting tag. The ending tag can be written using one of the following syntax examples:

```
<tag>body of tag</tag>
<tag></tag>
<tag />
```

The first example shows body text within the beginning and ending tags. The second example is the same but without the body text. (Some tags do not require or use the text within the beginning and ending tags.) The last example ends the tag within the starting tag.

An Action Tag Example

The following code is an example JSP action tag that specifies a BC4J application module:

```
<jbo:ApplicationModule definition="LocJSP.Locbc4jModule"  id="locAM"
    releasemode="Stateful"  />
```

This example shows the following parts of a JSP action tag.

Tag Library Prefix (jbo)   The first part of this tag (the *tag prefix*) refers to the alias for the tag library ("jbo") containing the code. This prefix is specified in another code line using a taglib directive such as the following, which appears in the JSP file before the action tag:

```
<%@ taglib  uri="/webapp/DataTags.tld"  prefix="jbo" %>
```

The `taglib` directive in this example specifies details about the location (uniform resource identifier or uri) of the *tag library descriptor* (an XML file with a .tld extension) that contains references to the classes, which implement the tags used in the JSP page.

Tag (ApplicationModule)   The tag is the name of an action caused by running a Java class file. The name is mapped to the class file in the tag library. The following listing is an excerpt from the DataTags.tld file referenced in the JSP directive. It is located in the JDEV_HOME\jdev\system\oc4j-config\applications\bc4j\webapp directory.

```
<tag>
  <name>ApplicationModule</name>
  <tagclass>oracle.jbo.html.jsp.datatags.ApplicationModuleTag
  </tagclass>
  <bodycontent>empty</bodycontent>
  <info>Creates an application module instance to service
        HTTP requests.</info>
… descriptive information
  <attribute>
    <name>id</name>
    <required>true</required>
  </attribute>
  <attribute>
    <name>definition</name>
    <required>false</required>
    <rtexprvalue>true</rtexprvalue>
  </attribute>
… more attributes
</tag>
```

This listing contains a reference to the class file (ApplicationModuleTag) and the Java path location of that file. It also contains a definition of all attributes that can be used with this tag. The class file is located in a Java Archive (JAR) file that is placed into the CLASSPATH so that the compiler and runtime can find it. This particular class is contained in datatags.jar in the JDEV_HOME\BC4J\lib directory. Figure 21-1 shows the tag references to the tag library. The tag library contains an entry that refers to a class in a JAR file. This class implements the code for the tag's functionality.

Attributes (definition, id, and releasemode) The other component of the JSP tag is a set of attributes that provide details for the tag. The attribute values are passed to the Java class file that represents the tag. In this example, the `definition` attribute identifies the client data definition model that designates the BC4J application module. The `id` attribute gives this tag a name. The id is used in the Java code as the name for this ApplicationModule object. The `releasemode` attribute allows you to specify whether the application module information will be held in memory between page requests and for the HTTP session. A value of "Stateful" means that the application module will be held in memory between page navigations.

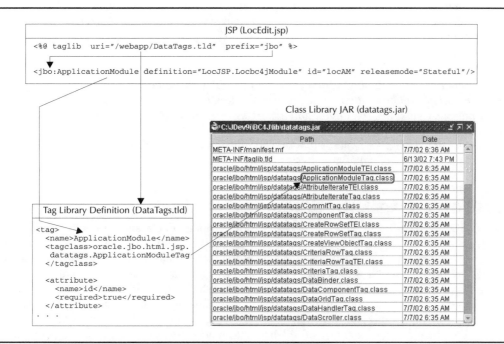

FIGURE 21-1. *References from JSP tag to tag library to class library*

Summary of JSP Tag Delimiters

The following table summarizes the tag format introduced in this section:

Type of Tag	Format
Actions	`<prefix:action_name />`
Declaration	`<%! %>`
Directive	`<%@ directive_name %>`
Expression	`<%= %>`
Page comment	`<%-- --%>`
Scriptlet	`<% %>`

Scriptlets can be used for normal Java comments that are written into the servlet. You would use the following format to define a Java scriptlet comment:

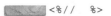 `<%// %>`

Other than the action tag type, the delimiters are self-closing and do not require a separate tag to close them. Action tags can use the single tag form where one tag includes both opening and closing tags ("`< tag />`"). If you use this form, be sure to include a space right before the end symbol "`/>`".

NOTE
It is important to remember as you code JSP pages that the code you are including will be written into a Java servlet. Remembering how scriptlets, expressions, directives, and action tags are converted to code in the servlet will help you avoid or fix syntax errors. The JDeveloper Code Editor features for code completion help with this task as do curly brace and parenthesis matching.

Custom Tag Libraries

The tags discussed earlier in this chapter (expression, scriptlet, declaration, directive, and action) are all part of the standard set of tags supported by the JSP container. In addition to standard tags, you can incorporate libraries of custom tag classes that are used as action tags. These *custom tag libraries* extend the core JSP technology in the same way that Java class libraries extend the standard Java language. Oracle provides a number of custom tag libraries that you can use to build JSP applications. It is useful to get an idea of the available libraries that are supported and their purposes. This should give you an idea of which tag library you may want to use for a particular application requirement. The sidebar "Information Sources for Custom Tag Libraries" provides hints for obtaining details about the custom tag libraries.

One of the main strengths of a tag is that it can incorporate a large amount of functionality. Since a custom tag is based on a Java class file, the base class file can encapsulate complex functionality into a single line of code in the JSP page. Custom tags fall into the category of action

Information Sources for Custom Tag Libraries

The main source of information about the Oracle custom tag libraries is supplied by the JDeveloper online documentation (help system). You can browse detailed descriptions of the tags and view some examples. You can also view the Javadoc for a particular tag's class in the online documentation.

In addition, you can dig into the source code. This requires finding the tag library entry for the tag and looking at the class name and location of the class. For example, the DataTags.tld tag library in the JDEV_HOME\jdev\system\oc4j-config\applications\ bc4j\webapp directory contains an entry for ApplicationModule and lists the class as oracle.jbo.html.jsp.datatags.ApplicationModuleTag. You can add that fully qualified class name to a Java file and select Go to Declaration from the right-click menu in the Code Editor. If that does not work, you then need to look for a source code file in the JDEV_HOME directory (usually named containing the string "src"). In this example, the source code file is bc4jhtmlsrc.zip, and it is located in the JDEV_HOME\BC4J\src directory. In that Zip file is ApplicationModuleTag.java, which you can open and browse for additional information.

As always, the Oracle Technology Network website, otn.oracle.com, offers discussion forums, documentation, white papers, and technique descriptions that may help.

tags. Therefore, they are just single-line calls to Java class files, rather than tags that include low-level Java code (as are the standard tags included with the JSP engine such as the scriptlet, expression, declaration, and directive). An example of a custom tag follows:

```
<jbo:ApplicationModule definition="LocJSP.Locbc4jModule"  id="locAM"
    releasemode="Stateful"  />
```

This code is an action tag (identifiable because of its "*prefix:tag*" syntax) that contains a prefix ("jbo"), a tag name ("ApplicationModule"), and attributes to that tag (definition, id, and releasemode) but no Java code.

JSP Tag Library Support

JDeveloper supports working with any JSP tag library, and it has incorporated a number of libraries into its wizards and work areas. Although it is likely that more libraries will be added in the future, at this writing, the following lists the main custom JSP tag libraries and frameworks that JDeveloper supports through its wizards and Component Palette pages. (Frameworks are further explained in the sidebar "What Is a Framework?")

- **BC4J Data Tags Library**   This library leverages the BC4J components that you can use with all styles of Java applications in JDeveloper. It contains data manipulation tags as well as presentation layer tags, both of which work with objects created in a BC4J project.

■ **OJSP tag libraries**   These JSP libraries are included with Oracle Containers for J2EE (OC4J)—a part of the Oracle9i Application Server. These libraries offer a number of utility functions such as database access, email and file manipulation, web object cache maintenance, and web services invocation.

■ **uiXML framework**   The User Interface XML (uiXML) is an Oracle framework that focuses on using XML to define the presentation layer. uiXML (also called "native UIX") is closely integrated with BC4J for the data layer. uiXML files are run in a controller servlet that handles events and accesses Java classes to render the user interface in the Oracle Browser look-and-feel. The Oracle Browser look-and-feel is used by the Oracle Applications (E-Business Suite).

■ **UIX JSP**   The UIX JSP tag library accesses the same Java classes as uiXML to draw components that use the Oracle Browser look-and-feel. UIX JSP is a standard JSP environment that is focused on development with the UIX classes (beans). UIX JSP files are run in a standard JSP container process and not within a servlet.

■ **Struts framework**   JDeveloper has incorporated work area support for the Struts framework by Apache Software Organization. Struts is a popular framework that offers ease of use and maintenance by separating the presentation tags (HTML and JSP tags that display data) from the action tags (Java and JSP scriptlets).

Generally, you decide on one type of tag library or framework for a particular project because each implies a specific method of operation and often a specific look-and-feel. All of these frameworks and libraries are capable of accessing data through BC4J objects, and JDeveloper makes the binding to BC4J relatively simple. The idea is that you are free to develop a solid business logic and data access layer in the BC4J project and use it to supply data and local caching to different styles of front-end applications such as Java applications and JSP pages.

What Is a Framework?

A tag library can be part of a *framework,* an architecture that provides a conceptual foundation upon which to build an application. A framework offers a complete set of interrelated, highly integrated classes with which you can create an application. You create applications from a framework by extending the base classes and adding the specific functionality that you need for a particular requirement. The base classes handle the details of the architecture such as communication between objects, data access, and UI presentation.

Generally, the application-specific information is stored in XML files that use a schema (format) readable by the base classes. You can tune the behavior of the base classes to a large extent using these definition XML files but, to fulfill the requirements of an application, it is usually necessary to create Java code to supplement or replace the functionality of the base classes. This is the model that BC4J uses and is the reason that it is considered a framework.

JSP Development Requirements

In addition to familiarity with JSP coding as discussed earlier in this chapter, other language skills are necessary. The developer also needs to have an understanding of how JSP compilation and runtime works.

Required Language Skills

Working with Java applications and applets requires knowledge of the Java language (in addition to database languages) and the BC4J framework, if you are working with JDeveloper. Working with JSP applications not only requires knowledge of Java, but also requires familiarity with HTML, JavaScript, cascading style sheets, and tag language syntax. All of these are very approachable languages or concepts, but may require a bit of study and a good reference book before you become fully fluent and comfortable with them.

In addition to the discussion of basic JSP tags earlier in this chapter, you can read an introduction to HTML, cascading style sheet, and JavaScript languages in Appendix D. This chapter assumes that you understand HTML and cascading style sheets at the basic level discussed in that appendix. In addition, free online resources are readily available from the originators of the languages, as follows:

Language	Resource	Online Location
HTML and cascading style sheets	World Wide Web Consortium	www.w3.org
Java and JSP tags	Sun Microsystems	java.sun.com
JavaScript	Netscape	developer.netscape.com

To supplement the information from the originator of the language, use your favorite Internet search engine to find other online reference guides. You can find a wealth of information about these languages on the Internet.

NOTE
Cascading style sheets are used to modify the display of standard HTML tags and can assist you in creating and using look-and-feel standards. It is important to spend time creating the styles that you will apply to the tags in your application.

Understanding JSP Compilation and Runtime

While working with JSP pages, it is helpful to keep in mind the mechanism used to run the JSP page. As a review of the JSP architecture introduced in Chapter 7, the application server (Web Tier) accepts an HTTP request from a browser. It interprets the type of file (using the file extension or type information embedded in the file) and sends the file to the JSP container (JVM). The first time the JSP page is run, the JSP container generates a *servlet*—a standard Java file that does not contain any raw HTML—and compiles it into a .class (bytecode) file. The transformation and compilation takes a bit of time. When the JSP page is requested again, the server finds the compiled code and does not need to generate the .java and .class files so the JSP page will run a bit faster. The JSP container then runs the .class file, which outputs HTML that is sent back to the browser. Figure 21-2 depicts this mechanism.

The JSP container generates a Java servlet with the same name as the JSP file (except with an underscore "_" prefix and a .java extension). The servlet contains one main method, _jspService(). This method acts like the main() method in a Java application since it is automatically executed when the class file is called. The servlet contains all of the code that is required to interact with the HTTP session and to assemble a complete HTML page that is sent to the browser.

> **NOTE**
> When you run a JSP file inside JDeveloper, the Embedded OC4J
> Server plays the roles of the Application Server and JSP container.
> It creates virtual ports that handle the HTTP requests and HTML
> return. It also processes the JSP file as just described.

Developing JSP Pages in the JDeveloper IDE

JDeveloper contains rich support for developing JSP applications. It provides wizards, component palettes, code libraries, and editor features that help you create JSP pages. In addition, JDeveloper allows you to run the JSP pages in a "real world" server process that provides a true JSP runtime. This server process, the *Embedded OC4J Server,* starts the OC4J (Oracle Containers for J2EE) runtime inside JDeveloper without the need to install the OC4J server or Oracle9i Application Server.

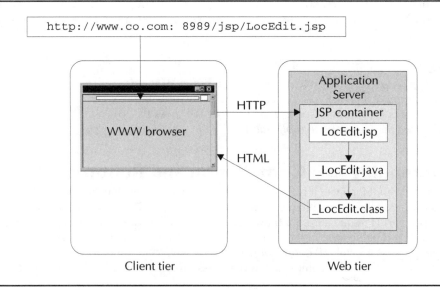

FIGURE 21-2. *JSP compilation and runtime*

Editing JSP Files

Developing JSP applications in JDeveloper is inherently different from developing Java client applications (Java applications and applets). Java applications and applets have a graphical design element to them. You drag and drop objects from the Component Palette into the Structure window or UI Editor. You can view and manipulate the properties of the components using the UI Editor and Property Inspector.

When you use JDeveloper to work with a JSP application, you do not work with the JSP page visually in JDeveloper. Most of the work you do is in the Code Editor. As mentioned in Chapter 2, the Code Editor is a full-featured, configurable text editor that offers features such as the following:

- **Code highlighting** shows language elements from user-defined elements.

- **Syntax checking** is performed as you are editing, and errors are displayed in the Structure window before compiling.

- **End Tag Completion** fills in tag endings (such as "</h2>") for HTML and JSP tags.

- **Code Insight** for HTML tags, JSP tags, and scriptlets presents a list of valid attributes for the tag languages and for Java code inside *scriptlets* (Java fragments inside JSP tags).

Many of these features are configurable in the Preferences dialog (**Tools | Preferences**). In addition, the Structure window works with the Code Editor to display the nesting of tags as shown in Figure 21-3. The Structure window also shows a representation of the tag attributes and their values. This gives you an accurate picture of how a JSP or HTML page is constructed. As with other types of files, you can double click a node in the Structure window to navigate to its code in the Code Editor.

The Code Editor excels in standard text code editing. However, in some instances you may want to view the visual layout of the JSP page without having to run it with the Embedded OC4J Server. In these cases, since JSP pages contain HTML tags for the visual elements, you can load the JSP file into an HTML editing tool such as Macromedia Dreamweaver or Microsoft FrontPage and work on the layout. You then save the file and return to JDeveloper to add the data access elements. While you are working in the HTML editor, you are not viewing data, and while you are working in JDeveloper, you are not viewing layout. To view both data and layout together, you must run the file in the Embedded OC4J Server or in another JSP container.

Although you can work with JSP pages completely within JDeveloper and can view the HTML layout within JDeveloper (using the JSP Viewer described later), you cannot edit the HTML in a visual way. Therefore, you may want to set up JDeveloper so that you can load the JSP code into an external HTML editor and work with this editor in conjunction with JDeveloper. The next section describes this technique.

TIP

Context-sensitive help is available in the Code Editor for the custom JSP tags supplied with JDeveloper. For example, if you place the cursor inside a BC4J tag such as "<jbo:ApplicationModule>" and press F1, *the help topic for ApplicationModule will be displayed.*

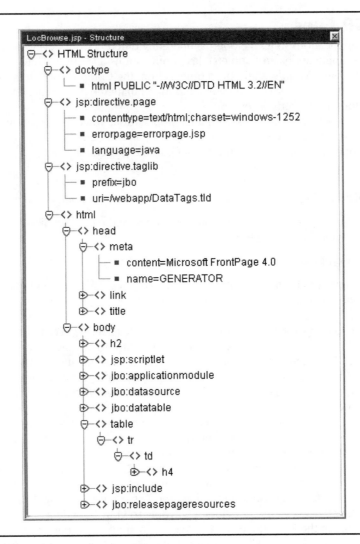

FIGURE 21-3. *Structure window display of a JSP file*

Setting Up an External HTML Editor

You can open an HTML editor session so that it is handy while you are working in JDeveloper.
When you need a visual editor, you save the file in JDeveloper, open it in the external HTML
editor, make changes, and save the file. When you return to JDeveloper, if the Code Editor was
open when you made the changes, it will immediately show those changes. If the Code Editor
was not open, it will show the changes you made in the HTML editor when you next open the
file. You have to be careful about saving the file in each tool before switching to the other tool.

To make it easier to call the HTML editor, you can set it up to appear as a toolbar button, Navigator or Code Editor right-click menu item, main Tools menu item, or any combination of these.

The following steps summarize how to incorporate a visual HTML editor into the JDeveloper menus and toolbar:

1. Select **Tools** | **External Tools**. Click the Add button. The following dialog will be displayed:

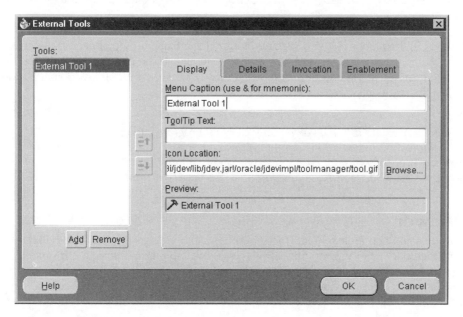

2. On the Display tab, fill in the *Menu Caption* and *ToolTip Text* fields (for example, "FrontPage"). If you want to change the default icon for this tool, you can enter a .gif file name in the *Icon Location* field.

3. On the Details tab, fill in the *Executable* field, using the Browse button to find the executable file (for example, in the C:\Program Files directory).

4. Click the >> button next to the *Run in Directory* field, and select "File parent directory" to specify that the working directory for the editor will be the directory that stores the file you are editing.

5. Click Add under the Arguments pane. A dialog will pop up where you can select "File name" to specify that the file name is sent as an argument to the executable program.

6. On the Invocation tab, select which menu (or toolbar) you would like to have display the new tool.

7. On the Enablement tab, specify when the menu item or toolbar button should be available for selection (that is, enabled). Select *Filename Matches Regular Expression*,

and fill in the field with "=*.jsp" so that the item will only be available when the cursor has clicked on or in a JSP file. If you want other file types to be opened as well, you could add their extensions to the expression.

Additional Information: An alternative syntax for the expression uses the format "\.extension$". Therefore, you could specify a JSP file extension by using the expression "\.jsp$". If you need to open more than one file type, separate the symbols with a "|" character. For example, to make either CSS or JSP files available to an editor, specify the expression as "\.css$|\.jsp$". Be sure that there are no spaces in the expression.

8. Click OK to dismiss the dialog. Click Save All.

9. Look in the places that you specified for the FrontPage item to appear. If the item is disabled, open a JSP file and look at the menu again. The new toolbar button is enabled and disabled at the appropriate time. You can check the hint on the toolbar button to see the text that you specified.

NOTE
You can incorporate into JDeveloper any external program such as Adobe Photoshop (www.adobe.com) for image editing or TopStyle Lite (www.bradsoft.com) for cascading style sheet editing into JDeveloper using the technique just described for the HTML editor.

JSP Viewer

In addition to setting up an external HTML editor, you can view a simulation of the HTML layout in JDeveloper's JSP Viewer. The JSP Viewer is available from the  in the Navigator and Code Editor. It shows some of the visual aspects of the JSP page and adds icons for the JSP tags; you can only view the JSP page in that window, although visual editing may be provided in future releases of JDeveloper. For example, the JSP Viewer shown next is a depiction of the JSP code that follows it:

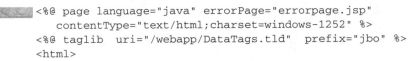
```
<%@ page language="java" errorPage="errorpage.jsp"
    contentType="text/html;charset=windows-1252" %>
<%@ taglib  uri="/webapp/DataTags.tld"  prefix="jbo" %>
<html>
```

```
<head>
  <META NAME="GENERATOR" CONTENT="Microsoft FrontPage 4.0">
  <LINK REL=STYLESHEET TYPE="text/css" HREF="bc4j.css">
  <TITLE>Browse Form</TITLE>
</head>
<body>
<h2>Locations</h2>
<% int numAttributes = 6; %>
<jbo:ApplicationModule definition="LocJSP.Locbc4jModule"  id="am"
   releasemode="Stateful"  />
<jbo:DataSource id="locData"  rangesize="6"  appid="am"
   viewobject="LocationsView1"  />
<jbo:DataTable datasource="locData"  edittarget="LocEdit.jsp" />
<table>
  <tr>
    <td>
    <h4><a class="clsToolbarButton" href="LocQuery.jsp">
        Find Location</a></h4>
    </td>
  </tr>
</table>
</body>
</html>
```

The HTML tags (such as headings and tables) are displayed in the viewer in a similar way to how they will appear when the JSP page is run. Styles in cascading style sheets that the JSP page references are incorporated. JSP tags are displayed with icons that suggest the type of code they represent (for example, JSP tag, page directive, or scriptlet). Double clicking an icon moves the cursor to its line of code in the Code Editor window. Tooltips on the icons show the tag.

> **CAUTION**
> *The JSP Viewer may be case sensitive to names of global styles in the style sheet. For example, if your CSS file contains a style called ".CODE", the reference in the JSP file requires the reference to be all uppercase (for example, "<body class="CODE">"). Otherwise, the JSP Viewer may not display the style correctly. Other styles that replace standard tags (such as H2 and TD) do not need to be case sensitive. This restriction may be eliminated in future releases.*

BC4J Admin Utility

JDeveloper contains a JSP application that allows you to examine the BC4J application modules that are in memory on the server. The *BC4J Admin Utility* (also called the *BC4J JSP Web Monitor*), shown in Figure 21-4, displays the status of the server, a list of application module pools, and links that display the Java runtime parameters and the BC4J runtime parameters. You can start this utility by accessing the following page after starting the application server:

```
http://localhost:8988/webapp/wm/bc4j.jsp
```

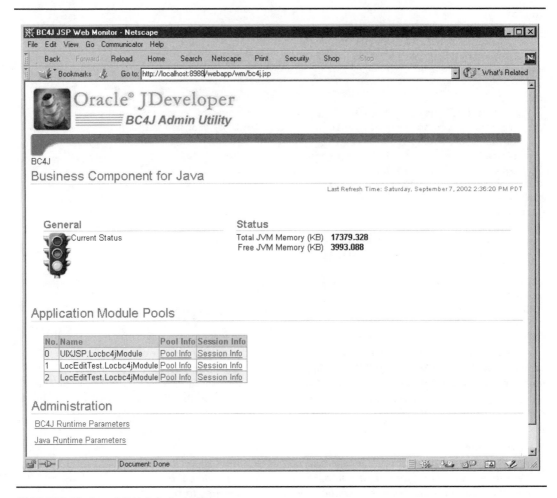

FIGURE 21-4. *BC4J Admin Utility*

Specify appropriate host and port numbers if you are running the application server on a machine other than your local machine.

TIP
When you click the Pool Info link for a particular application module pool, you will see a list of application module instances that are available. The "Total Number of View Objects" column in this list is a link to a page that contains details about the view objects in the application module instance. This page also allows you to browse the SQL queries and attributes in the application module instance.

JDeveloper JSP Directory Structure

As mentioned in Chapter 1, JDeveloper creates subdirectories under the project directory that are used to organize the many files that comprise a project. You can define the names and locations of the directories for source code and HTML code on the project level (when you create the project or in the project settings dialog). However, the default locations should work for most purposes.

You use the same kind of project structure for a JSP application as you do for a Java client application (that uses Java applications or applets). That is, you create a BC4J project with the business logic layer and an application project for the user interface code. When you develop a JSP application, part of the default directory structure is built to comply with Java 2 Platform, Enterprise Edition (J2EE) standards. A typical directory structure is shown here:

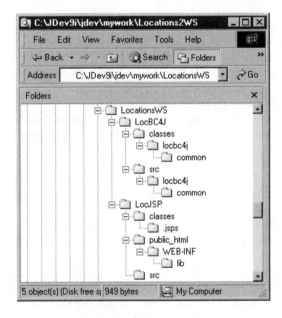

The workspace directory (LocationsWS) is the top level shown here. The two directories under the workspace contain the BC4J project and application project files.

BC4J Project Directory

This directory (in this example, LocBC4J) appears under the workspace directory. The BC4J directory structure consists of the following subdirectories:

classes   This directory contains the package subdirectory (in this case locbc4j) and the connections.xml file that stores the database and other server connections available to this project. The package subdirectory contains the compiled .class (bytecode) files and .xml files that provide application-specific properties to the BC4J framework. The package subdirectory also contains a subdirectory called "common" that contains the bc4j.xcfg configuration file and some compiled resource files.

src This directory contains the source code version of most of the same files as in the classes subdirectory. It is set up with the same subdirectory structure.

JSP Project Directory

The JSP project directory (LocJSP in this example) also appears under the workspace directory. It contains the following three directories.

classes This directory contains the same connections.xml file as in the BC4J project. It also contains a .cpx file that contains the client data model definition used by the data tags. A subdirectory called .jsps stores all of the JSP servlets (.java files) and compiled bytecode (.class files). The .jsps directory fills the same role as the package directory in the BC4J project's classes directory.

public_html This directory contains the JSP source code files (.jsp) and the default cascading style sheet file (bc4j.css). Files in this directory are available to any user when this project is deployed. This directory also contains the WEB-INF directory that is a standard J2EE deployment directory. When the project is deployed, files in the WEB-INF directory are either not viewable by users or are available only to authenticated users. WEB-INF stores the web.xml file, the J2EE standard Web Application Deployment Descriptor that contains parameters for the application server. If the application is large or needs additional organizational levels, you can add directories under public_html (considered the "root" directory) for JSP files.

This directory also contains a lib directory containing the tag libraries that your project requires. A *tag library* is a JAR or Zip file containing classes that implement the tags used in the JSP file. For example, if the project used BC4J Data Component Tags, the lib directory might contain datatags.jar, a JAR file that stores the compiled .class files for tags such as ApplicationModuleTag.class.

The public_html directory may also contain a directory called "classes" that holds other Java classes that you build or that are required for the application but that are not in libraries in the lib directory.

The Data Page Wizard automatically loads a number of files and subdirectories under a directory called "cabo" (the code name for the pre-production UIX project) in the public_html directory. These extra files (such as .gif image files, JavaScript code, and cascading style sheets) are then available to the components that you build in the project.

src The .jsp files stored in the public_html directory are the source code files, so the files stored here are miscellaneous code files such as the deployment profile and another copy of the client data model definition (in the .cpx file).

You might construct more than one JSP project within the same workspace, and those projects would each have their own project directories and subdirectories under the workspace directory.

Hands-on Practice: Build a Simple JSP Page

The practices thus far in the book have used the JSP wizards to create working code that accesses data in the database. Although JSP applications you write will normally require data from the database, this practice focuses on a nondata JSP page so that you can get an idea about how basic JSP tags work and how you develop and run JSP pages in JDeveloper. You will use standard

HTML, scriptlet, and expression tags in this practice. Scriptlets and expressions are introduced earlier in this chapter, and HTML is discussed in Appendix D.

The JSP page that you develop in this practice displays a "times table" that shows the multiplication of numbers from 1 to 9 inside an HTML table as shown in Figure 21-5.

This practice contains the following phases:

   I. Create a workspace, project, and default JSP page

   II. Modify the JSP page

   III. Apply a cascading style sheet

   IV. Run the JSP page

I. Create a Workspace, Project, and Default JSP Page

The first phase creates the JDeveloper workspace and project and adds a default JSP page file to the project. This JSP page contains basic HTML tags and some placeholder text that you will replace.

   I. Select the Workspaces node in the Navigator, and select New Workspace from the right-click menu.

   2. Name the workspace and its directory "SimpleJSPWS." Leave the *Add a New Empty Project* checkbox checked. Click OK.

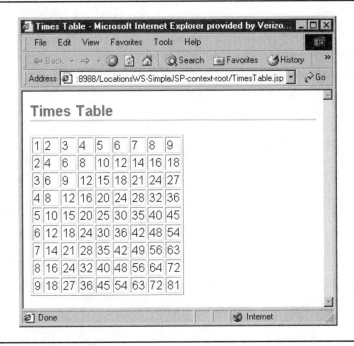

FIGURE 21-5. *Simple JSP page running in the browser*

3. In the New Project dialog, name the project and its directory "SimpleJSP."

4. Click OK. Click Save All.

5. On the SimpleJSP project node, select New from the right-click menu to display the New gallery.

6. Double click the JSP Page item in the Web Tier\JavaServer Pages (JSP) category. This displays the New JSP dialog.

7. Do not change the directory name. Change the *File Name* to "TimesTable" and click OK. The .jsp extension will automatically be added to the file name. Click Save All.

What Just Happened?   This phase created the JDeveloper containers for the JSP file and added a default JSP page to the project.

II. Modify the JSP Page

You can now modify the JSP page by replacing the placeholder information and adding your own code.

1. Double click the TimesTable.jsp file in the Navigator if it is not already open in the Code Editor.

2. Change the text between the "`<title></title>`" tags to "Times Table." This text will be displayed in the window title when the JSP page is run.

3. Change the text between the "`<h2></h2>`" tags to "Times Table." This text provides a heading on the page.

4. Delete the "`<p></p>`" tags and the text between them.

5. In a blank line between the "`</h2>`" tag and the "`</body>`" tag, add the following code:

```
<table border="1">
<%
  for (int i = 1; i < 10; i++) {
    %><tr><%
    for (int j = 1; j < 10; j++) {
      %><td><%= i * j %></td><%
    }
    %></tr><%
  }
%>
</table>
```

6. Double check that you have entered all the code to match the listing.

7. Click Save All. (You will run this file in a later phase.)

What Just Happened?   This phase modified the contents of the default JSP file and added Java code and HTML tags. This code contains the definition of an HTML table that contains the results of multiplication in a nested loop. At first glance, this code seems a bit cryptic. The main things to remember when reading this code are that anything inside "<% %>" markers is pure Java code, and that anything inside "<%= %>" markers is a Java expression that you could place inside a print statement such as `System.out.println()`. The following is an annotated guide to the code for the HTML table. The code is repeated here with line numbers added for the purpose of reference:

```
01: <table border="1">
02: <%
03:    for (int i = 1; i < 10; i++) {
04:       %><tr><%
05:       for (int j = 1; j < 10; j++) {
06:          %><td><%= i * j %></td><%
07:       }
08:       %></tr><%
09:    }
10: %>
11: </table>
```

Line 01 starts the HTML table and specifies a visible table border for the cells.

Line 02 opens a Java scriptlet. Anything within the "<% %>" tags is Java code that will be copied into the servlet when the JSP page is compiled.

Line 03 is a standard Java statement for the start of a loop that counts (using the counter i) from 1 to 9 corresponding to the rows that will appear in the times table.

Line 04 ends the scriptlet. Anything outside the scriptlet markers is treated as standard HTML or another type of JSP tag. This line also starts another scriptlet. This code formatting (placing the scriptlet start and close markers on the same line as an embedded HTML tag) is commonly used in the JDeveloper code. The HTML tag "<tr>" starts a row in the table.

Line 05 is another standard Java statement for the nested loop (using the counter j) that creates columns within each row.

Line 06 ends the scriptlet and starts and ends a table cell using the "<td></td>" tags. Inside the table cell tag is an expression whose results will be displayed on the page. In this case, the expression is the multiplication of the two counters.

Line 07 is the end of the inner loop.

Line 08 ends the scriptlet, embeds an HTML table row ending tag, and starts another scriptlet.

Line 09 is the end of the outer loop.

Line 10 is the end of the scriptlet.

Line 11 is the HTML table closing tag.

III. Apply a Cascading Style Sheet

You now have a working JSP file with a standard look-and-feel. This phase adds a cascading style sheet to the project so that you can incorporate a standard appearance for your application. (Cascading style sheets are described further in Appendix D.) The style sheet used in this phase is jdeveloper.css, which is distributed in the JDEV_HOME\jdev directory. It will provide the same appearance as the JDeveloper help system.

I. On the TimesTable.jsp node in the Navigator, select JSP Viewer from the right-click menu. The JSP Viewer window will appear, as shown here:

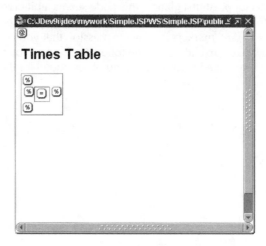

Additional Information: The JSP Viewer shows the text that will appear in the browser as well as styles that you apply to the text. It does not show the results of any Java code or the output from any data tag.

2. On the project node, select **File | Import** to display the Import dialog.

3. Select "Existing Sources" and click OK to display the Import Existing Sources Wizard. Click Next if the Welcome page appears.

4. Click the Add button and click the Home button to navigate to the JDEV_HOME\jdev directory (where JDEV_HOME is the directory in which JDeveloper is installed).

5. Click the jdeveloper.css file and click Open to copy the file name into the *Refine Files to Be Added* pane.

6. Check the *Copy Files to Project Directory* checkbox, and change the directory name to "public_html" instead of "src."

Additional Information: The full directory name should be "JDEV_HOME\jdev\mywork\SimpleJSPWS\SimpleJSP\public_html."

7. Click Next and Finish. The file will be copied and added to the project.

8. Check the location and name of the file in the JDeveloper status bar to be sure that it is in the public_html directory under your project. If it is not, select **File | Erase from Disk** and repeat this phase.

9. Add the following line of code on a line before the `<title>` tag in the TimesTable.jsp file:

```
<LINK REL=STYLESHEET TYPE="text/css" HREF="jdeveloper.css">
```

Additional Information: This line references the cascading style sheet file and makes its styles available to the JSP page.

10. On the TimesTable.jsp node in the Navigator, select JSP Viewer from the right-click menu. The JSP Viewer will display the page using the styles in the style sheet, as shown here:

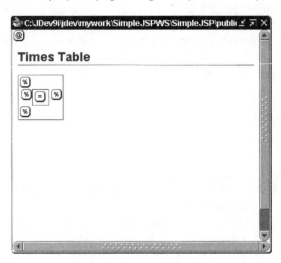

11. Click Save All.

What Just Happened?   This phase added an existing cascading style sheet to the project and referenced the style sheet in the JSP code. You also used the JSP Viewer to get an idea about what the HTML tags would display in the browser. The jdeveloper.css file contains styles that apply to standard tags such as the <h2> tag in this example. It also contains other styles that you can apply using the class attribute (for example, "<p class="GlossaryItem">").

IV. Run the JSP Page

You have now created a JSP page that will display an HTML table with the multiplication table. This phase runs the JSP page.

1. Click the SimpleJSP.jpr project node in the Navigator and click Rebuild SimpleJSP. Fix any compilation errors that appear in the Log window.

2. Click the TimesTable.jsp file node in the Navigator and click Run. The Embedded OC4J Server will start, and your browser will display the HTML page shown in Figure 21-5.

3. Examine the HTML source by selecting View Source from the right-click menu on the page. Identify all the code in the source with the code in your JSP page.

TIP
*If View Source does not work in Internet Explorer, you may need to clear out your Temporary Internet Files (file cache). Select **Tools** | **Internet Options** and click Delete Files.*

What Just Happened?   You ran the simple JSP page in the JDeveloper Embedded OC4J Server. If you are interested in exercising your Java language and JSP skills, you can try variations on this JSP page such as highlighting and bolding the first row and first column of the HTML table. This requires more than additional HTML tags; you will need to think a bit about where to begin and end scriptlets and expressions. To solve this problem, you need to know that the HTML attribute bgcolor will change the background color of the table cell. For example, the "text here" string within the following tag will be displayed inside a yellow cell:

```
<td bgcolor= "yellow">text here</td>
```

A possible answer appears in the sidebar "Solution to Times Table Highlighting Problem" at the end of this chapter.

Hands-on Practice: Create a Simple JSP Form

This practice uses a JSP page to create an HTML form containing an input text field and two buttons for Submit and Reset. The Submit button passes the input value to a Java scriptlet, which draws another times table for numbers between one and the number input. For example, if the user inputs the number "12," the table will show all multiplications between one and 12. The practice demonstrates how Java inside a JSP page can handle input from a standard HTML form. It also shows how to use some of the controls on the HTML page of the Component Palette.

This practice contains the following phases:

   I. **Create a default JSP page and add form code**

   II. **Add table logic and run the JSP page**

I. Create a Default JSP Page and Add Form Code

This phase creates a default JSP page and adds HTML form code to it. HTML forms enclose input fields and buttons. When the user runs the form by clicking the Submit button, the routine defined in the action attribute of the form tag is run. In this example, the action calls the same page.

   1. On the SimpleJSP project node, select New from the right-click menu to display the New gallery.

   2. Double click the JSP Page item in the Web Tier\JavaServer Pages (JSP) category. This displays the New JSP dialog.

   3. Do not change the directory name. Change the *File Name* to "TimesTableInput" and click OK. The .jsp extension will automatically be added to the file name.

   4. Change the text within the "`<title>`" tags to "Times Table Input," and remove the "`<h2>`" and "`<p>`" tags and text within those tags.

   5. Place the cursor in a blank line between "`<body>`" and "`</body>`" tags, and click the Form icon in the HTML page of the Component Palette.

   6. In the Insert Form dialog, fill in the *Action* as "TimesTableInput.jsp" and the *Method* as "post." Leave the other fields as the default. Click OK to add the tag to the JSP page.

Post is a type of HTTP request that sends parameters in the body of the form instead of on the URL line. The *get* HTTP method constructs a URL containing the parameter names and values. You use post when there could be "side effects" such as updating a database. Get could be used when you are doing a data query.

7. Press ENTER twice to create a blank line between the beginning and ending "<form>" tags. Insert two spaces as an indent. Type "Last number: " in the blank line. This will be a prompt for the text field.

8. Insert two spaces to indent the next piece of code. With the cursor on the same line as the prompt, click the Text Field icon in the HTML page of the Component Palette.

9. In the Insert Text Field dialog, fill in the *Name* as "inputNum" and the *Size* as "5." Click OK to add the tag to the JSP page.

10. Add a blank line before the "</form>" tag and, with the cursor in that blank line, click the Submit Button in the Component Palette.

11. In the Insert Submit Button dialog, fill in the *Name* as "Submit" and the *Caption* as "Submit." Click OK to add the tag to the JSP page.

12. The code between <body> tags in the JSP page should look like the following:

```
<form action="TimesTableInput.jsp" method="post">
  Last number: <input type="text" name="inputNum" size="5">
  <input type="submit" name="Submit" value="Submit">
</form>
```

13. Click Save All.

What Just Happened?   This phase created a default JSP page and added an HTML form with a text field and Submit button. If you were to run the form at this point, you would see the following:

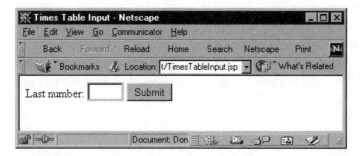

You can interact with this form by typing in a value and clicking the Submit button. The form will reload when you click the Submit button, but nothing will happen until you write code to interpret the parameters sent to the form.

II. Add Table Logic and Run the JSP Page

This phase adds the code you need to display a table based upon the value input into the text field.

I. Add a blank line after the form closing tag. Type the following code after the blank line:

```
<%
  String[] params = request.getParameterValues("inputNum");
  int lastNum;
  if (params != null) {
    lastNum = Integer.parseInt(params[0]);
  }
  else {
    lastNum = 9;
  }
%>
```

Additional Information: This scriptlet code defines variables that will be used in the times table code. The `params` variable is a String array that contains the value of the `inputNum` text field. If multiple values are typed into the text field (delimited by spaces), the array will contain more than one element. When the form is submitted, the text field value will be loaded into a parameter that will be passed back to the JSP page. The `request` object is created in the servlet into which the JSP page is compiled. Its `getParameterValues()` method returns the String array. The rest of the code defines a lastNum variable that is loaded with the first value in the String array (the only one that matters to this JSP page). If there is no value in the parameter (as is the case the first time the page is called), the variable defaults to "9."

2. Add a blank line under this code, and add the following under the blank line:

```
<h2>Times Table for <%= "1 to " + lastNum %></h2>
```

Additional Information: This code adds a standard HTML heading that contains an expression with the value of the lastNum variable.

3. Return to the Code Editor session for TimesTable.jsp, and copy into the clipboard (CTRL-C) all text between the "`<table>`" start and end tags (including the table tags).

4. Return to the Code Editor session for TimesTableInput.jsp. Add a blank line under the code you just added. In the blank line, paste (CTRL-V) the text from TimesTable.jsp that you copied into the clipboard.

5. Change the copied text so that it appears as follows. (The only difference is that "`<= lastNum`" replaces the hard-coded "10" in both loop statements.)

```
<table border="1">
<%
  for (int i = 1; i  <= lastNum; i++) {
    %><tr><%
    for (int j = 1; j <= lastNum; j++) {
      %><td><%= i * j %></td><%
    }
```

```
   %></tr><%
 }
%>
</table>
```

6. With the cursor in the TimesTableInput.jsp file, click Save All and click Run. The
   following will appear:

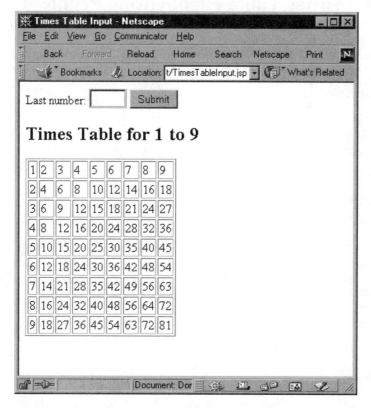

Additional Information: The first time that this JSP page appears, there is no value in
the form parameter, so the default of "9" is used as the top value in the loops. When
you type in another number and click the Submit button, the form will be submitted
and the parameter loaded with the new value. The times table will be sized accordingly.

What Just Happened? You added code to accept parameters and display the table
appropriately. If this were a production form, you would need to add logic to check the user
input so that the form accepts only numbers and not null values. At this point, both of these
inputs will cause the form to fail. You might also want to limit the maximum number that the
user can enter so that the times table does not become too large. You might also want to add
a reference to the cascading style sheet that you used in the preceding practice.

This practice demonstrates a page that fulfills its own request. It is also possible to use another
page to process the values from the page containing the form. For example, if the TimesTable.jsp
were written to process input parameters, you could call that page from the form tag instead of

calling the TimesTableInput.jsp page. In this case, you could either call the TimesTable.jsp or include it in the page using the following code:

```
<jsp:include page="TimesTable.jsp" />
```

Solution to Times Table Highlighting Problem

The first hands-on practice in this chapter ("Build a Simple JSP Page") posed the question of how to highlight and bold the first row and column in the times table. The table header ("`<tr>`") tag automatically bolds the text within it, and you can apply bold to the other cells using the bold ("`<b>`") tag. The following code would replace the table definition in TimesTable.jsp:

```
<table border="1">
<%
  // Header loop
  for (int i = 1; i < 10; i++) {
    %><th bgcolor="yellow" >
    <%= i %>
    </th><%
  }
  %></th><%

  // Body nested loops from row 2 to 9
  for (int i = 2; i < 10; i++) {
    // first column
    %><tr><td bgcolor="yellow"><b><%= i %></b></td><%
    for (int j = 2; j < 10; j++) {
      // columns 2 to 9
      %><td>
      <%= i * j %>
      </td><%
    }
    %></tr><%
  }
%>
</table>
```

The HTML table created by this code looks like the following:

1	2	3	4	5	6	7	8	9
2	4	6	8	10	12	14	16	18
3	6	9	12	15	18	21	24	27
4	8	12	16	20	24	28	32	36
5	10	15	20	25	30	35	40	45
6	12	18	24	30	36	42	48	54
7	14	21	28	35	42	49	56	63
8	16	24	32	40	48	56	64	72
9	18	27	36	45	54	63	72	81

CHAPTER
22

Constructing JSP Pages
with BC4J Data Tags

Hark! Hark! The dogs do bark,
The beggars are coming to town;
Some in rags, some in tags;
And some in velvet gowns.

—Nursery Rhyme, *Hark! Hark!*

ow that you have been introduced to JSP coding and development in JDeveloper, it is useful to examine how to work with a tag library. Since BC4J is an important feature of JDeveloper, this book concentrates on the BC4J Data Tags Library, which is built to maximize efficiency when programming JSP pages that access BC4J objects. The BC4J Data Tags Library consists of a set of tags that use BC4J objects as their data source. The tags are written so that you can easily bind them to existing BC4J objects. This chapter provides an overview of the tags and gives details about how to work with them in JDeveloper.

The bulk of this chapter is devoted to letting you experience the development methods for these tags in the hands-on practices. The practices create JSP pages that use the higher-level component tags. The JSP pages you develop are similar to those created by the JDeveloper Data Page Wizard.

Chapter 23 discusses other techniques for modifying the defaults and working with the tags. Chapter 24 examines the tags in more detail and concentrates on some of the low-level tags.

Introduction to the BC4J Data Tags Library

This section briefly introduces the BC4J Data Tags Library. The other tag libraries offer different tags, but the methods for creating applications are similar, as is the support in JDeveloper's wizards, Component Palette, Code Editor, and Embedded OC4J Server. The BC4J Data Tags Library consists of a number of tags that can be categorized into the following types:

Connection Tags   As with Java applications and applets, the BC4J application module forms the connection point from the user interface components to the BC4J view usages. An ApplicationModule tag is used to specify the BC4J application module that will be used for the connection to the database. The DataSource tag provides a declaration of the view usage for a particular component.

Database Operation Tags   These tags call transaction operations in the database (Commit, Rollback, and PostChanges).

Data Access and Presentation Tags   These tags cause a loop through rows (RowSetIterate) or through all attributes in the view object (AttributeIterate). Some tags show values of view object attributes on the page (ShowValue and RenderValue). You can use SetAttribute to update values or to insert a value into a new record.

Form Element Tags   Tags for presenting HTML form elements are connected to view usages to make the form elements data aware. For example, tags such as InputText, InputTextArea, InputDate, and InputLOVSelect present an HTML field that is linked to a view object attribute.

Presentation Form Component Tags   BC4J Component tags connect to a view usage in the application module and present fields or values from a row in that view usage. For example, the DataEdit tag presents an edit form with a field for each attribute in the view object. Components are available for DataTable (a multi-record display) and DataQuery (for a set of query fields). In addition, there are navigation components (DataScroller and DataNavigate).

The components package a large amount of functionality into a single tag. Another file, a *component JSP file,* which is generated when you enter the data component tag, contains the code that implements the logic for these tags. This concept is explained further in the section "Working with Data Tag Component JSP Files" in Chapter 23.

Other Tags   The library contains tags to help you embed interMedia objects (such as audio, video, or images) into the page that allow you to update and insert these objects in the database.

The WebBean and DataWebBean objects in the Component Palette are available for backwards compatibility with previous versions of JDeveloper. WebBeans present non-data-aware controls or displays. DataWebBeans are connected to BC4J objects and contain the same kind of functionality as the component tags. However, the DataWebBean requires more Java code in the JSP file. Oracle recommends using the component tags for new applications instead of the WebBean and DataWebBean tags, because component tags are simpler to use for default functionality and do not require scriptlet and method calls as do the WebBean and DataWebBean tags.

NOTE
The BC4J data tags are well documented in the JDeveloper online documentation, and you can refer to that source for complete details about each tag. To access this documentation, look for the topic "Reference: BC4J Data Tags Library" after clicking "BC4J data tags" on the Index tab. This topic is also available under the node "Developing Web Applications\Working with JSP Pages for Business Components" in the Contents tab.

Development Methods Using the BC4J Data Tags Library

You can develop JSP pages in JDeveloper in several ways by using the BC4J Data Tags Library. Although you can certainly hand-code JSP pages by typing into the Code Editor, this method is not as productive or as easy as starting with a skeleton page, as shown in this chapter. Regardless of the method you use to create the code, you will need to write custom code to fulfill application-specific requirements. It is always good to watch for code that seems to recur throughout the application. That code may be a candidate for inclusion in a common "include" file, custom tag library, or even a modification to the JDeveloper wizards.

General Development Steps

The general sequence for developing a JSP application in JDeveloper follows:

   I.   Create a BC4J project or open an existing BC4J project in a workspace.

2. Add an empty project that will contain the JSP page to the same workspace.

3. On the JSP project node, select New from the right-click menu (or use **File | New**) to run a JDeveloper wizard or dialogs (described later in the section "JSP Wizards and Dialogs") to create code that you can use as a starting point.

4. Click Save All to save the files.

5. Compile the JSP project using Rebuild <projectname> in the toolbar. Although the next step would compile any uncompiled files by default, fully compiling the project now will allow you to examine warnings and errors in a more controlled way.

6. When the files compile without errors, run the file that starts the JSP application by selecting it in the Navigator (or active Code Editor window) and clicking Run in the toolbar.

7. The Embedded OC4J Server will start, and the page will load in your default browser. Watch the messages that appear in the Log window, indicating the port numbers that are assigned and the URL that the server is calling.

   Additional Information: The following listing shows an example of these messages with line numbers added. Code without numbers would be written on the same code line as the line above it.

```
1: C:\JDev9i\jdk\bin\javaw.exe -ojvm -classpath C:\JDev9i\j2ee\home\oc4j.jar
    -Doracle.j2ee.dont.use.memory.archive=true com.evermind.server.OC4JServer
    -config C:\JDev9i\jdev\system\oc4j-config\server.xml
2: [Starting OC4J using the following ports: HTTP=8989,RMI=23892,JMS=9228.]
3: [waiting for the server to complete its initialization...]
4: Embedded OC4J startup time: 4927 ms.
5: Oracle9iAS (9.0.3.0.0) Containers for J2EE initialized
6: Target URL --
    http://localhost:8989/DataPageJSP/CountriesView1_StarterPage.jsp
```

   Line 1 shows the full runtime command for the OC4J server. Lines 2–5 display the status of the server with the port numbers assigned to it. Once the ports have been initialized, you can access them from any browser session while the Embedded OC4J Server is active, even if it is started outside of JDeveloper or on another machine on the same network.

8. Test the JSP operations and verify that the database actions have been committed or rolled back appropriately. Leave the browser open if you want to make modifications.

9. If necessary, modify the appearance of the JSP page. Use an HTML editor or make changes to the cascading style sheet to address common look-and-feel issues.

10. Add other data tags if needed, and test the file using the Run button again to check the modifications. Alternatively, if the embedded server is still active, you can compile the files and run the files by typing the name in the URL location field in the browser.

11. Add other JSP pages to the project, and provide links between the files.

12. Test the new files by running them using the Run toolbar icon.

13. When all development and testing is complete, prepare and deploy the package as described in Chapter 7.

TIP
Changes to the BC4J objects may be cached in the server and might not be available to the project until you restart the Embedded OC4J Server. You can stop the server by selecting Terminate from the right-click menu on the server name in the Run Manager window. If the Run Manager window is not displayed, select **View** *|* **Run Manager***.*

JSP Wizards and Dialogs

The wizards and dialogs that create JSP files are started by selecting items under the Web Tier node in the New gallery. A number of categories under the Web Tier node will create different types of files. The JavaServer Pages (JSP) node contains wizards or dialogs that will create generic JSP files (not specific to any tag library or framework). In that node, the JSP Page item creates a standard JSP page with basic HTML tags and some default text. The JSP Document item creates a JSP 1.2 document that will contain XML-style code. The JSP Page and JSP Document display a dialog that only requires a name. There are also wizards in that node for creating Web Beans and tag libraries.

The BC4J data tags are supported by the JSP for Business Components category under the Web Tier node. This category contains options for creating a full application or for creating data pages. There are similar nodes under the Web Tier for other types of application server code. The BC4J data tag wizards require a bit of explanation.

CAUTION
The exact location and names of these wizards may change over time, so explore the nodes in the New gallery if you do not find the locations or names used in this book.

Business Components JSP Application Wizard

The New gallery item Complete JSP Application (in the Web Tier\JSP for Business Components category) runs the Business Components JSP Application Wizard (also called the BC4J JSP Application Wizard). The wizard requires minimal input: the client-data model definition that specifies the application module, and view object and view link usages for which you need pages in the application. You can specify whether you want browse, query, and edit pages for each view usage. You can also specify whether you want a page for each view link. The wizard creates a fully functional application, as shown in the hands-on practice in Chapter 1.

For production systems, you will need to go beyond the defaults, and modify the code that the wizard creates. You can modify the cascading style sheet, JSP file component and HTML tags, and the component JSP files to change the behavior and appearance of the application.

The application wizard provides the "quick and dirty" application that may serve to demonstrate BC4J object editing, data administration, and even as a starting point for a more user-friendly application.

Data Page Wizard

The Data Page Wizard is triggered from the New gallery items Browse & Edit Form, Browse Form, Query Form, and Starter Data Page (in the JSP for Business Components category). The wizard will create a page (or pages) that connects to a single view usage. All modes of the Data Page Wizard copy a number of supporting files (such as the cascading style sheet file) into the project and create complete, working pages. The pages that the Data Page Wizard creates are similar to those that the Business Components JSP Application Wizard creates.

This wizard gives you a more controlled way to build an application. Each page is complete but, as with the Business Components JSP Application Wizard, you will need to modify its look-and-feel to fulfill your application requirements. You can build pages around the output from this wizard, or embed the pages that the wizard creates inside other pages.

Each of the modes of the wizard creates a page with the following characteristics.

Browse & Edit Form   The Browse & Edit Form selection creates a browse page such as the following that displays rows from a view usage in multi-record, grid table form with scroller links (Previous and Next).

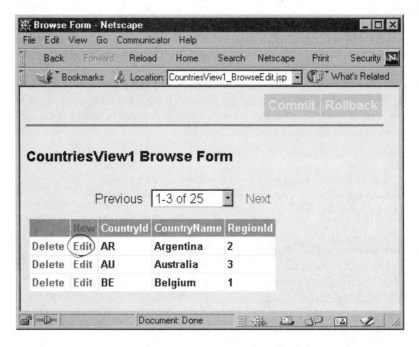

Each row has a link for Delete and Edit. The Delete function deletes the row. The Edit function displays an edit form page that contains editable fields loaded with the values from that row such as the following:

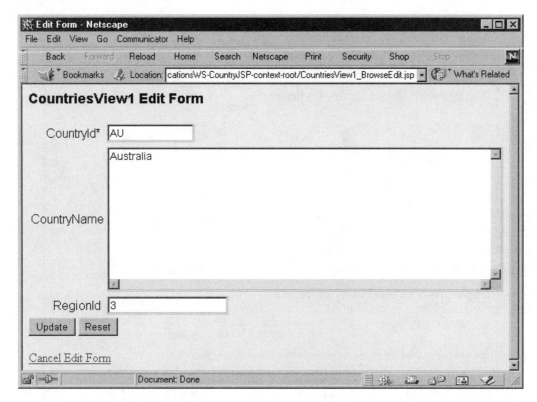

The edit page returns to the browse page, where you can commit or rollback the changes. The browse page also contains a New link that loads the same edit form (with empty fields) where the user can enter a new row.

Browse Form   The Browse Form selection creates the same browse form without New, Edit, and Delete links. The browse form has scroller links for Previous and Next but no Commit and Rollback links.

Query Form   The Query Form selection creates a form with fields where the user can enter query criteria and search for matches. After the user clicks Search, a data table appears at the bottom of the page with the results as shown here:

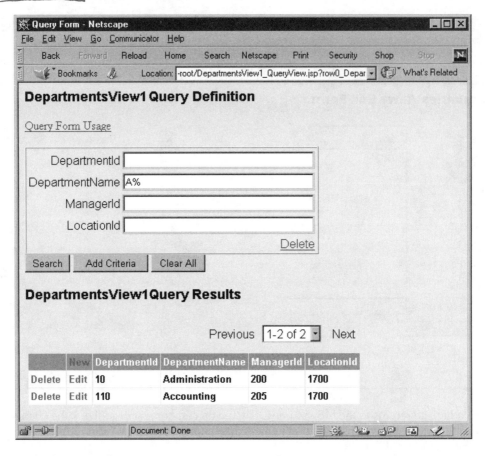

By default, there are no Edit, Delete, or New links on the browse area, but, if you create an edit page (or run the Data Page Wizard in Browse & Edit Form mode), you can link that page to the DataTable component by specifying the name of the edit form in the DataTable attribute *edittarget*.

Starter Data Page   The Starter Data Page selection creates a page containing ApplicationModule and DataSource tags but with no specific data component tag. Therefore, if you run this JSP page, you will see nothing on the page. The purpose of this page is to give you a starting point for entering data component tags that is farther along than the file, which the generic JSP Page dialog creates.

TIP

It is useful to examine the code that the Data Page Wizard and Business Components JSP Application Wizard create to determine how JSP pages are constructed with these tags.

Working with BC4J Data Tags in the Code Editor

Although you can type the code for BC4J data tags directly in the Code Editor, JDeveloper offers two tools that help ensure the correct spelling and syntax: the Component Palette and the JSP Data Binding tool.

TIP

As mentioned in Chapter 21, the Code Editor offers context-sensitive help for custom JSP tags supplied with JDeveloper. For example, if you place the cursor inside a BC4J tag (such as "<jbo:ApplicationModule>") and press F1, the help topic for ApplicationModule will be displayed.

Component Palette

The Component Palette displays pages appropriate to JSP work when the topmost Code Editor window contains a JSP file. To activate a page, you select it from the pulldown list in the Component Palette bar. If the Component Palette is not visible, select **View** | **Component Palette**.

When you select a tag, a wizard will appear that steps you through filling out the required properties. When you click Finish, the wizard will enter the tag text at the cursor location in the Code Editor and will add attributes to the tag based on the properties that you completed in the wizard. You cannot run the wizard on an existing tag in the Code Editor. If you run the wizard again, you will have to fill in the tag properties again.

TIP

If you want to replace a tag entry in the Code Editor, select the tag's text and click the tag in the Component Palette. After you fill out the wizard properties and click Finish, the new tag will overwrite the selected text.

Component Palette Placement and Appearance The Component Palette anchors by default on the right side of the IDE window. If you want more horizontal space in the Code Editor, you can drag the Component Palette to the top of the IDE (for example, under the Document Bar). This frees up the right side of the IDE so that you can expand the Code Editor. The Component Palette will appear with icons and names, as in the following example:

If you select Icon View from the right-click menu on the Component Palette, the names will be hidden, and you will just see the icons for each component, as in the following example:

If you have not memorized the meaning of the icons, this particular view of the Component Palette may slow down your development, so you may want to leave the names displayed. You can switch back to the name and icon display by selecting List View from the right-click menu on the Component Palette.

TIP
Remember that the Component Palette offers the ability to "pin" the buttons. If you hold the SHIFT *key while clicking a button, the tag will stay selected so that you can add more than one without reselecting the button. To unpin the button, click the Pointer button.*

Code Snippets   One of the Component Palette pages available to JSP pages is the Code Snippets page. This page allows you to select code that you have stored and named. For example, although the link to a cascading style sheet is not available on the HTML page of the Component Palette, you can add this to the Code Snippets page using the following steps:

1. Highlight the following line in the Code Editor window for a JSP page that you generated using the Data Page Wizard (or just type the line into an existing JSP page):

   ```
   <LINK REL=STYLESHEET TYPE="text/css" HREF="bc4j.css">
   ```

2. In the Code Editor, select Add Code Snippet from the right-click menu. The following dialog will appear:

Add Code Snippet   ✕

What are the details of your code snippet?

Name of code snippet: [   ]

code snippet: [<LINK REL=STYLESHEET TYPE="text/css" HREF="bc4j.   ]

[Help]   [OK]   [Cancel]

3. Fill in the *Name of code snippet* field with the name, in this case "bc4j.css Reference." The code snippet will be added to the Component Palette's Code Snippets page.

To use a code snippet, place the cursor where you want the code to appear in the Code Editor, and click the code snippet's button in the Component Palette. The code will be added to the file at the cursor position.

You can also create code snippets by selecting Add Component from the right-click menu on the Code Snippets page of the Component Palette. The right-click menu also contains selections for removing a component and displaying the properties of all components in all pages of the Component Palette. The properties dialog also allows you to modify the code in the code snippet.

JSP Data Binding Tool

The JSP Data Binding tool (shown in Figure 22-1) was new with release 9.0.3. It provides another method for adding BC4J data tags to the JSP file. Since it bypasses the wizard pages, you may find

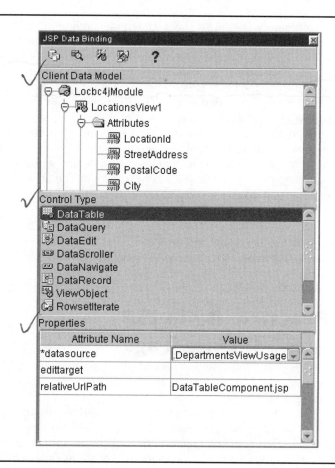

FIGURE 22-1. *JSP Data Binding tool*

it faster for entering tags once you know the required elements and are familiar with the purpose of the tag. The JSP Data Binding tool appears by default on the right side of the screen when you select **View** | **JSP Data Binding**. You can close this window using the close window ("X") icon in the top right corner of the palette window.

This palette contains the following panes:

- **Client Data Model**   This pane provides a hierarchical view of all client data model definitions available to the project. You use this pane to browse the view usages and their attributes. When you select a node in this pane, the Control Type pane is loaded with the components appropriate to that node.

- **Control Type**   This pane contains the appropriate component tags for the node selected in the Client Data Model pane. When you select a control type, the Properties pane changes to display the properties of that control.

- **Properties**   This pane allows you to set values for the selected control's properties.

There are buttons in the toolbar for creating a client data model definition, editing the BC4J object selected in the Client Data Model pane, creating view objects and view links, and help.

To add a tag to the JSP file, you click the appropriate object in the Client Data Model pane, select the tag in the Control Type pane, fill out the properties, and drag the component from the Control Type pane to the place in the Code Editor where you want the tag to appear. After you drag the tag into the Code Editor, the properties will remain in the properties window in case you want to add another tag with the same properties.

One advantage of the JSP Data Binding tool over the Component Palette is that it bypasses the wizard, which may save you time. This tool also allows you to interact with the BC4J data tags by starting with the application module element instead of starting with the tag. Another advantage is that you can drag the tag and drop it where you want. The tag does not need to be placed at the cursor location as it does with the Component Palette.

NOTE
Although the Component Palette offers tags from all frameworks and tag libraries, the JSP Data Binding tool only provides support for the BC4J Data Tags Library.

Hands-on Practice: Build JSP Pages Using BC4J Data Tags

The hands-on practice in Chapter 1 demonstrates how to generate a complete BC4J JSP application using the JSP Application Wizard. Chapter 3 contains a hands-on practice that introduces the method for creating individual JSP pages using the BC4J Data Tags Library. Chapter 7 contains a brief practice for creating a JSP page using the Data Page Wizard. As discussed earlier in this chapter, those are some of the main ways of creating JSP pages in JDeveloper.

This practice expands on the Chapter 3 practice and digs deeper into the data component tags. It steps through creating browse and edit pages for the LocationsView data. It re-creates most of the functionality of the Browse and Edit Form JSP pages that are generated by the Data

Page Wizard. This practice will give you experience with the functionality of the BC4J Data Tags Library and how you can use them to build an application. It also provides information about modifying the default behavior and appearance of the default tags. The tags that you use in this practice are further described in Chapter 23.

This practice contains the following phases:

I. Set up the workspace and projects

II. Create the browse page using the Component Palette

■ Create a starter data page

■ Add the interface components

■ Modify the cascading style sheet

III. Create an edit page using the JSP Data Binding tool

■ Create a default JSP page

■ Modify the default JSP page

I. Set Up the Workspace and Projects

This phase creates the workspace and projects in preparation for holding the JSP files. This phase also creates a default BC4J project and an empty JSP project in which you will place JSP files.

1. On the Workspaces node in the Navigator, select New Workspace from the right-click menu.

2. Change the *Directory Name* and the *File Name* fields to "LocationsWS." Leave the check mark on the *Add a New Empty Project* checkbox, and click OK to create the workspace file.

3. In the New Project dialog, enter the *Directory Name* and *File Name* as "LocJSP." Click OK to create the project file for the JSP files that you will add in the next phase.

4. Click Save All.

5. On the LocationsWS.jws node in the Navigator, select New Project from the right-click menu.

6. From the General\Project category in the New gallery, double click "Project Containing New Business Components."

7. Click Next if the Welcome page appears. Fill in the *Directory Name* and *File Name* as "LocBC4J" and click Next.

8. On the Paths page, fill in the *Default Package* as "locbc4j," and click Next and Finish to create the project. The Business Components Package Wizard will display.

9. Click Next if the Welcome page appears. Be sure that the *Package Name* is "locbc4j." Click Next to display the Connection page.

10. Be sure the HR connection is selected in the Connection Name field and click Next.

11. On the Business Components page, select COUNTRIES, DEPARTMENTS, and LOCATIONS, and move them to the Selected pane using the right-arrow button. Click Finish. The wizard will create default BC4J objects in the new project.

12. Click Save All.

What Just Happened?   This phase sets up the workspace and projects that you will use to house the JSP files. The BC4J project provides the application module and view objects that are required by the JSP pages as data sources. If you had a BC4J project with the same objects defined, you have opened that project in the new workspace instead of creating a new BC4J project. This practice modifies the BC4J objects; so, if you were using the project in another workspace, you would need to ensure that the changes you make would not adversely affect the projects in the other workspace.

II. Create the Browse Page Using the Component Palette

This phase uses the BC4J Data Tags Library to create a page that browses the LocationsView data. It uses the Component Palette to enter the data component tags. The next phase uses the JSP Data Binding tool to enter the tags so that you can experience both techniques.

The main tasks in this phase are adding the data component tags, adding the user interface tags that access data, and modifying some of the styles in the cascading style sheet. These are typical tasks for JSP development.

Create a Starter Data Page

The first tags in the file need to reference the application module and data source (view object) that the interface components require. The application module is contained in the BC4J project in this workspace. The data source is the locations view object usage within the application module. This phase takes a shortcut offered with release 9.0.3. Instead of using a new JSP Page from the New gallery and adding the data tags as in the Chapter 3 practice, this section uses the Data Page Wizard to create a starter data page that already contains the application module and data source tags. The Data Page Wizard also creates a number of other useful files.

1. On the LocJSP.jpr node, select New from the right-click menu.

2. In the Web Tier\JSP for Business Component category, double click "Starter Data Page." The Starter Data Page Wizard dialog will appear. Click Next if the Welcome page appears.

3. Click New to create a data model definition. Click Next if the Welcome page appears in the BC4J Client Data Model Definition Wizard.

   Additional Information: The *BC4J client data model definition* (contained in the .cpx file) connects the client interface code (in the JSP page) to the BC4J application module. This definition is discussed further in Chapter 17. This definition is required for JSP as well as Java client applications.

4. Select "LocBC4J.jpr" in the *Business Components Project* pulldown if it is not already selected. Click Next.

5. Click Next in the Definition Name page to accept the default name. Click Finish to create the data definition.

6. Select "LocationsView1" and click Next to display the Finish page. Click Next and Finish to create the starter data page JSP page.

   Additional Information: Notice that a number of other files appeared under the project along with the starter data page JSP page:

   ■   **bc4j.css**   This file contains the cascading style sheet that the starter data page JSP page references. The data component tags reference styles defined in this file.

   ■   **errorpage.jsp**   This file supplies error text inside the page that is being displayed so that the user can see the cause of any problems. The file is tailored specifically for BC4J application errors.

   ■   **globalinclude.html**   This HTML file contains instructions that will be compiled into the servlet for each JSP page in this project. It allows you to make application-wide changes in one place. By default, this file contains a scriptlet call to set the encoding scheme that defines the number of bytes used for each character sent to the browser. This is important if non-Western character sets need to be supported. You can add or modify this text if you need different instructions for all JSP pages in the project.

   ■   **LocJSP_jpr_War.deploy**   This file defines the deployment profile for the web application archive (WAR) file—an archive file (like a JAR file) that is generated by the deployment utilities and used to deploy the application to the server.

   ■   **LocJSP.cpx**   Many application modules could be defined in this workspace. This is the configuration file that contains the client data model definition. The client data model definition declares which application module is used for this project.

   ■   **ojsp-global-include.xml**   This file defines parameters used by the OC4J JSP server to modify the runtime. For example, the default version of this file contains a reference to the globalinclude.html file described earlier.

   ■   **web.xml**   This is a standard J2EE file known as the *Web Application Deployment Descriptor.* It provides parameters and other application-specific information to the application server.

   Although some of these files are also generated by other methods such as the Business Components JSP Application Wizard, you would normally need to create or copy files such as the error page and cascading style sheet into the project directory. For example, if the Data Page Wizard had not copied the cascading style sheet, you would need to add it using **File | Import** and navigating to the JDEV_HOME\jdev\system\templates\common\misc directory (where JDEV_HOME is the JDeveloper installation directory, for example, C:\JDev9i). The bc4j.css file that the JDeveloper wizards copy is housed here. In production installations, you would probably want to use a central location for CSS files so that all JSP pages access the same styles. Similarly, the master errorpage.jsp file is located in the

JDEV_HOME\jdev\system\templates\common\tagcomp directory along with the master component JSP files.

TIP
*To add a file to the project, use **File | Import**
to find and copy or reference the required file.*

7. Click Save All. Select LocationsView1_StarterPage.jsp and click Run.

    Additional Information: The Embedded OC4J Server will run and display the page in your browser. You will not see anything but a background color and window title, but this test verifies that the basic file works and can read the BC4J application module.

    You now need to rename the file that the wizard created. Renaming the file will allow you to run the Data Page Wizard again and not overwrite the customization in the file.

8. Click LocationsView1_StarterPage.jsp and select **File | Rename**. Fill in the *File name* as "LocBrowse." (The .jsp extension will be added automatically.) Click Save.

CAUTION
*If the Rename menu item is disabled, select the file
again in the Navigator and retry the menu item.*

9. Open LocBrowse.jsp in the Code Editor if it is not already open. You will see the application module and data source tags already entered by the Data Page Wizard.

10. Change the title between `<title>` tags to "Browse Locations."

11. Under the opening `<body>` tag, add the following heading:

    ```
    <h2>Browse Locations</h2>
    ```

    Additional Information: If you pause after typing "`<h2>`," End Tag Completion will add the ending tag, "`</h2>`."

12. Change the *rangesize* attribute of the DataSource tag to "6" and the id to "locData" so the tag reads as follows:

    ```
    <jbo:DataSource id="locData" appid="Locbc4jModule" viewobject=
        "LocationsView1" rangesize="6"/>
    ```

    Additional Information: The *rangesize* attribute specifies how many records are displayed in multi-record components such as DataTable. The id for this and other tags identifies the usage so that it can be referenced in other code. The Data Page Wizard defined an id of "ds," which does not help distinguish the view usage. If you have more than one view object in the JSP page, it is important to provide distinguishing ids for each one. If you required more than one view object in this JSP page, you would add a data source tag for each additional view usage.

NOTE
You can define more than one usage for a view object in your application module's data model. For example, DepartmentsView can appear as a master (top-level) usage as well as a detail usage (linked to a LocationsView usage). Each of these usages is different, so you need to define a separate data source for each usage if they will appear together within the same JSP page.

Add the Interface Components

The default starter data page contains tags for the application module and data source (view object) that this page will use. In this section, you add user interface components and transaction controls using the Component Palette.

1. The JSP Component Palette appears on the right side of the IDE by default. If the Component Palette is not visible, select **View | Component Palette** to display it.

2. Select the BC4J Component Tags page from the Component Palette pulldown. Click the cursor in a blank line after the `jbo:DataSource` tag, and click DataHandler in the Component Palette.

   Additional Information: The DataHandler tag is required to coordinate the processing of events for a component such as a data scroller that has Next and Previous actions. You will add a data scroller in later steps.

3. Select "Locbc4jModule" in the appid pulldown as shown next:

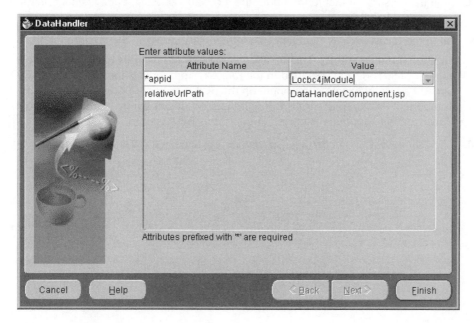

4. Click Finish to add the data handler tag.

5. With the cursor in a blank line after the jbo:DataHandler tag, click DataTransaction in the Component Palette. Select "Locbc4jModule" in the appid pulldown and click Finish. The DataTransaction tag will be added to the file.

Additional Information: The DataTransaction tag adds Commit and Rollback buttons to the page so that the changes can be sent from the cache to the database or undone in the cache, respectively. Notice that a DataTransactionComponent.jsp file was also added to the project. If you open that file, you will see code that defines an HTML table with two text buttons. This is the file that actually implements the functionality of the DataTransaction tag. It is a partial JSP file that must be included in a complete JSP page so that the HTML tags are complete. Similar files will be added in the next steps as you add data component tags.

6. With the cursor in a blank line after the `jbo:DataTransaction` tag, click DataTable in the Component Palette.

7. In the DataTable dialog, select "locData" in the *datasource* field and the *edittarget* as "LocEdit.jsp." The LocEdit.jsp file will be built in subsequent phases. Click Finish to add the tag.

Additional Information: The DataTable tag presents rows from the view usage in an HTML table (rows and columns). The number of records in this table is controlled by the *rangesize* property of the data source tag. A DataTableComponent.jsp file will be added to the project.

8. With the cursor in a blank line under the jbo:DataTable tag, click DataScroller in the Component Palette.

9. Fill in the *datasource* as "locData," and click Finish to write the tag into the file.

Additional Information: The DataScroller component scrolls back and forth the number of records you specified in the *rangesize* property of the data source tag. You can add a DataNavigate component (in the BC4J Data Components pulldown of the Component Palette) that scrolls through the rows one at a time and highlights each row. However, that capability is not required for this JSP page.

10. Click Save All. Run LocBrowse.jsp. Something like the following will appear:

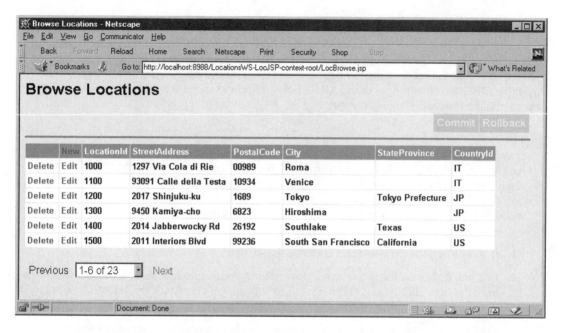

11. Test the scrolling capabilities by selecting from the record pulldown and by clicking the Previous and Next links. The pulldown and links are created by the DataScroller component.

12. Test the Delete link on one of the records, and click Rollback to restore the record.

13. Notice that the data table contains Delete and Edit links on each row. Hold the mouse cursor over an Edit link, and examine the URL in the browser status bar.

    Additional Information: The page that the Edit link refers to is the text you filled in for the data table *edittarget* property ("LocEdit.jsp"). You will see a similar URL on the New link at the top of the data table.

14. Leave the browser open. You can make changes to the file and refresh the browser to see the effect of the change.

TIP
You may need to hold the SHIFT *key when clicking Refresh or Reload in the browser to override any cached pages that the browser stores.*

Modify the Cascading Style Sheet

The cascading style sheet that the Data Page Wizard copied to this project (bc4j.css) is also used by other JDeveloper wizards. Suppose you decide that the font for the commit/rollback buttons is too large and that the color of the H2 heading tags should be similar to the heading bar of the data table. The steps that follow demonstrate how to find the style that you need to change and how to change the cascading style sheet.

TIP

Special editors are available to assist in creating and modifying cascading style sheets. These editors (such as TopStyle Lite from www.bradsoft.com) provide a visual display of the style and property lists that help you enter the correct syntax. Cascading style sheet editing is also available within some HTML editors.

1. If you closed the browser, run LocBrowse.jsp again.

2. In a blank spot on the browser window (where there is no link text), select View Source from the right-click menu. Another window will appear containing the HTML text displayed in the browser.

3. Find the <h2> tag at the top of the file. Notice that there is no *class* attribute for that tag (that is, the code does not read "<h2 class=classname>"), which means that the style sheet contains an entry that modifies the <h2> tag without requiring the style name in the HTML code. You may have to scroll down in the file to see this text.

4. Search for the word "commit" by using CTRL-F. You will see it in a block of code such as the following that is created by the DataTransactionComponent.jsp:

```
<table class="clsToolBar" cellspacing="1" cellpadding="5"
   border="0" width="100%">
   <tr>
      <td width="100%"> </td>
      <td class="clsToolBarButton">Commit</td>
      <td class="clsToolBarButton">Rollback</td>
   </tr>
</table>
```

5. This code defines an HTML table that contains commit and rollback text buttons. Notice that the name of the style that is applied to the "Commit" text is "clsToolBarButton."

6. Close the view source window. Double click bc4j.css in the Navigator to open it in the Code Editor.

7. Search for "clsToolBarButton" in the file. You will find a block of code such as the following:

```
.clsToolBarButton
{
   font-family:Arial, Helvetica, Geneva, sans-serif;
   color:#EFEFEF;
   font-size:13PT;
   font-weight:bold;
```

```
background-color:#CCCCCC;
}
```

Additional Information: The period prefix indicates that "clsToolBarButton" is a *global* style, which can be applied to any tag by including an attribute in that tag for "class=clsToolBarButton," for example, "<body class=clsToolBarButton>."

8. Change the text "13PT" in the *font-size* property to "10PT." This will reduce the font size by three points.

9. Search for the definition of the H2 style. It appears at the top of the file as a combined style definition for the H1, H2, H3, and TD tags. Add another style for H2 under this block that specifies the blue color (color number "336699") used by clsTitleBody.

10. Modify this entry to add the blue color so the style definition appears as follows:

```
H1, H2, H3, TD
{
    font-family:Arial, sans-serif;
}

H2
{
    color: #336699;
}
```

Additional Information: Both H2 style entries will be used. The first defines the font family, and the second specifies the color.

11. Click Save All. Examine the changes by clicking Reload (for Netscape) or Refresh (Internet Explorer) to rerun the JSP page. Notice the changed heading color and smaller commit/rollback text.

    Additional Information: You can also select Refresh or Reload from the View menu to reload the browser.

NOTE
You do not need to rebuild the project or JSP pages, because these changes are applied to the cascading style sheet that is not compiled and is read dynamically by the JSP pages.

12. Do not close the browser.

CAUTION
Browsers such as Internet Explorer and Netscape do not always render a JSP or HTML page in the same way. Fonts and spacing may look different in different browsers. If your application must support different browsers, it is important to test the application in those browsers. The sidebar "Testing JSP Pages in a Nondefault Browser" describes how to run JSP Pages in different browsers so that you can test the code in different environments.

Testing JSP Pages in a Nondefault Browser

Running a JSP page within the JDeveloper IDE starts the Embedded OC4J Server and opens the browser that is set up as the default in your operating system. You can use the following steps to run another browser session with the same JSP page so that you can test the visual aspects. If you want to permanently change the default browser, follow the steps in the sidebar "Changing Your Default Browser."

1. Run the JSP page from JDeveloper. Your default browser (such as Internet Explorer) will open with the JSP page loaded.

2. Copy the text from the URL *Address* (or *Location*) text field at the top of the browser.

3. Run a different browser (such as Netscape). It does not matter if the first browser is closed or open.

4. Paste the text you copied in step 2 into the *Address* or *Location* field of the different browser and press ENTER. The application will appear in the browser.

The virtual port (8988) for the OC4J server remains open once you start it. You can verify that it is running by looking in Run Manager (**View** | **Run Manager**). Run Manager allows you to terminate the server session (from the right-click menu or from **Run** | **Terminate** | **Embedded OC4J Server**). Once the server is started and the virtual port is open, you can open or close any browser (from any networked machine) and reconnect using the URL in the *Address* or *Location* field.

What Just Happened?   You defined a complete browse page with record scrolling, transaction control, and links to an edit page. The pre-built functionality of the tags made this process relatively easy. If you want to check your work, the following should appear in the JSP page between the "</h2>" tag and the "</body>" tag:

```
<jbo:ApplicationModule id="Locbc4jModule" definition="LocJSP.Locbc4JModule"
    releasemode="Stateful" />
<jbo:DataSource id="locData" appid="Locbc4jModule" viewobject=
    "LocationsView1" rangesize="6"/>
<jbo:DataHandler appid="Locbc4jModule" />
<jbo:DataTransaction appid="Locbc4jModule" />
<jbo:DataTable datasource="locData"  edittarget="LocEdit.jsp" />
<jbo:DataScroller datasource="locData" />
<jbo:ReleasePageResources />
```

Figure 22-2 shows the main visual elements in the JSP page and where they appear in the browser. In addition to the visible components, the JSP page requires the ApplicationModule, DataSource, and DataHandler component tags to support the other tags.

Your project now contains a dozen files even though you only selected one JSP file from the New gallery. In addition to the files described before that the Data Page Wizard generated, the editor generated separate JSP files for the DataHandler, DataScroller, DataTable, and DataTransaction component tags.

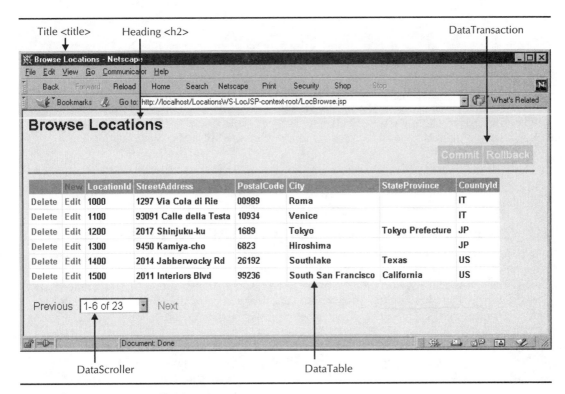

Title <title>   Heading <h2>   DataTransaction

FIGURE 22-2. *Tags in the browse page*

Changing Your Default Browser

If you want to change the browser that JDeveloper uses by default, you can specify the browser in the Preferences dialog (**Tools | Preferences**) Web Browser/Proxy page. Enter the executable name and path in the *Browser Command Line* field, and this browser will be used for all projects.

You can also change the browser that the operating system calls by default. In the Windows environments (Windows 95 or 98, Windows NT, Windows XP, and Windows 2000), the default browser is associated with the .html file type. Therefore, changing that association will change the browser that JDeveloper uses to open files in its Embedded OC4J Server if you have not set the preference mentioned before. In Windows operating systems, associating file types with a program is an operation of Windows Explorer (Tools

Options or View Options dialog). Consult the help files to determine how to change the file association.

Note that once the Embedded OC4J Server is started, you can open and close any browser and connect to the URL specified in the Log window. Therefore, if you just want to test another browser, but not change the default browser, you can open the other browser and copy the URL from the default browser or from the Log window into the other browser. You can also run a browser on another machine that is networked to your machine.

III. Create an Edit Page Using the JSP Data Binding Tool

The browse page is completely functional for browsing and deleting records. You now need a page that will allow users to edit or insert Location records when they click Edit or New in the browse page, respectively. This phase creates an edit page that also allows inserting records. You use the JSP Data Binding tool to enter the tags. The preceding phase uses the Component Palette to enter the tags. At the end of this phase, you will be able to compare the two techniques.

NOTE
The page flow model in BC4J data tag applications relies on HTML links between pages. As of this writing, a new effort called "JavaServer Faces" is under way at Sun Microsystems. JavaServer Faces is aimed at improving ease of development, integration with existing systems using APIs, and flexibility of page flow.

Create a Default JSP Page
You will use the Data Page Wizard to create a starter data page.

1. On the LocJSP.jpr node, select New from the right-click menu. In the Web Tier\JSP for Business Components category, double click Starter Data Page. The Data Page Wizard will appear.

2. Click Next if the Welcome page appears. Select LocationsView1 and click Next and Finish.

3. The Data Page Wizard will repeat the process of creating the starter data page and all of its supporting files. Since the supporting files are already created, you will see one or more confirmation dialogs that ask if you want to overwrite the existing files. Click No in each of these dialogs.

Modify the Default JSP Page

This section adds the components needed to present the edit page.

1. Select the LocationsView1_StarterPage.jsp file and select **File** | **Rename**. In the *File name* field, enter "LocEdit" (the .jsp extension is optional) and click Save.

2. Open LocEdit.jsp in a Code Editor window. Change the data source *id* property to "locData."

3. Change the title to "Edit Location." Add a heading 2 tag under the <body> tag for "Edit Location" ("<h2>Edit Location</h2>").

4. If the JSP Data Binding tool is not open (in a tab next to the Component Palette), open it by selecting **View** | **JSP Data Binding**.

5. Click LocationsView1 in the Client Data Model pane. The *Control Type* pane will display a list of tags appropriate to a view object as shown in Figure 22-3.

6. Click the DataEdit component in the *Control Type* pane. The properties for the DataEdit data component tag will display in the Properties pane as shown in Figure 22-3. Select "locData" in the *datasource* property pulldown. If there is no pulldown, type in "locData."

7. Drag the DataEdit component from the *Control Type* pane to the Code Editor. The cursor will change and show the position that the tag will take when you release the mouse button as shown here:

```
10 <h2>Edit Location</h2>
11 <jbo:ApplicationModule id="am" definition="LocJSP.Locbc4JMo
12 <jbo:DataSource id="locData" appid="am" viewobject="Locatio:
13 |
14
15 <jbo:ReleasePageResources />
16 </body>
17 </html>
```

8. Drop the control under the data source tag. The tag will appear in the Code Editor and the DataEdit component JSP file added to the project.

NOTE

If the tag is simple, you can also just type it into the editor. The component JSP file will be added when you complete the tag (with "/>").

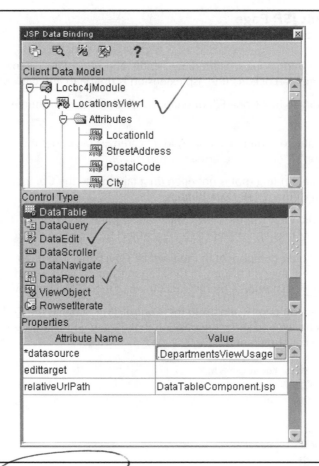

FIGURE 22-3. *JSP Data Binding tool*

9. Click Save All. Click Rebuild LocJSP.jpr.

10. If you closed the browser, click LocBrowse and click Run. If the browser still has LocBrowse running, click Reload or Refresh in the browser toolbar.

    Additional Information: The LocBrowse page supplies the parameters to the LocEdit page, so you need to run it first.

11. When the new browse page is displayed, click Edit on Location number 1000. The edit page such as that shown below opens with the record for 1000 loaded. Make a change to this record (by adding a province name, for example).

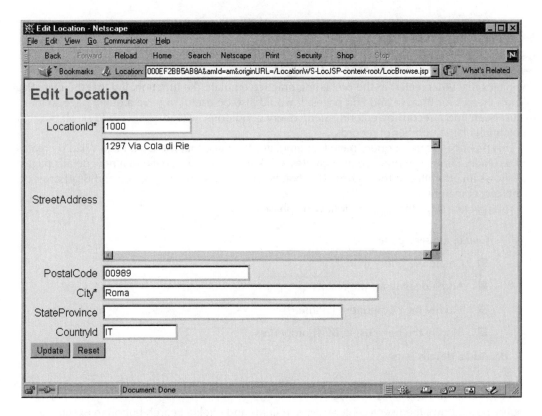

12. Click Reset to see that the form changes the values back to the retrieved values. Make the change again and click Update. The form returns to the LocBrowse page and refreshes with the modified value.

   Additional Information: Although you can see the new values in the browse page, they are not yet committed. The Commit and Rollback buttons are now enabled, which indicates a noncommitted change. If you click Rollback, the change you made on the previous page will be reversed. If you click Commit, the change will be saved to the database.

13. Click Rollback to reverse the change.

What Just Happened? You defined an edit page using the BC4J Data Component Tags. You started by running the Data Page Wizard to create a starter data page into which you placed the DataEdit component tag. This tag presents a set of edit fields for the attributes in a view object. The edit page is called from the browse page, and context information about which record needs to be edited is passed to it. The page can also be called in insert mode for new records.

Hands-on Practice: Build Query and Details Pages

The pages that you created in the preceding practice emulate the functionality that the Data Page Wizard creates for Browse and Edit pages. It would also be useful to have a query page so that the user can find a record by entering some query conditions instead of having to scroll through a potentially large number of records.

This practice creates a query page that emulates the page that the Data Page Wizard creates for the Query Form. The practice also creates a link from the query page to a new details page that shows all attributes of the record. This practice uses the same workspace and BC4J project as the preceding practice.

The practice steps through the following phases:

I. Create a query page

- Create the query fields

- Add a display for the results

- Modify the component JSP file

- Modify the page using BC4J properties

II. Add a details page

I. Create a Query Page

A *query page* allows the user to enter values in fields and click a Search button to execute a query that uses the values as query criteria. This phase creates the query page by adding tags to a starter data page. The resulting page emulates the Query Form page that the Data Page Wizard creates. Normally, the Data Page Wizard would be a faster development method, but this phase will show you how this kind of page is built from scratch and give you practice using the BC4J data tags.

Create the Query Fields

Since you had experience in the preceding practice with adding component tags using the JSP Data Binding tool and the Component Palette, you can choose either of (or both) those techniques for this section. The abbreviated steps here will present the task and allow you to accomplish it using either technique:

1. If you did not finish Phase I of the preceding practice that creates the BC4Jproject, return to that practice and complete the BC4J project.

2. Use the Data Page Wizard to create a starter data page for LocationsView1 in the LocationsWS workspace and LocJSP project. Rename the starter data page (using **File | Rename**) to "LocQuery.jsp."

    Additional Information: The Starter Data Page is an option in the New gallery (**File | New**) Web Tier\JSP for Business Components category. Refer to the steps in the preceding practice if you need further help with details. Be sure to rename the file and to change the *id* of the data source tag to "locData" to make the data source reference clearer (in case you add other data sources to your JSP page later).

3. Run LocQuery.jsp to ensure that your starting file is correct. You will not see any data, but will see a window title.

4. In the Code Editor, change the *rangesize* property of the data source to "6." This property defines how many rows will be displayed on the screen for a multi-record control such as DataTable.

5. Change the title to "Find Locations," and add heading 2 text at the beginning of the HTML body for "Find Locations."

6. After the DataSource tag, add a DataHandler tag and specify "Locbc4jModule" for the appid.

   Additional Information: This tag points to the application module instance that was created in the ApplicationModule tag. The DataHandler is required to process events for database transactions and for scrolling.

7. Add a DataQuery tag with a *datasource* property of "locData." This component presents a form with fields for each view object attribute and buttons for search operations.

8. Make and run this file. You should see something like the following:

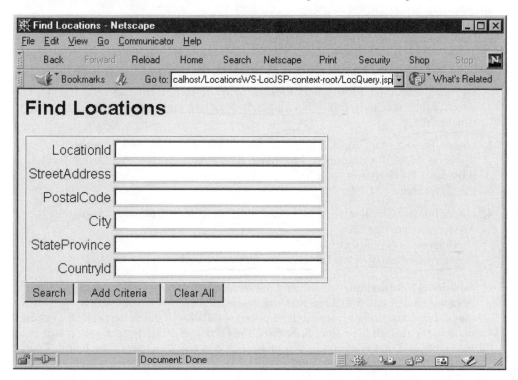

Additional Information: The buttons in this JSP page will not function until you complete the next section. However, running the JSP page at this stage gives you a sense of what the query form looks like and ensures you that the code compiles.

9. Leave the browser open.

Add a Display for the Results

This section adds code to the component JSP file so that you can display the results of the search on the same page. It adds the same DataTable component that you used in the preceding practice to create the browse page.

1. Under the DataQuery tag, add an OnEvent tag (from the BC4J Events page of the Component Palette). Specify the *datasource* as "locData" and the *list* as "Search, FirstSet, NextSet, PreviousSet, LastSet, GotoSet." If you are using the Component Palette, click Finish to dismiss the dialog and add the tag.

   Additional Information: The OnEvent tag provides the ability to add or modify elements on the page when an event such as navigation or a database transaction statement occurs. It is a conditional tag that will only execute for the events that you specify in the *list* attribute.

   CAUTION
   You may have to change the event list if you are using JSP pages created by the Data Page Wizard in earlier versions of JDeveloper 9.0.3, because the GotoSet event is spelled as "Goto."

2. Move the `</jbo:OnEvent>` closing tag to a new line, and on a blank line before that tag, enter a heading 2 for "Query Results" ("`<h2>Query Results</h2>`"). When an event in the list occurs, this and all other code before the closing OnEvent tag will be processed.

3. Under the `<h2>` tag, add a DataScroller tag (if you are using the Component Palette, this is on the BC4J Component Tags page) with a *datasource* of "locData." This tag provides a Previous and Next link that allows the user to scroll through record sets in the DataTable.

4. Under the DataScroller tag, add a DataTable tag with the following properties:
   datasource of "locData"
   edittarget of "LocRecord.jsp"
   relativeUrlPath of "DataTableQueryComponent.jsp"

   Additional Information: Specifying the *relativeUrlPath* with a file name that is different from the default will add a file with that name to the project. You can change this new file and not affect other DataTable component JSP files in the same project, because they point to the default file name. Specifying the *edittarget* property adds two columns to the data table grid that contain links—one for Edit and one for Delete. The Edit link runs the file specified in the *edittarget* attribute.

5. Click Finish. Make, save, and run (or refresh the browser for) the LocQuery.jsp file. When you click Search, a data table area will appear beneath the query fields as in Figure 22-4. When you click Clear All, the table will disappear and the query fields will clear. Try adding criteria and modifying the query conditions to see what the query mechanism will display.

The following is an example of the code between body tags of your JSP page. The application module name may be different in your case.

```
<h2>Find Locations</h2>
<jbo:ApplicationModule id="Locbc4jModule" definition="LocJSP.LocModule"
   releasemode="Stateful" />
<jbo:DataSource id="locData" appid="Locbc4jModule" viewobject="LocationsView1"
   rangesize="6"/>
<jbo:DataHandler appid="Locbc4jModule" />
<jbo:DataQuery datasource="locData" />
<jbo:OnEvent datasource="locData"
   list="Search, FirstSet, NextSet, PreviousSet, LastSet, GotoSet" >
<h2>Query Results</h2>
<jbo:DataScroller datasource="locData" />
<jbo:DataTable datasource="locData"  edittarget="LocRecord.jsp"
   relativeUrlPath="DataTableQueryComponent.jsp" />
</jbo:OnEvent>
<jbo:ReleasePageResources />
```

Modify the Component JSP File

The *component JSP file* is a file created when you add a component tag to a JSP page. For example, adding the DataQuery tag to this JSP page added a component JSP file to the project called DataQueryComponent.jsp. This file contains low-level functionality that is called by the main JSP page. The file is a copy of a template in one of the JDeveloper install directories. You can modify your local copy to fit your requirements. In this case, the query results should not display the street and postal code attributes. Also, the results table should not contain Delete, New, and Edit links, but does require a Details link that loads a page containing all of the attributes for a particular record.

Making these kinds of changes requires a basic understanding of HTML. The View Source feature of the browser (accessed from the right-click menu of the browser page) will display the underlying HTML. You should be able to find HTML tags in the main JSP page or in the component JSP file that match the HTML in the browser. This will give you a clue about where to make these kinds of changes.

For the requirements of this section, you have studied the HTML source and decide to make the following changes:

- Remove the New link in the second column header.

- Remove the Delete link for each row.

- Specify that the street address and postal code be hidden.

- Change the Edit link to a Details link. You already specified the target as LocDetails so that the link will be built with the parameters for presenting the appropriate record.

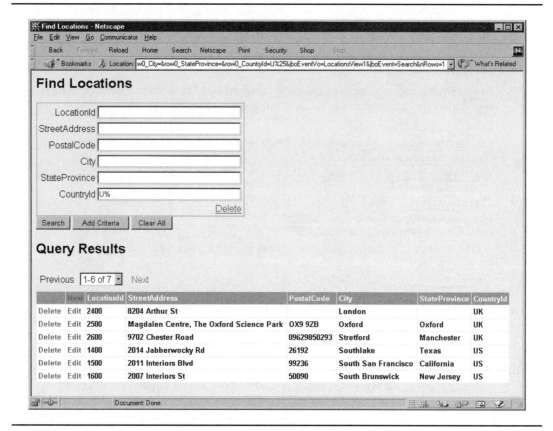

FIGURE 22-4. *Query page with results table*

The steps here implement these changes:

1. Open the DataTableQueryComponent.jsp file in the Code Editor. This file contains the low-level tags that create the HTML table.

2. Find the first table header—a tag starting with "<th". You will find something like the following:

```
<th class="clsTableHeader"> </th>
<th class="clsTableHeader"><a href="<jbo:UrlEvent targeturlparam=
    'edittarget' event='Create' datasource='dsBrowse' extraparameters=
    '<%="originURL=" + params.getParameter("originURL")%>'/>">
    New</a></th><%
```

Additional Information: This code constructs a blank cell for the first column and a New link in the second cell. Since you only need one of these columns and do not need the one with the New link, you can delete that one.

3. Delete the line with the New link (shown on multiple lines in the earlier code) up to the opening scriptlet tag "<%". The resulting code should appear as follows:

```
<th class="clsTableHeader"> </th>
<%
```

4. Look for the AttributeIterate starting tag ("<jbo:AttributeIterate ... />") just below this area that displays the attribute headings. Add a *hideattributes* attribute to this tag so that it looks like the following (on one line):

```
<jbo:AttributeIterate id="df" datasource="dsBrowse"
  hideattributes="StreetAddress, PostalCode">
```

Additional Information: The AttributeIterate tag normally steps through all BC4J view attributes in the view usage. The *hideattributes* attribute defines the BC4J view attributes that the AttributeIterate tag will skip.

5. Add the same *hideattributes* attribute to the other starting jbo:AttributeIterate tag that appears toward the end of the file. This tag displays the row values in the table.

6. Make the file and reload the browser (if the browser is still open with the LocQuery.jsp), or run the file (if the browser is displaying another page or is not open).

Additional Information: You should see a heading row that has three missing column headers. The next steps will remove the row values for the three deleted column headings.

7. Look for the table data ("<td>") code. You will find something like the following:

```
<td> <a href="<jbo:UrlEvent targeturlparam='originURL' event='Delete'
    datasource='dsBrowse' addrowkey='true'/>">Delete</a> </td>

<td> <a href="<jbo:UrlEvent targeturlparam='edittarget' event='Edit'
    datasource='dsBrowse' addrowkey='true' extraparameters='
  <%="originURL=" + params.getParameter("originURL")%>'/>">Edit</a>
</td><%
```

8. Delete the first row that contains the "Delete" event. (This spans multiple lines in the example just shown.) This will remove the column for Delete in the table.

9. Change the text at the end of the remaining tag from ">Edit</a>" to ">Details</a>".

10. Make the file. Run it by refreshing the browser or by clicking Run if you closed the browser. The results area should appear as follows:

Previous	1-6 of 23 ▾	Next		
	LocationId	**City**	**StateProvince**	**CountryId**
Details	1000	Roma		IT
Details	1100	Venice		IT
Details	1200	Tokyo	Tokyo Prefecture	JP
Details	1300	Hiroshima		JP
Details	1400	Southlake	Texas	US
Details	1500	South San Francisco	California	US

11. Leave the browser and OC4J server running.

Modify the Page Using BC4J Properties

Querying the street address attribute could cause slow performance because there is no index for the STREET_ADDRESS column in the table. Therefore, you do not want to allow the user to search using the address attribute. You also want to change the default label for this field to "Street."

1. Under the LocBC4J.jpr project in the Navigator, select the LocationsView node.

2. In the Structure window, double click the StreetAddress attribute to display the Attribute Wizard.

3. On the View Attribute page, uncheck the *Queriable* checkbox. When this property is not checked, the attribute cannot be used for queries. Therefore, the DataEdit component will not draw it.

4. Click the Control Hints node in the Attribute Wizard navigator, and change the *Label Text* to "Street." This text will be shown instead of the attribute name for data components that read the control hint.

5. Click OK. Open the Attribute Wizard for LocationID and change the Label Text to "LocID."

6. Click Save All and Rebuild LocBC4J.jsp. Close the browser and terminate the Embedded OC4J Server session.

7. Select LocQuery.jsp and click Run. The browser will show the modified query form without the *Street* field and with a modified LocationId prompt as shown in the following image:

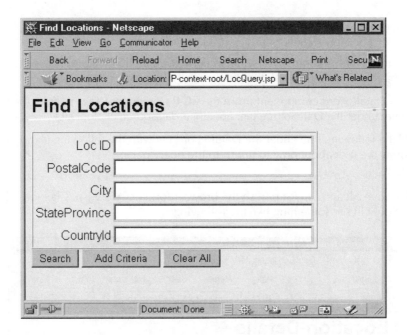

What Just Happened?   You created a complete query page that allows users to search for records based upon values that they enter. You also modified the component JSP code to remove some default columns and to link to a page that you will create next. Modifying the JSP page is a matter of studying the HTML that needs to be changed and finding that HTML in the main JSP page or component JSP file.

The modifications that you made to the code occurred in two general locations: BC4J attribute properties and JSP component code. Another location for visual modification is the cascading style sheet. Chapter 23 discusses other ways to modify BC4J data tags JSP pages.

II. Add a Details Page

Often, tables contain more columns than you want to display on a query form. The user needs to view data from all columns in the entire row after finding it. This phase uses the DataRecord component to dispay a record with all columns. DataRecord shows a form view of a row (instead of the table grid view that DataTable displays). As before, the steps for creating the JSP page are abbreviated, and you can refer to the preceding practice if you need more details.

1. Create another starter data page in the LocJSP project for the LocationsView1 view usage. Rename the file to "LocRecord.jsp."

2. Change the *id* property of the DataSource object to "locData."

3. Change the title to "Location Details," and add an h2 header in the HTML body with the text "Location Details."

Additional Information: To try the End Tag Completion feature, pause after typing "<h2>"; the End Tag Completion feature will fill in the "</h2>" tag.

4. Add a DataRecord component (from the BC4J Component Tags page of the Component Palette) under the DataSource tag. Specify a *datasource* of "locData."

5. Add the following line under the DataRecord tag with the following text. This text informs the user about how to return to the query page:

```
Click Back in the browser window to query locations
```

6. Click Save All and run (or refresh the browser for) LocQuery.jsp. Click on a Details link, and you will see something like the following:

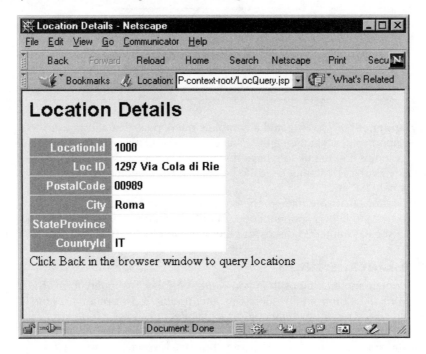

This page shows all attributes for a record, but has no insert, update, or delete features.

What Just Happened? You used the DataRecord component to construct a page that displays a single record. This kind of page is useful if you have a table with many columns that needs a full page to display all details.

CHAPTER
23

BC4J Data Tag
Techniques

Life is nothing but rags and tags and filthy rags at that.
— Christina Stead (1902–1983), *The Man Who Loved Children*

 ust as Java class libraries offer unlimited extensibility to the base Java language, tag libraries allow you to extend the standard JSP tags. These extensions are written in Java and are automatically supported by the JSP container. As mentioned in Chapter 22, this book concentrates on the BC4J Data Tags Library as an example of how to use JDeveloper with a framework. JDeveloper also contains integrated IDE support for tag libraries and frameworks such as OC4J JSP (OJSP), Struts, and User Interface XML (UIX).

This chapter builds on the discussions of developing JSP pages and how JSP tags work (Chapter 21) as well as the discussion about how to use BC4J tags in JDeveloper (Chapter 22). It discusses techniques that you can use to modify the behavior of the tags in this library and explores the role and function of the component JSP files. The hands-on practice at the end of the chapter demonstrates the methods that you might incorpoate into the standard templates provided by the BC4J Data Tags Library. Chapter 24 provides details about all of the BC4J Data Tags Library components and how some of the low-level tags work.

BC4J Data Tags Library Development Techniques

Working with BC4J data tag JSP pages in JDeveloper requires an awareness of all of these tags as well as of the page concepts mentioned in previous chapters. There are several techniques that you can use to be more effective when working with JSP pages.

Ordering Connection Tags and Component Tags

If you begin a JSP page using the Starter Data Page item in the New gallery, the ApplicationModule tag and a DataSource tag (connection tags) will be written into the JSP page. If you start developing a JSP page from scratch, you need to add the connection tags and component tags. There are some dependencies between the data component tags, and the tags need to appear in a certain order, as in the following list:

1. **ApplicationModule** This tag defines the application module that will be used as the source of the data objects.

2. **DataSource** This tag declares a name for the view object in the application module that will be used in other tags. It requires the ID of the ApplicationModule object and the name of the view usage.

3. **DataHandler** This tag is required to process events on the page. For example, it is required for the scroll and commit functions.

4. **Component tags** The last level of component tag assembly is the specific data component tag, for example, DataTable, DataEdit, and DataQuery.

You can define more than one ApplicationModule and DataSource tag, depending upon the requirements of the page. A single ApplicationModule tag can serve many data sources, and a single DataSource tag can serve many component tags. For example, the following code would appear in your JSP file:

```
<jbo:ApplicationModule definition="LocJSP.Locbc4jModule" id="locAM"
   releasemode="Stateful" />
<jbo:DataSource id="countriesData" appid="locAM"
   viewobject="CountriesView1" rangesize="6" />
<jbo:DataHandler appid="locAM" />
<jbo:DataQuery datasource="countriesData" />
<jbo:DataTable datasource="countriesData" edittarget="CountriesEdit.jsp" />
```

The DataSource and DataHandler tags refer to the ID of the ApplicationModule tag to give them a context. Similarly, the DataQuery and DataTable tags refer to the ID of the DataSource tag to link them to a view object. Figure 23-1 displays this relationship in diagrammatic form.

Working with Data Tag Component JSP Files

When you enter a BC4J data tag component in the Code Editor by using the Component Palette or the JSP Data Binding tool or just by typing it in, a data tag component JSP file will be created. A *component JSP file* (component JSP) contains logic to implement a high-level tag. It follows the recommended design practice of offloading complex operations to smaller files that can be shared among different JSP pages. This strategy simplifies the main JSP page so that most data component tags can be one line of code that represents a large amount of functionality contained in another file (the component JSP).

For example, if you enter a DataTable tag, the Code Editor creates a JSP file in your project that contains the lower-level tags that provide the function that the component tag represents. The component JSP file uses a default file name of the name of the component with a suffix "Component." For example, the DataTable tag automatically copies a component JSP called DataTableComponent.jsp from the templates directory into the project. The component JSP is generically written to provide the functionality that the tag suggests. In the DataTable example,

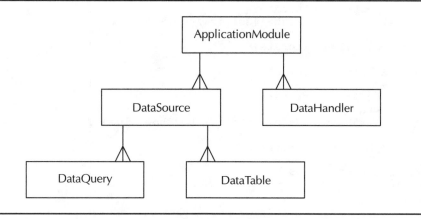

FIGURE 23-1. *Data connection and component tag relationships*

the component JSP loops through the attributes of the view object and creates a header row in an HTML table. It then iterates through the rows and writes all attribute values from a row to cells in the HTML table. You can view and modify this code in the component JSP. Figure 23-2 shows the process of copying a component JSP file from the templates directory to the project.

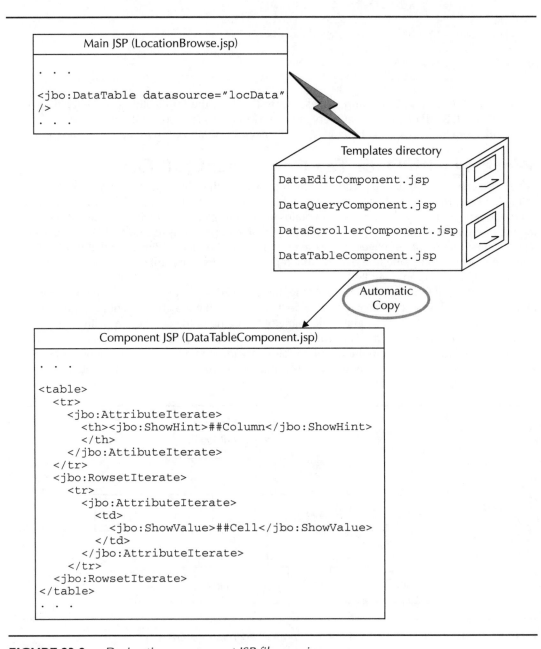

FIGURE 23-2. *Design time component JSP file copying*

When you run the main JSP file, the component JSP file creates another Java servlet that is called by the main JSP page's servlet file when the main file reaches the call to the component.

NOTE
The "##Column" and "##Cell" in this example are placeholders that are not used for processing. They help identify the HTML cell when you view the JSP page in an HTML viewer.

Using a Nondefault Component JSP

You can name the component JSP differently than the default when you create the component tag by using the *relativeUrlPath* property available in the data component properties dialog. You might want to use a different name if you have more than one of the same component tags in the page and want to alter the behavior of some of those tags but not the others. Since the component JSP is shared by the tags of the same name by default, customizing functionality for one tag requires a separate component JSP file. A good rule of thumb is to rename the component JSP if you need to make changes to it.

If you decide to make changes after completing the properties dialog, use **File | Rename** to change the name of the file, and add *relativeUrlPath* attributes to the applicable tags that are already in the file. If there is no *relativeUrlPath* attribute, the default component JSP is implied. For example, DataTableComponent.jsp is implied for the DataTable tag if it has no *relativeUrlPath* attribute.

When you create a component tag that already appears in the file (such as when you add a second DataTable component to a file that contains a DataTable component), a new component JSP will not be copied into the project unless you specify a different name in the *relativeUrlPath* attribute. If you specify a different name in the *relativeUrlPath* attribute, a file with the new name will be copied into the project directory. In the following example, the component JSP file, EmpDataTableComponent.jsp, will be copied into the project instead of the default DataTableComponent.jsp:

```
<jbo:DataTable datasource="locData"
   relativeUrlPath="EmpDataTableComponent.jsp" />
```

The Templates Directory

The files in the templates directory (JDEV_HOME\jdev\system\templates\common\tagcomp) are the master copies of component JSPs that are copied into the projects as component tags are entered. You can alter the master copy of any component if you want to affect all JSP pages that will be generated in the future.

CAUTION
Be sure to make a backup copy of the original template file if you modify it in the common templates directory, so that you can restore the backup if there are problems with your modifications. Also be aware that the default behavior of applications generated from the wizards may change if they use a file that you have modified.

Modifying the Component JSP

The component JSP supplies much of the low-level logic to the main component tag. You can alter the default behavior by changing the code in this file. As mentioned, if the change is something that needs to be standard for all pages, you can change the template in the JDEV_HOME\jdev\ system\templates\common\tagcomp directory.

As a simple example of a change, assume that you want to modify the buttons at the bottom of the DataEdit form to read "Post" and "Undo" instead of "Update" and "Reset." You can change the text on the buttons in the `<input>` tags at the end of the template file. For example, the Post button would be created by the following JSP/HTML code:

```
<input type="submit" value="Post">
```

Some other methods for modifying the way that a component JSP works are contained in the later section "Modifying JSP Attribute Behavior and Appearance" and in the hands-on practice. Many of these techniques can be used to modify the template files.

Before you make any kind of change to the component JSP, it is necessary to examine and understand the logic used. The following section discusses a sample component JSP.

> **CAUTION**
> *When you upgrade JDeveloper, be sure to save any template files that you have modified so that you can install them into the upgraded directories. In fact, you will want to work these templates into your source control process because they are part of the application code set.*

Annotated Component JSP Example   To get a sense of how to modify a component JSP, consider the component JSP used by the DataEdit tag. This tag is the core user component for an edit page such as the one shown here:

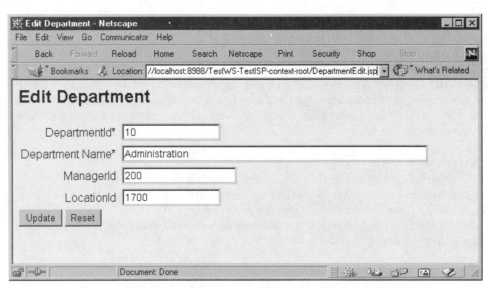

The component JSP file (DataEditComponent.jsp) contains the following logic, which has been simplified for illustration purposes. (The line numbers are not part of the JSP file.)

```
01: <jbo:DataSourceRef id="dsEdit" reference="<%=dsParam%>" />
02: <form name="<%=formName%>" >
03: <jbo:Row id="rowEdit" datasource="dsEdit" rowkeyparam="jboRowKey"
        action="<%=rowAction%>">
04:   <table border="0">
05:   <jbo:AttributeIterate id="def" datasource="dsEdit">
06:     <tr>
07:       <td title="<jbo:ShowHint hintname='TOOLTIP'/>" align="right">
08:         <jbo:ShowHint hintname="LABEL" />
09:       </td>
10:       <td title="<jbo:ShowHint hintname='TOOLTIP'/>">
11:         <jbo:InputRender datasource="dsEdit" formname="<%=formName%>" />
12:       </td>
13:     </tr>
14:   </jbo:AttributeIterate>
15:   </table>
16: </jbo:Row>
17:
18: <input type="submit" value="Update">
19: <input type="reset" value="Reset">
20: </form>
```

The top of this file also contains page directives, parameter loading, and a reference to the data source in the main JSP page. The following logic or code appears in this snippet:

- **Line 01** declares the data source view object (called "dsEdit") based upon a parameter passed from the main JSP page.

- **Lines 02 and 20** define the HTML form. This JSP file is included in the main JSP page so no starting and ending <html> tags are required. The form name is passed in as a parameter.

- **Line 03** (which wraps to two lines in the code listing) calls the data tag <jbo:Row> that receives a single row of data from the BC4J data source (dsEdit). It uses a parameter, rowAction, that specifies whether the form will be used for update (which presents a row with data on the screen) or insert (which presents a blank form). Line 16 ends this row access.

- **Lines 04 and 15** define the HTML table.

- **Lines 05 and 14** define a data tag, AttributeIterate, which loops through the list of attributes in the view object identified by dsEdit (in this case, DepartmentsView). The start of the loop is the starting AttributeIterate tag, and the end of the loop is the ending AttributeIterate.

NOTE
The AttributeIterate tag provides tag attributes ("displayattributes," "hideattributes," and "queryonly") that allow you to specify the attribute list. Also, although the attribute iterator is a generic way to handle the rendering of a page with data controls, it is not necessary to use it. You can build a page by specifying the controls (renderers) individually for the attributes that you need.

- **Lines 06 and 13** define an HTML table row.

- **Line 07** places the Tooltip control hint of the current attribute in the table data tag as a label of that tag. This is useful for applications that require disabled-access compatibility, because all screen elements must have names that can be audibly read. In addition, the tooltip will show in some browsers (like Internet Explorer) when the mouse cursor pauses over the field. (Control hints are discussed in the next section.)

- **Line 08** prints the Label control hint as the prompt for the field. If there is no Label control hint, the attribute name will be printed. For example, if the Label control hint were "Manager ID" and the Tooltip were "Manager's employee ID," lines 07–08 would generate the following HTML:

```
<td title="Manager's employee ID" align="right">Manager ID
```

- **Line 09** ends the first table data cell.

- **Lines 10–12** define another table data cell containing an HTML field. This field is drawn by the InputRender data tag.

- **Lines 18–19** declare the form buttons for submit and reset.

The AttributeIterate tag will loop for all attributes in the view object, and a row in the HTML table will be created for each. The first cell of the row contains the label, and the second cell contains the field.

Modifying JSP Attribute Behavior and Appearance

You can use a number of ways to modify how attributes are displayed or how they behave by default. Although this is not a complete list of techniques, it will give you an idea of where you should look when you need to modify a JSP attribute. All these techniques can help you in changing the code created by the JSP wizards.

About Control Hints

Normally, display attributes are stored in properties on UI objects. BC4J data tags offer both data access and display functions and are highly integrated with the BC4J objects. *Control hints* are properties of BC4J entity object attributes and view object attributes. Control hints alter the display behavior for all attributes displayed from the BC4J objects where they are defined. Since they are set on the entity object or view object level, they provide a way to make all pages built from the same BC4J layer consistent.

For example, if you set control hints for the Employees entity object attributes, all user interfaces that use view objects based upon the Employees entity object will take advantage of the settings on the entity object. You can also set control hints on the view object level, which is more specific. Control hints are used by BC4J (and UIX) JSP pages as well as by rich-client Java applications and applets.

Accessing Control Hints   You can edit control hints from the Attribute Wizard. Select the entity object or view object node in the BC4J project. Then select Edit from the right-click menu on an attribute in the Structure window. Click the Control Hints node, and you will see something like the following:

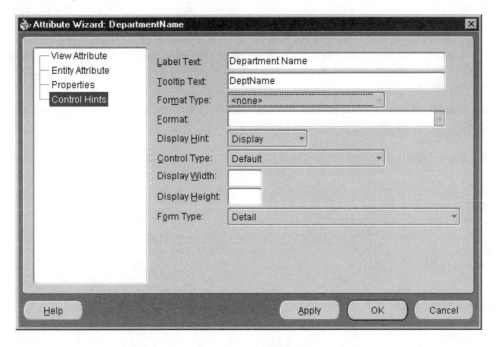

Control Hints   The control hints currently offered follow:

■ **Label Text** is displayed as a prompt for the attribute item.

■ **Tooltip Text** is displayed when the mouse pauses over an item. It will be written into the ALT attribute that HTML offers as a short description of a graphic.

■ **Format Type** shows which formatter will be used to display the item. A *formatter* is a set of format masks.

TIP
You can define your own formatters as described in the online help topic "Defining a Formatter and Format Masks for the UI." (On the Index tab, select "control hints: setting formatters.")

- **Format** is the actual format mask from the formatter's set that will be used for the attribute.

- **Display Hint** defines whether the attribute will be displayed.

- **Control Type** declares what type of user interface object (renderer) will be used for the field based upon the attribute type. "Default" means that a renderer appropriate to the item will be selected. For example, an item based on a date attribute will display a date field that has a date LOV button. An item based on a character attribute will be displayed using a text field (single line) if it is short; a text area (multiline field) will be displayed for the attribute if the character length is longer (for example, over 30). The "Edit" control type presents a standard input field that allows the user to type into and edit the field. If the attribute is set to non-updateable (in the BC4J attribute properties) and the control type is set to "Edit," the input field will still be displayed (whereas using the Default control type will display a non-editable area). A control type of "Date" offers a popup calendar to assist in entering dates. The Edit control type allows the user to modify the field. The default control type automatically selects the control most appropriate to the attribute.

- **Display Width** sets the number of characters of horizontal space that a field will take.

- **Display Height** stores the number of rows of vertical space that the field will take.

- **Form Type** is not used for JSP pages. It defines Detail mode (long form) or Summary (short form) for the attribute in a Java client program (Java application or applet).

NOTE
Control hints are stored as text strings in a Java class file under the entity object or view object node in the BC4J project. This file has a suffix of "ImplMsgBundle" and is compiled and deployed with the rest of the BC4J files.

Hiding Attributes
The following are some techniques for hiding attributes:

- **Display Hint property**   This property on the Control Hints page of the Attribute Wizard allows you to hide the attribute for all component tags.

- **Delete the attribute**   As an alternative to hiding the attribute, you can delete it from the view object (using the View Object Wizard). This will make the attribute unavailable for use by the component tags.

- **Queriable property**   This property on the View Properties page of the Attribute Wizard hides the attribute from the DataQuery component as demonstrated in the hands-on practice in Chapter 22.

- **hideattributes**   The AttributeIterate tag used in a number of component tag JSP pages offers a *hideattributes* attribute (property). If you list the attributes that you want to hide in this property (for example, "<jbo:AttributeIterate id="ai" datasource="ds" hideattributes="StreetAddress,CountryId" >"), all attributes except for those in the list (StreetAddress and CountryId in this example) will be processed. You can use a corresponding *displayattributes* property to list the attributes to show. For uses such as the query page, the *queriableonly* property can be used to filter out the attributes that have the *Queriable* property unchecked.

It is good to remember that mandatory (NOT NULL) properties must be displayed and enterable for an edit form that is used to create a new record. Therefore, you would not want to hide mandatory attributes for new records unless a default value were provided by BC4J code or database trigger code.

NOTE
The word "attribute" is overloaded in the area of JSP development. BC4J attributes correspond to individual data elements in a view object. HTML or JSP tag attributes are "properties" of the tag that alter its behavior or appearance. It is usually easy to distinguish between these forms of the word from the context in which they appear.

Change the View Object or the Entity Object?

The view object and related entity object contain many of the same attribute properties. Normally, the view object's properties will override the similar properties in the associated entity object. However, if you set an entity object property, the view object property may override it even if it has not been set differently from the default. For example, if the entity object attribute's *Queriable* property is unchecked, the corresponding view object attribute's *Queriable* property will be disabled so that you cannot change it. However, if the view object's *Queriable* property was checked before you changed the entity object, the attribute will appear in the query form regardless of whether the property is enabled or disabled, because the view object's property is checked, and it overrides the entity object setting.

Disabling Attributes with the Updateable Property

The *Updateable* property on the View Attribute page of the Attribute Wizard provides control for disabling the attribute in several situations. It may be set to the following values:

- **Always**   This value means that the user can fill in the attribute's field when inserting a record and can modify the attribute's field when updating the record.

- **While New**   This value means that the attribute will be disabled during updates. This is a useful setting for primary key attributes.

- **Never**   This setting means that users cannot fill in the attribute's field during inserts or updates. This setting has the same concern as hiding the attribute; if the attribute is mandatory, the user needs to be able to enter a value into it while inserting a record unless the value is provided by BC4J or the database.

A setting of "While New" or "Never" of the entity object attribute property forces the same setting on the view object attribute.

Formatting Data

The methods for formatting data in a JSP page follow standard Java mechanisms. The Control Hints page in the Attribute Wizard allows you to specify an existing format mask or to enter a new mask. *Formatters* (formatting masks) are stored in the formatinfo.xml file in the JDEV_HOME\ jdev\system directory so that they are available to other projects. Each formatter is associated with a datatype (such as Date, Number, or Integer) in this file.

The following discussion explains how dates and numbers may be formatted. Phase II of the "Traverse View Links and Change Data" hands-on practice in Chapter 14 contains another example of formatting data.

Applying a Date Format Mask

You can also specify a format for the renderer on the Control Hints page of the attribute or domain object using the following steps:

1. Select the entity object or view object node in the BC4J project (for example, Employees).

2. On the attribute node (for example, HireDate) in the Structure window, select Edit from the right-click menu to display the Attribute Wizard.

3. Select "Simple Date" in the *Format Type* field, and enter the format mask in the *Format* field as shown here:

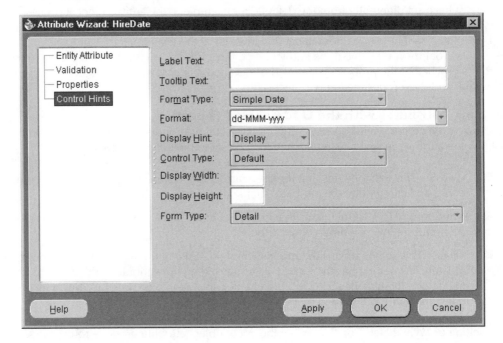

4. Click OK to dismiss the dialog. This writes the display hint into a file called <entity>ImplMsgBundle.java, where "<entity>" is the entity name.

Additional Information: If the MsgBundle class has compile errors, you will not be able to dismiss this dialog. Cancel the dialog and fix the errors before continuing.

5. Test the new BC4J project using the Business Component Browser. You will be able to see the new format in the browser.

When you run a JSP page built from this BC4J object, the new date format will appear as in the following example:

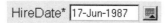

Date Format Strings   The format strings used for a date object are documented in the Javadoc for the java.text.SimpleDateFormat class. Some of the valid format characters follow. All format masks are case sensitive.

Format Character	Meaning
M	Unpadded month number
MM	Padded month number
MMM	Three-letter month name
MMMM	Full month name
dd	Day of the month
yyyy	Year
kk	Hour in 24-hour form
hh	Hour in 12-hour form
mm	Padded minute
ss	Second
aa	AM or PM

CAUTION
As of this writing, the date format mask is ignored when the user is querying data. The date format mask is applied to the display, but the user needs to query using the "yyyy-MM-dd" format. This limitation may be removed in future releases.

Formatting Number Fields

Number fields use the same formatting strategy as date fields. You can specify a format in the Control Hints of the attribute or domain to which the attribute belongs. Two default format types (Currency and Number) have several default masks as shown in the following example from the Attribute Wizard:

For this example, the Salary field will appear as follows:

The group separator (",") is optional for this use of the number format mask.

Number Format Strings   The format strings used for a number field are documented in the Javadoc for java.text.DecimalFormat. Some of the valid format characters follow:

Format Character	Meaning
0	Padded single number
#	Unpadded number that will not show if it is zero
%	Multiply by 100 and show with percentage symbol
;	Separates negative and positive format masks
.	Decimal separator
,	Group separator
E	Separates the two parts of a scientific notation number

TIP
If you change an attribute datatype in the Attribute Wizard, the formatters for that type may not be immediately accessible on the Control Hints page. Close the Attribute Wizard and reload it to apply the formatter.

The BC4J Cascading Style Sheet

Most BC4J data tags use the bc4j.css cascading style sheet included with JDeveloper. The classes that implement the BC4J data tags are coded to generate HTML, which specifies styles in this file. The practice in this chapter shows how to modify the HTML output by modifying this file.

The bc4j.css file is copied into projects in which you run the JSP application wizard or Data Page Wizard. The master file is located in the JDEV_HOME\system\templates\common\misc directory. You can make changes to that file and affect all projects created by the wizards.

You can use other style sheets included with JDeveloper as starting points for your style sheet: blaf.css is located in the same directory and offers the colors and fonts of the Oracle Browser look-and-feel that is used by the UIX libraries; jdeveloper.css is located in the JDEV_HOME\jdev directory and provides styles used by the online documentation (help system).

NOTE
In previous releases of JDeveloper, the bc4j.css file was contained in the webapp.war archive file in the JDEV_HOME\BC4J\redist directory.

Hands-on Practice: Modify a Data Page Wizard JSP Page

The practices in Chapters 21 and 22 show how to create and modify JSP pages. This practice supplies additional ways to modify a JSP page created by the Data Page Wizard. The principles demonstrated in this practice are also useful when you need to create JSP pages outside of the wizards.

This practice contains the following phases:

   I. Add to the BC4J project

  II. Create employee browse and edit forms

     ■ Create the forms

     ■ Specify the display attributes

 III. Modify the edit page

     ■ Modify the BC4J properties

     ■ Apply field styles—Method 1

     ■ Apply field styles—Method 2

I. Add to the BC4J Project

This phase adds an entity object, view object, and associations and link objects for the EMPLOYEES table to the BC4J project that you created in Chapter 22. If you do not need the step-by-step instructions in Chapter 22, you can use the Business Components Package Wizard to create a BC4J project called "LocBC4J" (in the LocationsWS workspace) that contains default objects for COUNTRIES, DEPARTMENTS, EMPLOYEES, and LOCATIONS tables in a package called "locbc4j." You can then skip to Phase II of this practice. Otherwise, follow the abbreviated steps in this phase to add the EMPLOYEES table to your BC4J project from Chapter 22.

    1. In the LocBC4J project, select New Entity Object from the right-click menu on the locbc4j package node.

    2. Select EMPLOYEES in the *Schema Object* pulldown on the Name page.

3. Use all the defaults on other pages to create an entity object from the Employees table. Be sure that the *Generate Default View Object* checkbox is checked on the Generate page, so that the EmployeesView view object will be created.

4. Verify that the Employees entity object, EmployeesView view object, and EmpDeptFkAssoc association have been created.

   Additional Information: If any of these objects is missing, add it by selecting the appropriate wizard from the right-click menu on the package node.

5. To add a view link between DepartmentsView and EmployeesView, select New View Link from the right-click menu on the locbc4j package node. Name the link "EmpDeptFkLink."

6. Select DepartmentsView as the source view object and EmployeesView as the destination view object. Use the EmpDeptFkAssoc association to define the link on the Source Attributes and Destination Attributes pages. On the View Link SQL page, click Finish.

7. On the Locbc4jModule node, select Edit from the right-click menu.

8. Add the EmployeesView to the Data Model pane (after selecting the module name in the Data Model pane). Add EmployeesView via EmpDeptFkLink to the Data Model pane after selecting DepartmentsView1. The Data Model area should look something like the following:

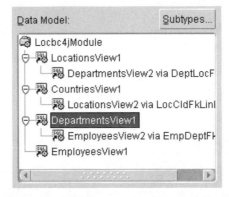

   Additional Information: Your view objects may display in a different order and have different number suffixes.

9. Click OK in the Application Module Wizard, and click Run to test the project in the Business Component Browser. Be sure that the EmployeesView and the EmpDeptFkLink objects work in the browser.

What Just Happened?   You added the Employees entity object to the BC4J project. You also created a view object and view link for the Employees object and made them available to the workspace by adding them to the application module. When you create objects in a BC4J project, you also need to add them to the application module so that they are available to projects in the same workspace.

II. Create Employee Browse and Edit Forms

In this phase, you use the Data Page Wizard to create a browse form for the EmployeesView view object. You modify this form to display the employee records that are related to the department being displayed. This modification results in a master-detail form such as the one demonstrated in the hands-on practice in Chapter 3.

NOTE
This practice uses the Component Palette for entering data component tags. You can also use the JSP Data Binding tool as discussed in Chapter 22.

Create the Forms

The first section uses the Data Page Wizard to create browse and edit forms for employees. The browse form would probably be called from a query form that passes in conditions for a subset of records to browse. The hands-on practice in Chapter 22 demonstrates how to build these two pages manually. The wizard is used here because the objective of this practice is to demonstrate how to modify some of the low-level settings and code in a BC4J JSP page.

1. On the LocJSP project node, select New from the right-click menu, and double click Browse & Edit Form in the Web Tier/JSP for Business Components category.

2. Select EmployeesView1 usage that is at a master level in the Data Definition page. If you had more than one client data model, you could select the appropriate model on this page.

3. Click Next and Finish. The JSP pages will be created in the project.

4. Open the EmployeesView1_BrowseEdit.jsp file in the Code Editor if it is not already open. Change the title (between "`<title>`" tags) to "Employees" and the text inside the first set of "`<h3>`" tags to "Employee Records."

5. Modify the rangesize on the `jbo:DataSource` tag to "6." Add an *orderbyclause* attribute for LAST_NAME so that it reads as follows:

```
<jbo:DataSource id="ds" appid="Locbc4jModule" viewobject="EmployeesView1"
   rangesize="6" itermode="LastPagePartial"
   orderbyclause="LAST_NAME"/>
```

Additional Information: The *itermode* attribute specifies how the last range of records will be displayed. If this is set to "LastPagePartial," the user may see a partial page. For example, if rangesize is set to "6" and the last range in the record set only contains five records, the user will see five records after selecting the last set of records. If the itermode is "LastPageFull," the user will see six records even though one of those six is in the record set before the last set.

6. Open the EmployeesView1_Edit.jsp file in the Code Editor. Change the title and h3 text to "Edit Employee."

7. Click Save All and click Rebuild. Click Run on EmployeesView1_BrowseEdit.jsp to test the browse form functions.

8. Click the Edit link and try editing an employee record. Notice that the HireDate field displays a button that loads a calendar LOV window. This LOV functionality is part of the BC4J date field renderer.

Specify the Display Attributes

The employee data display is intended to be used for identifying a specific employee so that the record can be edited. A number of the attributes that the DataTable displays are not required. This section removes these attributes.

1. Click the DataTableComponent.jsp file in the Navigator and select **File | Rename**. Fill in the name as "EmpDataTableComponent.jsp" and click Save.

   Additional Information: It is good practice to change the name of the default component JSP file if you make changes to it. Then, if you add another instance of the same component to the JSP file, the additional instance will include another default copy of the component JSP and will not be affected by the customizations you made. If the additional component requires the same customizations, you can specify the *relativeURLpath* of the new component to be the customized component JSP file.

2. In the EmployeesView1_BrowseEdit.jsp file, change the `jbo:DataTable` tag to include the name of the new file in the relativeUrlPath attribute. The complete tag should appear as follows:

   ```
   <jbo:DataTable datasource="ds" edittarget="EmployeesView1_Edit.jsp"
       relativeUrlPath="EmpDataTableComponent.jsp" />
   ```

3. Click Save and Rebuild. Run the file (or refresh or reload the browser) to ensure that the component JSP file is being used.

4. Open the EmpDataTableComponent.jsp file in the Code Editor and search for AttributeIterate tags. There should be one that displays the table header cells and one that displays the table data. Add a *displayattributes* attribute to each tag so that it displays the employee's ID, names, and email. The tags should look like the following. (One will contain a different *id* attribute.)

   ```
   <jbo:AttributeIterate id="df"   datasource="dsBrowse"
       displayattributes="EmployeeId,FirstName,LastName,Email">
   ```

5. Click Save All and Make the project. Refresh or reload the browser if it is open, or click Run for EmployeesView1_BrowseEdit.jsp. You will see a page that displays the specified attributes as shown here:

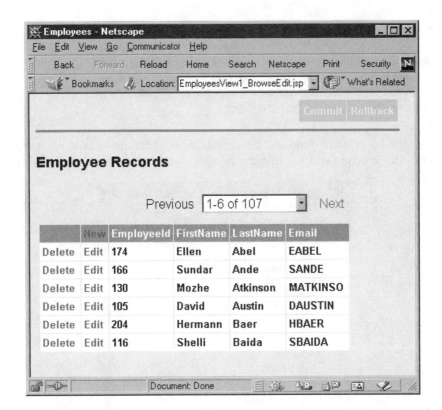

What Just Happened?   You built browse and edit pages using the Data Page Wizard. You also modified the browse page component JSP file to reduce the number of attributes displayed.

III. Modify the Edit Page

This phase creates an edit page that is the target for the link in the employee data table included in the previous phase.

Modify the BC4J Properties

You now have two functional pages and full DML capabilities for the employees data. The next step is to make the edit form more user friendly. The user should not be able to update the EmployeeId attribute, because this value may be linked to foreign key columns in other tables (such as a SALARY_HISTORY table). Therefore, the field should not be editable when the record is being updated, but should be editable when the record is new. In addition, you need to change some of the prompts to more user-friendly values and narrow the email field. You also need to hide salary and commission information and reorder the fields.

Since the data tags are closely tied to BC4J objects and read the BC4J definitions for the text, size, and updateable properties, you need to make these changes in the BC4J control hints.

NOTE
You can apply BC4J control hints and updateable settings at the entity object level or view object level. If you apply settings to an entity object, all view objects built from that entity object will inherit the settings. If you need to override the settings for a specific view object, you would change the settings on the view object.

1. Open the LocBC4J.jpr node and select Employees under the locbc4j application module node. The Structure window displays all attributes for this entity object as shown here:

2. Double click EmployeeId to display the Attribute Wizard. This wizard allows you to edit the properties of the entity object attribute.

3. On the Entity Attribute node, select "While New" in the *Updateable* radio group.

   Additional Information: This setting specifies that the attribute may be modified (filled in) only when the record is new. If the record is being updated, this attribute will not be updateable. The change you make in the properties will affect all applications built from the same BC4J project.

4. In the Control Hints page, type "ID" in the *Label Text* field and "Employee number" in the *Tooltip Text* field. This will change the field's prompt and tooltip (text that appears when the mouse cursor is held over the field). Click OK to close the wizard and save the change.

5. Repeat step 4 to change the *Label Text* property of the FirstName and LastName to "First Name" and "Last Name," respectively. Specify *Tooltip Text* values as "Employee's first name" and "Employee's last name," respectively.

6. Open the Attribute Wizard for the Email attribute, and specify its *Display Width* control hint as "10" so that the length of the field will be reduced.

7. Specify labels and tooltips for any other attributes that you would like to change.

TIP

If a field in the edit form appears to be too high, change the Control Type control hint to "Edit." This changes the control to a text field (single line) instead of a text area (multi-line). You can alternatively try changing the Height control hint, although this is not effective with the JDeveloper release as of this writing.

8. You do not want the employee's salary and commission to be displayed. Double click the Salary field to display the Attribute Wizard.

9. On the Control Hints page, select "Hide" for the *Display Hint* property. Click OK. Repeat this setting for the CommissionPct attribute.

10. You also want to change the order of the attributes. Double click the EmployeesView view object in the BC4J project and click the Attributes node in the View Object Wizard.

    Additional Information: So far, you have made changes to the entity object attributes so that all view objects built from the entity objects will be affected. The view objects inherit the properties of the entity object. This change is applied at the view object level because the view object default attribute order overrides any special order set on the entity object level. Therefore, even if you change the attribute order on the entity object, the order will be whatever order (default or not) that the view object specifies.

11. Select the JobId attribute in the right-hand *Selected* pane. Click the Move Up button until JobID follows the LastName attribute. Move the Email attribute after the PhoneNumber attribute. Click OK to save the changes.

12. Click Save All. Select the BC4J project and click Rebuild.

CAUTION

If you click Rebuild after selecting the JSP project node, you may receive an error message that the component JSP file, DataTableComponent.jsp (which you renamed), is not in the project node. Click Make for the project instead.

13. Refresh the browse form file if the browser is open, or click Run for the EmployeesView1_BrowseEdit.jsp file. You need to start the application from the browse form because it passes row ID information to the edit form.

    Additional Information: If your changes do not appear, you need to shut down the Embedded OC4J Server by selecting Terminate from the right-click menu on the process in the Run Manager window. If the Run Manager is not displayed, select **View | Run Manager**. Then run the JSP page again.

14. Look for the following changes:

    ■ The *Email* field is narrower because you changed the *Display Width* property to 10.

■ The *ID* field is not editable when you are updating a record as shown next.

■ The Salary and CommissionPct attributes are not displayed. Look at the source for the HTML page (select View Source from the right-click menu), and verify that the attributes are not in the HTML source code.

■ The *JobId* field appears after the *Last Name* field and *Email* appears after *PhoneNumber*.

■ The field labels you modified are visible.

■ Tooltips appear on some fields. Some versions of Netscape will not display tooltips.

The page will appear as follows:

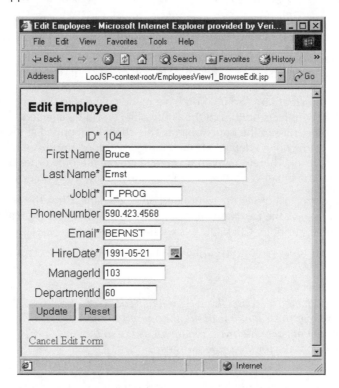

15. Click Cancel Edit Form to return to the browse page. Click New to view the edit page in insert mode. You will see that the *ID* field is enterable because you set the *Updateable* property of the EmployeeId attribute to "When New."

Apply Field Styles—Method 1

The edit form generates a style sheet reference for each field. For example, the following HTML code is created for the *FirstName* field:

```
<INPUT VALUE TYPE="TEXT" MAXLENGTH="20" NAME="FirstName" SIZE="25"
CLASS="clsFirstName">
```

You can add styles to the cascading style sheet that are named using this same naming convention. This section provides an example of how to add customized field styles.

1. Open the bc4j.css file under the LocJSP project node.

2. Add the following in a blank line after a closing curly bracket:

```
.clsLastName,
.clsEmployeeId,
.clsEmail,
.clsHireDate,
.clsJobId {
    background-color:yellow;
}
```

3. This code changes the background color to yellow for the mandatory fields in the edit form. An asterisk "*" is already added to all mandatory fields by the DataEditComponent.jsp.

4. Click Save All and Make the project. Run the edit form or reload the browser to see the change. The fields with styles defined in the style sheet will be shown with a background color as suggested in the following excerpt from the browser page:

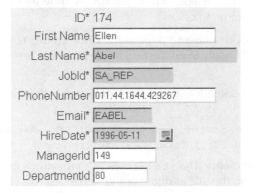

CAUTION
The preceding technique may not work in Netscape. If the Netscape version that your users run does not support the "class" attribute on an input field, you can use the highlighting workaround mentioned next.

Apply Field Styles—Method 2

The preceding method for changing the field style is useful for a specific set of fields. However, if you wanted to change all mandatory fields on all pages in the project, you could make a change in the template for DataEditComponent.jsp. The following steps explain how to make this kind of change. If this is a standard that you require in other projects, you can change the template files as described earlier in this chapter.

This technique may not work in some versions of Netscape because styles applied to an input field do not display. If you are using a version of Netscape that has this problem, you can apply the style to the `<td>` tag before the `<input>` tag so that there will be a highlight around the field as shown here:

The steps that follow explain the technique from the standpoint of a browser that supports applying a style to an input field:

1. In the bc4j.css file, remove the list of field class names, and insert the name "requiredField" in the bc4j.css file so the block of code appears as shown here:

```
.requiredField {
   background-color:yellow;
}
```

2. Click Save All and run the edit form or refresh the browser to check that the required fields have no background color.

3. Open the DataEditComponent.jsp file in the Code Editor. You are going to edit this file, but this change will apply to all the files in the project. Therefore, you do not need to rename the file.

4. Navigate to the InputRender tag. (There is only one in this file.) It is in the following line of code:

```
<td title="<jbo:ShowHint hintname='TOOLTIP'/>"><jbo:InputRender
   datasource="dsEdit" formname="<%=formName%>" />
```

Additional Information: The `jbo:ShowHint` tag returns the tooltip control hint text, which is assigned to the title attribute of the `<td>` tag. The `jbo:InputRender` tag creates an input field with a hidden value for the value. The HTML output for the LastName field follows:

```
<td title="Employee's last name">
<INPUT VALUE="Weiss" TYPE="TEXT" MAXLENGTH="25" NAME="LastName"
   SIZE="30" CLASS="clsLastName">
<INPUT VALUE="Weiss" TYPE="HIDDEN" NAME="_LastName">
```

You need to insert some logic to check for the mandatory attribute. There is scriptlet code right above this "`<td>`" tag in the component JSP that inserts the asterisk conditionally based upon the mandatory property of the view attribute. You can repeat this code and use it to apply the requiredField style to mandatory fields.

5. Change the code shown in step 4 to the following:

```
<td title="<jbo:ShowHint hintname='TOOLTIP'/>">
<%
```

```
if (def.isMandatory())
{ %>
  <jbo:InputRender datasource="dsEdit" formname="<%=formName%>" >
    <jbo:SetHtmlAttribute name="CLASS" value="requiredField" />
  </jbo:InputRender ><%
} else { %>
  <jbo:InputRender datasource="dsEdit" formname="<%=formName%>"
  /><%
} %>
```

Additional Information: The first line of this code that uses the hint is unchanged from the original component JSP. The next piece of code is a scriptlet that performs an if-else test on the mandatory attribute. If the attribute is mandatory, it uses a `jbo:InputRender` tag with the class attribute set to the name of your new style. Otherwise, it uses a `jbo:InputRender` tag without the style setting. Notice that you are only replacing the opening "`<td>`" tag and some of the code after it. The closing "`<td>`" tag already appears in the code.

6. Make the project and rerun (or refresh) the edit page. The background color of the mandatory fields will change as suggested here:

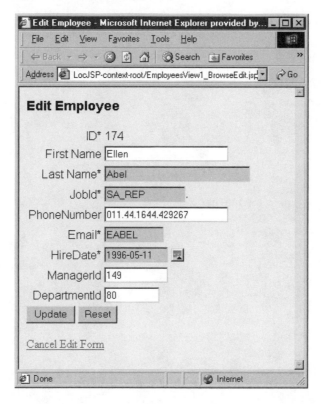

Additional Information: The HTML for nonrequired fields will be the same as before. The HTML for required fields will appear as follows:

```
<td title="Employee's last name">
<INPUT VALUE="Weiss" TYPE="TEXT" MAXLENGTH="25" NAME="LastName"
  SIZE="30" CLASS="requiredField">
<INPUT VALUE="Weiss" TYPE="HIDDEN" NAME="_LastName">
```

The class attribute is not a normal attribute for the jbo:InputRender tag. The jbo:SetHtmlAttribute tag adds this attribute to the HTML input tag.

What Just Happened? The changes you made to this page were accomplished using a combination of techniques such as changing the BC4J properties, modifying the cascading style sheet, and adding code to the component JSP files. Since the BC4J objects are shared among many JSP pages, all JSP pages are affected by changes to BC4J properties. To view the changes, you may have had to shut down the Embedded OC4J Server so that the cached application module could be refreshed. The changes made to the style sheet are also universally available (although they do not require a restart of the OC4J server). These are key techniques that you will use to build standard templates and style sheets that can create a common look-and-feel for your JSP applications.

CHAPTER
24

A Closer Look at BC4J
Data Tags

A spear, a spike,
A stake, a nail,
A drip, a drop,
The end of the tale...
It's the moon floating free
It's the curve of the slope
It's an ant, it's a bee
It's a reason for hope

— Antonio Carlos Jobim (1927–1994), *The Waters of March*

he last three chapters have supplied introductions to JSP pages as well as technical details about the BC4J Data Tags Library. This chapter provides a brief description of the tags in the BC4J Data Tags Library so that you can get a feel for the range of operations that you can perform with these tags. The hands-on practice in this chapter explores several of the lower-level tags and provides more techniques for creating JSP code using JDeveloper.

BC4J Data Tags Library

The BC4J Data Tags Library is a set of tags built from Java classes that work closely with BC4J objects. The following builds on the introduction to the BC4J Data Tags Library presented in Chapter 22. Before providing a quick tour of the BC4J data tags, it is useful to review some of the concepts at the core of JSP pages.

BC4J JSP Page Concepts

When you work with BC4J JSP pages in JDeveloper, the tags you use follow specific processing for rendering data, processing query criteria, and handling events. Before discussing all tags available in the BC4J Data Tags Library, it is useful to briefly explore how these areas work.

Rendering Data

Inputting and updating data in an HTML page requires that the proper user interface controls are available to the user. This requirement is met by HTML renderers. An *HTML renderer* (also called a *renderer*) is a user interface object that provides special functionality to display or to allow editing of text or data. The BC4J data tags associate a specific renderer with each datatype. For example, the date renderer displays a formatted date inside a field. It automatically adds a button next to the field that, when clicked, displays a date calendar window as shown here:

The main browser page is disabled when the date calendar is displayed and re-enabled after the user selects a date.

There are two types of renderers: one that is used for editing (called an *EditRenderer*) and one that is used for displaying (a *Renderer*). A default EditRenderer and Renderer are associated with each datatype offered by BC4J.

You can create a renderer class that implements some required functionality. You can then associate the renderer with an attribute or domain. In addition to renderers that implement a type of special field, the values in fields can be formatted in a certain way. The section "Formatting Data" in Chapter 23 discusses formatting techniques.

TIP
A how-to document on otn.oracle.com (currently called "How to Use BC4J HTML Field Renderers") demonstrates how you can write your own renderer and use it in a JSP page.

Querying Data

Although you can preset the WHERE clause on a view object or in the DataSource component tag, you may also want to allow users to search for records by completing a query form (using a process that is sometimes called "query by example"). When users enter values into fields on a query form, the JSP page uses these values to build a WHERE clause for the view object that will retrieve the records. A *criteria* is a part of the WHERE clause that is derived from the value that the user types into a query field, for example, "EMPLOYEE_ID = 101." The data tags take care of assembling the criteria based upon what is typed into the field. The following table shows examples of different types of data and how the criteria will be constructed based upon the value in the field.

Field	Value in the Field	Criteria
EmployeeID	100	EMPLOYEE_ID = 100
HireDate	1987-06-25	TO_CHAR(Employees.HIRE_DATE, 'yyyy-mm-dd') = '1987-06-25'
FirstName	David	Employees.FIRST_NAME LIKE 'David'
LastName	K%	Employees.LAST_NAME LIKE 'K%'
Salary	< 5000	Employees.SALARY < 5000
HireDate	> '1987-06-25'	TO_CHAR(Employees.HIRE_DATE, 'yyyy-mm-dd') > '1987-06-25'

Number field values are compared using an equal sign "=." Date field values are converted to character field values and compared using an equal sign. Character field values are compared using the LIKE operator. If the user precedes the value with a comparison operator (such as "<" or ">"), the default operator for the field will be overridden (as shown with Salary in the example).

All criteria are grouped programmatically into a *criteria row*. The criteria within that row are combined using the AND keyword. The user can add criteria rows to the query. Each row contains one or more criteria. The set of criteria rows is called a *criteria view*. The criteria view represents the entire WHERE clause of a query.

Query forms can contain more than one "row" (set of query fields) as shown here:

EmployeeId			
FirstName	Dav%		
LastName			
Email			
PhoneNumber			
HireDate		OR	> '1987-06-17'
JobId			
Salary	< 5000		
CommissionPct			
ManagerId			
DepartmentId			
	Delete		Delete

Search	Add Criteria	Clear All

The row of fields represents a criteria row, and criteria rows are combined using the OR keyword. When the Search button is pressed, the JSP page constructs the entire WHERE clause by assembling the criteria into criteria rows (using AND) and the criteria rows into a criteria view (using OR). For example, the query form just shown will construct the following WHERE clause:

```
WHERE ( ((Employees.FIRST_NAME LIKE 'Dav%') AND (Employees.SALARY <
    5000) ) OR ( (TO_CHAR(Employees.HIRE_DATE, 'yyyy-mm-dd') >
    '1987-06-17') ) )
```

CAUTION
The formatter that you apply to a date field (discussed in the "Formatting Data" section in Chapter 23) will not be applied to the query fields. Therefore, even if users see a date in the format "dd-MMM-yyyy" (such as "17-Jan-1987"), they must enter it into the field using the format "yyyy-MM-dd." This is the Java date mask, which is case sensitive. The SQL date mask (as shown inside the TO_CHAR() function) is not case sensitive.

Handling Events

When users work in a JSP page, they interact with the page using links or buttons that initiate page events. Events require a definition that names them and associates them with the link or button. They also require code to handle the event.

The BC4J Data Tags Library tags can create and process HTML form events as well as predefined events that are known to the BC4J data tags. HTML form events are defined and named by the developer. BC4J events have predefined names. Both types of events need to be associated with an HTML object or core process that will cause the event code to occur.

The JSP pages that the Data Page Wizard creates contain many examples of HTML form events and BC4J events. Table 24-1 lists the BC4J events that are available to the developer. This list contains two main types of events:

- **Navigation events**   These events occur when the user requests changing the display of a record or set of records. For example, a data table grid can show a set of records. When the user requests a set of records before or after the displayed set, a navigation event occurs.

- **Database events**   When the user requests a DML operation, commit, or rollback, a database event occurs.

Event Name	Description
FirstSet	This event indicates navigation to the starting set of records in a query. This is used for multi-record displays such as the display presented by the DataTable tag. The number of records in a set is determined by the *rangesize* attribute of the DataSource tag.
NextSet	This event is used like the FirstSet event for multi-record displays, but it navigates to the following set of records in a query.
PreviousSet	This event is used like the FirstSet event for multi-record displays, but it navigates to the preceding set of records in a query.
LastSet	This event is used like the FirstSet event for multi-record displays, but it navigates to the ending set of records in a query.
GotoSet	This event is used like the FirstSet event for multi-record displays, but it navigates to a specified set of records in a query.
First	This event is typically associated with a single-record display such as that presented by the DataRecord tag. It can also be used for multi-record displays. The event navigates to the starting record in a set.
Last	This event is used like the First event, but it navigates to the final record in a set.
Next	This event is used like the First event, but it navigates to the following record in a set.
Previous	This event is used like the First event, but it navigates to the prior record in a set.
Insert	This event is a database transaction event that issues an INSERT statement to the database with the values in the HTML form.
Update	This event is another database transaction event that issues an UPDATE statement to the database with the values in the HTML form.

TABLE 24-I.   *Predefined BC4J Events*

Event Name	Description
Delete	This event is another database transaction event that is responsible for issuing a DELETE statement to the database for the record in the HTML form.
Commit	This event issues a COMMIT to the database for the changed record in the BC4J cache. The changed records in the "transaction" will not be saved unless the user requests this event. There is no specific event for posting data.
Rollback	This event reverses the changes in the "transaction." It is required if the user needs to restore the state of the records before the Update and Delete events that occurred since the last Commit.

TABLE 24-1. *Predefined BC4J Events* (continued)

Setting Release Mode and State

When a JSP application requests BC4J objects, an application module instance is created to interact with the user interface. Each user receives an application module instance that is defined by a set of parameters. You can set or change parameters for the application module in an XML *configuration file* called *bc4j.xcfg* created by default in the BC4J project. You can edit and add configuration details by selecting Configurations from the right-click menu on the BC4J project's application module node. Parameters for the application module appear in the Properties tab of this dialog, as shown here:

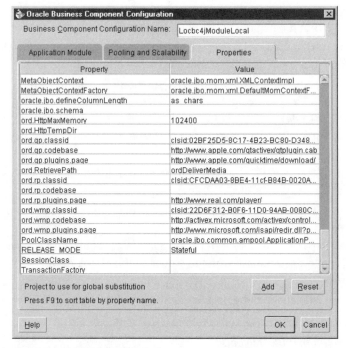

Chapter 16 discusses configurations in more detail.

As described in Chapter 14, the release mode property sets the *state* of the application module instance, which determines if and how the information about a specific application module instance is preserved across multiple page requests. If the application module is preserved, the application can store information about the transaction across multiple pages. This is necessary for a page such as the browse page, which contains a scroller control. In this case, it is important to know which records were previously queried so that the next or previous set of records can be accessed based upon that information.

The information about which records were previously queried is stored in the state information for an application module (resident in a file or in the PS_TXN database table for the connection user). If state is not preserved, the application module will be reinitialized for each page request, and transaction information will not carry over from one page to the next. The following are the alternatives for the release mode setting:

- **Stateful** This is the default release mode and is preferred for standard JDBC connections. "Stateful" means that the application module instance's state information is stored in a file or in the database until the user sends another page request to the application module. This option adds the processing overhead of storing and retrieving the state, but it allows functions such as browsing records. After an application module instance state is stored, that instance can be available to other users. When the primary user makes another call to the application module, the state information is read, and the application module is reinstated. Since the information is stored in a persistent location, this option provides *failover*—the ability to reestablish a session even if the container is stopped and restarted.

- **Stateless** This mode means that the application module instance is released between page requests. Thus, when a page finishes, the application module will be released, and no information about the state of the application module will be stored. Stateless mode provides better support for a large number of users because resources are released, not held as they are in a stateful connection. This option is therefore a bit faster, because there is no overhead to store and retrieve the state. It is good for a one-time retrieval of information on the page such as a display of reference data that will not change during the application (for example, product categories on an online orders page).

- **Reserved** This mode saves the application module instance during the entire browser session. Each client receives an application module instance. When the browser closes, the instance is terminated. This option is good for non-JDBC connections, but does not provide failover. Also, it takes more memory than the other options because application module instances are not shared. With a small set of users this is the best mode from performance and data integrity standpoints because the state is preserved, and there is no storage and retrieval of state required. However, the more users, the more memory is used on the server, and the memory of the server needs to match the requests. Therefore, this is not the choice to use for a large number of users.

A good example of preserving state between page requests is the Browse application that is generated by the Data Page Wizard with a stateful mode. When the user clicks Next to retrieve the next set of records, the page is redrawn with the new records. The state of the application module instance includes information about which records have been retrieved. When the user requests the next set of records, a NextSet event is sent to the application module instance, which sends the next set of records based on which records have been retrieved. Since the application module saves the state of the current record, it can navigate among records when the user clicks Next or Previous. If the application module is placed into a stateless mode, proper navigation will not occur.

Application module instances are distributed from a *pool,* a number of application module instances available in memory. The stateless mode releases application modules back to the pool immediately. Stateful mode releases the application module to the pool after storing the state information. Reserved mode does not release the application module until the end of the browser session. Chapter 15 provides details on the application module pool.

You can specify a different release mode for the application module instance in a particular JSP page. The *releasemode* attribute of the ApplicationModule tag allows you to specify the release mode for the page.

Quick Tour of the BC4J Data Tags

The JDeveloper online help documentation contains full syntax definitions and descriptions of each of the Component Palette elements, including reference information with examples. However, this section provides a brief description of each tag, so you can get a taste for the tools that you have available when working with the BC4J Data Tags Library. The tags are described in the order in which they are presented in the Component Palette pages that are available when you are editing a JSP file.

The BC4J Data Tags Library tags use the prefix "jbo" by convention (for example, "`<jbo:DataTable datasource="deptData" />`"). The library prefix is assigned in the taglib directive in the JSP page, and you can use any prefix that you want. However, the wizards generate code with a "jbo" prefix so, to be consistent, the code that you add should use the same convention for the library prefix.

> **NOTE**
> *The starting point for documentation about the BC4J Data Tags Library is in the Index page of the help system under the index entry "BC4J data tags: tag reference."*

BC4J Component Tags

Most of these tags are used to construct user interface objects.

DataEdit   This tag displays a set of edit fields for a view object as shown next:

DepartmentId*	10
Department Name*	Administration
ManagerId	200
LocationId	1700

Update   Reset

It can be called in insert mode to display blank fields or in update mode to display data from a row.

DataHandler   This tag does not draw specific interface objects, but is required for scrolling and transaction events in other components.

DataNavigate   This tag presents First, Previous, Next, and Last buttons (as shown here) for scrolling between records:

First Previous Next Last

This component is usually associated with a single record display such as that presented by DataRecord. However, if you associate this control with a data source that feeds a DataTable (multi-record component), the row highlight will change to indicate the "current" row. For example, the following shows a data table control after clicking the Next button:

	New	DepartmentId	Department Name	ManagerId	LocationId
Delete	Edit	10	Administration	200	1700
Delete	Edit	20	Marketing	201	1800
Delete	Edit	30	Purchasing	114	1700
Delete	Edit	40	Human Resources	203	2400
Delete	Edit	50	Shipping	121	1500
Delete	Edit	60	IT	103	1400
Delete	Edit	70	Public Relations	204	2700
Delete	Edit	80	Sales	145	2500

DataQuery   This tag constructs a set of query fields and buttons as shown here:

DepartmentId	
DepartmentName	
ManagerId	
LocationId	

Search   Add Criteria   Clear All

The user can enter data to be matched and click Search to return a row set that can be displayed in a component such as DataTable. The Add Criteria function allows the user to create OR conditions for searching.

DataRecord   This tag displays data for a single record as shown next. The tag offers no native insert or update function, but you could link to another component page that contains that functionality, if needed.

DepartmentId	10
Department Name	Administration
ManagerId	200
LocationId	1700

DataScroller   This tag (shown here) presents links to scroll a number of records using a Previous link, Next link, or a pulldown list with a record range. The increment for the number of records is defined in the DataSource tag.

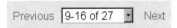

DataTable   This tag displays a grid of rows and columns. The number of records displayed is defined in the DataSource tag. If you define an *edittarget* attribute, the Delete and Edit links will be shown as in this example. If that attribute is missing, there will be no Delete or Edit links.

	New	DepartmentId	Department Name	ManagerId	LocationId
Delete	Edit	170	Manufacturing		1700
Delete	Edit	180	Construction		1700
Delete	Edit	190	Contracting		1700
Delete	Edit	200	Operations		1700
Delete	Edit	210	IT Support		1700
Delete	Edit	220	NOC		1700
Delete	Edit	230	IT Helpdesk		1700
Delete	Edit	240	Government Sales		1700

DataTransaction   This tag displays Commit and Rollback links with a horizontal line (as shown here) to separate the links from other elements on the page. Commit and Rollback are used to save or undo the changes made in the session to the database. The transaction is defined for each application module in the JSP page.

NOTE
A common attribute for the BC4J Component tags is targetURL. This attribute specifies the page that handles the submit request by the JSP page. If there is no targetURL attribute, the current page is used.

BC4J Connections
This category of tags is responsible for database operations or for connecting the components or data access tags to the database through BC4J objects.

ApplicationModule   This tag declares which BC4J application module will be used in the JSP page. You can use more than one application module for each JSP page by repeating this tag. One of the attributes for this tag specifies the release mode of the application module session. The earlier section "Setting Release Mode and State" explains how this setting works.

Commit   This tag issues a COMMIT statement to the database for the data changes made to objects in the application module.

CreateViewObject   Normally, you identify a data source with an existing view object in the application module. This tag allows you to dynamically define a SELECT statement as a view object for the application module. You then create a data source object based upon that view object. Using scriptlets, you can build a SELECT statement for this tag within the JSP logic, which provides dynamic SQL capabilities to the JSP page. This is useful for one-time uses of a query statement or for a query statement that needs to be built dynamically.

DataSource   You use this tag to define which view object usages you will be using within the application module. You can define more than one DataSource tag for one application module tag. A *data source* is the JSP page representation of a view usage in the application module.

DataSourceRef   This tag references an already defined data source. It is used in the component JSP pages to reference data sources in the main JSP page.

PostChanges   This tag issues a POST statement to the database for data changes made to objects in the application module. POST saves the data in the database so that it can be re-queried or rolled back before a full commit.

RefreshDataSource   This tag re-executes the database query for a specific data source after a post or commit operation and reloads the new data into the application module.

ReleasePageResources   This tag releases the application module instance. You use it at the end of a JSP page that contains data access. Although you can set the release mode for the application module state using this tag, it is better to set the release mode in the ApplicationModule tag to ensure that the correct mode is used.

Rollback   This tag issues a ROLLBACK statement to the database to reverse data changes made to objects in the application module.

BC4J Data Access
The tags in this category work on a lower level than the tags in the other pages. Some of them act at a view object level; others act at the attribute level. These are not primarily user interface tags, but some will display data.

AttributeIterate   This tag loops through the list of attributes in a data source (view object). The loop ends with the </jbo:AttributeIterate> tag. You can specify that certain attributes be processed with the *displayattributes* tag attribute. You can specify that certain attributes not be processed with the *hideattributes* tag attribute. The *queriableony* tag attribute specifies that only queriable attributes (which have the Attribute Wizard *Queriable* checkbox checked) be processed.

Criteria   As mentioned before (in the section "Querying Data"), a criteria is a value or expression that will be used in a WHERE clause for a query. The value is a relational expression (such as "> 300") and is used to create a piece of the WHERE clause. This tag is used in a query page to construct a WHERE clause for retrieving data. Multiple criteria are combined using the AND operator.

CriteriaRow   A *criteria row,* also mentioned before, is a set of attribute/value pairs all of which will form the WHERE clause of a SELECT statement. The CriteriaRow tag creates a criteria row object from the criteria created by the Criteria tag. Multiple criteria rows are combined using the OR operator.

ExecuteSQL   This tag allows you to issue SQL statements to the database dynamically. You can issue DDL or DML (except for SELECT) statements. Dynamic SELECT statements should use the CreateViewObject tag.

RenderValue   This tag displays the data from an attribute using the renderer appropriate to the datatype of the attribute (for example, a date renderer with the calendar selection button for date attributes). Text within the beginning and ending tags is not processed by the tag.

Row   This tag returns an instance of one row for a particular data source object. You can specify one of a number of operations that will occur on the row (such as Create, Delete, Lock, and Update).

RowsetIterate   This tag loops (iterates) through a set of rows for a data source. The number of rows is specified by the *rangesize* attribute of the data source. You perform whatever actions are required on each row inside the iterator tags.

RowsetNavigate   This tag changes the current row pointer. This process is referred to as "changing the currency." The tag supports operations such as First, Last, Previous, Next, FirstSet, LastSet, PreviousSet, NextSet, and GotoSet.

SetAttribute   This tag changes the value of an attribute. The tag must be placed inside a Row tag so that the attribute has the context of a row.

ShowCriteria   This tag displays the criteria (query value) for an attribute. This needs to occur inside a ViewCriteria or ViewCriteriaIterate tag to provide a context.

ShowDefinition   This tag displays metadata information (properties) of an attribute such as its name, column name, Java type, and SQL type.

ShowHint   This tag displays the control hints for an attribute that store information about how the attribute is displayed. See the section "About Control Hints" in Chapter 23 for more information about control hints. Text between the beginning and ending tags is not processed by the tag.

ShowValue   This tag displays the data value of the attribute in a data source. It does not use a field renderer as does RenderValue.

ViewCriteria   This tag creates a view criteria object for a data source. The view criteria object contains criteria rows that have attribute/value pairs. The criteria rows are concatenated into a WHERE clause for the query. You can also use the *whereclause* attribute of the DataSource tag.

ViewCriteriaIterate   This tag loops through all criteria rows in a view criteria object. The ShowCriteria tag will display separate criteria for each row.

> **NOTE**
> *You will notice that the page wizards write placeholder text such as "##Cell" or "##Column" between the beginning and ending of tags such as RenderValue and ShowHint. These placeholders will not display anything at runtime, but are handy for seeing what is inside a cell by using a visual HTML editor or viewer. For example, the following shows the JSP Viewer display of the DataTableComponent.jsp file, which contains ShowHint and RenderValue tags. The "##Column" placeholder text is displayed inside the ShowHint tags so that you know where the hint will be displayed. The "##Cell" placeholder text is inside a RenderValue tag.*

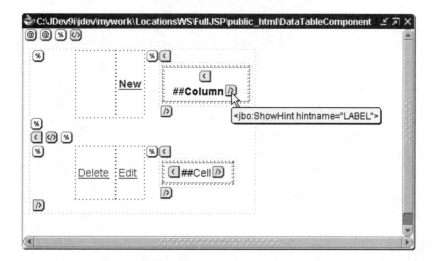

BC4J Events

The BC4J Events category offers tags that allow you to create and manage code that is triggered by the user interacting with the JSP page.

FormEvent   This tag allows you to add parameters to the normal HTML form event. This tag needs to be placed inside an HTML form tag. An attribute of this tag identifies the event that will be sent to the page that processes the HTML form. Table 24-1 (shown earlier) lists the predefined BC4J events. The names are not case sensitive.

OnEvent   This tag handles events declared by FormEvent and UrlEvent. It provides the ability to add or modify elements on the page when an event such as navigation or a database transaction statement occurs. It is a conditional tag that will only execute for the events that you specify in the list attribute.

UrlEvent   This tag allows you to create an event from a link on the HTML page. UrlEvent is used for the link behind buttons such as Next or Previous that initiates an event when the link is clicked. You can use a predefined form event such as those listed in Table 24-1, or you can name an event that will be processed by the OnEvent tag.

BC4J Forms

The BC4J Forms category of tags offers controls that you can use to draw and process input from HTML forms objects on the page.

InputDate   This tag creates an input field with a button that displays a calendar window when clicked. The user can select the date from the calendar window, and the selected date will populate the field. This field can be formatted using control hints in the BC4J attribute definitions.

InputHidden   This tag adds a hidden field to the page. The field can have a value, but will not be seen by the user unless the user displays the HTML source code of the page.

InputPassword   This tag adds an HTML field to the form that displays an asterisk ("*") character for each character input by the user. This tag must be within the HTML form tags if the user will be using Netscape.

InputRender   This tag adds an input renderer that is appropriate to the type of data in the field. If a renderer is defined in the attribute's properties, this tag will present that renderer.

InputSelect   This tag presents a list of values from which the user can select one or more. You can specify that the control is able to accept only one value. The control will appear as a multi-line selection text box or a single-line text box with a pulldown (combobox) list.

InputSelectGroup   This tag allows the user to select one or more values that are presented in a radio group list (single selection) or checkbox group (multiple selection).

InputSelectLOV   This tag presents a text field with a button next to it. When the user clicks the button, a list of values (LOV) window opens to allow the user to select a value that will be returned to the field.

InputText   This tag presents a single-line text item (field) where the user can enter a value.

InputTextArea   This tag presents a multiple-line text item (field) where the user can enter a value. You can specify the height and width of this control using the *rows* and *cols* attributes, respectively.

SetDomainRenderer   This tag assigns a specific renderer to a domain. This action affects the field types for all attributes that share the domain. The duration of this assignment can be set to the page, the request, the session, or the application.

SetFieldRenderer   This tag assigns a specific renderer to an attribute. This reassignment lasts for the duration of the JSP page.

SetHtmlAttribute   This tag allows you to add attributes available in HTML to the tag. For example, if you use an InputText tag to display a field, you can apply the HTML attribute *class* (style sheet style) to that field even though InputText does not offer such an attribute.

BC4J interMedia

The BC4J interMedia tags manage rich content objects such as images, video, and audio. *Oracle interMedia* is a feature of the Oracle9i database that provides services for storing, retrieving, and presenting these extended forms of data. JDeveloper's BC4J interMedia tags integrate with these services.

AnchorMedia   This tag inserts an HTML anchor tag ("<a>") in the page that links to an interMedia object such as a video. When the user clicks the link, the object will be retrieved from the database and displayed in the browser.

EmbedAudio   This tag inserts an HTML object tag ("<object>") that calls a plugin (such as Windows Media Player) to play an audio object. You can specify whether the audio plays automatically by setting the autoplay attribute. Although Netscape cannot always read the "<object>" tag, the nested "<embed>" tags are interpreted by Netscape.

EmbedImage   This tag inserts an HTML image tag ("<img>") to display an image object from the database.

EmbedVideo   This tag works like the EmbedAudio tag to render a video object stored in the database using a plugin such as Windows Media Player. It creates an "<object>" tag with nested "<embed>" tags.

FileUploadForm   This tag creates an HTML form that allows the user to upload a file to the web server (and potentially, to the database). You add tags between the beginning and ending FileUploadForm tags to display an input field and submit button to browse the local file system ("<input type="file" and input type="submit"").

MediaUrl   This tag retrieves multimedia content from the database and displays it in the HTML page. Unlike the other tags that display interMedia objects, MediaUrl does not create a link or an embedded plugin display. Instead, it displays the object in a page that is included in the main HTML. The included page, by default ordPlayMedia.jsp, displays the media content.

BC4J Web Beans

The tags in this category are included in JDeveloper for backwards compatibility with releases before 9i. In older releases, JDeveloper relied on the JSP tag "<jsp:useBean>" (as mentioned in Chapter 21) to include references to classes (Web Beans) with BC4J integration. The *Web Object*

Manager shown here allows you to add, modify, and remove classes that the Component Palette offers in the DataWebBean and WebBean categories:

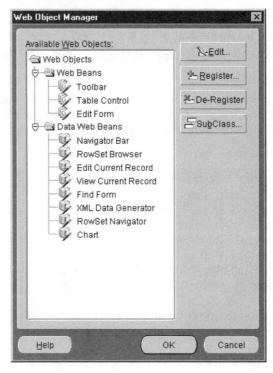

Development work with Web Beans is different from work with the rest of the BC4J Data Tags Library, because it requires coding inside the useBean tag calls to methods in the web bean class. The other BC4J Data Tags Library tags supply all the functionality of the web bean classes, but allow you to work more directly with HTML tags and attributes.

Therefore, Oracle recommends that new development use the other BC4J Data Tags Library elements. The online documentation provides hints about how to convert Web Beans to BC4J data and component tags.

DataWebBean   This tag allows you to include a class that creates HTML elements in the page that contain data loaded by BC4J. For example, a data Web Bean, RowSetBrowser, displays a table of records in the HTML page (like the DataTable component).

WebBean   This tag allows you to include a class that creates HTML such as a toolbar, table control, and edit form.

Hands-on Practice: Experiment with Form and Data Access Tags

This practice steps through the partial creation of an edit page containing input fields for selected attributes. It does not use the high-level, generic BC4J component tags (such as DataEdit), so you will get an idea about how much greater control you have when working on a lower level. Although the edit page will not be complete, the practice demonstrates how to use and modify the appearance of some of the BC4J form and data access tags provided in JDeveloper.

This practice contains the following phases:

I. Create the JSP file and add data sources

II. Define the HTML form and fields

III. Refine the edit page

■ Align the labels

■ Apply number and date formatters

IV. Construct a data table

I. Create the JSP File and Add Data Sources

This phase creates the file that you will use to experiment with some of the low-level tags. You start by using the Data Page Wizard to create a starter data page and provide the project with a style sheet, other related files, an application module, and data source tags. You then add data sources for the Department ID list of values field and for the Job ID selection list.

1. If you did not finish Phase I of the practice that creates the BC4J project in Chapter 22, return to that practice and complete the BC4J project. In addition, you need to add BC4J objects for the EMPLOYEES table (as in Phase I of the Chapter 23 hands-on practice.)

2. On the LocationsWS workspace node, select New Empty Project from the right-click menu. Name the project and directory "EmpDeptJSP." Click OK.

3. On the project node, select New from the right-click menu. Double click the Starter Data Page item in the Web Tier\JSP for Business Components category.

4. Create a data model definition using the New button. Leave all defaults in the Data Model Wizard and finish the wizard.

5. On the Data Definition page, select EmployeesView1 usage that is a parent-level view usage under the module as shown here:

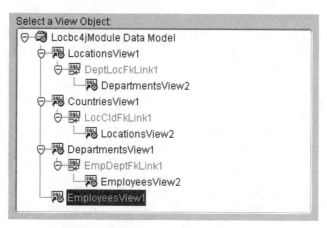

CAUTION
*All your view objects may not be visible in the Select a View Object
pane. If you cannot see a view object or view link, expand the height
of the window.*

6. Click Next and Finish. The JSP pages and other files will be created in the project.

7. Rename EmployeesView1_StarterPage.jsp to "EmpEdit" using **File** | **Rename**. The ".jsp" extension will be filled in automatically.

8. Click Save All.

9. Open the EmpEdit.jsp file in the Code Editor if it is not already open. Change the title (between "`<title>`" tags) to "Employee." Add the following after the first "`<body>`" tag:

   `<h2>Employee Edit</h2>`

10. Examine the `jbo:ApplicationModule` tag and the `jbo:DataSource` tag to verify their attributes.

11. Change the id attribute for the DataSource to "empData." The default id for a data source is "ds," which does not identify the source uniquely when the page supports more than one view object.

12. Click the cursor in a blank line after the `jbo:DataSource` tag, and click DataSource in the BC4J Connections page of the Component Palette.

13. Select DepartmentsView1 (parent-level node) as the source. Click Next and enter an *id* of "deptData" and an *orderbyclause* of "DEPARTMENT_NAME." Click Finish and the tag will be added to the code.

14. In a blank line under the deptData data source, click the CreateViewObject in the BC4J Connections page of the Component Palette.

15. In the CreateViewObject dialog, fill in the following attribute values:
    appid as "Locbc4JModule"
    name as "jobView"
    SQL SELECT as "SELECT job_id, job_title FROM jobs ORDER BY job_title"

16. Click Finish to add the tag.

17. In a blank line after the closing CreateViewObject tag, type in the following code:
    "`<jbo:DataSource appid="Locbc4jModule" id="jobData"`
    `viewobject="jobView" />`".

    Additional Information: You need to type in the DataSource tag because the Component Palette DataSource dialog in the current release has no support for a view object created using the CreateViewObject tag. The CreateViewObject tag allows you to define a view object instance that exists for the duration of the JSP page. The table or view does not need to be represented in the BC4J application module. The attributes of this dynamically created view object are named the same as the column names of the table (in uppercase). The SELECT statement for this view object could be built dynamically using scriptlets in the JSP code based upon user input or other conditions. The statement could then be passed to the tag in an expression such as in the following code extract:

```
<%
  String sqlStatement =
    "SELECT job_id, job_title FROM jobs ORDER BY job_title";
%>
<jbo:CreateViewObject appid="am" name="jobView2" >
  <%= sqlStatement %>
</jbo:CreateViewObject>
```

In this example, sqlStatement could be built dynamically from the code in the JSP page.

19. Click Save All.

What Just Happened? This phase adds to a starter data page created by the Data Page Wizard. It adds data source tags for lookup ID values (JobId and DepartmentId). One of the data sources is a SELECT statement that builds a view object on the page.

CAUTION
The problem with dynamic creation of view objects that occurs when you use the CreateViewObject tag is that user interface and data code merge. Separate view (user interface) and model (data access) layers are a main tenet of the MVC design pattern upon which most code in JDeveloper is built. Since the view object creation is embedded in the user interface code, no other user interface can reuse that code. Therefore, it is important to limit the use of this technique.

II. Define the HTML Form and Fields
This project now contains a cascading style sheet (bc4j.css) and a JSP file (EmpEdit.jsp) that refers to it. The body and headings will take their styles from the style sheet. The file also contains definitions for the data sources required by the field tags. The next step is to add the field tags inside an HTML form tag. The fields will be placed inside an HTML table structure.

1. In an empty line under the last data source tag, click the Form icon in the HTML page of the Component Palette. You will see the Insert Form dialog as shown here:

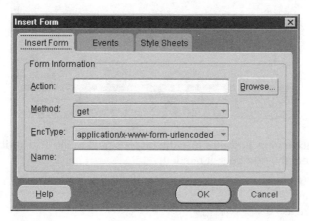

2. Specify the following attributes:

   Action as "/LocationsWS-EmpDeptJSP-context-root/EmpEdit.jsp"
   Method as "post"
   EncType as "multipart/form-data"
   Name as "emp_form"

3. Click OK. The tag will be written with its attributes into the JSP page.

4. Add two lines before the ending form tag ("`</form>`"). Place the cursor in the blank line before the ending form tag. Click the Table icon in the HTML page of the Component Palette. The Insert Table dialog will open where you can provide attributes for the table component as shown here:

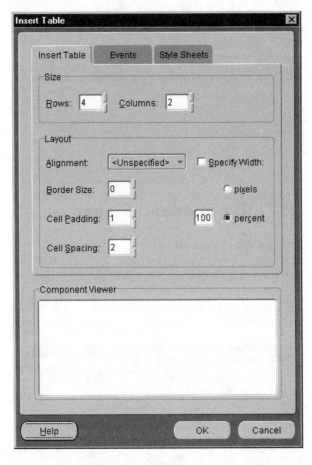

5. Specify the following attributes (use the buttons next to the size attributes to increment and decrement the numbers, if needed):

   Rows as "6"
   Columns as "2"
   Border Size as "0"

6. Click OK. The HTML table tags will be added to the file.

7. The "`<tr>`" tags define table rows and the "`<td>`" tags define data columns within the rows. Add a label text for the Employee ID, Last Name, Job, Hire Date, Salary, and Department ID in each row between the first pair of "`<td>`" tags. For example, the first row (defined by "`<tr>`" tags) would appear as follows:

```
<tr>
    <td>Employee ID</td>
    <td></td>
</tr>
```

The second pair of "`<td>`" tags in each row will hold the renderers (fields).

8. Click between the empty "`<td>`" tag pair in the first row under the "Employee ID" label.

9. Click InputRender in the BC4J Forms page of the Component Palette. The InputRender dialog will display as shown here:

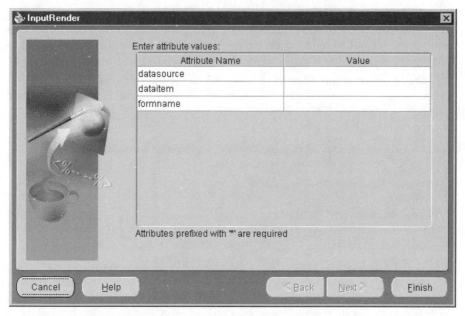

10. Fill in the following attributes:

> *datasource* as "empData"
> *dataitem* as "EmployeeId"
> *formname* as "emp_form"

Click Finish to add the tag to the code. The code for the first row will now appear as follows:

```
<tr>
    <td>Employee ID</td>
    <td>
      <jbo:InputRender datasource="empData"  dataitem="EmployeeId"
```

```
        <formname="emp_form" </jbo:InputRender>
    </td>
</tr>
```

Additional Information: An InputRender tag will draw a field renderer appropriate to the datatype of the attribute it is displaying. For normal number and character attributes, the renderer is a standard text input field such as that displayed using the InputText tag. For date attributes, the InputRender tag will display a date renderer. You can also use the InputDate tag for the same purpose, but InputRender is more generic to the datatype.

If you change the BC4J *Updateable* property of the attribute to "While New" (as the hands-on practice in Chapter 23 demonstrates), the field that the InputRender tag draws will not be editable for an existing record, but will be editable for a new record. The InputText tag does not offer this functionality, and it presents the same input field for new and existing records regardless of the *Updateable* property setting.

The *formname* attribute is optional for simple input attributes such as a number or character attributes, but is required for date attributes.

11. Repeat steps 8 and 9 to add InputRender tags under the labels for Last Name, Hire Date, and Salary. All tags have the same *datasource* ("empData") and appropriate dataitems. The *formname* attribute is optional for all but the Hire Date attribute.

    Additional Information: The Hire Date attribute will display a field and a button. When the user clicks the button, a date calendar window will be displayed where the user can select a date. This window was discussed in the "BC4J JSP Page Concepts" section earlier in this chapter.

12. For the *Job* field, use an InputSelect tag and specify the following attributes:

    multiple as "false"
    datasource as "empData"
    dataitem as "JobId"
    displaydatasource as "jobData"
    displaydataitem as "JOB_TITLE" (you will need to type in this value)
    displayvaluedataitem as "JOB_ID" (you will need to type in this value)

    Additional Information: The values are case sensitive, so enter them as shown in this step. This tag presents a pulldown list from which the user can select a name that represents a number. In this case, the pulldown list will contain the JOB_TITLE column from the dynamically created view object based on JOBS. The value behind the title will be the JOB_ID, which populates the JobId attribute of the employee record being edited. The attribute names that are prefixed with "display" represent the information used from the JOBS table. The *datasource* and *dataitem* attributes act the same way they do in InputRender; they are the data source of the record being edited and the attribute of that data source, respectively.

13. Click Finish. For the Department ID attribute, use an InputSelectLOV tag and specify the following attributes:

    datasource as "empData"
    dataitem as "DepartmentId"

displaydatasource as "deptData"

displaydataitem as "DepartmentName,DepartmentId" (Type this value in the field instead of selecting from the list. Be sure there is no space after the comma.)

displayvaluedataitem as "DepartmentId"

formname as "emp_form" (you will need to type in this value)

14. Click Finish.

Additional Information: You will notice that adding this tag copies a file called lovcomp.jsp into the project. This file is responsible for presenting an LOV window when the user clicks the button next to the field. The LOV window contains records from the *displaydatasource* view object. The user can select a value, and the field will be populated with the selected value. You can display more than one item in the LOV (by including a list of the attribute names in the *displaydataitem* attribute). The following shows the LOV window that this field will display when the button is clicked:

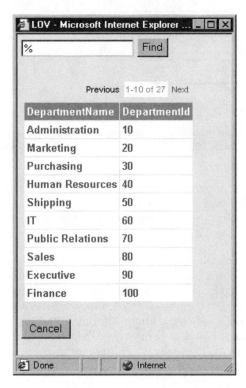

The *Find* field allows users to reduce the list in the LOV. The field searches all columns that are displayed for the value or pattern that users enter. Users can enter the multi-character wildcard "%" or a single-character wildcard "_" to find a pattern. For example, "A%" in the *Find* field will search all columns displayed for a value starting with "A" containing any number of characters.

15. Make the project and run the form. Try the selection buttons for each field and notice that the Employee ID field is not editable for the existing record. The application should appear as follows:

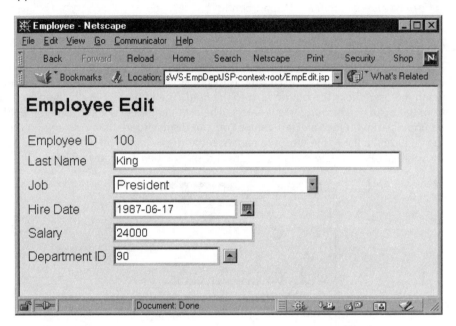

NOTE
If you are using Netscape and the fields do not appear when you run the JSP page, be sure that your code contains an HTML "<form>" tag and that the field and tables are within the "<form>" tags. Also, check the Structure window to see if it lists any HTML errors for the page.

What Just Happened?   This phase adds an HTML table to the page and assigns labels and fields to each row. HTML tables are a popular layout tool for maintaining alignment and order in a page. Until they are replaced by new HTML structures that separate content and layout, it is helpful to become accustomed to their use. The component JSP pages assign all fields using the default renderers or renderers associated with the attributes. Building a page a field at a time as shown in this practice provides you with control over the field renderers that are assigned to attributes. You can also more easily specify which attributes are displayed, the order in which they are displayed, and how they are sized.

III. Refine the Edit Page
You have completed a partially working edit form to practice using the field renderers. To complete this form, you would need to add event buttons and event processing. The best place to start with this work is by studying a fully developed application created by the Data Page Wizard. With the introduction provided in this book, you will be able to understand the code that the wizard creates. You will see the Update and Reset button code as well as the events that the generated JSP pages process. To round out the experimentation with this application, this phase will show how to refine the page.

Align the Labels
The labels in a Data Page Wizard application are right justified so that they directly adjoin their fields. The preceding phase used the default left alignment, but you can change this alignment.

1. In the EmpEdit.jsp, add an align attribute to the label cells in the HTML table. For example, the first row of the HTML page would appear as follows:

```
<tr>
  <td align="right">Employee ID</td>
  <td>
    <jbo:InputRender datasource="empData"  dataitem="EmployeeId" >
    </jbo:InputRender>
  </td>
</tr>
```

2. Complete all other rows in the same way.

3. When you make and reload the page, the browser will appear as follows:

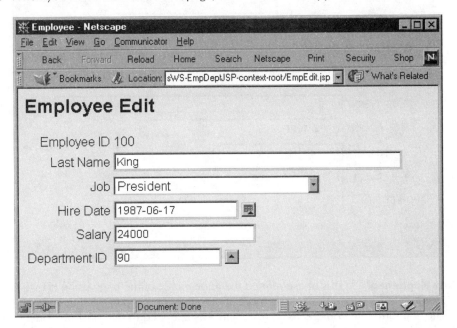

Apply Number and Date Formatters
This section applies formatters to the *Salary* and *Hire Date* fields. You apply formatters in the BC4J attribute properties.

1. Click the Employees entity object in the BC4J project in the Navigator. Double click the Salary attribute in the Structure window to display the Attribute Wizard.

2. Navigate to the Control Hints page, and set the *Format Type* to "Currency" and the *Format* to "$0000.00;$(0000.00)." This format will show a leading "$" and display the

amount with two decimal places and comma separators. Negative numbers will be surrounded by parentheses.

3. Click OK to close the wizard. Open the Attribute Wizard for the HireDate attribute.

4. On the Control Hints page, set the *Format Type* to "Simple Date," and type into the *Format* field the string "dd-MMM-yyyy." The format string is case sensitive.

5. Click OK to close the wizard. Rebuild the BC4J project.

6. If the OC4J server is started, terminate it using the Run Manager window. You need to restart the Embedded OC4J Server to see the effect of these changes in the BC4J project.

7. Click the EmpEdit.jsp and click Run. The application will appear with the new formats as follows:

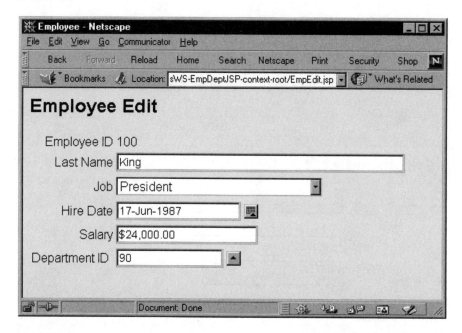

What Just Happened?   This phase refined the appearance of the page using HTML attributes and BC4J properties. Chapter 23 explains more about affecting JSP pages using BC4J property settings. The edit form that you create in this practice is intended to demonstrate some of the principles involved with the data tags and form tags. The finished file would need to be part of a complete application and include event handlers.

IV. Construct a Data Table

You can use this JSP page to test the attribute and row tags. These tags allow you to create an HTML table for a data source.

1. Comment out the entire form code block in the EmpEdit.jsp file by adding a JSP opening comment symbol ("<%--") before the form opening and a JSP closing comment symbol ("--%>") after the closing form tag.

2. Make and run the JSP page to be sure that the comments are in the right place. You will see a JSP page with only a heading.

3. Place the cursor before the commented code, and type the following heading code:

```
<h4>Jobs</h4>
```

4. Use the icons on the BC4J Data Access page of the Component Palette to enter the BC4J tags in the following code. For the HTML table code, type in the code or use the HTML Component Palette page Table icon. Run the JSP page when the code is complete.

```
<table class="clsTable" >
  <tr class="clsTableRow">
    <jbo:AttributeIterate id="jobHeader"  datasource="jobData" >
    <th class="clsTableHeader">
      <jbo:ShowHint hintname="LABEL"></jbo:ShowHint>
    </th>
    </jbo:AttributeIterate>
  </tr>
  <jbo:RowsetIterate datasource="jobData" >
    <tr class="clsTableRow">
      <jbo:AttributeIterate id="jobBody"  datasource="jobData" >
        <td>
          <jbo:RenderValue datasource="jobData" ></jbo:RenderValue>
        </td>
      </jbo:AttributeIterate>
    </tr>
  </jbo:RowsetIterate>
</table>
```

Additional Information: The entire structure is inside an HTML table. The first row of the table represents the header. The AttributeIterate tag loops through all attributes (in this case, two attributes) and shows the label control hint (using ShowHint) for each. In this case, there are no hints, because the data source is built from a SELECT statement in the JSP page. If the label control hint is not set, ShowHint displays the name of the attribute (the column name).

The code then iterates through all rows and displays the value (using RenderValue) for each of the attributes. A new row in the HTML table starts for each row in the view object. The attributes are separated by "<td>" tags. This builds up the table. The *class* attributes apply styles from the cascading style sheet. The following image shows the output of this code.

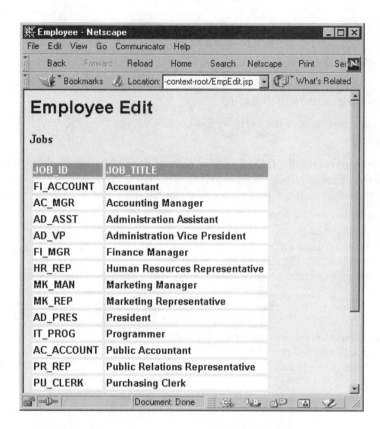

What Just Happened?   This phase uses iterator and other data access tags to display the data from a view object inside an HTML table. This is a short version of the method that the DataTableComponent.jsp uses to construct the data table. You also practiced commenting out code using JSP comments.

PART
V

APPENDIXES

APPENDIX
A

Wizards and Dialogs

Seek unto them that have familiar spirits,
and unto wizards that peep and that mutter. . .

—The Bible, Isaiah viii 19

Developer contains many wizards, dialogs, and automated features to help you create and edit the files needed for your applications. Some wizards (referred to in this book as "high-level wizards") allow you to create entire applications or large portions of applications. Others (referred to as "low-level wizards") help you create individual components of applications.

Wizards differ from dialogs in that a wizard has multiple pages (starting with a Welcome page). Many wizards are re-entrant, so that you can use the wizard to edit the definition after you create it. The pages of the re-entrant view of the wizard are usually the same as the pages in the creation view of the wizard, but in the re-entrant version, there are no Next and Previous buttons. Instead, the wizard displays a hierarchical tree navigator on the left to allow you to navigate to a specific page.

Dialogs consist of a single page where information is entered. Dialog windows cannot be resized. Wizard and dialog windows are *modal.* That is, when a wizard or dialog window is open, you cannot make any other selections in JDeveloper. All wizards and dialog pages include a Help button, which navigates to the online help system topic for the page of the wizard or dialog you are viewing.

The New Gallery

Most wizards and dialogs are accessible from the *New gallery,* a dialog containing items that will create files with default code. Display the New gallery, shown in Figure A-1, by selecting **File | New**. The hint text in the lower-right corner of the window describes the item and mentions when the item is available for selection (for example, after selecting the project node). You can view additional help text for an item by selecting it in the New gallery and clicking Help.

CAUTION
Some items are available in the New gallery by selecting the top-level node in the navigator. (For example, Database Connection is only available after selecting the Database Tier node.)

In addition to using the **File | New** menu selection to access the New gallery, you can access many of the same wizards and dialogs by clicking the appropriate project, package, or file in the Navigator and selecting Edit <item name> or New <item type name> from the right-click menu.

CAUTION
Figure A-1 shows the New gallery in JDeveloper release 9.0.3, build 988. The New gallery in your version of JDeveloper may differ somewhat from Figure A-1. **Help | About** *displays a dialog with version information.*

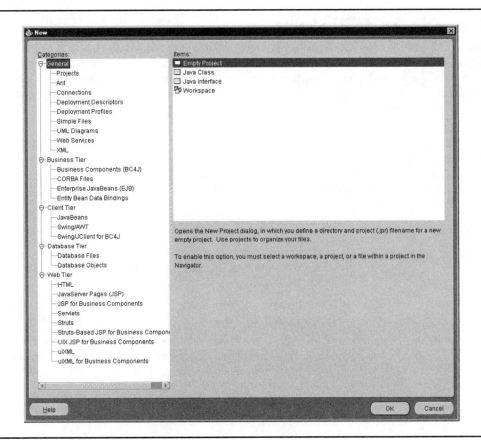

FIGURE A-1. *Oracle9i JDeveloper New gallery*

NOTE
Although many JDeveloper project components can be created with a wizard, some of the properties associated with them cannot be set using the creation wizards. You will need to select Edit from the item's right-click menu in order to edit its associated properties. For example, you can create a view link with the View Link Wizard, and you select Edit from the right-click menu to modify some of the view link properties.

Wizards and Dialogs

The following table lists the wizards and dialogs available in JDeveloper. The list is organized alphabetically by the item created. Some files that the wizards create or manipulate (such as the web.xml configuration file) have standard names, but most wizards and dialogs allow you to specify the name of the file you are creating. You can rename files that do not have standard names using **File | Rename**.

NOTE
As with Figure A-1, this table reflects the names and functionality of the wizards and dialogs for JDeveloper release 9.0.3, build 988. The item names may be slightly different in later builds.

Item Name	Description
Action	This displays the New Struts Action dialog, which creates an action class that defines an application-specific operation called from a JSP page.
ActionForm	This displays the New Struts Form Bean dialog, which creates a JavaBean class file that will be mapped to a Struts action.
Activity Diagram	This displays the Create New Activity Diagram dialog, which creates a UML Activity Diagram that you can use to document business processes and generate Oracle Workflow code.
Applet	This displays the New Applet dialog, which creates a Java class file to subclass JApplet. This file is used to run inside a browser's JVM.
Applet HTML File	This displays the Applet HTML File Wizard, which creates a .html file containing an applet tag that runs the specified applet.
Applet HTML Page	See "Applet HTML File."
Application	This displays the New Application dialog, which creates a Java Application file and optionally starts the New Frame dialog to create a frame (JFrame) Java class file.
Application Client Deployment Descriptor (application-client.xml)	This automatically generates a skeleton application-client.xml file in the selected project that you can use to specify information about deploying to J2EE servers.
Application Client Deployment Descriptor for OC4J (orion-application-client.xml)	This automatically generates a skeleton orion-application-client.xml file that you can use to specify information about deploying to OC4J.

Item Name	Description
Application Module	This displays the Application Module Wizard, which creates a new BC4J object that makes view objects and view links available to client applications.
Application Server Connection	This displays the Connection Wizard, which creates a definition for an OC4J, Oracle9iAS, or WebLogic host and user.
Association	This displays the Association Wizard, which creates a new link between entity objects and sets the properties including the cardinality. Associations usually represent foreign key constraints in the database.
Bean	This displays the New Bean dialog, which creates a blank Java file to which you can add code.
BeanInfo	This displays the New BeanInfo dialog, which allows you to supplement or provide bean information to the automatic information created by Java introspection about an existing JavaBean.
Browse & Edit Form	This displays the Data Page Wizard, which creates a JSP page for viewing and a JSP page for modifying data from a specific view object.
Browse Form	This displays the Data Page Wizard, which creates a JSP page to display data from a specific view object.
Buildfile from Existing XML File	This displays the Choose Ant Buildfile dialog to add an existing Ant XML build file to the project. This file supplies compile information to the Ant utility described earlier.
Buildfile Generated from Active Project Configuration	This displays the New Ant Buildfile from Active Project Configuration dialog, which creates an XML file for the Ant utility (described earlier) based upon project settings.
Business Components Client Data Model	This displays the BC4J Client Data Model Definition Wizard, which creates a .cpx file containing information about an application module in the same workspace. This file is required to connect BC4J to a Java client or web client application.
Business Components Archive	This displays the Simple Archive Files dialog, which creates a deployment profile, which allows you to deploy a BC4J project to a JAR or Zip archive file.
Business Components CORBA Server for VisiBroker	This displays the CORBA Server for VisiBroker dialog, which creates a .deploy file that you can use to specify information about deploying a BC4J project to a CORBA VisiBroker server.

Item Name	Description
Business Components EJB Session Bean	This displays the Business Components EJB Deployment Wizard, which creates a deployment file for the session Bean EJBs in a BC4J project.
Business Components Package	This displays the Business Components Package Wizard, (sometimes called the Package Wizard) which creates a directory to hold the selected business components for a project.
Business Components Project	See "Project Containing New Business Components."
Class Diagram	This displays the Create New Class Diagram dialog, which creates a blank diagram that you can use to model Java, BC4J, and EJB classes.
Class Diagrams from XMI Import	This displays the Import UML XMI dialog, which allows you to specify the name of an .xml file that contains one or more diagrams and that is written in the XMI format (for example, from another UML modeling tool). This dialog is only accessible from an empty project.
Client JAR File – J2EE Client Module	This displays the Save Deployment Profile – Client JAR File – J2EE Client Module dialog, which creates a J2EE deployment file (*.deploy) for a client application JAR file.
Complete uiXML Application	This displays the Business Components uiXML Application Wizard, which creates a set of uiXML forms for insert, update, and delete operations on a set of view objects defined in an existing BC4J application module.
Complete JSP Application	This displays the Business Components JSP Application Wizard, which creates JSP forms (for insert, update, and delete operations) for maintaining data in all view objects of BC4J client data model.
Complete Struts-Based JSP Application	This displays the Business Components Struts JSP Application Wizard, which creates a set of JSP pages (for insert, update, and delete operations) based on the Struts framework for an existing BC4J client data model.
Complete UIX JSP Application	This displays the Business Components UIX JSP Application Wizard, which creates a full set of JSP pages (for insert, update, and delete operations) based on the BC4J client data model.
Customizer	This displays the New Customizer dialog, which creates a customizer for a specific JavaBean. The customizer can allow several properties to be set at the same time.
Data Sources Descriptor for OC4J (data-sources.xml)	This automatically generates a standard OC4J information file in XML format (data-sources.xml). This file contains database connection information.

Item Name	Description
Database Connection	This displays the Connection Wizard, which allows you to create a definition for a JDBC database host and user.
Dialog	This displays the New Dialog dialog, which allows you to create a Java file that will serve as a dialog (message box).
Domain	This displays the Domain Wizard, which creates types that can be applied to BC4J entity attributes and view attributes.
EAR File – J2EE Application	This displays the Save Deployment Profile – EAR File – J2EE Application dialog, which creates a J2EE deployment file for an Enterprise Application Archive (EAR) file.
EJB Application Module	This displays the EJB Application Module Wizard, which creates an Enterprise JavaBean (EJB) session Bean that is remotely deployable.
EJB Deployment Descriptor (ejb-jar.xml)	This automatically generates a skeleton ejb-jar.xml file in a standard J2EE format. This file contains specifics about how the EJB is deployed.
EJB Deployment Descriptor for JBoss (jboss.xml)	This automatically generates a skeleton jboss.xml file that you can use to specify details about EJB deployment to the JBoss EJB container.
EJB Deployment for OC4J Descriptor (orion-ejb-jar.xml)	This automatically generates a skeleton orion-ejb-jar.xml file that you can use to specify details about deploying your EJBs to OC4J.
EJB Deployment for WebLogic Descriptor (weblogic-ejb-jar.xml)	This automatically generates a skeleton weblogic-ejb-jar.xml file that you can use to specify details about deploying your EJBs to a BEA WebLogic server.
EJB Entity Facade	This displays the EJB Entity Facade Wizard, which creates a data transfer object (entity facade) based on an entity Bean.
EJB Finder View Link	This displays the EJB Finder View Link Wizard, which creates an EJB Finder view link that connects two EJB Finder view objects.
EJB Finder View Object	This displays the EJB Finder View Object Wizard, which creates EJB Finder view objects for a BC4J project.
EJB JAR File – J2EE EJB Module	This displays the Save Deployment Profile – EJB JAR File – J2EE EJB Module window that creates a deployment (ejb*.deploy) file for an EJB JAR file.
Empty Buildfile	This displays the New Ant Buildfile dialog, which creates an XML file containing compiler information for the Ant utility. The *Ant utility* allows you to add compiler instructions to the project so that additional actions occur when you click the Make or Rebuild buttons.

Item Name	Description
Empty Form	This displays the JClient Empty Form Wizard, which creates an empty Java application file that is linked to BC4J projects through a client data model definition.
Empty Panel	This displays the JClient Empty Panel Wizard, which extends JPanel and which is linked to the existing BC4J client data model.
Empty Project	This displays the New Project dialog, which creates a project file and, optionally, creates a project directory in the file system.
Entity Bean	This displays the Enterprise JavaBean Wizard, which creates an Enterprise JavaBean that manages data transactions and persistence.
Entity Beans from Tables – Container-Managed Persistence	This displays the Create CMP Entity Beans from Tables Wizard, which creates an Enterprise JavaBean from a database table, and which is defined to use container-managed persistence.
Entity Constraint	This displays the Entity Constraint Wizard, which creates a new entity constraint along with its associated attributes and validation.
Entity Object	This displays the Entity Object Wizard, which creates a BC4J entity object.
EventSet	This displays the Event Set dialog, which generates a class file, which allows you to define events not provided by AWT or JFC.
Form	This displays the JClient Form Wizard, which creates single-table or master-detail Java applications using existing business components in the workspace.
Frame	This displays the New Frame dialog, which creates a class based on JFrame (a Swing window). Optionally, a title, menu bar, toolbar, status bar, and About box can be added by checking the appropriate checkbox(es) in this dialog.
HTML File	This displays the New HTML File dialog, which creates a skeleton Hypertext Markup Language (.html) file.
HTML Page	See "HTML File."
HTTP Servlet	This displays the HTTP Servlet Wizard, which creates a skeleton servlet file containing default methods.
IDL File	This displays the New IDL File dialog, which creates a blank file that you can use as a CORBA Interface Definition Language file.
Import Existing Sources	This allows you to add files to your project from any existing sources. It is accessible from the File menu. An example of how to do this is included in the third hands-on practice in Chapter 3.

Item Name	Description
Import EAR File	This allows you to import an Enterprise Application Archive (EAR) file into your project.
Import from WAR File	This allows you to add files to your project from an existing WAR file.
J2EE Application Deployment Descriptor (application.xml)	This automatically generates an application.xml file that contains application-specific settings for deploying to J2EE-compliant servers.
J2EE Application Deployment Descriptor for OC4J	See "Application Client Deployment Descriptor for OC4J."
JAR File – Simple Archive	This displays the Save Deployment Profile – JAR File – Simple Archive dialog, which creates a deployment (.deploy) file for a Java Archive (JAR) file.
Java Class	This displays the New Class dialog, which creates a blank .java file optionally containing a main method and constructor.
Java Interface	This displays the New Interface dialog, which creates a file that you can use as an interface (a Java file that contains method signatures and constants but no code).
Java Web Service	This displays the Web Service Publishing Wizard, which creates a deployment descriptor file and a Web Services Description Language (WSDL) document so that you can publish Java code as a Web Service.
Java Web Start (JNLP) Files	Displays the Java Web Start Wizard, which creates files that allow your Java application files to be distributed using the Java Web Start utility. You need to create an archive file before running this wizard.
Java Web Start (JNLP) Files for JClient	This displays the JClient Java Web Start Wizard, which creates the files required for distributing Java application files using Java Web Start.
JSP Document	This displays the New JSP Document dialog, which creates a skeleton JSP document (a JSP 1.2 page written in XML syntax).
JSP Page	This displays the New JSP dialog, which creates a skeleton JavaServer Page file.
JSP Tag Library	This displays the JavaServer Page Tag Library Wizard, which creates a tag library (.tld file) containing tag names with references to Java classes that implement the tags.
JSP Tag Library Descriptor	See "JSP Tag Library."

Item Name	Description
Loadjava and Java Stored Procedures	This displays the Save Deployment Profile – Loadjava and Java Stored Procedures dialog, which creates a deployment (.deploy) file for installing Java stored procedures into the Oracle9i database.
Message Driven Bean	This displays the Enterprise JavaBean Wizard, which creates an Enterprise JavaBean that is used to manage stateless messages between clients.
Oracle Forms Pluggable Java Component	This displays the New Oracle Forms Pluggable Java Component dialog, which generates the skeleton code for a class that can be used inside Oracle Forms as a Pluggable Java Component (PJC). You can specify an existing Oracle Forms component to be subclassed or build a component from scratch.
Panel (Swing/JClient for BC4J)	This displays the JClient Panel Wizard, which creates a class based on JClientPanel that presents fields and prompts for a specified view object.
Panel (Swing/AWT)	This displays the New Panel dialog, which creates a class file based on the JPanel component.
Panel with Graph	This displays the JClient Graph Wizard based on JClientPanel that displays a graph (in one of six formats) for a view object.
PL/SQL Program	This displays the New PL/SQL Procedure dialog, which creates a skeleton code unit in the Oracle database.
PL/SQL Web Service	This displays the PL/SQL Web Service Publishing Wizard, which generates the deployment descriptor and WSDL document required to publish PL/SQL stored procedures as a web service.
Project Configured for a New Web Module	This displays the Project with Web Module Wizard, which creates a project with Java and HTML paths set for directories that you specify in the wizard.
Project Configured for Remote Debugging and Profiling	This displays the Remote Debugging and Profiling Project Wizard, which creates a project set up for remote debugging. Remote debugging allows you to run the JDeveloper debugger on project files that are running outside of JDeveloper.
Project Containing a New Application	This displays Application Project Wizard, which creates a project and then runs the New Application dialog, which creates a Java application file. The New Application dialog allows you to add a frame class to the project by running the New Frame dialog.
Project Containing New Business Components	This displays the Business Components Project Wizard, which creates a project for BC4J objects. This wizard automatically launches the Business Components Package Wizard.

Item Name	Description
Project from an Existing WAR (.war) File	This displays the Project from War File Wizard, which creates a project using the contents of an existing Web Archive (WAR) file. The WAR file packages the application and the associated files for deployment purposes.
Project from Existing Source Code	This displays the Project from Existing Source Wizard, which creates a project and allows you to specify the files to include in the project.
Property Editor	This displays the Property Editor dialog, which creates a skeleton Java file that will make it easier to manipulate JavaBean properties.
Query Form	This displays the Data Page Wizard, which creates a JSP page that allows the user to search in and view results of the search for a specific BC4J view object.
Servlet Filter	This displays the Servlet Filter Wizard, which creates a Java file that you can supplement to modify the request to a servlet or to perform some action before or after the servlet is run.
Servlet Listener	This displays the Listener Wizard, which creates code that you can supplement to monitor and react to events that occur in a servlet.
Session Bean	This displays the Enterprise JavaBean Wizard, which creates an Enterprise Java Bean to implement business methods and manage the server session from a user interface.
SOAP Server Connection	This displays the SOAP Server Connection Wizard, which creates a definition for a Simple Object Access Protocol (SOAP) host and user.
SQL File	This displays the New SQL File dialog, which allows you to create an empty file to which you will add SQL statements.
SQLJ Class	This displays the New SQLJ Class dialog, which creates a skeleton Java class file to which you can add SQLJ code. Optionally, you can select public, constructor, and/or main method attributes in this dialog.
Starter Application	This displays a confirmation dialog that will add properties and configuration files to a project so that the project can be used for Struts application files.
Starter Data Page	This displays the Starter Data Page Wizard, which creates a skeleton JSP that is linked to a view object in the client data model.
Struts Starter Page	This displays the Struts Starter Page Wizard, which creates a JSP page that uses the Struts framework to access a BC4J client data model.

Item Name	Description
Table	This displays the Create Table Wizard, which creates a database table in the selected schema including storage parameters and tablespace definitions.
Taglib JAR File – Tag Library for JSP	This displays the Save Deployment Profile – Taglib JAR File – Tag Library for JSP dialog, which creates a deployment (.deploy) file for a JSP tag library.
Trigger	This displays the Create Trigger Wizard, which adds a PL/SQL trigger to the database in the schema selected in the dialog.
UDDI Registry Connection	This displays the UDDI Registry Connection Wizard, which creates a definition for a Universal Description, Discovery and Integration (UDDI) host from which you can obtain web services.
UIX JSP Browse & Edit Form	This displays the Data Page Wizard, which creates one JSP form for browsing records in a view object and another JSP form for modifying the records in that view object.
UIX JSP Browse Form (with Hide/Show)	This displays the Data Page Wizard, which creates a form to browse existing records in a view object and to allow you to toggle UINodes on the form to be hidden or shown.
UIX JSP Starter Page	This displays the Data Page Wizard, which creates a UIX JSP page including application module information, data source, and default layout tags.
uiXML Browse & Edit Form	This displays the uiXML Browse and Edit Form Wizard, which creates uiXML pages to view and modify data in a single BC4J view object.
uiXML Page	This displays the New uiXML Page dialog, which creates a simple uiXML page.
uiXML Page Based on Existing uiXML Template (UIT)	This displays the uiXML Template (UIT) Customizer Wizard, which creates a uiXML page based on a UIT (template) file that you created with the uiXML Template (UIT) Wizard.
uiXML Page with Header, Footer, and Navigation	This displays the uiXML Page Wizard, which creates a uiXML file with built-in layout elements for navigation and header and footer sections.
uiXML Template (UIT)	This displays the New uiXML Template (UIT) dialog to create a blank uiXML template that you can use as a starting point for uiXML pages.

Item Name	Description
uiXML Template (UIT) with Header, Footer, and Navigation	This displays the uiXML Template (UIT) Wizard to create a uiXML template that you can use as a starting point for uiXML. This template contains some default elements for tabs and navigation buttons as well as header and footer definitions.
User	This displays the New Database User dialog, which creates a database user account. The connection user that is active when you open the New gallery must have administrator privileges to enable this item.
View	This displays the Create View dialog, which adds a view object to the selected schema folder or JDBC database connetion object.
View Link	This displays the View Link Wizard, which creates a view link that forms a relationship between two view objects or between a view object and itself.
View Object	This displays the View Object Wizard, which creates a view object that represents a SQL query.
WAR File – J2EE Web Module	This displays the Save Deployment Profile – WAR File – J2EE Web Module dialog that creates a deployment (.deploy) file for a J2EE Web Application Archive (WAR) file.
Web Bean	This displays the New Web Bean dialog, which creates a .java file. You can use this file to create a class that you can call from a JSP useBean tag.
Web Deployment Descriptor	This automatically generates a web.xml file that includes J2EE web deployment information.
Web Deployment Descriptor for OC4J (orion-web.xml)	This automatically generates a skeleton orion-web.xml descriptor file that you can use to specify OC4J deployment information.
Web Deployment Descriptor for WebLogic (weblogic.xml)	This automatically generates a skeleton weblogic.xml descriptor file that you can use to specify BEA WebLogic deployment information.
Web Service Stub/Skeleton	This displays the Web Service Stub/Skeleton Wizard, which generates a Java stub that calls a web service and a Java skeleton that implements a web service. The wizard requires a WSDL document as input.

Item Name	Description
Workspace	This displays the New Workspace dialog, which creates a JDeveloper workspace that contains a specific set of projects. This dialog allows you to create a project using the *Add a New Empty Project* checkbox.
WSDL Document	This displays the New WSDL Document dialog, which creates an XML file that describes the location and calling interface for web services.
XML Document	This displays the New XML File dialog, which creates a blank .xml file in your project.
XML Schema	This displays the New XML Schema file dialog, which creates an .xsd file that defines a set of XML tags.
XSL Stylesheet	This displays the New XSL File dialog, which allows you to create an .xsl file that provides a display format for data in your XML files.
XSQL Page	This automatically adds a skeleton.xsql file to your project. XSQL files allow you to embed SQL statements inside an XML file.

APPENDIX
B

Other Resources

I concluded that he laughed in derision of my efforts, confident of his own resources.
—Henry David Thoreau (1817–1862), *Walden*

 sing JDeveloper effectively requires many resources beyond those available from Oracle and this book. While the following is by no means a comprehensive list, the authors have found these resources to be helpful when working in the JDeveloper environment.

Books

The following books are useful references when working with JDeveloper:

- *The Java Tutorial: A Short Course on the Basics, Third Edition,* Mary Campione and Kathy Walrath, Addison-Wesley, 2000.

- *The Java Tutorial, Continued,* Campione, Walrath, Huml, et al., Addison-Wesley, 1998.

- *The JFC Swing Tutorial: A Guide to Constructing GUIs,* Kathy Walrath and Mary Campione, Addison-Wesley, 1999.

- *Oracle8 Design Using UML Object Modeling,* Paul Dorsey and Joseph Hudicka, Oracle Press, 1998.

- *Java 2: The Complete Reference, Fifth Edition,* Herbert Schildt, Osborne McGraw-Hill, 2002.

- *Refactoring: Improving the Design of Existing Code,* Martin Fowler et al., Addison-Wesley, 1999.

Websites

Free online resources are readily available from the originators of the languages (Java, HTML, JavaScript). The following websites have information that can assist you in your development efforts in JDeveloper:

URL	Website Description
developer.netscape.com/tech/javascript	Netscape JavaScript developer's website.
java.sun.com	Sun Microsystems website (Java and JSP tags).
java.sun.com/docs/books/tutorial	Sun website location for the *Java Tutorial,* which provides an introduction to the language. It is the online version of the book listed earlier and is downloadable so that you can run it without being connected to the Internet.
java.sun.com/features/1998/05/birthday.html	Information about the release announcement of the Java language.

URL	Website Description
java.sun.com/j2ee/ java.sun.com/j2se/ java.sun.com/j2me/	Sun website information about Java 2 Platform, Enterprise Edition; Java 2 Platform, Standard Edition; and Java 2 Platform, Micro Edition, respectively.
java.sun.com/products/javawebstart/ java.sun.com/products/plugin/	Sun website information about plugins for Java Web Start and browser Swing class support, respectively.
java.sun.com/products/jlf/ed1/dg/higm.htm	Sun website information about menus and toolbars in Java applications and applets.
java.sun.com/products/jsp/	Sun website information about JavaServer Pages.
otn.oracle.com	Oracle Technology Network, which includes white papers, how-tos, sample code, and documentation that serve as valuable reference material.
www.ioug.org	Website of the International Oracle Users Group, which contains discussion forums and a technical repository of tips and white papers from users of Oracle technology.
www.odtug.com	Website for the Oracle Development Tools User Group, which contains a page to sign up for list serves as well as presentations and white papers from conferences focused on Oracle development tools.
www.omg.org	Website for the Object Management Group, who developed and provide specifications for UML and other object-oriented technologies.
www.opensource.org	The website for Open Source Initiative, which promotes the concept of free access to source code, no-cost licenses, and the ability for others to extend products that are built upon open source concepts.
www.rational.com	Contains a full discussion of UML and all of its diagrams; see the UML Documentation on the Rational website.
www.sys-con.com/java/	Java Developer's Journal website, which contains numerous archived articles from past issues of the printed version of this popular journal.
www.theserverside.com	A news source and developer community centered around J2EE and middleware issues.

URL	Website Description
www.w3c.org	The website for the World Wide Web Consortium (W3C), who developed and maintain standards for, among others, the HTML and Cascading Style Sheets languages.

Many websites offer information about building computer applications with Java and other technologies. Use your favorite web search engine to gain access to these websites. However, always consider the source and reliability of the information.

APPENDIX
C

UML Class
Diagram Syntax

Class isn't something you buy. Look at you.
You have a $500 suit on and you're still a lowlife.

—Roger Spottiswoode, *48 Hours* (1983)

o use the JDeveloper Class Modeler, it is important to be familiar with some of the basic Unified Modeling Language (UML) class modeling diagram conventions and concepts. More information about the Class Modeler and a hands-on practice can be found in Chapters 8 and 11.

Even though UML class diagrams superficially resemble Entity Relationship Diagrams (ERDs), they do not necessarily represent the same types of objects. ERDs have only been used to act as logical representations of relational tables. Logical data modelers may assert that ERDs do not even explicitly represent these tables.

However, UML class diagrams are most often used to represent Java classes. A class diagram is merely a picture. Currently, in JDeveloper, a class diagram can represent Java classes, BC4J entity objects, web services, and Enterprise JavaBeans (EJBs). In the future, JDeveloper will likely use class diagrams to model database objects just as ERDs are used in Oracle Designer.

Classes

Those familiar with Entity Relationship Diagrams and relational modeling can think of a class as equivalent to an entity. *Classes* represent things of interest in a system or represent abstractions of things of interest. In an ERD, entities and instances of entities translate into tables and rows. In UML, classes and objects within the class are similar to the associated elements in ERDs, although they may translate into different types of components. Just like entities, classes also have attributes.

Attributes

Class attributes look and behave in a way similar to entity attributes. They both represent elemental pieces of information about the object or entity instance. Attributes can be required, and the values are restricted by a domain.

Associations

Associations link classes to one another. They are similar to relationships in ERDs. In ERDs, the typical notation includes naming both sides of the relationship. For example, a one-to-many relationship between Department and Employee would be modeled in an ERD as shown here:

The relationship in an ERD is read in a bidirectional way. For example, the association shown in this diagram means that each employee must work for one and only one department, and each department may employ any number of (or no) employees.

In UML, the situation is different. Typically, UML associations are named with a single verb phrase that is unidirectional. The diagram shown here would be used to represent the same relationship in UML:

Association Roles

In addition, in UML, you can also place nouns called *association roles* on the ends of the association. The association itself is typically named with a verb and preposition.

As mentioned in *The UML Notation Guide OMG UML v.1.3,* the end of the association indicates "the role played by the class attached to the end of the path near the role name." This concept of a role works well in many cases. For example, between Department and Person, for the employment association between the two using the full UML notation, you would create the diagram shown here:

This diagram reads as follows: "The department acting as employer may employ any number of persons acting as employees. An employee need not work for any department." However, you could just as easily have written the same relationship with the arrow going in the opposite direction, as shown next, from the employee's perspective and calling the association "works for." For example, the association would read: "Any number of employees may work for a department. An employee need not work for any department."

This notational scheme holds up fairly well. However, sometimes it is difficult to determine the appropriate word or words to describe the roles of the objects.

Naming Associations

Usually, using a single verb phrase (without roles) is enough to name an association. For example, an association between Person and Committee classes could be named "member of" with no role descriptors on the ends of the association at all. However, to use full UML syntax with this example, you might use a diagram like the following.

Which naming of the association would make the most sense in this case? *The UML Notation Guide* suggestion with the simple "member of" name seems much clearer than using the full notational standard. The sentence "Any number of persons acting as members may belong to any number of committees when acting as committees" is certainly no clearer than the sentence "Any number of persons can be members of any number of committees." On one hand, a consistent set of standards should be used to name associations. On the other hand, the purpose of naming the associations is to effectively communicate the data-related business rules. The ultimate test of whether an association is adequately named is whether the diagram communicates the association accurately to whoever is working with it.

The authors recommend using an *association phrase* consisting of a noun or verb followed by a preposition, for example, "works for."

Additionally, if required to enhance the clarity of the diagram, use roles on the association ends. Note that in using this association phrase in the case of a one-to-many association, it is usually more descriptive to name the association from the child (many) side to the parent (one) class. For example, to describe the Dept/Emp example, "works for" usually is easier to understand than "employer of."

You may use role names even if the logical naming of the association does not require them. This convention is very useful to adopt in JDeveloper since there is no way to indicate the directionality of the association verb phrase in the tool. The arrowheads on association lines in JDeveloper can be on both sides of the line and usually refer to the visibility of accessors. It should be noted that this suggestion is only for the "logical" description of the association. Various products (including JDeveloper) use these names to specify parts of the generated code. When using UML in JDeveloper's Class Modeler as a code generator, you need to know exactly how each element will be used and what kind of code it will generate.

Association Cardinality (Multiplicity)

Association *cardinality* (also called *multiplicity*) syntax (which describes how many instances or objects of one side occur for how many objects of the other side) is quite different from that of ERDs. UML cardinality notation goes back to the original ERD notation as specified in *The Entity Relationship Model—Toward A Unified View of Data* by Peter Pin-Shan Chen (ACM Transactions on Database Systems, Vol. 1, No. 1, March 1976). In this paper, Chen explained that the number of objects in each class that can be associated with each other is explicitly declared.

In UML, basic associations are also drawn differently than they are in ERDs. A standard mandatory one-to-many association (where the "many" side must have one and only one of the "one" side entities) is drawn as shown here in UML and ERD:

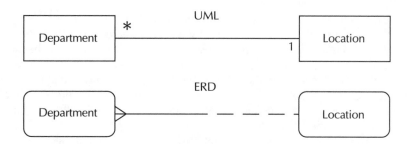

An optional one-to-many association would be drawn as follows in UML notation. The "0" shows that the side is optional.

This notation will take some getting used to for experienced relational database modelers since the visual indication for a normal one-to-many mandatory relationship occurs on the "one" side in UML rather than on the "many" side in ERDs.

Close Associations

An association indicates that one object has a link to another object. It does not tell anything about the nature of that link. Sometimes it is useful to model a tighter association between objects. You might want to say that one object is part of another, or that an object is partially defined by its associations to other objects. Such associations between classes are called *close associations* to distinguish them from regular associations.

From a modeling perspective, the association between a purchase order and a purchase order detail is quite different from the association between a project and an employee who is acting as project manager. In the purchase order/purchase order detail case, it does not make sense to have a purchase order detail without a purchase order. The detail is part of the parent object. A purchase is, to some extent, defined by its details. The details indicate what was purchased. In addition, details about purchase orders never move from one purchase order to another.

The association between a project and its project manager is quite different. Projects are independent objects. They are of interest to the organization regardless of who manages them. A project is not defined by who the manager is; and managers can easily be replaced on projects. Similarly, project managers are simply employees who, as one of their roles, can act as a manager of a project. An employee can also have other roles. An employee need not even be associated with any project and can manage several projects at once.

The relationship between a purchase order and its purchase order details is an example of a *close association,* because the child cannot exist without the parent. That is, they are closely related. From an implementation perspective, close associations are interesting because items that are close associations may have different requirements. Objects built from closely associated classes should be retrieved together, so they should be stored in such a way that makes retrieval of those objects efficient. Once a class is closely associated, you may want to prevent the changing of that link or to create, update, and delete closely associated objects together, so having them stored as some kind of grouped object makes sense.

The next sections will review dependent relationships from relational theory. Next, the concepts of aggregation and composition as they are used in the UML will be explained.

Dependent Associations

An association from ERDs is used when the child object (in this case the purchase order detail) is dependent upon the parent object (in this case the purchase order) as shown here using UML syntax. "Dependent" means that the child object has no meaning outside of the context of the parent object.

Dependent associations are primarily used in two contexts. The first is illustrated by the purchase order/purchase order detail example. Whenever there is a line item on a document (or something similar), it is modeled using a dependent association.

The second place that such associations are frequently used is with intersection entities that arise from many-to-many associations. Instances of intersection entities have no meaning without their parent objects, so a dependent association is appropriate. For example, it does not make any sense to talk about an enrollment of a Student in a Course Offering without knowing who the Student is and what Course he or she is taking. This association is shown here in ERD format (the UML form is discussed later in this appendix). Note that an entity may be dependent upon more than one parent entity.

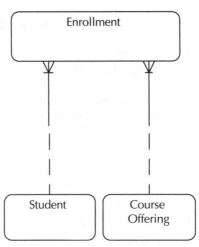

The way in which the dependence association is typically implemented is by making the primary key of the master table (for example, Enrollment just shown) part of the primary key of the detail table (Course Offering). This means that the Course Offering is "dependent" on the Enrollment. Using the UML, there are two different types of close associations between object classes:

- Aggregation (sometimes called "weak aggregation")
- Composition (sometimes called "strong aggregation")

Composition and *aggregation* are new concepts for ER modelers and will require careful explanation. In entity relationship modeling, one entity being closely related to another is expressed in the dependent relationship represented by a UID bar on the relationship in an ERD, as shown here:

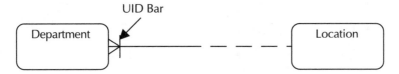

Aggregation

In the UML *aggregation* association, objects from one class collectively define the objects in the aggregation class. Class A is said to be an aggregation of class B if an object in class A is defined as a collection of objects from class B. Objects from class B need not be attached to any object from class A. The classic example of this kind of association is the one between a committee and a person, in that a committee is made up of the people on the committee. A committee can be defined as a collection of people.

Aggregation does not correspond to any concept in entity relationship modelling. This is a new concept of a relationship that is much weaker than the dependency relationship. Aggregation means that the two classes are more strongly related than a simple association, but they can still exist independently.

In the relational dependent relationship, the child object cannot be thought of outside the context of its parent. In aggregation, the parent usually cannot be thought of outside the context of its children. The aggregation is represented by an unfilled diamond in UML. Some classic examples of aggregation relationships in UML are shown here:

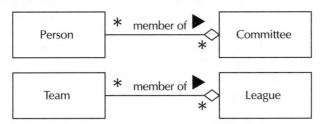

The other aspect of an aggregation association is that the details (Person and Team in these examples) have relevance outside of the context of their masters (Committee and League).

Sometimes, aggregation is used because of a unique workflow. One system encountered by one of the authors included some government contract change requests. These requests came

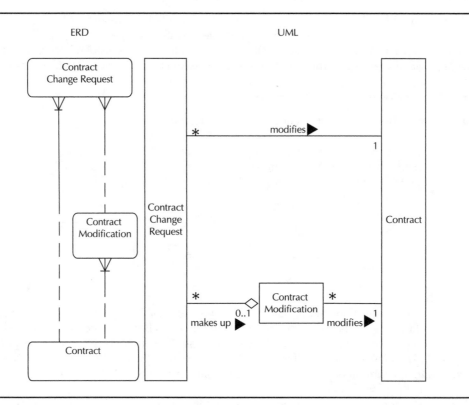

FIGURE C-1. *Aggregation example in ERD and UML formats*

in individually over an extended period and were eventually bundled together into a contract modification, as shown in Figure C-1.

The structure shown in Figure C-1 can be used in a similar situation. A system must be versioned, and system enhancement requests are received over time. These must be prioritized and associated with a particular system version. The appropriate model is shown in Figure C-2 in both ERD and UML formats. Note that it is still important to show multiplicity (cardinality in an ER world) when using aggregations.

If you show an aggregation in your class model, what does this mean for the generated structure? This is a difficult question to answer. The child object is closely associated with the apparent object, but may also exist independently. Depending upon the context in which the UML class model is used, there may or may not be any implementation impact.

Directed aggregations in JDeveloper refer to making accessors visible and are shown by placing an arrowhead on the association.

Composition
Composition (also called "strong aggregation") is similar to aggregation. Class A is said to be a *composition* of class B if each object of class B is a part of an object of class A. Objects of class B

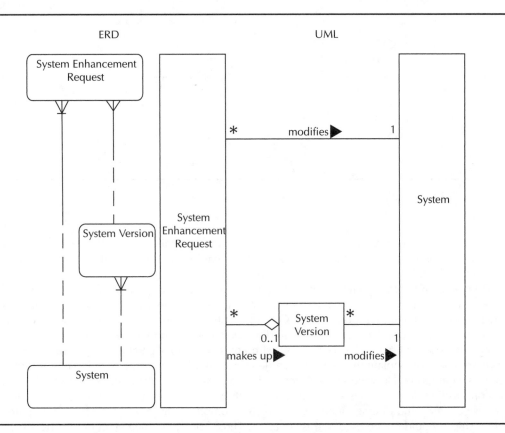

FIGURE C-2. *System enhancement request model in ERD and UML formats*

may not exist unless they are part of a specific object from class A. Class B objects may not exist independently. An object from class B may not be a composition child of more than one object at a time, whether it is from class A or another class. In an aggregation association, the master is composed of its details, but the details can be independent of the master. In a composition association, the master is still composed of the details, but these details cannot be thought of outside the context of the master. The dependency examples of PO and PO Detail can be used to illustrate this, as shown in the ERD and UML diagrams in Figure C-3.

The formal rule in the UML is that the detail can exist independently of the master until it is attached to a master. However, from that point forward, the detail must always be associated with some master. The distinction suggested here between aggregation and composition is a more restrictive condition than required by the formal UML syntax, but is more logically clean and consistent with the way in which databases interact with these constructs.

The definition of composition is similar to the dependency relationship in ERDs, but a bit more restrictive than ERD dependency.

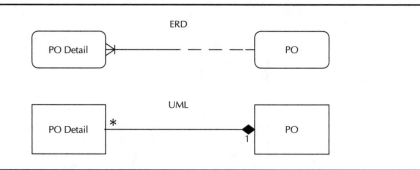

FIGURE C-3. *Simple composition association*

Composition is only used to indicate that objects in the detail object class always belong to one and only one master and have no independent meaning apart from that master. Therefore, PO/PO Detail association is a good example of composition.

Composition in UML is slightly more restrictive than dependency in an ERD. For example, in an ERD you might want to say that a Course at a university is dependent upon the Department where it is offered. Furthermore, specific Offerings of this course are dependent upon the Course, as shown in Figure C-4. However, this would not be a composition in the UML.

Notice how the UML in Figure C-4 uses simple association. Actually, using composition in this case would not violate the composition definition in UML, nor would it violate our more restrictive definition. However, in practice, object-oriented designers only use composition when the composition detail objects are created and destroyed at the same time as the parent object. Because Courses and Course Offerings are created completely independently from their parents, composition should not be used in this situation. Thus, from an implementation perspective, you might want to use composition even though UML tradition would argue against it.

Generalization

The generalization association is a concept similar to that of a supertype/subtype relationship in an ERD. For example, an Employee can be either hourly or salaried as shown in this ERD:

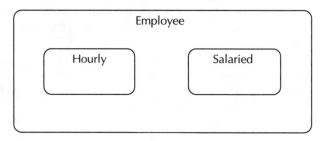

In UML, the same concept can be represented as shown here:

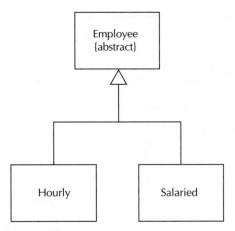

This UML diagram indicates that you have an Employee class. The "{*abstract*}" constraint indicates that the class cannot have any independent objects. (Constraints are described later in

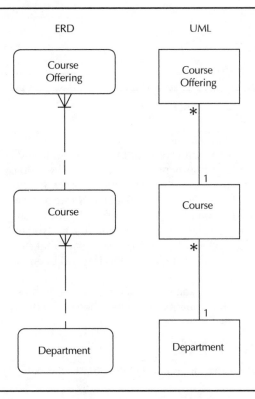

FIGURE C-4.   *Composition (UML) Dependency (ERD) comparison*

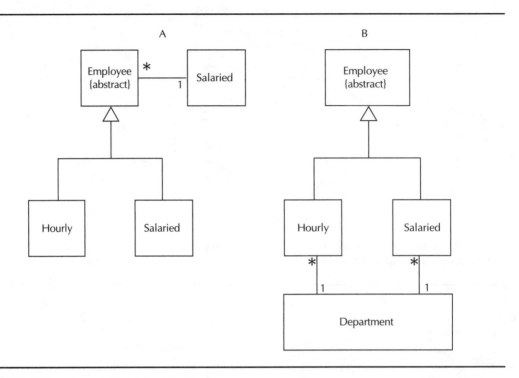

FIGURE C-5. *Association inheritance*

this appendix.) If the abstract constraint were omitted, this would indicate that it is possible to have an employee who is neither hourly nor salaried. Since the employee class cannot have any objects, what is its purpose? If there are attributes defined for the Employee class, they are inherited by the Hourly and Salaried classes. For example, a First Name and Last Name attribute defined for the Employee class would automatically be inherited by the Hourly and Salaried classes.

Associations to the Employee class are also inherited. An association between Employee and Department as shown in diagram A of Figure C-5 also means that the salaried and hourly classes inherit the association to the department class just as if it had been drawn as shown in diagram B of Figure C-5.

Methods are also inherited. For example, defined methods such as "Hire," "Fire," or "Give Raise" in the Employee class would automatically be inherited by the Hourly and Salaried classes.

Extending the UML

UML is explicitly extensible using three different constructs: stereotypes, constraints, and keywords.

Stereotypes

Stereotypes designated by these guillemets << >> symbols extend or redefine an element. Users can create their own stereotypes to alter or extend the semantics of the UML. JDeveloper uses stereotypes to indicate what a class represents, such as a BC4J entity, Java class, or Java interface.

Constraints

Constraints designated with curly brackets ({ }) limit the functionality of the UML object. There are native constraints defined by the UML such as the {or} constraint for connecting associations or the {abstract} constraint on classes (as shown in Figure C-5). Users may define additional constraints such as:

- ■ **{singleton}**   A class may only have a single object in it.
- ■ **{history}**   Objects in the class may be logically deleted but not removed.

Keywords (Tagged Values)

Keywords are a notational way of representing metamodel names. Tagged values are what the user/architect defines in a profile. Keywords are the user-defined properties of an object. They allow you to extend an object by adding a descriptor (with or without a value) to an object. Keywords look the same as constraints (they use curly brackets).

Properties of classes not supported by standard UML could be represented as keywords. If you wanted to generate the entity object class "Employee" to the table EMP, you could use a table keyword with the value EMP as shown here:

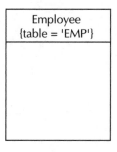

Employee
{table = 'EMP'}

TIP
For more information about UML, visit the Object Management Group website: www.omg.org.

Interfaces and Realizations

The notions of interfaces and realizations (classes implement interfaces) are primarily object-oriented Java/C++ coding elements and are not typically part of logical class models. They are discussed in Chapter 4.

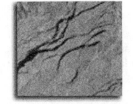

APPENDIX
D

Overview of HTML and Cascading Style Sheets

*An author arrives at a good style
when his language performs
what is required of it without shyness.*

—Cyril Connolly, (1903–1974), *Enemies of Promise*

ork with JSP pages and other browser-centric technologies requires skills with Hypertext Markup Language (HTML) and often with the cascading style sheet language. This appendix introduces these subjects in case you are unfamiliar with the concepts. A complete discussion of these subjects is the topic of entire books and websites. You can refer to those sources for additional and more complete information. The discussion in this appendix is intended to start you thinking about the subjects with an assumption that you will continue to study them using other resources.

HTML

HTML is a tag language. "Hypertext" in the name of the language refers to the ability to click a word or phrase and open a new page. You navigate hypertext pages in a nonlinear way as your interest dictates. This navigation method differs from the linear way in which you read printed information such as this book. "Markup" in the name of the language refers to the process of adding tags to plain text. The tags are separated from the text with angled brackets ("<" and ">"), and each tag designates a specific format for the text within it.

HTML is a product of the World Wide Web Consortium (W3C), and complete information about the language, including links to tutorials and examples, is available on the W3C website, www.w3c.org.

Editing HTML

HTML files are standard ASCII text files that you can edit using any text editor. Many visual HTML editors allow you to view and modify the page as it will look when it is presented in the browser. Macromedia Dreamweaver and Microsoft FrontPage are two popular visual HTML editors. A number of low-cost shareware editors are also available; a quick search on the Web will give you a starting point for such shareware. In addition, some standard word processing tools, such as Microsoft Word, will save files in an HTML format and allow rudimentary visual editing. However, dedicated HTML editors are usually the best choice.

HTML Tags

HTML tags are usually paired to have a starting tag and an ending tag, inside of which you embed text or other content (such as graphics or JavaScript). The starting and ending tags have the same name and are distinguished with the ending tag containing a slash "/." For example, the starting tag used to apply the bold style to text is "<b>," and the ending tag is "</b>." The tag delimiters "< >" set the tag apart from the text that is inside it. The tag name is not case sensitive, so "<B>" is the same as "<b>." Tags define how the browser should display the content as shown here:

```
<b>This is bold. </b>This is not bold.
```

The browser will interpret the <b> tag and display everything between it and the matching closing tag </b> in boldface as in the following illustration:

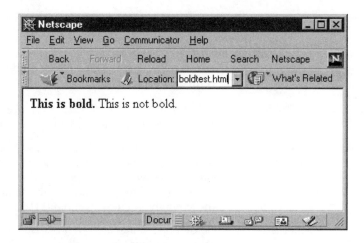

Table D-1 lists some common tags, roughly in the order in which they would appear in a file. An example containing these tags appears later in Figure D-1. As mentioned, tags are not case sensitive, so "<b>" and "<B>" will produce the same results.

Opening Tag	Ending Tag	Purpose
<html>	</html>	Declares the beginning and end of the page. Anything outside of these tags will not be placed on the page.
<head>	</head>	Page heading that will not print on the page. This section of the page can contain code such as JavaScript and a reference to the cascading style sheet. The text in this section is not printed on the page.
<title>	</title>	Displays the text inside the tags as the window title. It is placed inside the page heading "<head>" tags.
<body>	</body>	Anything inside these tags is treated as display content for the page.
<h1>	</h1>	Heading level 1, which displays text in a larger font. There are also <h2> through <h6> tags (with corresponding closing tags) for nested heading levels. You can align the heading (left, right, or center) with the ALIGN attribute.
<p>	</p> (optional)	The paragraph tag. Hard returns in HTML code are ignored, so you need to define the return by enclosing the text in paragraph tags (or by placing a "<p>" at the end of the paragraph).

TABLE D-I. *Common HTML Tags*

Opening Tag	Ending Tag	Purpose
` `	(none)	Inserts a line break. Line breaks insert a smaller vertical space between lines than do paragraph tags.
`<b>`	`</b>`	Displays the text in boldface.
`<i>`	`</i>`	Displays the text in italics.
`<a>`	`</a>`	An anchor that links to another file, page, or location on the same page. The most common attribute for this tag is `href`, which defines a hyperlink to another page or to another location on the same page as shown in the section "Sample HTML Code."
`<!--`	`-->`	Comments, which are not processed. Comments, as well as other tags, are displayed when the user selects View Source from the right-click menu on the browser page.
`<ul>`	`</ul>`	An unordered list. These tags surround a list of paragraphs that are bulleted and surrounded by a `<li></li>` (list item) tag pair. Use `<ol>` and `</ol>` for an "ordered list," where list items are numbered.
`<hr>`	`</hr>` (optional)	A hard rule (horizontal line). Code in the section "Sample HTML Code" shows two `<hr>` attributes: `align` and `width`.

TABLE D-1. *Common HTML Tags* (continued)

NOTE
Extra spaces in the body section are ignored. For example, three spaces between letters are compressed to one space. You can specify the display of a space character using the special character reference " " (nonbreaking space). There are other special characters called "character entity references" that you can use to display symbols such as "<" (less than), ">" (greater than), and "&" (ampersand). The special characters are "<", ">", and "&", respectively.

Attributes

Many tags have documented *attributes* that refine how the tag is interpreted. Attributes appear in the opening tag just before the closing ">". For example, the heading tag "<h1 align=center>" contains an align attribute that signals the browser to center the heading text within the browser window. When the window width is changed, the text is re-centered within the new size. The attributes for each tag are documented in the HTML language reference manuals available on the Web or in many books.

The HTML Form

The *HTML form* is a construct that allows users to input values and click a Submit or Reset button. It is a standard HTML feature and does not require a processing language. Form tags contain input fields and buttons. When a button is clicked, the form information is sent to the process or procedure defined in the form tag. The form is useful for HTML pages that accept input from the user (for example, an edit or input page). A page can contain more than one form.

> **NOTE**
> *Different versions of HTML offer different tags and attributes. The W3C website discusses HTML versions (www.w3.org/MarkUp/ #previous) and the elements available for each.*

Sample HTML Code

The following is a sample of HTML code that demonstrates the tags in Table D-1:

```
<html>
  <head>
    <title>Sample HTML Tags</title>
  </head>
  <body>
    <h1 align=center>Samples of Basic HTML Tags</h1>
    The font for plain body text depends on the browser settings.
    <b>This is bold. </b>
    <i>This is italic. </i>This is not.
    <b><i>This is both.</b></i>

    <p>New paragraph before this sentence.<br>Line break before this sentence.

    <br>Extra spaces            without special characters are ignored.
```

```
   <p>Line breaks
   in
   the code are ignored.
   <p>

   <!-- A comment: the anchor tag has several attributes.
       HREF is one -->
   JDeveloper is a product of
   <a href="http://www.oracle.com">Oracle Corporation.</a>

   <hr width=80% align=center />
   <b>Unordered List</b>
   <ul>
       <li>An item in a list </li>
       <li>Another item in a list </li>
       <li>Yet another item in a list </li>
   </ul>
 </body>
</html>
```

Notice that the `<hr>` tag does not surround text, so it can be closed within the opening tag using the "/" character preceded by a space. The `<hr>` line is equivalent to "`<hr width=80% align=center></hr>`." As with any programming language, you can indent HTML code to show its structure. This makes the code more readable and maintainable. Since the browser will ignore hard returns and extra spaces, the code formatting will not be displayed.

Figure D-1 shows how this code will display in the browser.

CAUTION
Some browsers may format a page improperly if a tag that can be closed is not closed. Therefore, it is good programming practice to write closing tags for all tags that can be closed even if the closing tag is optional.

JavaScript in HTML

You can extend the functionality of HTML by embedding code written in *JavaScript,* an object-based scripting language created by Netscape but supported in all browsers. For example, you can use JavaScript to perform data validation on the client side, which saves network traffic. Although it is beyond the scope of this book to describe any of the basics of JavaScript, the following sample will help you become familiar with what JavaScript looks like. You will then be able to recognize it in the code that JDeveloper creates. As mentioned earlier, the Web is an

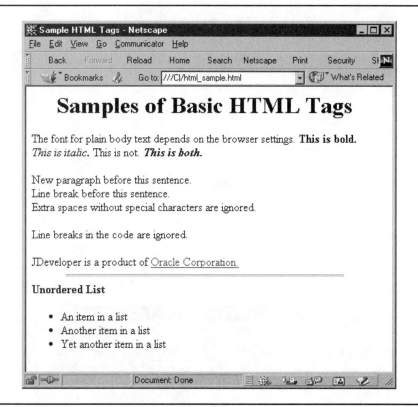

FIGURE D-1.   *Output of sample HTML code*

excellent source of information. Start with the JavaScript pages on the Netscape JavaScript developer's website, developer.netscape.com/tech/javascript.

```
<html>
<head>
  <script language="JavaScript">
  <!--
  function checkRequired(which) {
    if (which.fname.value == '') {
      alert("The Name field is required.");
      return false;
```

```
      }
    else {
      alert("The Name = \"" + which.fname.value +"\"");
      which.fname.value = which.fname.value.toUpperCase();
      return true;
      }
    }
  -->
  </script>
</head>

<body>
  <form onsubmit="return checkRequired(this)">
  First Name:  <input type="text" name="fname">
  <p><input type=submit value="Save">
  </form>
</body>
</html>
```

The HTML tags in the body section display a label, a text item, and a button, as shown here:

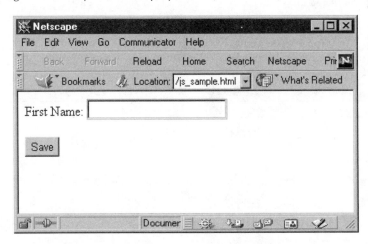

In this example, the source code for JavaScript appears in a comment in the heading section. Alternatively, you can refer to a central JavaScript source code file in the heading using the script tag as shown in the following example:

```
<script src="jdevscript.js" language="JavaScript"></script>
```

In the preceding example, the `<form>` tag defines the form as well as what happens when the button that is labeled "Save" (and defined by the "`input type=submit`" tag) is clicked. When the button is clicked, the JavaScript function `checkRequired()`, defined in a comment in the page header, is executed. If a value is input into the field, the `checkRequired()` function converts the value to uppercase and returns a Boolean true; the submit feature of the form calls the page again and passes it a parameter of the field value. (This value will appear in the URL.)

If no value is input, the `checkRequired()` function displays an error message and returns a Boolean false; the form is not submitted in this case. This demonstrates one way that JavaScript is defined and called, but you will need to consult a JavaScript reference for further information.

CAUTION

As with HTML, JavaScript is not supported equally by all browsers, and it is important to test your application using the same browsers that your users will employ to access your application. If you do not know which browsers your users have, you need to test your application in both Netscape and Internet Explorer—the two most popular browsers. This is good advice to follow even if you do not use JavaScript because even HTML is not handled equally by all browsers.

Cascading Style Sheets

A cascading style sheet provides another way of extending HTML by enabling a set of common definitions to serve many uses within an HTML document. A *cascading style sheet* (CSS) is a set of named style definitions each of which has a list of visual attributes. The styles can be applied to text or tags in the HTML document to change the default appearance presented by the browser. You can define styles that change the appearance of a tag every time it appears in the page. You can also define styles that you can explicitly apply to a tag when needed. These styles can be limited to a particular tag or set of tags or can be *global* styles that are available to all tags.

The cascading style sheet styles can be embedded in the page heading of each HTML file. They can also be placed in a separate file (normally with a .css extension) that can be used by many pages. JDeveloper uses the separate file strategy because it is the most flexible and maintainable for multi-page applications. That strategy also reduces the size of the HTML page.

The JDeveloper sample .css files (bc4j.css and blaf.css) are located in the JDEV_HOME\ jdev\system\templates\common\misc directory (where JDEV_HOME is the JDeveloper installation directory, for example, C:\JDev9i). Each style sheet has a different set of fonts and colors.

Building a Cascading Style Sheet

A cascading style sheet is a standard ASCII text file that you can edit using a text editor. Some HTML editing tools provide assistance with this task and allow you to view samples of the style as you are editing it. There are also dedicated CSS editors such as TopStyle Lite (www.bradsoft .com).

A cascading style sheet allows you to define and name a set of attributes that you want to apply to HTML tags. The following is a sample of a small cascading style sheet file:

```
<!--
/*
||   demo.css style sheet
*/
```

```
H2 {
  font-family: Arial;
  font-style: italic;
  color: BLUE;
}

BODY
{
  background-color:#DDDDDD;
}

.emphasis
{
  color: black;
  font-weight: bold;
  font-style: italic;
}

P.codeText{
  font-family: Courier;
  color: BLACK;
  font-weight: BOLD;
  font-size: 10pt;
}

TH {
  color:WHITE;
  background-color:#888888;
  font-weight: BOLD;
}

TD {
  color:BLACK;
  background-color:WHITE;
}
-->
```

This example defines a global style: emphasis. The name of a *global style* is preceded by a ".", which means that the style may be applied to any tag.

You can also define styles for standard HTML tags (such as H2, BODY, TH, and TD in the example) so that each time the tag is used, the style will be applied. This simplifies the HTML coding a great deal because you do not have to keep applying the same style to the same tag. In the preceding example, the <h2> and <body> tags will always be shown with the styles defined in the style sheet.

There are also tag-specific styles that may only be applied to a specific tag (for example, codeText in the sample style sheet). The style name (codeText) is prefixed with the tag name (P) so that only the <p> tag may use the codeText style.

Using a Cascading Style Sheet

Using the cascading style sheet file is a matter of referencing the file location in the heading section of the HTML page and using the styles in the HTML tags by specifying the style name in the *class* attribute. The following HTML file uses the styles defined in the sample style sheet:

```html
<html>
  <head>
    <link rel=stylesheet type="text/css" href="demo.css">
  </head>
  <body>
    This is normal body text. The body background is gray.
    <p class=emphasis>
      This uses the EMPHASIS style.</class>
    </p>
      <p class=codeText>// Java code sample comment</p>
    <P>
    <h2>An H2 header is blue by default.</h2>
    <table border=0>
      <tr>
        <th class=tableHeader>ID<th>
        <th class=tableHeader>Name<th>
      </tr>
      <tr>
        <td>101<td>
        <td>Tiger<td>
      </tr>
      <tr>
        <td class=emphasis>102<td>
        <td class=emphasis>Dragon<td>
      </tr>
    </table>
  </body>
</html>
```

NOTE
This example shows an "HTML table" structure that represents rows and columns of data. It is useful to be familiar with this structure because it is used extensively for formatting pages in most applications.

The <link> tag references the style sheet file. The heading 2, body, table heading, and table data cell tags (<h2>, <body>, <th>, and <td>, respectively) default to the styles defined in the style sheet and do not require anything additional in the HTML file. Both a line in the top of the body and the table data (cells) in the second row of the table apply the global style "emphasis" by specifying a `class` attribute. The nature of the global style allows it to be used in two different tags. The text at the top of the file also applies the tag-specific style codeText. The following illustration shows how the HTML file will appear in the browser:

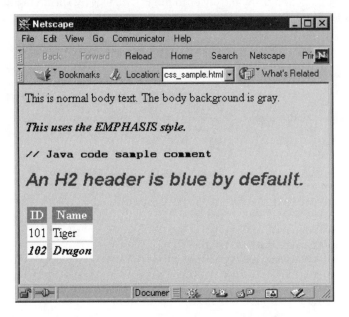

NOTE
The W3C group is also responsible for the creation of cascading style sheet language, and more information is available on the W3C CSS website, www.w3c.org/ Style/CSS.

Index

!-- HTML tag, 878
&AMP HTML tag, 878
&GT HTML tag, 878
&LT HTML tag, 878
  HTML tag, 878
< >, *See* HTML, tags
<% %>, *See* Scriplet
<%= %>, *See* Expression
* to *, *See* Many-to-many
0..1 to *, 105
3GL, xxxiv, 4, 22, 96, 136, 139, 169, 563, 565
1 to *, 105, 266
1 to 1, 266, 268, 270, 337
##Cell, 791
##Column, 791

A

A HTML tag, 878
Abbreviations, 173
Abstract Windowing Toolkit, *See* AWT
Accelerators, 57, 196, 628, 630, 631, 642
Access modifier, *See* Access specifier

Access specifier, 144
Accessors, 147, 281, 376, 482–483
    creating methods for associated entries, 333
    generating, 332–333
    traversing, 482
    view row, 472–473
    See also Getters; Setters
Action, 846
    Swing components, 591
    tag example, 726–727
Action tags, *See* Actions; Action, tag example; Actions, JSP action tags
ActionForm, 846
actionPerformed
    event handler, 65, 598, 643–644
Actions, 723–727
    JSP action tags, 723–725
Activity diagram, 846
Activity Diagrammer, 261
    See also Modelers, Activity
Add a New Empty Project, 24
Add CodeSnippet dialog, 582, 760
Add JavaBeans dialog, 617

Add to Diagram
    item on Model menu, 272
Add to project checkbox, 52, 56
Add Validation Rule dialog, 380, 381,
    382, 383, 384
Add Watch dialog, 216
Aggregation, 867–868
    directed strong, 266, 290, 299
Align
    diagram elements, 283
    menu, 685
    option on Model menu, 271
alignment
    property, 664, 673, 690
    x, 670
    y, 670
anchor, 680, 681
AnchorMedia tag, 827
Ant
    Buildfile dialog, 849
    utility, 849
Ant Buildfile from Active Project
    Configuration dialog, 847
Applet
    dialog, 846
    viewer, 246
Applet HTML File Wizard, 246, 846
Applet HTML Page, *See* Applet HTML
    File Wizard
Applets, 231–233, 245–247, 562,
    563–564
    .class file, 232
    calling sequence, 232
    creating, 245–246
    deploying, 246–247
    running, 247
    tags, 231

Application
    specific menus, 625
    See also Applications
Application architecture model for J2EE,
    224–225
Application Client Deployment
    Descriptor, 846
Application Client Deployment
    Descriptor for OC4J, 846
Application Module Wizard, 85,
    107–108, 109, 322, 349–351, 448,
    455–457, 465, 847
Application modules, 4, 12, 14, 308–309
    checking into and out of pool,
        522–524
    class, 464
    creating, 107–108
    instantiating with configuration,
        540–541
    instantiating, 468
    naming, 179
    nested, 447–448
    pooling, 519–520
    testing BC4J, 188, 439
Application Project Wizard, 852
Application server connection, 49, 178,
    847, 252
Application tier, 19
ApplicationModule tag, 788–789, 822
Applications, 4
    building using BC4J, 18–19
    deploying, 238–245
    Java, 4, 32–34, 111–129
    testing, 108–111
    See also Application; Java
        applications

Archive Viewer, 76
Arrays, 148, 155–156, 297
Association 1 to *
    element on BC4J Component
        Palette page, 267
    element on Java Component Palette
        page, 270
    See also Associations, one-to-many
        and 1 to *
Association Wizard, 105, 317, 334,
    344–346, 363, 847
Associations, 11, 12–13, 289–291, 299,
    305, 307, 847, 862–870
    cardinality, 864–865
    close, 864–870
    creating, 104–106, 296–297,
        333–335, 368–369
    deleting, 104
    dependent, 866–867
    directed, 289
    many-to-many, 337–338
    modeling, 358–359
    naming, 179, 863–864
    non-directed, 289
    one-to-many, 336
    one-to-one, 337
    role, 290
    roles, 279, 863
    traversing, 401–402
    See also Relationships
Attachment element on Component
    Palette, 266, 268, 270, 271
Attribute Wizard, 134, 795, 795, 796,
    797, 798, 800
AttributeIterate tag, 794, 823, 839
Attributes, 10, 146, 797, 862
    adding to diagram, 294–295
    calculating, 407–409
    changing values, 480–481
    class, 885
    definition, 727
    entity, 10, 415, 420
    hiding, 796–797
    HTML tag, 879
    id, 727
    mandatory, 342–343
    persistent, 352–353, 414–415,
        416–418
    read-only, 435
    releasemode, 727
    SQL-only, 376–415, 418
    transient, 341, 352–353, 400–401,
        414, 416, 420
    verify mappings, 437–438
    view, 10
    See also Attribute Wizard
Automatically Generate Java checkbox,
    261, 274, 284
Automatically Resize Shapes checkbox,
    272, 273
AWT, 578, 579–581, 660
    controls, 567
    Component Palette page, 579–581

B

B HTML tag, 878
background property, 671
Batch clients, 462
    creating, 471–480
    testing, 517–518

Batch files
    setvars.bat, 249
BC4J, xxxv, 6, 8–19, 304–326
    Admin Utility, 737–738
    API, 462
    approaches, 15–18
    associations, 278–279
    binding Swing components to,
        569–570, 596
    build a class diagram, 279–283
    building applications using, 18–19
    caching, 416, 503
    cascading style sheet, 800–801, *See*
        also bc4j.css
    Class Modeler and, 274–279,
        356–359
    client data model, 568, 847
    client-side architecture, 227,
        542–543
    Component Palette page, 264–266
    component tags, 820–822
    components, 10–12
    configurations, 538, *See also* .cpx;
        Configuration; Configurations
    connections, 822–823
    control hints, 608
    create a project, 27–31, 96–97,
        98–101
    creating applications with IDE tools,
        95–134
    data access tags, 823–825
    data tag techniques, 788–812
    Data Tags Library, 237, 729,
        752–762, 788–801, 814–828
    data validation strategy, 566
    default layer, 311–326

    deploy an application, 545–558
    deploying as Web Service, 544–545
    events, 825–826
    examine a default layer, 311–314
    forms, 826–827
    framework, 310, 400, 426, 465,
        507–508
    interMedia tags, 827
    JSP page concepts, 814–820
    layer, 103, 133, 227, 235, 274,
        359, 465–466, 534
    link to Java application project,
        32, 112
    local mode deployment, 239
    logical architecture, 12–14
    naming objects, 170, 178–180
    package, 20, 288–289
    project directory, 739–740
    renaming object, 97
    runtime properties, 540
    structure, 9–10
    testing application module, 188
    testing view object, 188
    using, 15
    WebBeans, 827–828
    why use, 304–305
BC4J Client Data Model Definition
    Wizard, 32–33, 35, 569, 847
BC4J Component Tags Component
    Palette page, 820–822
BC4J Connections Component Palette
    page, 822–823
BC4J Data Access Component Palette
    page, 823–825
BC4J Events Component Palette page,
    825–826

BC4J Forms Component Palette page, 826–827

BC4J interMedia Component Palette page, 827

BC4J Web Beans Component Palette page, 827–828

BC4J Data Tags Library, 237, 729, 752–762, 788–801, 814–828

BC4J JSP Web Monitor, 737–738

bc4j.css, 765, 809, 883, *See also* BC4J, cascading style sheet; Cascading style sheets

bc4j.xcfg, 104, 818

BeanInfo, 847
    dialog, 847

Bean-managed transactions, 550

Binding, 32, 575, 607
    JSP Data Binding tool, 761–762, 774, 776
    panels, 569–570
    Swing components to BC4J, 567, 569, 596

blaf.css, 801, 883

BluePrints, 138
    J2EE, 223–224

Body HTML tag, 877

Boolean
    datatype, 146, 154
    wrapper class, 156

Border object, 661

BorderLayout, 663, 666, 667–668, 692
    use the manager, 696–699
    uses for, 668, 698

bounds property, 705

BoxLayout2, 666, 668–670, 671, 692
    uses for, 670

BR HTML tag, 878

Breakpoint conditions, 199–200

Breakpoint groups, 198–199
    in Edit Breakpoint Group dialog, 201

Breakpoints
    actions, 200
    class, 198
    conditions, 199–200
    deadlock, 198
    debug window, 194, 195, 198–199, 215
    defining, 198
    Edit Breakpoint dialog, 199, 200
    exception, 198
    groups, 198–199
    method, 198
    source, 198
    window, 194

Bring to Front item
    on Model menu, 271

Browse & Edit Form, 756–757, 847
    create, 803–805

Browse Form, 252, 756, 757, 847

Browse Symbol, 57
    at Cursor, 57

Browsers, 771
    changing default, 773–774
    testing JSP pages in nondefault, 772

Build, *See* Rebuild

Buildfile from Existing XML File, 847

Buildfile Generated from Active Project Configuration dialog, 847

Business Component Browser, 31, 110, 323–326, 458, 512, 513

Business components, 176,
178–180, 310
deploying, 532–558
modeling, 356–359
testing, 323–326
Business Components Archive, 847
Business Components Client Data
Model, 847
Business Components CORBA Server for
VisiBroker, 847
Business Components Deployment
Wizard, 549
Business Components EJB Deployment
Wizard, 848
Business Components EJB Session
Bean, 848
Business Components for Java, *See* BC4J
Business Components JSP Application
Wizard, 755, 848
Business Components Package Wizard,
28, 101, 280, 312–313, 848
Business Components Project Wizard,
27, 28, 29, 852
Business Components Struts JSP
Application Wizard, 848
Business Components UIX JSP
Application Wizard, 848
Business Components uiXML Application
Wizard, 848
Business logic, 304–305, 377, 398
enforce at domain level, 396–397
in setters, 387–388
testing, 411–412
use and reuse, 423
using domains to add, 390–394

Business rules
adding to BC4J projects, 376–412
adding to source code, 386–390
Business Tier, 224, 532, 535
Business-logic tier approach, 17–18, 305
Button
AWT component, 580
code, 657
setting properties, 654–657
See also JButton
byte
class, 156
datatype, 154

C

.cpx, 32, 112, *See also* Configuration
C++, 140
Caching, 416, 509
query, 503
Cardinality, 105, 289, 864–865
CardLayout, 666, 671–672, 692
uses for, 672
Cascading style sheets, 236, 731,
743–745, 770–771, 808–812, 876–886
BC4J, 800–801
building, 883–884
using, 885–886
See also, bc4j.css
Case sensitivity, 144, 147, 172–173, 737
Casting
literals, 160
objects, 159
variables, 159
catch, 151
CGI, 233

Change indicators, 511
Change Indicator checkbox, 511
char, 154
Character, 156
Character entity references, 878
Check constraints, 330
Check mark menu item, 627
Checkboxes, 580
   Add a New Empty Project, 24
   Add to project, 52, 56
   Application Module, 312
   Automatically Generate Java, 261,
     274, 284
   AWT, 580
   Change Indicator, 511
   Composition association, 335
   Compress Archive, 241
   Create Deployment Profile for
     Applet, 246
   Data manipulation methods, 508
   Deferrable validation, 365
   Deploy Password, 26
   Disable validation, 365
   Discriminator, 403
   Enable validation, 365
   Expose Accessor, 279
   Generate a runnable panel, 571
   Generate Java File, 108, 464
   Generate Main Method, 165, 556
   Highlight all Occurrences, 57
   Include Debug Information, 81,
     193, 211, 212, 213
   Initially deferred validation, 365
   Java console enabled, 192
   Make Project, 45, 100, 211

Mandatory, 103, 342–343
Navigable, 296
Persistent, 342, 392
Primary Key, 103
Public, 164
Queriable, 10, 435, 784, 797
Selected in Query, 434
Show All Database Schemas, 50
TCP Packet Monitor, 63
Unique, 362
Update Imports, 572
Use Active Project Source Path by
   Default, xl
Validation Method, 393
View Links, 312
View Objects, 312
CheckboxGroup, 580
Choice
   AWT component, 580
Choose AntBuildfile dialog, 847
Class breakpoint, 198
Class diagrams, 261, 275
   adding elements, 262
   behavior, 278
   build BC4J, 279–283
   build Java, 291–298
   Component Palette pages, 264–271
   starting, 263–264
Class diagrams from XMI Import, 848
Class Editor, 73–74, 284
Class instances
   naming, 174
Class method, 148
Class model sample, 78
Class Modeler, 262–279, 356–359, 862
   for BC4J, 274–278

for Java elements, 283–291
using for database design, 298–299
visual properties, 273
window icons, 263
window, 276, 292
Class variables, 153
Classes, 140, 156–158, 739, 740, 862
application module, 464
creating Java, 162–166
debug window, 194
entity collection, 378
entity definition, 377–378
entity object, 376–377, 378
frame, 593
implementation, 465–467
naming, 174, 176, 177
SequenceImpl, 400
String, 157
StringBuffer, 157–158
subdirectory, 564
tracing, 214–216
variables, 148
view, 464
CLASSPATH, 244
Clear Highlighting, 57
Client data model, 32–33, 112,
568–569, 722
Client JAR Deployment Profile Settings
dialog, 240
Client JAR File-J2EE Client Module, 848
Client/server
application, 139
limitations of environment, 229
Client tier, 19, 224, 532, 535
Code
block, 145

deployment process, 149
development process, 149
highlighting, 733
Code Completion
templates, 64–68
See also End Tag Completion
Code Editor, 54, 65, 66–70, 126, 130,
184, 733
and BC4J data tags, 759–762
Preferences dialog, 67
Code Insight, 69–70, 126, 733
Code Snippets, 578, 581–582, 760–761
Code stub, 65
CodeCoach, 59, 79–82
Collections, 155
Columns
modifying width, 608–609
property, 682
Comment, 144, 718
Commit
changes, 515–517
cycle, 507
event, 818
method, 507–508
reports on operation, 516–517
tag, 822
Common Gateway Interface, *See* CGI
CompareValidator, 379–382
Compiling operation, 54, 55
Component JSP file, 753, 789–794,
817, 789
modifying, 792
nondefault, 791
Component Palette, 54, 64, 578–589,
759–761
adding a page, 616–617

BC4J, 265, 358
class diagram, 264–271
customizing, 612–622
EJB, 267–268
Java, 268–270
JSP, 759–760, 820–828
Web Service, 270–271
Component tags, 788
Components
adding interface to project,
572–575
menu, 681, 685
naming, 180
Composition, 279, 290, 335, 868–870
Composition Association checkbox, 335
Compress Archive checkbox, 241
Conditional branching, 150
Configuration, 92, 538–541
creating and editing, 538–539
file, 818
for JDeveloper windows, 60
using to instantiate application
module, 540–541
See also Configurations, .cpx
Configuration Manager, 539–540
Configurations
project setting, 60
Configure Palette menu item, 62
Connection tags, 752, 788
Connection Wizard, 25–26, 847, 849
Connections
application server, 252
creating, 25–26
database, 849
naming, 176, 178
pooling, 528–529

selecting, 101
testing and editing, 187
types, 49–50
Consistency
of naming conventions, 170–171
Console window, 189
Constants, 154
naming, 174
See also Variables, final
Constraint, 270
Constraints
check, 330
defining, 369–370
dialog, 675–676
entity, 364–365
foreign key, 363
in UML, 873
modifying, 676
NOT NULL, 331, 362
primary key, 331, 362
property, 117, 279, 663, 668, 670,
674, 706
representing column, 330–331, 392
unique, 330, 362
window, 681
Constructor, 146, 227
Containers, 233, 588, 591–595
web, 233
EJB, 233
J2EE, 532–533
layout, 576, 593
resizing, 662
objects, 591
layout guidelines, 592
Swing components, 591
Container-managed transactions, 550

Containment Hierarchy, 660–661
Context menu, 627
Context-root directory, 254
Continue Step menu item, 197
Control hints, 608, 794–796, 806
Control statements in Java, 149–152
    conditional branching, 150
    exception handling, 151–152
    iteration (looping), 151
    sequence, 150
Control type, 762, 807
Controller, 224, 589
Convert HTML, 63
CORBA Server for VisiBroker dialog, 847
Create CMP Entity Beans from Tables
    Wizard, 850
Create Deployment Profile for Applet
    checkbox, 246
Create New Activity Diagram dialog, 846
Create Table Wizard, 854
Create Trigger Wizard, 854
Create View dialog, 855
createRootApplicationModule( ),
    468, 475
CreateViewObject tag, 823, 830, 831
Criteria tag, 815, 823
Criteria row, 815, 824
Criteria view, 815
CriteriaRow tag, 824
CSS, *See* Cascading style sheets
Curly brackets, 145
Customizers, 65, 848

D

Data
    debug window, 194, 201
    formatting in a JSP page, 798–800,
        817–838, *See also* Formatters
    querying, 815
    rendering in a JSP, 814–815
    representing, 328–353
    Swing components, 591
Data access and presentation tags, 752
Data condition errors, 183
    correcting, 185
Data Manipulation Methods checkbox,
    508
Data models, 426–448
    application, 308–309
    traversing a ViewLink through, 482
    changing at runtime, 498–502
Data Page Wizard, 251–252, 740,
    756–759, 774, 847
    modify a JSP page using, 801–812,
        853, 854
Data source
    adding to project, 131–132
Data Sources Description for OC4J, 848
Data table, 838–840
Data tags
    adding to project, 131–132
Data window, 194, 201
Database
    connection, 49–50
    design using UML Class Modeler,
        298–299

generating tables, 359–361
operation tags, 752
tier, 20
transactions, 506–529
which to use, xxxix
Database-centric approach, 16–17
DataEdit tag, 820
DataHandler tag, 767, 788–789, 820
DataNavigate tag, 821
dataPanel, 583
DataQuery tag, 821
DataRecord tag, 785–786, 821
DataScroller tag, 768, 822
DataSource tag, 788, 823, 834
DataSourceRef tag, 823
DataTable tag, 768, 790–791, 822
DataTransaction tag, 768, 822
Datatypes
    changing, 329–330
    mapping, 329
    matching, 158–161
    primitive, 146, 154–155
    reference, 155–158
    See also, Variables
DataWebBean tag, 753, 828
DBTransactionImpl, 506
Deadlock breakpoint, 196
Debug
    <project>, 196
    <selected file>, 197
Debug menu, 197
Debugging, 182–219
    actions, 197–198
    help, 186
    in JDeveloper, 192–207
    menu, 60, 197

operations, 55
remote, 203
starting a session, 193–195
toolbar, 196
windows, 194–195
Declarations, 718
Default specifier, 145
Default values
    adding to entity attributes, 388–400
    dynamically calculated, 399–400
    static, 399
Deferrable validation checkbox, 365
Delete
    event, 818
    from disk, *See* Erase from Disk
Delete from Model, 289
Dependency, 357, 615
    add to BC4J layer, 474
    element on Class Modeler
        Component Palette, 266, 268,
        270, 271
Deploy Password checkbox, 26
Deployment, xxiv, 137, 149, 222,
    465, 546
    automated, 533
    BC4J application, 545–558
    business components, 532–558
    configuration independence, 472,
        473, 475, 489, 490, 542
    configurations, 538–541
    configurations for Java clients,
        533–535
    configurations for JSP clients,
        535–537
    creating profile, 240–241, 253–254,
        256, 546, 550

descriptor files, 74, 256
J2EE applications, 226
Java clients, 533–535
JSP clients, 535–537
switching modes, 541
Design considerations, 624–631
Design patterns, *See* BluePrints
Detail class, 595
Detach menu item, 197
Development process, 149
Diagrams
iconic format, 276
importing, 274
publishing, 273
symbolic format, 276
visual properties, 273, 282, 283
Dialog,
class, 190–191
Swing components, 591
Dialogs, 82–83, 844–856
Association, 296
Class, 290
Edit Renderer, 815
Edit Watch, 202
External Tools, 735
message, 189–190
Modify Value, 202, 219
New Application, 83, 846
New Bean, 613, 847
New Class, 162, 210, 851
New Database User, 855
New Dialog, 849
New Entity Attribute, 342
New Frame, 632
New Interface, 851
New JSP, 851

New JSP Document, 755, 851
New Library, 616
New Panel, 852
New PL/SQL Procedure, 852
New Project, 32
New XML Schema File, 856
New SQL File, 853
New SQLJ Class, 853
New uiXML Page, 854
New uiXML Template, 854
New WebBean, 855
New Workspace, 25, 99, 856
New WSDL Document, 856
New XML File, 856
New XML Schema File, 856
New XSL File, 856
Property Editor, 853
Save As, 704, 706
Search Files dialog, xli, 58
Subtypes, 448–449
Synchronize with Database
dialog, 332
Visual Properties dialog, 272, 276,
282, 283, 287
Directed Association 1 to *
element on BC4J Component
Palette page, 266
element on Java Component Palette
page, 270
Directed Association 1 to 1
element on BC4J Component
Palette page, 266
element on Java Component Palette
page, 270
Directed Relationship 1 to *
element on EJB Component Palette
page, 268

Directed Relationship 1 to 1
    element on EJB Component Palette
        page, 268
Directed Strong Aggregation
    element on Class Modeler
        Component Palette pages, 266,
        268, 270
Directives in JSP pages, 720–722
    page, 720
    include, 722
    taglib, 722
Directories, 101, 565–566
Disable validation checkbox, 365
Discriminator
    checkbox, 403
    column, 402–405
Display
    modifying, 51
Display Height control hint, 796
Display Hint control hint, 796
Display Width control hint, 796
Distribute item
    on Model menu, 271
Dockable windows, 43
Document
    bar, 70–71
    explicit, 71
    icons, 71
    implicit, 71
    numbers, 71
document property, 118, 567, 569, 574,
    596, 605
Document bar, 70–71
Dog-leg, adding to diagram, 290
Domain

DB sequence, 400
    element on BC4J Component
        Palette page, 266
Domain Wizard, 392, 396, 849
Domains, 11, 309–310
    coding with, 388–390
    custom, 338
    naming, 179
    using to add business logic,
        390–394
    validation, 398
Double
    class, 156
do-while
    loop statement, 151
Drag and drop, 52
Drag handles, 675
Drill Down
    item on Model menu, 272
Drill Up
    item on Model menu, 272

E

EAR
    file –J2EE application, 849
    files, 256, 851
Edit
    form, 757
    menu, 56, 625
    operations, 54
    page, 774, 805–812
Edit Rule tab, 610
Edit Watch dialog, 202
EditRenderer, 815

Editors
    class, 45, 73–74
    code, 45, 91
    in JDeveloper, 72–74
    UI, 45
    XML, 73
edittarget attribute, 758, 769, 780
EIS tier, 224, 532
EJB, 305, 542
    application module, 849
    Component Palette page, 267–268
    container, 233, 533
    entity facades, 306
    module editor, 74
EJB Deployment Descriptor, 849
EJB Deployment for OC4J
    Descriptor, 849
EJB Deployment for WebLogic
    Descriptor, 849
EJB Entity Facade, 849
EJB Entity Facade Wizard, 849
EJB Finder View Link Wizard, 849
EJB FinderViewObject, 849
EJB-JAR File-J2EE EJB Module, 849
EJB Local Ref
    element on EJB Component Palette
        page, 268
EJB Module Editor, 74–75
EJB Ref
    element on EJB Component Palette
        page, 268
Elbow
    adding to diagram, 290
EmbedAudio tag, 827
Embedded OC4J Server, 237

    See also OC4J
EmbedImage tag, 827
EmbedVideo tag, 827
Empty Buildfile, 849
Empty Panel, 850
Empty Panel Wizard, 113
Empty Project, 850
Enable validation, 365
Encapsulation, 143
End Tag Completion, 73, 766
    See also Code Completion
Enterprise application archive, *See* EAR
Enterprise Information System, *See*
    EIS tier
Enterprise JavaBean, *See* EJB
Enterprise JavaBean Wizard, 267, 268,
    850, 852, 853
Entity associations, 179
Entity attributes, 10, 270, 306,
    328–332, 397
    adding, 328–329
    adding default values, 398–400
    deleting, 328–329
    naming, 178
    See also attributes
Entity Bean, 850
    element on EJB Component Palette
        page, 268
Entity Beans from Tables –
    Container-Managed Persistence, 850
Entity cache, 378
Entity collection classes, 378
Entity Constraint Wizard, 364, 850
Entity constraints, 364–365
Entity definition classes, 377–378

Entity Object Wizard, 102–103, 315, 329–330, 343, 344, 360–362, 379, 391, 395, 399, 403–405, 508, 511, 850

Entity objects, 10, 12–13, 270, 305–307, 393, 443, 797, 807, 850
    adding to diagram, 281–283
    as base for view objects, 425–426, 499–500
    classes, 376–377, 378
    creating, 102–104, 366–368
    element on BC4J Component Palette, 265
    maintaining data in, 421–423
    modeling, 357–358
    naming, 178
    reference, 433
    representation in Class Modeler, 282
    synchronizing with database, 332

Entity Relationship Diagrams, *See* ERD

Erase from Disk, 289

ERDs, 862

Errors
    correcting logic, 185
    correcting resource, 185
    correcting syntax, 183–185
    logic, 183
    resource, 183
    syntax, 183
    types, 183–186

errorpage.jsp, 765

Events
    BC4J, 825–474
    code, 643–646, 648
    code for, 643–645
    database, 817
    defining, 596–598
    handling, 816–818
    listener, 596
    method, 596
    navigation, 817
    tab, 65, 73, 597–598, 644

EventSet, 850

Exception breakpoint, 198

Exception handling, 151–152

Exceptions
    naming, 174

ExecuteSQL tag, 824

executeQuery( ), 483

Execution point, 197

Expert mode, 424–426, 436–438

Explicit documents, 71

Expose Accessor checkbox, 279

Expressions in JSP pages, 715–716

Extend class, 142

extends
    clause, 163, 164, 298
    keyword, 21, 145, 154

Extension Manager
    page of Preferences dialog, 42

Extensions
    file, 176

External HTML Editor, 734–736

External Tools, 734–736
    dialog, 735
    menu item, 63

F

Facades service session, 542

Failover, 819

Fields, 146
    adding to application, 118–119
    page in Class Editor, 73
File
    extensions, 176
    list button, 52
    menu, 56
    operations, 54
File management, 21
File menu, 625
Files
    adding, 51
    editing, 51
    miscellaneous, 49
    opening using drag and drop, 52
    renaming, 51
FileUploadForm tag, 827
fill, 680, 681, 708, 709
final, 154
    variables, *See* Constants
finally keyword, 151
findApplicationModule( ), 468
findViewObject( ), 469
first( ), 469
First event, 817
FirstSet event, 817
Fit to Window icon
    in Class Modeler, 263
float
    datatype, 156
    wrapper class, 156
floatable property, 589, 634, 658
FlowLayout, 666, 672–674, 692
    use the manager, 699–703
    uses for, 674
for loop statement, 151

foreground property, 671
Foreign key
    constraints, 372–373
    representing relationships, 332–335
Format
    control hint, 796
    date strings, 799
    number fields, 800
Format masks
    date, 798–799, 837–838
    number, 800, 837–838
Format Type control hint, 795
Form element tags, 752
Formatters, 798, 800, 816, 837–838
    See also Format masks
Form Type control hint, 796
Forms Developer, *See* Oracle Forms
    Developer
FormEvent tag, 825
Forward-Only Mode, 503–504
Frame, 850
    class, 593
Framework, 730
    multi-tier, 10

G

Gallery
    new, *See* New gallery
Garbage Collection button, 196
Generalization, 279, 290–291, 299
    adding to diagram, 297–298
Generate
    business components, 275
    database objects, 299
    item on Model menu, 272

Generate a runnable panel, 571
Generate Accessor, 455
Generate BusinessComponents, 275
Generate Default Constructor
    checkbox, 164
Generate Javadoc, 61
Generate Java file checkbox, 464
Generate Main Method checkbox, 556
Generalization, 142, 357, 870–872
        changing into interface, 298
        element on BC4J Component
            Palette page, 266
        element on Java Component Palette
            page, 270
Generate Java checkbox, 274
get( ), 11
getAttribute( ), 480
Getters, 147, 376
        adding calculations to, 407–408
        See also get( )
Global style, 883
globalinclude.html, 765
GotoSet event, 817
Go to Java Class
        search feature, 57–58
Go to Source menu item, 272
GridBagLayout, 115, 663, 666, 674,
    678–679, 692
        align and size objects, 704–706
        constraints editor, 677
        use the manager, 703–709
        uses for, 682
gridheight property, 678
GridLayout, 666, 682–683, 692
        uses for, 683
gridwidth property, 678

gridx property, 677
gridy property, 678

H

H1 HTML tag, 877
Hands-on practices, xxxi–xxxii,
    xxxvii–xli
Head HTML tag, 877
Heap debug window, 194
Help
        context-sensitive, 733
        menu item, 63
        menu, 626
Help system, xlii, 42, 63, 86–88,
    645, 714
        displaying, 88
        run from centralized server, 88
hgap property, 664, 668, 672, 674,
    682, 690
hideattributes attribute, 783, 796
High-level wizards, 21, 97
Highlight all Occurrences checkbox, 57
horizontalFill property, 690
Hosted documentation, 88
HR HTML tag, 878
HR schema, 25
HTML, 139, 234, 237, 721, 731,
    836, 876
        creating file, 246
        external editor, 734–736
        file, 850
        form, 879
        JavaScript in, 880–883
        messages, 192
        naming files, 176

renderer, 814–815
sample code, 879–880
table, 743, 839
tag, 877
tags, 876–879
HTML File dialog, 850
HTML Viewer, 75
HTTP Servlet, 233, 850
See also Servlet
HTTP Servlet Wizard, 850

I

I HTML tag, 878
iconic format, 276
icons, 630, 653–654, 655
IDE, 40–93
menu bar, 55–64
right-click menu, 55
toolbar, 54–55
window, 42, 43
IDL File, 850
dialog, 850
if-else statement, 150
Image Viewer, 75
Immutable, 158
Implement Cascade Delete
checkbox, 335
Implement Interface
menu item, 63
Implicit documents, 71
Import classes, 144
Import menu item, 56
Import EAR File, 851
Import Existing Sources, 850

Import Existing Sources Wizard,
132–133, 614
Import from WAR File, 851
Import UML XMI dialog, 848
Import UML XML dialog, 848
Importing a diagram, 274
Imports tab, 68
Include Debug Information checkbox,
81, 193, 211, 212, 213
include directive, 722
includes, *See* Import
Incremental Search, 57
Index HTML file, 250
Inheritance, 142–143, 279
init( ), 150
Initially deferred validation checkbox,
365
In-place editing
in Class Modeler, 293, 294
InputDate tag, 826
InputHidden tag, 826
InputPassword tag, 826
InputRender tag, 826, 833, 834
InputSelect tag, 826, 834
InputSelectGroup tag, 826
InputSelectLOV tag, 826, 834–836
InputText tag, 826
InputTextArea tag, 826
Insert event, 817
Insert Form dialog, 831
Insert Table dialog, 832
inset property, 678
Inspector
debug window, 194, 202
See also Property Inspector
Instance variables, 148, 153

INSTEAD OF triggers, 13, 15
int datatype, 154
Integer wrapper class, 156
Integrated Development Environment,
   See IDE
Interface
   creating from generalization, 298
   element on Java Component Palette
     page, 269
Interfaces, 156, 286, 465–467, 873
   creating, 472
   custom, 466
   transaction, 506–507
interMedia, 583
Intersection table, 337
Intranet, 232
ipadx property, 679
ipady property, 679
Iteration, 151
itermode attribute, 803

J

_jspService( ), 718
jsp:fallback, 723
jsp:forward, 723
jsp:getproperty, 724
jsp:include, 724
jsp:param, 724
jsp:params, 724
jsp:plugin, 725
jsp:setProperty, 725
jsp:useBean, 725
J2EE, 138, 223–225, 532
   and JDeveloper, 225–233

application architecture model of,
   224–225
BluePrints, 223–224
compliance, 305
conceptual architecture model, 225
containers, 532–533
deploying applications in
   JDeveloper, 226
deployment file, 848
patterns, 223
software, 224
specifications, 224
summary, 222–225
J2EE Application Deployment
   Descriptor, 851
J2ME, 223
J2SE, 223
JAR Deployment Profile Settings, 547
JAR files, 239–245
   deploying to, 557–558
   install and test, 243–245
JAR File-Simple Archive, 851
Java, xxxiv, 8–9, 42, 136–166, 222, 310,
   590, 731
   Association dialog, 296
   benefits of using, 136–138
   case sensitivity, 144, 147
   Class dialog, 290
   classes, 284–285, 851
   code generation, 283–284
   comments in, 144
   component, 563
   development process, 40–41
   drawbacks of using, 138–139
   identifiers, 172
   language review, 143–147

naming elements, 147, 169–170
portability, 138
runtime, 144, 149, 244
transitioning to, 138–140
types, 329
Java 2 Platform, Enterprise Edition, 5
See also J2EE
Java 2 Platform, Micro Edition, *See* J2ME
Java 2 Platform, Standard Edition,
See J2SE
Java applications, 226–230, 562,
563–564
advantages of, 229
calling sequence, 228
creating, 32–34, 97–98, 111–119,
600–601
creating a shortcut for, 245
debugging, 207–219
deploying, 238–245
disadvantages of, 229
naming conventions, 168–169, 180
runtime architecture, 227
when to use, 228
See also Applications
Java archive, *See* JAR file
Java class
diagram building, 291–298
dialog, 290, 293, 295
element on Java Component Palette
page, 269
Java clients, 222, 562–576
architectures, 226–233, 565–567
deployment configurations,
533–535
local mode, 533, 535
remote mode, 533–535

Java Component Palette page, 268–270
Java console enabled checkbox, 192
Java Database Connectivity, *See* JDBC
Java Development Kit, *See* JDK
Java Interface, 851
Java Network Launching Protocol,
See JNLP
Java Source Path, 101
Java Virtual Machine, 42, 138, 230, 562
See also Runtime, Java
Java Web Service, 851
Java Web Start, 229, 230
Java Web Start (JNLP) Files, 851
Java Web Start (JNLP) Files for
JClient, 851
Java Web Start Wizard, 230, 851
JavaBeans, 579
add a custom, 616, 617–618
creating, 612–622
creating a library for, 615–616
deploying, 614–615
Javadoc, 59, 61, 157
JavaScript, 139, 731
in HTML, 880–883
JavaServer Page Tag Library Wizard, 851
JavaServer Pages, 149
architecture, 233–237
code, 222
See also JSP
JavaServer Pages specification, 715
JavaServer Pages Standard Tag Library
(JSTL), 717
jbo.ampool.maxavailablesize, 528
jbo.ampool.maxinactiveage, 528
jbo.ampool.minavailablesize, 528

JButton, 586
    See also Button
JCheckBox, 586
JClient, 305
    architecture, 567–570
    building a Java application,
        570–575
    controls, 578, 582–584
    form, 34
JClient attribute binding, 574
JClient Controls, 582–584
JClient data models
    naming, 178
JClient Empty Form Wizard, 600, 850
JClient Empty Panel Wizard, 571, 850
JClient Form, 34, 82, 97, 238–239, 632,
    644, 646, 850
JClient Form Wizard, 245, 565, 593,
    632, 635, 638, 644, 645, 649, 850
JClient Graph Wizard, 852
JClient Java Web Start Wizard, 851
JClient Panel Wizard, 852
JComboBox, 586
JDBC, 142
JDesktopPane, 591, 593
jdev.exe, xxxvii
jdevw.exe, xxxvii
JDEV_HOME, xxxvii–xxxviii
JDeveloper, xxxiv–xxxv
    arranging windows, 45
    creating application code in, 19–20
    debugger, 192–207
    directory structure, 20, 101,
        739–740
    environment, 42–93

file management, 21
help system, xlii, 42
IDE and JSP pages, 732–740
IDE window, 44
index file, 250
installing and running, xxxvii
layout managers, 692
main work areas, 47–82
menus and toolbars, 631–635
Profiler, 203–207
Readme (Release Notes), xlii
samples, xlii
screen layout, 23
Software Configuration
    Management, 42
specific naming conventions,
    175–180
System Navigator, 45
tutorials, xlii
wizards, 22, 42, 176, 592, 844–856
work areas, 42
JDK, 40, 224
    See also SDK
JEditorPane, 586
JFrame, 591, 592, 593, 693
JInternalFrame, 591
JLabel, 586
JList, 586
JMenuBar, 588
JNLP, 230
JOptionPane, 190
JPanel, 588, 592, 666
    adding to application, 123
JPasswordField, 586
JPopupMenu. 589
JProgressBar, 586

JRadioButton, 586
JScrollBar, 586
JScrollPane, 589, 592
JSeparator, 586, 655, 671
JSlider, 586
JSP, 36, 129–134, 149
    1.2 document, 715
    advantages, 235–236
    application wizard, 755
    architecture, 233–237
    attributes behavior, 794–797
    calling sequence, 236
    clients, 305, 462, 535–537
    Code Editor and, 759–762
    compilation and runtime, 731–732
    Component Palette pages,
      759–760, 820–828
    connection tags, 752
    container, 234
    create a form, 746–750
    create a project, 34–38
    creating, 6–7
    Data Binding Tool, 761–762,
      774, 776
    Data Page Wizard, 756–759
    database operations tags, 752
    development, 132, 714–750
    development requirements,
      731–732, 753–762
    disadvantages, 236–237
    document, 755, 851
    editing files, 743
    form element tags, 752
    handling events in, 816
    page, 715, 740–36

    presentation form component
      tags, 753
    project directory, 740
    project files, 37
    querying data in, 815–816
    rendering data in 814–789
    samples in JDeveloper, 250
    tag library, 851
    tags, 725–728, 731
    technology overview, 234–237
    translator, 234
    Viewer, 75, 736–737, 734
    when to use, 235
    wizards and dialogs, 755–759
JSP applications, 462, 848
    deploy, 247–257
    files and directories, 255
JSP Data Binding Tool, 761–762,
    774, 776
JSP document, 755, 851
JSP pages, 851
    build using BC4J data tags,
      752–786
    building, 741–746
    modify, 742–743, 775–777,
      801–812
    testing in browser, 772, 773–774
JSP tags, 725–728, 731
    delimiters, 728
    See also Tags; BC4J Data
      Tags Library
JSP Viewer, 75, 736–737, 734
JSplitPane, 589, 593
JTabbedPane, 589, 593, 602
JTable, 586
JTextArea, 587

JTextField, 587
JTextPane, 587
JToggleButton, 587
JToolBar, 589
    See also Toolbars
JTree, 587
JUArrayComboBox, 584
JUImage, 583
JULabel, 585
JUNavigationBar, 584
    See also Navigation bar
JURadioButtonGroupPanel, 584
JUStatusBar, 584
JVM, 42, 138, 230, 562
    See also Runtime, Java

K

Keyboard, 57, 196
Keywords, 873
    catch, 151
    extends, 145
    final, 154
    finally, 151
    public, 144–145
    static, 148
    throw, 151
    try, 151

L

Label
    AWT component, 580
Label Text control hint, 795
Labels
    adding to application, 115–117

aligning, 837
    modifying properties, 133–134
LAN, 229
Last
    event, 817
last( ), 469
LastSet event, 817
layout property, 229
    See also, Layout managers
Layout managers, 229, 660–709
    default, 663
    multiple, 692–695
    null, 665
    setting properties, 664
    sources, 666
Layouts for JDeveloper windows
    activating, 46
    JDeveloper feature, 46
    saving, 46
Layouts
    See also Layout managers
Libraries, 144
    aliasing names, 177
    naming, 176
List
    AWT component, 580
Listener Wizard, 853
ListValidator, 382–383
Literals
    casting, 160
Loadjava and Java Store Procedures
    dialog, 852
Local mode, 239, 533, 535
Locate in Navigator
    search feature, 57
LocJSP.cpx, 765

LocJSP-jpr-War.deploy, 765
Locking, 509–511
    optimistic, 509–510
    pessimistic, 509
    rows, 510
Log window, 24, 45, 66, 213
    messages, 184, 254, 754
Logic errors, 183
    correcting, 185
Logical operators, 150
long
    datatype, 154
    wrapper class, 156
Look-and-feel, 575, 602
    changing, 43, 45, 587
Looping, 151
    statements, 151
LOV, 584
    input field for JSPs, *See*
        InputSelectLOV tag
    window, 835
lovcomp.jsp, 835
Low-level wizards, 21

M

main( ), 150, 166, 227
Make button, 55
Make Project checkbox, 100, 211
Manage Libraries
    menu item, 62
Mandatory checkbox, 103
Many-to-many, 335–338
Master class, 594–595
Master-detail panel, 694
    naming, 180

maximumSize property, 670, 691
MDI, 43, 587, 591
MediaControl, 584
MediaUrl tag, 827
Member variables, 154
Memory Profiler window, 207
Menu Editor, 633–12
MenuBar
    AWT component, 580
Menus, 625–630
    build, 637–646
    enabling and disabling items, 630
    item code, 643–646
    item icons, 629
    multi-level, 626
    nested, 626
    objects, 633–634
    popup, 627, 646–650
Message Driven Bean, 852
    element on EJB Component Palette
        page, 268
Messages
    dialog, 189–190
    displaying, 186–192
    HTML, 192
Method breakpoint, 198
Methods, 389, 596, 872
    accessor, 147, 281
    createRootApplicationModule( ),
        468, 475
    exported, 465–467
    findApplicationModule( ), 468
    findViewObject, 469
    first( ), 469
    get( ), 11
    init( ), 150

last( ), 469
main( ), 150, 166
names for, 147
naming, 174
overloaded, 146
pack( ), 662
previous( ), 469
service, 488–490
set( ), 11
signature, 146
tab in Class Editor, 73
validate( ) 391–392
validateEntity( ), 392–394
MethodValidator, 384–385, 387–388
Minimize Pages item
on Model menu, 271
minimumSize property, 670, 691
Miscellaneous files
node, 49
Mnemonics, 628, 630, 641
Modal property, 191
Model menu, 62
in Class Modeler, 271–273
model property, 223, 567, 569, 583,
589, 596, 606, 607
Modelers
Activity, 78
Class, *See* Class Modeler
in JDeveloper, 78
Modeling
business components, 356–359
in JDeveloper, 260
Model-View-Controller, 6, 137,
223–224, 567, 589
Modify Value dialog, 202, 210
Monitor

resolution, 46–47
size, 46–47
Monitors debug window, 194
Multiple Document Interface, 591
See also MDI
Multiple table mapping, 279
Multiplicity, *See* Cardinality
mutable, 157
MVC, 137, 223
See also Model-View-Controller

N

Name, 688
Namespace, 284
Naming conventions, 168–180
general guidelines, 171–174
recognized Java, 174–175
Navigable checkbox, 296
Navigation bar, 635
adding to application, 115
See also JUNavigationBar
Navigator, 113
organization, 287
packages in, 287–289
searching, 51
Show Categories button, 51
system, 23, 48–53
toolbar, 51–53
See also System Navigator
Nested menus, 626
New
file menu option, 56
gallery, 27, 33, 84, 102, 285,
844–845, *See also* New gallery
New Application dialog, 83, 846

New Bean dialog, 613, 847
New Class dialog, 162, 210, 851
New Database User dialog, 855
New Dialog dialog, 849
New Entity Attribute dialog, 342
New Frame dialog, 632
New gallery, 84, 755–756, 844–845,
    See also New, gallery
New Interface dialog, 851
New JSP dialog, 853
New JSP Document dialog, 755, 851
New Library dialog, 616
New Panel dialog, 852
New PL/SQL Procedure dialog, 852
New Project dialog, 32
New SQL File dialog, 853
New SQLJ Class dialog, 853
New uiXML Page dialog, 854
New uiXML Template (UIT) dialog, 854
New WebBean dialog, 855
New Workspace dialog, 25, 99, 856
New WSDL Document dialog, 856
New XML File dialog, 856
New XML Schema File dialog, 856
New XSL File dialog, 856
Next event, 817
nextFocusableComponent property, 665
NextSet event, 817, 819
Node View item
    on Model menu, 272
Nonvisual Swing components, 591
Normal Size icon
    in Class Modeler, 263
NOT NULL, 331, 362, 369–370
Notes, 279

element on Class Modeler
    Component Palette page, 266,
    268, 270, 271
null layout manager, 665, 666,
    683–685, 692
    converting from, 676
    uses for, 685
Number class, 156

O

Object orientation, 260
    concepts, 140–143, 298
Object serialization, 141
Objects
    casting, 159
    naming, 169–171
    representing Oracle types, 338–339
OC4J, 237
    embedded server, 732, 755, 766
    set up, 248–251
    starting and stopping, 249–31
OJSP tag libraries, 730
ojsp-global-include.xml, 765
One-to-many relationship, 105, 266
One-to-one relationship, 266, 268, 270,
    327
OnEvent tag, 780, 825
Opaque property, 686
Optimistic locking, 510
    testing, 512, 513–515
Oracle Business Component
    Browser, 551
Oracle Business Component
    Configuration, 540, 818
Oracle Containers for J2EE, *See* OC4J

Oracle Forms Developer, 5, 7, 136, 139
Oracle Forms Pluggable Java Component
    dialog, 852
Oracle object types, 338–339
Oracle Portal, 5
Oracle User Groups, xliii
oracle.jbo.server.DBTransaction
    interface, 506, 507
oracle.jbo.Transaction
    interface, 506
Oracle9i SCM Workarea Wizard, 90
Oracle9iAS, 237
ORDER BY clause
    changing, 424
Other node
    in Navigator, 620
OverlayLayout2, 666, 686–687, 692
    uses for, 686–687
Overloaded methods, 146
Override Methods
    menu item, 62

P

P HTML tag, 877
Package
    item on Class Modeler Component
        Palette, 266, 270
Packages, 11, 28, 144, 566
    in diagrams, 287–289
    naming, 175
Page
    directive, 720–721
Panel
    AWT component, 581
    borders, 661

class, 594
    See also JPanel
PaneLayout, 666, 687–689, 692
Panels, 661, 852
    binding, 569–570
    class, 570–572
    resizing, 698–699
    with graph, 852
PATH
    environment variable, 243
    setting, 548
Pause button, 196
Persistence, 141
Persistent checkbox, 342, 392
Pessimistic locking, 509
    testing, 512–513
Pin icon, 43, 262, 760
PL/SQL, 139, 140
    editing, 70
    program, 852
PL/SQL Server Pages, 5
PL/SQL Web Service Publishing Wizard,
    852
PL/SQL Web Toolkit, 5
Polymorphism, 143
    view objects, 448
Pool Info, 738
PopulateAttribute( ), 401
Popup menu, 627, 646–650
PopupMenu
    AWT component, 580
Portability of Java, 138
Position, 689
Post, 747
PostChanges tag, 823

Preferences
        breakpoints, 201
        dialog, 42, 45, 46, 48, 67, 68, 70,
            195
        menu item, 63
preferredSize, 663, 668, 670, 674, 690
Presentation form component tags, 753
Previous event, 817
previous( ), 469
PreviousSet event, 817
Primary Key checkbox, 103
Primary Key Constraints, 331
        generating, 362
println( ) method, 234
private keyword, 144–145
Profiler, 203–207
        Event, 205–206, 207
        Execution, 205–206, 206
        Memory, 205, 207
        running, 204–205
Program Arguments, 212
Project from Existing Source Wizard, 853
Project from War File Wizard, 853
Project Settings, 80, 212, 479, 523, 525
        configurations in, 60
        dialog, 58–59, 60, 80, 189, 204,
            211, 523
Project with Web Module Wizard, 852
Projects, 19, 20, 565–566
        creating BC4J, 100–101
        menu, 58–59
        naming, 176, 177
Properties, 11, 663, 762
        alignment, 664, 690
        alignmentX, 670
        alignmentY, 670

anchor, 680, 708
axis, 668
background, 671
columns, 682
constraints, 663, 668, 674, 685,
        688–689, 706
fill, 680, 708, 709
floatable, 589, 634, 658
foreground, 671
gridheight, 678
gridwidth, 678
gridx, 677, 708
gridy, 678, 708
hgap, 664, 668, 690
horizontalFill, 690
inset, 678
ipadx, 679
ipady, 679
layout, 663
maximumSize, 670, 671, 691
minimumSize, 670, 691
modal, 191
name, 688
nextFocusableComponent, 665
opaque, 686
position, 689
preferredSize, 663, 668, 670,
        671, 690
proportion, 689
Queriable, 797
rootVisible, 611
splits, 689
verticalFill, 690
vgap, 664, 668, 690
Property Editor dialog, 853
Property Inspector, 64–66, 597
Position, 689

protected keyword, 145
PSPs
> *See* PL/SQL Server Pages
public
> checkbox, 164
> class, 145
> keyword, 144
public_html directory, 740
Publish Diagram item
> on Model menu, 272, 273

Q

Queriable checkbox, 435, 784, 797
queriableonly attribute, 823
Queries, 414–460
> at runtime, 462–504
> optimizing caching, 503–504
Query columns, 417
Query form, 758, 778–785, 816, 853
Query page, 778–785

R

Radio group menu items, 627
Ranges, 504
Rangesize attribute, 766, 779, 803,
> 817, 824
RangeValidator, 383–384
RDBMS, 141, 509
Read-only attributes, 435
Realization element
> on Java Component Palette page,
> 270
Realizations, 279, 286, 873
Rebuild, 55, 807

Recycle threshold, 525–527
Refactor, 21
> menu item, 56, 62
Refresh button, 52
RefreshDataSource tag, 823
Relational database system, 141–142
Relationship 1 to *
> element on EJB Component Palette
> page, 268
Relationships
> many-to-many, 335–338
> one-to-one, 335–337
> representing between query result
> sets, 441–443
> *See also* Associations
relativeUrlPath attribute, 780, 791, 804
Release mode, *See* Stateful release mode;
> Stateless release mode; Reserved
> release mode
releasemode attribute, 818–819, 820
ReleasePageResources tag, 823
Remote Debugging and Profiling
> Project, 852
Remote mode, 239, 533–535, 536, 537
Remove insets, 681
Remove padding, 681
Renaming, xli, 21, 644
> entity objects in Class Modeler, 283
> menu option, 56, 97
> table column, 369–370
Renderer, *See* HTML, renderer
RenderValue tag, 824, 839
Reopen, 56
Required Attribute Insertion, 73
Reserved release mode, 524, 819
Resource errors, 183

correcting, 171
Resources, xlii, 858–860
    books, 858
    information, 575–576
    websites, 858–860
Result sets
    navigating, 469
    stepping through, 469
Resume, 196
Right-click menu, 627
Rollback
    cycle, 509
    event, 818
    method, 507
    tag, 823
rootVisible property, 611
Row keys, 470–471
Row objects, 402
Row tag, 824
Rows
    creating, 481
    deleting, 481
    explicitly locking, 510
    property, 683
RowSet iterators
    secondary, 502
RowSetIterate tag, 824, 839
RowSetNavigate tag, 824
Run
    menu, 59–60
    operations, 54–55
Run Manager, 53
Run to Cursor, 197
Runtime
    Java, 144, 149, *See also* JVM

S

Save As dialog, 704, 706
Save Deployment Profile-Client JAR
    File-J2EE Client Module dialog, 848
Save Deployment Profile-EAR File-J2EE
    Application dialog, 849
Save Deployment Profile-EJB JAR
    File-J2EE EJB Module window, 849
Save Deployment Profile-JAR File-Simple
    Archive dialog, 851
Save Deployment Profile-Taglib JAR
    File-Tag Library for JSP dialog, 854
Save Deployment Profile-WAR File-J2EE
    Web Module dialog, 855
Schemas
    HR, xxxviii, 50
SCM, 89–93, 299
    features, 89
    other options, 93
    repository, 89
    See also Software Configuration
        Management
Scripting elements, 715–720
Scriptlets, 716–717
Scope of variables, 152–153
Scrollbar
    AWT component, 581
ScrollPane
    AWT component, 581
SDK, 40, 224
    See also JDK
Search
    files, xl, 58
    incremental backward, 57

incremental forward, 57
menu, 57–58
Search Files dialog, xli, 58
Selected in Query checkbox, 434
Send to Back item
on Model menu, 271
Separators, 629
Sequence Viewer, 77–78
SequenceImpl, 400, 407
Server Business Logic Rier, 224, *See also*
Business Tier
Server-side presentation tier, 224, 532
Service Methods, 488–490
row-level, 488
view object-level, 489
Service session facade, 542
Servlet Filter Wizard, 853
Servlet Listener, 853
Servlets, 6, 222, 233, 716, 718, 719, 728
HTTP, 233, 850
JSP-generated, 721
samples page, 250
Session ID, 521
SessionBean, 853
element on EJB Component Palette
page, 267
SessionCookies, 521
Set Next Statement, 197
Set Start Debugging Option, 196
set( ), 11, 386
setAttribute( ), 480–481
SetAttribute tag, 824
SetDomainRenderer tag, 826
SetFieldRenderer tag, 827
SetHtmlAttribute tag, 827

Setters, 147, 376–377, 387–388, 393,
408, *See also* set( )
setvars.bat, 249
setWhereClause( ), 483
short, 154
Shortcuts
for a Java application, 245
keyboard, 57
Show All Database Schemas checkbox,
50
Show All Files, 52
Show Categories, 287
Show Dependencies, 62
Show Execution Point, 197
Show Grid, 681
Show Implementation Files
item on Model menu, 272
Show Related Elements
item on Model menu, 272
Show rules tab, 610
Show Warnings, 211
ShowCriteria tag, 824
ShowDefinition tag, 824
ShowHint tag, 824, 839
ShowValue tag, 824
Signature, 146
Simple Archive Files dialog, 847
Simple Object Access Protocol server,
See SOAP server
Size and Space menu, 685
Size padding, 679
Smart Data window, 194, 201, 213
Snippets, 64, 581–582
SOAP Server, 544
connection, 50, 178, 853

SOAP Server Connection Wizard, 853
Software Configuration Management, 42,
    89–93
        See also SCM
Software Configuration Manager,
    See SCM
Software Development Kit, *See* SDK
Source breakpoint, 198
Source Control, 92
    connection, 50
    enabling, 89–90
        See also Software Configuration
        Management
Specialization, 142
Splits, 689
SQL, 139, 142
    file, 853
    types, 306–307
SQL Worksheet, 78–79
SQL*Plus, 62
SQLJ class, 853
SQL-only view objects, 424–425,
    431–432
        creating, 434–435, 499
        testing, 439–440
src subdirectory, 564, 740
Stack debug window, 194
Starter Application, 853
Starter Data Page, 758, 764–767, 853
Starter Data Page Wizard, 853
State
    setting, 818–819
Stateful release mode, 525–527, 819
Stateless release mode, 524, 819
static keyword, 148
Static Swing components, 591

Step Into, 196, 197
Step Out, 196, 197
Step Over, 196, 213
Step to End of Method, 196
Stereotypes, 873
Straighten Lines item
    in Model menu, 271
String class, 157
StringBuffer class, 157–158
Structure window, 23, 53–54, 114, 119,
    184, 603, 639, 734
Struts, 730
Struts Action dialog, 846
Struts FormBean dialog, 846
Struts Starter Page Wizard, 853
Struts-based JSP Application, 848
Stubs
    client-side Java, 556
Style sheets, 876–886
    applied to JSP, 133
    applying, 132–133
Subclass, 142
    file, 163–165
Subtypes dialog, 448–449
Suffixes, 172
Superclass, 142
Swing
    component categories, 591
    components, 560, 578, 584–587,
        590
    modifying components, 595–596
Swing containers, 578, 588–589
switch statement, 150
Symbolic format, 276
Synchronization, 421–422
Synchronize with Database dialog, 332

Syntax errors, 183–184
    checking, 733
    correcting, 183–185
    highlighting, 67, 184
    in the Structure window, 184
System Navigator, 23, 45, 48–53

T

Table Viewer, 76–77
Tables, 854
    constraints, 361
    generating, 359–361
    populating, 371–373
Tag Insight, 73
Tag library, *See* JSP, tag library
Tagged values, *See* Keywords
taglib directive, 722
Taglib JAR File-Tag Library for JSP, 854
Tags, 772–775
    AnchorMedia, 827
    ApplicationModule, 788–789, 822
    AttributeIterate, 794, 823, 839
    Commit, 822
    CreateViewObject, 823, 830, 831
    Criteria, 815, 823
    CriteriaRow, 824
    custom libraries, 728–730, 740
    DataEdit, 820
    DataHandler, 767, 788–789, 820
    DataNavigate, 821
    DataQuery, 821
    DataRecord, 785–786, 821
    DataScroller, 768, 822
    DataSource, 788, 823, 834
    DataSourceRef, 823

    DataTable, 768, 822
    DataTransaction, 768, 822
    DataWebBean, 753, 828
    EmbedAudio, 827
    EmbedImage, 827
    EmbedVideo, 827
    End Tag Completion, 733
    ExecuteSQL, 824
    FileUploadForm, 827
    FormEvent, 825
    HTML, 876–879
    InputDate, 826
    InputHidden, 826
    InputPassword, 826
    InputRender, 826, 833, 834
    InputSelect, 826
    InputSelectGroup, 826
    InputSelectLOV, 826
    InputText, 826
    InputTextArea, 826
    library prefix (jbo), 726
    MediaUrl, 827
    OnEvent, 780, 825
    PostChanges, 823
    RefreshDataSource, 823
    ReleasePageResources, 823
    RenderValue, 824, 839
    Rollback, 823
    Row, 824
    RowSetIterate, 824, 839
    RowSetNavigate, 824
    SetAttribute, 824
    SetDomainRenderer, 826
    SetFieldRenderer, 827
    SetHtmlAttribute, 827
    ShowCriteria, 824

ShowDefinition, 824
ShowHint, 824, 839
ShowValue, 824
UrlEvent, 826
ViewCriteria, 824
ViewCriteriaIterate, 825
See also Action, tag example;
    Actions, JSP Action tags
TCP Packet Monitor checkbox, 63
Templates directory, 791
Terminal server, 230
Terminate, 196
Testing, 121–122, 162–165, 182
    application, 479–480
    Business Component Browser,
        323–326
    default view objects, 347
text property, 628, 634–635, 642
TextArea
    AWT component, 581
TextField
    AWT component, 581
Threads
    debug window, 194
throw statement, 151
Toolbars, 630–631
    arrangements, 631
    build, 650–658
    debug, 196
    multiple, 630
    objects, 634–635
    UI Editor, 676
    vertical and floating, 658
    See also, JToolbar
Tools menu, 62
Tooltips, 629, 630

Tooltip Text, 795
Top-level container, 661–662
Tracing classes
    disabling, 214–216
    enabling, 214–216
TransactionEvents, 516
Transactions
    Bean-managed, 550
    committing, 507–508
    container-managed, 550
    managing multiple, 506–529
    rolling back, 507, 508–509
Transform to Business Components
    item on Model menu, 273, 274
Transient Attributes
    341, 352–353, 400–401
Tree structure, 609–610
Trigger, 854
Troubleshooting techniques, 187
try keyword, 151
Typesafe
    matching concept, 160–161

U

UDDI Registry Connection, 50, 178
UDDI Registry Connection Wizard, 854
UI
    naming components, 180
    See also User Interface
UI Editor, 72, 119, 604, 639
    tools, 664–665
    toolbar, 676
UIX, 305
UIX JSP Browse & Edit Form, 854

UIX JSP Browse Form (with Hide/Show), 854
UIX JSP Starter Page, 854
UIX JSP Application, 848
UIX JSP, 730
uiXML Application, 848
    framework, 730
uiXML Browse and Edit Form Wizard, 854
uiXML Page, 854
uiXML Page Wizard, 854
uiXML Template (UIT) Customer Wizard, 854
uiXML Template (UIT) Wizard, 855
UL HTML tag, 878
UML, 260
    class diagram syntax, 862–873
    class diagram, 356–359
    Class Modeler, 298–299
    creating a diagram, 280
    extending to support physical database design, 299
    extending, 872–873
    naming diagram elements, 180
    package, 288–289
Unified Modeling Language, *See* UML
Unique checkbox, 362
Unique constraints, 330, 362, 370
Universal Description, Discovery and Integration, *See* UDDI
Update event, 817
Update Imports, 572
Updateable property, 797, 834
UrlEvent tag, 826
Use Active Project Source Path by Default checkbox, xl

User Interface, 660, 661–663
    created a tabbed, 598–612
    See also UI

V

validate( ), 391
validateEntity( ), 392–394
Validation
    attribute-level, 392
    custom rules, 380
    domains, 392
    entity-level, 393
    failure, 385
    logic, 390, 409–411, 14
    of diagram elements, 294
    rules, 378–385
    strategy, 566
    testing rules, 397–388
Validation Method checkbox, 393
Variables, 140, 146, 147, 152, 194, 202, 748
    array, 289
    bind, 441
    Boolean, 189
    casting, 159
    class, 148, 153–154, 156
    CLASSPATH environment, 243, 244
    declaration, 152
    environment, 249
    examine value of, 218
    final, 154, 158
    instance, 148, 153, 156
    member, 154
    modify value of, 219
    mutable, 157

naming, 169, 174
scope, 151–152
type, 158, 203
See also, Constants; Datatypes;
Immutable
Vectors, 156
Version control, *See* SCM
verticalFill, 690
VerticalFlowLayout, 666, 689–691, 691,
692
vgap, 664, 668, 672, 674, 683, 690
View, 589, 855
menu, 625
View attributes, 10–11, 307–308,
414–423
naming, 179–180
View cache, 419
View link SQL, 441–442
View Link Wizard, 106, 320–321,
348–349, 442, 452–454, 855
View links, 11, 14, 307–308, 855
accessors, 443
bidirectional, 445
cardinality, 443–446
creating, 106–107, 347, 442–443
directionality, 443–446
many-to-many, 445–446,
454–455, 458
naming, 180
one-to-many, 445–446, 452–454,
458
one-to-one, 445–446
traversing, 482, 487–490
View object classes, 462, 463

View Object Wizard, 318–319, 424,
430, 437–439, 464, 484, 855
View objects, 11, 14, 307–308,
319–320, 414, 807, 855
abstract, 485–487
based on entity objects, 425–426,
499–452
create default, 346–347
creating, 426–441
naming, 179
polymorphic, 448–449
refining query, 423–426
SQL-only, 424–425, 431–432,
499, 797
synchronization, 423
testing, 188, 438–441
XML file, 320
View rows, 319
classes, 462, 463, 472–473
export accessors, 472–473
View usages, 308
detail, 447
instantiating, 468
linking at runtime, 500–502
View Whole Value
window, 203
ViewCriteria tag, 824
ViewCriteriaIterate tag, 825
Viewer
Archive, 76
HTML, 75
Image, 75
JSP, 75, 736–737, 734
Sequence, 77–78
Table, 76–77

windows, 75
Views, 13, 15, 17, 223
    menu, 58
Visual Properties
    in diagrams, 273
    dialog, 272, 276, 282, 283, 287
void keyword, 146

W

W3C group, 886
WAR Deployment Profile Settings, 253, 257
WAR files, 226, 253, 256, 765, 853, 855
    importing, 851
Watches, 202, 216
    debug window, 194, 202, 217
web.xml, 257, 740, 765, 855
Web Application Archive, *See* WAR files
Web-based Distributed Authoring and
    Versioning, *See* WebDAV
Web Bean, 855
Web container, 233, 533
Web Deployment Descriptor, 765, 855
Web Deployment Descriptor for
    OC4J, 855
Web Deployment Descriptor for
    WebLogic, 855
Web module mode, 535, 537
Web Object Manager, 827–828
    menu item, 63
Web Service Stub/Skeleton Wizard, 556, 855
Web Services, 544–545, 554–558
Web Service

Component Palette page, 270–271
    item on Model | Generate
        menu, 273
Web Services Publishing Wizard, 271, 555, 851
Web Tier, 224, 532
WebBean, 753, 828
WebDAV
    connection, 50
Websites, 729, 858–860
weight property, 679, 681
    x property, 679
    y property, 679
Welcome page, 25, 101
WHERE clauses, 815
    changing, 424, 483
    parameterized, 484–485
while loop statement, 151
Window
    menu, 625
    menu item, 63
    Navigator, 87
    topic, 87–88
Windows
    arranging JDeveloper, 45
    Data, 201
    dockable, 43
    docking, 43
    editor, 43
    IDE, 43
    Inspector, 202
    Log, 24, 45
    Navigator, 48, 53, 58, 87
    Smart Data, 201
    Structure, 53–54, 23
    undocking, 43–45

viewer, 43, 75–78
Watches, 202
See also Navigator; System
    Navigator
Wizards, 7, 22, 42, 82–83, 85, 111, 176,
    592, 844–856
    Applet HTML File Wizard, 246
    Application Module, 107–108, 322,
        349–351
    Association, 317, 334,
        344–346, 363
    Attribute, 134, 795, 797, 798, 800
    BC4J, 9, 31
    BC4J Client Data Model Definition,
        32–33, 569
    Business Components Deployment
        Wizard, 549
    Business Components Package, 28,
        101, 312–313
    Business Components Project, 27,
        333
    Connection, 25–26
    Data Page, 251–252, 740,
        756–759, 774, 847
    Domain, 392, 396
    Empty Panel, 113, 571
    Enterprise JavaBean Wizard, 267,
        268, 850, 852, 853
    Entity Constraint, 364
    Entity Object, 102–103, 314–315,
        329–330, 343, 360–361, 362,
        379, 391, 395, 399, 403–405,
        508, 511
    high-level, 21, 32

    Implement Cascade Delete, 335
    Import Existing Sources,
        132–133, 614
    Java Web Start Wizard, 230, 851
    JClient Empty Form Wizard,
        600, 850
    JClient Form, 34, 82, 97, 238–239,
        593, 632, 644, 646, 850
    JSP, 755–8
    low-level, 21, 97, 98
    modifying what is created by,
        85–86
    Oracle9i SCM Workarea, 90
    View Link, 106, 320–321, 348, 442
    View Object, 318–319, 424, 430,
        464, 484
    Web Service Stub/Skeleton Wizard,
        556, 855
Work area in JDeveloper's IDE, 24
Workareas in Oracle9i SCM, 90–91, 93
Workspaces, 12, 49, 565–566, 856
    create new, 24–25, 99, 161
    naming, 176
WSDL Document, 856

X

XML, 8–9, 139, 307, 310, 443, 568
    creating elements for associated
        entities, 332–333
    creating file for association, 333
    document, 856
    Editor, 73
    naming files, 176

validation roles, 378
view object file, 320
XML Document, 856
XML Schema, 856
XSL Stylesheet, 856
XSQL
    clients, 305
    page, 856
XYLayout, 666, 685, 691, 692
    uses for, 691

Z

Z-order, 664–665
Zoom
    submenu on Model menu, 272
Zoom in, 263
Zoom out, 263, 281, 292
Zoom to Selected, 263

INTERNATIONAL CONTACT INFORMATION

AUSTRALIA
McGraw-Hill Book Company Australia Pty. Ltd.
TEL +61-2-9900-1800
FAX +61-2-9878-8881
http://www.mcgraw-hill.com.au
books-it_sydney@mcgraw-hill.com

CANADA
McGraw-Hill Ryerson Ltd.
TEL +905-430-5000
FAX +905-430-5020
http://www.mcgraw-hill.ca

GREECE, MIDDLE EAST, & AFRICA
(Excluding South Africa)
McGraw-Hill Hellas
TEL +30-1-656-0990-3-4
FAX +30-1-654-5525

MEXICO (Also serving Latin America)
McGraw-Hill Interamericana Editores S.A. de C.V.
TEL +525-117-1583
FAX +525-117-1589
http://www.mcgraw-hill.com.mx
fernando_castellanos@mcgraw-hill.com

SINGAPORE (Serving Asia)
McGraw-Hill Book Company
TEL +65-863-1580
FAX +65-862-3354
http://www.mcgraw-hill.com.sg
mghasia@mcgraw-hill.com

SOUTH AFRICA
McGraw-Hill South Africa
TEL +27-11-622-7512
FAX +27-11-622-9045
robyn_swanepoel@mcgraw-hill.com

SPAIN
McGraw-Hill/Interamericana de España, S.A.U.
TEL +34-91-180-3000
FAX +34-91-372-8513
http://www.mcgraw-hill.es
professional@mcgraw-hill.es

UNITED KINGDOM, NORTHERN, EASTERN, & CENTRAL EUROPE
McGraw-Hill Education Europe
TEL +44-1-628-502500
FAX +44-1-628-770224
http://www.mcgraw-hill.co.uk
computing_neurope@mcgraw-hill.com

ALL OTHER INQUIRIES Contact:
Osborne/McGraw-Hill
TEL +1-510-549-6600
FAX +1-510-883-7600
http://www.osborne.com
omg_international@mcgraw-hill.com

Dulcian, Inc. provides a wide variety of consulting services, customized training and products for the Oracle environment. Services include new project development, auditing existing efforts and rescuing failed projects.

Led by Dulcian's founder and President, Dr. Paul Dorsey, we have consistently tried to be the thought leaders in the industry, keeping a step ahead of the rapidly changing Oracle development environment. Our object-relational approach to database design and business rule repository product suite (BRIM™) allow us to build extremely flexible and generic systems that can be easily adapted to accommodate changing business rules.

Why should you hire Dulcian?

Many of our consultants are recognized experts in their fields, frequently presenting at national conferences and publishing books and articles in leading industry journals.

Oracle Consulting Services
Web Application Development
Custom Training
Software Products

Dulcian brings a strong methodological background to all of our projects as evidenced by our best-selling Oracle Press technical books, co-authored by Dr. Paul Dorsey:

◢ Oracle Designer Handbook (2nd Edition) 1999

◢ Oracle8 Design Using UML Object Modeling, 1999

◢ Oracle Developer: Advanced Forms & Reports, 2000

◢ Oracle JDeveloper 3 Handbook, 2001

(732) 744-1116
FAX (732) 744-2896

WWW.DULCIAN.COM

GET YOUR FREE SUBSCRIPTION
TO ORACLE MAGAZINE

Oracle Magazine is essential gear for today's information technology professionals. Stay informed and increase your productivity with every issue of *Oracle Magazine*. Inside each free bimonthly issue you'll get:

- Up-to-date information on Oracle Database, E-Business Suite applications, Web development, and database technology and business trends
- Third-party news and announcements
- Technical articles on Oracle Products and operating environments
- Development and administration tips
- Real-world customer stories

Three easy ways to subscribe:

① Web
Visit our Web site at www.oracle.com/oraclemagazine. You'll find a subscription form there, plus much more!

IF THERE ARE OTHER ORACLE USERS AT YOUR LOCATION WHO WOULD LIKE TO RECEIVE THEIR OWN SUBSCRIPTION TO ORACLE MAGAZINE, PLEASE PHOTOCOPY THIS FORM AND PASS IT ALONG.

② Fax
Complete the questionnaire on the back of this card and fax the questionnaire side only to +1.847.647.9735.

③ Mail
Complete the questionnaire on the back of this card and mail it to P.O. Box 1263, Skokie, IL 60076-8263

Oracle Publishing

ORACLE®

FREE SUBSCRIPTION

○ Yes, please send me a FREE subscription to *Oracle Magazine*   ○ NO

To receive a free subscription to *Oracle Magazine*, you must fill out the entire card, sign it, and date it (incomplete cards cannot be processed or acknowledged). You can also fax your application to +1.847.647.9735.
Or subscribe at our Web site at www.oracle.com/oraclemagazine/

○ From time to time, Oracle Publishing allows our partners exclusive access to our e-mail addresses for special promotions and announcements. To be included in this program, please check this box.

○ Oracle Publishing allows sharing of our mailing list with selected third parties. If you prefer your mailing address not to be included in this program, please check here. If at any time you would like to be removed from this mailing list, please contact Customer Service at +1.847.647.9630 or send an e-mail to oracle@halldata.com.

signature (required)   date

X

name   title

company   e-mail address

street/p.o. box

city/state/zip or postal code   telephone

country   fax

YOU MUST ANSWER ALL NINE QUESTIONS BELOW

① WHAT IS THE PRIMARY BUSINESS ACTIVITY OF YOUR FIRM AT THIS LOCATION? (check one only)

- □ 01 Application Service Provider
- □ 02 Communications
- □ 03 Consulting, Training
- □ 04 Data Processing
- □ 05 Education
- □ 06 Engineering
- □ 07 Financial Services
- □ 08 Government (federal, local, state, other)
- □ 09 Government (military)
- □ 10 Health Care
- □ 11 Manufacturing (aerospace, defense)
- □ 12 Manufacturing (computer hardware)
- □ 13 Manufacturing (noncomputer)
- □ 14 Research & Development
- □ 15 Retailing, Wholesaling, Distribution
- □ 16 Software Development
- □ 17 Systems Integration, VAR, VAD, OEM
- □ 18 Transportation
- □ 19 Utilities (electric, gas, sanitation)
- □ 98 Other Business and Services

② WHICH OF THE FOLLOWING BEST DESCRIBES YOUR PRIMARY JOB FUNCTION? (check one only)

Corporate Management/Staff
- □ 01 Executive Management (President, Chair, CEO, CFO, Owner, Partner, Principal)
- □ 02 Finance/Administrative Management (VP/Director/ Manager/Controller, Purchasing, Administration)
- □ 03 Sales/Marketing Management (VP/Director/Manager)
- □ 04 Computer Systems/Operations Management (CIO/VP/Director/ Manager MIS, Operations)

IS/IT Staff
- □ 05 Systems Development/ Programming Management
- □ 06 Systems Development/ Programming Staff
- □ 07 Consulting
- □ 08 DBA/Systems Administrator
- □ 09 Education/Training
- □ 10 Technical Support Director/Manager
- □ 11 Other Technical Management/Staff
- □ 98 Other

③ WHAT IS YOUR CURRENT PRIMARY OPERATING PLATFORM? (select all that apply)

- □ 01 Digital Equipment UNIX
- □ 02 Digital Equipment VAX VMS
- □ 03 HP UNIX
- □ 04 IBM AIX

- □ 05 IBM UNIX
- □ 06 Java
- □ 07 Linux
- □ 08 Macintosh
- □ 09 MS-DOS
- □ 10 MVS
- □ 11 NetWare
- □ 12 Network Computing
- □ 13 OpenVMS
- □ 14 SCO UNIX
- □ 15 Sequent DYNIX/ptx
- □ 16 Sun Solaris/SunOS
- □ 17 SVR4
- □ 18 UnixWare
- □ 19 Windows
- □ 20 Windows NT
- □ 21 Other UNIX
- □ 98 Other
- 99 □ None of the above

④ DO YOU EVALUATE, SPECIFY, RECOMMEND, OR AUTHORIZE THE PURCHASE OF ANY OF THE FOLLOWING? (check all that apply)

- □ 01 Hardware
- □ 02 Software
- □ 03 Application Development Tools
- □ 04 Database Products
- □ 05 Internet or Intranet Products
- 99 □ None of the above

⑤ IN YOUR JOB, DO YOU USE OR PLAN TO PURCHASE ANY OF THE FOLLOWING PRODUCTS? (check all that apply)

Software
- □ 01 Business Graphics
- □ 02 CAD/CAE/CAM
- □ 03 CASE
- □ 04 Communications
- □ 05 Database Management
- □ 06 File Management
- □ 07 Finance
- □ 08 Java
- □ 09 Materials Resource Planning
- □ 10 Multimedia Authoring
- □ 11 Networking
- □ 12 Office Automation
- □ 13 Order Entry/Inventory Control
- □ 14 Programming
- □ 15 Project Management
- □ 16 Scientific and Engineering
- □ 17 Spreadsheets
- □ 18 Systems Management
- □ 19 Workflow

Hardware
- □ 20 Macintosh
- □ 21 Mainframe
- □ 22 Massively Parallel Processing

- □ 23 Minicomputer
- □ 24 PC
- □ 25 Network Computer
- □ 26 Symmetric Multiprocessing
- □ 27 Workstation

Peripherals
- □ 28 Bridges/Routers/Hubs/Gateways
- □ 29 CD-ROM Drives
- □ 30 Disk Drives/Subsystems
- □ 31 Modems
- □ 32 Tape Drives/Subsystems
- □ 33 Video Boards/Multimedia

Services
- □ 34 Application Service Provider
- □ 35 Consulting
- □ 36 Education/Training
- □ 37 Maintenance
- □ 38 Online Database Services
- □ 39 Support
- □ 40 Technology-Based Training
- □ 98 Other
- 99 □ None of the above

⑥ WHAT ORACLE PRODUCTS ARE IN USE AT YOUR SITE? (check all that apply)

Software
- □ 01 Oracle9i
- □ 02 Oracle9i Lite
- □ 03 Oracle8
- □ 04 Oracle8i
- □ 05 Oracle8i Lite
- □ 06 Oracle7
- □ 07 Oracle9i Application Server
- □ 08 Oracle9i Application Server Wireless
- □ 09 Oracle Data Mart Suites
- □ 10 Oracle Internet Commerce Server
- □ 11 Oracle interMedia
- □ 12 Oracle Lite
- □ 13 Oracle Payment Server
- □ 14 Oracle Video Server
- □ 15 Oracle Rdb

Tools
- □ 16 Oracle Darwin
- □ 17 Oracle Designer
- □ 18 Oracle Developer
- □ 19 Oracle Discoverer
- □ 20 Oracle Express
- □ 21 Oracle JDeveloper
- □ 22 Oracle Reports
- □ 23 Oracle Portal
- □ 24 Oracle Warehouse Builder
- □ 25 Oracle Workflow

Oracle E-Business Suite
- □ 26 Oracle Advanced Planning/Scheduling
- □ 27 Oracle Business Intelligence
- □ 28 Oracle E-Commerce
- □ 29 Oracle Exchange
- □ 30 Oracle Financials

- □ 31 Oracle Human Resources
- □ 32 Oracle Interaction Center
- □ 33 Oracle Internet Procurement
- □ 34 Oracle Manufacturing
- □ 35 Oracle Marketing
- □ 36 Oracle Order Management
- □ 37 Oracle Professional Services Automation
- □ 38 Oracle Projects
- □ 39 Oracle Sales
- □ 40 Oracle Service
- □ 41 Oracle Small Business Suite
- □ 42 Oracle Supply Chain Management
- □ 43 Oracle Travel Management
- □ 44 Oracle Treasury

Oracle Services
- □ 45 Oracle.com Online Services
- □ 46 Oracle Consulting
- □ 47 Oracle Education
- □ 48 Oracle Support
- □ 98 Other
- 99 □ None of the above

⑦ WHAT OTHER DATABASE PRODUCTS ARE IN USE AT YOUR SITE? (check all that apply)

- □ 01 Access
- □ 02 Baan
- □ 03 dbase
- □ 04 Gupta
- □ 05 BM DB2
- □ 06 Informix
- □ 07 Ingres
- □ 08 Microsoft Access
- □ 09 Microsoft SQL Server
- □ 10 PeopleSoft
- □ 11 Progress
- □ 12 SAP
- □ 13 Sybase
- □ 14 VSAM
- □ 98 Other
- 99 □ None of the above

⑧ DURING THE NEXT 12 MONTHS, HOW MUCH DO YOU ANTICIPATE YOUR ORGANIZATION WILL SPEND ON COMPUTER HARDWARE, SOFTWARE, PERIPHERALS, AND SERVICES FOR YOUR LOCATION? (check only one)

- □ 01 Less than $10,000
- □ 02 $10,000 to $49,999
- □ 03 $50,000 to $99,999
- □ 04 $100,000 to $499,999
- □ 05 $500,000 to $999,999
- □ 06 $1,000,000 and over

⑨ WHAT IS YOUR COMPANY'S YEARLY SALES REVENUE? (please choose one)

- □ 01 $500, 000, 000 and above
- □ 02 $100, 000, 000 to $500, 000, 000
- □ 03 $50, 000, 000 to $100, 000, 000
- □ 04 $5, 000, 000 to $50, 000, 000
- □ 05 $1, 000, 000 to $5, 000, 000

123101